WRITING SKILLS CURRICULUM LIBRARY

Ready-to-Use
PORTFOLIO DEVELOPMENT Activities

UNIT 6

JACK UMSTATTER

Illustrations by Maureen Umstatter

THE CENTER FOR APPLIED
RESEARCH IN EDUCATION
West Nyack, New York 10994

Library of Congress Cataloging-in-Publication Data

Umstatter, Jack.
    Writing skills curriculum library / Umstatter, Jack.
        p.   cm.
    Contents: Unit 1. Ready-to-use word activities
    ISBN 0-87628-482-9
    1. English language—Composition and exercises—Study and teaching
(Secondary)—United States.   2 Education, Secondary—Activity
programs—United States.   I. Title.
    LB1631.U49 1999
    808'.042'0712—dc21

99-21556
CIP

Printed in the United States of America

10 9 8 7 6 5 4 3 2 1

ISBN 0-87628-487-X

**The Center for Applied Research
in Education**
West Nyack, NY 10994

www.phedu.com

DEDICATED

To my publishing mentors and personal friends, Connie Kallback and Win Huppuch. You are so professional and knowledgeable. Every author should have the pleasure of working with you and learning from you. This library is a tribute to your skills and guidance.

ACKNOWLEDGMENTS

Thanks to my daughter Maureen for her artistic creativity and to my wife Chris for her many hours of work on this project. I couldn't have done it without you.

Thanks again to Connie Kallback and Win Huppuch for their support and encouragement with this series.

Appreciation and thanks to Diane Turso for her meticulous development and copyediting and to Mariann Hutlak, production editor, for her tireless attention throughout the project.

To current students, Lauren Dentone (Activities 6–21, "Airlines Tickets" [Part One] and 6–22, "Airlines Tickets" [Part Two]; Kristin Dillner (Activity 6–25, "Bricks"); Emily King (Activity 6–28, "Thinking and Writing Creatively"); and former students, Katie Wells (Activity 6–20, "Scooby Doo and Much More"); Kelly Grace (Activity 6–23, "The Summer Tradition"); Katie Megear (Activity 6–24, "Imitating Another Student's Writing"); Olivia Racanelli (Activities 6–26, "Before Thirty–Something" [Part One], 6–27, "Before Thirty-Something" [Part Two], and 6–64, "Hamlet—A Man of Action"); Marissa Heller (Activities 6–29, "Something New" [Part One] and 6–30, "Something New" [Part Two]; Alison DeVita (Activity 6–31, "Joey"), Adam Rohksar (Activities 6–32 through 6–35, "Your Town" [Parts One through Four]); Michelle Bellino (Activity 6–48, "Andrea Bocelli"); Craig Weiss (Activity 6–50, "A Teenager's Stressful Life"); Chris Olsen (Activity 6–59, "To Follow or Not to Follow—That Is the Question"); Chirag Badlani (Activity 6–65, "Hammer or Anvil?"); and Sasha Metznik (Activity 6–80, "Mr. Peacock")—thank you for your writings and for the pleasure of your company in English class each day.

Thanks to my students, past and present, who inspire these ideas and activities.

Thanks to Terry from WISCO COMPUTING of Wisconsin Rapids, Wisconsin 54495 for his programs.

Definitions for certain words are taken from *Webster's New World Dictionary, Third College Edition* (New York: Simon & Schuster, Inc., 1988).

ABOUT THE AUTHOR

Jack Umstatter has taught English on both the junior high and senior high school levels since 1972, and education and literature at Dowling College (Oakdale, New York) for the past nine years. He currently teaches English in the Cold Spring Harbor School District in New York.

Mr. Umstatter graduated from Manhattan College with a B.A. in English and completed his M.A. in English at S.U.N.Y.—Stony Brook. He earned his Educational Administration degree at Long Island University.

Mr. Umstatter has been selected Teacher of the Year several times and was elected to *Who's Who Among America's Teachers*. Most recently, he appeared in *Contemporary Authors*. Mr. Umstatter has taught all levels of secondary English classes including the Honors and Advanced Placement classes. As coach of the high school's Academic team, the Brainstormers, he led the team in capturing the Long Island and New York State championships when competing in the American Scholastic Competition Network National Tournament of Champions in Lake Forest, Illinois.

Mr. Umstatter's other publications include *Hooked on Literature!* (1994), *201 Ready-to-Use Word Games for the English Classroom* (1994), *Brain Games!* (1996), and *Hooked on English!* (1997), all published by The Center for Applied Research in Education.

ABOUT THE WRITING SKILLS CURRICULUM LIBRARY

According to William Faulkner, a writer needs three things—experience, observation, and imagination. As teachers, we know that our students certainly have these essentials. Adolescents love to express themselves in different ways. Writing is undoubtedly one of these modes of expression. We stand before potential novelists, poets, playwrights, columnists, essayists, and satirists (no comment!). How to tap these possibilities is our task.

The six-unit *Writing Skills Curriculum Library* was created to help your students learn the elements of effective writing and enjoy the experience at the same time. This series of progressive, reproducible activities will instruct your students in the various elements of the writing process as it fosters an appreciation for the writing craft. These stimulating and creative activities also serve as skill-reinforcement tools. Additionally, since the lesson preparation has already been done, you will be able to concentrate on guiding your students instead of having to create, develop, and sequence writing exercises.

- Unit 1, *Ready-to-Use Word Activities*, concentrates on the importance of word selection and exactness in the writing process. William Somerset Maugham said, "Words have weight, sound, and appearance; it is only by considering these that you can write a sentence that is good to look at and good to listen to." Activities featuring connotations, denotations, prefixes, roots, suffixes, synonyms, antonyms, and expressions will assist your students in becoming more conscientious and selective "verbivores," as Richard Lederer would call them. Diction, syntax, and specificity are also emphasized here.

- The renowned essayist, philosopher, and poet, Ralph Waldo Emerson, commented on the necessity of writing effective sentences. He said, "For a few golden sentences we will turn over and actually read a volume of four or five hundred pages." Knowing the essentials of the cogent sentence is the focus of Unit 2, *Ready-to-Use Sentence Activities*. Here a thorough examination of subjects, predicates, complements, types of sentences, phrases, clauses, punctuation, capitalization, and agreement situations can be found. Problems including faulty subordination, wordiness, split infinitives, dangling modifiers, faulty transition, and ambiguity are also addressed within these activities.

- "Every man speaks and writes with the intent to be understood." Samuel Johnson obviously recognized the essence of an effective paragraph. Unit 3, *Ready-to-Use Paragraph Writing Activities*, leads the students through the steps of writing clear, convincing paragraphs. Starting with brainstorming techniques, these activities also emphasize the importance of developing effective thesis statements and topic sentences, selecting an appropriate paragraph form, organizing the paragraph, introducing the paragraph, utilizing relevant supporting ideas, and concluding the paragraph. Activities focusing on methods of developing a topic—description, exemplification, process, cause and effect, comparison-contrast, analogy, persuasion, and definition—are included.

- "General and abstract ideas are the source of the greatest errors of mankind." Jean-Jacques Rousseau's words befit Unit 4, *Ready-to-Use Prewriting & Organization Activities*, for here the emphasis is on gathering and using information intelligently. Activities include sources of information, categorization, topics and sub-topics, summaries, outlines, details, thesis statements, term paper ideas, and formats.

- "Most people won't realize that writing is a craft." Katherine Anne Porter's words could be the fifth unit's title. Unit 5, *Ready-to-Use Revision & Proofreading Activities*, guides the students through the problem areas of writing. Troublesome areas such as verb tense, words often confused, superfluity, double negatives, and clarity issues are presented in interesting and innovative ways. Students will become better proofreaders as they learn to utilize the same methods used by professional writers.

- "Our appreciation of fine writing will always be in proportion to its real difficulty and its apparent ease." Charles Caleb Colton must have been listening in as Unit 6, *Ready-to-Use Portfolio Development Activities*, was developed. Students are exposed to many different types of practical writings including literary analyses, original stories and sketches, narratives, reviews, letters, journal entries, newspaper articles, character analyses, dialogue writing, college admission essays, and commercials. The goal is to make the difficult appear easy!

Whether you use these realistic classroom-tested activities for introduction, remediation, reinforcement, or enrichment, they will guide your students toward more effective writing. Many of the activities include riddles, hidden words and sayings, word-finds, and other devices that allow students to check their own answers. These activities will also help you to assess your students' progress.

So go ahead and make Mr. Faulkner proud by awakening the experience, observation, and imagination of your students. The benefits will be both theirs—and yours!

Jack Umstatter

ABOUT UNIT 6

Ready-to-Use Portfolio Development Activities, the sixth and final unit in the *Writing Skills Curriculum Library*, provides you with 90 creative and practical reproducible activities that will readily assist you and your students in developing and organizing their individual writing portfolios. Divided into five sections, the 90 activities will guide your students in this process as the students organize ideas about their portfolios, review the basics of writing, examine the skillful writing techniques of other writers, and then write about literature, the real world, and themselves. The activities can be implemented in many ways. They can be used as individual, partner, small-group, cooperative learning, or entire-class activities. Though they are writing activities, many can also be used as interesting discussion pieces. Some of these activities can fill a 15-minute space while others can be used for longer segments. They can be done in class or at home. The possibilities are many!

- Activities 6–1 through 6–19, "Working on the Basics," are preliminary activities for developing the portfolio. Here the portfolio log, writer's conference information, writing questions, brainstorming ideas, writing terminology, and a review of grammar, mechanics and usage are found.

- "Examining Writing Techniques," activities 6–20 through 6–35, presents the writings of 10 student writers. Personal narratives, grammar-based writings, reflective writings, creative writings, character sketches, and descriptions are the primary types of writings included in this section. Students will answer the questions that follow each writing and become more aware of effective writing techniques.

- Section Three, "Writing Away," includes activities 6–36 through 6–53. Eighteen writings including newspaper articles, writing directions, poetry writings, character sketches, comparison-contrast essays, persuasive essays, descriptive, and narration selections are here. In these activities students are asked to write their own pieces based on the techniques exemplified in these specific writings formats.

- "Looking at Literature," activities 6–54 through 6–72, encourages students to look closely at literature and its components. In these 19 literature-based activities, students, after examining the sample writings, will write character assessments, analyses, comparisons, plot synopses, descriptions, author interviews, dialogues, reader responses, movie reviews, poems, paraphrases, and more.

- Activities 6–73 through 6–90, "Living and Writing in Today's World," include18 activities that involve the students in real-life situations. Here the importance of strong and convincing writing is quite evident as the students become advice columnists, advertisement developers, reporters, quotation creators, punsters, letter writers, and journal writers—all real-world positions. Additionally, students will argue positions, relate a personal growth experience, write a thank-you to a former teacher, and complete a crossword puzzle about, who else, themselves.

Portfolios, these ordered compilations of students' chosen writings, should exhibit the students' skills and accomplishments and include various types of authentic, real-life writings. Portfolios should also contain the students' thoughts about their own writing abilities and an informative examination of and authentic practice in the writing process. With so many interesting and entertaining writings selections to choose from, *Ready-to-Use Portfolio Development Activities* will help you and your students decide which writings will ultimately be included in their portfolios. My students have done many of these activities—and have truly enjoyed the writing experience. These 90 helpful and entertaining activities will do the same for your students. May the ideas and words begin to flow. Write now!

Jack Umstatter

CONTENTS

SECTION ONE
WORKING ON THE BASICS

SECTION TWO
EXAMINING WRITING TECHNIQUES

SECTION THREE
WRITING AWAY

SECTION FOUR
LOOKING AT LITERATURE

SECTION FIVE
LIVING AND WRITING IN TODAY'S WORLD

TEACHER'S CORRECTION MARKS

ab	abbreviation problem		pr ref	pronoun reference problem
agr	agreement problem		pun	punctuation needed or missing
amb	ambiguous		reas	reasoning needs improvement
awk	awkward expression or construction		rep	unnecessary repetition
cap	capitalize		RO	run-on
case	error in case		shift	faulty tense shift
cp	comma problem		sp	incorrect spelling
cs	comma splice		thesis	improve the thesis
d	inappropriate diction		trans	improve the transition
det	details are needed		TX	topic sentence needed (or improved)
dm	dangling modifier		U	usage problem
dn	double negative		UW	unclear wording
frag	fragment		V	variety needed
ital	italics or underline		VAG	vague
lc	use lower case		VE	verb error
mm	misplaced modifier		VT	verb tense problem
num	numbers problem		w	wordy
^	insert		WC	better word choice
¶	new paragraph needed		WM	word missing
‖	faulty parallelism		WW	wrong word
,	insert comma			
pass	misuse of passive voice			

WORKING ON THE BASICS

6-1. YOUR PORTFOLIO LOG

As you select various writings to include in your portfolio, you should keep a log detailing vital information about the portfolio's contents. This page has been designed to do exactly that. After each writing, fill in the information requested below. Continue the comments under the title's line. An example is done for you.

Title	Date	Grade	Comments (yours, your teacher's, or a peer evaluator's)
Special Kids	9/26	A-	Good details and examples;

the opening paragraph attracts my attention; conclusion is well developed; watch for occasional pronoun problems

_____   _____ _____   _____
_____
_____

_____   _____ _____   _____
_____

_____   _____ _____   _____
_____
_____

_____   _____ _____   _____
_____
_____

6-2. PORTFOLIO WRITING CONSIDERATIONS

Writers benefit from reflecting about the writing process. They consider elements of their own writing, assess personal writing strengths and weaknesses, and look to improve their skills. Below are some ideas that you could utilize when looking at your writing since these kinds of responses and ideas will be helpful in both improving your writings and designing your portfolio.

   In the spaces provided, answer the following questions to improve your composition skills. If more space is needed, use the reverse side of this paper.

Title of writing _____

Date _____

Approximate length _____

Type of writing (circle one or more): (a) narrative   (b) description   (c) comparison–contrast
(d) persuasion   (e) process analysis   (f) cause-effect   (g) definition
(h) response   (i) letter   (j) ad   (k) free writing   (l) other (_____)

The purpose of this writing is _____
_____

Some aspects of this writing that I like are _____
_____
_____

Some aspects of this writing that I think could use improvement are _____
_____
_____

A few difficulties that I had composing this piece are _____
_____
_____

Some things that I learned about myself as a writer through working on this piece are _____
_____
_____

Some writing skills that I look to improve upon on the next writing are _____
_____
_____

Name _____ Date _____ Period _____

6-3. WRITING CONFERENCE SHEET

After making several copies of this writing conference sheet, use this information to assess and improve your writing. To save time, fill in as many of these answers before the conference. Even if you and your teacher do not conference with each writing, this information should be filled in to keep an accurate record of the items in your portfolio. Use the reverse side if needed.

Date of writing conference _____

Title of your writing _____

Type of writing _____

Approximate number of words in this writing _____

Purpose(s) of writing: _____

_____

What were some of the specifications (required items for inclusion) for this piece?

_____

What organizational pattern did you use? _____

_____

What problems did you have in writing this piece? _____

_____

How did you eventually solve this problem? _____

_____

What do you feel you did well in this writing? _____

_____

What improvements do you feel can be made in this writing? _____

_____

What are some of your teacher's remarks about the piece? _____

_____

If you shared this writing with another student (or more), what were some suggestions?

_____

Will you choose this writing as part of your portfolio? _____ Why or why not?

_____

Other ideas/suggestions concerning this writing: _____

_____

Name _____ Date _____ Period _____

6-4. HOW MUCH ARE YOU THE SAME?

How typical are you when you start to think of yourself as a student writer? Do you share the same concerns as other writers? Are your writing problems the same as those of others your age? Do you have suggestions on how to improve student writing? Below are four writing situations and the responses given by students your age. Place a check next to those situations that apply to you. Discuss your findings with your classmates.

What are some problems you have starting your writing?

_____ I cannot think of what to say.

_____ I cannot think of a good beginning.

_____ I have difficulty finding the words to express what I want to say.

_____ I lack confidence as a writer, so I generally do not think I can write effectively.

_____ Coming up with an idea for the composition is hard for me.

What types of writings do you enjoy creating?

_____ creative

_____ personal narratives

_____ science fiction

_____ topics that apply to people my age

How can you improve your writing?

_____ Have a better vocabulary.

_____ Know grammar better.

_____ Read the writings of professional writers.

_____ Spell better.

_____ Have more time to write.

_____ Proofread more carefully.

What is the most difficult part of the writing process?

_____ getting started

_____ organizing my composition

_____ being pleased with the final product

_____ writer's block

6-5. FOLLOWING THE BRAINSTORM

On a separate sheet of paper, trace the logic of the five sets of brainstorms listed below. Thus, in the first set, you could write that the *business world* contains *companies* and that *officers* head companies, and so on. Your explanations do not have to be in complete sentences, but they should be logically connected. Share your answers with your classmates. How common are your explanations with those of your classmates?

SET ONE: business world / companies / officers / Bill Gates / Microsoft / computers / printers / repairs / ordering parts / factories / deliveries / methods of transportation / drivers

SET TWO: beach / walkers / bathing suits / muscles / fitness / working out / weightlifting / aerobics / eating properly / diet / calories / fat content / body fat / scales / doctors / hospitals

SET THREE: newspapers / sections / classifieds / jobs / wages / raises / bosses / qualifications / education / college / location / cost / loans / major / minor / professors

SET FOUR: literature / reading / speed / comprehension / interest level / vocabulary level / book's length / favorite writers / J.D. Salinger / *Catcher in the Rye* / Holden Caulfield / teen rebel / Phoebe / innocent sister

SET FIVE: summer / backyards / barbecues / hot dogs / hamburgers / aroma / salads / potato chips / pretzels / sodas / games / families / teams / video cameras / memories / reunions / school classes / becoming adults

6-6. BRAINSTORMING IDEAS

On a separate piece of paper, brainstorm five of the following 25 topics. In a logical flow of thoughts, go wherever your thoughts take you. Allow approximately five minutes per topic. After completing your five topics, share your ideas with another student who selected the same topic. What do your brainstorms have in common? How are they different?

cartoons	pets
children's television	professional sports
compact discs	relatives
department stores	retirement
dictionaries	science class
editorials	snow
fads	space exploration
hairstyles	summer
jail	toys
jewelry	tragedies
jingles	vacations
ocean liners	your five senses
Olympics	

Name _____ Date _____ Period _____

6-7. VOCABULARY JOURNAL

The skilled writer is astute with words. Knowing when to use a specific word is essential for successful writing. Even the most talented writers know they must have a good vocabulary. They add words to their vocabulary through reading newspapers, novels, magazines, and other literary forms. Additionally, they then incorporate these new words into their writings and daily conversations. You should do the same. On the lines below write a new word, its definition, and that new word in an illustrative sentence. An example is done for you.

(*word*) benign: (*definition*) gentle, harmless, innocuous   (*illustrative sentence*) Callie, our benign dog, did not attack the youngster who was teasing her.

1. _____

_____

2. _____

_____

3. _____

_____

4. _____

_____

5. _____

_____

6. _____

_____

7. _____

_____

8. _____

_____

9. _____

_____

10. _____

_____

6-8. VOCABULARY DEXTERITY

Each word listed below has at least two different meanings. Use each word in two illustrative sentences to show you clearly know that the specific word has at least two different meanings. Each word can be used as different parts of speech.

1. chum _____

_____

2. dark _____

_____

3. dart _____

_____

4. grill _____

_____

5. mesh _____

_____

6. plot _____

_____

7. rank _____

_____

8. ring _____

_____

9. spell _____

_____

10. tread _____

_____

6-9. GROUPING THE PIECES OF INFORMATION

Fourteen bits of information concerning Duke Ellington, a jazz composer, orchestra leader, and pianist, are listed below. On a separate piece of paper, place these items in their proper groups. Give each group a title. To save time, write the number next to each piece of information under the proper group's title. The information bits are not in complete sentences.

1. One of the first jazz writers to work in longer forms of music

2. By 1918 he was a successful bandleader in Washington

3. Born in Washington, DC in 1899

4. By the time he was fifty years old, he earned so much money that he no longer had to travel to do shows

5. A superb innovator in every jazz style he adopted

6. From 1927–1931, he and his orchestra starred at the Cotton Club in New York City

7. Began studying piano at the age of six

8. Most prolific composer in jazz history

9. Wrote "Solitude," "Sophisticated Lady," and "Mood Indigo"

10. Wrote more than 100 short pieces

11. His 1933 European tour brought Ellington international fame

12. Collaborated with Billy Strayhorn

13. Considered by many to be the most important figure in the history of jazz

14. Wrote for the particular strengths of his orchestra members

6-10. YOU AS THE EDITOR

This writing below needs immediate improvement. There are numerous errors in this piece including spelling, sentence, mechanical, and usage errors. Wordiness is also quite apparent here. In the lines below the piece, rewrite it correcting the errors and making it much more readable and interesting for the next reader. If you need more space, continue on the reverse side of this paper.

Tennis is one of my favoritest sports to play. Their is several reasons why I feel this way about the sport that everybody calls tennis. It is grate exercize. If you play for half a hour, one gets a good work out. I love to sweet and, tennis makes me do that alot. Second of all, the competition is another thing about tennis that I like after the first thing that I like about tennis, the sport. I like to challenge others and this helps me to do it. I remember one teriffic match I had. This competiton with the other player in this match was exiting. Third, too, is the fun tennis brings and gives to me at the same time. What a good way to spend moments!

I hop you see how and that tennis and me are a match! Exercize, competting, and fun is why I like to and do play regularly tennis.

_____

_____

_____

_____

_____

_____

_____

_____

_____

© 1999 by The Center for Applied Research in Education

6-11. DON'T GO BELLY UP HERE!

Good writers often frown upon using idioms because there are more effective ways to express the same idea. Yet, some idioms are so much a part of our language that they often very clearly express what the author wants to say. Match the 25 idioms with their meanings by placing the number in its proper box in the Magic Square. If all your answers are correct, each row, column, and diagonal will add up to the same number. Good luck!

A=	B=	C=	D=	E=
F=	G=	H=	I=	J=
K=	L=	M=	N=	O=
P=	Q=	R=	S=	T=
U=	V=	W=	X=	Y=

Idioms

A. olive branch
B. talk a blue streak
C. ballpark estimate
D. run the gamut
E. hocus pocus
F. fly off the handle
G. on hold
H. heart of the matter
I. hang in
J. up a creek
K. pay through the nose
L. go belly up
M. face the music
N. out of touch
O. make short work of
P. smell a rat
Q. pull some strings
R. raise the roof
S. stole the show
T. go haywire
U. Achilles heel
V. caught red-handed
W. on the nose
X. beat around the bush
Y. break the ice

Meanings

1. detected in an act of stealth
2. out of control
3. take on an unpleasant task
4. become angry
5. do the entire range
6. magic
7. exactly
8. be suspicious
9. losing contact
10. postponement
11. main part
12. peace symbol
13. evade
14. use influence
15. dispose of quickly
16. exorbitant cost
17. persevere
18. speak quickly
19. start
20. cause trouble
21. was the star
22. to become bankrupt
23. seemingly inescapable dilemma
24. approximation
25. weakest point

6-12. SENTENCE WARM-UP

Five groups of words are fragments (FR); five are run-ons (RO); and five are complete sentences (CS). Use the two-letter designation for each group of words. Counting each question number as that number of points, the fragments total 36; the run-ons total 38; and the sentences total 46. Check to see if your answers are correct.

1. _____ Even though they practiced for many hours each day.

2. _____ Let us start the match over, Martin.

3. _____ They passed them by, they arrived fifteen minutes late.

4. _____ Running along the tracks as quickly as possible.

5. _____ This is one of the most complicated problems.

6. _____ Seeing her family in the crowd of people, Samantha waved to them, they were happy for her.

7. _____ These stamps are valuable, you should store them in a very safe place.

8. _____ Whenever the opportunity presented itself to Tim.

9. _____ Flood waters ruined the downtown area, the townspeople are emotionally spent.

10. _____ There is a big piece of gum stuck to the bottom of your shoe.

11. _____ The thing called love that they all talk about.

12. _____ The best week of my life at camp.

13. _____ Brenda enjoys renting movies, she has rented over two hundred movies during the last two years.

14. _____ I am.

15. _____ Stop!

6-13. PUNCTUATION REVIEW

The fifteen sentences below are poorly punctuated. Each sentence contains at least one punctuation error. Place the correct marks of punctuation in their proper positions. If a punctuation mark has been improperly placed, cross it out and insert the correct mark.

1. The tall handsome man lives in Altoona Pennsylvania.

2. Are there any birds outside the classroom window.

3. In my opinion the suggestions should be brought up at the next council meeting?

4. On March 24 1980 an important event took place on Long Island.

5. Kasheema asked are you the only person who will attend the special conference.

6. Henry Kissinger the former U.S. Secretary of State will be the keynote speaker.

7. Because we will arrive after you leave the key under the mat.

8. The manuscript was found by the archaeologist and now she will analyze its contents.

9. At fifteen when Jeremiah went to the Special Olympics he won three medals.

10. Mr. Fennelly cannot go to Spain with the family, because he has several business commitments.

11. Her gardens are very impressive, however; few people have seen them.

12. Whenever you kick the ball out of bounds Caroline said you should retrieve it

13. The one eighth inch board should be nailed to the wall very carefully.

14. Larrys brother/in/law visited the family on January 14 1988.

15. First they mapped out their route then they packed the car, and finally they set off on their journey.

© 1999 by The Center for Applied Research in Education

6-14. PUNCTUATING DIALOGUE

Perhaps a career as a novelist is in your future. Even if your aspirations will take you elsewhere, knowing how to punctuate dialogue is a skill that requires honing and patience. A dialogue between two fourteen-year-olds, Mitch and Frank, appears below. The problem is that it has not been punctuated properly. On the lines below, correct the punctuation problems and make this dialogue come alive in the proper grammatical fashion. Remember to indent each time the speaker changes. (Use the reverse side of this paper if you need more space.)

I never wanted to come here in the first place said Frank as he looked nervously down the alley in this tough part of the city what are we doing here tonight you have heard about this area and what happens here lets go back out and get on the train to go home now oh come on now said his friend Mitch whats there to be scared about here youre just imagining what is probably not going to happen hey thats wishful thinking Mitch we could easily get killed by who knows what in this place im leaving before something happens to us you know the other guys will hear about what a chicken you are Frank do you think they would behave this way i dont care what you tell them Mitch youre just as scared as I am but youre pretending to be tough i bet that if some group of tough guys came down this alley right now you would run out of here faster than you have ever run before do what you want Mitch but im out of here

_____

_____

_____

_____

_____

_____

_____

_____

_____

_____

6-15. GRAMMAR, MECHANICS, AND USAGE REVIEW

Each of these 20 groups of words contains a mistake in either grammar, mechanics, or usage. On a separate sheet of paper, correct the mistake. Then, after each correction, briefly state the rule that applies to that particular sentence's problem.

1. The day after Mario broke the track record.

2. Yesterday all my troubles seemed so far away, now they are not.

3. Several pieces of cake had been left out on the counter all night this morning they were too hard to eat.

4. Each of the girls has their own prom dress.

5. That could of been the best way to solve this dilemma.

6. Unfortunately, these computers are the worstest I have ever used.

7. Roberta, our lead guitar player, is the more talented of the three musicians who auditioned for the band.

8. Their are many young people who would like to be in your position right now.

9. Do you feel that our class has choosed the most efficient method?

10. Yuri was happy receiving the award.

11. Gertrude is the type of an aunt who likes to visit often.

12. All of the delicious loaves of bread had been ate before the weekend concluded.

13. These dogs so bad want to go out, but since it is raining, I will keep them inside.

14. It took the police approximately sixteen minutes to get to the sceane of the crime.

15. Our attendance officer has dislike of those students who are truant from school that often.

16. The flag is risen each morning at exactly 7 A.M.

17. Is there much sense in you becoming a sales clerk at that particular department store this late in the summer?

18. Can you disagree with the end result of this debate, Mildred?

19. When Brandi told her sister about the problem, she was upset.

20. I prefer studying biology over chemistry.

6-16. ESSENTIAL TERMS

Twenty-three terms that are necessary to know in order to address specific writing concerns are the answers to this puzzle. Fill in the 20 answers and remember these important terms. Several letters have already been placed within the puzzle.

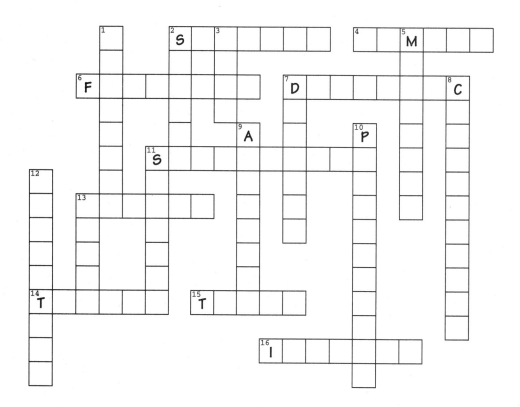

ACROSS

2. time and place of a story
4. something that represents itself and something else simultaneously
6. a group of words that do not form a complete sentence because it lacks either a verb, subject, or a complete thought
7. writing intended to instruct
11. the dictionary definition of a word
13. word or sentence arrangement
14. position that the author hopes to prove
15. main thought expressed by the author
16. images within the writing

DOWN

1. the author's placement of elements to achieve a desired effect
2. comparison using "like," "as," or "than"
3. usually described by an adjective, it is how an author expresses his or her thoughts
5. comparison between two things or people
7. word choice
8. implications of a word or phrase
9. author's disposition toward the subject
10. author's vantage point in telling the story
11. specifics included within the writing
12. arrangement of the work's elements
13. mode of expression by the author

6-17. HALF AND HALF

Writers should be good spellers. If they are not, the dictionary and the spell check device are other sources to check on spelling exactness.

Of the 40 words listed below, half are spelled correctly and half are spelled incorrectly. Circle the misspelled words and next to each, spell that word correctly. Use whatever sources you need in order to spell *all* these words correctly.

_____ 1. buffalos	_____ 21. churches
_____ 2. radioes	_____ 22. Belgian
_____ 3. megaphone	_____ 23. forgetton
_____ 4. obsesive	_____ 24. grammer
_____ 5. businesses	_____ 25. tongue
_____ 6. commitee	_____ 26. husbend
_____ 7. bouquit	_____ 27. marraige
_____ 8. experience	_____ 28. necesary
_____ 9. imaginary	_____ 29. administer
_____ 10. vicinity	_____ 30. provisional
_____ 11. recomend	_____ 31. governor
_____ 12. occasionally	_____ 32. labortory
_____ 13. tekniques	_____ 33. foundation
_____ 14. stupify	_____ 34. warrent
_____ 15. temporary	_____ 35. wrinkled
_____ 16. repetition	_____ 36. independant
_____ 17. schedule	_____ 37. historical
_____ 18. violence	_____ 38. vengeance
_____ 19. documents	_____ 39. rapiddly
_____ 20. responsibilty	_____ 40. succesfully

6-18. PLAYING WITH WORDS THAT ARE NOT WORDS

As far as we know, the following ten combinations of letters are not English words—or words in any language for that matter. However, today, with your creativity and writing talent, you will assign each combination a definition.

Often, words give off a "sense" of what they mean. *Melody* sounds like what it means. So do *itchy* and *gruesome*. At other times words that have two or more different meanings do not always sound like what they mean. *Swell* is swell when something good happens to you. However, *swell* is not so *swell* when your ankle *swells* or when a *swell* of water is heading for your rowboat.

Directions: On the lines provided, write your own definition for these combinations of letters (We will call them words even though they have not yet made it into the language.) Make them nouns, verbs, adjectives, or whatever else you want them to be. If asked, be ready to say why you gave it the definition you did. Most importantly, have fun!

1. wertpoke _____

   _____

2. legploy _____

   _____

3. gholkicky _____

   _____

4. huvob _____

   _____

5. paslew _____

   _____

6. oufouf _____

   _____

7. trahnques _____

   _____

8. mouhrde _____

   _____

9. wosogol _____

   _____

10. difgo _____

    _____

6-19. TIME FOR A BREAK

Writer's block is a common problem for both experienced and inexperienced writers. So here is a way to relieve the frustration and anxiety of writer's block. Using the letters in the words WRITING and PORTFOLIOS, form as many 4- or more letter words as possible. No word may end with the letter S. Come up with as many words as possible. If you can form over 30, you have probably conquered writer's block. Write your words on the lines provided. Good luck.

SECTION TWO

EXAMINING WRITING TECHNIQUES

Name _____ Date _____ Period _____

6-20. SCOOBY DOO AND MUCH MORE

Student writer Katie Wells gives us an insider's look at who she is in this introspective writing that combines serious and humorous elements. Katie focuses on one specific characteristic. On a separate sheet of paper: (1) Summarize each paragraph including its purpose. (2) Cite each paragraph's topic sentence. (3) List two humorous aspects and two serious aspects Katie includes. Finally, write your own introspective piece that allows the reader to see who you are. You might consider, as Katie does, emphasizing one personal characteristic and combining some humorous and some serious aspects.

(1) There is this thing in the back of my head that gnaws at me when I'm watching *Scooby Doo*. (2) It taunts, "Katie, oh, Katie, remember your calc homework? (3) You don't want to see Mr. Chartan's face turn red again, do you?" (4) I guess you could say that I am a compulsive worrier. (5) Just the other night I went to bed anxious after madly studying for my first AP Economics test. (6) Around 3:30 A.M., I woke up out of a half-doze in which I was reciting supply and demand gibberish in my dreams. (7) And this is an improvement! (8) Usually I would have lain awake half the night brooding over production possibility curves. (9) Dad always says how much I am like him in this respect, but I bet Dad never worried about whether his hair would become overrun by split ends, or whether terrorists would take all of New York hostage.

(10) The realization that I was a worrier came after a traumatic event. (11) When I was ten, my mother had a double mastectomy, although at the time I had no idea what this was, let alone how to pronounce it. (12) But as I got older and more aware, I began to worry about the implications of this reality. (13) What if Mom wasn't okay? (14) And after studying genetics, I wondered, "Would it happen to me?" (15) These questions haunted me at night when I lay in bed thinking. (16) One sleepless night, my fear became too much for me to handle alone. (17) As I told my parents about my anxieties, I began to sob uncontrollably. (18) Mom and Dad told me I had no reason to be so upset. (19) "You are so young," they said. (20) You shouldn't have to worry about *anything*, let alone cancer. (21) This is when it hit me. (22) I was stunned looking back at how ridiculous I had been. (23) I was like Vada in *My Girl*. (24) In the opening line of the movie, she says, "My left breast is developing much quicker than my right. (25) It can only mean one thing—cancer" (this is the audience's cue to break out in laughter). (26) Like Vada, I had exaggerated worries—so exaggerated as to be laughable. (27) Now when I hear that line, I laugh too.

(28) But despite all of its I-want-to-pull-my-hair-out-I'm-going-crazy side effects, I have come to think positively about this whole worrying thing. (29) Sometimes I wonder if I would get all my work done if I didn't worry about it—I will even wait until I finish writing this paper to meet with my friends. (30) In this way, I think worrying gives me a certain discipline. (31) I don't need Mom to tell me to do my homework or to write this essay. (32) It's just in me to do these things, and to do them as best I can. (33) Because I know that if I don't study, I'll fail the test, never get into college, never get a job, become the epitome of a failure, and the whole world will run askew of its orbit.

(34) Now I try not to fret so much about the petty stuff. (35) I am simply attempting to become carefree again, like before all of this worrying nonsense, when tree climbing was considered hard work. (36) However, I could be sitting in class worrying about the wobbly tire on my car, biting my nails at the prospect that at any time I could go careening off into the woods. (37) So I guess I'm not entirely cured.

6-21. AIRLINE TICKETS (PART ONE)

Student writer Lauren Dentone's assignment was to create a story that includes specific types of phrases, clauses, transitions, and more. The first half of Lauren's composition is reprinted here. Read it and then answer the questions that follow. Write your answers on the lines provided for you.

(1) This summer Tracy wanted to earn enough money to see her cousins in Vermont. (2) In order to go to Vermont, she needed a job that would allow her to earn enough money for the air fare. (3) A round trip ticket would cost her $500. (4) Reaching her goal would not be easy.

(5) Tracy thought the mall would be a good place to look for a job. (6) She wanted to be the first person at the mall when it opened, so she woke up early in the morning. (7) Walking around the mall, Tracy noticed there were many job opportunities. (8) Tracy was very used to being supported by her siblings, and she felt nervous without her sister.

(9) Tracy wandered around the mall for a while until she came to a restaurant. (10) Waitressing seemed like a good way to earn the money. (11) Tracy saw that the manager was talking to the waitress, and she wanted to introduce herself. (12) Tracy tapped the manager on the shoulder and ran from the restaurant completely frustrated. (13) She was very embarrassed seeing her former boyfriend as the manager.

1. There are two infinitive phrases in the first sentence. List both of them.

   _____

2. What is the adjective clause in sentence 2?

   _____

3. What is the gerund phrase in sentence 4? _____

4. What type of clause is "when it opened" in sentence 6? _____

5. What is the participial phrase in sentence 7? _____

6. What type of prepositional phrase is "to a restaurant" in sentence 9?

   _____

7. What is the gerund in sentence 10? _____

8. What type of clause is "that the manager was talking to the waitress," in sentence 11?

   _____

9. What are the two prepositional phrases in sentence 12?

   _____

10. What is the adverb in sentence 13? _____

© 1999 by The Center for Applied Research in Education

6-22. AIRLINE TICKETS (PART TWO)

Student writer Lauren Dentone's assignment was to create a story that includes specific types of phrases, clauses, transitions, and more. The second portion of Lauren's composition appears below. After you have read it, answer the questions that follow on the lines provided for you. When necessary, include line numbers in your answers.

(1) Tracy was now so upset that all she wanted to do was shop. (2) She was spending her money faster than she could ever make it. (3) The Gap was Tracy's favorite store and it had a great sale. (4) All who were in the store were looking at the merchandise. (5) At The Gap, the clerk with the high-heel shoes at the counter could tell that she was upset, and she almost forgot that her mother had asked her to go to the grocery store.

(6) Traveling to the store was boring. (7) Tracy stopped at a newsstand. (8) She was looking for the classified magazine. (9) An ad in the magazine caught her eye immediately. (10) The advertisement was for a local travel agency. (11) Tracy knew that this job would be perfect. (12) She would now be able to get the plane ticket to Vermont. (13) Tracy went to the travel agency at once and got the job. (14) They told her if she worked diligently she would get airline tickets for almost nothing. (15) So she worked very hard because she desperately wanted to see her cousins.

(16) The air fare, now a great bargain, would need to be booked two weeks in advance. (17) So out of all Tracy's disappointments she was able to work hard enough to get the airline tickets.

(18) This was a summer that Tracy will never forget.

1. Which sentence in the first paragraph begins with a prepositional phrase? _____

2. Which sentence in the first paragraph contains an adjective clause? _____

3. What is the noun reference to "it" in sentence 3? _____

4. What type of prepositional phrase is "with the high-heel shoes" in sentence 5?

   _____

5. Which sentence in the first paragraph contains two noun clauses? _____

6. Which sentence in the first paragraph is classified as a compound sentence? _____

7. Traveling to the store (sentence 6) is what type of verbal phrase? _____

8. In line 8 is "looking" part of a verb phrase or a participial phrase? (Circle the answer.)

9. What is the infinitive phrase in sentence 12? _____

10. What part of speech is "So" in sentence 15? _____

11. List two infinitive phrases found in the third paragraph. _____

12. What type of clause is "that Tracy will never forget" in sentence 18? _____

6-23. THE SUMMER TRADITION

In this reminiscence told in the present tense, student writer Kelly Grace tells of a favorite summer tradition. In this writing intended to entertain and inform, Kelly includes at least four necessary components of effective narration and reminiscence—specific descriptive details, dialogue, active verbs, and a prevalent tone or mood.

First, discuss these four techniques with your classmates. Then, on a separate piece of paper, write a combination narration and reminiscence piece imitating Kelly's style. Include the same writing techniques, including present tense verbs, that she does.

(1) "Hurry up!" yells Brad as he grabs his clothes and hops the fence for the next house, the next pool. (2) Chrissy and I giggle because Trey's pants get caught on the rhododendron as he lands, and he scrapes himself trying to disentangle them. (3) Trey mutters to himself, cursing the bush as Brad slowly dives into the aqua tranquillity of #37. (4) Brad takes the lead, gaining the advantage of the first dive, and therefore the position of the most probable escapee in case of capture. (5) That's the way it used to be anyway before we could drive. (6) The danger in this late night expedition, as in many of our other rituals, has since decreased. (7) It's amazing how our lives were so different then; yet, our fundamental worries and happiness are the same today as they were before we hit junior high. (8) It has been a long and knee-scraping road, but somehow, together, we have made it through. (9) Tonight is a night of reflection and reminiscence; (10) as we examine our scars, the road shows its presence, and a sense of age and wisdom permeates the practice of one of our silliest traditions.

(11) Trey follows a few seconds after Brad and gains points for courage in the form of a whooping cannonball. (12) In this contest, points are awarded for speed, courage, creativity, and transition. (13) As Trey has just fallen behind in transition and speed, he must attempt to compensate with a taboo holler. (14) It's a little dig at Brad to let him know his opponent is still in the game. (15) Victory on this block has yet to be declared. (16) Chrissy shoots me a glance, and we both smile, thinking about the announcement of the winner and the awards later. (17) We are driving the getaway Jeep, which, we have recently discovered, can be even more amusing than actually participating in the midnight madness. (18) It is the last week of summer and this is our final celebration of a five-year pool hopping tradition. (19) We four will be splitting up in a few days, each of us going his separate way to start a new life and form new friendships in new homes at new schools. (20) This is our farewell to reckless teenage rebellion and our acceptance of full-fledged half-way-adulthood. (21) We have been together for so long that we forget what it is like not to have one another. (22) In this gentle moonlight we say unspoken good-byes to innocence and to our family of four. (23) This is our last night together, an end to eight years of best-friendship, and we have chosen this, our most-favored ritual, as our final memory of being together.

© 1999 by The Center for Applied Research in Education

Name _____ Date _____ Period _____

6-24. IMITATING ANOTHER STUDENT'S WRITING

Student writer Katie Megear has entitled her writing "Black and White Movie Romance." What are you expecting with this title? This is the first trace of Katie's skill as a writer since through her title, she has captured your attention. This excerpt is the initial portion of Katie's composition.

Directions: First, read this selection paying close attention to Katie's writing style. Then, on a separate sheet of paper, comment on Katie's use of narrative techniques, sensory images, word choice, and total effect. Then, again on another sheet of paper, add another 200 words to complete Katie's story in your own way. Your goal in this writing is to imitate, as best as you can, Katie's writing style. Compare your endings with those of your classmates.

Black and White Movie Romance

(1) I have this memory.
(2) And it makes me feel sick and shuddery as if I'm sitting in a corner and my best friend is about to burst into tears and I don't know why but I do know—that whatever it is, it is going to pierce like ice straight into me. **(3)** Only it's that sick that other things can do to you. **(4)** Things that are sweet and amazing and completely, utterly, out of your control.
(5) The moment flows like black and white tape recording, the slow motion button painfully jammed. **(6)** It's December eighteenth. **(7)** And outside is that December dusk that all the poets seem to forget about. **(8)** It hits the grayness of Madison Avenue buildings the way you're scared to put down on paper—put into actual words. **(9)** Paints it like a picture that translates into the sound of horror movie suspense music.
(10) It's six twenty-two according to a fluorescent pink clock above the door but I—I don't know that. **(11)** He tells me this later in a letter that makes me feel the same sweet corner-sick. **(12)** I'm facing the back of the cafe right now, and he's sitting dead across. **(13)** Pensive and reflective. **(14)** It's not really a cafe; **(15)** it's a diner/coffee house on sixty-third and the window panes are shower-mirror musty except for the pane right behind me, adjacent to the door.
(16) It's bright and lazy and conversationally full enough not to let things fall into awkwardness when we're silent. **(17)** He takes big gulps of his hot chocolate, smiling questioningly between gulps. **(18)** He's trying to find my eyes.
(19) I am trying to hear them hit against the glass. **(20)** Tiny white flakes just bordering extra-heavy rain-drops. **(21)** I shudder and breathe out slowly. **(22)** I'm cold . . . and this—is romantic.

6-25. BRICKS

Student writer Kristin Dillner was asked to write an essay having the title "A Lost Art." She decided to write about bricklaying, and she writes of the bricklaying experience her family had. On a separate sheet of paper, write your own comments about Kristin's writing. Consider style, tone, sentence structure, sentence starter variety, point of view, interest level, structure, appropriate vocabulary, and imagery. Discuss your thoughts with your classmates.

(1) When I think of the world and its history, it is difficult to grasp a true feeling of all the different cultures and customs that once were or are now present. (2) Many things have either been lost, taken over, improved, or forgotten. (3) For me, a lost art is bricklaying.

(4) Bricklaying is an art dating back to the Egyptians and the Pyramids. (5) One might question the actual labor that went into creating the Great Pyramids. (6) Until last summer, I also was one that questioned the fact until my family decided to lay a brick patio.

(7) Just to pick the brick desired, one has to consider the color, shape, size, texture, thickness, and composition. (8) One might ask, "But why? They all look the same." (9) Not if you're my father, because, according to Dad, each brick has to be exactly like one another—to the point of perfection. (10) Transporting the bricks—stacking, laying, and moving—is a task of its own. (11) With each brick weighing over 5 pounds, just try to imagine 5,600 of them. (12) Before laying the bricks, one must level the ground and make it smooth and pitched enough for water runoff. (13) Don't forget the three inches of stone dust and two inches of sand compacted to create a foundation on which 5,600 bricks will lay on for the next two months. (14) Last summer under the blazing sun, we measured pitch and height over time and time again running string lines to ensure accuracy. (15) Once we were satisfied, we began to lay the bricks. (16) The easy part one might say? (17) This was just as difficult as the previous part. (18) Was making sure the columns and rows were symmetrical—mind no chipped edges, carrying the bricks here and there until our hands were chapped and chafed from the rough sand paper-like texture, and the unfortunate dropping of bricks on fingers and toes, the "easy part"? (19) I think not. (20) My father had to saw bricks at different points in time to "make them fit" as we went along the courses. (21) Hearing protectors had to be worn due to the extremely shrill whine of the saw bearing a fourteen-inch blade. (22) I can still picture it now, the water spraying everywhere and the orange dust soaring throughout the air like a sunset cloud.

(23) This work over the summer was tiresome, and by the last brick we were all relieved to see the finished masterpiece. (24) We conquered this task as a family—a gratification of its own.

(25) Since you have heard my story, you might ask, "Why didn't you just hire someone?" (26) But wouldn't you know, we've lined our driveway with 408 cobblestones and this fall we put in another walkway of 2,000 bricks. (27) Bricklaying, a lost art, was revived at my house last summer.

Name _____ Date _____ Period _____

6-26. BEFORE THIRTY-SOMETHING (PART ONE)

In this reflective writing, student writer Olivia Racanelli recounts an experience she had with her younger sister, Rachel. First, read the excerpt, the first of her essay's two parts. Then answer the questions in the spaces provided. These questions are intended to make you think about what constitutes effective writing.

(1) Rachel, with her scraped knees and tangled hair, had always been my very much younger sister. (2) Our individual stages while growing up had never seemed to coincide or even overlap.

(3) When I was eleven and she was six, I decided that she might be ready to solve my greatest problem in life. (4) I needed her to sit on the opposite end of the board games for which I had a great passion, but never a willing partner. (5) My mother, in fact, could not stand them, my dad had a proclivity only for playing cards, and my brother, at a grand thirteen, had more important things on his mind than *Snakes and Ladders*, namely video games. (6) So that left young Rachel. (7) "Little Rachie" had nothing better or more important to do. (8) I counted so desperately on her young brain's understanding of the complexities of a board game. (9) Unfortunately, she could not yet figure a sum of the dots on a pair of settled dice. (10) She could not slide her piece the correct number of squares either, and after a while of instructing (if not outright performing) her every move, I realized that I was playing a two-player game from only one side of the beloved board.

(11) When I was twelve and she was seven, I would create a highly organized art studio out of our kitchen table. (12) I would have many perfect bottles of paint set in a line, sheets of white paper—clean and crisp in a pile, and new brushes lined up for easy access. (13) Before my brush could take its first paint-bottle bath, Rachel's voice would come from behind my chair. (14) "Whatcha doing and can I do it too?" (15) So I would set a place for Rachel and cringe at her every move. (16) The truth was that Rachel still made a good finger-painting candidate while I sought to paint skies with clouds. (17) I preferred white clouds, and not the kind made from the green and orange streaks in my white paint jar.

1. What is the purpose of the first paragraph? _____
   _____

2. Within the initial five lines of her piece, Olivia introduces the reader to her family members. What do we know about each person?

   _____

3. Rachel is characterized well in the initial paragraphs. List several traits of Rachel as shown there. _____

4. What is the purpose of the third paragraph? _____

   _____

5. What is the tone of the piece? _____ Give several examples to support your answer. _____

   _____

6. List some descriptions you like. _____

   _____

6-27. BEFORE THIRTY-SOMETHING (PART TWO)

This is the second excerpt of student writer Olivia Racanelli's composition about her relationship with her sister, Rachel. Read this concluding excerpt and answer the questions on the lines provided. Then, on the reverse side of this paper, list five aspects of Olivia's writing that you admire. For each aspect, give a supporting example from Olivia's composition.

(1) Even last summer, the differences were blatantly obvious. (2) We would seek relief from a hot sun together by the pool. (3) At first, Rachel would entertain herself for a while keeping her head below the surface more than above while I sat by the side reading my book, jumping in occasionally. (4) After a while, a while never failing to be right smack in the middle of a chapter, she would ask me to come in and play some games. (5) We would have diving contests and races, but unlike her, I did not want to be in the water until my fingertips and toes pruned anymore. (6) I was always the one to get out and put an end to the fun. (7) Rachel would get frustrated with me and my "stupid books" and send flying drops of water my way. (8) I would ignore her as the pages of my book turned slowly into wrinkled prunes themselves.

(9) As time passed, I began losing hope in our becoming close. (10) I would hear my friends speaking of their younger sisters as their best friends and wish that Rachel and I could be that close. (11) We were, of course, older sister–younger sister, but not teenage sisters, or high school sisters. (12) We couldn't quite connect.

(13) On an August night, I had just had an argument with my mom over spending a summer weekend away with one of my friends, and her reluctantly granted permission left me in the smothering depths of despair. (14) Since Rachel's bedroom walls were a freshly painted sky-blue, she would be spending the night with me. (15) I was feeling so guilt-stricken and desperate to vent to someone that I actually decided to try Rachel out for some sympathy. (16) I didn't expect her to understand at all, but figured that at the very worst, I could at least be soothing myself out loud. (17) So I went for it. (18) I spilled everything. (19) "*I* wouldn't feel bad because *I'm* insensitive," she said. (20) The combination of humor and frankness with which she stated this made me laugh. (21) She continued, "Besides, daughters are supposed to torture their mothers every once in a while. Even *Mom* admits to that!"

(22) That night, Rachel, by the foot of my bed, helped me to sleep more easily. (23) Something in what she said was exactly what I needed to hear from someone's voice other than my own. (24) She had convinced me that maybe we wouldn't have to wait until our thirties, the age I had previously predicted would make our five years seem less than a lifetime, to connect—older sister to older sister.

1. List three transitions Olivia employs. _____
   _____

2. Which paragraph *most obviously* points out the writer's dilemma regarding her relationship with her sister at that time in their lives? _____

3. Sentences 12, 17, and 18 are quite short in comparison to the other sentences. What effect do these shorter sentences have? _____
   _____

4. How did Rachel surprise the writer? _____
   _____

5. How does Olivia tie in her composition's title to the story? _____
   _____

© 1999 by The Center for Applied Research in Education

6-28. THINKING AND WRITING CREATIVELY

In this composition student writer Emily King considers the creative and thought-provoking situation *If Rocks Could Talk*. Both her approach to the topic and the details she includes are interesting. Before reading Emily's piece, consider how you would approach this situation. Then answer the questions that follow her composition. Finally, on the reverse side of this paper, write at least three hypothetical situations, like this one here, and then brainstorm how you would write a composition about each situation. What would you include? Why?

(1) Rocks have been a significant part of my world. **(2)** If rocks could talk, what would they say? **(3)** Maybe, "Get off me; you are too heavy," or "Stop throwing me, I don't like it!" **(4)** I could think of numerous things.

(5) When I was younger, I visited the beach often. **(6)** At the beach was a rock on which I spent many hours. **(7)** This rock was huge. **(8)** It had a "staircase." **(9)** I was a princess when I embarked upon this rock. **(10)** My sister joined me on the rock many times, but, of course, I was still the princess. **(11)** Sometimes when both my sister and I were on the rock, I would order her to go capture the "bad people"—our parents. **(12)** I wonder what the rock would say if I asked it about those times in my life.

(13) On our visits to the beach, my father and I would have rock-skipping contests. **(14)** I was young when my father taught me how to skip a rock. **(15)** "Bend your knees, and get real low to the ground," he would say to me. **(16)** We had competitions every time we went down to that beach. **(17)** It was not until about age 14 that I finally won one of those contests. **(18)** I was so excited. **(19)** To this day, when we visit the beach, we still have those silly competitions. **(20)** All those rocks we have skipped over the years, I really wonder what they would say about these competitions between my father and me.

(21) If rocks could talk, they probably would not have much to say to me. **(22)** I have thrown them, walked all over them, and claimed them as mine, taking away their freedom. **(23)** I would love to hear what rocks would say if they could talk. **(24)** They would have more stories than I could imagine.

1. What organizational structure does Emily employ (chronological, large to small, small to large, grouping)? _____

   _____

2. Is Emily's story told in the first- or third-person narration? _____

3. Comment on the author's tone in this composition. _____

   _____

4. Comment on Emily's writing style. What aspects do you like? Why? _____

   _____

5. Pretend you are one of the rocks used by Emily in one of her many rock-skipping contests. On the reverse side of this paper, write a one-paragraph response to what Emily says in this piece.

6-29. SOMETHING NEW (PART ONE)

In this paragraph Marissa Heller, a high school senior at the time she wrote this piece, envisions an important moment in her life—leaving the comforts of her own home and moving on to the initially unfamiliar environment of college. In this section of the two-part activity, Marissa reflects upon the topic of moving on to college. In her writing that makes up the next activity, she writes about moving-in day at college.

Here you will do the same. First, on the lines provided, answer the questions. Then, on a separate sheet of paper, reflect on a time either when something new *happened* to you or when something new *will happen* to you. In your paragraph include some of the writing techniques Marissa uses here.

(1) I assumed that life was its own preparation. (2) Somehow, life naturally prepared us for the next, larger step. (3) But I never expected that step to be such a leap. (4) You figure that in high school, we all learn how to become real, to cope and experience reality in its pure, raw form. (5) But life in high school is still very sheltered. (6) You see the same people and know the same not-knowings. (7) When you go to college, there is always someone new, something you did not know, some new life experience. (8) For the most part, my friends and I spent most of our time and energy finding a way to rebel against our sheltered lives. (9) Yet when I went to college, I missed the old, regulated way of life I was used to. (10) Perhaps it became easier to adapt to college life because I was able to enjoy the freedom it had to offer. (11) I had previously visited what was to be my new home, but I had not seen it as that, a home. (12) Like the first day of grade school, college was a little scary at first glance. (13) I wondered if I would find happiness here. . . .

1. Other than introducing the topic, what is the purpose of sentence 1?

   _____

   _____

2. What effect does Marissa hope to attain with her third sentence? _____

   _____

3. What techniques does the writer employ to make the reader feel comfortable with the topic? _____

4. List two contrasts found in the paragraph. _____

   _____

5. Provide an adjective that depicts the tone of the paragraph. Support your choice.

   _____

   _____

© 1999 by The Center for Applied Research in Education

Name _____ Date _____ Period _____

6-30. SOMETHING NEW (PART TWO)

In the second portion of this two-part activity, high school student Marissa Heller envisions the happenings of her freshman moving-in day at college. This chronological narration includes dialogue, internal monologue, sensory details, appropriate level of vocabulary, and character description.

On a separate sheet of paper, recount (or imagine) a day in which you took on "something new." Include the same writing tools that Marissa does in this narration. Your teacher will set some other guidelines (including length) for this writing. You may want to share your writings with your classmates. (Sentences 14–78 pick up where the first portion of this writing, "Something New (Part One)," left off.

(14) I promise myself I will not cry. (15) It is hard to leave my old friends and family when they are all I know. (16) My parents and I pull up in front of my dorm. (17) My mother opens the car door for me as if I am some Hollywood big-shot, her own secret superstar. (18) I can see her eyes sparkling with pride. (19) Her wet tears make them glisten in the sun. (20) I step outside. (21) Looking back, I expect to fall into the arms of my past, hoping to be taken home. (22) But with their hidden tears, they smile to assure my success in this new world. (23) Saying goodbye is especially hard for my mother.

(24) "I can't believe my baby has grown so much."

(25) "Gosh Mom, I'll be back in a few weeks."

(26) "There'll be no one else in the house now that you're gone."

(27) I know this is hard for her. (28) I am her only child. (29) She feels the signs of aging moving faster now. (30) The slow hand on the clock is winding up, ready to speed up at any moment. (31) It is very unsettling. (32) I want to assure her that things will be all right, but that is her job. (33) Looking into her eyes, I am glad that I have gotten to know her so well over these last few years.

(34) My father doesn't say much. (35) I don't think he has much to add to the list of lessons I have already been taught. (36) He leans over and gives me a kiss on the cheek.

(37) "You'll be fine. (38) You'll find that college is a breeze."

(39) My dad makes me laugh when he says things like that. (40) Yeah right, like college is really going to be that easy. (41) He thinks everything is easy for me. (42) I keep telling him I hate him for thinking that way. (43) I don't want him to think that I don't work hard.

(44) "Shut up, Dad." (45) I start to laugh, but the tears are running down my cheeks. (46) They feel like icicles. (47) I don't know where all this pain suddenly came from.

(48) "We love you so much. (49) We are very proud of you." (50) My parents give me these last words to remember. (51) They hug me so tightly I can feel my breath pause. (52) I wish I could hold them tighter. (53) I watch them walk slowly toward the car. (54) My mother is still turning around every other step, just to make sure I am still watching her leave. (55) They wave goodbye. (56) I can still feel their smiles.

(57) I turn around and pick up my bags. (58) There are so many people here. (59) It makes me feel small, almost insignificant. (60) Looking around in my new environment, I am scared. (61) I know it is normal to be nervous, but it is difficult to accept what is normal.

(62) My room is on the third floor. (63) It is a good thing that there is an elevator. (64) I have probably over-packed, but I want to make a good impression. (65) Once I am in my room, I find my roommate already settled in. (66) She is putting up posters.

(67) "If you want to use them, I brought these to decorate the room." (68) I point to my bundle of Red-Hot-Chili-Peppers' lights.

(69) She smiles. (70) "Those are really cool. (71) My name is Jamie; you must be Marissa."

(72) "Yeah. (73) How long have you been here?"

(74) "I just got here a few hours ago."

(75) Immediately my heart has stopped racing. (76) Her smile is so securing. (77) It shows an element of fear, just as mine does. (78) It proves she is human.

6-31. JOEY

Student writer Ali DeVita writes a character sketch of her friend Joey. Notice what Ali chooses to present and how she presents that material. First, number the paragraphs 1–6 in the left margin. Then, on a separate sheet of paper, answer the six questions. Finally, on another sheet of paper, using some of the same techniques Ali does here, write a character sketch about a friend, celebrity, literary character, or another interesting person.

(1) She was a senior, and I was a freshman. (2) I didn't think we had anything in common. (3) She was the editor-in-chief, and I could barely manage to put two sentences together. (4) She had mastered several instruments, and I was a novice in two. (5) She spoke her mind with confidence while I often found myself tongue-tied. (6) Who would have thought we had anything in common? (7) Who would have thought we would end up best friends?

(8) I first met her at the newspaper. (9) She was tall, had long black hair, and an intense gaze that exuded confidence. (10) She did most of the talking, telling us what to do and how to do it. (11) I could manage a couple of words, which made sense in my mind, but by the time they got to my mouth, they came out jumbled. (12) Instead of making fun of me, she thought I was funny. (13) We had one friend in common, and we began to run into each other outside of school. (14) We quickly became very close friends.

(15) Once I got to really know her, I discovered we were so similar we could have been sisters. (16) We liked the same clothes and would often come to school dressed alike. (17) We enjoyed the same music, and even played the same instruments. (18) We both played soccer and, best of all, she shared my love of the beach.

(19) Most importantly, she was different from my other friends. (20) She never viewed me as inferior, even though she was better than I was at most things. (21) She accepted me for who I was and, for the first time, I didn't have to pretend. (22) I could be myself. (23) And she liked me for me.

(24) As our friendship deepened, I realized that she was human and had faults, just like me. (25) Although on the surface she seemed to have it all together, underneath she, too, was unsure of many things. (26) Together, we learned that it was okay not to be perfect, to have doubts, to be silly, to be scared. (27) Together, we learned what it was like to really let a friend inside, to the place that no one else was permitted to go. (28) At first it was scary, to have someone know me so well. (29) But it was wonderful to know that there was someone in the world who really understood me—and liked me just the way I was.

(30) Joey is one of the most amazing people I have ever met. (31) And while I am sure I will meet many people and have many different friends, no one will ever fill her shoes.

1. Write the purpose (no more than one sentence) for each of the six paragraphs.

2. What writing techniques does Ali employ in the first paragraph?

3. Which two paragraphs are stylistically similar?

4. Make up a title for the fifth paragraph.

5. Why does Ali repeat "She" (first paragraph) and "We" (third paragraph) as often as she does?

6-32. YOUR TOWN (PART ONE)

Here student writer Adam Rohksar tells us about his town, Cold Spring Harbor. This excerpt is the first of four sections from Adam's composition. The original assignment Adam was given was to emulate the style used by Albert Camus in his novel *The Plague*. Camus opens this novel by telling the reader about Oran, a large French port on the Algerian coast. Adam did a wonderful job in imitating Camus' style, and Camus would be proud of his efforts.

Directions: Answer the following questions regarding Adam's writing, and then, on a separate piece of paper, copy Adam's style by writing two paragraphs as you tell us about your town. (The number in parentheses indicates the sentence's number in this two-paragraph excerpt.)

(1) The stories that color the town of Cold Spring Harbor are hardly apparent at a first glance. (2) Indeed, no more than a first glance may be deemed necessary by the casual observer. (3) But the impatient eye often errs, as it would if it were to write Cold Spring Harbor away as a quaint town by the water.

(4) There is no denying the physical allure of the town. (5) Its single main street is lined by small shops stocked with oddities and trinkets to catch the eyes. (6) The early morning sleepiness doesn't fade with the climbing of the sun, and you cannot help but feel comfortable walking the town's cracked sidewalks. (7) But to solely detail the town itself would be a gross oversight, for it is the water that distinguishes Cold Spring Harbor. (8) It lies as the centerpiece of the town, the source of its breath and spirit. (9) On some days, you might find it calming; more than one soul has stopped to gaze upon the gentle lapping, the ripples of sunlight that touches areas unknown. (10) Or, if you come on a more troubled day, it may quietly seize you with its restless waves and gray depths.

1. What is the purpose of the first sentence? _____
   _____

2. What specific images back up Adam's claim in the fourth sentence?
   _____

3. According to Adam, what is Cold Spring Harbor's most prominent aspect?
   _____

4. What effects does the water have on people? _____
   _____

5. Point out two transitional words/phrases Adam uses. Give the specific function of these transitions. _____
   _____

6. Select three adjectives and explain why they are used effectively.
   _____
   _____

6-33. YOUR TOWN (PART TWO)

In this second excerpt from his composition emulating Albert Camus' style in the opening pages of *The Plague*, student writer Adam Rohksar writes about the various seasons of the year evident in his hometown, Cold Spring Harbor. This group of eight sentences is the second paragraph of Adam's composition; the initial section is found in the activity "Your Town (Part One)." After reading this passage, answer the five questions and then, on a separate piece of paper, write about the seasons in your hometown. Compare your writings with those of your classmates.

(1) The smell of water accompanies you throughout your ventures here, a lingering reminder that stretches back to the days of the fishermen and sailing vessels. (2) The smell remains even as the seasons come to and fro bearing changes on the wind. (3) Summer brings huge blue skies and the taste of green newness. (4) The hot sidewalks become crowded with travelers and locals, all loud and eager to explore the stores or the parks. (5) With autumn, there is the ever-present crunching of leaves, the melancholy branches of trees that seem to yearn for the sky. (6) When winter descends, it is not entirely unbelievable to think that you have stumbled into a storybook wonderland, complete with gently smoking chimneys and snow-covered shops. (7) Winter here is the only season when the sun is small and not as present as during the other seasons. (8) Spring, on the other hand, is announced by the sun's return, the scent of rebirth and possibility in the young leaves.

1. Which sentence is the topic sentence of this excerpt? Why? _____

_____

2. Many of Adam's adjectives have strong sensory appeal. Select two that appeal to the sense of hearing. _____

3. Select two adjectives that appeal to the sense of sight. _____

_____

_____

4. List the transitions that Adam employs to move from one season to another.

_____

_____

5. Which of the season's description is your favorite? Why? _____

_____

_____

© 1999 by The Center for Applied Research in Education

Name _____ Date _____ Period _____

6-34. YOUR TOWN (PART THREE)

Student writer Adam Rohksar's third excerpt from his composition about his town contains the following 14 sentences. Answer the five questions in the spaces provided and then, on a separate piece of paper, write a paragraph describing the type of people living in your town. As Adam does, show what influences your community members to be the way they are.

(1) The inhabitants of Cold Spring Harbor are generally thinkers. (2) This haphazard generalization may seem ambiguous, perhaps even erroneous, but once you've walked our streets and broken first impressions, you may well find some truth to it. (3) This is not to say that we produce a plethora of geniuses. (4) Granted, the Cold Spring Harbor Laboratories may attract a certain type of learner, but this is not the type of thought prevalent in our town. (5) Rather, it is a type of thinker who thinks because he, quite simply, is often left alone. (6) Cold Spring Harbor is a town that can almost be identified by its silence. (7) A solitary moment by the park or near the water may come when you least expect it, and moments like these have left a lasting impression on our citizens. (8) We are forced to be alone at times, to think without the regimented direction of conversation. (9) Perhaps the word "thinker" is as accurate as "explorer," a sort of explorer of the self. (10) However, we must not exaggerate. (11) We are not a town of spiritual wanderers or soul seekers. (12) Rather, we are simply a people given something that many others lack—time and a chance to be alone. (13) We are surrounded by answers that may come in the form of whispering tides or calling gulls. (14) Though many of us never find the answers we seek (or indeed even be aware that we were seeking at all), we are aware of things that often get trodden in the busy streets of a metropolis.

1. What is Adam's intention in this paragraph? Give examples to support your answer.

   _____

   _____

2. Is the topic sentence stated or implied? _____

3. What specifics does Adam offer to show what influences the people of his town?

   _____

   _____

4. What are some words used by Adam to display his sophisticated vocabulary? Give the definitions of some of the words you did not know.

   _____

   _____

5. List the different types of people inhabiting Cold Spring Harbor. _____

   _____

   _____

6-35. YOUR TOWN (PART FOUR)

In this final excerpt from student writer Adam Rohksar, the author concludes his thoughts about Cold Spring Harbor, his hometown. Answer the four questions on the lines provided, then make up two of your own questions and answer them. Finally, on the reverse side of this page, give two ways in which this excerpt fittingly concludes Adam's composition.

(1) The more tangible results of these thoughts is that there is not a soul in Cold Spring Harbor without a story. (2) This is hardly unique; (3) every town has a thousand stories to tell. (4) But at Cold Spring Harbor the stories are more present in the mind of its people, simply because they have more time to be thought about. (5) In other towns, lives are often lived without the time needed to reflect, to internalize, and to draw conclusions. (6) There is no shortage of this time here. (7) You may find that in the course of a seemingly casual exchange, your new acquaintance has just revealed wounds years deep for you to see without a second thought. (8) At first, you may find this practice odd, and perhaps even a bit disconcerting. (9) Soon, however, you will see that there are stories to tell in our town. (10) It is freeing for us, sharing pieces of our lives with near strangers. (11) The stories that we make are different from those of other towns, if only because our citizens tell them.

1. What would be an appropriate title for this single paragraph?

   _____

2. What is a contrast Adam utilizes here? _____

   _____

   _____

3. Comment on the types of sentences found in this paragraph. Are they simple sentences? Sophisticated? Why? _____

   _____

   _____

4. Adam speaks of the inhabitants' dependency on others. Where does he show this to be true? _____

   _____

   _____

© 1999 by The Center for Applied Research in Education

SECTION THREE

WRITING AWAY

6-36. REACHING THEM

Audience. Plain and simple. Audience. As a writer, you must know your audience members and use the proper writing techniques to reach them. Vocabulary that is either far beyond or below the readers could be a problem. So could literary or historical allusions that are unfamiliar to your readers. The structure and length of your sentences must be appropriately chosen to suit your reading (or listening) audience.

Consider Shakespeare's dilemma. Here is a playwright whose audience consisted of rich and poor, royal and commoner, literate and nearly illiterate. Which audience did he try to reach? His language was quite sophisticated, and some of his images included nature, historical, and other bits of required knowledge not familiar to the typical Elizabethan audience member. Perhaps several of his plays' early scenes including three witches (*Macbeth*), a brawl (*Romeo and Juliet*), and a ghost returning to seek revenge (*Hamlet*) exemplify how Shakespeare had to capture the attention of the groundlings, the unsophisticated, and often, unintelligent and uneducated, members of his audience. He probably felt that once he had their attention (and quieted their talking and curbed their possible misbehaviors!), he could move on to the higher-level concepts of refined language and debatable actions and themes.

Directions: Today you will experience what all writers experience—reaching the intended audience. You will pretend that you are writing a speech for various audiences. First, select two of the scenarios below. Then, on a separate sheet of paper, write the opening paragraph of the speech for those two particular audiences. Pay attention to vocabulary, sentence structure, sentence length, allusions, opening sentences, and tone. Compare your writings with those of your classmates.

- *Scenario #1:* You must deliver a speech on AIDS. Your two audiences are (A) a fourth-grade class and (B) a senior high school biology class.

- *Scenario #2:* You must deliver a speech about why there is day and why there is night. Your two audiences are (A) a second-grade class and (B) a tenth-grade class.

- *Scenario #3:* You will deliver a speech in which you state reasons why some people are in favor of the death penalty. Your two audiences are (A) a fifth-grade class and (B) a senior high school social studies class.

- *Scenario #4:* You must deliver a speech on why _____ is your favorite writer (or actor or musician or painter or celebrity or . . .). Your two audiences are (A) your last three English teachers and (B) your closest friends.

6-37. TAYLOR'S BUCKET

Would you like to write for your school newspaper or your future college newspaper? Perhaps you could even have a career as a writer for a local or city paper. Today's activity might help you to decide.

Below is a typical sports story that could appear in a newspaper. It recounts a high school basketball game and, in particular, one player's accomplishments. First, read some newspaper articles to see the usual format. Take notice of the various writers' styles including angle (or focus), details, quotes, and more. Decide which type of article you would like to write. Will it be a news story, a feature story, a sports story, or some other type? Then, on a separate piece of paper, invent a story (as the one below is), and write a newspaper account of it.

Taylor's Bucket Captures Victory For Stevenson

Here we are in the depths of January, snow piled up all over the city, and Jeremiah Taylor is thinking about July. Not next July—last July. Recalling those dog days, Taylor remembers the shooting drill he practiced day after day at Kenny Loudon's Basketball Camp. Summer's work has turned into winter's rewards.

Last night Stevenson High School moved into first place in the Presidential League with its last-second 62–61 victory over rival Truman at the City Center. The hero of the game was Jeremiah Taylor, Stevenson's 6'2" shooting guard. Taylor's 27 points were eclipsed only by his last-minute heroics as he dribbled the length of the court and sank a fifteen-foot jump shot just before the buzzer sounded. The crowd of 1,650 erupted as Taylor's swish shot trickled through the net. Taylor, carried off the court on his teammates' shoulders, raised both arms and waved ecstatically to Stevenson's fans.

Last summer Taylor was one of 150 high school boys who attended Loudon's camp, a two-week session in July where the campers work on various aspects of their game. Coming into the camp, Taylor was a fair shooter. "He could shoot the ball as well as about half the boys there," Ralph Wilson, the camp's shooting coach remarked. "He needed to work on his stamina, and he had to learn to shoot the ball more consistently." Wilson worked with Taylor, devising a 45-minute shooting drill that would not only increase Taylor's stamina, but it would also give him better range and shooting opportunities.

Needless to say, what the spectators saw at the City Center last night did not happen overnight—or without much hard work and determination. Taylor performed Wilson's shooting drill twice a day during Loudon's camp and has done the same every day since. The once fair shooter has become a fine shooter. In the locker room after the game, Taylor reflectively said, "Coach says he wants the ball in my hands in a clutch situation. Last night was the payoff for all the time I have spent knocking down those shots in practice. The camp was the start of even better things to come because I still have a long way to go with my shooting if I want to be an outstanding college player."

Stevenson's win on a night when the thermometer did not go above the freezing mark had its beginnings in a 99-degree gymnasium last July. Just ask Jeremiah Taylor. He remembers July.

6-38. YOU GIVE AND THEY FOLLOW

Clear directions are a joy to behold. Unclear directions can be the ruination of one's day.

These two sentences sum up most people's feelings regarding directions. Well-written directions make one's life trouble-free. The opposite holds true for those badly written directions. So write those directions clearly and concisely!

Select one of the ten procedures below and write accurate and understandable directions for completing that procedure. Though your directions may initially be written in a list format, write the final copy in prose. Make proper use of transitions and other linking words. After you have finished writing your final set of directions, test them out to ensure that they are accurate and understandable.

Write the directions (or procedures) for:

1. getting from your school to your house

2. applying eyeliner

3. brushing your teeth properly

4. tying your shoes

5. making waffles

6. fixing a flat on a bicycle

7. successfully completing a lay-up in basketball (starting with dribbling the ball from near the foul line)

8. bowling a strike (starting with picking up the ball from the ball-return area)

9. making a peanut butter and jelly sandwich (starting with unopened jars of peanut butter and jelly)

10. writing the word *universality* in script (instructing someone who has a limited knowledge of how to write in script)

6-39. FRENCH OR SPANISH?

The choice is yours today. You can write a story using words the English language has borrowed from the French or those words borrowed from the Spanish. This work of fiction should have either ten words from the French, ten words from the Spanish, or five from each. Your teacher will tell you the story's length. Write this story on a separate piece of paper.

French Words	Spanish Words
alliance	banana
attorney	barbecue
authority	bonanza
bizarre	cafeteria
charity	cannibal
clergy	canyon
detail	chili
essay	fiesta
explore	hammock
government	lariat
judge	macho
jury	mosquito
mayor	potato
religion	pronto
ticket	sombrero
trophy	stampede
verdict	tobacco

6-40. THE POET IN YOU

The object of this activity is to write a poem that has 26 lines. Start the first line with a word that begins with an A, the second line with a B, and so forth, all the way to Z. For more of a challenge, try the following. Since there are 26 lines, the line starting with the A word should have one word in it; the line starting with the B word should have two words in it; the line starting with the C word should have three words in it, all the way to the concluding line of the poem that should have 26 words it. The following poem, "War," is given as an example. Share your poem with your classmates.

War

"Attack"

Be prepared.

Could it be?

Did he hear correctly?

Everybody's on his own, again.

Fusillades fell quickly all around him.

Grenades and missiles filled the darkened skies.

Hit by the bullet, the soldier fell forward.

Injuries are all too common when wars are fought.

Justice, they say, is seldom found on these bloody battlefields.

Kindness, care, and concern for your enemy are scorned upon here.

Looking at his bloodied and shattered leg, the soldier began to cry.

Months of training for such a situation did not help him much now.

Never before had he felt such awful pain or wanted so much to live.

On many occasions he had imagined himself in this situation, struggling hard to stay alive.

"Perhaps," he thought, "this is how life and dreams will end, shattered on this horrendous battlefield."

Quietly, he thought about why he was here now, why he was dying, why he had lived.

Ruefully, the soldier began to prepare for death by giving in to the excruciating pain, hoping to die.

Slowly, this hurt began to slip away and a comfort, one that he had never felt before, overwhelmed him.

To die in such an inhumane way, bloodied and alone on this distant battlefield, was not what he had imagined.

Untimely death, unwarranted death, that death that poets and mystics acclaim and even revere, has the devil's print all over it.

Villainous leaders who seek to win glory for their country (and themselves) will never know who he was or what he did.

"When they bury me far from this horrible place," he thought, "they'll talk of honors and victories and all that kind of stuff."

"X" is my name to those men whose medals won't tell of the blood and guts and more we left here on the fields.

Youth has been wasted for the glory of the select few who spent the war in plush restaurants and slept comfortably through the air attacks.

Zero in, my friends, and know well this monster called war is a living hell that few of you will know as this dead soldier has.

6-41. THE NEIGHBOR

The following story sketches a character. Using techniques such as details, first-person narration, transitions, vivid description, diction, and syntax, the writer creates this look at Mr. Frank Monahan.

On a separate piece of paper, create a story about a character. Include the same techniques (and more) that were used here. Make your story both creative and memorable.

Nobody had ever seen the inside of Mr. Monahan's garage—until last night. For the past thirty years, Mr. Frank Monahan had lived in our middle-class neighborhood outside Boston. We knew very little about his present life—and nothing about his past. He was a soft spoken, elderly man who had lost his wife to bone cancer about twenty summers ago. Childless and living alone, Mr. M., as we called him, seldom came outside his house except to collect his mail from the black mailbox located just outside his front door.

Monahan was certainly not in the best physical condition. Arthritis had severely curtailed Mr. M.'s movement. Generally, trudging stooped-shouldered with head bent toward the ground, Monahan found each step a task. Yet, still capable of driving, Monahan would leave for about an hour each Friday evening. Quietly, Mr. M. would back his car out of his driveway and proceed slowly down our long street heading toward the local supermarket. Without fail, he would return an hour later with two small bags of groceries—supposedly enough to keep him fed until next Friday evening when the ritual was repeated.

Never had we seen his garage door open. He always entered and exited his house through a dilapidated gray-stained front door. When not in use, Monahan's car, a rather old two-door model with numerous dents and scratches, not to mention the rust, was always parked in his driveway. The garage door was also terribly weather-beaten, and its three small cob-webbed windows were so dirty that it would take a good hour's worth of hard scrubbing to make them somewhat presentable enough to see into the garage. Assuredly, the small wheels and iron tracks along which this garage door traveled back and forth as it was raised or lowered were in terrible need of serious oiling. Maybe that was why Monahan never used the door. Yes, we thought, it was probably too hard to manipulate for this frail man.

Last night Mr. M. died. The newspaper reported that he was 82. We thought he was 100. When neighbors saw his mail starting to pile up, they called the police. That night, a rookie cop broke into Monahan's house around midnight. She found him in his den—slumped dead in his favorite chair. His television was still blaring with some infomercial about life insurance.

A few hours later, two police officers went to check out Mr. M.'s garage. Not surprisingly, the door had to be smashed in with a sledgehammer before they could enter. Shining her flashlight, the female cop was the first to see what had been a mystery to an entire neighborhood for many years. There, hanging on the back wall, was the front page of an old newspaper. Now quite worn, dusty, and ripped in spots, the page showed a handsome, muscular runner standing atop the Olympic podium with his first-place medal being placed around his neck. The faded letters of the picture's caption read, "U.S. Olympian Frank Monahan Sets World Marathon Record."

6-42. MEET THE TRIPPS

In this piece you will learn about the members of the Tripp family, especially Daddy and Nathan. Read the short piece. Then, considering the elements that go into effectively describing a character, rate the story 1–10 with 10 as the highest possible rating. Justify why you gave it this rating. Use the reverse side of this paper for that purpose. Finally, on another sheet of paper, complete this story by adding another 150–200 words to it. Share your endings with your classmates.

His father had abandoned the family when Nathan, the oldest of six children, was only eight years old. Nathan's mother, uneducated and accustomed to a life of poverty and dreams that never came true, never spoke about the day Daddy Tripp left—never to return to their decaying three-room, tar-roofed shack along the banks of the Chicot River.

Momma Tripp had married Daddy when she was only sixteen in her attempt to, as she would always say, "get some of the good life." He had promised her that—and more. Nathan arrived exactly six months after his parents, in the company of a Justice of the Peace, vowed "to love one another for better or for worse." Better never appeared; worse was their constant companion. Jobs were scarce those days, and Daddy Tripp's love of liquor did not help him gain favor with his bosses—seven or so in just ten years. Daddy had a mind of his own and found taking orders almost impossible. Thus, he would seldom hold down a job for more than a few months—the longest three hundred two days with Mista Merkel, a man who barely paid a living wage but treated his workers like family—picnics, turkeys at Thanksgiving, and a few birthday toys at Christmas for the "little uns."

Ever since he was quite young, Nathan had watched and listened to what Daddy did and said, vowing to himself that now that Daddy was gone, poverty and want would never again set foot in the "Tripp Place," as the townsfolk called it. Responsibility had robbed Nathan of his youth, but this Tripp was determined to make a name for himself and his family. Nothing—and no one—were going to stop him.

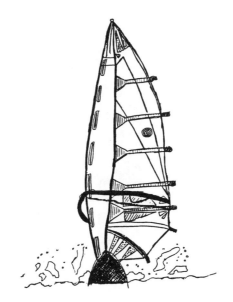

6-43. STORY STARTERS

Here are the first lines of ten possible stories. Use any one of them to start your 300-word story. Make the plot interesting by including a conflict, good details, and effective character development. Write your story on a separate piece of paper. Share your story with your classmates.

1. Uncle Ted had warned us.

2. Our teacher, Mr. Terrinn, slammed the door and scowled at the two students who had given the substitute teacher a hard time yesterday.

3. Joan never saw the other car coming.

4. You never truly know everything about someone.

5. His mother's voice told it all.

6. It was early December.

7. She shuffled her deck of cards.

8. The names of those selected for the team had been posted an hour ago.

9. This place gives me the creeps.

10. A crisp autumn wind blew through the trees.

© 1999 by The Center for Applied Research in Education

6-44. NEW YORK AND PARIS

As a writer, you could be asked to compare and/or contrast two subjects such as two animals, two jobs, or two cities, let's say, New York and Paris. Comparing is showing how New York and Paris are similar, and contrasting is showing how New York and Paris are different.

You can organize this New York–Paris comparison–contrast essay through a couple of different methods. One is the *subject-by-subject* (New York vs. Paris) comparison method in which you discuss aspects about New York, and then, usually in another paragraph, discuss aspects of Paris. Thus, each city should get its own paragraph. The last portion of this essay, usually another paragraph, should emphasize the two cities' greatest similarity or difference.

Another method is the *point-by-point* or *topic-by-topic* comparison. Here you would select several topics for both New York and Paris and then arrange these topics in some intelligent and logical order. Each topic, e.g., location, cultural attractions, or hotel accommodations, is usually given its own paragraph and features a discussion of the first topic (location) for New York and then a discussion of that same topic (location) for Paris. An effective topic sentence and clear examples are necessary here. Either of these standard comparison–contrast methods is equally acceptable.

Directions: Select one of the situations below. On a separate piece of paper, write a comparison–contrast essay in which you compare and/or contrast the two subjects. Brainstorm and outline the essay first. Then start your first draft.

- Two fast-food restaurants

- The park in your town on a sunny day and then on a rainy day

- Two cars your family has owned

- Two current rock groups

- Your bedroom and a friend's bedroom

- Your current home and your former home

- Two newspaper or magazine articles about your country's current leader

- This year's social studies class and last year's social studies class

- Two geometric figures

- Two relatives

- Your relationship with two of your friends

- College sports and professional sports

6-45. INTERPRETING QUOTATIONS

Good writers are usually intelligent readers. Reading the words of wise men and women will help you become a better writer. Not only will you observe how cleverly these writers use words to attain their purpose, but you will also see how well they choose their words.

This activity invites you to paraphrase the words of these craftsmen. On the line(s) beneath each quote, write what you think the writer is saying. Compare your answers with those of your classmates.

1. "Learning is its own exceeding great reward." (*William Hazlitt*)

_____

_____

2. "The first prerogative of an artist in any medium is to make a fool of himself." (*Pauline Kael*)

_____

_____

3. "The reward of a thing well done is to have done it." (*Ralph Waldo Emerson*)

_____

_____

4. "If misery loves company, misery has company enough." (*Henry David Thoreau*)

_____

_____

5. "Anger as soon as fed is dead—'Tis starving makes it fat—." (*Emily Dickinson*)

_____

_____

6-46. HUMPTY DUMPTY

In this persuasive essay the writer analyzes the nursery rhyme "Humpty Dumpty." The humorous tone gives life to this essay. On a separate piece of paper, select a nursery rhyme character and, using many of the same techniques utilized in this Humpty Dumpty essay, write a humorous analysis of a nursery rhyme. What is funny about it? Point out the rhyme's illogical elements and other interesting aspects. "Jack and Jill," "Little Miss Muffet," and "Old King Cole" are some possible rhymes.

> Humpty Dumpty sat on a wall,
> Humpty Dumpty had a great fall;
> All the king's horses and all the king's men
> Couldn't put Humpty together again.

There is this idea going around that Humpty Dumpty is an egg. Where in this four-line poem does it say that? Just because all those illustrators depict Mr. Dumpty as an egg does not mean that he is definitely an egg. After all, how can an egg balance itself atop a wall? Would that not be defying the laws of physics? And how would an egg get up there? Okay, if Humpty has legs, as I see in this illustration, he would be the first egg to have legs. That would defy the laws of biology! Chickens have legs, but eggs don't have legs. Be reasonable—please.

Now let us take a look at this fall that Humpty had. Again, our friendly illustrators want us to believe that this Mr. Humpty Dumpty, this legged-egg, cracked when he fell from this wall's heights. Nonsense. This fall could be an emotional breakdown. This fall could be a fall from grace akin to the misdeeds of one in a prominent and conspicuous position. And what was so great about this fall I ask you? Have you ever had a great fall? Unless it is the season that follows summer, I have never had a great fall and probably never will have a great fall. I leave those *great falls* for those downhill skiers who think that careening down a sharp mountain at breakneck speed is fun.

Now when I am told that all the king's horses and all the king's men couldn't put Humpty together again, I become a bit suspicious. Exactly where did all this mending thing happen? If I am to believe that Humpty is an egg, how can I begin to believe that *all* these men were gathered at one place at one time? How many men were there working on Dumpty? I cannot imagine many guys working on poor Dumpty at the exact same time. Would legions of soldiers and innumerable royal confidants attempt to repair Mr. Dumpty at once? Never. They are too busy trying to make the king happy. And what would these guys use to mend the broken Humpty? Exactly how does one put a cracked egg back together? Do you see the logic here? Horses trying to put Humpty Dumpty back together again? I don't think so. What would a horse do? Would it become glue in order to mend the broken egg? What horse would give his life for an egg that was stupid enough to climb up a wall, sit on it, and then fall from it? I wouldn't, and I hope to think that a horse, though not so intelligent as a human being, but apparently more intelligent than Dumpty, would not sacrifice himself for this spastic egg.

So the next time you think about Humpty Dumpty, don't let those illustrators fool you. He was not the poor egg they make him out to be. Instead, he was one who made an error in judgment, attempted to defy the laws of nature, and paid the price for his foolishness. End of story—and end of Humpty!

6-47. KIDS' TV

An article by Nick Gillespie, the executive editor of *Reason* magazine, appeared on page A17 in the July 6, 1999, edition of *The New York Times*. His article "Does Kids' TV Have to Be Edifying?" addresses the educational value of children's television. Gillespie takes issue with the findings of the Annenberg Public Policy Center, a group that conducted the research on children's television.

Directions: Pretend you are Mr. Gillespie and write a 200-word essay that includes at least three reasons why children's television is not so harmful as some people think. An excerpt from *The New York Times* article appears below. Write your essay on a separate piece of paper.

"...the Annenberg Public Policy Center at the University of Pennsylvania has concluded that there's little of value in children's television. The authors found that 28 percent of children's programs contained four or more acts of violence, that 45 percent contained 'problematic' language and that only a third of shows classified as 'educational' under guidelines set by the Federal Communication Commission were in fact 'highly educational.' The others, said the researchers, were only 'moderately' or 'minimally' so."

—*The New York Times*, July 6, 1999, p. A17

© 1999 by The Center for Applied Research in Education

6-48. ANDREA BOCELLI

In this assignment student writer Michelle Bellino was asked to relate Gerard Bauer's quote, "The voice is a second face," to something or someone in her life. She chose the singer Andrea Bocelli. On a separate piece of paper, take on the role of a writing instructor and comment on the aspects of Michelle's writing that you enjoy. Consider tone, vocabulary, sentence length, sentence structure, sentence variety, sensory images, transitions, and voice. Essentially, how well does Michelle connect the quote to her experience with Andrea Bocelli? If your teacher asks you, use Bauer's quote and follow the rules that Michelle did here. Good luck and write well!

(1) His name is Andrea Bocelli, and I am in love with his voice. (2) I only heard him a few days ago, but I cannot remember what music was like before I heard his voice. (3) It is a different kind of music for me. (4) But it is more than the music; (5) it is the way he sings. (6) He sings in Italian, and I cannot understand the words or sing along, so it forces me to listen, completely unarmed and open-minded. (7) Though I do not know what his words mean, they carry in them so much passion that I can feel his undying love, his insides all twisted up over this girl whom he cannot be without. (8) Each morning I wake myself up to "Con te Partiró," beginning my day with something so beyond me in its wonder; (9) it makes me believe that there are still so many masterpieces not yet created. (10) I cannot imagine what it must feel like to be able to create music with your voice, saying words that have all been said a million times before, notes that have already been sung. (11) How does one hear the music, that sensitive poetry of the ear, and know enough to give his voice to it, to give himself to the music? (12) As I listen, I am in pain with him; (13) I feel what is meant for me to feel; (14) I need not understand the words. (15) That I don't know what the words mean makes it all so much more beautiful.

(16) I ride through Cold Spring Harbor, windows open, Andrea Bocelli dominating the midday sounds of the road. (17) Heads turn to look at me, the one with that strange music. (18) Even for that one moment that people hear his voice, seeping out the slits of open window and escaping into the air, they too know this power; (19) they are in awe at this magic the same way I was when it first found me.

(20) Still, I like to keep him a secret, tell only those who will understand his greatness. (21) My favorite place to listen to his songs is in my bedroom, door closed, volume high, and Bocelli captures the entire room, sound bouncing off the walls like I am at a symphony. (22) The words fill me until drunk with them. "Con te partiró. Paesi che non ho mai veduto e vissuto con te, adesso si li vivró." (23) His voice makes me tremble. (24) It makes me want to know the world and my roots; (25) it makes me yearn for Italy.

(26) I will probably never hear Andrea Bocelli sing in a real opera or meet him on the street, but I do not need to see his face to know his power.

6-49. AMERICAN GOTHIC

Describing a scene is not as easy as it seems, particularly if your reader has never seen the scene. What pattern of description should the writer use? Is a top-to-bottom, left-to-right, or middle-to-sides approach the best way to describe the scene? Is there a best way? Does it depend on the scene itself?

Directions: In the following three paragraphs, the writer describes Grant Wood's *American Gothic.* First read his description. You might even attempt to sketch the painting based on his description. Then find the painting in an art book and see how accurate his description is. Finally, select a piece of artwork, a painting or a sculpture, and, as the writer does here, describe it as precisely as possible. Share the artwork and your writing with your classmates.

American Gothic, an oil painting by American artist Grant Wood, depicts a stern, solemn-faced, staid farm couple with their farmhouse and barn behind them. The long-faced, balding man holds a pitchfork in his huge right hand. The farmer's dark protruding eyes, round-rimmed glasses, and tight lips contribute to his austere appearance. He is wearing a dark sweater that partially covers his overalls and white shirt.

His dour-looking female companion, standing left and a bit behind him, looks simultaneously off into the distance and at the man. Her hair, pulled tightly against her head, is parted down the middle. She wears a white-collared black dress, a calico-designed apron with rickrack at the top, and a cameo.

Their barn, located to the right and rear of the couple, is typical for its day. The same can be said for their Carpenter Gothic farmhouse with its A-framed roof, two long rectangular windows on the first level, and the customary front and side porches. The upstairs front of the house is white and has a Gothic-style curtained window in the middle.

6-50. A TEENAGER'S STRESSFUL LIFE

In this persuasive essay, student writer Craig Weiss expresses his opinion as to what contributes to the stress in the lives of today's teenagers. Following a standard five-paragraph approach, Craig uses the first paragraph as introduction, the middle three paragraphs as supporting examples, and the short final paragraph as conclusion.

Directions: On a separate piece of paper, argue one of the following issues using the same format Craig does. **(A)** Cell phones should not be used while one is operating a motor vehicle. **(B)** Students who average A- or better in a specific course should be exempt from that course's final examination. **(C)** CDs containing profanity and other vulgarity cannot be sold to anyone under sixteen years of age. **(D)** Too much emphasis is placed on standardized tests such as state tests, SATs, and ACTs.

The life of today's teenager is a very trying time. At one minute, one can be sitting on top of the world and the next minute that same person can be having suicidal tendencies. Being a teenager in this decade can be summed up in one word—*stress.* Teens are exposed to many different pressures throughout their lives. The origins of the tensions vary. They can range from school, to the athletic fields, to at-home responsibilities.

A teen's responsibility in school is probably the main source of stress. Probably the worst feeling a teen can experience is the one that arrives on a Sunday night. This is one of pure, unadulterated apprehension. The typical teenager has a horrible habit of procrastination; thus, he or she saves school work for the wee hours of Sunday night. This intense feeling of anxiety is also at its strongest when a report, project, or presentation is due or when there is an important examination approaching. Also, this junior year of our high school career is greatly significant because it is when we take those dreaded SATs. The amount of preparation that is necessary for these tests is tremendous because they may determine whether or not one is accepted into a certain college. Today's teenager withstands such pressures throughout the school year.

However, one would think that the pressures would decline at the stroke of 2:25 P.M. This is false for this is when the pressures of varsity sports take over. The day of a big game in soccer, lacrosse, or whatever sport it may be, can be greatly stressful. This stress can take over the mental and physical aspects of the body. Some athletes endure mental stress and physical pains such as stomach aches, nausea, and "the jitters" due to the stress that the big game brings.

Finally, the pressures of one's social life take over the weekend. Pressure is dramatically increased when one has a girlfriend or a boyfriend. This is primarily because of the conflict between spending time with that girlfriend or boyfriend or a group of friends. Also, at this time of our junior year, the stress that comes with the Junior Prom can be tremendous, especially on females. They worry much about who is going to ask them or if they are going to be asked at all. The significance of the dance is blown out of proportion by many—both males and females.

These, and numerous unmentioned stresses, burden the lives of the majority of today's teenagers.

6-51. THE RECALL

An expository writing explains or informs since it presents and clarifies information such as facts, terms, and other concepts. In this five-paragraph essay, the writer discusses the political device known as the recall. Included here are specific facts and an explanation of the process known as the recall.

Directions: On a separate sheet of paper, select a topic, such as the recall, and write an essay about that topic. Be sure to explain the process as fully as possible through details, examples, and other supporting explanations.

The *recall* is a political device that enables voters to remove a person from state or local public office before his or her term is completed. This removal is effected through the means of a special vote of the citizens. This recall also provides the means to elect a new public official through a special election. This system was initially developed in the first two decades of the twentieth century mostly because of what was thought to be the undue influence of special-interest groups including the railroads, manufacturers, and banks.

In order for the recall to be legal, a petition, signed by a number of displeased voters—usually between 10 to 25 percent of the voters who voted in the previous election—must be filed. This percent is considered substantial enough to rule out a frivolous recall. These signatures are checked for accuracy and validity. There does not have to be any evidence of wrongdoing by this official. Though the official may also voluntarily opt to resign from the elected position, if he or she does not, candidates for this office may file petitions to run for office in the usual way. Then a special election is held between the official in question and the candidates who filed such petitions. He or she who receives the most votes in this election will then serve out the remainder of the term.

Because the recall is an attempt to have greater direct popular control over government, several elected officials have been the victims of the recall system. More than several hundred cities and at least 15 states have used the recall system. In 1921 the governor of North Dakota was recalled. Eight years later the same happened to the mayor of Detroit, and nine years after that, the mayor of Los Angeles was removed through this process.

Often the recall is a reflection of two different philosophies regarding the purpose of elected officials. Some believe that an elected official should have the freedom to vote as he or she deems appropriate, and others feel that an elected official should always represent the wishes of those who elected him or her into office. The most common reasons why the recall system has been implemented are dishonesty, incompetence, and disregard of public opinion.

Essentially, the recall, as part of our democratic political system, allows the people to have a more direct control over government.

6-52. AN UNPLEASANT SITUATION

In this narrative the writer relates a yearly ritual that he does not look forward to each summer. Read the following story told in the first person, and then on the reverse side of this paper, write down three images that you remember from this story. Finally, write your own account of an unpleasant situation you have experienced. Be aware of setting, tone, narration, details, character sketches, and any other techniques that make for effective writing. Write your story on another piece of paper.

Going back to school each fall is definitely not the most exciting event of my year. Yet, the days preceding that fateful September morning are even more anxiety-ridden. Worse still is the day my mom takes me shopping for new school clothes. I usually try to talk my way out of going, but it is no use. I am doomed!

Each year, Mom and I enter the clothing store and the same salesman, Mr. Thompson, greets us with his big smile and a cheery, "How's our big guy today?" Same line every year. I keep on thinking that when I do go to college, I'll never have to see Mr. Thompson again. Anyway, it is now time to start looking for school pants. "Thirty-three thirty," Mr. Thompson tells Mom. Then after ten minutes' worth of shuffling hangers and placing pants against my body, Mr. Thompson and Mom decide that I should try on these three pairs of pants. With a disgruntled look, I head for the dressing room. If there were an exit out the back of the dressing room, I would leave and never come back. However, believing that moms and clothing store people have a conspiracy against students, I find no such possible exit. Ugh!

After a few measurements, some white chalk marks, and some rolled-up pants' legs, I am ready for Mr. Thompson's next torture drill—fitting me for a sports jacket. Another six hundred or so seconds of sifting through a seemingly countless number of sports jackets before Mom selects two—both blue with gold buttons. "Try them on, Billy, and stand there in front of the mirror where we can see you." Completely bored and detecting that my frustration level is rising, I generally start to pose like those guy models in the fashion magazines. I first give it the "thoughtful" pose, then the "look at the watch" look, and finally the "look into the distance" gaze before I hear Mom say, "Billy, please behave so we can get you some nice clothes for school."

A believer in the proverb "If you can't beat 'em, join 'em," I concede and start to cooperate. After all, the sooner they approve of the clothes, the sooner I can get out of this store. So, fifteen minutes later and a handsome credit-card charge, Mom and I are on our way home—or so I think. "Billy, you know you could really use some new school shoes."

I think you know the rest!

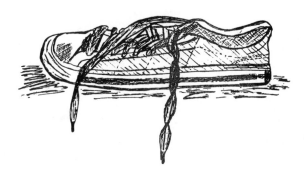

© 1999 by The Center for Applied Research in Education

6-53. A REAL PROBLEM

In this narration, the writer tells about a television show he watched. The first paragraph is mostly narration, and the other two paragraphs are more reflective. In addition to using a chronological narration and sufficient details (the *what?*, *when?*, *where?*, *who?*, *why?*, and *how?* of the situation), the writer also gives his insight into a dilemma featured on the show.

Directions: On a separate piece of paper, recount an event you witnessed. In the first paragraph, explain what happened. In the next two paragraphs, offer your thoughts about what you saw. Use clear and effective transitions, details, sentence structure, and vocabulary to gain your reader's interest.

Last night I watched an episode of the television show *The Real World.* The focus of the program was a group member (we will call her Gretchen) who has a problem with alcohol. Her housemates were concerned with her drinking problem and tried, to some extent, to help her stop her unhealthy behavior. Their worst fears about Gretchen's problem came true. On this particular night, Gretchen spent a few hours at a club and consumed too much alcohol. She then drove her car rather recklessly along the streets of a resort town. This action was so upsetting to the show's crew that two *Real World* officials spoke with her about this problem. They gave her an ultimatum. She could either attend counseling sessions or resign from the show. Wisely, Gretchen opted to go for counseling.

Gretchen was brave to remain on the show since some of her therapy sessions were taped for all to see. Apparently, because she had had a somewhat difficult childhood, she had problems that needed to be resolved. In front of many viewers, the troubled girl was asked some very personal and embarrassing questions by the counselor. Although Gretchen did not answer these questions exactly as the counselor probably wished, she nevertheless dealt with the situation bravely.

Each of us can learn from this episode. All people have problems. Some are easy to overcome, and some pose greater difficulties. Alcohol-related problems are not easy to resolve. Gretchen's predicament affected both her and those around her—especially those on the road that night since she could have hurt or killed herself and others. Now, Gretchen has taken the first step to recovery. Hopefully, with the help of counselors and her own self-determination, this problem will be solved.

LOOKING AT LITERATURE

6-54. THE LITERARY ME

How often have you seen yourself in a literary character you have encountered? Is there a little bit of Holden in you? How much do you resemble Gatsby? Is honest John Proctor your mirror-image? Are you tired and worn-out like Willy Loman?

Here is your chance to take a closer look at your literary soul mate(s). First, select a character (or two characters at the most) whose personal characteristics are quite similar to yours. Then select three similar personality traits.

The format is five paragraphs. The initial paragraph should include the character's (characters') name(s), the work in which s/he is found, the work's author, and the work's genre (novel, full-length play, short story, . . .). Make the opening lines attractive by avoiding the mundane start. Interest the reader with a clever initial few sentences. Do not allow the reader to know what qualities you will address just yet. Hold him/her in suspense!

The second, third, and fourth paragraphs in this *comparison* type of writing should illustrate the similarities you and the character(s) share. A clear topic sentence which includes the trait is advisable. Talk about the character first, and then talk about yourself. Be honest about yourself since only you and your teacher will know what you have written. Interesting and concise details should be included. Repeat this format for the third and fourth paragraphs as well.

The fifth paragraph ties the first four together. It should not be lengthy, but it should include some clever method to make the reader feel satisfied.

Some of the *connective* transitional words and phrases include *another, another way, besides, first, second,* and *third.* These words and phrases will be used to *link one paragraph with another.* Use variety in selecting these words and phrases.

Some of the *comparison* transitional words and expressions you might include are *like, similarly, in like manner, for example, for instance, likewise,* and *thus.* These would be used to *link the character's trait explanation and your trait explanation.* Again, use variety in selecting these words and phrases.

Invent a catchy title. Check that there are no misspellings, that there are only complete sentences, that you have used good transitions, and that you have proofread for possible errors. Your teacher will determine the essay's length.

Write the essay on another sheet of paper

6-55. TRAGIC CHARACTERS

Many works of literature trace the tragic downfall of a character. The Greek tragedians gave us the very first glimpse of tragic characters in their dramatic presentations. Shakespeare, of course, was a master at this with the likes of Hamlet, Macbeth, Romeo and Juliet, Julius Caesar, Othello, and more.

   Here we will compare tragic heroes you have encountered in literature and ask you to ascertain to what extent he or she is comparable to a tragic Shakespearean tragic character. Select a tragic character from your reading and then place a check next to any of the characteristics he or she possesses. Then, on a separate sheet of paper, write a two-paragraph composition showing specifically how your tragic character is more *like* or *unlike* the typical literary tragic characters. Use at least three points of comparison or contrast.

_____ 1. The tragic figure meets his/her death during the literary work.

_____ 2. The tragic figure is a conspicuous person, a person of high degree.

_____ 3. The tragic figure's suffering and calamity are exceptional. Often the suffering is unexpected and is a strong contrast to previous happiness experienced by the tragic figure.

_____ 4. The fall of the character extends beyond the character himself/herself.

_____ 5. The tragic character should not be perfect. He/She has faults that make him/her human.

_____ 6. The tragic figure's disaster is inevitable.

_____ 7. The tragic figure fights for a noble cause.

_____ 8. Pride is often the main cause of the character's downfall.

6-56. SKETCHING A LITERARY CHARACTER

As a reader, learning how to assess literary characters is a valuable skill. Knowing how to start your character assessment is important. One suggestion is to vertically write down the letters of the character's full name. Then, for each letter, write a quality of the character that begins with that letter. Finally, next to that quality, write an instance from the literary work that exemplifies that particular characteristic.

In the appropriate space, choose a literary character and do as suggested. Have fun!

Character's name _____

Literary work _____

Author _____

Letter	Characteristic	Example
_____	_____	_____
_____	_____	_____
_____	_____	_____
_____	_____	_____
_____	_____	_____
_____	_____	_____
_____	_____	_____
_____	_____	_____
_____	_____	_____
_____	_____	_____
_____	_____	_____

6-57. MATCHING THE CHARACTER AND THE QUOTE

For each of the five quotes below, select a different literary character who, in your opinion, is connected to the quote. In a paragraph of several sentences, exemplify how the character is connected to the quote. Write the answers to the first two quotes on this sheet and the answers to the remaining three quotes on a separate sheet of paper. An example is done for you. Share your answers with your classmates.

"The weaknesses of the many make the leader possible." (*Elbert Hubbard*)

In Henrik Ibsen's play, *An Enemy of the People*, Dr. Stockmann is a man who discovers that the rejuvenating municipal baths of his small Norwegian town are infected. Knowing that these baths are a major source of revenue for the community, yet knowing that people who use them can easily become deathly sick, Stockmann fights against the "compact majority," who, in this instance, show how selfish and small-minded they are. Thus, Stockmann is the leader who tries to convince these weak people of what they should be doing.

1. "Reason can wrestle and overthrow terror." (*Euripides*)

   _____

   _____

   _____

   _____

   _____

2. "Human history is the sad result of each one looking out for himself." (*Julio Cortázar*)

   _____

   _____

   _____

   _____

   _____

3. "I think of a hero as someone who understands the degree of responsibility that comes with his freedom." (*Bob Dylan*)

4. "No, when the fight begins within himself, a man's worth something." (*Robert Browning*)

5. "It is the confession, not the priest, that gives us absolution." (*Oscar Wilde*)

6-58. PERSONAL CHARACTERISTICS

Whether you are writing an essay about a literary character, looking at your own characteristics, or considering the traits of others, this list of 50 personal attributes will be valuable. Most of the adjectives are positive in nature. Of course, you should be able to use each adjective's opposite, if necessary.

On a separate sheet of paper, list five adjectives (or their opposites) that describe a character from a literary work you have recently read. For each adjective, cite an instance from the literary work that displays how that word clearly befits the literary character. Do this for three different characters.

active	educated	individualistic	natural	short
agile	eloquent	inquisitive	old	simple
athletic	friendly	insightful	open-minded	sociable
brave	generous	intelligent	poor	tall
charitable	handsome	introspective	pretty	trusting
cheerful	hardworking	lean	proud	unusual
confident	helpful	loving	reliable	wealthy
cultured	honorable	mature	reserved	willful
dedicated	humble	muscular	respected	young
eager	humorous	naive	serious	zealous

6-59. TO FOLLOW OR NOT TO FOLLOW— THAT IS THE QUESTION

In this persuasive essay, student writer Chris Olsen argues that Prince Hamlet would not be an effective king of Denmark. In these opening two paragraphs of his essay, Chris immediately gains the reader's attention through his thesis statement, clearly argues his side of the issue, displays some of the opposition's side of the argument, and includes detailed facts and examples. Note that his initial paragraph states the three examples he will use to support his belief that Prince Hamlet would not make a laudable king. All of these are effective techniques for writing convincing persuasive essays.

First, select a controversial topic from one of the literary works you have read and discussed during the past two years. Then, on a separate sheet of paper, state your thesis statement. Next, list three points that will strongly support your opinion. Finally, as Chris does below, write the opening first two paragraphs of your essay. If your teacher requests, write three more paragraphs—two with more supporting details and examples and the last one as your concluding paragraph—to form the traditional five-paragraph approach.

Idealistically, Prince Hamlet would be a laudable ruler, but if he were to become king, he would be unable to rule efficiently and control his domain. He is the portrait of a citizen king because at heart he is a caring and generous person, but a leader cannot be constantly dragged down by his/her conscience as Prince Hamlet is. Also, his melancholia is even worse than his supposed insanity because unlike insanity, melancholia shows a weakness in his character that makes him unable to carry out tasks. Furthermore, Prince Hamlet tries to do too much. By exceeding his capabilities as a man, he turns a problem that can be resolved into a complicated degradation of the royal court of Denmark. Before the play, Prince Hamlet seems to have been an admirable, honest, and smart person. While not repudiating his honesty or intelligence, we see his deficiencies as a leader throughout the tragedy.

It has been proven throughout history that a good ruler does not have to be the most conscientious, honest, or caring person. In fact, in Machiavellian terms, these characteristics are exactly what a king should not have. A character's downfall because of too much thinking and worrying is clearly evident in *Hamlet*. This downfall gives us a glimpse of what could happen if Prince Hamlet were given the kingdom. The most obvious example of this indecisiveness is when he is unable to kill the reigning king, Claudius, the uncle who poisoned and killed Hamlet's father, King Hamlet. Yet, there is a deeper root than his religiousness; Prince Hamlet cannot kill Claudius at the altar because he is unsure of what Claudius' fate will be. Anything that is not finite or clear-cut causes anxiety and fret in Hamlet's mind.

6-60. MORE THAN A PEEP OF BO-PEEP

Writing a character analysis can be very interesting. Today is your opportunity to analyze and profile Little Bo-Peep, from the nursery rhyme of the same title, one of literature's more famous personalities. Be careful—for she may be far more complex than you think!

First, read the nursery rhyme printed below. Then, on a separate piece of paper, write five questions you have about this female literary character. These questions can deal with what she did, what she thought, what the narrator thought of her, whether or not she was an admirable person, or any other valid question. Have a classmate write his or her responses to these questions. After that, discuss these questions and answers. Finally, write a composition (your teacher will determine its length) analyzing Little Bo-Peep. Use a clear thesis statement, effective supporting details and examples from the nursery rhyme, and a fitting conclusion. Share these writings with your classmates.

Little Bo-Peep has lost her sheep,
And can't tell where to find them;
Leave them alone, and they'll come home,
And bring their tails behind them.

Little Bo-Peep fell fast asleep,
And dreamt she heard them bleating;
But when she awoke, she found it a joke,
For they were still all fleeting.

Then up she took her little crook,
Determined for to find them;
She found them indeed, but it made her heart bleed,
For they'd left all their tails behind 'em.

It happened one day, as Bo-Peep did stray
Unto a meadow hard by
There she espied their tails side by side,
All hung on a tree to dry.

She heaved a sigh and wiped her eye,
And over the hillocks she raced;
And tried what she could, as a shepherdess should,
That each tail should be properly placed.

Name _____ Date _____ Period _____

6-61. THE CRUCIBLE

The following composition is a synopsis of Arthur Miller's play *The Crucible*. Within the five paragraphs, the writer introduces us to the setting, plot, characters, and themes. On a separate piece of paper, do the same. Select a novel, play, or short story you have read. Then, include the same elements as found here, and write a synopsis of your work. Your teacher will decide the writing's length.

In 1953, *The Crucible*, a four-act play by Arthur Miller, hit the Broadway stage. The drama recounts the dark period of American history surrounding the 1692 Salem witchcraft trials. The denial of one's freedom of conscience and the wrongful accusation and subsequent persecution of individuals are major wrongs Miller challenges in this disturbing play.

During the latter part of the seventeenth century, an intolerable lot of English people immigrated to the New World and settled in New England, specifically Salem, Massachusetts. Fearing the possible corruptive influence of others outside their immediate group, these predominantly close-minded individuals sought to maintain community unity through state and religious control. Unfortunately, this attempt to maintain order and discipline within the Salem community fails when thinking contrary to the "established beliefs" begins to emerge. Panic sets in as formerly respected individuals are accused of either being witches or keeping the company of witches. The witch trials provide the means to identify these wayward individuals.

John Proctor, a farmer, is the most visibly attacked during these dreadful witch hunts. A married farmer in his thirties, Proctor, who has been intimate and sinned with the evil 17-year-old Abigail Williams during his marriage, has a sickly wife, Elizabeth. Abigail, unable to seduce John again, is now more determined than ever to inflict pain upon John and his family. Not only has Elizabeth been the victim of John's infidelity, but now she is also accused of witchcraft and jailed—most likely through Abigail's influence upon a group of young girls who scream out the names of women who have had "knowledge" of the devil. In less than two weeks, nearly 40 women are arrested based on the mere accusations of these frenzied young girls who keep company with Abigail. Essentially, if these girls make an accusation against an individual, that person is incarcerated.

After Elizabeth is jailed, John convinces one of the young girls, Mary Warren, to confess that the girls have perpetrated this hoax that has turned Salem into a frenzied state of affairs. However, Warren does not have the courage to stand up and admit this fraud in the presence of the Salem's three trial judges, citizens—and especially in front of the vicious Abigail Williams.

In an interesting sequence of events, John, accused of being anti-Christ and anti-authority, confesses to witchcraft only because it will save Elizabeth's life. Unwilling to make charges against any other people, John also refuses to sign his confession paper that will be hung upon the church door. Rather than give the judges and some rabid townspeople that satisfaction, John chooses to preserve his name and reputation and die honestly.

6-62. EVALUATION STRATEGIES

Writers expand their knowledge as they read more and more. They evaluate, analyze, and synthesize the material they read and perhaps use some of these facts and ideas in their own writings. After you have read any type of literature—whether it is a magazine article, short story, novel, play, essay or any other writing—it is wise to share your ideas and feelings about what you have read. Perhaps keeping a literary journal suits your needs.

Directions: Here are some ideas that are popular with students after they have finished reading a novel, play, or short story. On a separate piece of paper, answer each of the first four assignments in 100 words or more. For the other two assignments, use your judgment as to the length of each response. Keep this activity sheet in your folder or notebook for future readings and responses.

1. Summarize the work's plot.

2. Describe a memorable character.

3. Discuss two problems encountered by this memorable character.

4. Did the work satisfy your expectations? How?

5. Create an ad—television, radio, or print—about this work.

6. Devise three questions that you would like to ask the author. Then, switching roles, pretend you are the author and answer these questions.

6-63. A WORTHWHILE CONVERSATION

It is fun (and educational) to find out how the book or play you have just finished reading came to be. One way to find out is to speak directly to the author or playwright. Since that is not always possible, another suggestion is to write a letter to this writer posing some interesting questions for him or her to answer. Below are some questions that you could use in your letter. Feel free to add to or delete questions from this list. Often, the letter can be sent to the publisher who will, in turn, forward it to the writer. When these questions have been answered by the writer, share his or her responses with your classmates. Good luck!

1. How did the idea for this work come about?

2. How close to your own life are the lives of any of the characters?

3. Are there characters in this work who resemble people in your personal life?

4. Does the work's setting resemble any setting familiar to you?

5. What message, if any, do you want to deliver to your readers?

6. What difficulties, if any, did you have in writing this work? How did you overcome these difficulties?

7. Were there any disagreements between you and the publisher or editor of this work? If so, what was the situation?

8. How long did it take you to write this work? Were there any extended breaks in your writing?

9. What changes did you make from the way you originally intended the work to be written?

10. What is the age group of your intended readers?

11. Did you originally have another ending in mind? If so, how did it differ from the work's published ending?

12. What was the most difficult chapter or scene to write? Why?

13. What did you hope to accomplish by starting the work with that particular opening scene?

14. To what extent do you agree or disagree with the work's critical reviews?

15. Do you have plans for a sequel? Could you share a bit of the plot?

© 1999 by The Center for Applied Research in Education

6-64. HAMLET - A MAN OF ACTION

Student writer Olivia Racanelli writes about one of literature's most famous characters, Hamlet. Read her paragraph and then, on the lines provided, answer the questions.

(1) In William Shakespeare's tragic play *Hamlet*, the main character, Hamlet, the prince of Denmark, is a man of action. (2) Throughout the play Hamlet is driven by a strong, deep-rooted desire for avenging his father's untimely death. (3) From the start of the play, Hamlet is preoccupied with the death of his father and is a great man of action until he achieves the ultimate revenge of killing his father's murderer. (4) Hamlet first shows that he is a man of action by pursuing, then speaking with, an apparition he is told about by the night watchmen of the castle. (5) By planning a play that will reenact his father's death, as the ghost reveals it, Hamlet is taking action to seek the truth about the possible past misdeeds of his uncle, Claudius, with respect to the death of King Hamlet of Denmark. (6) Hamlet also takes action by confronting his mother, Queen Gertrude, with the tragic news involved in her former husband's death and her new sinful marriage. (7) Again proving himself a man of action, Hamlet takes the life of Polonius in a hasty fit of rage. (8) Hamlet, while in his last moments of life, carries out his mission in a noble fit of action and anger by killing Claudius and thereby finally avenging his father's death.

1. What was the question Olivia had to answer in this paragraph? _____

_____

2. What organizational pattern does Olivia use? _____

_____

_____

3. What transitions are used? _____

_____

_____

4. Is the topic sentence stated or implied? _____

5. On the reverse side of this paper, write an outline that Olivia might have used as her guide.

6-65. HAMMER OR ANVIL?

In this assignment student writer Chirag Badlani was asked to relate the Henry Wadsworth Longfellow quote, "In this world a man must be either a hammer or an anvil," to a literary work covered in his English class. He selected Ken Kesey's novel *One Flew Over the Cuckoo's Nest*. Read the opening two paragraphs of Chirag's composition and then answer the questions.

(1) A man is an anvil when he takes the pounding from others and handles the incessant thrashes and beatings without a dent on his body or soul. (2) A man is a hammer when he is one who delivers this pounding, when he is the one who unsuccessfully tries to damage the heart of another. (3) In Ken Kesey's *One Flew Over the Cuckoo's Nest*, the roles of anvil and hammer are not clearly defined; rather, the characters switch their positions throughout the novel. (4) The two characters who do exchange the roles of anvil and hammer are Nurse Ratched, otherwise known as Big Nurse, and Randle Patrick McMurphy.

(5) McMurphy establishes his role as the hammer early in the novel. (6) He places bets with the other inmates that he can beat Nurse Ratched at her own game. (7) He says, "Just what I said: any of you sharpies here willing to take five bucks that says I can get the best of that woman—before the week's up—without her getting the best of me?" (68) (8) McMurphy, without "cussing" or losing his temper, attempts to "hammer" Nurse Ratched, and, she, as a result, becomes the anvil. (9) McMurphy uses such tactics as brushing his teeth before the scheduled time, singing in the latrine, and walking around with no more than a towel around his waist. (10) He challenges her authority, pushes the rules, and "beats" and "strikes" Big Nurse, attempting to damage her character. (11) However, because of the strong and sturdy make-up of an anvil, Big Nurse does not yield, even as McMurphy pounds away.

1. What is an anvil? _____
   _____

2. What is Chirag's purpose in his opening paragraph? _____
   _____

3. What support does Chirag offer for McMurphy as the hammer? _____
   _____

4. What do you think Chirag's purpose is in his third paragraph (which does not appear here)?
   _____

5. What does (68) mean at the end of the seventh sentence? _____
   _____

6. What is the purpose of the eleventh sentence? _____
   _____

7. Name a literary character who you feel is a hammer and give two reasons why you feel this way. _____
   _____

8. Name a literary character who you feel is an anvil and give two reasons why you feel this way.
   _____

6-66. THE READER'S MIND

In a reader-response approach to literature, what goes on in the reader's mind as he or she reads the literary work is the most important facet. *What* and *how* we read are the principal considerations. A reader-response is essentially a reading of the reader who comes to the work with his or her own assumptions about how the world functions. As the reader encounters the work's characters, settings, vocabulary, images, themes, tone, and other elements, his or her consciousness is hard at work assessing what is going on in the text—*and* in his or her own mind. Social and cultural values will influence how the reader responds to what is happening in the text.

Select a recent read and just let your thoughts flow freely about what went on in the work. Do not restrict yourself as you think about people, places, actions, and things that you encountered. If more space is needed, use the reverse side of this paper.

Title of literary work: _____

Author: _____

Type of work: novel   play   short story   (Circle one.)

Number of pages: _____

_____

_____

_____

_____

_____

_____

_____

_____

_____

_____

_____

_____

_____

6-67. STEPPING INTO THE WORK

How often have you wished you could step into a book, play, or story and talk to a character? Perhaps you wanted to give him or her some advice, help out with a troublesome situation, or simply talk to the character about life and things in general. Well, today your wish comes true because here is your chance to have a conversation/dialogue with the character of your choice.

Select a character from a literary work you have read. Now select a particularly interesting aspect of the character's personality or demeanor. Maybe you want to explore some action he or she took—or did not take. You start the conversation and then he or she will respond to your question or comment. Then just continue as a normal conversation would. Obviously, you are writing both ends of the dialogue, but more importantly, you are thinking seriously about this character. Insert the character's name in the blank spaces. Write the conversation as a play's script and do not worry about the quotation marks that would normally appear in a conversation. It is more important to have a meaningful conversation. If you need more space, continue the conversation on the reverse side.

Me: _____

_____

: _____

Me: _____

_____

: _____

Me: _____

_____

: _____

Me: _____

_____

: _____

Me: _____

_____

: _____

Me: _____

_____

: _____

Me: _____

_____

: _____

_____

6-68. DEAD POETS SOCIETY

A movie review, such as the one for *Dead Poets Society* below, should include several important aspects of the movie. Some of the more prominent actors, their roles, other movies that they have acted in (or produced or directed), the basic plot, a conflict or two, and a few opinions about the actors' performances are usually found in a movie review.

Directions: Select a movie you have seen and, on a separate piece of paper, write a movie review. The length of the review will be determined by your teacher. Exchange your review with your classmates.

Dead Poets Society, a 1989 movie directed by Peter Weir (*Witness*), examines the high school experience of several students and their charismatic English teacher at the prestigious, male Welton Academy during the latter part of the 1950s. For years Welton has been an outstanding preparatory school for young men who primarily enter the lucrative fields of business, finance, medicine, and law. Now the eccentric teaching methods of former Welton student-turned-teacher, John Keating, played by Robin Williams (*Good Morning, Vietnam*), and his influence on some of the boys he teaches (primarily Robert Sean Leonard and Ethan Hawke) come under attack from the school's conservative administration and wealthy parents.

Keating's exhortations of "Carpe Diem" (Seize the day) and "Make your lives extraordinary" become the operative phrases for his students who create a poetry reading group similar to the Dead Poets Society, the poetry group Keating and his cronies began during their Welton days. The passionate Keating urges the boys to select creativity over conformity, thinking quite contrary to that promoted by Welton Academy. Expectedly, problems arise and Keating takes the brunt of the attack. The other major conflict pits Neil Perry (Leonard) against his father (Kurtwood Smith). The younger Perry's wish to involve himself in a local Shakespearean production is contrary to his father's career path plan for his son. The outcome of this friction provides the impetus for the movie's subsequent action.

Williams is brilliant in his role as the nonconformist teacher. Memorable performances are turned in by relative newcomers Leonard, Hawke (Todd Anderson), and Josh Charles (Knox Overstreet). Smith, as the inflexible, success-driven parent, is outstanding. *The Los Angeles Times* calls the movie "Remarkable!" and *The New York Times* hails it as "Exceptional!" *Dead Poets Society* is a movie that makes you think about your education, your life's philosophy, and yourself!

6-69. THE GRAMMATICALLY CORRECT POEM

Today you will be a poet. Better yet, you will be a grammatically perfect poet since you will follow the directions below. Have some fun and enjoy this poetic experience! On a separate piece of paper, write your poem following the directions under the heading **YOUR POEM.** An example poem (**HER POEM**) that has followed another set of directions has been done for you.

HER POEM: (1) The poem should be five lines. (2) Label the proper noun (PN) in the first line. (3) Label the common noun (CN) in the second line. (4) Underline the simile in the third line. (5) Label the conjunction (C) in the fourth line. (6) Circle the parallel structure in the fifth line. (7) Label the preposition (PREP) in the simile. (8) Label the two adjectives (ADJ) in the second line (9) Draw a box around the verb in the fourth line. (10) Label the pronoun (PRO) in the third line.

```
        PN       PN
The Rocky Mountains are heavenly.

        CN        ADJ        ADJ
Their tops are snow-covered and majestic

                    PREP   PRO
Like an angelic piece of art, they tower above the land.

              C
The rivers and valleys [pay] homage to these peaks

(So breathtaking) and (so magnificent.)
```

YOUR POEM: (1) The poem should be five lines. (2) Label the proper noun (PN) in the third line. (3) Label the common noun (CN) in the first line. (4) Underline the simile in the fourth line. (5) Label the conjunction (C) in the second line. (6) Circle the parallel structure in the fifth line. (7) Label the article (ART) in the simile. (8) Label the two adjectives (ADJ) in the third line (9) Draw a box around the verb in the fourth line. (10) Label the pronoun (PRO) in the last line.

6-70. ROMEO AND JULIET

Shakespeare wrote the tragedy *Romeo and Juliet* during the 1590s. Though the play is written in English, the English of that day and the English we speak today are quite different. "Translating" the sixteenth-century language is both challenging and educational.

    The "Prologue" to *Romeo and Juliet* is reprinted below. On the lines below the "Prologue," write its modern-day translation. If you have not seen the play or the movie version of *Romeo and Juliet*, you might have to research some of the information contained in the fourteen lines of poetry written in iambic pentameter verse. The lines are numbered for easy reference. Use the reverse side of this paper if you need more space.

1. Two households both alike in dignity,
2. In fair Verona, where we lay our scene,
3. From ancient grudge break to new mutiny,
4. Where civil blood makes civil hands unclean.
5. From forth the fatal loins of these two foes
6. A pair of star-crossed lovers take their life,
7. Whose misadventured piteous overthrows
8. Do with their death bury their parents' strife.
9. The fearful passage of their death-marked love,
10. And the continuance of their parents' rage,
11. Which, but their children's end, naught could remove,
12. Is now the two hours' traffic of our stage;
13. The which if you with patient ears attend,
14. What here shall miss, our toil shall strive to mend.

_____

_____

_____

_____

_____

6-71. PARAPHRASING THE CONSTITUTION

The Founding Fathers of the United States of America were no weaklings when it came to writing. In Article V of the Constitution, the words are quite challenging. Not only is the vocabulary rather difficult, but the sentence structure can also be troublesome for the average person.

Here you will paraphrase the words of the Founding Fathers. First, define the thirteen words found in this article. Then, on a separate piece of paper, paraphrase Article V. Compare your answers with those of your classmates.

"No person shall be held to answer for a capital, or otherwise infamous crime, unless on a presentment or indictment of a Grand Jury, except in cases arising in the land or naval forces, or in the Militia, when in actual service in time of War or public danger; nor shall any person be subject for the same offense to be twice put in jeopardy of life or limb; nor shall be compelled in any criminal case to be a witness against himself, nor be deprived of life, liberty, or property, without due process of law; nor shall private property be taken for public use without just compensation." *Constitution of the United States of America, Article V*

capital _____
_____

infamous _____
_____

presentment _____
_____

indictment _____
_____

Grand Jury _____
_____

Militia _____
_____

offense _____
_____

jeopardy _____
_____

limb _____
_____

compelled _____
_____

deprived _____
_____

liberty _____
_____

compensation _____
_____

Name _____ Date _____ Period _____

6-72. SHAPING UP YOUR SHAKESPEARE

Attending a play is certainly the way to go since plays were meant to be seen and heard. Yet, at times, you will be asked to read a play for class. Most students will read a Shakespearean play and some of the play will be read at home or in class.

Romeo and Juliet is one of Shakespeare's most famous tragedies. Here is your opportunity to work with the Bard's words to see how well you understand his language and style. On the lines beneath each quote, write your interpretation of what these words from *Romeo and Juliet* mean. As you read the quotations, remember that the two families have been feuding for many years. Discuss your interpretations with your classmates.

1. **Romeo**   O, she (Juliet) doth teach the torches to burn bright!
It seems she hangs upon the cheek of night
Like a rich jewel in an Ethiop's ear;
Beauty too rich for use, for earth too dear!

_____

_____

_____

2. **Juliet**   O be some other name!
What's in a name? that which we call a rose
By any other name would smell as sweet;
So Romeo would, were he not Romeo call'd,
Retain that dear perfection which he owes
Without that title. Romeo, doff thy name,
And for thy name, which is no part of thee,
Take all myself.

_____

_____

_____

3. **Juliet**   If that thy bent of love be honourable,
Thy purpose marriage, send me word to-morrow,
By one that I'll procure to come to thee,
Where and what time thou wilt perform the rite,
And all my fortunes at thy foot I'll lay,
And follow thee, my lord, throughout the world.

_____

_____

_____

LIVING AND WRITING IN TODAY'S WORLD

6-73. ADVICE COLUMNIST

Abigail Van Buren (Dear Abby) and Ann Landers, two syndicated newspaper advice columnists, have given good suggestions to many people for many years. These two women usually seem to say the right thing as they give people good suggestions on how to solve problems. Here you will do the same. Two students have submitted their letters asking for your advice. Give them some sound advice on how to resolve their dilemmas. Be logical and caring. After writing your responses on separate pieces of paper, share these suggestions with your classmates.

I am a thirteen-year-old girl and have a nine-year-old sister. Usually, we get along pretty well, but lately she has been getting on my nerves. She just comes into my room and "borrows" whatever she needs whether it is a CD, my Walkman, or jewelry. When I ask her not to "borrow" these, she runs to my mother who really doesn't do much to solve the problem I am having. So the problem really doesn't go away. Most recently, she tries to listen in when I am on the telephone with my friends, especially my boyfriend, Chad. What should I do?—*Monique Karstan*

Some of the students in our English class copy homework and cheat on tests and quizzes. They never get caught doing these things. They even go so far as to brag about it to their friends in other classes. Because they copy and cheat so well, they have higher averages than some of the other students who would not copy or cheat. Though we have told these cheaters we don't think it is cool to do what they are doing, they have not stopped. I am not sure if we should let our teacher know what is going on, but many of us are getting tired of it all. What should we do?—*Ralph Ermanns*

6-74. TEN TOUGH PROPOSALS

Good writers argue well. You are no exception! Ten proposals that can be argued equally well on both sides of the issue appear below. For four of these proposals, list three arguments for and three arguments against the proposal. An example is done for you. Use a separate sheet of paper for your answers. Then share (and argue) these proposals with your classmates.

PROPOSAL: *School facilities should be open seven nights a week for students' use.*

For: (a) Students can have a safe common meeting place.

(b) Students can use the athletic, computer, theatrical, and other facilities to improve their skills.

(c) Parents will feel confident that their children are safe and enjoying themselves.

Against: (a) Students will probably not want to come back to school at night after they have been there at least six hours each day for five days each week.

(b) The cost of insurance and supervision for this program may be too expensive.

(c) There are not enough different activities to do in this program. Students will become bored after a while.

1. The school year should be extended by 25 days.

2. There should only be 4 days of school per week.

3. Gym classes should be eliminated from your schedule.

4. Each classroom should have at least ten computer stations.

5. Gym classes should not be co-ed.

6. The state should allow 15-year-olds to be fully licensed.

7. Hats should be allowed in school.

8. Retired people should have a 20% price reduction on everything they buy.

9. Store owners should not allow students to work over 10 hours a week.

10. Store owners should give a 20% price reduction on items purchased by students who make the school's honor roll.

6-75. THREE FAVORITES

Writers often look to others for wisdom. There is much to be gained from leafing through a book of quotations and learning about life from the perspectives of other people. Their words and viewpoints can be helpful to any writer who desires a broader view of life's mysteries and intricacies.

The three quotes below are some of one writer's favorites, for they teach valuable lessons about life. As the writer does here, with the help of a book of quotations, select three quotes. **(A)** Paraphrase the quote and then **(B)** explain either what each quote teaches you or why you agree or disagree with the quote. Use your own paper for this activity.

Quote #1: "Ideal conversation must be an exchange of thought, and not, as many of those who worry most about their shortcomings believe, an eloquent exhibition of wit or oratory."—*Emily Post*

(A) The best conversation is a simple sharing of ideas and not a showcase for people to show off their knowledge and ability to speak well. **(B)** Often we are intimidated by what others might say or what others might think about what we have to say. We should feel confident enough to engage in conversation with other people and not be concerned about looking silly in their eyes. In turn, our conversation partners should not attempt to display their smarts and verbal sharpness.

Quote #2: "Reflection makes men cowards."—*William Hazlitt*

(A) Thinking about the pros and cons of an issue makes us shy away from action. This is probably because the dangers outweigh other issues in this matter. **(B)** Reflection often makes us do what we think is the right or moral thing to do. Yes, thinking about an intended action can make us fearful of doing that action, but just as often, this reflection helps us find direction and cause to do what is correct.

Quote #3: "The greatest pleasure of a dog is that you may make a fool of yourself with him and not only will he not scold you, but he will make a fool of himself too."—*Samuel Butler*

(A) A dog not only unconditionally accepts the fact that we do silly things, but he will also make us feel less silly by showing us his own foolish side. **(B)** Too frequently we are afraid to make mistakes because of what others may say and think about us. The dog allows for our shortcomings and foolish behaviors without comment. He will even do much the same silly things. Too bad more people are not like dogs in this way.

6-76.   THE VERY NECESSARY ___

Alexander Graham Bell move over. Thomas Alva Edison step aside. Here is the new invention called the _____, something the world has needed for a long time . . .

If you were to write a print ad or 30-second radio commercial for a new product, one that the population truly needs, what would you write or say? Perhaps the italicized words above would be an interesting beginning to catch the reader's or listener's attention. What do you think?

Today you will write an ad for this new product. Follow the directions below, be as creative as you can, and have a good time as you instantly become part of the advertising world.

What is the name of this product? _____

Describe what this product does. _____

_____

_____

Specifically, how will this product benefit a specific group or the population in general?

_____

_____

_____

How will you capture the reader's or listener's attention from the start?

_____

_____

How will you make sure the audience or reader does not forget the product's name?

_____

_____

What is the price of this product? _____

Where/How can people obtain this product? _____

_____

What aspects of the product will you emphasize and how will you do this? _____

_____

_____

How will you conclude the ad? _____

_____

_____

Now, using all this information, write the print ad or 30-second radio commercial on a separate piece of paper.

6-77. CLEVER ADVERTISING LINES

Advertisers try to capture a potential customer's attention with clever lines promoting their product. Creating these smart lines takes some talent and today you will show your skill in this area. After reading the advertising lines below, write an ad line for each of the five types of businesses given to you. Then, below those lines, think of five other types of businesses, list each business and write an advertising line for each one. Share your answers with your classmates.

> *Laser Surgery:* "You'll see the difference."
>
> *Hair Cutters:* "We're a cut above the rest."
>
> *Diamond Sellers:* "Put some sparkle in your life."
>
> *Podiatrists:* " We stand on our reputation."
>
> *Moving Company:* "We take you where you want to go."

Dentist: _____

Auto Repair Company: _____

Swimming Pool Installers: _____

Child Care Service: _____

Crayon Manufacturers: _____

Business: Advertising line

_____

_____

_____

_____

_____

_____

_____

_____

_____

_____

_____

6-78. PUNS

A pun is a play on words. So when the headlines read "Smoking in Public Building a Hot Issue," the newspaper writer is using a pun since the reader is supposed to almost groan after connecting the words *hot issue* with *smoking*.

Several puns are listed below. On the lines following the puns, make up your own ten headlines that contain puns. If you feel the need to explain a pun, please do so.

"*Chicago* is Now in New York" (The play *Chicago* is on Broadway in New York City.)

"*The Lion King* Roars Into Another Year on Broadway" (*The Lion King* is a play on Broadway.)

"Open Door Policy Is a Closed Issue" (Open and close[ed] are opposites.)

"*Lake Placid* Disturbs Viewers" (*Lake Placid* is a scary movie. Placid means peaceful.)

"Wells Digs Deep for Latest Win" (David Wells is a major league pitcher and people dig deep wells.)

Write your own puns here.

_____

_____

_____

_____

_____

_____

_____

_____

_____

_____

6-79. THE PERSONAL CROSSWORD PUZZLE

Here is a rather unique crossword puzzle that will make you do some thinking about someone close to you—*yourself!* There are no clues and no absolutely correct answers. Only the puzzle's numbers and spaces are given to you. Since this activity is entitled "The Personal Crossword Puzzle," you must come up with the puzzle's clues and their answers. Best of all, they must all be about YOU!! Remember, it is *The Personal Crossword Puzzle*. Have fun!!!

ACROSS	DOWN
1. _____	2. _____
3. _____	3. _____
5. _____	4. _____
6. _____	5. _____
8. _____	6. _____
10. _____	7. _____
13. _____	9. _____
14. _____	10. _____
18. _____	11. _____
19. _____	12. _____
21. _____	15. _____
22. _____	16. _____
23. _____	17. _____
	20. _____

6-80. MR. PEACOCK

Often colleges require high school seniors to write a personal statement as part of the college application process. You probably will be asked to write one. Essentially, a personal statement allows you the opportunity to tell the college admissions officers something about yourself. Usually, this statement relates some incident or experience that shows how you learned something new and interesting about yourself.

Student writer Sasha Metznik masterfully writes about a growth experience that occurred during her eleventh-grade social studies class. Her personal statement immediately captures the reader's interest. It is also detailed, introspective, and grammatically and mechanically correct— all important aspects of an effective personal statement.

Even though you might not have to write a personal statement for college just yet, recount an experience that contributed to your personal growth. Include some of the strong writing techniques that Sasha does here. Use a separate sheet of paper for your work.

His name was Peacock, Lenwood Peacock. He so admired Alexander Hamilton that he named his son Alexander Hamilton Peacock. He began his class with a shrill blow of a police whistle. The mug on his desk read, "Ronnie Rules." He was a passionate Republican, an unabashed male chauvinist, and to my initial horror, my U.S. History teacher. To a naive junior like myself, he was the teacher from hell. He was also one of the greatest influences in my high school career.

On the first day of class, I learned Peacock's Policy: "There is a right way, a wrong way, your way, and my way. Do it my way." Judging from my first grade, I must have done it "the wrong way." In hindsight, I can safely say that it was the very wrong way, and herein lies the significance of my time with Mr. Peacock.

Mr. Peacock demanded excellence. He wanted insight, he insisted upon understanding, and he was determined that I extract meaning and significance from his lessons. For my part, I was exceptionally good at—let me be painfully honest with you—regurgitating the facts.

His style, like his name, was somewhat unorthodox. He was an intellectual antagonist. He used his macho demeanor and any of a dozen upsetting expressions to goad students to a better way of thinking. Pity the poor student ("you lollipop-sucking-democrat-wimp") who gave an inadequate answer to one of his challenges.

In the beginning, of course, I was devastated. "Weak and superficial" was written on top of my first essay. Then a strange and wonderful thing happened. I determined to beat him at his own game. I would out-think him. I would annihilate his condescending attitude with brilliant insights. I would anticipate his objections and destroy his intellectual smugness. Slowly, painfully slowly, I came to realize he was demolishing my limited way of thinking and was excavating a new foundation on which to build.

The payoff came quickly. The next essay said, "Interesting thesis"; the next showed, "Well written and argued." The culmination of my efforts came one day after a particularly lengthy and thought-provoking discussion with Mr. Peacock. He looked up at me and said, "You know, Metznik, you have a great mind, a great mind."

I will always remember that day. Something changed inside of me. I had earned his respect. It was as if he had pinned a medal on me. I had moved to a higher level, the level of a truly inquiring mind.

I consider my experience with Mr. Peacock to be the most significant in my life with respect to academic growth. He taught me (perhaps I should say I was pulled kicking and screaming) to question and to challenge statements and even facts. I no longer sat on the fence on issues. He made the fence too uncomfortable. And the challenge to state and defend a position was too enticing.

This happened last year. I wish it had happened much earlier. I never thought after first hearing the whistle that began class that I would miss hearing it. Nor did I ever think that I would miss Mr. Peacock's self-assurance. But that's the point; I never thought. And now I do.

6-81. CLOTHES MAKE THE MAN (OR WOMAN OR BOY OR GIRL)

An old expression says, "Clothes make the man." Well, to be politically correct, we have expanded the quote as you can see by the activity's title. Often what we wear tells much about us. Do you usually wear "designer clothing"? Do you refuse to wear anything that has a name on it because you choose not to do free advertising for that company? Are you making a statement by what you wear? Could you care less about what it is that you wear?

On the lines below, characterize yourself by the clothes you wear. As much as you might not think you are telling everyone something about yourself by what you wear, you really are. So, think, be honest, and tell us (and yourself) how your clothes tell who you are.

_____

_____

_____

_____

_____

_____

_____

_____

_____

_____

_____

_____

_____

_____

_____

_____

6-82. IF I WERE ___ FOR A DAY

Have you ever imagined if you were someone or something else—just for a day? Would that day be more or less interesting, have more or fewer problems, bring you more or less satisfaction? Why?

Listed below are some people, animals, and things. Select one person, one animal, and one thing. On a separate piece of paper, brainstorm what that day as a different person, animal, and thing would be like. You certainly can comment on whether or not this alternate existence would be better or worse, but, more important, describe how it would be similar and/or different from your current existence. Finally, select one of these three choices you have worked on and write a composition (the length is up to your teacher) detailing the day's events. Be as creative as possible. Share your writing with your classmates.

People	Animals	Things
army recruiter	cat	button
carpenter	dog	crowbar
farmer	elephant	drill
police officer	ferret	fountain
pop musician	giraffe	jaw
race car driver	hyena	mirage
surgeon	lion	playground
teacher	panda	steeple
television host	walrus	umbrella
truck driver	whale	yo-yo

6-83. IT DOES NOT WORK AND SO . . .

Your computer has been giving you problems. Unfortunately, the company you bought it from tells you that you must deal with the computer's manufacturer. And even more unfortunately, the manufacturer's fee of $35 per phone call to deal with your problems is a bit expensive. As a result, you must write a letter to the manufacturer about this situation. Include the following problems in your letter. The company is *The Wonderful World of Computers* and its address is *560 Neptune Road, Download, CT 00000.* Use your home address as your mailing address. Use the typical business letter format and write the letter on a separate sheet of paper.

The problems include: (a) the speakers are blown; (b) you cannot save to the disc so you must always save to the hard drive; (c) the machine often freezes up and you must turn it off and reboot it; and (d) the machine makes this annoying noise after it has been on for one hour or longer.

6-84. DEAR MRS. WILKER

Too often people are quick to criticize, but they seldom remember to compliment others. This *Dear Mrs. Wilker* activity is a favorite for students and teachers alike. Select a former teacher or coach who has helped you in some way. Write a letter to him or her explaining what he or she did that was so memorable to you. Your current teacher and you can work out the details on how to get this letter to your former teacher or coach. A sample letter appears below. The holiday season has been a very appropriate time to send such a letter.

Dear Mrs. Wilker,

I hope you remember me. My name is Richard Olson, and I was a student in your second-grade class ten years ago. I was the little boy who would "help" you play the piano during our Music Appreciation period. You allowed me to sit next to you on the piano bench. My time with you at Fountain Lane School seems so long ago. Now a senior in high school, I want to thank you for what you did for me during my year in second grade.

I have been thinking back on my school years and often I think of your class. Whether it was dressing up for our holiday pageants, making arts and crafts projects, or our reading circles, you were always helpful and smiling. (If you were not smiling, we never saw it!) Where did you ever get the patience to care for all 26 of us? I will always remember how you listened to our long-winded stories about relatives, Little League, or even hamsters. Your smile and kind welcome each morning told us how much you enjoyed your time with children. You made us want to come to your classroom each day, and all of us wanted to do our best to please you. Whenever your name came up at our dinner table at home, all five Olson children who had been one of your students one time or another would smile and relate yet another Mrs. Wilker story. I promise they were all good ones!

As for me, I will graduate next month and head to college in late August. I think I want to major in music with a concentration in piano. Who knows? Perhaps that second-grade boy who "helped" you play the piano will have a young student who wants to "help" him play the piano in the years ahead. Assuredly, your musical influence is a big part of my music major.

I thank you again for who you are and what you did for me as one of your second graders. You are a great teacher and a very special person.

6-85. JOURNAL ENTRY

Journal writing helps you get in touch with your feelings. Though the process can take only ten or fifteen minutes a day, the results are well worth the time. So find a comfortable spot, take out your notebook (or journal log or word processor or computer), write the date of the journal entry at the top of the page, think, and then write about anything that is important to you. For once, grammar and mechanics are not going to be graded. So write well, but just as importantly, write to explore what is going on in your life.

Keep these entries and read them over every once in a while. They will prove to be very interesting! Perhaps they can even be used for future writings. An example journal entry appears below.

© 1999 by The Center for Applied Research in Education

> Today I walked along the shoreline. I wanted to do some thinking about things that have been going on in my life. It probably would have been better had there been no other people on the beach, but I was still able to do some serious thinking. School is only a month away, and already I am feeling the pressure of grades and college and the other important decisions that I will have to make before too long. This upcoming year is supposed to be so stressful. With six major classes, three sports, and a couple of extracurricular activities, I will hardly have time to do anything else. Why can't the school year be shorter and summer be longer? Well, we will see what happens . . .
>
> As I walked along the beach today, I saw many different people. There were a few guys surfing, a couple of girls throwing Frisbees, and many swimmers. Little kids were building sand castles and digging tunnels with the help of their parents. This world truly amazes me. Here in this small area of this huge planet are all sorts of people, young and old, just hanging out and doing what makes them happy. I wonder if I will be happy when I am fifty or sixty years old. I surely hope so. After all, most of my family lives to be pretty old so I better take good care of myself.
>
> Tomorrow is my parents' twentieth wedding anniversary. As far as parents go, they are pretty cool. They don't really hassle me about too many things because they trust that I will usually do the right things. Since I don't want to disappoint them, I will try to do the right thing. Who wants parents who don't trust you? That could be a major problem!!!

6-86. JUST AS THE EDITOR ORDERED

Pretend that you are working for a newspaper editor who is quite demanding. Your work must meet the editor's requirements and standards. Today you have been given an assignment that must include the 15 specifics listed below. On a separate sheet of paper, write a story about the topic of your choice that includes these specifics. Underline each specific and place the appropriate number after it. Thus, you should place 1 after the rhetorical question that begins the story since that is the first specific.

1. Begin the story with a rhetorical question.

2. Include an adjective phrase.

3. Include an adverb phrase.

4. Include three colors.

5. Include at least one simple sentence.

6. Include at least one complex sentence.

7. Include at least one compound sentence.

8. Include an interrupting expression.

9. Include a quotation.

10. Include at least three adjectives.

11. Include at least three adverbs.

12. Include an appositive.

13. Include one example of parallel structure.

14. Include one semicolon.

15. Include a date that includes the month, day, and year.

6-87. WHAT'S IN A NAME?

As a writer, the names you assign to people and places can affect how your readers view them. Here is some practice to see if you feel that a particular name is appropriate. The names of ten cars appear in bold letters. Write each definition on the line next to the car's name. Then decide what "impression" the car manufacturer wants to give off by selecting that particular name. Write that answer on the line below the definition.

1. Ford **Mustang** _____

_____

2. Cadillac **Eldorado** _____

_____

3. Olds **Cutlass Supreme** _____

_____

4. Ford **Taurus** _____

_____

5. Chevrolet **Celebrity** _____

_____

6. Jeep **Wrangler** _____

_____

7. Plymouth **Voyager** _____

_____

8. Dodge **Ram Charger** _____

_____

9. Ford **Explorer** _____

_____

10. GMC **Safari** Van _____

_____

6-88. RESEARCHING THE AWARDS

The awards bestowed upon people in your school, town, county, state, and nation are often named in honor of outstanding individuals. These people usually accomplished great deeds, possessed notable traits, or represented some important aspect of the organization conferring this award. The Nobel Prize, the Cy Young Award, and the Academy Awards are examples of such awards on an international level.

First, research the history of several awards given to people either in your school, town, or nation. Who is this person after whom the award has been named? What is his or her background? What did he or she do that was so outstanding? How many years has this award been given out? Who are some of the past recipients? Then, on a separate piece of paper, write a short composition that includes this information. Organize it in an interesting and logical manner. Use the example below as a guide.

The Alfred B. Nobel Prize

Alfred B. Nobel, who was born in 1833 and died in 1896, was a chemist and the inventor of dynamite. He bequeathed most of his $9,000,000 estate to be set up as a fund to be distributed yearly to those people judged to have benefited mankind in physics, chemistry, medicine–physiology, literature, and the promotion of peace. The first Nobel prizes were awarded in 1901. Famous recipients include Theodore Roosevelt (Peace), Ernest Hemingway (Literature), Marie Curie (Chemistry), and Toni Morrison (Literature).

6-89. WHAT'S GOING ON AROUND YOU

Writers need to be aware of what is happening around them. You are no exception. During the next three days, record some of the interesting statements and incidents you hear and witness. Look for incidents or dialogues that are funny, deep, interesting, or rather unique. Allow some of your findings to be the genesis for some future writings. You might even want to share some of these observations with your classmates.

Day 1:

_____
_____
_____
_____
_____
_____
_____
_____

Day 2:

_____
_____
_____
_____
_____
_____
_____
_____

Day 3:

_____
_____
_____
_____
_____
_____
_____
_____

6-90. WORDS TO LIVE BY

Often authors write a particular sentence or phrase, and their readers truly appreciate the wisdom of these words. Notice how frequently writers like William Shakespeare and Mark Twain are quoted. Writers do leave their marks on their readers!

Directions: Today you will pen some words of wisdom—some words to live by. Several examples appear below. Just let your ideas flow across the page as this writer does. Share your words with your classmates. Most of all, enjoy yourself and live by your own words . . .

Eat good foods as often as you can. Try to donate something to the poor during the holiday season. Take your local recycling program seriously. Take a walk in the rain. Turn off violent television shows. Make believe your parents' music is tolerable. Don't be afraid to cry. Clean your room without being asked to. Call your grandparents without being asked to. Help a small child solve what seems to be a big problem. Be quiet in libraries. Do without a cell phone for the next 24 hours. Ask the shy boy or girl to dance. Tell your teacher you enjoyed the day's lesson. Be honest. Care about others.

_____

_____

_____

_____

_____

_____

_____

_____

_____

_____

_____

_____

_____

_____

_____

_____

_____

_____

ANSWER KEY

6-1.   Your Portfolio Log

Answers will vary.

6-2.   Portfolio Writing Considerations

Answers will vary.

6-3.   Writing Conference Sheet

Answers will vary.

6-4.   How Much Are You The Same?

Answers will vary.

6-5.   Following The Brainstorm

Answers will vary.

6-6.   Brainstorming Ideas

Answers will vary.

6-7.   Vocabulary Journal

Answers will vary.

6-8.   Vocabulary Dexterity

These are sample answers.

1. **(a)** Harry spends much time fishing and playing cops and robbers with his favorite *chum*, Bert.
   (b) Jill used *chum* and other types of bait to attract fish to her pole.
2. **(a)** Because it was too *dark* to play, the softball game was suspended. **(b)** The weird family concealed many *dark* family secrets that would scare most normal people.
3. **(a)** The rabbit had to *dart* across the road to avoid getting run over by the automobile.
   (b) Kenny threw the *dart* at the board and earned 50 points for his effort.

4. **(a)** The detectives chose to *grill* the suspect for more than three hours in their attempt to get a confession. **(b)** Dad loves to cook hot dogs and hamburgers on the outdoor *grill*.

5. **(a)** Members of the team found it easy to *mesh* with one another throughout the three weeks at camp. **(b)** Heidi wore *mesh* stockings to complement her outfit.

6. **(a)** The story's *plot* contained many twists and other surprises to keep the audience involved. **(b)** Many people visited the renowned politician's *plot* in the local cemetery.

7. **(a)** What is her *rank* in the United States Navy? **(b)** The *rank* smell of the stale milk made us nauseous.

8. **(a)** The best man passed the wedding *ring* to the groom. **(b)** We heard the bell *ring* to signal the end of recess.

9. **(a)** Can a witch cast a *spell* on anyone? **(b)** Can you *spell* the word "thespian"?

10. **(a)** His tire *tread* marks were clearly visible on the country road. **(b)** How long can the average swimmer *tread* water before extreme fatigue sets in?

6-9. Grouping the Pieces of Information

Answers will vary.

6-10. You as the Editor

Answers will vary.

6-11. Don't Go Belly Up Here!

A=12	B=18	C=24	D=5	E=6
F=4	G=10	H=11	I=17	J=23
K=16	L=22	M=3	N=9	O=15
P=8	Q=14	R=20	S=21	T=2
U=25	V=1	W=7	X=13	Y=19

6-12.   Sentence Warm Up

1. FR	6. RO	11. FR
2. CS	7. RO	12. FR
3. RO	8. FR	13. RO
4. FR	9. RO	14. CS
5. CS	10. CS	15. CS

Fragments (1, 4, 8, 11, and 12) total 36; Run-ons (3, 6, 7, 9, and 13) total 38; Complete sentences (2, 5, 10, 14, and 15) total 46.

6-13.   Punctuation Review

1. The tall, handsome man lives in Altoona, Pennsylvania.

2. Are there any birds outside the classroom window?

3. In my opinion, the suggestions should be brought up at the next council meeting.

4. On March 24, 1980, an important event took place on Long Island.

5. Kasheema asked, "Are you the only person who will attend the special conference?"

6. Henry Kissinger, the former U.S. Secretary of State, will be the keynote speaker.

7. Because we will arrive after you, leave the key under the mat.

8. The manuscript was found by the archaeologist, and now she will analyze its contents.

9. At fifteen, when Jeremiah went to the Special Olympics, he won three medals.

10. Mr. Fennelly cannot go to Spain with the family because he has several business commitments.

11. Her gardens are very impressive; however, few people have seen them.

12. "Whenever you kick the ball out of bounds," Caroline said, "you should retrieve it."

13. The one-eighth-inch board should be nailed to the wall very carefully.

14. Larry's brother-in-law visited the family on January 14, 1988.

15. First they mapped out their route, then they packed the car, and finally they set off on their journey.

6-14.   Punctuating Dialogue

"I never wanted to come here in the first place," said Frank as he looked nervously down the alley in this tough part of the city. "What are we doing here tonight? You have heard about this area and what happens here. Let's go back out and get on the train to go home now."

"Oh, come on now," said his friend Mitch. "What's there to be scared about here? You're just imagining what is probably not going to happen."

"Hey, that's wishful thinking, Mitch. We could easily get killed by who knows what in this place. I'm leaving before something happens to us."

"You know the other guys will hear about what a chicken you are, Frank. Do you think they would behave this way?"

"I don't care what you tell them, Mitch. You're just as scared as I am, but you're pretending to be tough. I bet that if some group of tough guys came down this alley right now, you would run out of here faster than you have ever run before. Do what you want, Mitch, but I'm out of here."

6-15. Grammar, Mechanics, and Usage Review

These are possible answers. Numbers 2 and 3 could use semicolons.

1. **Fragment.** The day after Mario broke the record, he received a cash award.

2. **Comma splice.** Yesterday all my problems seemed so far away. Now they are not.

3. **Run-on.** Several pieces of cake had been left out on the counter all night. This morning they were too hard to eat.

4. **Pronoun number problem.** *Each* of the girls has *her* own prom dress.

5. **Wrong word.** That could *have* been the best way to solve this dilemma.

6. **Wrong comparison word.** Unfortunately, these computers are the *worst* I have ever used.

7. **Wrong comparison word.** Roberta, our lead guitar player, is the *most* talented of the three musicians who auditioned for the band.

8. **Wrong word.** *There* are many young people who would like to be in your position right now.

9. **Incorrect verb.** Do you feel that our class has *chosen* the most efficient method?

10. **Wrong tense.** (Use the present infinitive *to receive* since the main verb, *was*, is in the past tense.) Yuri received the award after he felt happy about receiving it.

11. **Idiom error.** Gertrude is the type of aunt who likes to visit often.

12. **Wrong verb tense.** All of the delicious loaves of bread had been *eaten* before the weekend concluded.

13. **Wrong adverb.** These dogs so *badly* want to go out, but since it is raining, I will keep them inside.

14. **Misspelling.** It took the police approximately sixteen minutes to get to the *scene* of the crime.

15. **Idiom error.** Our attendance officer has dislike *for* those students who are truant from school that frequently.

16. **Wrong verb.** The flag is *raised* each morning at exactly 7 A.M.

17. **Wrong pronoun.** (Since *becoming* is a gerund, a noun, it is modified by an adjective. The pronoun *your* is the correct modifier.) Is there much sense in *your* becoming a sales clerk at that particular department store this late in the summer?

18. **Idiom error.** (The phrase *end result* is redundant.) Can you disagree with the *result* of this debate, Mildred?

19. **Unclear pronoun.** (Is Brandi or her sister the one who is upset?) Brandi was upset when she told her sister about the problem.

20. **Idiom error.** (The standard usage is *prefer to*.) I prefer studying biology *to* studying chemistry.

6-16. Essential Terms

```
¹S       ²S E ³T T I N G        ⁴S Y ⁵M B O L
 T         I     O                     E
⁶F R A G M E N T      ⁷D I D A C T I C   ⁸C
 A         I     E         I           A    O
 T         L    ⁹A    C  ¹⁰P            P    N
           ¹¹D E N O T A T I O N        H    N
¹²S    G    E     T    I    N           O    O
 T ¹³S Y N  T A X  I    O                R    T
 R  T       A      T    N                     A
 U  Y       I      U                          T
 C  L       L      D                          I
¹⁴T H E S I S   ¹⁵T H E M E                   O
 U                      V                     N
 R             ¹⁶I M A G E R Y
 E                      W
```

6-17. HALF AND HALF

1. buffaloes
2. radios
4. obsessive
6. committee
7. bouquet
11. recommend
13. techniques
14. stupefy
20. responsibility
22. Belgian (or Belgium)
23. forgotten
24. grammar
26. husband
27. marriage
28. necessary
32. laboratory
34. warrant
36. independent
39. rapidly
40. successfully

6-18. Playing with Words that are Not Words

Answers will vary.

6-19. Time for a Break

Here are possible words.

fling	front	pistol	sling	tint
flip	frost	poor	slip	tort
flit	frown	port	solo	trip
floor	gift	print	song	troop
flop	going	prior	snoop	twin
florist	golf	proof	spilt	twirl
flown	grown	prow	split	twist
foil	inflow	prowl	spoil	wing
foist	iris	rift	spool	wisp
folio	iron	ring	spoon	writ
fooling	lift	roil	sport	wring
foot	lifting	rotor	sting	wrist
forgot	ping	rowing	strip	wrong
fort	pinto	silo	swing	

6-20. Scooby Doo and Much More

1. The purpose of each paragraph is as follows: *first paragraph:* to introduce the fact that Katie is a worrier; *second paragraph:* how a traumatic event confirmed Katie's fear that she is a habitual worrier though she has become more relaxed today; *third paragraph:* worrying has helped Katie in some ways; *fourth paragraph:* though she has improved and become more relaxed, Katie is not entirely cured of worrying.

2. The topic sentences are numbers 4, 10, 28, and 37.

3. Humorous aspects include the juxtaposition of Scooby Doo and calculus, her worrying about her split ends (though her dad does not), Vada's quote (line 24), her lists of cause and effects that conclude the third paragraph, and her imagining (during class) that her car will careen off into the woods. The serious aspects include her mother's traumatic event, Katie's wanting to be successful in school, the knowledge that worrying has some positive effects, and Katie's understanding that she is not entirely cured of her worrying.

6-21. Airline Tickets (Part One)

1. to earn enough money, to see her cousins in Vermont
2. that would allow her to earn enough money for the air fare
3. Reaching her goal
4. adverbial or subordinate clause
5. Walking around the mall
6. adverbial phrase

7. Waitressing

8. noun clause

9. on the shoulder, from the restaurant

10. completely

6-22.   Airline Tickets (Part Two)

1. sentence 5 (At The Gap)

2. sentence 4 (who were in the store)

3. The Gap

4. adjective phrase

5. sentence 5 (that she was upset, that her mother had asked her to go to the grocery store)

6. sentence 3

7. gerund

8. verb phrase

9. to get the plane ticket to Vermont

10. conjunction

11. Infinitive phrases include "to be booked two weeks in advance," "to work hard enough," and "to get the airline tickets."

12. adjective clause

6-23.   The Summer Tradition

Answers will vary.

6-24.   Imitating Another Student's Writing

Answers will vary.

6-25.   Bricks

Answers will vary.

6-26.   Before Thirty-Something (Part One)

1. The first paragraph sets up the distance between Olivia and her sister mostly because of the age difference.

2. Olivia's mother does not enjoy board games; her father likes to play cards; her brother enjoys video games; Rachel, bored, is looking for things to do.

3. Rachel is a playful good sport who is not yet ready for the board games that Olivia wants to play.

4. Olivia points out how, at this time, she and Rachel are at different stages of maturity.

5. The tone is reflective as Olivia explains how Rachel and she were different at this time. The author tolerates her sister and depends upon her at the same time as seen in their playtimes together.

6. Answers will vary.

6-27.   Before Thirty-Something (Part Two)

1. "Even last summer" (1), "At first" (3), "After a while" (4), "As time passed" (9), "On an August night" (13), and "That night" (22) are transitions.

2. paragraph 2

3. These shorter sentences give more variety to the piece and also serve as a contrast to the longer ones. The reader will pay greater attention to these shorter sentences because of their placement within the composition.

4. Rachel had the solution to Olivia's dilemma.

5. The concluding paragraph shows that the two sisters do not have to wait until they are thirty-something in order to have a relationship and appreciate each other.

6-28.   Thinking and Writing Creatively

1. chronological

2. first person

3. Answers will vary.

4. Answers will vary.

5. Answers will vary.

6-29.   Something New (Part One)

Answers will vary.

6-30.   Something New (Part Two)

Answers will vary.

6-31. Joey

These are possible answers.

1. *Paragraph One:* Ali says that despite their differences, Joey and she became best friends. *Paragraph Two:* Ali gives a glimpse back at how she and Joey met and how she and Joey began to bond. *Paragraph Three:* These sentences show the girls' similarities. *Paragraph Four:* Ali states how Joey was different from other people in that she was very accepting of Ali. *Paragraph Five:* Ali admits that Joey had her own issues, and together the two girls became trusting friends. *Paragraph Six:* Here Ali tells how special—and unique—Joey is.

2. Ali makes good use of comparison–contrast techniques in showing how she and Joey were initially so seemingly unlike. She also uses two rhetorical questions to make the reader more curious about how this relationship works out.

3. Answers will vary.

4. Answers will vary.

5. Ali repeats "She" to emphasize Joey's qualities (as contrasted to her own) and repeats "We" to emphasize how similar the two girls really were.

6-32. Your Town (Part One)

1. The first sentence sets the mood for the rest of the excerpt. It adds some enticement and mystery to what is ahead.

2. The single main street has cute shops containing oddities and trinkets, and the town gives one a comforting feeling.

3. Cold Spring Harbor's most distinguishing aspect is its water.

4. Adam writes that the water is calming and beautiful. It can also quietly seize a person on a troubling day.

5. "But" (sentence 3) shows a change of appearance from the previous two sentences. "Or" (sentence 10) allows the reader to see yet another aspect of Cold Spring Harbor's water.

6. Answers will vary.

6-33. Your Town (Part Two)

1. Sentence 2 is the excerpt's topic sentence because it introduces the concept of the town's changing seasons.

2. Two adjectives that appeal to the sense of hearing are the "loud" travelers and locals (sentence 4) and the "ever-present crunching of leaves" (sentence 5).

3. Sight images include "huge blue skies" (3), "melancholy branches of leaves" (5), "gently smoking chimneys" and "snow-covered shops" (6), and the "small sun" (7).

4. These transitions include "Summer brings" (3), "With autumn" (4), "When winter descends" (6), and "Spring, on the other hand," (8).

5. Answers will vary.

6-34. Your Town (Part Three)

1. Adam discusses the different types of people who live in Cold Spring Harbor.
2. The topic sentence, sentence 1, is stated.
3. Influences on the town inhabitants include Cold Spring Harbor Laboratories (4), ones "left alone" (5), the town's "silence" (6), the "park" and "water" (7), "time" (12), and "whispering tides" and "calling gulls" (13)
4. Answers will vary though typical words include haphazard (2), erroneous (2), plethora (3), prevalent (4), regimented (7), metropolis (14).
5. Inhabitants include thinkers (1), certain type of learner (4), the thinker who is left alone (4), "explorers of the self" (8), and people who have time and a chance to be alone (11).

6-35. Your Town (Part Four)

1. Answers will vary.
2. Cold Spring Harbor residents have more time to reflect, internalize, draw conclusions, and share stories than residents of other places do.
3. The sentences are sophisticated.
4. The inhabitants' dependency is noted in sentence 6 and beyond.

Additional answers will vary.

6-36. Reaching Them

Answers will vary.

6-37. Taylor's Bucket

Answers will vary.

6-38. You Give and They Follow

Answers will vary.

6-39. French or Spanish?

Stories will vary.

6-40. The Poet in You

Answers will vary.

6-41. The Neighbor

Answers will vary.

6-42. Meet the Tripps

Answers will vary.

6-43. Story Starters

Answers will vary.

6-44. New York and Paris

Answers will vary.

6-45. Interpreting Quotations

Answers will vary.

6-46. Humpty Dumpty

Answers will vary.

6-47. Kids' TV

This is a sample answer.

In the article Gillespie argues that children's television (a) does not have to be educational in the first place because schools and parents take care of a child's education; (b) children spend more time than ever before in educational settings; (c) children are busy—as busy—as their parents; and (d) children do learn from TV. They learn real-life lessons.

6-48.   Andrea Bocelli

Answers will vary.

6-49.   American Gothic

Answers will vary.

6-50.   A Teenager's Stressful Life

Answers will vary.

6-51.   The Recall

Answers will vary.

6-52.   An Unpleasant Situation

Answers will vary.

6-53.   A Real Problem

Answers will vary.

6-54.   The Literary Me

Answers will vary.

6-55.   Tragic Characters

Answers will vary.

6-56.   Sketching a Literary Character

Answers will vary.

6-57.   Matching the Character and the Quote

Answers will vary.

6-58.   Personal Characteristics

Answers will vary.

6-59.   To Follow or Not to Follow—That is the Question

Answers will vary.

6-60.   More Than a Peep of Bo-Peep

Answers will vary.

6-61.   The Crucible

Answers will vary.

6-62.   Evaluation Strategies

Answers will vary.

6-63.   A Worthwhile Conversation

Answers will vary.

6-64.   Hamlet—A Man of Action

1. "How Is Hamlet a man of action?" is a possible question.
2. Olivia organized her paragraph chronologically, starting from the play's beginning and working up to its conclusion.
3. Transitions include "throughout the play" (2), "From the start of" (3), "first shows" (4), "Again proving himself" (7), and "while in the last moments of his life" (8).
4. The topic sentence (#1) is stated.
5. The outline should include the topic sentence and the chronology of Hamlet's actions showing he is a man of action.

6-65. Hammer or Anvil?

1. An anvil is an iron or steel block on which metal objects are hammered into shape.

2. In this introductory paragraph, Chirag explains when a man is an anvil and when he is a hammer. He tells which novel he will use, and then he shows how the two characters, McMurphy and Ratched, exchange the roles of anvil and hammer.

3. McMurphy is a hammer when he places bets with the inmates in order to rile Ratched. The tactics listed in sentence 9 also help McMurphy to be the hammer. Finally, he challenges her authority by pushing the rules.

4. In the next paragraph Chirag will discuss how Ratched is either the anvil or the hammer.

5. (68) is the page number on which the quote Chirag uses is found.

6. The eleventh sentence's purpose is to show that Ratched, the anvil in the examples of the second paragraph, is no easy match for McMurphy.

7. Answers will vary.

8. Answers will vary.

6-66. The Reader's Mind

Answers will vary.

6-67. Stepping into the Work

Answers will vary.

6-68. Dead Poets Society

Answers will vary.

6-69. The Grammatically Correct Poem

Answers will vary.

6-70. Romeo and Juliet

The following is an acceptable translation.

1. Two families both of equal honor,

2. Live in lovely Verona (an Italian town), this play's setting,

3. An old family feud has now broken out into new rioting.

4. And public blood makes civilized hands unclean.

5. From forth the deadly bodies of these two enemies

6. A pair of lovers doomed by the stars are killed,

7. Because of their unfortunate adventures leading to their pitiful deaths

8. Their families' feuding ceases.

9. The horrible progress of their ill-fated love,

10. And the suspension of their parents' rage

11. Which, except for their children's deaths, nothing could eliminate

12. Is now the business of our two-hour play;

13. And if you listen patiently and carefully,

14. What information you did not hear here, our work on this stage will make clearer.

6-71. Paraphrasing the Constitution

capital: involving or punishable by death

infamous: punishable by imprisonment in a penitentiary

presentment: notice taken or report made by a Grand Jury of an offense on the basis of the jury's own knowledge and observation and without a bill of indictment

indictment: formal charging of one or more persons with the commission of a crime

Grand Jury: a special jury of a statutory number of citizens, usually more than 12, that investigates accusations against persons charged with crime and indicts them for trial before a jury—if there is sufficient evidence

Militia: military force

offense: breaking of the law

jeopardy: danger

limb: arm or leg

compelled: forced

deprived: kept from having

liberty: freedom

just: fair

compensation: something given as an equivalent

Here is an acceptable paraphrasing of Article V of the Constitution of the United States:

No person shall be held for either a crime punishable by death or a crime punishable by imprisonment in a penitentiary unless on a notice taken or report made by a Grand Jury of an offense on the basis of the Jury's own knowledge and observation and without a bill formally charging that person (or more than that one person) with the commission of a crime. The exception to this is in cases originating in the land or water forces, or the Militia, during one's actual services in time of War or public danger. No person shall be tried twice for the same offense. No person shall be forced to be a witness against himself or be deprived of his life, freedom, or property without due process of the law. None of his private property shall be taken from him for public use unless he is fairly compensated for that property.

6-72. Shaping Up Your Shakespeare

These are possible interpretations.

1. Juliet's beauty radiates so. She is like a piece of jewelry on an Ethiop's ear. Her beauty transcends the earth and is "out of this world."

2. Don't have the name (Romeo Montague). A name is unimportant since it really means nothing. A rose still has its perfection no matter what it is called. Romeo, take on another name (besides Montague) since it doesn't suit you. Give up your name and take me instead.

3. If you truly love me and want to marry me, let me know tomorrow when I send someone to find out where and when our marriage will take place. From then on, I will give you all that I have and go with you everywhere you go in this world.

6-73. Advice Columnist

Answers will vary.

6-74. Ten Tough Proposals

Answers will vary.

6-75. Three Favorites

Answers will vary.

6-76. The Very Necessary _____

Answers will vary.

6-77. Clever Advertising Lines

Answers will vary.

6-78. Puns

Answers will vary.

6-79. The Personal Crossword Puzzle

Answers will vary.

6-80.   Mr. Peacock

Answers will vary.

6-81.   Clothes Make the Man (or Woman or Boy or Girl)

Answers will vary.

6-82.   If I Were _____ For a Day

Answers will vary.

6-83.   It Does Not Work and So . . .

Answers will vary.

6-84.   Dear Mrs. Wilker

Answers will vary.

6-85.   Journal Entry

Answers will vary.

6-86.   Just as the Editor Ordered

Answers will vary.

6-87.   What's in a Name?

These are the definitions.

1. A mustang is a small wild horse.
2. Eldorado is a legendary country in South America, supposedly rich in gold and precious stones.
3. A cutlass is a short, thick, curving sword, formerly used especially by sailors. Supreme means the highest degree of something.
4. A taurus is a bull.

5. A celebrity is a famous person.

6. A wrangler is a cowboy who herds livestock, especially saddle horses.

7. A voyager is one who is on a journey.

8. A ram is a male sheep known to charge its opponent.

9. An explorer loves to travel into unknown places.

10. A safari is a journey or hunting exhibition.

6-88.   Researching the Awards

Answers will vary.

6-89.   What's Going on Around You

Answers will vary.

6-90.   Words to Live By

Answers will vary.

CONTENTS

iii

online preparation resource

indicates an option.

indicates an optional segment

23⅝ 24

4⅝ 4¹¹⁄₁₆

5½ 5½ − ⅜

5½ 2¹³⁄₁₆ − ⅛

20⅝ 2¹³⁄₁₆ − ⅛

17⅜ 18⅛ + ⅞

6½ 6½ − ½

7¼ 3¹⁄₃₂ − ⅛

15⁄16

9⁄16 ⅝

1¹⁵⁄₃₂ 7¹⁵⁄₁₆

7¹⁵⁄₁₆ 7¹³⁄₁₆ 7¹⁵⁄₁₆

2⅝ 2¹¹⁄₃₂ 2½ +

27 2¾ 2¼ 2¼

6⅞ 12¹⁄₁₆ 11⅜ 11¾ +

87 33¾ 33 33¹⁄₁₆ −

6⅜ 25⅝ 24⁹⁄₁₆ 25⅝ +

833 12 11⅝ 11⅝ +

16 10½ 10½ 10⅝ −

78 15⅞ 15¹³⁄₁₆ 15⅞ −

508 9¹⁄₁₆ 8¼ 8⅜ +

11¼ 10⅝ 10⅜

HOW TO USE THE CFA PROGRAM CURRICULUM

Congratulations on your decision to enter the Chartered Financial Analyst (CFA®) Program. This exciting and rewarding program of study reflects your desire to become a serious investment professional. You are embarking on a program noted for its high ethical standards and the breadth of knowledge, skills, and abilities it develops. Your commitment to the CFA Program should be educationally and professionally rewarding.

The credential you seek is respected around the world as a mark of accomplishment and dedication. Each level of the program represents a distinct achievement in professional development. Successful completion of the program is rewarded with membership in a prestigious global community of investment professionals. CFA charterholders are dedicated to life-long learning and maintaining currency with the ever-changing dynamics of a challenging profession. The CFA Program represents the first step towards a career-long commitment to professional education.

The CFA examination measures your degree of mastery of the assigned CFA Program curriculum. Therefore, the key to your success on the examination is reading and studying the CFA Program curriculum. The remaining sections provide background on the Candidate Body of Knowledge (CBOK™), the organization of the curriculum and tips for developing an effective study program.

Curriculum Development

The CFA Program curriculum is grounded in the practice of the investment profession. Utilizing the Global Body of Investment Knowledge (GBIK) collaborative website, CFA Institute performs a continuous practice analysis with investment professionals around the world to determine the knowledge, skills, and abilities that are relevant to the profession. Regional panels and targeted surveys are conducted annually to verify and reinforce the continuous feedback. The practice analysis process ultimately defines the Candidate Body of Knowledge (CBOK). The CBOK consists of four components:

▶ A broad topic outline that lists the major knowledge areas

▶ Topic area weights that indicate the relative exam weightings of the top-level topic areas

▶ Learning Outcome Statements (LOS) that advise candidates as to what they should be able to do with this knowledge (LOS are provided in candidate study sessions and at the beginning of each reading)

▶ The curriculum of material that candidates receive upon exam registration and are expected to master

A committee made up of practicing charterholders, in conjunction with CFA Institute staff, designs the CFA Program curriculum to deliver the CBOK to candidates. The examinations, also written by practicing charterholders, are designed to allow you to demonstrate your mastery of the CBOK as set forth in the CFA Program curriculum. As you structure your personal study program, you should emphasize mastery of the CBOK and the practical application of that knowledge. For more information on the practice analysis, CBOK, and development of the CFA Program curriculum, please visit www.cfainstitute.org/toolkit.

Organization of the Curriculum

The Level I CFA Program curriculum is organized into 10 topic areas. Each topic area begins with a brief statement of the material and the depth of knowledge expected.

Each topic area is then divided into one or more study sessions. These study sessions—18 sessions in the Level I curriculum—should form the basic structure of your reading and preparation.

Each study session includes a statement of its structure and objective, and is further divided into specific reading assignments. The outline on the inside front cover of each volume illustrates the organization of these 18 study sessions.

The reading assignments are the basis for all examination questions, and are selected or developed specifically to teach the CBOK. These readings are drawn from CFA Program-commissioned content, textbook chapters, professional journal articles, research analyst reports, and cases. Readings include problems and solutions as well as appendices to help you learn.

Reading-specific Learning Outcome Statements (LOS) are listed at the beginning of each reading. These LOS indicate what you should be able to accomplish after studying the reading. We encourage you to review how to properly use LOS, and the descriptions of commonly used LOS "command words," at www.cfainstitute.org/toolkit. The command words signal the depth of learning you are expected to achieve from the reading. You should use the LOS to guide and focus your study, as each examination question is based on an assigned reading and one or more LOS. However, the readings provide context for the LOS and enable you to apply a principle or concept in a variety of scenarios. The candidate is responsible for the entirety of all of the required material in a study session, the assigned readings as well as the end-of-reading questions and problems.

Features of the Curriculum

- ► **Required vs. Optional Segments** - You should read all of the pages for an assigned reading. In some cases, however, we have reprinted an entire chapter or article and marked those parts of the reading that are not required as "optional." The CFA examination is based only on the required segments, and the optional segments are included only when they might help you to better understand the required segments (by seeing the required material in its full context). When an optional segment begins, you will see an icon and a solid vertical bar in the outside margin that will continue until the optional segment ends, accompanied by another icon. *Unless the material is specifically marked as optional, you should assume it is required.* Keep in mind that the optional material is provided strictly for your convenience and will not be tested. You should rely on the required segments and the reading-specific LOS in preparing for the examination.

- ► **Problems/Solutions** - *All questions and problems in the readings as well as their solutions (which are provided directly following the problems) are part of the curriculum and required material for the exam.* When appropriate, we have included problems within and after the readings to demonstrate practical application and reinforce your understanding of the concepts presented. The questions and problems are designed to help you learn these concepts and may serve as a basis for exam questions. Many of the questions are adapted from past CFA examinations.

- ► **Margins** - The wide margins in each volume provide space for your note-taking.

▶ **Two-Color Format** - To enrich the visual appeal and clarity of the exhibits, tables, and text, the curriculum is printed in a two-color format.

▶ **Six-Volume Structure** - For portability of the curriculum, the material is spread over six volumes.

▶ **Glossary and Index** - For your convenience, we have printed a glossary and index in each volume. Throughout the curriculum, a **bolded blue** word in a reading denotes a term defined in the glossary.

▶ **Source Material** - The authorship, publisher, and copyright owners are given for each reading for your reference. We recommend that you use this CFA Institute curriculum rather than the original source materials because the curriculum may include only selected pages from outside readings, updated sections within the readings, and has problems and solutions tailored to the CFA Program.

▶ **LOS Self-Check** - We have inserted checkboxes next to each LOS that you can use to track your progress in mastering the concepts in each reading.

Designing Your Personal Study Program

Create a Schedule - An orderly, systematic approach to examination preparation is critical. You should dedicate a consistent block of time every week to reading and studying. Complete all reading assignments and the associated problems and solutions in each study session. Review the LOS both before and after you study each reading to ensure that you have mastered the applicable content and can demonstrate the knowledge, skill, or ability described by the LOS and the assigned reading. Use the new LOS self-check to track your progress and highlight areas of weakness for later review.

You will receive periodic e-mail communications that contain important study tips and preparation strategies. Be sure to read these carefully.

CFA Institute estimates that you will need to devote a minimum of 10–15 hours per week for 18 weeks to study the assigned readings. Allow a minimum of one week for each study session, and plan to complete them all at least 30–45 days prior to the examination. This schedule will allow you to spend the final four to six weeks before the examination reviewing the assigned material and taking online sample and mock examinations.

At CFA Institute, we believe that candidates need to commit to a *minimum* of 270–300 hours reading and reviewing the curriculum and end-of-reading questions and problems. Many candidates have also incorporated the online sample examinations into their preparations during the final weeks before the exam. This recommendation, however, may substantially underestimate the hours needed for appropriate examination preparation depending on your individual circumstances, relevant experience, and academic background. You will undoubtedly adjust your study time to conform to your own strengths and weaknesses, and your educational and professional background.

You will probably spend more time on some study sessions than on others, but on average you should plan on devoting 15 hours per study session. You should allow ample time for both in-depth study of all topic areas and additional concentration on those topic areas for which you feel least prepared.

Preliminary Readings - The reading assignments in Economics assume candidates already have a basic mastery of the concepts typically presented in introductory university-level economics courses. Information on suggested readings to improve your knowledge of these topics precedes the relevant study sessions.

Candidate Preparation Toolkit - We have created the online toolkit to provide a single comprehensive location with resources and guidance for candidate preparation. In addition to in-depth information on study program planning, the CFA Program curriculum, and the online sample and mock examinations, the toolkit also contains curriculum errata, printable study session outlines, sample examination questions, and more. Errata that we have identified in the curriculum are corrected and listed periodically in the errata listing in the toolkit. We encourage you to use the toolkit as your central preparation resource during your tenure as a candidate. Visit the toolkit at www.cfainstitute.org/toolkit.

Online Sample Examinations - CFA Institute online sample examinations are intended to assess your exam preparation as you progress toward the end of your study. After each question, you will receive immediate feedback noting the correct response and indicating the relevant assigned reading, so you'll be able to identify areas of weakness for further study. The 120-minute sample examinations reflect the question formats, topics, and level of difficulty of the actual CFA examinations. Aggregate data indicate that the CFA examination pass rate was higher among candidates who took one or more online sample examinations than among candidates who did not take the online sample examinations. For more information on the online sample examinations, please visit www.cfainstitute.org/toolkit.

Online Mock Examinations - In response to candidate requests, CFA Institute has developed mock examinations that mimic the actual CFA examinations not only in question format and level of difficulty, but also in length. The three-hour online mock exams are intended to be taken after you complete your study of the full curriculum, so you can test your understanding of the CBOK and your readiness for the exam. To further differentiate, feedback is provided at the end of the exam, rather than after each question as with the sample exams. CFA Institute recommends that you take these mock exams at the final stage of your preparation toward the actual CFA examination. For more information on the online mock examinations, please visit www.cfainstitute.org/toolkit.

Tools to Measure Your Comprehension of the Curriculum

With the addition of the online mock exams, CFA Institute now provides three distinct ways you can practice for the actual CFA exam. The full descriptions are above, but below is a brief summary of each:

End-of-Reading Questions and Problems - These are found at the end of each reading in the printed curriculum, and should be used to test your understanding of the concepts.

Online Sample Exams - Available in Fall 2010, online sample exams are designed to assess your exam preparation, and can help you target areas of weakness for further study.

Online Mock Exams - In contrast to the sample exams, mock exams will be available in Spring 2011. Mock exams are designed to replicate the exam day experience, and should be taken near the end of your study period to prepare for exam day.

Preparatory Providers - After you enroll in the CFA Program, you may receive numerous solicitations for preparatory courses and review materials. When considering a prep course, make sure the provider is in compliance with the CFA Institute Prep Provider Guidelines Program. Just remember, there are no shortcuts to success on the CFA examinations; reading and studying the CFA curriculum is the key to success on the examination. The CFA examinations reference only the CFA Institute assigned curriculum—no preparatory course or review course materials are consulted or referenced. For more information on the Prep Provider Guidelines Program, visit www.cfainstitute.org/cfaprog/resources/prepcourse.html.

SUMMARY

Every question on the CFA examination is based on specific pages in the required readings and on one or more LOS. Frequently, an examination question is also tied to a specific example highlighted within a reading or to a specific end-of-reading question and/or problem and its solution. To make effective use of the curriculum, please remember these key points:

1. All pages printed in the Custom Curriculum are required reading for the examination except for occasional sections marked as optional. You may read optional pages as background, but you will not be tested on them.

2. All questions, problems, and their solutions - printed at the end of readings - are part of the curriculum and required study material for the examination.

3. You should make appropriate use of the CFA Candidate Toolkit and the online sample/mock examinations.

4. You should schedule and commit sufficient study time to cover the 18 study sessions, review the materials, and take sample/mock examinations.

5. **Note:** Some of the concepts in the study sessions may be superseded by updated rulings and/or pronouncements issued after a reading was published. Candidates are expected to be familiar with the overall analytical framework contained in the assigned readings. Candidates are not responsible for changes that occur after the material was written.

Feedback

At CFA Institute, we are committed to delivering a comprehensive and rigorous curriculum for the development of competent, ethically grounded investment professionals. We rely on candidate and member feedback as we work to incorporate content, design, and packaging improvements. You can be assured that we will continue to listen to your suggestions. Please send any comments or feedback to curriculum@cfainstitute.org. Ongoing improvements in the curriculum will help you prepare for success on the upcoming examinations, and for a lifetime of learning as a serious investment professional.

$4\frac{5}{8}$ $4\frac{11}{16}$ $-\frac{3}{8}$

$5\frac{1}{2}$ $5\frac{1}{2}$ $-$

$5\frac{1}{2}$ $21\frac{3}{16}$ $-\frac{1}{16}$

$20\frac{5}{8}$ $21\frac{3}{16}$ $+\frac{7}{8}$

$17\frac{3}{8}$ $18\frac{1}{8}$ $+$

$6\frac{1}{2}$ $6\frac{1}{2}$ $-\frac{1}{2}$

$7\frac{1}{4}$ $6\frac{1}{2}$ $31\frac{1}{32}$ $-\frac{1}{8}$

$\frac{15}{16}$

$9\frac{1}{8}$

$9\frac{1}{16}$ $9\frac{1}{8}$

$\frac{1}{32}$

$7\frac{13}{16}$ $7\frac{15}{16}$

$7\frac{15}{16}$ $7\frac{13}{16}$ $7\frac{15}{16}$

$2\frac{5}{8}$ $2\frac{11}{32}$ $2\frac{1}{2}$ $+$

$2\frac{3}{4}$ $2\frac{1}{4}$ $2\frac{1}{4}$

$6\frac{1}{8}$ $12\frac{1}{16}$ $11\frac{3}{8}$ $11\frac{3}{4}$ $+$

87 $33\frac{3}{4}$ 33 $33\frac{1}{8}$ $-$

$6\frac{7}{32}$ $25\frac{5}{8}$ $24\frac{9}{16}$ $25\frac{3}{8}$ $+$

833 12 $11\frac{5}{8}$ $11\frac{7}{8}$ $+$

16 $10\frac{1}{2}$ $10\frac{1}{2}$ $10\frac{1}{2}$ $-$

78 $15\frac{1}{8}$ $15\frac{13}{16}$ $15\frac{1}{8}$ $-$

$8\frac{1}{8}$ $+$

4608 $9\frac{1}{16}$ $8\frac{1}{4}$

430 $11\frac{1}{4}$ $10\frac{1}{8}$

ECONOMICS

STUDY SESSIONS

TOPIC LEVEL LEARNING OUTCOME

The candidate should be able to demonstrate a thorough knowledge of macroeconomic and microeconomic principles, including the key components of economic activity, and macroeconomic theory and policy.

4⅝ 4¹¹/₁₆ — ⅜
5½ 5½ — ⅜
5½ 2¹³/₁₆ — ⅛
20⅝ 21³/₁₆ + ⅞
17⅜ 18⅛ +
18½ 6½ 6½ — ½
7¼ 6½ 31/32 —
15/16 9/16
9/16
7¹⁵/₃₂ 7¹³/₁₆ 7¹⁵/₁₆
2⅝ 2¹¹/₃₂ 2½ +
2¾ 2¼ 2¼
6⅛ 12¹/₁₆ 11⅜ 11¾ +
33¾ 33 33⅛ — ⅛
25⅝ 24⁹/₁₆ 25⅝ +
12 11⅝ 11⅝ +
16 10½ 10½ 10⅝ —
78 15⅝ 15¹³/₁₆ 15⅞ —
9¹/₁₆ 8¼ 8⅛ +
11¼ 10⅛

Preparing to Study the CFA Curriculum Materials on Economics

Before beginning the reading assignments, candidates should have a basic mastery of the concepts typically presented in introductory college-level economics courses. The primary source of reading assignments in the CFA Curriculum is *Economics*, 8th edition, by Michael Parkin.

Reading assignments assume candidates are already knowledgeable in economics and understand the following important subjects:

- ► For Microeconomics (Study session 4)
  - ► The laws of supply and demand and factors causing shifts in or movements along the supply and demand curves;
  - ► The operation of market forces in resource and funds markets; and
  - ► Effects on economic activity of price controls and taxes.
- ► For Market Structure and Macroeconomics (Study session 5)
  - ► Price determination, market equilibrium, and the behavior of market participants;
  - ► Using national income, output, and price measures to track the performance of national economies. For example,
    - ► Approaches to measuring gross domestic product (GDP);
    - ► Difference between real and nominal GDP;
    - ► Problems encountered when measuring GDP;
    - ► How changes occur over time; and
    - ► Components of alternative measures (GNP, national income, personal income, and disposable income) and how they relate to each other.
  - ► Factors affecting aggregate demand and supply, and how markets adjust to anticipated and unanticipated changes in these factors;
  - ► Self correcting mechanisms that may help stabilize the market economy;
  - ► Major theoretical and practical considerations of macroeconomic models.

If you have not taken an introductory economics course within the past few years, we strongly encourage you to consider additional study of introductory course material related to the above mentioned topics. Although examination questions are drawn only from the reading assignments, studying the additional introductory material will strengthen candidates' understanding of the required concepts. *Economics,* 8th edition, by Michael Parkin, is available from Pearson Addison-Wesley. At a minimum, we recommend that candidates study the following chapters:

- ► Chapter 3, Demand and Supply
- ► Chapter 7, Utility and Demand
- ► Chapter 21, Measuring GDP and Economic Growth
- ► Chapter 23, At Full Employment: The Classical Model
- ► Chapter 28, Expenditure Multipliers: The Keynesian Model

Many economics textbooks and courses provide similar coverage and will enable you to master the concepts and principles discussed in the Parkin text.

If you do not have a strong background in economics, please take some extra time before you begin your study program to review economic concepts and principles.

23⅜ 24

4⅝ 4¹¹⁄₁₆

5⅛ 5½ 5½ — ⅜

20⅝ 2¹³⁄₁₆ — ¹⁄₁₆

17⅜ 18⅛ + ⅞

6½ 6½ — ½

7¼ 15⁄₁₆ 3¹⁄₃₂ — ⅛

9⁄₁₆ ⅞

⁹⁄₃₂ 7¹³⁄₁₆ 7¹⁵⁄₁₆

7¹⁵⁄₁₆ 2¹¹⁄₃₂ 2½ +

2⅝ 2¼ 2¼

2¾

6⅛ 12¹⁄₁₆ 11⅜ 11¾ +

87 33¾ 33 33⅛ —

502 25⅝ 24⁹⁄₁₆ 25⅜ +

833 12 11⅝ 11⅞ +

16 10½ 10½ 10½ —

78 15⅞ 15¹³⁄₁₆ 15⅞ —

508 9¹⁄₁₆ 8¼ 8⅛ +

11⅛ 10⅛ 10

STUDY SESSION 4
ECONOMICS:
Microeconomic Analysis

This study session focuses on microeconomic concepts and how firms are affected by these concepts. One of the main concepts related to the equilibrium between demand and supply is elasticity, which measures the rate of changes on the equilibrium price level. A second key concept is efficiency, which is a measure of the firm's "optimal" output given its cost and revenue functions. Understanding these concepts enables analysts to differentiate among various firms on an individual level and to determine their attractiveness for an investor.

READING ASSIGNMENTS

Reading 13   Elasticity
            Economics, Eighth Edition, by Michael Parkin

Reading 14   Efficiency and Equity
            Economics, Eighth Edition, by Michael Parkin

Reading 15   Markets in Action
            Economics, Eighth Edition, by Michael Parkin

Reading 16   Organizing Production
            Economics, Eighth Edition, by Michael Parkin

Reading 17   Output and Costs
            Economics, Eighth Edition, by Michael Parkin

5

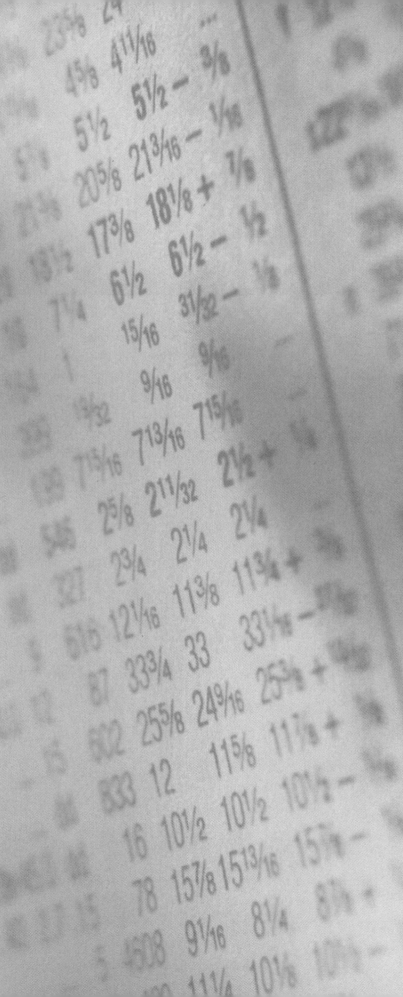

ELASTICITY
by Michael Parkin

LEARNING OUTCOMES

The candidate should be able to:	Mastery
a. calculate and interpret the elasticities of demand (price elasticity, cross elasticity, and income elasticity) and the elasticity of supply, and discuss the factors that influence each measure;	☐
b. calculate elasticities on a straight-line demand curve, differentiate among elastic, inelastic, and unit elastic demand, and describe the relation between price elasticity of demand and total revenue.	☐

WHEN PRICES TUMBLE, DOES REVENUE GROW?

The personal computer industry is operating in fiercely competitive conditions. The prices of notebooks tumbled to average less than $1,000 in 2006. Desktop computer prices also tumbled in 2006 to average less than $500. As the prices of personal computers fell, the quantity of computers bought increased. But did the revenues of Acer, Apple, Gateway, Dell, Hewlett-Packard, and the other computer makers grow?

When computer prices fall, the total revenue of computer producers might still grow. But for revenue to grow, the percentage increase in the quantity of computers sold must exceed the percentage fall in the price. Does this happen? And what determines the effect of a change in the price on the quantity sold and revenue? Find the answer in this reading.

In this reading, you will learn about a tool that helps us to answer many questions about the changes in prices and quantities traded in markets. You will

Economics, Eighth Edition, by Michael Parkin. Copyright © 2008 by Pearson Education. Reprinted with permission of Pearson Education, publishing as Pearson Addison Wesley.

learn about the elasticities of demand and supply. At the end of the reading, we'll return to the market for personal computers and see whether lower-priced computers lower or raise the revenues of computer producers.

2   PRICE ELASTICITY OF DEMAND

You know that when supply increases, the equilibrium price falls and the equilibrium quantity increases. But does the price fall by a large amount and the quantity increase by a little? Or does the price barely fall and the quantity increase by a large amount?

The answer depends on the responsiveness of the quantity demanded to a change in price. You can see why by studying Fig. 1, which shows two possible scenarios in a local pizza market. Figure 1(a) shows one scenario, and Fig. 1(b) shows the other.

In both cases, supply is initially S_0. In part (a), the demand for pizza is shown by the demand curve D_A. In part (b), the demand for pizza is shown by the demand curve D_B. Initially, in both cases, the price is $20 a pizza and the quantity of pizza produced and consumed is 10 pizzas an hour.

Now a large pizza franchise opens up, and the supply of pizza increases. The supply curve shifts rightward to S_1. In case (a), the price falls by an enormous $15 to $5 a pizza, and the quantity increases by only 3 to 13 pizzas an hour. In contrast, in case (b), the price falls by only $5 to $15 a pizza and the quantity increases by 7 to 17 pizzas an hour.

The different outcomes arise from differing degrees of responsiveness of the quantity demanded to a change in price. But what do we mean by responsiveness? One possible answer is slope. The slope of demand curve D_A is steeper than the slope of demand curve D_B.

In this example, we can compare the slopes of the two demand curves. But we can't always do so. The reason is that the slope of a demand curve depends on the units in which we measure the price and quantity. And we often must compare the demand curves for different goods and services that are measured in unrelated units. For example, a pizza producer might want to compare the demand for pizza with the demand for soft drinks. Which quantity demanded is more responsive to a price change? This question can't be answered by comparing the slopes of two demand curves. The units of measurement of pizza and soft drinks are unrelated. The question can be answered with a measure of responsiveness that is independent of units of measurement. Elasticity is such a measure.

The **price elasticity of demand** is a units-free measure of the responsiveness of the quantity demanded of a good to a change in its price when all other influences on buyers' plans remain the same.

Calculating Price Elasticity of Demand

We calculate the *price elasticity of demand* by using the formula:

$$\text{Price elasticity of demand} = \frac{\text{Percentage change in quantity demanded}}{\text{Percentage change in price}}.$$

To use this formula, we need to know the quantities demanded at different prices when all other influences on buyers' plans remain the same. Suppose we

FIGURE 1   How a Change in Supply Changes Price and Quantity

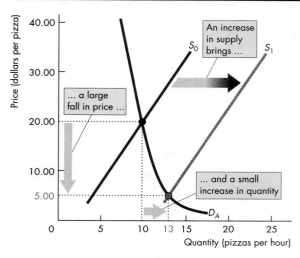

(a) Large price change and small quantity change

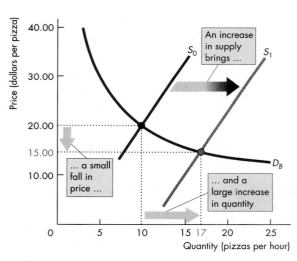

(b) Small price change and large quantity change

Initially the price is $20 a pizza and the quantity sold is 10 pizzas an hour. Then supply increases from S_0 to S_1. In part (a), the price falls by $15 to $5 a pizza, and the quantity increases by 3 to 13 pizzas an hour. In part (b), the price falls by only $5 to $15 a pizza, and the quantity increases by 7 to 17 pizzas an hour. The price change is smaller and the quantity change is larger in case (b) than in case (a). The quantity demanded is more responsive to price in case (b) than in case (a).

have the data on prices and quantities demanded of pizza and we calculate the price elasticity of demand for pizza.

Figure 2 zooms in on the demand curve for pizza and shows how the quantity demanded responds to a small change in price. Initially, the price is $20.50 a pizza and 9 pizzas an hour are sold—the original point in the figure. The price then falls to $19.50 a pizza, and the quantity demanded increases to 11 pizzas an hour—the new point in the figure. When the price falls by $1 a pizza, the quantity demanded increases by 2 pizzas an hour.

To calculate the price elasticity of demand, we express the changes in price and quantity demanded as percentages of the *average price* and the *average quantity*. By using the average price and average quantity, we calculate the elasticity at a point on the demand curve midway between the original point and the new

FIGURE 2   Calculating the Elasticity of Demand

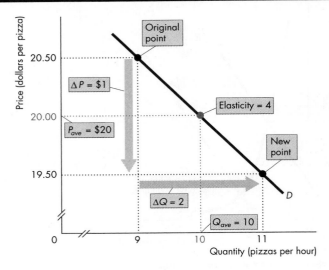

The elasticity of demand is calculated by using the formula:*

$$\text{Price elasticity of demand} = \frac{\text{Percentage change in quantity demanded}}{\text{Percentage change in price}}$$

$$= \frac{\%\Delta Q}{\%\Delta P}$$

$$= \frac{\Delta Q/Q_{ave}}{\Delta P/P_{ave}}$$

$$= \frac{2/10}{1/20}$$

$$= 4.$$

This calculation measures the elasticity at an average price of $20 a pizza and an average quantity of 10 pizzas an hour.

---

*In the formula, the Greek letter delta (Δ) stands for "change in" and %Δ stands for "percentage change in."

---

point. The original price is $20.50 and the new price is $19.50, so the average price is $20. The $1 price decrease is 5 percent of the average price. That is,

$$\Delta P/P_{ave} = (\$1/\$20) \times 100 = 5\%.$$

The original quantity demanded is 9 pizzas and the new quantity demanded is 11 pizzas, so the average quantity demanded is 10 pizzas. The 2 pizza increase in the quantity demanded is 20 percent of the average quantity. That is,

$$\Delta Q/Q_{ave} = (2/10) \times 100 = 20\%.$$

So the price elasticity of demand, which is the percentage change in the quantity demanded (20 percent) divided by the percentage change in price (5 percent) is 4. That is,

$$\text{Price elasticity of demand} = \frac{\%\Delta Q}{\%\Delta P}$$

$$= \frac{20\%}{5\%} = 4.$$

Average Price and Quantity

Notice that we use the *average* price and *average* quantity. We do this because it gives the most precise measurement of elasticity—at the midpoint between the original price and the new price. If the price falls from $20.50 to $19.50, the $1 price change is 4.9 percent of $20.50. The 2 pizza change in quantity is 22.2 percent of 9 pizzas, the original quantity. So if we use these numbers, the price elasticity of demand is 22.2 divided by 4.9, which equals 4.5. If the price rises from $19.50 to $20.50, the $1 price change is 5.1 percent of $19.50. The 2 pizza change in quantity is 18.2 percent of 11 pizzas, the original quantity. So if we use these numbers, the price elasticity of demand is 18.2 divided by 5.1, which equals 3.6.

By using percentages of the *average* price and *average* quantity, we get the same value for the elasticity regardless of whether the price falls from $20.50 to $19.50 or rises from $19.50 to $20.50.

Percentages and Proportions

Elasticity is the ratio of two percentage changes. So when we divide one percentage change by another, the 100s cancel. A percentage change is a *proportionate* change multiplied by 100. The proportionate change in price is $\Delta P/P_{ave}$, and the proportionate change in quantity demanded is $\Delta Q/Q_{ave}$. So if we divide $\Delta Q/Q_{ave}$ by $\Delta P/P_{ave}$ we get the same answer as we get by using percentage changes.

A Units-Free Measure

Now that you've calculated a price elasticity of demand, you can see why it is a *units-free measure*. Elasticity is a units-free measure because the percentage change in each variable is independent of the units in which the variable is measured. And the ratio of the two percentages is a number without units.

Minus Sign and Elasticity

When the price of a good *rises*, the quantity demanded *decreases* along the demand curve. Because a *positive* change in price brings a *negative* change in the quantity demanded, the price elasticity of demand is a negative number. But it is the magnitude, or *absolute value*, of the price elasticity of demand that tells us how responsive—how elastic—demand is. To compare price elasticities of demand, we use the magnitude of the elasticity and ignore the minus sign.

Inelastic and Elastic Demand

Figure 3 shows three demand curves that cover the entire range of possible elasticities of demand. In Fig. 3(a), the quantity demanded is constant regardless of the price. If the quantity demanded remains constant when the price changes, then the price elasticity of demand is zero and the good is said to have a **perfectly inelastic demand**. One good that has a very low price elasticity of demand

FIGURE 3   Inelastic and Elastic Demand

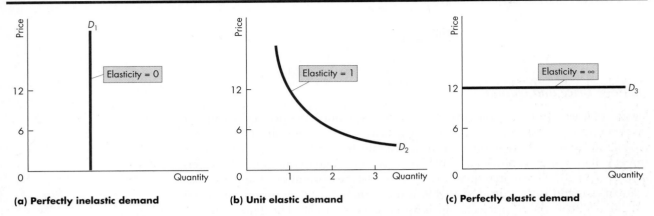

(a) Perfectly inelastic demand   **(b) Unit elastic demand**   **(c) Perfectly elastic demand**

Each demand illustrated here has a constant elasticity. The demand curve in part (a) illustrates the demand for a good that has a zero elasticity of demand. The demand curve in part (b) illustrates the demand for a good with a unit elasticity of demand. And the demand curve in part (c) illustrates the demand for a good with an infinite elasticity of demand.

(perhaps zero over some price range) is insulin. Insulin is of such importance to some diabetics that if the price rises or falls, they do not change the quantity they buy.

If the percentage change in the quantity demanded equals the percentage change in price, then the price elasticity equals 1 and the good is said to have a **unit elastic demand**. The demand in Fig. 3(b) is an example of unit elastic demand.

Between the cases shown in Fig. 3(a) and Fig. 3(b) is the general case in which the percentage change in the quantity demanded is less than the percentage change in price. In this case, the price elasticity of demand is between zero and 1 and the good is said to have an **inelastic demand**. Food and housing are examples of goods with inelastic demand.

If the quantity demanded changes by an infinitely large percentage in response to a tiny price change, then the price elasticity of demand is infinity and the good is said to have a **perfectly elastic demand**. Figure 3(c) shows a perfectly elastic demand. An example of a good that has a very high elasticity of demand (almost infinite) is a soft drink from two campus machines located side by side. If the two machines offer the same soft drinks for the same price, some people buy from one machine and some from the other. But if one machine's price is higher than the other's, by even a small amount, no one will buy from the machine with the higher price. Soft drinks from the two machines are perfect substitutes.

Between the cases in Fig. 3(b) and Fig. 3(c) is the general case in which the percentage change in the quantity demanded exceeds the percentage change in price. In this case, the price elasticity of demand is greater than 1 and the good is said to have an **elastic demand**. Automobiles and furniture are examples of goods that have elastic demand.

Elasticity along a Straight-Line Demand Curve

Elasticity and slope are not the same, but they are related. To understand how they are related, let's look at elasticity along a straight-line demand curve—a demand curve that has a constant slope.

FIGURE 4   Elasticity along a Straight-Line Demand Curve

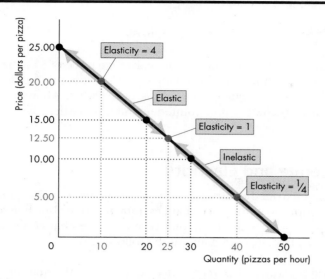

On a straight-line demand curve, elasticity decreases as the price falls and the quantity demanded increases. Demand is unit elastic at the midpoint of the demand curve (elasticity is 1). Above the midpoint, demand is elastic; below the midpoint, demand is inelastic.

Figure 4 illustrates the calculation of elasticity along a straight-line demand curve. First, suppose the price falls from $25 to $15 a pizza. The quantity demanded increases from zero to 20 pizzas an hour. The average price is $20 a pizza, and the average quantity is 10 pizzas. So

$$\text{Price elasticity of demand} = \frac{\Delta Q / Q_{ave}}{\Delta P / P_{ave}}$$

$$= \frac{20/10}{10/20}$$

$$= 4.$$

That is, the price elasticity of demand at an average price of $20 a pizza is 4.

Next, suppose that the price falls from $15 to $10 a pizza. The quantity demanded increases from 20 to 30 pizzas an hour. The average price is now $12.50 a pizza, and the average quantity is 25 pizzas an hour. So

$$\text{Price elasticity of demand} = \frac{10/25}{5/12.50}$$

$$= 1.$$

That is, the price elasticity of demand at an average price of $12.50 a pizza is 1.

Finally, suppose that the price falls from $10 to zero. The quantity demanded increases from 30 to 50 pizzas an hour. The average price is now $5 and the average quantity is 40 pizzas an hour. So

$$\text{Price elasticity of demand} = \frac{20/40}{10/5}$$
$$= 1/4.$$

That is, the price elasticity of demand at an average price of $5 a pizza is 1/4.

You've now seen how elasticity changes along a straight-line demand curve. At the mid-point of the curve, demand is unit elastic. Above the mid-point, demand is elastic. Below the mid-point, demand is inelastic.

Total Revenue and Elasticity

The **total revenue** from the sale of a good equals the price of the good multiplied by the quantity sold. When a price changes, total revenue also changes. But a rise in price does not always increase total revenue. The change in total revenue depends on the elasticity of demand in the following way:

▶ If demand is elastic, a 1 percent price cut increases the quantity sold by more than 1 percent and total revenue increases.

▶ If demand is inelastic, a 1 percent price cut increases the quantity sold by less than 1 percent and total revenue decreases.

▶ If demand is unit elastic, a 1 percent price cut increases the quantity sold by 1 percent and so total revenue does not change.

Figure 5 shows how we can use this relationship between elasticity and total revenue to estimate elasticity using the total revenue test. The **total revenue test** is a method of estimating the price elasticity of demand by observing the change in total revenue that results from a change in the price, when all other influences on the quantity sold remain the same.

▶ If a price cut increases total revenue, demand is elastic.

▶ If a price cut decreases total revenue, demand is inelastic.

▶ If a price cut leaves total revenue unchanged, demand is unit elastic.

In Fig. 5(a), over the price range from $25 to $12.50, demand is elastic. Over the price range from $12.50 to zero, demand is inelastic. At a price of $12.50, demand is unit elastic.

Figure 5(b) shows total revenue. At a price of $25, the quantity sold is zero, so total revenue is zero. At a price of zero, the quantity demanded is 50 pizzas an hour and total revenue is again zero. A price cut in the elastic range brings an increase in total revenue—the percentage increase in the quantity demanded is greater than the percentage decrease in price. A price cut in the inelastic range brings a decrease in total revenue—the percentage increase in the quantity demanded is less than the percentage decrease in price. At unit elasticity, total revenue is at a maximum.

Your Expenditure and Your Elasticity

When a price changes, the change in your expenditure on the good depends on *your* elasticity of demand.

FIGURE 5 Elasticity and Total Revenue

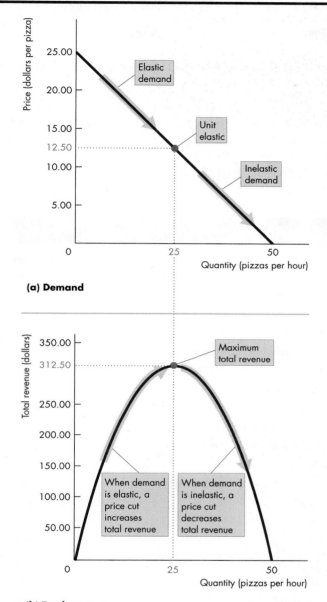

(a) Demand

(b) Total revenue

When demand is elastic, in the price range from $25 to $12.50, a decrease in price (part a) brings an increase in total revenue (part b). When demand is inelastic, in the price range from $12.50 to zero, a decrease in price (part a) brings a decrease in total revenue (part b). When demand is unit elastic, at a price of $12.50 (part a), total revenue is at a maximum (part b).

▶ If your demand is elastic, a 1 percent price cut increases the quantity you buy by more than 1 percent and your expenditure on the item increases.

▶ If your demand is inelastic, a 1 percent price cut increases the quantity you buy by less than 1 percent and your expenditure on the item decreases.

▶ If your demand is unit elastic, a 1 percent price cut increases the quantity you buy by 1 percent and your expenditure on the item does not change.

So if you spend more on an item when its price falls, your demand for that item is elastic; if you spend the same amount, your demand is unit elastic; and if you spend less, your demand is inelastic.

The Factors That Influence the Elasticity of Demand

Table 1 lists some estimates of actual elasticities in the real world. You can see that these real-world elasticities of demand range from 1.52 for metals, the item with the most elastic demand in the table, to 0.05 for oil, the item with the most inelastic demand in the table. What makes the demand for some goods elastic and the demand for others inelastic?

TABLE 1   Some Real-World Price Elasticities of Demand

Good or Service	Elasticity
Elastic Demand	
Metals	1.52
Electrical engineering products	1.39
Mechanical engineering products	1.30
Furniture	1.26
Motor vehicles	1.14
Instrument engineering products	1.10
Professional services	1.09
Transportation services	1.03
Inelastic Demand	
Gas, electricity, and water	0.92
Chemicals	0.89
Drinks (all types)	0.78
Clothing	0.64
Tobacco	0.61
Banking and insurance services	0.56
Housing services	0.55
Agricultural and fish products	0.42
Books, magazines, and newspapers	0.34
Food	0.12
Oil	0.05

Sources: Ahsan Mansur and John Whalley, "Numerical Specification of Applied General Equilibrium Models: Estimation, Calibration, and Data," in *Applied General Equilibrium Analysis,* eds. Herbert E. Scarf and John B. Shoven (New York: Cambridge University Press, 1984), 109, and Henri Theil, Ching-Fan Chung, and James L. Seale, Jr., *Advances in Econometrics, Supplement 1, 1989, International Evidence on Consumption Patterns* (Greenwich, Conn.: JAI Press Inc., 1989), and Geoffrey Heal, Columbia University, website.

The magnitude of the elasticity of demand depends on

► The closeness of substitutes
► The proportion of income spent on the good
► The time elapsed since a price change

Closeness of Substitutes

The closer the substitutes for a good or service, the more elastic is the demand for it. For example, oil from which we make gasoline has substitutes but none that are currently very close (imagine a steam-driven, coal-fueled car). So the demand for oil is inelastic. Plastics are close substitutes for metals, so the demand for metals is elastic.

The degree of substitutability between two goods also depends on how narrowly (or broadly) we define them. For example, a personal computer has no really close substitutes, but a Dell PC is a close substitute for a Hewlett Packard PC. So the elasticity of demand for personal computers is lower than the elasticity of demand for a Dell or a Hewlett Packard.

In everyday language we call some goods, such as food and housing, *necessities* and other goods, such as exotic vacations, *luxuries*. A necessity is a good that has poor substitutes and that is crucial for our well-being. So generally, a necessity has an inelastic demand. In Table 1, food and oil might be classified as necessities.

A luxury is a good that usually has many substitutes, one of which is not buying it. So a luxury generally has an elastic demand. In Table 1, furniture and motor vehicles might be classified as luxuries.

Proportion of Income Spent on the Good

Other things remaining the same, the greater the proportion of income spent on a good, the more elastic is the demand for it.

Think about your own elasticity of demand for chewing gum and housing. If the price of chewing gum doubles, you consume almost as much gum as before. Your demand for gum is inelastic. If apartment rents double, you shriek and look for more students to share accommodation with you. Your demand for housing is more elastic than your demand for gum. Why the difference? Housing takes a large proportion of your budget, and gum takes only a tiny proportion. You don't like either price increase, but you hardly notice the higher price of gum, while the higher rent puts your budget under severe strain.

Figure 6 shows the price elasticity of demand for food and the proportion of income spent on food in 10 countries. This figure confirms the general tendency we have just described. The larger the proportion of income spent on food, the larger is the price elasticity of demand for food. For example, in Tanzania, a nation where average incomes are 3.3 percent of incomes in the United States and where 62 percent of income is spent on food, the price elasticity of demand for food is 0.77. In contrast, in the United States, where 12 percent of income is spent on food, the price elasticity of demand for food is 0.12.

Time Elapsed since Price Change

The longer the time that has elapsed since a price change, the more elastic is demand. When the price of oil increased by 400 percent during the 1970s,

FIGURE 6   Price Elasticities in 10 Countries

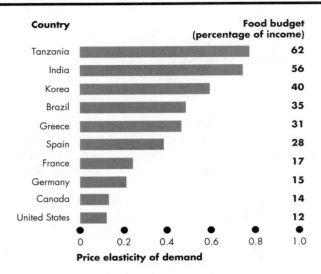

As income increases and the proportion of income spent on food decreases, the demand for food becomes less elastic.

Source: Henri Theil, Ching-Fan Chung, and James L. Seale, Jr., _Advances in Econometrics, Supplement 1, 1989, International Evidence on Consumption Patterns_ (Greenwich, Conn.: JAI Press, Inc., 1989).

people barely changed the quantity of oil and gasoline they consumed. But gradually, as more efficient auto and airplane engines were developed, the quantity consumed decreased. The demand for oil has become more elastic as more time has elapsed since the huge price hike. Similarly, when the price of a PC fell, the quantity of PCs demanded increased only slightly at first. But as more people have become better informed about the variety of ways of using a PC, the quantity of PCs bought has increased sharply. The demand for PCs has become more elastic.

You've now completed your study of the _price_ elasticity of demand. Two other elasticity concepts tell us about the effects of other influences on demand. Let's look at these other elasticities of demand.

3   MORE ELASTICITIES OF DEMAND

Back at the pizzeria, you are trying to work out how a price rise by the burger shop next door will affect the demand for your pizza. You know that pizzas and burgers are substitutes. And you know that when the price of a substitute for pizza rises, the demand for pizza increases. But by how much?

You also know that pizza and soft drinks are complements. And you know that if the price of a complement of pizza rises, the demand for pizza decreases. So you wonder by how much will a rise in the price of a soft drink decrease the demand for your pizza?

To answer these questions, you need to calculate the cross elasticity of demand. Let's examine this elasticity measure.

Cross Elasticity of Demand

We measure the influence of a change in the price of a substitute or complement by using the concept of the cross elasticity of demand. The **cross elasticity of demand** is a measure of the responsiveness of the demand for a good to a change in the price of a substitute or complement, other things remaining the same. We calculate the *cross elasticity of demand* by using the formula:

$$\text{Cross elasticity of demand} = \frac{\text{Percentage change in quantity demanded}}{\text{Percentage change in price of a substitute or complement}}.$$

The cross elasticity of demand can be positive or negative. It is *positive* for a *substitute* and *negative* for a *complement*.

Substitutes

Suppose that the price of pizza is constant and 9 pizzas an hour are sold. Then the price of a burger rises from $1.50 to $2.50. No other influence on buying plans changes and the quantity of pizzas sold increases to 11 an hour.

The change in the quantity demanded is +2 pizzas—the new quantity, 11 pizzas, minus the original quantity, 9 pizzas. The average quantity is 10 pizzas. So the quantity of pizzas demanded increases by 20 percent (+20). That is,

$$\Delta Q / Q_{ave} = (+2/10) \times 100 = +20\%.$$

The change in the price of a burger, a substitute for pizza, is +$1—the new price, $2.50, minus the original price, $1.50. The average price is $2 a burger. So the price of a burger rises by 50 percent (+50). That is,

$$\Delta P / P_{ave} = (+1/2) \times 100 = +50\%.$$

So the cross elasticity of demand for pizza with respect to the price of a burger is

$$\frac{+20\%}{+50\%} = 0.4.$$

Figure 7 illustrates the cross elasticity of demand. Pizza and burgers are substitutes. Because they are substitutes, when the price of a burger rises, the demand for pizza increases. The demand curve for pizza shifts rightward from D_0 to D_1. Because a *rise* in the price of a burger brings an *increase* in the demand for pizza, the cross elasticity of demand for pizza with respect to the price of a burger is *positive*. Both the price and the quantity change in the same direction.

Complements

Now suppose that the price of pizza is constant and 11 pizzas an hour are sold. Then the price of a soft drink rises from $1.50 to $2.50. No other influence on buying plans changes and the quantity of pizzas sold falls to 9 an hour.

FIGURE 7   Cross Elasticity of Demand

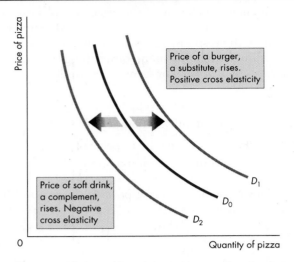

A burger is a *substitute* for pizza. When the price of a burger rises, the demand for pizza increases and the demand curve for pizza shifts rightward from D_0 to D_1. The cross elasticity of the demand is *positive*.

Soft drinks are a *complement* of pizza. When the price of a soft drink rises, the demand for pizza decreases and the demand curve for pizza shifts leftward from D_0 to D_2. The cross elasticity of the demand is *negative*.

The change in the quantity demanded is the opposite of what we've just calculated: The quantity of pizzas demanded decreases by 20 percent (−20).

The change in the price of a soft drink, a complement of pizza, is the same as the percentage change in the price of a burger that we've just calculated: The price rises by 50 percent (+50). So the cross elasticity of demand for pizza with respect to the price of a soft drink is

$$\frac{-20\%}{+50\%} = -0.4.$$

Because pizza and soft drinks are complements, when the price of a soft drink rises, the demand for pizza decreases. The demand curve for pizza shifts leftward from D_0 to D_2. Because a *rise* in the price of a soft drink brings a *decrease* in the demand for pizza, the cross elasticity of demand for pizza with respect to the price of a soft drink is *negative*. The price and quantity change in *opposite* directions.

The magnitude of the cross elasticity of demand determines how far the demand curve shifts. The larger the cross elasticity (absolute value), the greater is the change in demand and the larger is the shift in the demand curve.

If two items are close substitutes, such as two brands of spring water, the cross elasticity is large. If two items are close complements, such as movies and popcorn, the cross elasticity is large.

If two items are somewhat unrelated to each other, such as newspapers and orange juice, the cross elasticity is small—perhaps even zero.

Income Elasticity of Demand

Suppose the economy is expanding and people are enjoying rising incomes. This prosperity is bringing an increase in the demand for most types of goods and services. But by how much will the demand for pizza increase? The answer depends on the **income elasticity of demand**, which is a measure of the responsiveness of the demand for a good or service to a change in income, other things remaining the same.

The income elasticity of demand is calculated by using the formula:

$$\text{Income elasticity of demand} = \frac{\text{Percentage change in quantity demanded}}{\text{Percentage change in income}}.$$

Income elasticities of demand can be positive or negative and fall into three interesting ranges:

- ▶ Greater than 1 (*normal* good, income elastic)
- ▶ Positive and less than 1 (*normal* good, income inelastic)
- ▶ Negative (*inferior* good)

Income Elastic Demand

Suppose that the price of pizza is constant and 9 pizzas an hour are sold. Then incomes rise from $975 to $1,025 a week. No other influence on buying plans changes and the quantity of pizzas sold increases to 11 an hour.

The change in the quantity demanded is +2 pizzas. The average quantity is 10 pizzas, so the quantity demanded increases by 20 percent. The change in income is +$50 and the average income is $1,000, so incomes increase by 5 percent. The income elasticity of demand for pizza is

$$\frac{20\%}{5\%} = 4.$$

The demand for pizza is income elastic. The percentage increase in the quantity of pizza demanded exceeds the percentage increase in income. *When the demand for a good is income elastic, as income increases, the percentage of income spent on that good increases.*

Income Inelastic Demand

If the income elasticity of demand is positive but less than 1, demand is income inelastic. The percentage increase in the quantity demanded is positive but less than the percentage increase in income. *When the demand for a good is income inelastic, as income increases, the percentage of income spent on that good decreases.*

Inferior Goods

If the income elasticity of demand is negative, the good is an *inferior* good. The quantity demanded of an inferior good and the amount spent on it *decreases* when income increases. Goods in this category include small motorcycles, potatoes, and rice. Low-income consumers buy most of these goods!

TABLE 2 Some Real-World Income Elasticities of Demand	
Elastic Demand	
Airline travel	5.82
Movies	3.41
Foreign travel	3.08
Electricity	1.94
Restaurant meals	1.61
Local buses and trains	1.38
Haircuts	1.36
Automobiles	1.07
Inelastic Demand	
Tobacco	0.86
Alcoholic drinks	0.62
Furniture	0.53
Clothing	0.51
Newspapers and magazines	0.38
Telephone	0.32
Food	0.14

Sources: H. S. Houthakker and Lester D. Taylor, *Consumer Demand in the United States* (Cambridge, Mass.: Harvard University Press, 1970), and Henri Theil, Ching-Fan Chung, and James L. Seale, Jr., *Advances in Econometrics, Supplement 1, 1989, International Evidence on Consumption Patterns* (Greenwich, Conn.: JAI Press, Inc., 1989).

Real-World Income Elasticities of Demand

Table 2 shows estimates of some real-world income elasticities of demand. The demand for a necessity such as food or clothing is income inelastic, while the demand for a luxury such as transportation, which includes airline and foreign travel, is income elastic.

But what is a necessity and what is a luxury depends on the level of income. For people with a low income, food and clothing can be luxuries. So the *level* of income has a big effect on income elasticities of demand. Figure 8 shows this effect on the income elasticity of demand for food in 10 countries. In countries with low incomes, such as Tanzania and India, the income elasticity of demand for food is high. In countries with high incomes, such as the United States, the income elasticity of demand for food is low.

You've now completed your study of the *cross elasticity* of demand and the *income elasticity* of demand. Let's look at the other side of the market and examine the elasticity of supply.

4 ELASTICITY OF SUPPLY

You know that when demand increases, the price rises and the quantity increases. But does the price rise by a large amount and the quantity increase by a little? Or does the price barely rise and the quantity increase by a large amount?

FIGURE 8   Income Elasticities in 10 Countries

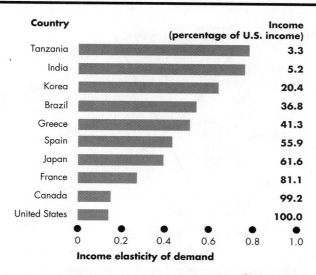

Country		Income (percentage of U.S. income)
Tanzania		3.3
India		5.2
Korea		20.4
Brazil		36.8
Greece		41.3
Spain		55.9
Japan		61.6
France		81.1
Canada		99.2
United States		100.0

0   0.2   0.4   0.6   0.8   1.0

Income elasticity of demand

As income increases, the income elasticity of demand for food decreases. Low-income consumers spend a larger percentage of any increase in income on food than do high-income consumers.

Source: Henri Theil, Ching-Fan Chung, and James L. Seale, Jr., *Advances in Econometrics, Supplement 1, 1989, International Evidence on Consumption Patterns* (Greenwich, Conn.: JAI Press, Inc., 1989).

The answer depends on the responsiveness of the quantity supplied to a change in price. You can see why by studying Fig. 9, which shows two possible scenarios in a local pizza market. Figure 9(a) shows one scenario, and Fig. 9(b) shows the other.

In both cases, demand is initially D_0. In part (a), the supply of pizza is shown by the supply curve S_A. In part (b), the supply of pizza is shown by the supply curve S_B. Initially, in both cases, the price is $20 a pizza and the quantity produced and consumed is 10 pizzas an hour.

Now increases in incomes and population increase the demand for pizza. The demand curve shifts rightward to D_1. In case (a), the price rises by $10 to $30 a pizza, and the quantity increases by only 3 to 13 pizzas an hour. In contrast, in case (b), the price rises by only $1 to $21 a pizza, and the quantity increases by 10 to 20 pizzas an hour.

The different outcomes arise from differing degrees of responsiveness of the quantity supplied to a change in price. We measure the degree of responsiveness by using the concept of the elasticity of supply.

Calculating the Elasticity of Supply

The **elasticity of supply** measures the responsiveness of the quantity supplied to a change in the price of a good when all other influences on selling plans remain the same. It is calculated by using the formula:

$$\text{Elasticity of supply} = \frac{\text{Percentage change in quantity supplied}}{\text{Percentage change in price}}.$$

FIGURE 9   How a Change in Demand Changes Price and Quantity

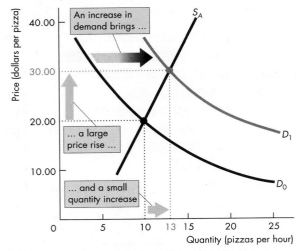

(a) Large price change and small quantity change

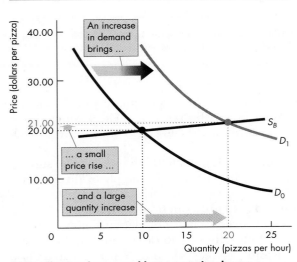

(b) Small price change and large quantity change

Initially, the price is $20 a pizza, and the quantity sold is 10 pizzas an hour. Then increases in incomes and population increase the demand for pizza. The demand curve shifts rightward to D_1. In part (a) the price rises by $10 to $30 a pizza, and the quantity increases by 3 to 13 pizzas an hour. In part (b), the price rises by only $1 to $21 a pizza, and the quantity increases by 10 to 20 pizzas an hour. The price change is smaller and the quantity change is larger in case (b) than in case (a). The quantity supplied is more responsive to price in case (b) than in case (a).

We use the same method that you learned when you studied the elasticity of demand. Let's calculate the elasticity of supply along the supply curves in Fig. 9.

In Fig. 9(a), when the price rises from $20 to $30, the price rise is $10 and the average price is $25, so the price rises by 40 percent of the average price. The quantity increases from 10 to 13 pizzas an hour, so the increase is 3 pizzas, the average quantity is 11.5 pizzas an hour, and the quantity increases by 26 percent. The elasticity of supply is equal to 26 percent divided by 40 percent, which equals 0.65.

FIGURE 10   Inelastic and Elastic Supply

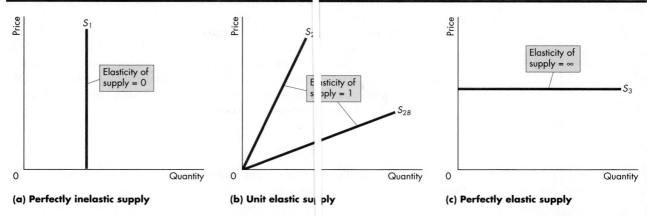

Each supply illustrated here has a constant elasticity. The supply curve in part (a) illustrates the supply of a good that has a zero elasticity of supply. The supply curve in part (b) illustrates the supply of a good with a unit elasticity of supply. All linear supply curves that pass through the origin illustrate supplies that are unit elastic. The supply curve in part (c) illustrates the supply of a good with an infinite elasticity of supply.

In Fig. 9(b), when the price rises from \$20 to \$21, the price rise is \$1 and the average price is \$20.50, so the price rises by 4.9 percent of the average price. The quantity increases from 10 to 20 pizzas an hour, so the increase is 10 pizzas, the average quantity is 15 pizzas, and the quantity increases by 67 percent. The elasticity of supply is equal to 67 percent divided by 4.9 percent, which equals 13.67.

Figure 10 shows the range of elasticities of supply. If the quantity supplied is fixed regardless of the price, the supply curve is vertical and the elasticity of supply is zero. Supply is perfectly inelastic. This case is shown in Fig. 10(a). A special intermediate case is when the percentage change in price equals the percentage change in quantity. Supply is then unit elastic. This case is shown in Fig. 10(b). No matter how steep the supply curve is, if it is linear and passes through the origin, supply is unit elastic. If there is a price at which sellers are willing to offer any quantity for sale, the supply curve is horizontal and the elasticity of supply is infinite. Supply is perfectly elastic. This case is shown in Fig. 10(c).

The Factors That Influence the Elasticity of Supply

The magnitude of the elasticity of supply depends on

► Resource substitution possibilities
► Time frame for the supply decision

Resource Substitution Possibilities

Some goods and services can be produced only by using unique or rare productive resources. These items have a low, even perhaps a zero, elasticity of supply. Other goods and services can be produced by using commonly available resources that could be allocated to a wide variety of alternative tasks. Such items have a high elasticity of supply.

A Van Gogh painting is an example of a good with a vertical supply curve and a zero elasticity of supply. At the other extreme, wheat can be grown on land that is almost equally good for growing corn. So it is just as easy to grow wheat as corn, and the opportunity cost of wheat in terms of forgone corn is almost constant. As a result, the supply curve of wheat is almost horizontal and its elasticity of supply is very large. Similarly, when a good is produced in many different countries (for example, sugar and beef), the supply of the good is highly elastic.

The supply of most goods and services lies between these two extremes. The quantity produced can be increased but only by incurring a higher cost. If a higher price is offered, the quantity supplied increases. Such goods and services have an elasticity of supply between zero and infinity.

Time Frame for the Supply Decision

To study the influence of the length of time elapsed since a price change, we distinguish three time frames of supply:

1. Momentary supply

2. Long-run supply

3. Short-run supply

When the price of a good rises or falls, the *momentary supply curve* shows the response of the quantity supplied immediately following a price change.

Some goods, such as fruits and vegetables, have a perfectly inelastic momentary supply—a vertical supply curve. The quantities supplied depend on crop-planting decisions made earlier. In the case of oranges, for example, planting decisions have to be made many years in advance of the crop being available. The momentary supply curve is vertical because, on a given day, no matter what the price of oranges, producers cannot change their output. They have picked, packed, and shipped their crop to market, and the quantity available for that day is fixed.

In contrast, some goods have a perfectly elastic momentary supply. Long-distance phone calls are an example. When many people simultaneously make a call, there is a big surge in the demand for telephone cables, computer switching, and satellite time, and the quantity bought increases. But the price remains constant. Long-distance carriers monitor fluctuations in demand and reroute calls to ensure that the quantity supplied equals the quantity demanded without changing the price.

The *long-run supply curve* shows the response of the quantity supplied to a change in price after all the technologically possible ways of adjusting supply have been exploited. In the case of oranges, the long run is the time it takes new plantings to grow to full maturity—about 15 years. In some cases, the long-run adjustment occurs only after a completely new production plant has been built and workers have been trained to operate it—typically a process that might take several years.

The *short-run supply curve* shows how the quantity supplied responds to a price change when only *some* of the technologically possible adjustments to production have been made. The short-run response to a price change is a sequence of adjustments. The first adjustment that is usually made is in the amount of labor employed. To increase output in the short run, firms work their labor force overtime and perhaps hire additional workers. To decrease their output in the short run, firms either lay off workers or reduce their hours of work. With the passage of time, firms can make additional adjustments, perhaps training additional workers or buying additional tools and other equipment.

The short-run supply curve slopes upward because producers can take actions quite quickly to change the quantity supplied in response to a price change. For example, if the price of oranges falls, growers can stop picking and leave oranges to rot on the trees. Or if the price rises, they can use more fertilizer and improved irrigation to increase the yields of their existing trees. In the long run, they can plant more trees and increase the quantity supplied even more in response to a given price rise.

You have now learned about the elasticities of demand and supply. Table 3 summarizes all the elasticities that you've met in this reading. In the next reading, we study the efficiency of competitive markets. But first study *Reading Between the Lines*, which puts the elasticity of demand to work and looks at the market for personal computers that we described at the beginning of this reading.

TABLE 3   A Compact Glossary of Elasticities

Price Elasticities of Demand

A Relationship Is Described As	When Its Magnitude Is	Which Means That
Perfectly elastic	Infinity	The smallest possible increase in price causes an infinitely large decrease in the quantity demanded*
Elastic	Less than infinity but greater than 1	The percentage decrease in the quantity demanded exceeds the percentage increase in price
Unit elastic	1	The percentage decrease in the quantity demanded equals the percentage increase in price
Inelastic	Greater than zero but less than 1	The percentage decrease in the quantity demanded is less than the percentage increase in price
Perfectly inelastic	Zero	The quantity demanded is the same at all prices

Cross Elasticities of Demand

A Relationship Is Described As	When Its Value Is	Which Means That
Close substitutes	Large	The smallest possible increase in the price of one good causes an infinitely large increase in the quantity demanded of the other good
Substitutes	Positive	If the price of one good increases, the quantity demanded of the other good also increases
Unrelated goods	Zero	If the price of one good increases, the quantity demanded of the other good remains the same
Complements	Negative	If the price of one good increases, the quantity demanded of the other good decreases

(Table continued on next page . . .)

TABLE 3   (continued)

Income Elasticities of Demand

A Relationship Is Described As	When Its Value Is	Which Means That
Income elastic (normal good)	Greater than 1	The percentage increase in the quantity demanded is greater than the percentage increase in income
Income inelastic (normal good)	Less than 1 but greater than zero	The percentage increase in the quantity demanded is less than the percentage increase in income
Negative income elastic (inferior good)	Less than zero	When income increases, quantity demanded decreases

Elasticities of Supply

A Relationship Is Described As	When Its Magnitude Is	Which Means That
Perfectly elastic	Infinity	The smallest possible increase in price causes an infinitely large increase in the quantity supplied
Elastic	Less than infinity but greater than 1	The percentage increase in the quantity supplied exceeds the percentage increase in the price
Inelastic	Greater than zero but less than 1	The percentage increase in the quantity supplied is less than the percentage increase in the price
Perfectly inelastic	Zero	The quantity supplied is the same at all prices

*In each description, the directions of change may be reversed. For example, in this case, the smallest possible *decrease* in price causes an infinitely large *increase* in the quantity demanded.

READING BETWEEN THE LINES   5

The Elasticities of Demand for Notebook and Desktop Computers

THE NEW YORK TIMES, May 27, 2006

Timing the Electronics Market for the Best Deal on a New PC

Lower prices are part of the natural order in the world of electronics. Sometimes, though, the slow but relentless drop in price turns into a torrent. That's happening now in personal computers. . . .

The lower-priced notebooks are pushing desktop prices down, too. "I would expect even more intense price competition," said Charles Smulders, an analyst with Gartner, another market research firm. . . .

When an electronic device breaks through the $1,000 psychological barrier, sales take off. Samir Bhavnani, director for research at Current Analysis, said 37 percent more notebooks have been sold so far this year. About 60 percent of all notebook computers sold last month were priced below $1,000. He credits Dell, saying, "They love getting down in the mud." . . .

Another statistic will tell you just how good consumers have it. While the number of notebooks sold is up 37 percent, revenue growth in the period is up only 15.5 percent, Mr. Bhavnani said. Companies are making less money on each notebook. Desktop computers are literally being given away. Retailers sold 14.8 percent more of them in the first five months of the year, but revenue declined 4 percent, Mr. Bhavnani said. Half of the computers sold for less than $500. . . .

Source: Copyright 2006 The New York Times Company. www.nytimes.com. Reprinted with permission. Further reproduction prohibited.

Essence of the Story

► About 60 percent of notebook computers are priced at less than $1,000.

► The lower price of a notebook has pushed down the price of a desktop and half of the desktops are priced at less than $500.

► When an electronic device breaks through the $1,000 psychological barrier, sales take off.

► The quantity of notebooks sold increased by 37 percent in 2006, and the total revenue from the sale of notebooks increased by 15.5 percent.

► The quantity of desktop computers sold increased by 14.8 percent in 2006, and the total revenue from desktops decreased by 4 percent.

Economic Analysis

► This news article provides information about the changes in quantities and total revenue in the markets for notebook and desktop computers.

► Other things remaining the same, the information about the change in the quantity and total revenue is sufficient to calculate the price elasticity of demand.

► If the price falls and total revenue increases (as in the market for notebooks), demand is elastic.

► And if the price falls and total revenue *decreases* (as in the market for desktops), demand is inelastic.

► But other things did not remain the same in the markets for notebooks and desktops.

► Notebook and desktop computers are *substitutes*. If the price of a notebook falls, the demand for desktops decreases. And if the price of a desktop falls, the demand for notebooks decreases.

► Figure 11 illustrates the market for notebook computers *assuming* that the price elasticity of demand is 4 and given the information in the news article.

FIGURE 11   The Market for Notebook Computers

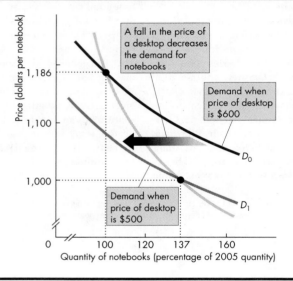

► When the price of a desktop is $600, the demand for notebooks is D_0, and when the price of a desktop is $500, the demand for notebooks decreases to D_1.

► In 2006, the price of a notebook decreased from almost $1,200 to about $1,000 (on the average) and the quantity bought increased by 37 percent.

► If we assumed that there was no change in the demand for notebooks, the demand curve would be the light blue curve and the price elasticity of demand would be estimated to be 1.83.

► Figure 12 illustrates the market for desktop computers *assuming* that the price elasticity of demand is 4 and given the information in the news article.

► When the price of a notebook is $1,186, the demand for desktops is D_0, and when the price of a notebook is $1,000, the demand for desktops decreases to D_1.

► In 2006, the price of a desktop decreased from about $600 to about $500 (on the average) and the quantity bought increased by almost 15 percent.

FIGURE 12   The Market for Desktop Computers

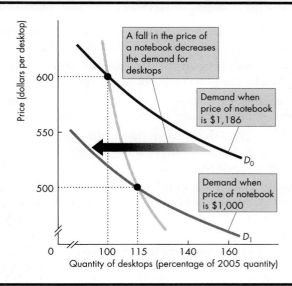

▶ If we assumed that there was no change in the demand for desktops, the demand curve would be the light blue curve and the price elasticity of demand would be estimated to be 0.77.

▶ Because other things do not remain the same, there is insufficient information in this news article to calculate the price elasticities of demand for personal computers.

▶ But other information suggests that the demand for computers is elastic. And the news article says that demand becomes highly elastic at prices below $1,000—what is called the "psychological barrier" below which "sales take off."

SUMMARY

▶ Elasticity is a measure of the responsiveness of the quantity demanded of a good to a change in its price, other things remaining the same.

▶ Price elasticity of demand equals the percentage change in the quantity demanded divided by the percentage change in price.

▶ The larger the magnitude of the price elasticity of demand, the greater is the responsiveness of the quantity demanded to a given change in price.

▶ Price elasticity of demand depends on how easily one good serves as a substitute for another, the proportion of income spent on the good, and the length of time elapsed since the price change.

▶ If demand is elastic, a decrease in price leads to an increase in total revenue. If demand is unit elastic, a decrease in price leaves total revenue unchanged. And if demand is inelastic, a decrease in price leads to a decrease in total revenue.

▶ Cross elasticity of demand measures the responsiveness of demand for one good to a change in the price of a substitute or a complement, other things remaining the same.

▶ The cross elasticity of demand with respect to the price of a substitute is positive. The cross elasticity of demand with respect to the price of a complement is negative.

▶ Income elasticity of demand measures the responsiveness of demand to a change in income, other things remaining the same. For a normal good, the income elasticity of demand is positive. For an inferior good, the income elasticity of demand is negative.

▶ When the income elasticity of demand is greater than 1 (income elastic), the percentage of income spent on the good increases as income increases.

▶ When the income elasticity of demand is less than 1 (income inelastic and inferior), the percentage of income spent on the good decreases as income increases.

▶ Elasticity of supply measures the responsiveness of the quantity supplied of a good to a change in its price.

▶ The elasticity of supply is usually positive and ranges between zero (vertical supply curve) and infinity (horizontal supply curve).

▶ Supply decisions have three time frames: momentary, long run, and short run.

▶ Momentary supply refers to the response of sellers to a price change at the instant that the price changes.

▶ Long-run supply refers to the response of sellers to a price change when all the technologically feasible adjustments in production have been made.

▶ Short-run supply refers to the response of sellers to a price change after some of the technologically feasible adjustments in production have been made.

PRACTICE PROBLEMS FOR READING 13

1. For a particular company's product, the percent change in quantity demanded is smaller than the percent change in price that caused the change in quantity demanded. If the company increased the price of that product, total revenue from sales of that product would *most likely*:

  A. increase more in the short run than in the long run.

  B. increase more in the long run than in the short run.

  C. decrease more in the short run than in the long run.

2. For a particular product produced by a firm, the quantity at which demand is unit elastic is *most likely* the quantity that maximizes:

  A. total profit from the product but not total revenue from the product.

  B. total revenue from the product but not total profit from the product.

  C. both total profit from the product and total revenue from the product.

3. For a particular company's product, the percent change in quantity demanded is smaller than the percent change in price that caused the change in quantity demanded. If the company increased the price of that product, total revenue from sales of that product would *most likely*:

  A. increase and demand is elastic.

  B. decrease and demand is elastic.

  C. increase and demand is inelastic.

4. Clemens News sells both the *Wall Street Journal* (WSJ) and the *Financial Times* (FT). Proprietor Stan Clemens noticed that when he raised the price of the WSJ from $1.50 per copy to $2 per copy, the number of FT that he sold rose from 22 to 28. The cross-elasticity of demand is *closest* to:

  A. −0.08.

  B. 0.84.

  C. 1.19.

5. Susan Jahlberg, CFA recognizes that the expanding economy of China is increasing prosperity and the demand for many types of goods and services. To estimate the demand for a particular item, which of the following elasticities of demand would be the *best* choice for Jahlberg to calculate?

  A. The price elasticity.

  B. The income elasticity.

  C. The cross-elasticity.

6. The price elasticity of furniture has been reported at 1.26. Lee's Furniture Emporium decides to raise prices by 3%. What is your *most appropriate* conclusion?

  A. Demand is elastic and total revenue will increase.

  B. Demand is elastic and total revenue will decrease.

  C. Demand is inelastic and total revenue will increase.

7. An analyst has determined that when the price of product X increases from $10 to $12, the quantity demanded declines from 30 units to 28 units. The price elasticity of demand for product X is *closest* to:

  A. 0.38.

  B. 0.67.

  C. 1.50.

8. If the income elasticity of demand for product Y is negative, then product Y is *most likely* a:

   A. normal good.

   B. inferior good.

   C. substitute good.

9. Which of the following is *least likely* to influence the elasticity of supply?

   A. Resource substitution possibilities.

   B. Time frame for the supply decision.

   C. Proportion of income spent on the product.

10. When the price of a cup of coffee is a constant Kenya Shillings (KES) 70 per cup, 10 cups of coffee are sold each hour at the Habari Café. However, when the price of tea falls from KES 70 per cup to KES 50 per cup, the quantity of coffee sold falls to 5 cups per hour. Assuming no other influences, the cross elasticity of demand for coffee with respect to the price of tea is *closest* to:

   A. 0.57.

   B. 1.75.

   C. 2.00.

SOLUTIONS FOR READING 13

1. A is correct. The price elasticity of demand for the product is inelastic (absolute value of elasticity coefficient is less than one). An increase in price will increase total revenue in the short run. The longer the time that has elapsed since a price change, the more elastic is demand. In the long run consumers will reduce their consumption by a larger amount than in the short run.

2. B is correct. A firm maximizes its revenue at the price (or quantity) where demand is unit elastic. This price or quantity is not the one that maximizes profit unless output can be increased at zero cost (no marginal costs).

3. C is correct. The price elasticity of demand for the product is inelastic (absolute value of elasticity coefficient is less than one). When demand is inelastic, an increase in price will increase total revenue.

4. B is correct.

The cross-elasticity of demand for a substitute = Percentage change in quantity demanded/Percentage change in price of substitute $= \dfrac{\Delta Q/Q_{ave}}{\Delta P/P_{ave}}$

$\Delta Q/Q_{ave} = (28 - 22)/[(28 + 22)/2] = 6/25 = 0.24$

$\Delta P/P_{ave} = (\$2.00 - \$1.50)/[(\$2.00 + \$1.50)/2] = 0.5/1.75 = 0.2857$

$0.24/0.2857 = 0.84$

5. B is correct. The income elasticity of demand measures the effect of income changes on demand and is the appropriate measure in this case. The price elasticity of demand measures the effect of price changes on demand. The cross-elasticity of demand measures the effect of price changes in substitutes and complementary products on demand.

6. B is correct. Price elasticities greater than one indicate elasticity of demand. Any percentage increase in price will result in a correspondingly greater percentage decrease in demand. This will decrease total revenue.

7. A is correct. The price elasticity of demand equals the percentage change in quantity demanded divided by the percentage change in price. The percentage change in quantity demanded (based on average quantity) is $2/[(30+28)/2] = 2/29 = 6.90\%$. The percentage change in price (based on average price) is $2/[(10 + 12)/2] = 2/11 = 18.18\%$. The price elasticity of demand is $6.90\%/18.18\% = 0.38$.

8. B is correct. The income elasticity of demand is negative for an inferior good because as incomes increase, the demand for the good decreases.

9. C is correct. The elasticity of supply for a product is influenced by resource allocation possibilities and the time frame to make the supply decision.

10. C is correct. The formula for the cross elasticity of demand is as follows:

Cross elasticity of demand = Percentage change in quantity demanded/Percentage change in price of a substitute or complement.

Therefore the cross elasticity of demand for coffee with respect to the price of tea is:

Percentage change in quantity demanded $= (5 - 10)/((10 + 5)/2) \times 100 = -5/7.5 \times 100 = -66.67.0\%$

Percentage change in price of a substitute $= (50 - 70)/((50 + 70)/2) = -20/60 = -33.33.0\%$

Cross elasticity of demand $= -66.67\%/-33.33\% = 2.00$

23⅝ 24 ...
4⅝ 4 11/16 3/8
5½ 5½ − 3/8
5½ 5½ − 3/16
20⅝ 21 13/16 − 3/16
17⅜ 18⅛ + ⅞
13½ 6½ 6½ − ½
7¼ 6½ 31/32 − ⅛
15/16
9/16 9/16
1 13/32 7 13/16 7 15/16
7 15/16 7 13/16 7 15/16
2⅝ 2 11/32 2½ +
2¾ 2¼ 2¼
6⅝ 12 1/16 11⅜ 11¾ +
87 33¾ 33 33¼ +
502 25⅝ 24 9/16 25⅜ +
833 12 11⅝ 11⅞ +
16 10½ 10½ 10½ −
78 15⅝ 15 13/16 15⅞ +
4608 9 1/16 8¼ 8⅞ +
11¼ 10⅝ 10⅝

EFFICIENCY AND EQUITY
by Michael Parkin

LEARNING OUTCOMES

The candidate should be able to:	Mastery
a. explain the various means of markets to allocate resources, describe marginal benefit and marginal cost, and demonstrate why the efficient quantity occurs when marginal benefit equals marginal cost;	☐
b. distinguish between the price and the value of a product and explain the demand curve and consumer surplus;	☐
c. distinguish between the cost and the price of a product and explain the supply curve and producer surplus;	☐
d. discuss the relationship between consumer surplus, producer surplus, and equilibrium;	☐
e. explain 1) how efficient markets ensure optimal resource utilization and 2) the obstacles to efficiency and the resulting underproduction or overproduction, including the concept of deadweight loss;	☐
f. explain the two groups of ideas about the fairness principle (utilitarianism and the symmetry principle) and discuss the relation between fairness and efficiency.	☐

SELF-INTEREST AND THE SOCIAL INTEREST   1

Every time you buy a pair of sports shoes or a textbook, fill your gas tank, download some MP3 files, burn a CD, order a pizza, check in at the airport, or even just take a shower, you express your view about how scarce resources should be used. You try to spend your income and your time in ways that get the most out of *your* scarce resources—you make choices that further your *self-interest*. And markets coordinate your decisions along with those of everyone else. But do markets do a good job? Do they enable us to allocate resources between shoes, books, gasoline, music, CD-Rs, pizza, airline services, water, and all the other things we buy in the *social interest*? Could we as a society be better off if we spent more on some things and less on others?

The market economy generates huge incomes for some people and miserable pickings for others. For example, software sales by Microsoft have generated enough profit over the past ten years to rocket Bill Gates, one of its founders, into the position of being one of the richest people in the world. Is it *fair* that Bill Gates is so incredibly rich while others live in miserable poverty?

The social interest has the two dimensions that we've just discussed: efficiency and fairness (or equity). So our central question in this reading is: Does the market achieve an efficient and fair use of resources?

At the end of the reading, in *Reading Between the Lines*, we discuss the use of the world's water resources. Do we use markets and other arrangements that allocate the world's scarce water efficiently?

2 RESOURCE ALLOCATION METHODS

The goal of this reading is to evaluate the ability of markets to allocate resources efficiently and fairly. But to see whether the market does a good job, we must compare it with its alternatives. Resources are scarce, so they must be allocated somehow. And trading in markets is just one of several alternative methods.

Resources might be allocated by

▶ Market price
▶ Command
▶ Majority rule
▶ Contest
▶ First-come, first-served
▶ Lottery
▶ Personal characteristics
▶ Force

Let's briefly examine each method.

Market Price

When a market price allocates a scarce resource, the people who are willing and able to pay that price get the resource. Two kinds of people decide not to pay the market price: those who can afford to pay but choose not to buy and those who are too poor and simply can't afford to buy.

For many goods and services, distinguishing between those who choose not to buy and those who can't afford to buy doesn't matter. But for a few items, it does matter. For example, poor people can't afford to pay school fees and doctors' fees. Because poor people can't afford items that most people consider to be essential, these items are usually allocated by one of the other methods.

Command

A **command system** allocates resources by the order (command) of someone in authority. In the U.S. economy, the command system is used extensively inside firms and government departments. For example, if you have a job, most likely someone tells you what to do. Your labor is allocated to specific tasks by a command.

A command system works well in organizations in which the lines of authority and responsibility are clear and it is easy to monitor the activities being performed. But a command system works badly when the range of activities to be monitored is large and when it is easy for people to fool those in authority. The system works so badly in North Korea, where it is used extensively in place of markets, that it fails even to deliver an adequate supply of food.

Majority Rule

Majority rule allocates resources in the way that a majority of voters choose. Societies use majority rule to elect representative governments that make some of the biggest decisions. For example, majority rule decides the tax rates that end up allocating scarce resources between private use and public use. And majority rule decides how tax dollars are allocated among competing uses such as education and health care.

Majority rule works well when the decisions being made affect large numbers of people and self-interest must be suppressed to use resources most effectively.

Contest

A contest allocates resources to a winner (or a group of winners). Sporting events use this method. Tiger Woods competes with other golfers, and the winner gets the biggest payoff. But contests are more general than those in a sports arena, though we don't normally call them contests. For example, Bill Gates won a contest to provide the world's personal computer operating system.

Contests do a good job when the efforts of the "players" are hard to monitor and reward directly. When a manager offers everyone in the company the opportunity to win a big prize, people are motivated to work hard and try to become the winner. Only a few people end up with a big prize, but many people work harder in the process of trying to win. So total output produced by the workers is much greater than it would be without the contest.

First-Come, First-Served

A first-come, first-served method allocates resources to those who are first in line. Many casual restaurants won't accept reservations. They use first-come, first-served to allocate their scarce tables. Highway space is allocated in this way too: the first to arrive at the on-ramp gets the road space. If too many vehicles enter the highway, the speed slows and people wait in line for some space to become available.

First-come, first-served works best when, as in the above examples, a scarce resource can serve just one user at a time in a sequence. By serving the user who arrives first, this method minimizes the time spent waiting for the resource to become free.

Lottery

Lotteries allocate resources to those who pick the winning number, draw the lucky cards, or come up lucky on some other gaming system. State lotteries and casinos reallocate millions of dollars worth of goods and services every year.

But lotteries are more widespread than jackpots and roulette wheels in casinos. They are used to allocate landing slots to airlines at some airports and have been used to allocate fishing rights and the electromagnetic spectrum used by cell phones.

Lotteries work best when there is no effective way to distinguish among potential users of a scarce resource.

Personal Characteristics

When resources are allocated on the basis of personal characteristics, people with the "right" characteristics get the resources. Some of the resources that matter most to you are allocated in this way. For example, you will choose a marriage partner on the basis of personal characteristics. But this method is also used in unacceptable ways. Allocating the best jobs to white, Anglo-Saxon males and discriminating against visible minorities and women is an example.

Force

Force plays a crucial role, for both good and ill, in allocating scarce resources. Let's start with the ill.

War, the use of military force by one nation against another, has played an enormous role historically in allocating resources. The economic supremacy of European settlers in the Americas and Australia owes much to the use of this method.

Theft, the taking of the property of others without their consent, also plays a large role. Both large-scale organized crime and small-scale petty crime collectively allocate billions of dollars worth of resources annually.

But force plays a crucial positive role in allocating resources. It provides the state with an effective method of transferring wealth from the rich to the poor, and it provides the legal framework in which voluntary exchange in markets takes place.

A legal system is the foundation on which our market economy functions. Without courts to enforce contracts, it would not be possible to do business. But the courts could not enforce contracts without the ability to apply force if necessary. The state provides the ultimate force that enables the courts to do their work.

More broadly, the force of the state is essential to uphold the principle of the rule of law. This principle is the bedrock of civilized economic (and social and political) life. With the rule of law upheld, people can go about their daily economic lives with the assurance that their property will be protected—that they can sue for violations against their property (and be sued if they violate the property of others).

Free from the burden of protecting their property and confident in the knowledge that those with whom they trade will honor their agreements, people can get on with focusing on the activity at which they have a comparative advantage and trading for mutual gain.

In the next sections, we're going to see how a market can achieve an efficient use of resources, examine the obstacles to efficiency, and see how sometimes an alternative method might improve on the market. After looking at efficiency, we'll turn our attention to the more difficult issue of fairness.

DEMAND AND MARGINAL BENEFIT   `3`

Resources are allocated efficiently when they are used in the ways that people value most highly. This outcome occurs when marginal benefit equals marginal cost. So to determine whether a competitive market is efficient, we need to see whether, at the market equilibrium quantity, marginal benefit equals marginal cost. We begin by seeing how market demand reflects marginal benefit.

Demand, Willingness to Pay, and Value

In everyday life, we talk about "getting value for money." When we use this expression, we are distinguishing between *value* and *price*. Value is what we get, and the price is what we pay.

The value of one more unit of a good or service is its marginal benefit. And we measure marginal benefit by the maximum price that is willingly paid for another unit of the good or service. But willingness to pay determines demand. *A demand curve is a marginal benefit curve.*

In Fig. 1(a), Lisa is willing to pay $1 for the 30th slice of pizza and $1 is her marginal benefit from that slice. In Fig. 1(b), Nick is willing to pay $1 for the 10th slice of pizza and $1 is his marginal benefit from that slice. But for what quantity is the economy willing to pay $1? The answer is provided by the market demand curve.

Individual Demand and Market Demand

The relationship between the price of a good and the quantity demanded by one person is called *individual demand.* And the relationship between the price of a good and the quantity demanded by all buyers is called *market demand.*

FIGURE 1   Individual Demand, Market Demand, and Marginal Social Benefit

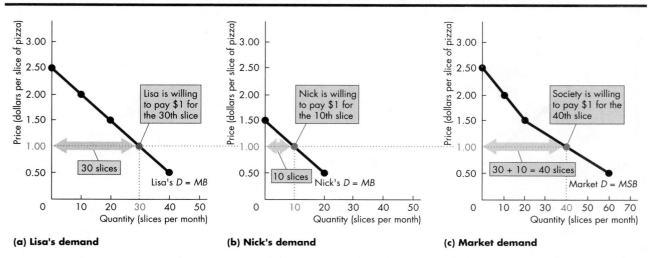

(a) Lisa's demand   **(b) Nick's demand**   **(c) Market demand**

At a price of $1 a slice, the quantity demanded by Lisa is 30 slices and the quantity demanded by Nick is 10 slices, so the quantity demanded by the market is 40 slices. Lisa's demand curve in part (a) and Nick's demand curve in part (b) sum horizontally to the market demand curve in part (c). The market demand curve is the marginal social benefit (MSB) curve.

The market demand curve is the horizontal sum of the individual demand curves and is formed by adding the quantities demanded by all the individuals at each price.

Figure 1(c) illustrates the market demand for pizza if Lisa and Nick are the only people. Lisa's demand curve (part a) and Nick's demand curve (part b) sum horizontally to the market demand curve in part (c).

At a price of $1, Lisa demands 30 slices and Nick demands 10 slices, so the quantity demanded by the market at $1 a slice is 40 slices.

So from the market demand curve, we see that the economy (or society) is willing to pay $1 for 40 slices a month. *The market demand curve is the economy's marginal social benefit (MSB) curve.*

Although we're measuring the price in dollars, think of the price as telling us the number of *dollars' worth of other goods and services willingly forgone* to obtain one more slice of pizza.

Consumer Surplus

We don't always have to pay what we are willing to pay—we get a bargain. When people buy something for less than it is worth to them, they receive a consumer surplus. A **consumer surplus** is the value (or marginal benefit) of a good minus the price paid for it, summed over the quantity bought.

Figure 2(a) shows Lisa's consumer surplus from pizza when the price is $1 a slice. At this price, she buys 30 slices a month because the 30th slice is worth only $1 to her. But Lisa is willing to pay $2 for the 10th slice, so her marginal benefit from this slice is $1 more than she pays for it—she receives a *consumer surplus* of $1 on the 10th slice.

Lisa's consumer surplus is the sum of the surpluses on *all of the slices she buys*. This sum is the area of the gray triangle—the area below the demand curve and above the market price line. The area of this triangle is equal to its base

FIGURE 2   Demand and Consumer Surplus

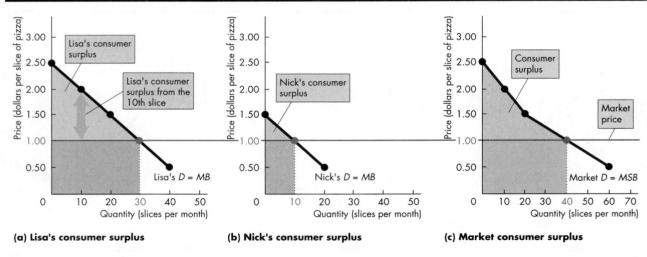

(a) Lisa's consumer surplus   **(b) Nick's consumer surplus**   **(c) Market consumer surplus**

Lisa is willing to pay $2.00 for her 10th slice of pizza (part a). At a market price of $1 a slice, Lisa receives a consumer surplus of $1 on the 10th slice. The gray triangle shows her consumer surplus on the 30 slices she buys at $1 a slice. The gray triangle in part (b) shows Nick's consumer surplus on the 10 slices that he buys at $1 a slice. The gray area in part (c) shows the consumer surplus for the economy. The blue rectangles show the amounts spent on pizza.

(30 slices) multiplied by its height ($1.50) divided by 2, which is $22.50. The area of the blue rectangle in Fig. 2(a) shows what Lisa pays for 30 slices of pizza.

Figure 2(b) shows Nick's consumer surplus, and part (c) shows the consumer surplus for the economy. The consumer surplus for the economy is the sum of the consumer surpluses of Lisa and Nick.

All goods and services, like pizza, have decreasing marginal benefit. So people receive more benefit from their consumption than the amount they pay.

SUPPLY AND MARGINAL COST   4

We are now going to see how market supply reflects marginal cost. This section closely parallels the related ideas about market demand and marginal benefit that you've just studied. Firms are in business to make a profit. To do so, they must sell their output for a price that exceeds the cost of production. Let's investigate the relationship between cost and price.

Supply, Cost, and Minimum Supply-Price

Making a profit means receiving more from the sale of a good or service than the cost of producing it. Just as consumers distinguish between value and price, so producers distinguish between cost and price. Cost is what a producer gives up, and the price is what a producer receives.

The cost of producing one more unit of a good or service is its marginal cost. And marginal cost is the minimum price that producers must receive to induce them to offer to sell another unit of the good or service. But the minimum supply-price determines supply. *A supply curve is a marginal cost curve.*

In Fig. 3(a), Max is willing to produce the 100th pizza for $15, his marginal cost of that pizza. In Fig. 3(b), Mario is willing to produce the 50th pizza for $15,

FIGURE 3   Individual Supply, Market Supply, and Marginal Social Cost

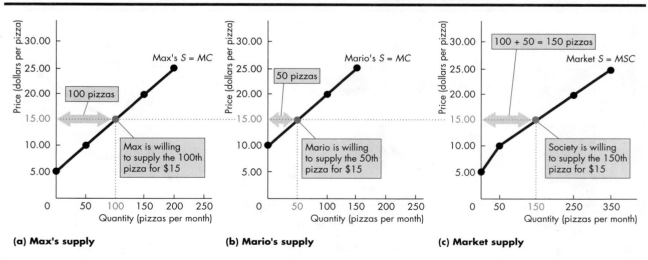

At a price of $15 a pizza, the quantity supplied by Max is 100 pizzas and the quantity supplied by Mario is 50 pizzas, so the quantity supplied by the market is 150 pizzas. Max's supply curve in part (a) and Mario's supply curve in part (b) sum horizontally to the market supply curve in part (c). The market supply curve is the marginal social cost (*MSC*) curve.

his marginal cost of that pizza. But what quantity is the economy willing to produce for $15 a pizza? The answer is provided by the *market supply curve*.

Individual Supply and Market Supply

The relationship between the price of a good and the quantity supplied by one producer is called *individual supply*. And the relationship between the price of a good and the quantity supplied by all producers is called *market supply*.

The market supply curve is the horizontal sum of the individual supply curves and is formed by adding the quantities supplied by all the producers at each price.

Figure 3(c) illustrates the market supply if Max and Mario are the only producers. Max's supply curve (part a) and Mario's supply curve (part b) sum horizontally to the market supply curve in part (c).

At a price of $15 a pizza, Max supplies 100 pizzas and Mario supplies 50 pizzas, so the quantity supplied by the market at $15 a pizza is 150 pizzas.

So from the market supply curve, we see that the economy (or society) is willing to produce 150 pizzas a month for $15 each. *The market supply curve is the economy's marginal social cost (MSC) curve.*

Again, although we're measuring price in dollars, think of the price as telling us the number of *dollars' worth of other goods and services that must be forgone* to obtain one more pizza.

Producer Surplus

When price exceeds marginal cost, the firm receives a producer surplus. A **producer surplus** is the price received for a good minus its minimum supply-price (or marginal cost), summed over the quantity sold.

Figure 4(a) shows Max's producer surplus from pizza when the price is $15 a pizza. At this price, he sells 100 pizzas a month because the 100th pizza costs him

FIGURE 4   Supply and Producer Surplus

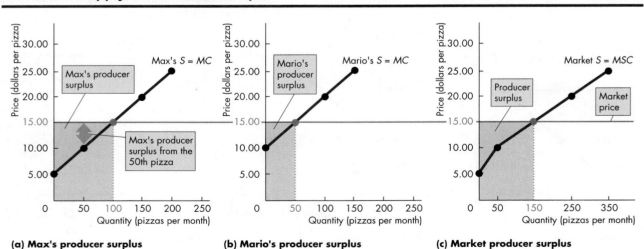

(a) Max's producer surplus   **(b) Mario's producer surplus**   **(c) Market producer surplus**

Max is willing to produce the 50th pizza for $10 (part a). At a market price of $15 a pizza, Max gets a producer surplus of $5 on the 50th pizza. The blue triangle shows his producer surplus on the 100 pizzas he sells at $15 each. The blue triangle in part (b) shows Mario's producer surplus on the 50 pizzas that he sells at $15 each. The blue area in part (c) shows producer surplus for the economy. The gray areas show the cost of producing the pizzas sold.

$15 to produce. But Max is willing to produce the 50th pizza for his marginal cost, which is $10. So he receives a *producer surplus* of $5 on this pizza.

Max's producer surplus is the sum of the surpluses on each pizza he sells. This sum is the area of the blue triangle—the area below the market price and above the supply curve. The area of this triangle is equal to its base (100) multiplied by its height ($10) divided by 2, which is $500. The gray area in Fig. 4(a) below the supply curve shows what it costs Max to produce 100 pizzas.

Figure 4(b) shows Mario's producer surplus and part (c) shows the producer surplus for the economy. The producer surplus for the economy is the sum of the producer surpluses of Max and Mario.

Consumer surplus and producer surplus can be used to measure the efficiency of a market. Let's see how we can use these concepts to study the efficiency of a competitive market.

IS THE COMPETITIVE MARKET EFFICIENT?   5

Figure 5(a) shows the market for pizza. The market forces pull the pizza market to its equilibrium price of $15 a pizza and equilibrium quantity of 10,000 pizzas a day. Buyers enjoy a consumer surplus (gray area), sellers enjoy a producer surplus (blue area), but is this competitive equilibrium efficient?

Efficiency of Competitive Equilibrium

You've seen that the demand curve tells us the marginal benefit from pizza. If the only people who benefit from pizza are the people who buy it, then the demand curve for pizza measures the marginal benefit to the entire society from pizza. We call the marginal benefit to the entire society, marginal *social* benefit, *MSB*. In this case, the demand curve is also the *MSB* curve.

You've also seen that the supply curve tells us the marginal cost of pizza. If the only people who bear the cost of pizza are the people who produce it, then the supply curve of pizza measures the marginal cost to the entire society of pizza. We call the marginal cost to the entire society, marginal *social* cost, *MSC*. In this case, the supply curve is also the *MSC* curve.

So where the demand curve and the supply curve intersect in part (a), marginal social benefit equals marginal social cost in part (b). This condition delivers an efficient use of resources for the entire society.

If production is less than 10,000 pizzas a day, the marginal pizza is valued more highly than its opportunity cost. If production exceeds 10,000 pizzas a day, the marginal pizza costs more to produce than the value that consumers place on it. Only when 10,000 pizzas a day are produced is the marginal pizza worth exactly what it costs.

The competitive market pushes the quantity of pizza produced to its efficient level of 10,000 a day. If production is less than 10,000 pizzas a day, a shortage raises the price, which increases production. If production exceeds 10,000 pizzas a day, a surplus lowers the price, which decreases production. So a competitive pizza market is efficient.

When the efficient quantity is produced, *total surplus* (the sum of consumer surplus and producer surplus) is maximized. Buyers and sellers acting in their self-interest end up promoting the social interest.

FIGURE 5   An Efficient Market for Pizza

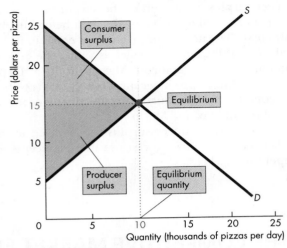

(a) Equilibrium and surpluses

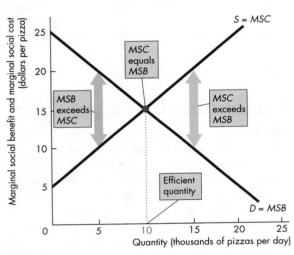

(b) Efficiency

Competitive equilibrium in part (a) occurs when the quantity demanded equals the quantity supplied. Consumer surplus is the area under the demand curve and above the price—the gray triangle. Producer surplus is the area above the supply curve and below the price—the blue triangle.

Resources are used efficiently in part (b) when marginal social benefit, *MSB*, equals marginal social cost, *MSC*.

The efficient quantity in part (b) is the same as the equilibrium quantity in part (a). The competitive pizza market produces the efficient quantity of pizza.

The Invisible Hand

Writing in his *Wealth of Nations* in 1776, Adam Smith was the first to suggest that competitive markets send resources to the uses in which they have the highest value. Smith believed that each participant in a competitive market is "led by an invisible hand to promote an end [the efficient use of resources] which was no part of his intention."

© The New Yorker Collection 1985
Mike Twohy from cartoonbank.com. All Rights Reserved.

You can see the invisible hand at work in the cartoon. The cold drinks vendor has both cold drinks and shade. He has an opportunity cost of each and a minimum supply-price of each. The reader on the park bench has a marginal benefit from a cold drink and from shade. You can see that marginal benefit from shade exceeds the price but the price of a cold drink exceeds its marginal benefit. The transaction that occurs creates a producer surplus and a consumer surplus. The vendor obtains a producer surplus from selling the shade for more than its opportunity cost, and the reader obtains a consumer surplus from buying the shade for less than its marginal benefit. In the third frame of the cartoon, both the consumer and the producer are better off than they were in the first frame. The umbrella has moved to its highest-valued use.

The Invisible Hand at Work Today

The market economy relentlessly performs the activity illustrated in the cartoon and in Fig. 5 to achieve an efficient allocation of resources. And rarely has the market been working as hard as it is today. Think about a few of the changes taking place in our economy that the market is guiding toward an efficient use of resources.

New technologies have cut the cost of producing computers. As these advances have occurred, supply has increased and the price has fallen. Lower prices have encouraged an increase in the quantity demanded of this now less costly tool. The marginal social benefit from computers is brought to equality with their marginal social cost.

A Florida frost cuts the supply of oranges. With fewer oranges available, the marginal social benefit increases. A shortage of oranges raises their price, so the market allocates the smaller quantity available to the people who value them most highly.

Market forces persistently bring marginal cost and marginal benefit to equality and maximize total surplus (consumer surplus plus producer surplus).

Underproduction and Overproduction

Inefficiency can occur because either too little of an item is produced—underproduction—or too much is produced—overproduction.

Underproduction

In Fig. 6(a), the quantity of pizza produced is 5,000 a day. At this quantity, consumers are willing to pay $20 for a pizza that costs only $10 to produce. The quantity produced is inefficient—there is underproduction.

The scale of the inefficiency is measured by **deadweight loss,** which is the decrease in total surplus that results from an inefficient level of production. The light gray triangle in Fig. 6(a) shows the deadweight loss.

Overproduction

In Fig. 6(b), the quantity of pizza produced is 15,000 a day. At this quantity, consumers are willing to pay only $10 for a pizza that costs $20 to produce. By producing the 15,000th pizza, $10 of resources are wasted. Again, the light gray triangle shows the deadweight loss. The total surplus (the sum of consumer surplus and producer surplus) is smaller than its maximum by the amount of the deadweight loss. The deadweight loss is borne by the entire society. It is not a loss for the consumers and a gain for the producer. It is a *social* loss.

Obstacles to Efficiency

The obstacles to efficiency that bring underproduction or overproduction are

► Price and quantity regulations
► Taxes and subsidies
► Externalities
► Public goods and common resources
► Monopoly
► High transactions costs

FIGURE 6   Underproduction and Overproduction

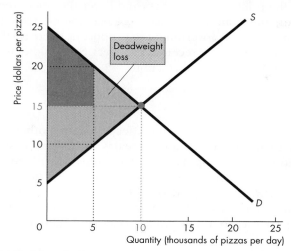

(a) Underproduction

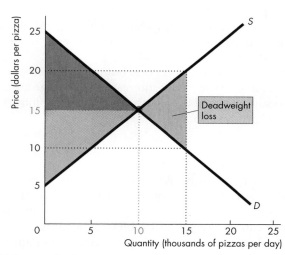

(b) Overproduction

If pizza production is cut to only 5,000 a day, a deadweight loss (the light gray triangle) arises (part a). Total surplus (the dark gray and blue areas) is reduced. At 5,000 pizzas, the benefit from one more pizza exceeds its cost. The same is true for all levels of production up to 10,000 pizzas a day.

If production increases to 15,000, a deadweight loss arises (part b). At 15,000 pizzas a day, the cost of the 15,000th pizza exceeds its benefit. The cost of each pizza above 10,000 exceeds its benefit. Total surplus equals the sum of the dark gray and blue areas minus the deadweight loss.

Price and Quantity Regulations

Price regulations that put a cap on the rent a landlord is permitted to charge and laws that require employers to pay a minimum wage sometimes block the price adjustments that balance the quantity demanded and the quantity supplied and lead to underproduction. *Quantity regulations* that limit the amount that a farm is permitted to produce also lead to underproduction.

Taxes and Subsidies

Taxes increase the prices paid by buyers and lower the prices received by sellers. So taxes decrease the quantity produced and lead to underproduction. *Subsidies,* which are payments by the government to producers, decrease the prices paid by buyers and increase the prices received by sellers. So subsidies increase the quantity produced and lead to overproduction.

Externalities

An *externality* is a cost or a benefit that affects someone other than the seller or the buyer of a good. An electric utility creates an external cost by burning coal that brings acid rain and crop damage. The utility doesn't consider the cost of pollution when it decides how much power to produce. The result is overproduction. An apartment owner would provide an *external benefit* if she installed a smoke detector. But she doesn't consider her neighbor's marginal benefit when she is deciding whether to install a smoke detector. There is underproduction.

Public Goods and Common Resources

A *public good* is a good or service that is consumed simultaneously by everyone even if they don't pay for it. Examples are national defense and law enforcement. Competitive markets would underproduce a public good because of a *free-rider problem*: It is in each person's interest to free ride on everyone else and avoid paying for her or his share of a public good.

A *common resource* is owned by no one but used by everyone. Atlantic salmon is an example. It is in everyone's self-interest to ignore the costs of their own use of a common resource that fall on others (called the *tragedy of the commons*), which leads to overproduction.

Monopoly

A *monopoly* is a firm that is the sole provider of a good or service. Local water supply and cable television are supplied by firms that are monopolies. The self-interest of a monopoly is to maximize its profit. And because the monopoly has no competitors, it can set the price to achieve its self-interested goal. To achieve its goal, a monopoly produces too little and charges too high a price. It leads to underproduction.

High Transactions Costs

Stroll around a shopping mall and observe the retail markets in which you participate. You'll see that these markets employ enormous quantities of scarce labor and capital resources. It is costly to operate any market. Economists call the opportunity costs of making trades in a market **transactions costs**.

To use market price as the allocator of scarce resources, it must be worth bearing the opportunity cost of establishing a market. Some markets are just too costly to operate. For example, when you want to play tennis on your local "free" court, you don't pay a market price for your slot on the court. You hang around until the court becomes vacant, and you "pay" with your waiting time. When transactions costs are high, the market might underproduce.

You now know the conditions under which resource allocation is efficient. You've seen how a competitive market can be efficient, and you've seen some impediments to efficiency. But can alternative allocation methods improve on the market?

Alternatives to the Market

When a market is inefficient, can one of the alternative nonmarket methods that we described at the beginning of this reading do a better job? Sometimes it can.

Often, majority rule might be used in a number of ways in an attempt to improve the allocation of resources. But majority rule has its own shortcomings. A group that pursues the self-interest of its members can become the majority. For example, a price or quantity regulation that creates a deadweight loss is almost always the result of a self-interested group becoming the majority and imposing costs on the minority. Also, with majority rule, votes must be translated into actions by bureaucrats who have their own agendas based on their self-interest.

Managers in firms issue commands and avoid the transactions costs that they would incur if they went to a market every time they needed a job done. First-come, first-served saves a lot of hassle in waiting lines. These lines could have markets in which people trade their place in the line—but someone would have to enforce the agreements. Can you imagine the hassle at a busy ATM if you had to buy your spot at the head of the line?

There is no one efficient mechanism for allocating resources efficiently. But markets, when supplemented by majority rule, by command systems inside firms, and by occasionally using first-come, first-served, do an amazingly good job.

Is an efficient allocation of resources also a fair allocation? Does the competitive market provide people with fair incomes for their work? Do people always pay a fair price for the things they buy? Don't we need the government to step into some competitive markets to prevent the price from rising too high or falling too low? Let's now study these questions.

IS THE COMPETITIVE MARKET FAIR?   6

When a natural disaster strikes, such as a severe winter storm or a hurricane, the prices of many essential items jump. The reason the prices jump is that some people have a greater demand and greater willingness to pay when the items are in limited supply. So the higher prices achieve an efficient allocation of scarce resources. News reports of these price hikes almost never talk about efficiency. Instead, they talk about equity or fairness. The claim that is often made is that it is unfair for profit-seeking dealers to cheat the victims of natural disaster.

Similarly, when low-skilled people work for a wage that is below what most would regard as a "living wage," the media and politicians talk of employers taking unfair advantage of their workers.

How do we decide whether something is fair or unfair? You know when you *think* something is unfair. But how do you *know*? What are the *principles* of fairness?

Philosophers have tried for centuries to answer this question. Economists have offered their answers too. But before we look at the proposed answers, you should know that there is no universally agreed upon answer.

Economists agree about efficiency. That is, they agree that it makes sense to make the economic pie as large as possible and to bake it at the lowest possible cost. But they do not agree about equity. That is, they do not agree about what are fair shares of the economic pie for all the people who make it. The reason is that ideas about fairness are not exclusively economic ideas. They touch on politics, ethics, and religion. Nevertheless, economists have thought about these issues and have a contribution to make. So let's examine the views of economists on this topic.

To think about fairness, think of economic life as a game—a serious game. All ideas about fairness can be divided into two broad groups. They are

▶ It's not fair if the *result* isn't fair.

▶ It's not fair if the *rules* aren't fair.

It's Not Fair if the *Result* Isn't Fair

The earliest efforts to establish a principle of fairness were based on the view that the result is what matters. And the general idea was that it is unfair if people's incomes are too unequal. It is unfair that bank presidents earn millions of dollars a year while bank tellers earn only thousands of dollars a year. It is unfair that a store owner enjoys a larger profit and her customers pay higher prices in the aftermath of a winter storm.

There was a lot of excitement during the nineteenth century when economists thought they had made the incredible discovery that efficiency requires equality of incomes. To make the economic pie as large as possible, it must be cut into equal pieces, one for each person. This idea turns out to be wrong, but there is a lesson in the reason that it is wrong. So this nineteenth century idea is worth a closer look.

Utilitarianism

The nineteenth century idea that only equality brings efficiency is called *utilitarianism*. **Utilitarianism** is a principle that states that we should strive to achieve "the greatest happiness for the greatest number." The people who developed this idea were known as utilitarians. They included the most eminent thinkers, such as Jeremy Bentham and John Stuart Mill.

Utilitarians argued that to achieve "the greatest happiness for the greatest number," income must be transferred from the rich to the poor up to the point of complete equality—to the point at which there are no rich and no poor.

They reasoned in the following way: First, everyone has the same basic wants and a similar capacity to enjoy life. Second, the greater a person's income, the smaller is the marginal benefit of a dollar. The millionth dollar spent by a rich person brings a smaller marginal benefit to that person than the marginal benefit that the thousandth dollar spent brings to a poorer person. So by transferring a dollar from the millionaire to the poorer person, more is gained than is lost. The two people added together are better off.

Figure 7 illustrates this utilitarian idea. Tom and Jerry have the same marginal benefit curve, *MB*. (Marginal benefit is measured on the same scale of 1 to 3 for both Tom and Jerry.) Tom is at point *A*. He earns $5,000 a year, and his marginal benefit of a dollar of income is 3. Jerry is at point *B*. He earns $45,000 a year, and his marginal benefit of a dollar of income is 1. If a dollar is transferred from Jerry to Tom, Jerry loses 1 unit of marginal benefit and Tom gains 3 units. So together, Tom and Jerry are better off. They are sharing the economic pie more efficiently. If a second dollar is transferred, the same thing happens: Tom gains more than Jerry loses. And the same is true for every dollar transferred until they both reach point *C*. At point *C*, Tom and Jerry have $25,000 each, and

FIGURE 7   Utilitarian Fairness

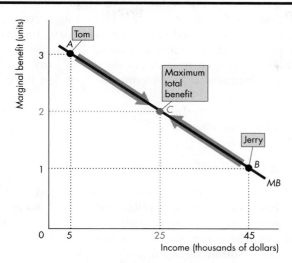

Tom earns $5,000 and has 3 units of marginal benefit at point *A*. Jerry earns $45,000 and has 1 unit of marginal benefit at point *B*. If income is transferred from Jerry to Tom, Jerry's loss is less than Tom's gain. Only when each of them has $25,000 and 2 units of marginal benefit (at point *C*) can the sum of their total benefit increase no further.

each has a marginal benefit of 2 units. Now they are sharing the economic pie in the most efficient way. It is bringing the greatest attainable happiness to Tom and Jerry.

The Big Tradeoff

One big problem with the utilitarian ideal of complete equality is that it ignores the costs of making income transfers. Recognizing the costs of making income transfers leads to what is called the **big tradeoff**, which is a tradeoff between efficiency and fairness.

The big tradeoff is based on the following facts. Income can be transferred from people with high incomes to people with low incomes only by taxing the high incomes. Taxing people's income from employment makes them work less. It results in the quantity of labor being less than the efficient quantity. Taxing people's income from capital makes them save less. It results in the quantity of capital being less than the efficient quantity. With smaller quantities of both labor and capital, the quantity of goods and services produced is less than the efficient quantity. The economic pie shrinks.

The tradeoff is between the size of the economic pie and the degree of equality with which it is shared. The greater the amount of income redistribution through income taxes, the greater is the inefficiency—the smaller is the economic pie.

There is a second source of inefficiency. A dollar taken from a rich person does not end up as a dollar in the hands of a poorer person. Some of it is spent on administration of the tax and transfer system. The cost of tax-collecting agencies, such as the IRS, and welfare-administering agencies, such as the Health Care Financing Administration, which administers Medicaid and Medicare, must be paid with some of the taxes collected. Also, taxpayers hire accountants, auditors, and lawyers to help them ensure that they pay the correct amount of taxes.

These activities use skilled labor and capital resources that could otherwise be used to produce goods and services that people value.

You can see that when all these costs are taken into account, taking a dollar from a rich person does not give a dollar to a poor person. It is even possible that with high taxes, people with low incomes end up being worse off. Suppose, for example, that highly taxed entrepreneurs decide to work less hard and shut down some of their businesses. Low-income workers get fired and must seek other, perhaps even lower-paid work.

Because of the big tradeoff, those who say that fairness is equality propose a modified version of utilitarianism.

Make the Poorest as Well Off as Possible

The philosopher, John Rawls, proposed a modified version of utilitarianism in a classic book entitled *A Theory of Justice*, published in 1971. Rawls says that, taking all the costs of income transfers into account, the fair distribution of the economic pie is the one that makes the poorest person as well off as possible. The incomes of rich people should be taxed, and after paying the costs of administering the tax and transfer system, what is left should be transferred to the poor. But the taxes must not be so high that they make the economic pie shrink to the point at which the poorest person ends up with a smaller piece. A bigger share of a smaller pie can be less than a smaller share of a bigger pie. The goal is to make the piece enjoyed by the poorest person as big as possible. Most likely, this piece will not be an equal share.

The "fair results" idea requires a change in the results after the game is over. Some economists say that these changes are themselves unfair and propose a different way of thinking about fairness.

It's Not Fair if the *Rules* Aren't Fair

The idea that it's not fair if the rules aren't fair is based on a fundamental principle that seems to be hardwired into the human brain: the symmetry principle. The **symmetry principle** is the requirement that people in similar situations be treated similarly. It is the moral principle that lies at the center of all the big religions and that says, in some form or other, "Behave toward other people in the way you expect them to behave toward you."

In economic life, this principle translates into *equality of opportunity*. But equality of opportunity to do what? This question is answered by the philosopher Robert Nozick in a book entitled *Anarchy, State, and Utopia*, published in 1974.

Nozick argues that the idea of fairness as an outcome or result cannot work and that fairness must be based on the fairness of the rules. He suggests that fairness obeys two rules:

1. The state must enforce laws that establish and protect private property.
2. Private property may be transferred from one person to another only by voluntary exchange.

The first rule says that everything that is valuable must be owned by individuals and that the state must ensure that theft is prevented. The second rule says that the only legitimate way a person can acquire property is to buy it in exchange for something else that the person owns. If these rules, which are the only fair rules, are followed, then the result is fair. It doesn't matter how unequally the economic pie is shared, provided that the pie is baked by people, each one of whom voluntarily provides services in exchange for the share of the pie offered in compensation.

These rules satisfy the symmetry principle. And if these rules are not followed, the symmetry principle is broken. You can see these facts by imagining a world in which the laws are not followed.

First, suppose that some resources or goods are not owned. They are common property. Then everyone is free to participate in a grab to use these resources or goods. The strongest will prevail. But when the strongest prevails, the strongest effectively *owns* the resources or goods in question and prevents others from enjoying them.

Second, suppose that we do not insist on voluntary exchange for transferring ownership of resources from one person to another. The alternative is *involuntary* transfer. In simple language, the alternative is theft.

Both of these situations violate the symmetry principle. Only the strong acquire what they want. The weak end up with only the resources and goods that the strong don't want.

In a majority rule political system, the strong are those in the majority or those with enough resources to influence opinion and achieve a majority.

In contrast, if the two rules of fairness are followed, everyone, strong and weak, is treated in a similar way. Everyone is free to use their resources and human skills to create things that are valued by themselves and others and to exchange the fruits of their efforts with each other. This set of arrangements is the only one that obeys the symmetry principle.

Fairness and Efficiency

If private property rights are enforced and if voluntary exchange takes place in a competitive market, resources will be allocated efficiently if there are no

1. Price and quantity regulations
2. Taxes and subsidies
3. Externalities
4. Public goods and common resources
5. Monopolies
6. High transactions costs

And according to the Nozick rules, the resulting distribution of income and wealth will be fair. Let's study a concrete example to examine the claim that if resources are allocated efficiently, they are also allocated fairly.

Case Study: A Water Shortage in a Natural Disaster

An earthquake has broken the pipes that deliver drinking water to a city. Bottled water is available, but there is no tap water. What is the fair way to allocate the bottled water?

Market Price

Suppose that if the water is allocated by market price, the price jumps to $8 a bottle—five times its normal price. At this price, the people who own water can make a large profit by selling it. People who are willing and able to pay $8 a bottle get the water. And because most people can't afford the $8 price, they end up either without water or consuming just a few drops a day.

You can see that the water is being used efficiently. There is a fixed amount available, some people are willing to pay $8 to get a bottle, and the water goes to those people. The people who own and sell water receive a large producer surplus and total surplus (the sum of consumer surplus and producer surplus) is maximized.

In the rules view, the outcome is also fair. No one is denied the water they are willing to pay for. In the results view, the outcome would most likely be regarded as unfair. The lucky owners of water make a killing, and the poorest end up the thirstiest.

Nonmarket Methods

Suppose that by a majority vote, the citizens decide that the government will buy all the water, pay for it with a tax, and use one of the nonmarket methods to allocate the water to the citizens. The possibilities now are

Command   Someone decides who is the most deserving and needy. Perhaps everyone is given an equal share. Or perhaps government officials and their families end up with most of the water.

Contest   Bottles of water are prizes that go to those who are best at a particular contest.

First-come, first-served   Water goes to the first off the mark or to those who place the lowest value on their time and can afford to wait in line.

Lottery   Water goes to those in luck.

Personal characteristics   Water goes to those with the "right" characteristics. Perhaps the old, the young, or pregnant mothers get the water.

Except by chance, none of these methods delivers an allocation of water that is either fair or efficient. It is unfair in the rules view because the tax involves involuntary transfers of resources among citizens. And it is unfair in the results view because the poorest don't end up being made as well off as possible.

The allocation is inefficient for two reasons. First, resources have been used to operate the allocation scheme. Second, some people are willing to pay for more water than they have been allocated and others have been allocated more water than they are willing to pay for.

The second source of inefficiency can be overcome if, after the nonmarket allocation, people are permitted to trade water at its market price. Those who value the water they have at less than the market price sell, and people who are willing to pay the market price to obtain more water buy. Those who value the water most highly are the ones who consume it.

Market Price with Taxes

Another approach is to allocate the scarce water using the market price but after the redistribution of buying power by taxing the sellers of water and providing benefits to the poor.

Suppose water owners are taxed on each bottle sold and the revenue from these taxes is given to the poorest people. People are then free, starting from this new distribution of buying power, to trade water at the market price.

Because the owners of water are taxed on what they sell, they have a weaker incentive to offer water for sale and the supply decreases. The equilibrium price rises to more than $8 a bottle. There is now a deadweight loss in the market for water—similar to the loss that arises from underproduction on p. 48. (We study the effects of a tax and show its inefficiency in the reading on markets in action.)

So the tax is inefficient. In the rules view, the tax is also unfair because it forces the owners of water to make a transfer to others. In the results view, the outcome might be regarded as being fair.

This brief case study illustrates the complexity of ideas about fairness. Economists have a clear criterion of efficiency but no comparably clear criterion of fairness. Most economists regard Nozick as being too extreme and want a fair tax in the rules. But there is no consensus about what would be a fair tax.

You've now studied the two biggest issues that run through the whole of economics: efficiency and equity, or fairness. In the next reading, we study some sources of inefficiency and unfairness. At many points throughout this volume—and in your life—you will return to and use the ideas about efficiency and fairness that you've learned in this reading. *Reading Between the Lines* looks at an example of an inefficiency in our economy today.

7   READING BETWEEN THE LINES

Inefficiency in Water Use

THE NEW YORK TIMES, SEPTEMBER 30, 2006

India Digs Deeper, but Wells Are Drying Up, and a Farming Crisis Looms

. . . Across India, where most people still live off the land, the chief source of irrigation is groundwater, at least for those who can afford to pump it.

Indian law has virtually no restrictions on who can pump groundwater, how much and for what purpose. Anyone, it seems, can—and does—extract water as long as it is under his or her patch of land. That could apply to homeowner, farmer or industry. . . .

"We forgot that water is a costly item," lamented K. P. Singh, regional director of the Central Groundwater Board, in his office in the city of Jaipur. "Our feeling about proper, judicious use of water vanished."

. . . On a parched, hot morning . . . a train pulled into the railway station at a village called Peeplee Ka Bas.

Here, the wells have run dry and the water table fallen so low that it is too salty even to irrigate the fields.

The train came bearing precious cargo: 15 tankers loaded with nearly 120,000 gallons of clean, sweet drinking water.

The water regularly travels more than 150 miles, taking nearly two days, by pipeline and then by rail, so that the residents of a small neighboring town can fill their buckets with water for 15 minutes every 48 hours.

It is a logistically complicated, absurdly expensive proposition. Bringing the water here costs the state about a penny a gallon; the state charges the consumer a monthly flat rate of 58 cents for about 5,300 gallons, absorbing the loss . . .

Source: Copyright 2006 The New York Times Company. www.nytimes.com. Reprinted with permission. Further reproduction prohibited.

Essence of the Story

► In India, groundwater is the chief source of irrigation.

► Indian law has few restrictions on who can pump groundwater.

► A regional director of the Central Groundwater Board laments that Indians are behaving as if water were a free resource.

► Where the wells have run dry, water is delivered by pipeline and then by train.

► Water is rationed by permitting residents to fill their buckets with water for 15 minutes every 48 hours.

► Transporting water costs 1 cent per gallon, but consumers pay about 11 cents per 1,000 gallons.

Economic Analysis

▶ Water is one of the world's most vital resources, and it is used inefficiently.

▶ Markets in water are not competitive. They are controlled by governments or private producers, and they do not work like the competitive markets that deliver an efficient use of resources.

▶ The major problem in achieving an efficient use of water is to get it from the places where it is most abundant to the places in which it has the most valuable uses.

▶ Some places have too little water, and some have too much.

▶ The news article tells us that the owners of land that has groundwater under it pump the water and sell it and pay little attention to the fact that they will pump the well dry.

▶ Figure 8 illustrates this situation. The curve *D* shows the demand for water and its marginal social benefit *MSB*. The curve *S* shows the supply of water and its marginal social cost *MSC*.

FIGURE 8   Overproduction where Wells Are Not Dry

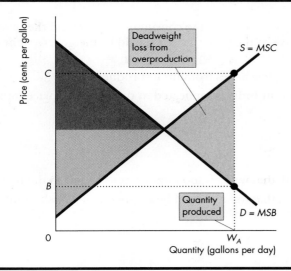

▶ Ignoring the high marginal social cost, land owners produce W_A gallons a day, which is greater than the efficient quantity. Farmers are willing to pay *B*, which is less than the marginal social cost *C* but enough to earn the land owner a profit.

▶ A deadweight loss arises from overproduction.

▶ Figure 9 shows the situation in places where the wells have run dry.

▶ A limited quantity of water, W_B, is transported in, and each consumer is restricted to the quantity that can be put into a bucket in 15 minutes every 48 hours.

▶ Consumers are willing to pay *B* per gallon, which is much more than the marginal social cost *C*.

FIGURE 9   Underproduction where Wells Run Dry

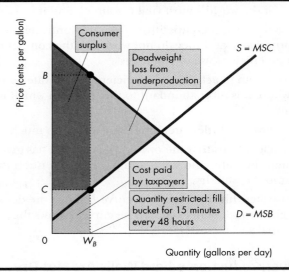

► The dark gray area shows the consumer surplus, and the blue rectangle shows the cost of the water, which is paid by the government and borne by the taxpayers.

► A deadweight loss arises from underproduction.

► The situation in India is replicated in thousands of places around the world.

You're the Voter

► Do you think that water is too important to be left to the market to allocate?

► Do you think that water should be shipped from Washington, Alaska, and Canada to California?

SUMMARY

► Because resources are scarce, some mechanism must allocate them.

► The alternative allocation methods are market price; command; majority rule; contest; first-come, first-served; lottery; personal characteristics; and force.

► Marginal benefit determines demand, and a demand curve is a marginal benefit curve.

► The market demand curve is the horizontal sum of the individual demand curves and is the marginal social benefit curve.

► Value is what people are *willing to* pay; price is what people *must* pay.

► Consumer surplus equals value minus price, summed over the quantity bought.

► The minimum supply-price determines supply, and the supply curve is the marginal cost curve.

► The market supply curve is the horizontal sum of the individual supply curves and is the marginal social cost curve.

► Opportunity cost is what producers pay; price is what producers receive.

► Producer surplus equals price minus opportunity cost, summed over the quantity sold.

► In a competitive equilibrium, marginal social benefit equals marginal social cost and resource allocation is efficient.

► Buyers and sellers acting in their self-interest end up promoting the social interest.

► The sum of consumer surplus and producer surplus is maximized.

► Producing less than or more than the efficient quantity creates deadweight loss.

► Price and quantity regulations; taxes and subsidies; externalities; public goods and common resources; monopoly; and high transactions costs can create inefficiency and deadweight loss.

► Ideas about fairness can be divided into two groups: fair *results* and fair *rules.*

► Fair-results ideas require income transfers from the rich to the poor.

► Fair-rules ideas require property rights and voluntary exchange.

PRACTICE PROBLEMS FOR READING 14

1. If voluntary exchange occurs in a competitive market, which of the following will encourage efficient resource allocation?
   A. Price ceilings.
   B. External benefits.
   C. Private property rights.

2. The value of one more unit of a product is equivalent to that unit's marginal:
   A. cost.
   B. benefit.
   C. revenue.

3. Overproduction is *most likely* associated with which of the following obstacles to efficiency?
   A. Taxes.
   B. Public goods.
   C. External costs.

4. All else equal, if the elasticity of demand and the elasticity of supply both increase, which of the following is *most likely*?
   A. Consumer surplus will increase and producer surplus will increase.
   B. Consumer surplus will decrease and producer surplus will increase.
   C. Consumer surplus will decrease and producer surplus will decrease.

SOLUTIONS FOR READING 14

1. C is correct. Private property rights encourage efficient resource allocation. Price ceilings and external benefits impede the efficient allocation of resources.

2. B is correct. The value of one more unit of a good or service is its marginal benefit.

3. C is correct. External costs will lead to the overproduction of a product because the supply curve for the product does not reflect all the costs.

4. C is correct. If both the elasticity of demand and elasticity of supply increase, then both the demand curve and the supply curve will become more horizontal. The space between the curves to the left of the equilibrium quantity will become smaller and both consumer and producer surplus will decrease.

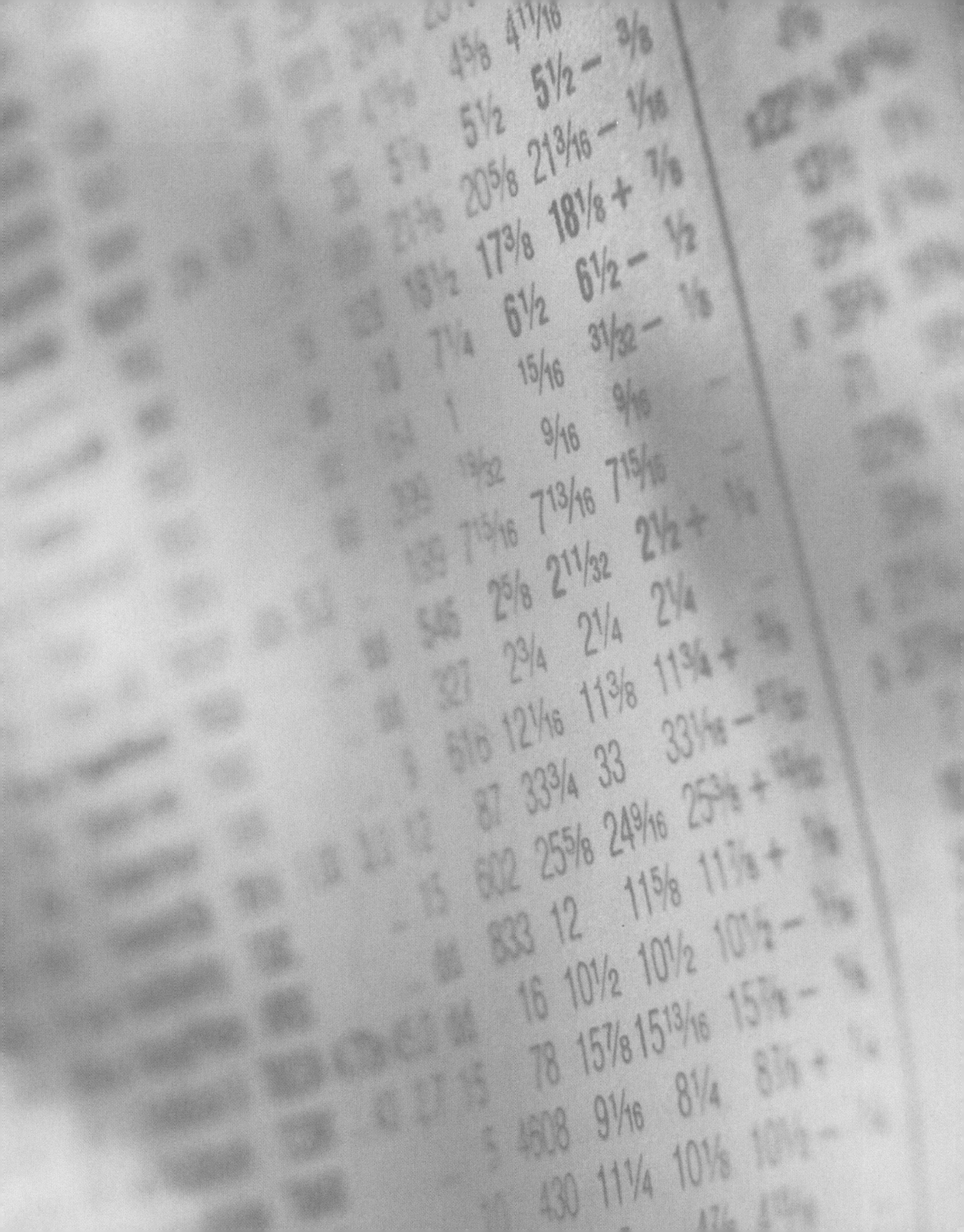

4⅝ 4¹¹/₁₆
5½ 5½ − ⅜
5½ 5½ − ¹/₁₆
20⅝ 21³/₁₆ − ⅛
17⅜ 18⅛ + ⅞
19½ 17⅜
6½ 6½ − ½
7¼ 31³/₃₂ − ⅛
15/₁₆
9/₁₆ ⅝
1¹/₃₂
7¹⁵/₁₆ 7¹³/₁₆ 7¹⁵/₁₆
2⅝ 2¹¹/₃₂ 2½ +
2¾ 2¼ 2¼
12¹/₁₆ 11⅜ 11⅝ +
333¾ 33 33⅛ −
25⅝ 24⁹/₁₆ 25⅜ +
12 11⅝ 11⅝ +
16 10½ 10½ 10⅞ −
78 15⅞ 15¹³/₁₆ 15⅞ −
9¹/₁₆ 8¼ 8⅜ +
430 −11¼ 10⅝

MARKETS IN ACTION
by Michael Parkin

LEARNING OUTCOMES

The candidate should be able to:	Mastery
a. explain market equilibrium, distinguish between long-term and short-term effects of outside shocks, and describe the effects of rent ceilings on the existence of black markets in the housing sector and on the market's efficiency;	☐
b. describe labor market equilibrium and explain the effects and inefficiencies of a minimum wage above the equilibrium wage;	☐
c. explain the impact of taxes on supply, demand, and market equilibrium, and describe tax incidence and its relation to demand and supply elasticity;	☐
d. discuss the impact of subsidies, quotas, and markets for illegal goods on demand, supply, and market equilibrium.	☐

TURBULENT TIMES   1

Apartment rents are skyrocketing in Washington, and people are screaming for help. Can the government limit rent increases to help renters live in affordable housing?

Almost every day, a new machine is invented that replaces some workers and increases productivity. Take a look at the machines in McDonald's that have replaced some low-skilled workers. Can we protect low-skilled workers with minimum wage laws that enable people to earn a living wage?

Almost everything we buy is taxed. Beer is one of the most heavily taxed items. How much of the beer tax is paid by the buyer and how much by the seller? Do taxes help or hinder the market in its attempt to move resources to where they are valued most highly?

In 2003, ideal conditions brought record yields and global grain production increased. But in 2000 and 2001, yields were low and global grain production decreased. How do farm prices and revenues react to such output fluctuations and how do subsidies and production quotas affect farmers?

Trading drugs and sharing downloaded music files are illegal activities. How do laws that make trading in a good or service illegal affect its price and the quantity bought and sold?

In this reading, we use the theory of demand and supply and the concepts of elasticity and efficiency to answer questions like those that we've just posed. In *Reading Between the Lines* at the end of the reading, we explore the challenge of limiting the illegal downloading and sharing of music files.

2   HOUSING MARKETS AND RENT CEILINGS

To see how a housing market works, let's transport ourselves to San Francisco in April 1906, as the city is suffering from a massive earthquake and fire. You can sense the enormity of San Francisco's problems by reading a headline from the April 19, 1906, *New York Times* about the first days of the crisis:

> Over 500 Dead, $200,000,000 Lost in San Francisco Earthquake
>
> Nearly Half the City Is in Ruins and 50,000 Are Homeless

The commander of federal troops in charge of the emergency described the magnitude of the problem:

> Not a hotel of note or importance was left standing. The great apartment houses had vanished . . . two hundred-and-twenty-five thousand people were . . . homeless.[1]

Almost overnight, more than half the people in a city of 400,000 had lost their homes. Temporary shelters and camps alleviated some of the problem, but it was also necessary to utilize the apartment buildings and houses left standing. As a consequence, they had to accommodate 40 percent more people than they had before the earthquake.

The *San Francisco Chronicle* was not published for more than a month after the earthquake. When the newspaper reappeared on May 24, 1906, the city's housing shortage—what would seem to be a major news item that would still be of grave importance—was not mentioned. Milton Friedman and George Stigler describe the situation:

> *There is not a single mention of a housing shortage!* The classified advertisements listed sixty-four offers of flats and houses for rent, and nineteen of

---

[1] Reported in Milton Friedman and George J. Stigler, "Roofs or Ceilings? The Current Housing Problem," in *Popular Essays on Current Problems*, vol. 1, no. 2 (New York: Foundation for Economic Education, 1946), pp. 3–159.

houses for sale, against five advertisements of flats or houses wanted. Then and thereafter a considerable number of all types of accommodation except hotel rooms were offered for rent.[2]

How did San Francisco cope with such a devastating reduction in the supply of housing?

The Market before and after the Earthquake

Figure 1 shows the market for housing in San Francisco. The demand curve for housing is *D*. There is a short-run supply curve, labeled *SS*, and a long-run supply curve, labeled *LS*.

Short-Run Supply

The short-run supply curve shows the change in the quantity of housing supplied as the rent changes while the number of houses and apartment buildings remains constant. The short-run supply response arises from changes in the intensity with which existing buildings are used. The higher the rent, the greater is the incentive for families to rent out some of the rooms that they previously used themselves.

Long-Run Supply

The long-run supply curve shows how the quantity of housing supplied responds to a change in price after enough time has elapsed for new apartment buildings and houses to be erected or for existing ones to be destroyed. In Fig. 1, the long-run supply curve is *perfectly elastic*. The marginal cost of building is the same regardless of the number of houses and apartments in existence. And so long as the rent exceeds the marginal cost of building, developers have an incentive to keep on building. So long-run supply is perfectly elastic at a rent equal to marginal cost.

Equilibrium

The equilibrium rent and quantity are determined by demand and *short-run* supply. Before the earthquake, the equilibrium rent is $16 a month and the quantity is 100,000 units of housing.

Figure 1(a) shows the situation immediately after the earthquake. Few people died in the earthquake, so demand remains at *D*. But the devastation decreases supply and shifts the short-run supply curve *SS* leftward to *SS*$_A$. If the rent remains at $16 a month, only 44,000 units of housing are available. But with only 44,000 units of housing available, the maximum rent that someone is willing to pay for the last available apartment is $24 a month. So rents rise. In Fig. 1(a), the rent rises to $20 a month.

As the rent rises, the quantity of housing demanded decreases and the quantity supplied increases to 72,000 units. These changes occur because people economize on their use of space and make spare rooms, attics, and basements available to others. The higher rent allocates the scarce housing to the people who value it most highly and are willing to pay the most for it.

But the higher rent has other, long-run effects. Let's look at these long-run effects.

---

[2] *Ibid.*, p. 3.

FIGURE 1 The San Francisco Housing Market in 1906

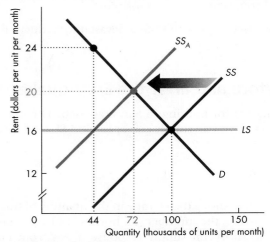

(a) After earthquake

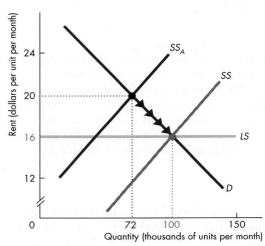

(b) Long-run adjustment

Part (a) shows that before the earthquake, 100,000 housing units were rented at $16 a month. After the earthquake, the short-run supply curve shifts from *SS* to *SS*$_A$. The rent rises to $20 a month, and the quantity of housing decreases to 72,000 units.

  With rent at $20 a month, there is profit in building new apartments and houses. As the building proceeds, the short-run supply curve shifts rightward (part b). The rent gradually falls to $16 a month, and the quantity of housing increases to 100,000 units—as the arrowed line shows.

Long-Run Adjustments

With sufficient time for new apartments and houses to be constructed, supply increases. The long-run supply curve tells us that in the long run, housing is supplied at a rent of $16 a month. Because the rent of $20 a month exceeds the long-run supply price of $16 a month, there is a building boom. More apartments and houses are built, and the short-run supply curve shifts gradually rightward.

  Figure 1(b) shows the long-run adjustment. As more housing is built, the short-run supply curve shifts gradually rightward and intersects the demand curve at lower rents and larger quantities. The market equilibrium follows the arrows down the demand curve. The building boom comes to an end when there is no further profit in building new apartments and houses. The process ends when the rent is back at $16 a month, and 100,000 units of housing are available.

We've just seen how a housing market responds to a decrease in supply. And we've seen that a key part of the adjustment process is a rise in the rent. Suppose the government passes a law to stop the rent from rising. What happens then?

A Regulated Housing Market

We're now going to study the effects of a price ceiling in the housing market. A **price ceiling** is a regulation that makes it illegal to charge a price higher than a specified level. When a price ceiling is applied to housing markets, it is called a **rent ceiling**. How does a rent ceiling affect the housing market?

The effect of a price (rent) ceiling depends on whether it is imposed at a level that is above or below the equilibrium price (rent). A price ceiling set above the equilibrium price has no effect. The reason is that the price ceiling does not constrain the market forces. The force of the law and the market forces are not in conflict. But a price ceiling below the equilibrium price has powerful effects on a market. The reason is that the price ceiling attempts to prevent the price from regulating the quantities demanded and supplied. The force of the law and the market forces are in conflict, and one (or both) of these forces must yield to some degree. Let's study the effects of a price ceiling that is set below the equilibrium price by returning to San Francisco. What would have happened in San Francisco if a rent ceiling of $16 a month—the rent before the earthquake—had been imposed?

Figure 2 enables us to answer this question. A rent that exceeds $16 a month is in the gray-shaded illegal region in the figure. At a rent of $16 a month, the quantity of housing supplied is 44,000 units and the quantity demanded is 100,000 units. So there is a shortage of 56,000 units of housing.

FIGURE 2   A Rent Ceiling

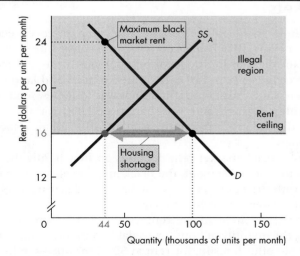

A rent above $16 a month is illegal (in the gray-shaded illegal region). At a rent of $16 a month, the quantity of housing supplied after the earthquake is 44,000 units. Someone is willing to pay $24 a month for the 44,000th unit. Frustrated renters spend time searching for housing and they make deals with landlords in a black market.

But the story does not end here. Somehow, the 44,000 units of available housing must be allocated among people who demand 100,000 units. How is this allocation achieved? When a rent ceiling creates a housing shortage, two developments occur. They are

► Search activity
► Black markets

Search Activity

The time spent looking for someone with whom to do business is called **search activity**. We spend some time in search activity almost every time we buy something. You want the latest hot CD, and you know four stores that stock it. But which store has the best deal? You need to spend a few minutes on the telephone finding out. In some markets, we spend a lot of time searching. An example is the housing market in which we spend a lot of time checking the alternatives available before making a choice.

But when a price is regulated and there is a shortage, search activity increases. In the case of a rent-controlled housing market, frustrated would-be renters scan the newspapers, not only for housing ads but also for death notices! Any information about newly available housing is useful. And they race to be first on the scene when news of a possible supplier breaks.

The *opportunity cost* of a good is equal not only to its price but also to the value of the search time spent finding the good. So the opportunity cost of housing is equal to the rent (a regulated price) plus the time and other resources spent searching for the restricted quantity available. Search activity is costly. It uses time and other resources, such as telephones, cars, and gasoline that could have been used in other productive ways. A rent ceiling controls the rent portion of the cost of housing, but it does not control the opportunity cost, which might even be *higher* than the rent would be if the market were unregulated.

Black Markets

A **black market** is an illegal market in which the price exceeds the legally imposed price ceiling. Black markets occur in rent-controlled housing, and scalpers run black markets in tickets for big sporting events and rock concerts.

When rent ceilings are in force, frustrated renters and landlords constantly seek ways of increasing rents. One common way is for a new tenant to pay a high price for worthless fittings, such as charging $2,000 for threadbare drapes. Another is for the tenant to pay an exorbitant price for new locks and keys—called "key money."

The level of a black market rent depends on how tightly the rent ceiling is enforced. With loose enforcement, the black market rent is close to the unregulated rent. But with strict enforcement, the black market rent is equal to the maximum price that renters are willing to pay.

With strict enforcement of the rent ceiling in the San Francisco example shown in Fig. 2, the quantity of housing available remains at 44,000 units. A small number of people offer housing for rent at $24 a month—the highest rent that someone is willing to pay—and the government detects and punishes some of these black market traders.

FIGURE 3   The Inefficiency of a Rent Ceiling

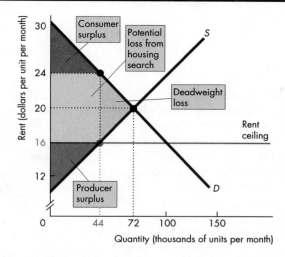

A rent ceiling of $16 a month decreases the quantity of housing supplied to 44,000 units. Producer surplus shrinks, and a deadweight loss arises. If people use no resources in search activity, consumer surplus is the dark gray triangle plus the light blue rectangle. But if people use resources in search activity equal to the amount shown by the light blue rectangle, the consumer surplus shrinks to the dark gray triangle.

Inefficiency of Rent Ceilings

In an unregulated market, the market determines the rent at which the quantity demanded equals the quantity supplied. In this situation, scarce resources are allocated efficiently. *Marginal social benefit* equals *marginal social cost.*

Figure 3 shows the inefficiency of a rent ceiling. If the rent is fixed at $16 per month, 44,000 units are supplied. Marginal benefit is $24 a month. The blue triangle above the supply curve and below the rent ceiling line shows producer surplus. Because the quantity of housing is less than the competitive quantity, there is a deadweight loss, shown by the light gray triangle. This loss is borne by the consumers who can't find housing and by producers who can't supply housing at the new lower price. Consumers who do find housing at the controlled rent gain. If no one incurs search costs, consumer surplus is shown by the sum of the dark gray triangle and the light blue rectangle. But search costs might eat up part of the consumer surplus, possibly as much as the amount shown by the light blue rectangle.

Are Rent Ceilings Fair?

Do rent ceilings achieve a fairer allocation of scarce housing? The reading on efficiency and equity explores the complex ideas about fairness. According to the *fair rules* view, anything that blocks voluntary exchange is unfair, so rent ceilings are unfair. But according to the *fair result* view, a fair outcome is one that benefits the less well off. So according to this view, the fairest outcome is the one that allocates scarce housing to the poorest. To see whether rent ceilings help to achieve a fairer outcome in this sense, we need to consider how the market allocates scarce housing resources in the face of a rent ceiling.

Blocking rent adjustments doesn't eliminate scarcity. Rather, because it decreases the quantity of housing available, it creates an even bigger challenge for the housing market. So somehow, the market must ration a smaller quantity of housing and allocate that housing among the people who demand it.

When the rent is not permitted to allocate scarce housing, what other mechanisms are available? Some possibilities are

► A lottery
► A queue
► Discrimination

Are these mechanisms fair?

A lottery allocates housing to those who are lucky, not to those who are poor. A queue (a method used to allocate housing in England after World War II) allocates housing to those who have the greatest foresight and who get their names on a list first, not to the poorest. Discrimination allocates scarce housing based on the views and self-interest of the owner of the housing. In the case of public housing, it is the self-interest of the bureaucracy that administers the allocation that counts.

In principle, self-interested owners and bureaucrats could allocate housing to satisfy some criterion of fairness. But they are not likely to do so. Discrimination based on friendship, family ties, and criteria such as race, ethnicity, or sex is more likely to enter the equation. We might make such discrimination illegal, but we would not be able to prevent it from occurring.

It is hard, then, to make a case for rent ceilings on the basis of fairness. When rent adjustments are blocked, other methods of allocating scarce housing resources operate that do not produce a fair outcome.

Rent Ceilings in Practice

London, New York, Paris, and San Francisco, four of the world's great cities, have rent ceilings in some part of their housing markets. Boston had rent ceilings for many years but abolished them in 1997. Many other U.S. cities do not have, and never have had, rent ceilings. Among them are Atlanta, Baltimore, Chicago, Dallas, Philadelphia, Phoenix, and Seattle.

We can test for the effects of rent ceilings by comparing the housing markets in cities with and without ceilings. We learn two main lessons from such a comparison.

First, rent ceilings definitely create a housing shortage. Second, they do lower the rents for some but raise them for others. A survey[3] conducted in 1997 showed that the rents of housing units *actually available for rent* were 2.5 times the average of all rents in New York but equal to the average rent in Philadelphia. The winners from rent ceilings are the families that have lived in a city for a long time. In New York, these families include some rich and famous ones. And it is the voting power of the winners that keeps the rent ceilings in place. The losers are the mobile newcomers.

The bottom line is that in principle and in practice, rent ceilings are inefficient and unfair. They prevent the housing market from operating in the social interest.

You now know how a price ceiling (rent ceiling) works. Next, we'll learn about the effects of a price floor by studying minimum wages in the labor market.

3   THE LABOR MARKET AND THE MINIMUM WAGE

For each one of us, the labor market is the market that influences the jobs we get and the wages we earn. Firms decide how much labor to demand, and the lower the wage rate, the greater is the quantity of labor demanded. Households decide

---

[3] William Tucker, "How Rent Control Drives Out Affordable Housing."

how much labor to supply, and the higher the wage rate, the greater is the quantity of labor supplied. The wage rate adjusts to make the quantity of labor demanded equal to the quantity supplied.

Equilibrium wage rates give some people high incomes but leave many more people with low incomes. And the labor market is constantly hit by shocks that often hit the lowest paid the hardest. The most pervasive of these shocks is the arrival of new labor-saving technologies that decrease the demand for low-skilled workers and lower their wage rates. During the 1980s and 1990s, for example, the demand for telephone operators and television repair technicians decreased. Throughout the past 200 years, the demand for low-skilled farm laborers has steadily decreased.

How does the labor market cope with this continuous decrease in the demand for low-skilled labor? Doesn't it mean that the wage rate of low-skilled workers is constantly falling?

To answer these questions, we must study the market for low-skilled labor in both the short run and the long run.

In the short run, there are a given number of people who have a given skill, training, and experience. The short-run supply of labor describes how the number of hours of labor supplied by this given number of people changes as the wage rate changes. To get them to work more hours, they must be offered a higher wage rate.

In the long run, people can acquire new skills and find new types of jobs. The number of people in the low-skilled labor market depends on the wage rate in this market compared with other opportunities. If the wage rate of low-skilled labor is high enough, people will enter this market. If the wage rate is too low, people will leave it. Some will seek training to enter higher-skilled labor markets, and others will stop working.

The long-run supply of labor is the relationship between the quantity of labor supplied and the wage rate after enough time has passed for people to enter or leave the low-skilled labor market. If people can freely enter and leave the low-skilled labor market, the long-run supply of labor is *perfectly elastic.*

Figure 4 shows the market for low-skilled labor. Other things remaining the same, the lower the wage rate, the greater is the quantity of labor demanded by firms. The demand curve for labor, *D* in part (a), shows this relationship between the wage rate and the quantity of labor demanded. Other things remaining the same, the higher the wage rate, the greater is the quantity of labor supplied by households. But the longer the period of adjustment, the greater is the *elasticity of supply* of labor. The short-run supply curve is *SS,* and the long-run supply curve is *LS.* In the figure, long-run supply is assumed to be perfectly elastic (the *LS* curve is horizontal). This market is in equilibrium at a wage rate of $5 an hour and 22 million hours of labor employed.

What happens if a labor-saving invention decreases the demand for low-skilled labor? Figure 4(a) shows the short-run effects of such a change. Before the new technology is introduced, the demand curve is the curve labeled *D.* After the introduction of the new technology, the demand curve shifts leftward to D_A. The wage rate falls to $4 an hour, and the quantity of labor employed decreases to 21 million hours. But this short-run effect on the wage rate and employment is not the end of the story.

People who are now earning only $4 an hour look around for other opportunities. They see many other jobs (in markets for other types of skills) that pay more than $4 an hour. One by one, workers decide to go back to school or take jobs that pay less but offer on-the-job training. As a result, the short-run supply curve begins to shift leftward.

Figure 4(b) shows the long-run adjustment. As the short-run supply curve shifts leftward, it intersects the demand curve D_A at higher wage rates and fewer hours employed. The process ends when workers have no incentive to leave the

FIGURE 4   A Market for Low-Skilled Labor

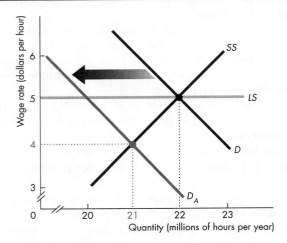

(a) After invention

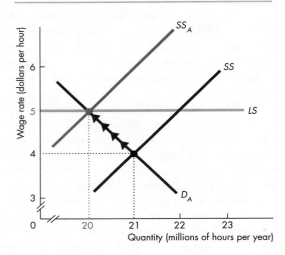

(b) Long-run adjustment

Part (a) shows the immediate effect of a labor-saving invention on the market for low-skilled labor. Initially, the wage rate is $5 an hour and 22 million hours are employed. A labor-saving invention shifts the demand curve from D to D_A. The wage rate falls to $4 an hour, and employment decreases to 21 million hours a year. With the lower wage rate, some workers leave this market, and the short-run supply curve starts to shift gradually leftward to SS_A (part b). The wage rate gradually increases, and the employment level decreases. In the long run, the wage rate returns to $5 an hour and employment decreases to 20 million hours a year.

low-skilled labor market and the short-run supply curve has shifted to SS_A. At this point, the wage rate has returned to $5 an hour and employment has decreased to 20 million hours a year.

Concerned about the incomes of low-paid workers, Congress has enacted a Federal minimum wage law. And many cities and states have introduced living wage regulations that require employers to pay higher wages than those determined by market forces.

Let's look at the effects of minimum wage and living wage regulations.

A Minimum Wage

A **price floor** is a regulation that makes it illegal to trade at a price lower than a specified level. When a price floor is applied to labor markets, it is called a **minimum wage**. If a minimum wage is set *below* the equilibrium wage, the minimum wage has no effect. The minimum wage and market forces are not in conflict. If a minimum wage is set *above* the equilibrium wage, the minimum wage is in conflict with market forces and does have some effects on the labor market. Let's study these effects by returning to the market for low-skilled labor.

Suppose that with an equilibrium wage of $4 an hour (Fig. 4a), the government sets a minimum wage at $5 an hour. Figure 5 shows the minimum wage as the horizontal dark gray line labeled "Minimum wage." A wage below this level is illegal, in the gray-shaded illegal region. At the minimum wage rate, 20 million hours of labor are demanded (point *A*) and 22 million hours of labor are supplied (point *B*), so 2 million hours of available labor are unemployed.

With only 20 million hours demanded, some workers are willing to supply that 20 millionth hour for $3. Frustrated unemployed workers spend time and other resources searching for hard-to-find jobs.

FIGURE 5   Minimum Wage and Unemployment

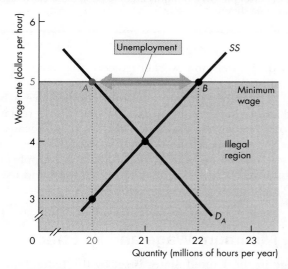

A wage below $5 an hour is illegal (in the gray-shaded illegal region). At the minimum wage of $5 an hour, 20 million hours are hired but 22 million hours are available. Unemployment—*AB*—of 2 million hours a year is created.

Inefficiency of a Minimum Wage

In an unregulated labor market, everyone who is willing to work for the going wage rate gets a job. And the market allocates the economy's scarce labor resources to the jobs in which they are valued most highly. The minimum wage frustrates the market mechanism and results in unemployment—wasted labor resources—and an inefficient amount of job search.

Figure 6 illustrates the inefficiency of the minimum wage. There is a deadweight loss because at the quantity of labor employed—20 million hours—the

FIGURE 6   The Inefficiency of a Minimum Wage

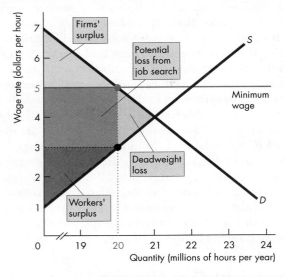

A minimum wage shrinks the firms' surplus (light blue area) and workers' surplus (dark gray area) and creates a deadweight loss (light gray area). If people use extra resources in job search, the dark blue area shows the potential loss from job search.

value to the firm of the marginal worker exceeds that wage rate for which that person is willing to work.

At this level of employment, unemployed people have a big incentive to spend time and effort looking for work. The dark blue rectangle shows the potential loss from this extra job search. This loss arises because someone who finds a job earns $5 an hour (read off from the demand curve) but would have been willing to work for $3 an hour (read off from the supply curve). So everyone who is unemployed has an incentive to search hard and use resources that are worth the $2-an-hour surplus to find a job.

The Federal Minimum Wage and Its Effects

A minimum wage in the United States is set by the federal government's Fair Labor Standards Act. In 2007, the federal minimum wage was $5.15 an hour. Some state governments have passed state minimum wage laws that exceed the federal minimum wage. The minimum wage has increased from time to time and has fluctuated between 35 percent and more than 50 percent of the average wage of production workers.

You saw in Fig. 5 that the minimum wage brings unemployment. But how much unemployment does it bring? Economists do not agree on the answer to this question. Until recently, most economists believed that the minimum wage was a big contributor to high unemployment among low-skilled young workers. But this view has recently been challenged and the challenge rebutted.

David Card of the University of California at Berkeley and Alan Krueger of Princeton University say that increases in the minimum wage have not decreased employment and created unemployment. From their study of minimum wages in California, New Jersey, and Texas, Card and Krueger say that the employment rate of low-income workers increased following an increase in the minimum wage. They suggest three reasons why higher wages might increase employment. First, workers become more conscientious and productive. Second, workers are less likely to quit, so labor turnover, which is costly, is reduced. Third, managers make a firm's operations more efficient.

Most economists are skeptical about Card and Krueger's suggestions. They ask two questions. First, if higher wages make workers more productive and reduce labor turnover, why don't firms freely pay wage rates above the equilibrium wage to encourage more productive work habits? Second, are there other explanations for the employment responses that Card and Krueger have found?

Card and Krueger got the timing wrong according to Daniel Hamermesh of the University of Texas at Austin. He says that firms cut employment *before* the minimum wage is increased in anticipation of the increase. If he is correct, looking for the effects of an increase *after* it has occurred misses its main effects. Finis Welch of Texas A&M University and Kevin Murphy of the University of Chicago say the employment effects that Card and Krueger found are caused by regional differences in economic growth, not by changes in the minimum wage.

One effect of the minimum wage, according to Fig. 5, is an increase in the quantity of labor supplied. If this effect occurs, it might show up as an increase in the number of people who quit school before completing high school to look for work. Some economists say that this response does occur.

A Living Wage

You've seen that the federal minimum wage probably causes unemployment and creates a deadweight loss. Despite these effects of a price floor in the labor market, a popular movement is seeking to create a more pervasive and much higher floor at a living wage. A **living wage** has been defined as an hourly wage rate that enables a person who works a 40-hour work week to rent adequate housing for not more than 30 percent of the amount earned. For example, if the going market rent for a one-bedroom apartment is $180 a week, the living wage is $15 an hour. (Check: 40 hours at $15 an hour is $600, and $180 is 30 percent of $600.)

Living wage laws already operate in St. Louis, St. Paul, Minneapolis, Boston, Oakland, Denver, Chicago, New Orleans, and New York City, and campaigns to expand the living wage are being mounted in many cities and states. The effects of the living wage can be expected to be similar to those of the minimum wage.

Next we're going to study a more widespread government action in markets: taxes. We'll see how taxes change prices and quantities. You will discover the surprising fact that while the government can impose a tax, it can't decide who will pay the tax! And you will see that a tax creates a deadweight loss.

TAXES   4

Everything you earn and almost everything you buy is taxed. Income taxes and Social Security taxes are deducted from your earnings and sales taxes are added to the bill when you buy something. Employers also pay a Social Security tax for their workers, and producers of tobacco products, alcoholic drinks, and gasoline pay a tax every time they sell something.

Who *really* pays these taxes? Because the income tax and Social Security tax are deducted from your pay, and the sales tax is added to the prices that you pay, isn't it obvious that *you* pay these taxes? And isn't it equally obvious that your employer pays the employer's contribution to the Social Security tax and that tobacco producers pay the tax on cigarettes?

You're going to discover that it isn't obvious who *really* pays a tax and that lawmakers don't make that decision. We begin with a definition of tax incidence.

Tax Incidence

Tax incidence is the division of the burden of a tax between the buyer and the seller. When the government imposes a tax on the sale of a good,[4] the price paid by the buyer might rise by the full amount of the tax, by a lesser amount, or not at all. If the price paid by the buyer rises by the full amount of the tax, then the burden of the tax falls entirely on the buyer—the buyer pays the tax. If the price paid by the buyer rises by a lesser amount than the tax, then the burden of the tax falls partly on the buyer and partly on the seller. And if the price paid by the buyer doesn't change at all, then the burden of the tax falls entirely on the seller.

Tax incidence does not depend on the tax law. The law might impose a tax on sellers or on buyers, but the outcome is the same in either case. To see why, let's look at the tax on cigarettes in New York City.

A Tax on Sellers

On July 1, 2002, Mayor Bloomberg of New York City raised the tax on the sale of cigarettes from almost nothing to $1.50 a pack. To work out the effects of this tax on the sellers of cigarettes, we begin by examining the effects on demand and supply in the market for cigarettes.

In Fig. 7, the demand curve is *D*, and the supply curve is *S*. With no tax, the equilibrium price is $3 per pack and 350 million packs a year are bought and sold.

FIGURE 7   A Tax on Sellers

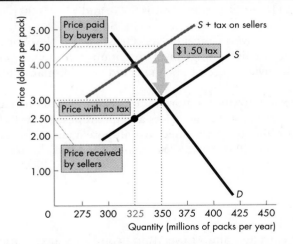

With no tax, 350 million packs a year are bought and sold at $3 a pack. A tax on sellers of $1.50 a pack shifts the supply curve leftward to *S + tax on sellers*. The equilibrium quantity decreases to 325 million packs a year, the price paid by buyers rises to $4 a pack, and the price received by sellers falls to $2.50 a pack. The tax raises the price paid by buyers by less than the tax and lowers the price received by sellers, so buyers and sellers share the burden of the tax.

---

[4] These propositions also apply to services and factors of production (land, labor, capital).

A tax on sellers is like an increase in cost, so it decreases supply. To determine the position of the new supply curve, we add the tax to the minimum price that sellers are willing to accept for each quantity sold. You can see that without the tax, sellers are willing to offer 350 million packs a year for $3 a pack. So with a $1.50 tax, they will offer 350 million packs a year only if the price is $4.50 a pack. The supply curve shifts to the dark gray curve labeled *S + tax on sellers*.

Equilibrium occurs where the new supply curve intersects the demand curve at 325 million packs a year. The price paid by buyers rises by $1 to $4 a pack. And the price received by sellers falls by 50¢ to $2.50 a pack. So buyers pay $1 of the tax and sellers pay the other 50¢.

A Tax on Buyers

Suppose that instead of taxing sellers, New York City taxes cigarette buyers $1.50 a pack.

A tax on buyers lowers the amount they are willing to pay the seller, so it decreases demand and shifts the demand curve leftward. To determine the position of this new demand curve, we subtract the tax from the maximum price that buyers are willing to pay for each quantity bought. You can see, in Fig. 8, that without the tax, buyers are willing to buy 350 million packs a year for $3 a pack. So with a $1.50 tax, they are willing to buy 350 million packs a year only if the price including the tax is $3 a pack, which means that they're willing to pay the seller only $1.50 a pack. The demand curve shifts to become the gray curve labeled *D – tax on buyers*.

Equilibrium occurs where the new demand curve intersects the supply curve at a quantity of 325 million packs a year. The price received by sellers is $2.50 a pack, and the price paid by buyers is $4.

FIGURE 8   A Tax on Buyers

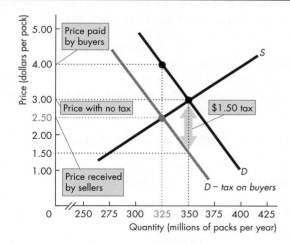

With no tax, 350 million packs a year are bought and sold at $3 a pack. A tax on buyers of $1.50 a pack shifts the demand curve leftward to *D – tax on buyers*. The equilibrium quantity decreases to 325 million packs a year, the price paid by buyers rises to $4 a pack, and the price received by sellers falls to $2.50 a pack. The tax raises the price paid by buyers by less than the tax and lowers the price received by sellers, so buyers and sellers share the burden of the tax.

Equivalence of Tax on Buyers and Sellers

You can see that the tax on buyers in Fig. 8 has the same effects as the tax on sellers in Fig. 7. In both cases, the equilibrium quantity decreases to 325 million packs a year, the price paid by buyers rises to $4 a pack, and the price received by sellers falls to $2.50 a pack. Buyers pay $1 of the $1.50 tax, and sellers pay the other 50¢ of the tax.

Can We Share the Burden Equally?

Suppose that Mayor Bloomberg wants the burden of the cigarette tax to fall equally on buyers and sellers and declares that a 75¢ tax be imposed on each. Is the burden of the tax then shared equally?

You can see that it is not. The tax is still $1.50 a pack. And you've seen that the tax has the same effect regardless of whether it is imposed on sellers or buyers. So imposing half the tax on one and half on the other is like an average of the two cases you've examined. (Draw the demand-supply graph and work out what happens in this case. The demand curve shifts downward by 75¢ and the supply curve shifts upward by 75¢. The new equilibrium quantity is still 325 million packs a year. Buyers pay $4 a pack, of which 75¢ is tax. Sellers receive from buyers $3.25, but must pay a 75¢ tax, so they net $2.50 a pack.)

The key point is that when a transaction is taxed, there are two prices: the price paid by buyers, which includes the tax; and the price received by sellers, which excludes the tax. Buyers respond only to the price that includes the tax, because that is the price they pay. Sellers respond only to the price that excludes the tax, because that is the price they receive.

A tax is like a wedge between the buying price and the selling price. It is the size of the wedge, not the side of the market on which the tax is imposed by the government, that determines the effects of the tax.

The Social Security Tax

The Social Security tax is an example of a tax that Congress imposes equally on both buyers and sellers. But the principles you've just learned apply to this tax too. The market for labor, not Congress, decides how the burden of the Social Security tax is divided by firms and workers.

In the New York City cigarette tax examples, the buyers bear twice the burden of the tax borne by sellers. In special cases, either buyers or sellers bear the entire burden. The division of the burden of a tax between buyers and sellers depends on the elasticities of demand and supply, as you will now see.

Tax Division and Elasticity of Demand

The division of the tax between buyers and sellers depends in part on the elasticity of demand. There are two extreme cases:

▶ Perfectly inelastic demand—buyers pay.
▶ Perfectly elastic demand—sellers pay.

Perfectly Inelastic Demand

Figure 9(a) shows the market for insulin, a vital daily medication of diabetics. Demand is perfectly inelastic at 100,000 doses a day, regardless of the price, as

FIGURE 9   Tax and the Elasticity of Demand

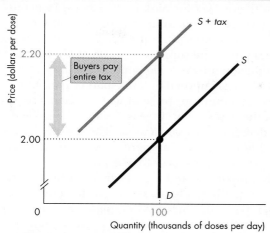

(a) Perfectly inelastic demand

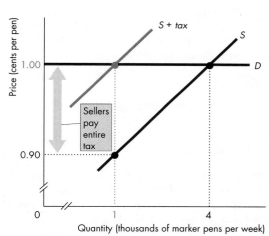

(b) Perfectly elastic demand

Part (a) shows the market for insulin, where demand is perfectly inelastic. With no tax, the price is $2 a dose and the quantity is 100,000 doses a day. A tax of 20¢ a dose shifts the supply curve to *S* + *tax*. The price rises to $2.20 a dose, but the quantity bought does not change. Buyers pay the entire tax.

Part (b) shows the market for pink pens, in which demand is perfectly elastic. With no tax, the price of a pen is $1 and the quantity is 4,000 pens a week. A tax of 10¢ a pink pen shifts the supply curve to *S* + *tax*. The price remains at $1 a pen, and the quantity of pink pens sold decreases to 1,000 a week. Sellers pay the entire tax.

shown by the vertical curve *D*. That is, a diabetic would sacrifice all other goods and services rather than not consume the insulin dose that provides good health. The supply curve of insulin is *S*. With no tax, the price is $2 a dose and the quantity is 100,000 doses a day.

If insulin is taxed at 20¢ a dose, we must add the tax to the minimum price at which drug companies are willing to sell insulin. The result is the new supply curve *S* + *tax*. The price rises to $2.20 a dose, but the quantity does not change. Buyers pay the entire sales tax of 20¢ a dose.

Perfectly Elastic Demand

Figure 9(b) shows the market for pink marker pens. Demand is perfectly elastic at $1 a pen, as shown by the horizontal curve *D*. If pink pens are less expensive than the others, everyone uses pink. If pink pens are more expensive than the others, no one uses pink. The supply curve is *S*. With no tax, the price of a pink marker is $1, and the quantity is 4,000 pens a week.

If a tax of 10¢ a pen is imposed on pink marker pens but not on other colors, we add the tax to the minimum price at which sellers are willing to offer pink pens for sale, and the new supply curve is *S + tax*. The price remains at $1 a pen, and the quantity decreases to 1,000 a week. The 10¢ tax leaves the price paid by buyers unchanged but lowers the amount received by sellers by the full amount of the tax. Sellers pay the entire tax of 10¢ a pink pen.

We've seen that when demand is perfectly inelastic, buyers pay the entire tax and when demand is perfectly elastic, sellers pay the entire tax. In the usual case, demand is neither perfectly inelastic nor perfectly elastic and the tax is split between buyers and sellers. But the division depends on the elasticity of demand. The more inelastic the demand, the larger is the amount of the tax paid by buyers.

Tax Division and Elasticity of Supply

The division of the tax between buyers and sellers also depends, in part, on the elasticity of supply. Again, there are two extreme cases:

► Perfectly inelastic supply—sellers pay.
► Perfectly elastic supply—buyers pay.

Perfectly Inelastic Supply

Figure 10(a) shows the market for water from a mineral spring that flows at a constant rate that can't be controlled. Supply is perfectly inelastic at 100,000 bottles a week, as shown by the supply curve *S*. The demand curve for the water from this spring is *D*. With no tax, the price is 50¢ a bottle and the 100,000 bottles that flow from the spring are bought.

Suppose this spring water is taxed at 5¢ a bottle. The supply curve does not change because the spring owners still produce 100,000 bottles a week even though the price they receive falls. But buyers are willing to buy the 100,000 bottles only if the price is 50¢ a bottle. So the price remains at 50¢ a bottle. The tax reduces the price received by sellers to 45¢ a bottle, and sellers pay the entire tax.

Perfectly Elastic Supply

Figure 10(b) shows the market for sand from which computer-chip makers extract silicon. Supply of this sand is perfectly elastic at a price of 10¢ a pound, as shown by the supply curve *S*. The demand curve for sand is *D*. With no tax, the price is 10¢ a pound and 5,000 pounds a week are bought.

If this sand is taxed at 1¢ a pound, we must add the tax to the minimum supply-price. Sellers are now willing to offer any quantity at 11¢ a pound along the curve *S + tax*. A new equilibrium is determined where the new supply curve intersects the demand curve: at a price of 11¢ a pound and a quantity of 3,000 pounds a week. The tax has increased the price buyers pay by the full amount of the tax—1¢ a pound—and has decreased the quantity sold. Buyers pay the entire tax.

FIGURE 10   Tax and the Elasticity of Supply

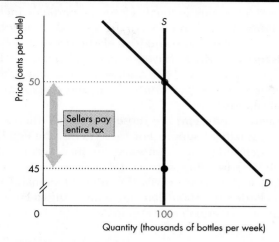

(a) Perfectly inelastic supply

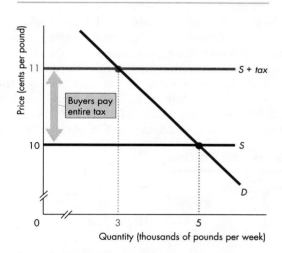

(b) Perfectly elastic supply

Part (a) shows the market for water from a mineral spring. Supply is perfectly inelastic. With no tax, the price is 50¢ a bottle. With a tax of 5¢ a bottle, the price remains at 50¢ a bottle. The number of bottles bought remains the same, but the price received by sellers decreases to 45¢ a bottle. Sellers pay the entire tax.

Part (b) shows the market for sand. Supply is perfectly elastic. With no tax, the price is 10¢ a pound. A tax of 1¢ a pound increases the minimum supply-price to 11¢ a pound. The supply curve shifts to *S + tax*. The price increases to 11¢ a pound. Buyers pay the entire tax.

We've seen that when supply is perfectly inelastic, sellers pay the entire tax and when supply is perfectly elastic, buyers pay the entire tax. In the usual case, supply is neither perfectly inelastic nor perfectly elastic and the tax is split between buyers and sellers. But how the tax is split depends on the elasticity of supply. The more elastic the supply, the larger is the amount of the tax paid by buyers.

Taxes in Practice

Supply and demand are rarely perfectly elastic or perfectly inelastic. But some items tend toward one of the extremes. For example, alcohol, tobacco, and gasoline have low elasticities of demand and high elasticities of supply. So the burden of these taxes falls more heavily on buyers than on sellers. Labor has a low elasticity of supply and a high elasticity of demand. So despite Congress's desire to split the Social Security tax equally between workers and employers, the burden of this tax falls mainly on workers.

The most heavily taxed items are those that have either a low elasticity of demand or a low elasticity of supply. For these items, the equilibrium quantity doesn't decrease much when a tax is imposed. So the government collects a large tax revenue and the deadweight loss from the tax is small.

It is unusual to tax an item heavily if neither its demand nor its supply is inelastic. With an elastic supply *and* demand, a tax brings a large decrease in the equilibrium quantity, and a small tax revenue.

Taxes and Efficiency

You've seen that a tax places a wedge between the price buyers pay and the price sellers receive. The price buyers pay is also the buyers' willingness to pay, which measures marginal benefit. And the price sellers receive is also the sellers' minimum supply-price, which equals marginal cost.

So because a tax places a wedge between the buyers' price and the sellers' price, it also puts a wedge between marginal benefit and marginal cost and creates inefficiency. With a higher buyers' price and a lower sellers' price, the tax decreases the quantity produced and consumed and a deadweight loss arises. Figure 11 shows the inefficiency of a tax on CD players. With a tax, both con-

FIGURE 11   Taxes and Efficiency

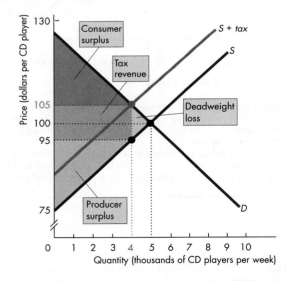

With no tax on CD players, 5,000 a week are bought and sold at $100 each. With a tax of $10 a CD player, the buyers' price rises to $105 a player, the sellers' price falls to $95 a player, and the quantity decreases to 4,000 CD players a week. Consumer surplus shrinks to the dark blue area, and the producer surplus shrinks to the light blue area. Part of the loss of total surplus (the sum of consumer surplus and producer surplus) goes to the government as tax revenue, the dark gray area, and a deadweight loss arises, the light gray area.

sumer surplus and producer surplus shrink. Part of each surplus goes to the government in tax revenue—the dark gray area. And part becomes a deadweight loss—the light gray area.

In the extreme cases of perfectly inelastic demand and perfectly inelastic supply, a tax does not change the quantity bought and sold and there is no deadweight loss. The more inelastic is either demand or supply, the smaller is the decrease in quantity and the smaller is the deadweight loss. When demand or supply is perfectly inelastic, the quantity remains constant and no deadweight loss arises.

Your next task is to study intervention in the markets for farm products. These markets have special problems and provide examples of two additional ways of changing market outcomes: subsidies and quotas.

SUBSIDIES AND QUOTAS   5

An early or late frost, a hot dry summer, and a wet autumn present just a few of the challenges that fill the lives of farmers with uncertainty and sometimes with economic hardship. Fluctuations in the weather bring big fluctuations in farm output. How do changes in farm output affect farm prices and farm revenues? And how might farmers be helped by government intervention in the markets for farm products? Let's look at some agricultural markets and see how they're affected.

Harvest Fluctuations

Figure 12 shows the market for wheat. In both parts, the demand curve for wheat is D. Once farmers have harvested their crop, they have no control over the quantity supplied and supply is inelastic along a *momentary supply curve*. With a normal harvest, the quantity produced is 20 billion bushels and the momentary supply curve is MS_0. The price is $4 a bushel, and farm revenue (price multiplied by quantity) is $80 billion.

Poor Harvest

In Fig. 12(a), a poor harvest decreases the quantity supplied to 15 billion bushels. The momentary supply curve shifts leftward to MS_1, the price rises to $6 a bushel, and farm revenue increases to $90 billion. A *decrease* in supply brings a rise in price and an *increase* in farm revenue.

Bumper Harvest

In Fig. 12(b), a bumper harvest increases the quantity supplied to 25 billion bushels. The momentary supply curve shifts rightward to MS_2, the price falls to $2 a bushel, and farm revenue decreases to $50 billion. An *increase* in supply brings a fall in price and a *decrease* in farm revenue.

Elasticity of Demand

Farm revenue and the quantity produced fluctuate in opposite directions because the demand for wheat is *inelastic*. The percentage change in the quantity

FIGURE 12   Harvests, Farm Prices, and Farm Revenue

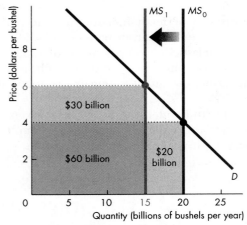

(a) Poor harvest: revenue increases

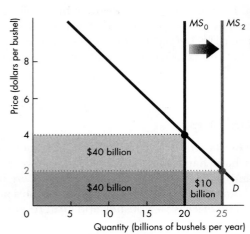

(b) Bumper harvest: revenue decreases

The demand curve is *D*. In normal times, the supply curve is MS_0 and 20 billion bushels are sold for $4 a bushel.

A poor harvest decreases the quantity supplied. The supply curve shifts to MS_1 (part a). The price rises to $6 a bushel, and farm revenue increases by $10 billion—the $30 billion increase from the higher price (light blue area) minus the $20 billion decrease from the smaller quantity (gray area).

A bumper harvest increases the quantity supplied. The supply curve shifts to MS_2 (part b). The price falls to $2 a bushel, and farm revenue falls by $30 billion—the $10 billion increase from the larger quantity (light blue area) minus the $40 billion decrease from the lower price (gray area).

demanded is less than the percentage change in price. In Fig. 12(a), the increase in revenue from the higher price ($30 billion—light blue area) exceeds the decrease in revenue from the smaller quantity ($20 billion—the gray area). In Fig. 12(b), the decrease in revenue from the lower price ($40 billion—the gray area) exceeds the increase in revenue from the larger quantity.

If demand is *elastic,* farm revenue and the quantity produced fluctuate in the same direction. Bumper harvests increase revenue, and poor harvests decrease it. But the demand for most agricultural products is inelastic, so the case we've studied is the relevant one.

Avoiding a Fallacy of Composition

Although *total* farm revenue increases when there is a poor harvest, the revenue of those *individual* farmers whose entire crop is wiped out decreases. Those whose crop is unaffected gain. So a poor harvest is not good news for all farmers.

Because the markets for farm products often confront farmers with low incomes, government intervention occurs in these markets. Price floors that work a bit like the minimum wage that we've already studied might be used. You've already seen that this type of intervention creates a surplus and is inefficient. These same conclusions apply to markets for farm products.

Two other methods of intervention are often used in markets for farm products. They are

► Subsidies
► Production quotas

Subsidies

The producers of peanuts, sugarbeets, milk, wheat, and many other farm products receive subsidies. A **subsidy** is a payment made by the government to a producer. To discover the effects of a subsidy, we'll look at a market for peanuts. Figure 13 shows this market. The demand for peanuts is *D* and the supply of peanuts is *S*. With no subsidy, the price is $40 a ton and the quantity is 40 million tons a year.

FIGURE 13   A Subsidy Increases Production

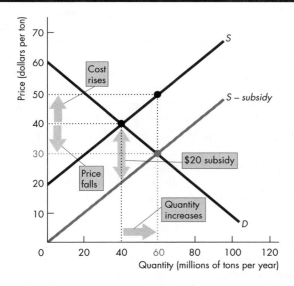

With no subsidy, 40 million tons a year are produced at $40 a ton. A subsidy of $20 a ton shifts the supply curve rightward to *S – subsidy*. The equilibrium quantity increases to 60 million tons a year, the price falls to $30 a ton, and the price plus subsidy received by farmers rises to $50 a ton. In the new equilibrium, marginal cost (on the supply curve) exceeds marginal benefit (on the demand curve) and a deadweight loss arises from overproduction.

Suppose that the government introduces a subsidy to peanut growers of $20 a ton. A subsidy is like a negative tax. You've seen that a tax is equivalent to an increase in cost. So a subsidy is equivalent to a decrease in cost. The subsidy brings an increase in supply.

To determine the position of the new supply curve, we subtract the subsidy from the farmers' minimum supply-price. Without a subsidy, farmers are willing to offer 40 million tons a year for $40 a ton. So with a subsidy of $20 a ton, they will offer 40 million tons a year if the price is as low as $20 a ton. The supply curve shifts to the gray curve labeled *S – subsidy*.

Equilibrium occurs where the new supply curve intersects the demand curve at 60 million tons a year. The price falls by $10 to $30 a ton. But the price plus subsidy received by farmers rises by $10 to $50 a ton.

Because the supply curve is the marginal cost curve, and the demand curve is the marginal benefit curve, a subsidy raises marginal cost above marginal benefit and creates a deadweight loss from overproduction.

Subsidies spill over to the rest of the world. Because they lower the price, subsidized farmers offer some of their output for sale on the world market, which lowers the price in the rest of the world. Faced with lower prices, farmers in other countries decrease production and receive smaller revenues.

Farm subsidies are a major obstacle to achieving an efficient use of resources in the global markets for farm products and are a source of tension between the United States, Europe, and poorer developing nations.

Production Quotas

The markets for sugarbeets, tobacco leaf, and cotton, (among others) have, from time to time, been regulated with production quotas. A **production quota** is an upper limit to the quantity of a good that may be produced in a specified period. To discover the effects of quotas, we'll look at a market for sugarbeets in Fig. 14. With no quota, the price is $30 a ton and 60 million tons of sugarbeets per year are produced.

Suppose that the sugarbeets growers want to limit total production to get a higher price. They persuade the government to introduce a production quota of 40 million tons of sugarbeets a year.

The effect of a production quota depends on whether it is set below or above the equilibrium quantity. If the government introduced a quota above 60 million tons a year, the equilibrium quantity in Fig. 14, nothing would change because sugarbeets growers are already producing less than the quota. But a quota of 40 million is less than the equilibrium quantity. Figure 14 shows the effects of this quota.

To implement the quota, each grower is assigned a production limit and the total of the production limits equals 40 million tons. Production that in total exceeds 40 million tons is illegal, so we've shaded the illegal region above the quota. Growers are no longer permitted to produce the equilibrium quantity because it is in the illegal region. As in the case of price ceilings and price floors, market forces and political forces are in conflict.

When the government sets a production quota, it does not regulate the price. Market forces determine it. In the example in Fig. 14, with production limited to 40 million tons a year, the market price rises to $50.

The quota not only raises the price, but also *lowers* the marginal cost of producing the quota because the sugarbeets growers slide down their supply (and marginal cost) curves.

FIGURE 14   A Quota Limits Production

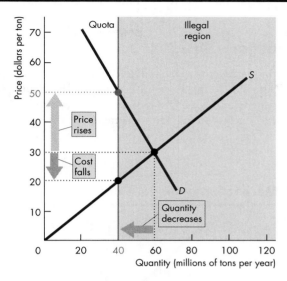

With no quota, 60 million tons a year are produced at $30 a ton. A quota of 40 million tons
a year restricts total production to that amount. The equilibrium quantity decreases to
40 million tons a year, the price rises to $50 a ton, and the farmers' marginal cost falls to $20
a ton. In the new equilibrium, marginal cost (on the supply curve) is less than marginal benefit
(on the demand curve) and a deadweight loss arises from underproduction.

A production quota is inefficient because it results in underproduction. At
the quota quantity, marginal benefit is equal to the market price and marginal
cost is less than the market price, so marginal benefit exceeds marginal cost.

Because of these effects of a quota, such arrangements are often popular
with producers and in some cases, producers, not governments, attempt to
implement them. But it is hard for quotas to work when they are voluntary. The
reason is that each producer has an incentive to cheat and produce a little bit
more than the allotted quota. You can see why by comparing the market price
and marginal cost. If one producer could get away with a tiny increase in production, her or his profit would increase. But if all producers cheat by producing
above the quota, the market moves back toward the unregulated equilibrium
and the gain for producers disappears.

Governments intervene in some markets by making it illegal to trade in a
good. Let's now see how these markets work.

MARKETS FOR ILLEGAL GOODS   6

The markets for many goods and services are regulated, and buying and selling
some goods is illegal. The best-known examples of such goods are drugs, such as
marijuana, cocaine, ecstasy, and heroin.

Despite the fact that these drugs are illegal, trade in them is a multibillion-
dollar business. This trade can be understood by using the same economic
model and principles that explain trade in legal goods. To study the market for
illegal goods, we're first going to examine the prices and quantities that would

prevail if these goods were not illegal. Next, we'll see how prohibition works. Then we'll see how a tax might be used to limit the consumption of these goods.

A Free Market for a Drug

Figure 15 shows the market for a drug. The demand curve, *D*, shows that, other things remaining the same, the lower the price of the drug, the larger is the quantity of the drug demanded. The supply curve, *S*, shows that, other things remaining the same, the lower the price of the drug, the smaller is the quantity supplied. If the drug were not illegal, the quantity bought and sold would be Q_C and the price would be P_C.

FIGURE 15   A Market for an Illegal Good

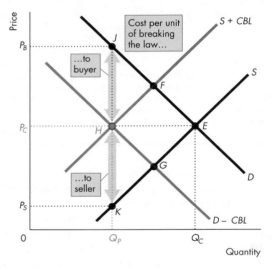

The demand curve for drugs is *D*, and the supply curve is *S*. If drugs are not illegal, the quantity bought and sold is Q_C at a price of P_C—point *E*. If selling drugs is illegal, the cost of breaking the law by selling drugs (*CBL*) is added to the minimum supply-price and supply decreases to *S + CBL*. The market moves to point *F*. If buying drugs is illegal, the cost of breaking the law is subtracted from the maximum price that buyers are willing to pay, and demand decreases to *D – CBL*. The market moves to point *G*. With both buying and selling illegal, the supply curve and the demand curve shift and the market moves to point *H*. The market price remains at P_C, but the market price plus the penalty for buying rises—point *J*— and the market price minus the penalty for selling falls—point *K*.

A Market for an Illegal Drug

When a good is illegal, the cost of trading in the good increases. By how much the cost increases and who incurs the cost depend on the penalties for violating the law and the effectiveness with which the law is enforced. The larger the penalties and the more effective the policing, the higher are the costs. Penalties might be imposed on sellers, buyers, or both.

Penalties on Sellers

Drug dealers in the United States face large penalties if their activities are detected. For example, a marijuana dealer could pay a $200,000 fine and serve a

15-year prison term. A heroin dealer could pay a $500,000 fine and serve a 20-year prison term. These penalties are part of the cost of supplying illegal drugs, and they bring a decrease in supply—a leftward shift in the supply curve. To determine the new supply curve, we add the cost of breaking the law to the minimum price that drug dealers are willing to accept. In Fig. 15, the cost of breaking the law by selling drugs (*CBL*) is added to the minimum price that dealers will accept and the supply curve shifts leftward to *S* + *CBL*. If penalties were imposed only on sellers, the market equilibrium would move from point *E* to point *F*.

Penalties on Buyers

In the United States, it is illegal to *possess* drugs such as marijuana, cocaine, ecstasy, and heroin. For example, possession of marijuana can bring a prison term of 1 year, and possession of heroin can bring a prison term of 2 years. Penalties fall on buyers, and the cost of breaking the law must be subtracted from the value of the good to determine the maximum price buyers are willing to pay for the drugs. Demand decreases, and the demand curve shifts leftward. In Fig. 15, the demand curve shifts to *D* − *CBL*. If penalties were imposed only on buyers, the market equilibrium would move from point *E* to point *G*.

Penalties on Both Sellers and Buyers

If penalties are imposed on both sellers *and* buyers, both supply and demand decrease and both the supply curve and the demand curve shift. In Fig. 15 the costs of breaking the law are the same for both buyers and sellers, so both curves shift leftward by the same amount. The market equilibrium moves to point *H*. The market price remains at the competitive market price P_C, but the quantity bought decreases to Q_P. The buyer pays P_C plus the cost of breaking the law, which equals P_B. And the seller receives P_C minus the cost of breaking the law, which equals P_S.

The larger the penalties and the greater the degree of law enforcement, the larger is the decrease in demand and/or supply. If the penalties are heavier on sellers, the supply curve shifts farther than the demand curve and the market price rises above P_C. If the penalties are heavier on buyers, the demand curve shifts farther than the supply curve and the market price falls below P_C. In the United States, the penalties on sellers are larger than those on buyers, so the quantity of drugs traded decreases and the market price increases compared with a free market.

With high enough penalties and effective law enforcement, it is possible to decrease demand and/or supply to the point at which the quantity bought is zero. But in reality, such an outcome is unusual. It does not happen in the United States in the case of illegal drugs. The key reason is the high cost of law enforcement and insufficient resources for the police to achieve effective enforcement. Because of this situation, some people suggest that drugs (and other illegal goods) should be legalized and sold openly but should also be taxed at a high rate in the same way that legal drugs such as alcohol are taxed. How would such an arrangement work?

Legalizing and Taxing Drugs

From your study of the effects of taxes, it is easy to see that the quantity of a drug bought could be decreased if the drug was legalized and taxed. A sufficiently high tax could be imposed to decrease supply, raise the price, and achieve the same decrease in the quantity bought as with a prohibition on drugs. The government would collect a large tax revenue.

Illegal Trading to Evade the Tax

It is likely that an extremely high tax rate would be needed to cut the quantity of drugs bought to the level prevailing with a prohibition. It is also likely that many drug dealers and consumers would try to cover up their activities to evade the tax. If they did act in this way, they would face the cost of breaking the law—the tax law. If the penalty for tax law violation is as severe and as effectively policed as drug-dealing laws, the analysis we've already conducted applies also to this case. The quantity of drugs bought would depend on the penalties for law breaking and on the way in which the penalties are assigned to buyers and sellers.

Taxes versus Prohibition: Some Pros and Cons

Which is more effective: prohibition or taxes? In favor of taxes and against prohibition is the fact that the tax revenue can be used to make law enforcement more effective. It can also be used to run a more effective education campaign against illegal drug use. In favor of prohibition and against taxes is the fact that prohibition sends a signal that might influence preferences, decreasing the demand for illegal drugs. Also, some people intensely dislike the idea of the government profiting from trade in harmful substances.

You now know how to use the demand and supply model to predict prices, to study government actions in markets, and to study the sources and costs of inefficiency. Before you leave this topic, take a look at *Reading Between the Lines* about the market for illegal music downloads.

READING BETWEEN THE LINES   7

The Market for Illegal Downloads

THE NEW YORK TIMES, August 5, 2006

Music Publishers Sue Owner of Web File-Sharing Program

A coalition of record companies sued the operators of the file-sharing program LimeWire for copyright infringement on Friday, claiming the company encouraged users to trade music without permission.

The Recording Industry Association of America said in a statement that it had sued the Lime Group, the corporation's executives, and the subsidiaries that designed and distributed LimeWire. The suit was filed in Federal District Court in Manhattan.

The case is the first piracy lawsuit brought against a distributor of file-sharing software since the Supreme Court ruled last year that technology companies could be sued for copyright infringement on the grounds that they encouraged customers to steal music and movies over the Internet.

The record companies—Sony BMG Music Entertainment, Vivendi's Universal Music Group, Time Warner's Warner Music Group and EMI Music—are seeking compensatory and punitive damages, including at least $150,000 for each instance in which a copyrighted song was distributed without permission.

In the complaint, the record companies contend that LimeWire's operators are "actively facilitating, encouraging and enticing" computer users to steal music by failing to block access to copyrighted works and building a business model that allows them to profit directly from piracy.

Like similar programs, LimeWire allows computer users to make files on their PCs available to a multitude of other people all connected to each other, a method known as peer-to-peer file-sharing.

The original Napster software first popularized such swapping of files online before it was forced to shut down in 2001 after record companies sued. . . .

Essence of the Story

► Napster, the software that popularized online music file swapping, was shut down in 2001 after being sued by record companies.

► Five years later, record companies claimed that LimeWire was earning a profit on software that enabled computer users to engage in peer-to-peer file sharing and to steal copyrighted music.

► The record companies sued LimeWire and sought damages, including at least $150,000 for each instance in which a copyrighted song was distributed without permission.

Economic Analysis

▶ Downloaded music is easily accessible to people with file-sharing programs.

▶ File-sharing programs are available on the internet.

▶ The marginal cost of a downloaded file is zero.

▶ In Fig. 16, the supply curve *S*, which is also the marginal cost curve, is horizontal along the *x*-axis.

FIGURE 16   Downloaders Face Cost of Breaking Law

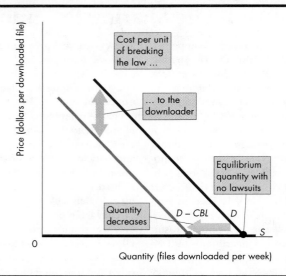

▶ The demand curve for downloaded music is the downward-sloping curve *D*.

▶ The equilibrium quantity occurs at an equilibrium price of zero, where the demand curve *D* touches the *x*-axis.

▶ If the record companies file lawsuits against downloaders, the downloaders are faced with the cost of breaking the law.

▶ The cost of breaking the law is subtracted from the value of the downloaded music to determine the maximum price that a person is willing to pay for a download.

▶ In Fig. 16, the demand curve shifts leftward from *D* to *D* − *CBL* and the vertical distance between the two curves is equal to the cost of breaking the law.

▶ The quantity of downloaded files decreases, but because the supply curve does not shift, the equilibrium price remains at zero.

▶ But if the record companies sue the creators of the file-sharing programs, as in the news article, the cost of breaking the law falls on the supply side of the market.

▶ In Fig. 17, the supply curve shifts upward from *S* to *S* + *CBL* when the creator of the file-sharing program is charged an amount *P* for each file that is illegally downloaded.

FIGURE 17   Downloaders and Program Creators Face Cost of Breaking Law

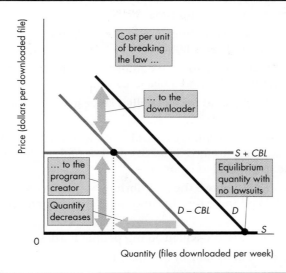

- ► If downloaders continue to face the cost of breaking the law, the demand curve *D – CBL* is the same as the curve in Fig. 16.
- ► When both creators of file-sharing programs and downloaders face the cost of breaking the law, the equilibrium quantity of downloaded files falls farther. The price of a download rises to equal the program creators' cost of breaking the law.

You're the Voter

- ► Why are record companies suing the creators of file-sharing programs rather than suing the downloaders and file sharers?
- ► Which do you think would be more effective: filing lawsuits against the creators of file-sharing software or against downloaders and file sharers?
- ► Would you support a change in the law that made file sharing legal? Explain why or why not.

SUMMARY

- ▶ A decrease in the supply of housing raises rents.
- ▶ Higher rents stimulate building, and in the long run, the quantity of housing increases and rents fall.
- ▶ A rent ceiling that is set below the equilibrium rent creates a housing shortage, wasteful search, and a black market.
- ▶ A decrease in the demand for low-skilled labor lowers the wage rate and reduces employment.
- ▶ The lower wage rate encourages people with low skills to acquire more skill, which decreases the supply of low-skilled labor and, in the long run, raises the wage rate of low-skilled labor.
- ▶ A minimum wage set above the equilibrium wage rate creates unemployment and increases the amount of time people spend searching for a job.
- ▶ A minimum wage hits low-skilled young people hardest.
- ▶ A tax raises price but usually by less than the tax.
- ▶ The shares of a tax paid by buyers and by sellers depend on the elasticity of demand and the elasticity of supply.
- ▶ The less elastic the demand or the more elastic the supply, the larger is the share of the tax paid by buyers.
- ▶ If demand is perfectly elastic or supply is perfectly inelastic, sellers pay the entire tax. And if demand is perfectly inelastic or supply is perfectly elastic, buyers pay the entire tax.
- ▶ Farm revenues fluctuate because supply fluctuates. Because the demand for most farm products is inelastic, a decrease in supply increases farm revenue, while an increase in supply decreases farm revenue.
- ▶ A subsidy is like a negative tax. It lowers the price and leads to inefficient overproduction.
- ▶ A quota leads to inefficient underproduction, which raises the price.
- ▶ Penalties on sellers of an illegal good increase the cost of selling the good and decrease its supply. Penalties on buyers of an illegal good decrease their willingness to pay and decrease the demand for the good.
- ▶ The higher the penalties and the more effective the law enforcement, the smaller is the quantity bought.
- ▶ A tax that is set at a sufficiently high rate will decrease the quantity of a drug bought, but there will be a tendency for the tax to be evaded.

PRACTICE PROBLEMS FOR READING 15

1. When a tax is imposed, which of the following would *most likely* lead to **sellers** bearing the cost?
   A. Elastic demand and elastic supply.
   B. Elastic demand and inelastic supply.
   C. Inelastic demand and elastic supply.

2. The *most likely* short-run effect on the housing market of a natural disaster such as a typhoon is a(n):
   A. decrease in supply.
   B. increase in demand.
   C. decrease in demand.

3. Compared to equilibrium in the labor market, the *most likely* result from setting the minimum wage above the equilibrium wage is a(n):
   A. increase in the workers' surplus.
   B. decrease in the deadweight loss.
   C. increase in potential loss from job search.

4. Compared to a producer, the consumer is *most likely* to pay the largest part of a tax increase if the elasticity of demand and elasticity of supply, respectively, are more:

	Elasticity of Demand	Elasticity of Supply
A.	Elastic	Elastic
B.	Elastic	Inelastic
C.	Inelastic	Elastic

5. In principle and in practice rent ceilings are *most likely* to:
   A. be fair.
   B. be efficient.
   C. prevent the housing market from operating in the social interest.

6. Setting a minimum wage above the equilibrium wage in a labor market *most likely*:
   A. creates a deadweight loss.
   B. increases the firms' surplus.
   C. increases the workers' surplus.

SOLUTIONS FOR READING 15

1. B is correct. The division of tax between buyers and sellers depends in part on the elasticity of demand and the elasticity of supply. In the extreme, sellers pay when the demand is perfectly elastic and the supply is perfectly inelastic.

2. A is correct. A natural disaster such as a typhoon that destroys a significant number of homes will most likely cause a leftward shift in the supply curve for housing—a decrease in supply.

3. C is correct. Setting a minimum wage above the equilibrium wage results in fewer workers employed and increased potential loss from job search.

4. C is correct. The buyer pays the largest portion of a tax when demand is more inelastic and supply is more elastic.

5. C is correct. In principle and in practice rent ceilings are inefficient and unfair. They prevent the housing market from operating in the social interest.

6. A is correct. The existence of a minimum wage set above the equilibrium wage in a labor market creates a deadweight loss, where the marginal worker exceeds that wage rate for which that person is willing to work, thus creating an inefficient labor market. Minimum wage also shrinks both the firms' surplus and the workers' surplus.

ORGANIZING PRODUCTION

by Michael Parkin

LEARNING OUTCOMES

The candidate should be able to:	Mastery
a. explain the types of opportunity cost and their relation to economic profit, and calculate economic profit;	☐
b. discuss a firm's constraints and their impact on achievability of maximum profit;	☐
c. differentiate between technological efficiency and economic efficiency and calculate economic efficiency of various firms under different scenarios;	☐
d. explain command systems and incentive systems to organize production, the principal-agent problem, and measures a firm uses to reduce the principal-agent problem;	☐
e. describe the different types of business organization and the advantages and disadvantages of each;	☐
f. calculate and interpret the four-firm concentration ratio and the Herfindahl-Hirschman Index, and discuss the limitations of concentration measures;	☐
g. explain why firms are often more efficient than markets in coordinating economic activity.	☐

SPINNING A WEB   1

In the fall of 1990, a British scientist named Tim Berners-Lee invented the World Wide Web. This remarkable idea paved the way for the creation and growth of thousands of profitable businesses. One of these businesses is Google, Inc. Built on the idea of two Stanford University graduate students, Larry Page and Sergey Brin, Google, Inc. opened its door for business—a garage door!—in 1998. In just a few years, Google became the world's most used, most efficient, and most profitable search engine.

How do Google and the other 20 million firms that operate in the United States make their business decisions? How do they operate efficiently?

One way in which firms seek to operate efficiently is by establishing incentives for their top executives, managers, and workers. What are the incentive schemes that firms use and how do they work?

Most of the firms that you know the names of don't make things. They buy and sell things. For example, most of the components of a Dell personal computer are made by other firms. Intel makes its processor chip, other firms make the hard drive, modem, the CD drive, sound card, and so on. Why doesn't Dell make its own computer components? How do firms decide what to make themselves and what to buy in the marketplace from other firms?

In this reading, we are going to learn about firms and the choices they make to cope with scarcity. In *Reading Between the Lines* at the end of the reading, we'll look at competition in the search engine business between Google and Yahoo!. But we begin by studying the economic problems and choices that are common to all firms.

2   THE FIRM AND ITS ECONOMIC PROBLEM

The 20 million firms in the United States differ in size and in the scope of what they do. But they all perform the same basic economic functions. Each **firm** is an institution that hires factors of production and organizes those factors to produce and sell goods and services. Our goal is to predict firms' behavior. To do so, we need to know a firm's goals and the constraints it faces. We begin with the goals.

The Firm's Goal

If you asked a group of entrepreneurs what they are trying to achieve, you would get many different answers. Some would talk about making a high-quality product, others about business growth, others about market share, and others about the job satisfaction of their work force. All of these goals might be pursued, but they are not the fundamental goal. They are means to a deeper goal.

A firm's goal is to maximize profit. A firm that does not seek to maximize profit is either eliminated or bought by firms that do seek to maximize profit. What exactly is the profit that a firm seeks to maximize? To answer this question, let's look at Sidney's Sweaters.

Measuring a Firm's Profit

Sidney runs a successful business that makes sweaters. Sidney's Sweaters receives $400,000 a year for the sweaters it sells. Its expenses are $80,000 a year for wool, $20,000 for utilities, $120,000 for wages, $5,000 for lease of a computer from

Dell, Inc., and $5,000 in interest on a bank loan. With receipts of $400,000 and expenses of $230,000, Sidney's Sweaters' annual surplus is $170,000.

Sidney's accountant lowers this number by $20,000, which he says is the depreciation (fall in value) of the firm's buildings and knitting machines during the year. (Accountants use Internal Revenue Service rules based on standards established by the Financial Accounting Standards Board to calculate the depreciation.) So the accountant reports that the profit of Sidney's Sweaters is $150,000 a year.

The accountant measures cost and profit to ensure that the firm pays the correct amount of income tax and to show the bank how its loan has been used. But we want to predict the decisions that a firm makes. These decisions respond to *opportunity cost* and *economic profit*.

Opportunity Cost

The *opportunity cost* of any action is the highest-valued alternative forgone. The action that you choose not to take—the highest-valued alternative forgone—is the cost of the action that you choose to take. For a firm, the opportunity cost of production is the value of the firm's best alternative use of its resources.

Opportunity cost is a real alternative forgone. But so that we can compare the cost of one action with that of another action, we express opportunity cost in money units. A firm's opportunity cost includes both

▶ Explicit costs
▶ Implicit costs

Explicit Costs

Explicit costs are paid in money. The amount paid for a resource could have been spent on something else, so it is the opportunity cost of using the resource. For Sidney's Sweaters, its expenditure on wool, utilities, wages, and interest are explicit costs.

Firms often lease capital—computers, photocopiers, earth-moving equipment, and so on. Sidney's Sweaters leases a computer and the payment it makes to Dell is also an explicit cost.

Implicit Costs

A firm incurs implicit costs when it forgoes an alternative action but does not make a payment. A firm incurs implicit costs when it

1. Uses its own capital.
2. Uses its owner's time or financial resources.

The cost of using capital owned by the firm is an implicit cost—and an opportunity cost—because the firm could have rented the capital to another firm. The rental income forgone is the firm's opportunity cost of using the capital it owns. This opportunity cost is called the **implicit rental rate** of capital.

If a firm uses the capital it owns, it incurs an implicit cost, which is made up of

1. Economic depreciation
2. Interest forgone

Economic depreciation is the change in the *market* value of capital over a given period. It is calculated as the market price of the capital at the beginning of the period minus its market price at the end of the period. For example, suppose that Sidney's Sweaters could have sold its buildings and knitting machines on December 31, 2005, for $400,000. If it can sell the same capital on December 31, 2006, for $375,000, its economic depreciation during 2006 is $25,000—the fall in the market value of the buildings and machines. This $25,000 is an implicit cost of using the capital during 2006.

The funds used to buy capital could have been used for some other purpose. And in their next best use, they would have earned an interest income. This forgone interest is part of the opportunity cost of using the capital. For example, Sidney's Sweaters could have bought bonds instead of a knitting factory. The interest forgone on the bonds is an implicit cost of operating the knitting factory.

Cost of Owner's Resources

A firm's owner often supplies entrepreneurial ability—the factor of production that organizes the business, makes business decisions, innovates, and bears the risk of running the business. The return to entrepreneurship is profit, and the return that an entrepreneur can expect to receive on the average is called **normal profit**.

The entrepreneur's normal profit is part of a firm's opportunity cost, because it is the cost of a forgone alternative—running another firm. If normal profit in the textile business is $50,000 a year, this amount is Sidney's normal profit and it is part of Sidney's Sweaters' opportunity costs.

As well as being the entrepreneur, the owner of a firm can supply labor, which earns a wage. The opportunity cost of the owner's labor is the wage income that the owner forgoes by not taking the best alternative job. Suppose that, in addition to being the entrepreneur, Sidney could supply labor to another firm and earn $40,000 a year. By working for his own business, Sidney forgoes $40,000 a year and this amount is part of Sidney's Sweaters' opportunity cost.

Economic Profit

What is the bottom line—the profit or loss of the firm? A firm's **economic profit** is equal to its total revenue minus its total cost. The firm's total cost is the sum of its explicit costs and implicit costs. And the implicit costs, remember, include *normal profit*. The return to entrepreneurial ability is greater than normal in a firm that makes a positive economic profit. And the return to entrepreneurial ability is less than normal in a firm that makes a negative economic profit—a firm that incurs an economic loss.

Economic Accounting: A Summary

Table 1 summarizes the economic accounting. Sidney's Sweaters' total revenue is $400,000. Its opportunity cost (explicit costs plus implicit costs) is $365,000. And its economic profit is $35,000.

To achieve the objective of maximum profit—maximum economic profit—a firm must make five basic decisions:

1. What goods and services to produce and in what quantities
2. How to produce—the techniques of production to use
3. How to organize and compensate its managers and workers
4. How to market and price its products
5. What to produce itself and what to buy from other firms

TABLE 1 Economic Accounting		
Item		**Amount**
Total Revenue		**$400,000**
Costs		
Wool	$80,000	
Utilities	20,000	
Wages paid	120,000	
Dell lease paid	5,000	
Bank interest paid	5,000	
Total Explicit Costs		$230,000
Sidney's wages forgone	40,000	
Sidney's interest forgone	20,000	
Economic depreciation	$25,000	
Sidney's normal profit	$50,000	
Total Implicit Costs		$135,000
Total Cost		**$365,000**
Economic Profit		**$35,000**

In all these decisions, a firm's actions are limited by the constraints that it faces. Our next task is to learn about these constraints.

The Firm's Constraints

Three features of its environment limit the maximum profit a firm can make. They are

► Technology
► Information
► Market

Technology Constraints

Economists define technology broadly. A **technology** is any method of producing a good or service. Technology includes the detailed designs of machines. It also includes the layout of the workplace. And it includes the organization of the firm. For example, the shopping mall is a technology for producing retail services. It is a different technology from the catalog store, which in turn is different from the downtown store.

It might seem surprising that a firm's profits are limited by technology because it seems that technological advances are constantly increasing profit opportunities. Almost every day, we learn about some new technological advance that amazes us. With computers that speak and recognize our own speech and cars that can find the address we need in a city we've never visited, we can accomplish more than ever.

Technology advances over time. But at each point in time, to produce more output and gain more revenue, a firm must hire more resources and incur greater costs. The increase in profit that the firm can achieve is limited by the technology available. For example, by using its current plant and work force, Ford can produce some maximum number of cars per day. To produce more cars per day, Ford must hire more resources, which increases its costs and limits the increase in profit that it can make by selling the additional cars.

Information Constraints

We never possess all the information we would like to have to make decisions. We lack information about both the future and the present. For example, suppose you plan to buy a new computer. When should you buy it? The answer depends on how the price is going to change in the future. Where should you buy it? The answer depends on the prices at hundreds of different computer shops. To get the best deal, you must compare the quality and prices in every shop. But the opportunity cost of this comparison exceeds the cost of the computer!

Similarly, a firm is constrained by limited information about the quality and effort of its work force, the current and future buying plans of its customers, and the plans of its competitors. Workers might slacken off when the manager believes they are working hard. Customers might switch to competing suppliers. Firms might have to compete against competition from a new firm.

Firms try to create incentive systems for workers to ensure that they work hard even when no one is monitoring their efforts. And firms spend millions of dollars on market research. But none of these efforts and expenditures eliminate the problems of incomplete information and uncertainty. And the cost of coping with limited information itself limits profit.

Market Constraints

What each firm can sell and the price it can obtain are constrained by its customers' willingness to pay and by the prices and marketing efforts of other firms. Similarly, the resources that a firm can buy and the prices it must pay for them are limited by the willingness of people to work for and invest in the firm. Firms spend billions of dollars a year marketing and selling their products. Some of the most creative minds strive to find the right message that will produce a knockout television advertisement. Market constraints and the expenditures firms make to overcome them limit the profit a firm can make.

In the rest of this reading, we study the decisions that firms make. We're going to learn how we can predict a firm's behavior as the response to both the constraints that it faces and to changes in those constraints. We begin by taking a closer look at the technology constraints that firms face.

3   TECHNOLOGICAL AND ECONOMIC EFFICIENCY

Microsoft employs a large work force, and most Microsoft workers possess a large amount of human capital. But the firm uses a small amount of physical capital. In contrast, a coal-mining company employs a huge amount of mining equipment (physical capital) and almost no labor. Why? The answer lies in the concept of efficiency. There are two concepts of production efficiency: technological efficiency and economic efficiency. **Technological efficiency** occurs when the firm produces a given output by using the least amount of inputs. **Economic efficiency** occurs when the firm produces a given output at the least cost. Let's explore the two concepts of efficiency by studying an example.

TABLE 2 Four Ways of Making 10 TV Sets a Day		
	Quantities of Inputs	
Method	**Labor**	**Capital**
A Robot production	1	1,000
B Production line	10	10
C Bench production	100	10
D Hand-tool production	1,000	1

Suppose that there are four alternative techniques for making TV sets:

A. *Robot production.* One person monitors the entire computer-driven process.

B. *Production line.* Workers specialize in a small part of the job as the emerging TV set passes them on a production line.

C. *Bench production.* Workers specialize in a small part of the job but walk from bench to bench to perform their tasks.

D. *Hand-tool production.* A single worker uses a few hand tools to make a TV set.

Table 2 sets out the amounts of labor and capital required by each of these four methods to make 10 TV sets a day.

Which of these alternative methods are technologically efficient?

Technological Efficiency

Recall that technological efficiency occurs when the firm produces a given output by using the least amount of inputs. Inspect the numbers in the table and notice that method *A* uses the most capital but the least labor. Method *D* uses the most labor but the least capital. Method *B* and method *C* lie between the two extremes. They use less capital but more labor than method *A* and less labor but more capital than method *D*. Compare methods *B* and *C*. Method *C* requires 100 workers and 10 units of capital to produce 10 TV sets. Those same 10 TV sets can be produced by method *B* with 10 workers and the same 10 units of capital. Because method *C* uses the same amount of capital and more labor than method *B*, method *C* is not technologically efficient.

Are any of the other methods not technologically efficient? The answer is no. Each of the other three methods is technologically efficient. Method *A* uses more capital but less labor than method *B*, and method *D* uses more labor but less capital than method *B*.

Which of the alternative methods are economically efficient?

Economic Efficiency

Recall that economic efficiency occurs when the firm produces a given output at the least cost. Suppose that labor costs $75 per person-day and that capital costs $250 per machine-day. Table 3(a) calculates the costs of using the different methods. By inspecting the table, you can see that method *B* has the lowest cost.

TABLE 3   The Costs of Different Ways of Making 10 TV Sets a Day

(a) Four ways of making TVs

Method	Labor Cost ($75 per Day)		Capital Cost ($250 per Day)		Total Cost	Cost per TV Set
A	$75	+	$250,000	=	$250,075	$25,007.50
B	750	+	2,500	=	3,250	325.00
C	7,500	+	2,500	=	10,000	1,000.00
D	75,000	+	250	=	75,250	7,525.00

(b) Three ways of making TVs: High labor costs

Method	Labor Cost ($150 per Day)		Capital Cost ($1 per Day)		Total Cost	Cost per TV Set
A	$150	+	$1,000	=	$1,150	$115.00
B	1,500	+	10	=	1,510	151.00
D	150,000	+	1	=	150,001	15,000.10

(c) Three ways of making TVs: High capital costs

Method	Labor Cost ($1 per Day)		Capital Cost ($1,000 per Day)		Total Cost	Cost per TV Set
A	$1	+	$1,000,000	=	$1,000,001	$100,000.10
B	10	+	10,000	=	10,010	1,001.00
D	1,000	+	1,000	=	2,000	200.00

Although method A uses less labor, it uses too much expensive capital. And although method D uses less capital, it uses too much expensive labor.

Method C, which is technologically inefficient, is also economically inefficient. It uses the same amount of capital as method B but 10 times as much labor. So it costs more. A technologically inefficient method is never economically efficient.

Although B is the economically efficient method in this example, method A or D could be economically efficient with different input prices.

Suppose that labor costs $150 a person-day and capital costs only $1 a machine-day. Table 3(b) now shows the costs of making a TV set. In this case, method A is economically efficient. Capital is now so cheap relative to labor that the method that uses the most capital is the economically efficient method.

Next, suppose that labor costs only $1 a person-day while capital costs $1,000 a machine-day. Table 3(c) shows the costs in this case. Method D, which uses a lot of labor and little capital, is now the least-cost method and the economically efficient method.

From these examples, you can see that while technological efficiency depends only on what is feasible, economic efficiency depends on the relative costs of resources. The economically efficient method is the one that uses a smaller amount of a more expensive resource and a larger amount of a less expensive resource.

A firm that is not economically efficient does not maximize profit. Natural selection favors efficient firms and opposes inefficient firms. Inefficient firms go out of business or are taken over by firms with lower costs.

Next we study information constraints that firms face and the diversity of organization structures they generate.

INFORMATION AND ORGANIZATION   4

Each firm organizes the production of goods and services by combining and coordinating the productive resources it hires. But there is variety across firms in how they organize production. Firms use a mixture of two systems:

▶ Command systems
▶ Incentive systems

Command Systems

A **command system** is a method of organizing production that uses a managerial hierarchy. Commands pass downward through the hierarchy, and information passes upward. Managers spend most of their time collecting and processing information about the performance of the people under their control and making decisions about what commands to issue and how best to get those commands implemented.

The military uses the purest form of command system. A commander-in-chief (in the United States, the President) makes the big decisions about strategic objectives. Beneath this highest level, generals organize their military resources. Beneath the generals, successively lower ranks organize smaller and smaller units but pay attention to ever-increasing degrees of detail. At the bottom of the managerial hierarchy are the people who operate weapons systems.

Command systems in firms are not as rigid as those in the military, but they share some similar features. A chief executive officer (CEO) sits at the top of a firm's command system. Senior executives who report to and receive commands from the CEO specialize in managing production, marketing, finance, personnel, and perhaps other aspects of the firm's operations. Beneath these senior managers might be several tiers of middle management ranks that stretch downward to the managers who supervise the day-to-day operations of the business. Beneath these managers are the people who operate the firm's machines and who make and sell the firm's goods and services.

Small firms have one or two layers of managers, while large firms have several layers. As production processes have become ever more complex, management ranks have swollen. Today, more people have management jobs than ever before. But the information revolution of the 1990s slowed the growth of management, and in some industries, it reduced the number of layers of managers and brought a shakeout of middle managers.

Managers make enormous efforts to be well informed. And they try hard to make good decisions and issue commands that end up using resources efficiently. But managers always have incomplete information about what is happening in the divisions of the firm for which they are responsible. It is for this reason that firms use incentive systems as well as command systems to organize production.

Incentive Systems

An **incentive system** is a method of organizing production that uses a market-like mechanism inside the firm. Instead of issuing commands, senior managers create compensation schemes that will induce workers to perform in ways that maximize the firm's profit.

Selling organizations use incentive systems most extensively. Sales representatives who spend most of their working time alone and unsupervised are induced to work hard by being paid a small salary and a large performance-related bonus.

But incentive systems operate at all levels in a firm. CEOs' compensation plans include a share in the firm's profit, and factory floor workers sometimes receive compensation based on the quantity they produce.

Mixing the Systems

Firms use a mixture of commands and incentives. And they choose the mixture that maximizes profit. They use commands when it is easy to monitor performance or when a small deviation from an ideal performance is very costly. They use incentives when monitoring performance is either not possible or too costly to be worth doing.

For example, it is easy to monitor the performance of workers on a production line. And if one person works too slowly, the entire line slows. So a production line is organized with a command system.

In contrast, it is costly to monitor a CEO. For example, what did Ken Lay (former CEO of Enron) contribute to the initial success and subsequent failure of Enron? This question can't be answered with certainty, yet Enron's stockholders had to put someone in charge of the business and provide that person with an incentive to maximize their returns. The performance of Enron illustrates the nature of this problem, known as the principal-agent problem.

The Principal-Agent Problem

The **principal-agent problem** is the problem of devising compensation rules that induce an *agent* to act in the best interest of a *principal*. For example, the stockholders of Enron are *principals*, and the firm's managers are *agents*. The stockholders (the principals) must induce the managers (agents) to act in the stockholders' best interest. Similarly, Bill Gates (a principal) must induce the programmers who are working on the next generation of Windows (agents) to work efficiently.

Agents, whether they are managers or workers, pursue their own goals and often impose costs on a principal. For example, the goal of stockholders of Citicorp (principals) is to maximize the firm's profit—its true profit, not some fictitious paper profit. But the firm's profit depends on the actions of its managers (agents), and they have their own goals. Perhaps a manager takes a customer to a ball game on the pretense that she is building customer loyalty, when in fact she is simply enjoying on-the-job leisure. This same manager is also a principal, and her tellers are agents. The manager wants the tellers to work hard and attract new customers so that she can meet her operating targets. But the workers enjoy conversations with each other and take on-the-job leisure. Nonetheless, the firm constantly strives to find ways of improving performance and increasing profits.

Coping with the Principal-Agent Problem

Issuing commands does not address the principal-agent problem. In most firms, the shareholders can't monitor the managers and often the managers can't monitor the workers. Each principal must create incentives that induce each agent to work in the interests of the principal. Three ways of attempting to cope with the principal-agent problem are

- ► Ownership
- ► Incentive pay
- ► Long-term contracts

Ownership

By assigning ownership (or part-ownership) of a business to a manager or worker, it is sometimes possible to induce a job performance that increases a firm's profits. Part-ownership schemes for senior managers are quite common, but they are less common for workers. When United Airlines was running into problems a few years ago, it made most of its employees owners of the company.

Incentive Pay

Incentive pay schemes—pay related to performance—are very common. They are based on a variety of performance criteria such as profits, production, or sales targets. Promoting an employee for good performance is another example of an incentive pay scheme.

Long-Term Contracts

Long-term contracts tie the long-term fortunes of managers and workers (agents) to the success of the principal(s)—the owner(s) of the firm. For example, a multiyear employment contract for a CEO encourages that person to take a long-term view and devise strategies that achieve maximum profit over a sustained period.

These three ways of coping with the principal-agent problem give rise to different types of business organization. Each type of business organization is a different response to the principal-agent problem. Each type uses ownership, incentives, and long-term contracts in different ways. Let's look at the main types of business organization.

Types of Business Organization

The three main types of business organization are

- ► Proprietorship
- ► Partnership
- ► Corporation

Proprietorship

A *proprietorship* is a firm with a single owner—a proprietor—who has unlimited liability. *Unlimited liability* is the legal responsibility for all the debts of a firm up to an amount equal to the entire wealth of the owner. If a proprietorship cannot pay its debts, those to whom the firm owes money can claim the personal property of the owner. Some farmers, computer programmers, and artists are examples of proprietorships.

The proprietor makes management decisions, receives the firm's profits, and is responsible for its losses. Profits from a proprietorship are taxed at the same rate as other sources of the proprietor's personal income.

Partnership

A *partnership* is a firm with two or more owners who have unlimited liability. Partners must agree on an appropriate management structure and on how to divide the firm's profits among themselves. The profits of a partnership are taxed as the personal income of the owners. But each partner is legally liable for all the debts of the partnership (limited only by the wealth of that individual partner). Liability for the full debts of the partnership is called *joint unlimited liability.* Most law firms are partnerships.

Corporation

A *corporation* is a firm owned by one or more limited liability stockholders. *Limited liability* means that the owners have legal liability only for the value of their initial investment. This limitation of liability means that if the corporation becomes bankrupt, its owners are not required to use their personal wealth to pay the corporation's debts.

Corporations' profits are taxed independently of stockholders' incomes. Stockholders pay a capital gains tax on the profit they earn when they sell a stock for a higher price than they paid for it. Corporate stocks generate capital gains when a corporation retains some of its profit and reinvests it in profitable activities. So retained earnings are taxed twice because the capital gains they generate are taxed. Until recently, dividend payments were also taxed twice but this anomaly has now been corrected.

Pros and Cons of Different Types of Firms

The different types of business organization arise as different ways of trying to cope with the principal-agent problem. Each has advantages in particular situations. And because of its special advantages, each type continues to exist. Each type also has its disadvantages, which explains why it has not driven out the other two.

Table 4 summarizes these and other pros and cons of the different types of firms.

The Proportions of Different Types of Firms

Figure 1(a) shows the proportions of the three main types of firms in the U.S. economy. The figure also shows that the revenue of corporations is much larger than that of the other types of firms. Although only 18 percent of all firms are corporations, they generate 86 percent of total revenue.

Figure 1(b) shows the percentage of total revenue generated by the different types of firms in various industries. Proprietorships in agriculture, forestry, and fishing generate about 40 percent of the total revenue in those sectors. Proprietorships in the service sector, construction, and retail trades also generate a

TABLE 4   The Pros and Cons of Different Types of Firms

Type of Firm	Pros	Cons
Proprietorship	▶ Easy to set up ▶ Simple decision making ▶ Profits taxed only once as owner's income	▶ Bad decisions not checked by need for consensus ▶ Owner's entire wealth at risk ▶ Firm dies with owner ▶ Cost of capital and labor is high relative to that of a corporation
Partnership	▶ Easy to set up ▶ Diversified decision making ▶ Can survive withdrawal of partner ▶ Profits taxed only once as owners' incomes	▶ Achieving consensus may be slow and expensive ▶ Owners' entire wealth at risk ▶ Withdrawal of partner may create capital shortage ▶ Cost of capital and labor is high relative to that of a corporation
Corporation	▶ Owners have limited liability ▶ Large-scale, low-cost capital available ▶ Professional management not restricted by ability of owners ▶ Perpetual life ▶ Long-term labor contracts cut labor costs	▶ Complex management structure can make decisions slow and expensive ▶ Retained profits taxed twice: as company profit and as stockholders' capital gains

FIGURE 1   The Proportions of the Three Types of Firms

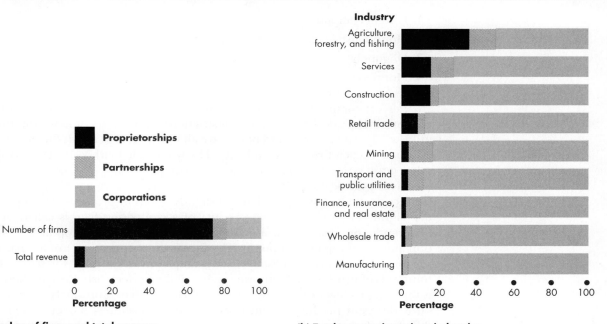

(a) Number of firms and total revenue

(b) Total revenue in various industries

Three quarters of all firms are proprietorships, almost one fifth are corporations, and only a twentieth are partnerships. Corporations account for 86 percent of total revenue (part a). But proprietorships and partnerships account for a significant percentage of total revenue in some industries (part b).

Source: U.S. Bureau of the Census, *Statistical Abstract of the United States: 2001.*

large percentage of total revenue. Partnerships in agriculture, forestry, and fishing generate about 15 percent of total revenue. Partnerships are more prominent in services; mining; and finance, insurance, and real estate than in other sectors. Corporations dominate all sectors and have the manufacturing field almost to themselves.

Why do corporations dominate the business scene? Why do the other types of business survive? And why are proprietorships and partnerships more prominent in some sectors? The answers to these questions lie in the pros and cons of the different types of business organization that are summarized in Table 4. Corporations dominate where a large amount of capital is used. But proprietorships dominate where flexibility in decision making is critical.

You've now seen how technology constraints and information constraints influence firms. We'll now look at market constraints and see how they influence the environment in which firms compete for business.

5 MARKETS AND THE COMPETITIVE ENVIRONMENT

The markets in which firms operate vary a great deal. Some are highly competitive, and profits in these markets are hard to come by. Some appear to be almost free from competition, and firms in these markets earn large profits. Some markets are dominated by fierce advertising campaigns in which each firm seeks to persuade buyers that it has the best products. And some markets display a warlike character.

Economists identify four market types:

1. Perfect competition
2. Monopolistic competition
3. Oligopoly
4. Monopoly

Perfect competition arises when there are many firms, each selling an identical product, many buyers, and no restrictions on the entry of new firms into the industry. The many firms and buyers are all well informed about the prices of the products of each firm in the industry. The worldwide markets for corn, rice, and other grain crops are examples of perfect competition.

Monopolistic competition is a market structure in which a large number of firms compete by making similar but slightly different products. Making a product slightly different from the product of a competing firm is called **product differentiation**. Product differentiation gives the firm in monopolistic competition an element of market power. The firm is the sole producer of the particular version of the good in question. For example, in the market for frozen foods, hundreds of firms make their own version of the perfect dish. Each of these firms is the sole producer of a particular brand. Differentiated products are not necessarily different products. What matters is that consumers perceive them to be different. For example, different brands of aspirin are chemically identical (acetylsalicylic acid) and differ only in their packaging.

Oligopoly is a market structure in which a small number of firms compete. Computer software, airplane manufacture, and international air transportation are examples of oligopolistic industries. Oligopolies might produce almost identical products, such as the colas produced by Coke and Pepsi. Or they might produce differentiated products such as Chevrolet's Lumina and Ford's Taurus.

Top left: Courtesy of PhotoDisc, Inc.; Bottom left: Courtesy of Beth Anderson; Top right: Courtesy of Dick Morton; Bottom right: Courtesy of Corbis.

Monopoly arises when there is one firm, which produces a good or service that has no close substitutes and in which the firm is protected by a barrier preventing the entry of new firms. In some places, the phone, gas, electricity, and water suppliers are local monopolies—monopolies restricted to a given location. Microsoft Corporation, the software developer that created Windows, the operating system used by PCs, is an example of a global monopoly.

Perfect competition is the most extreme form of competition. Monopoly is the most extreme absence of competition. The other two market types fall between these extremes.

Many factors must be taken into account to determine which market structure describes a particular real-world market. One of these factors is the extent to which the market is dominated by a small number of firms. To measure this feature of markets, economists use indexes called measures of concentration. Let's look at these measures.

Measures of Concentration

Economists use two measures of concentration:

▶ The four-firm concentration ratio
▶ The Herfindahl-Hirschman Index

The Four-Firm Concentration Ratio

The **four-firm concentration ratio** is the percentage of the value of sales accounted for by the four largest firms in an industry. The range of the concentration ratio is from almost zero for perfect competition to 100 percent for monopoly. This ratio is the main measure used to assess market structure.

Table 5 shows two calculations of the four-firm concentration ratio: one for tire makers and one for printers. In this example, 14 firms produce tires. The largest four have 80 percent of the sales, so the four-firm concentration ratio is 80 percent. In the printing industry, with 1,004 firms, the largest four firms have only 0.5 percent of the sales, so the four-firm concentration ratio is 0.5 percent.

TABLE 5   Concentration Ratio Calculations

Tire Makers		Printers	
Firm	**Sales (Millions of Dollars)**	**Firm**	**Sales (Millions of Dollars)**
Top, Inc.	200	Fran's	2.5
ABC, Inc.	250	Ned's	2.0
Big, Inc.	150	Tom's	1.8
XYZ, Inc.	100	Jill's	1.7
Largest 4 firms	700	Largest 4 firms	8.0
Other 10 firms	175	Other 1,000 firms	1,592.0
Industry	875	Industry	1,600.0

Four-firm concentration ratios:

Tire makers: $\dfrac{700}{875} \times 100 = 80$ percent

Printers: $\dfrac{8}{1,600} \times 100 = 0.5$ percent

A low concentration ratio indicates a high degree of competition, and a high concentration ratio indicates an absence of competition. A monopoly has a concentration ratio of 100 percent—the largest (and only) firm has 100 percent of the sales. A four-firm concentration ratio that exceeds 60 percent is regarded as an indication of a market that is highly concentrated and dominated by a few firms in an oligopoly. A ratio of less than 60 percent is regarded as an indication of a competitive market.

The Herfindahl-Hirschman Index

The **Herfindahl-Hirschman Index**—also called the HHI—is the square of the percentage market share of each firm summed over the largest 50 firms (or summed over all the firms if there are fewer than 50) in a market. For example, if there are four firms in a market and the market shares of the firms are 50 percent, 25 percent, 15 percent, and 10 percent, the Herfindahl-Hirschman Index is

$$\text{HHI} = 50^2 + 25^2 + 15^2 + 10^2 = 3,450.$$

In perfect competition, the HHI is small. For example, if each of the largest 50 firms in an industry has a market share of 0.1 percent, then the HHI is $0.1^2 \times 50 = 0.5$. In a monopoly, the HHI is 10,000. The firm has 100 percent of the market: $100^2 = 10,000$.

The HHI became a popular measure of the degree of competition during the 1980s, when the Justice Department used it to classify markets. A market in which the HHI is less than 1,000 is regarded as being competitive. A market in which the HHI lies between 1,000 and 1,800 is regarded as being moderately competitive. But a market in which the HHI exceeds 1,800 is regarded as being uncompetitive. The Justice Department scrutinizes any merger of firms in a market in which the HHI exceeds 1,000 and is likely to challenge a merger if the HHI exceeds 1,800.

Concentration Measures for the U.S. Economy

Figure 2 shows a selection of concentration ratios and HHIs for the United States calculated by the U.S. Department of Commerce.

Industries that produce chewing gum, household laundry equipment, light bulbs, breakfast cereal, and motor vehicles have a high degree of concentration and are oligopolies. The ice cream, milk, clothing, concrete blocks and bricks,

FIGURE 2   Concentration Measures in the United States

The industries that produce chewing gum, household laundry equipment, light bulbs, breakfast cereal, and motor vehicles are highly concentrated, while those that produce ice cream, milk, clothing, concrete blocks and bricks, and commercial printing are highly competitive. The industries that produce pet foods and cookies and crackers have an intermediate degree of concentration.

Source: *Concentration Ratios in Manufacturing* (Washington, D.C.: U.S. Department of Commerce, 1996).

TABLE 6	Market Structure			
Characteristics	Perfect Competition	Monopolistic Competition	Oligopoly	Monopoly
Number of firms in industry	Many	Many	Few	One
Product	Identical	Differentiated	Either identical or differentiated	No close substitutes
Barriers to entry	None	None	Moderate	High
Firm's control over price	None	Some	Considerable	Considerable or regulated
Concentration ratio	0	Low	High	100
HHI (approx. ranges)	Less than 100	101 to 999	More than 1,000	10,000
Examples	Wheat, corn	Food, clothing	Automobiles, cereals	Local water supply

and commercial printing industries have low concentration measures and are highly competitive. The pet food and cookies and crackers industries are moderately concentrated. They are examples of monopolistic competition.

Concentration measures are a useful indicator of the degree of competition in a market. But they must be supplemented by other information to determine a market's structure. Table 6 summarizes the range of other information, along with the measures of concentration that determine which market structure describes a particular real-world market.

Limitations of Concentration Measures

The three main limitations of using only concentration measures as determinants of market structure are their failure to take proper account of

▶ The geographical scope of the market
▶ Barriers to entry and firm turnover
▶ The correspondence between a market and an industry

Geographical Scope of Market

Concentration measures take a national view of the market. Many goods are sold in a *national* market, but some are sold in a *regional* market and some in a *global* one. The newspaper industry consists of local markets. The concentration measures for newspapers are low, but there is a high degree of concentration in the newspaper industry in most cities. The auto industry has a global market. The biggest three U.S. car producers account for 92 percent of cars sold by U.S. producers, but they account for a smaller percentage of the total U.S. car market (including imports) and a smaller percentage of the global market for cars.

Barriers to Entry and Firm Turnover

Concentration measures don't measure barriers to entry. Some industries are highly concentrated but have easy entry and an enormous amount of turnover of firms. For example, many small towns have few restaurants, but there are no restrictions on opening a restaurant and many firms attempt to do so.

Also, an industry might be competitive because of *potential entry*—because a few firms in a market face competition from many firms that can easily enter the market and will do so if economic profits are available.

Market and Industry Correspondence

To calculate concentration ratios, the Department of Commerce classifies each firm as being in a particular industry. But markets do not always correspond closely to industries for three reasons.

First, markets are often narrower than industries. For example, the pharmaceutical industry, which has a low concentration ratio, operates in many separate markets for individual products—for example, measles vaccine and AIDS-fighting drugs. These drugs do not compete with each other, so this industry, which looks competitive, includes firms that are monopolies (or near monopolies) in markets for individual drugs.

Second, most firms make several products. For example, Westinghouse makes electrical equipment and, among other things, gas-fired incinerators and plywood. So this one firm operates in at least three separate markets. But the Department of Commerce classifies Westinghouse as being in the electrical goods and equipment industry. The fact that Westinghouse competes with other producers of plywood does not show up in the concentration numbers for the plywood market.

Third, firms switch from one market to another depending on profit opportunities. For example, Motorola, which today produces cellular telephones and other communications products, has diversified from being a TV and computer chip maker. Motorola no longer produces TVs. Publishers of newspapers, magazines, and textbooks are today rapidly diversifying into Internet and multimedia products. These switches among industries show that there is much scope for entering and exiting an industry, and so measures of concentration have limited usefulness.

Despite their limitations, concentration measures do provide a basis for determining the degree of competition in an industry when they are combined with information about the geographical scope of the market, barriers to entry, and the extent to which large, multiproduct firms straddle a variety of markets.

Market Structures in the U.S. Economy

How competitive are the markets of the United States? Do most U.S. firms operate in competitive markets or in non-competitive markets?

Figure 3 provides part of the answer to these questions. It shows the market structure of the U.S. economy and the trends in market structure between 1939 and 1980. (Unfortunately, comparable data for the 1980s and 1990s are not available.)

In 1980, three quarters of the value of goods and services bought and sold in the United States was traded in markets that are essentially competitive—markets that have almost perfect competition or monopolistic competition. Monopoly and the dominance of a single firm accounted for about 5 percent of sales. Oligopoly, which is found mainly in manufacturing, accounted for about 18 percent of sales.

Over the period covered by the data in Fig. 3, the U.S. economy became increasingly competitive. You can see that the competitive markets have

FIGURE 3　The Market Structure of the U.S. Economy

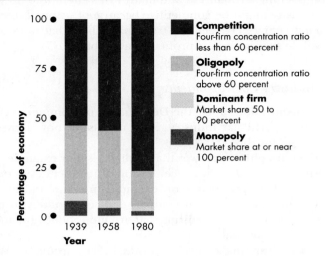

Three quarters of the U.S. economy is effectively competitive (perfect competition or monopolistic competition), one fifth is oligopoly, and the rest is monopoly. The economy became more competitive between 1939 and 1980. (Professor Shepherd, whose 1982 study remains the latest word on this topic, suspects that although some industries have become more concentrated, others have become less concentrated, so the net picture has probably not changed much since 1980.)

Source: William G. Shepherd, "Causes of Increased Competition in the U.S. Economy, 1939–1980," *Review of Economics and Statistics*, November 1982, pp. 613–626. © MIT Press Journals.

expanded most (the blue areas) and the oligopoly markets have shrunk most (the gray areas).

But also during the past decades, the U.S. economy has become much more exposed to competition from the rest of the world. Figure 3 does not capture this international competition.

You now know the variety of market types and the way we classify firms and industries into the different market types. Our final question in this reading is: What determines the things that firms decide to buy from other firms rather than produce for themselves?

6　MARKETS AND FIRMS

A firm is an institution that hires factors of production and organizes them to produce and sell goods and services. To organize production, firms coordinate the economic decisions and activities of many individuals. But firms are not the only coordinators of economic decisions. Markets also coordinate decisions. They do so by adjusting prices and making the decisions of buyers and sellers consistent—making the quantity demanded equal to the quantity supplied for each good and service.

Market Coordination

Markets can coordinate production. For example, markets might coordinate the production of a rock concert. A promoter hires a stadium, some stage equipment, audio and video recording engineers and technicians, some rock groups, a superstar, a publicity agent, and a ticket agent—all market transactions—and sells tickets to thousands of rock fans, audio rights to a recording company, and video and broadcasting rights to a television network—another set of market transactions. Alternatively, if rock concerts were produced like cornflakes, the firm producing them would own all the capital used (stadiums, stage, sound and video equipment) and would employ all the labor needed (singers, engineers, and salespeople).

Outsourcing, buying parts or products from other firms, is another example of market coordination. Dell uses outsourcing for all the components of the computers it produces. The major automakers use outsourcing for windshields and windows, gearboxes, tires, and many other car parts.

What determines whether a firm or markets coordinate a particular set of activities? How do firms decide whether to buy from another firm or manufacture an item themselves? The answer is cost. Taking account of the opportunity cost of time as well as the costs of the other inputs, firms use the method that costs least. In other words, they use the economically efficient method.

Firms coordinate economic activity when they can perform a task more efficiently than markets can. In such a situation, it is profitable to set up a firm. If markets can perform a task more efficiently than a firm can, firms will use markets, and any attempt to set up a firm to replace such market coordination will be doomed to failure.

Why Firms?

Firms are often more efficient than markets as coordinators of economic activity because they can achieve

► Lower transactions costs
► Economies of scale
► Economies of scope
► Economies of team production

Transactions Costs

The idea that firms exist because there are activities in which firms are more efficient than markets was first suggested by University of Chicago economist and Nobel Laureate Ronald Coase. Coase focused on the firm's ability to reduce or eliminate transactions costs. **Transactions costs** are the costs that arise from finding someone with whom to do business, of reaching an agreement about the price and other aspects of the exchange, and of ensuring that the terms of the agreement are fulfilled. Market transactions require buyers and sellers to get together and to negotiate the terms and conditions of their trading. Sometimes, lawyers have to be hired to draw up contracts. A broken contract leads to still more expenses. A firm can lower such transactions costs by reducing the number of individual transactions undertaken.

Consider, for example, two ways of getting your rattling car fixed.

Firm coordination: You take the car to the garage. The garage owner coordinates parts and tools as well as the mechanic's time, and your car gets fixed. You pay one bill for the entire job.

Market coordination: You hire a mechanic, who diagnoses the problems and makes a list of the parts and tools needed to fix them. You buy the parts from the local wrecker's yard and rent the tools from ABC Rentals. You hire the mechanic again to fix the problems. You return the tools and pay your bills—wages to the mechanic, rental to ABC, and the cost of the parts used to the wrecker.

What determines the method that you use? The answer is cost. Taking account of the opportunity cost of your own time as well as the costs of the other inputs that you would have to buy, you will use the method that costs least. In other words, you will use the economically efficient method.

The first method requires that you undertake only one transaction with one firm. It's true that the firm has to undertake several transactions—hiring the labor and buying the parts and tools required to do the job. But the firm doesn't have to undertake those transactions simply to fix your car. One set of such transactions enables the firm to fix hundreds of cars. Thus there is an enormous reduction in the number of individual transactions that take place if people get their cars fixed at the garage rather than going through an elaborate sequence of market transactions.

Economies of Scale

When the cost of producing a unit of a good falls as its output rate increases, **economies of scale** exist. Automakers, for example, experience economies of scale because as the scale of production increases, the firm can use cost-saving equipment and highly specialized labor. An automaker that produces only a few cars a year must use hand-tool methods that are costly. Economies of scale arise from specialization and the division of labor that can be reaped more effectively by firm coordination rather than market coordination.

Economies of Scope

A firm experiences **economies of scope** when it uses specialized (and often expensive) resources to produce a *range of goods and services*. For example, Microsoft hires specialist programmers, designers, and marketing experts and uses their skills across a range of software products. As a result, Microsoft coordinates the resources that produce software at a lower cost than an individual can who buys all these services in markets.

Economies of Team Production

A production process in which the individuals in a group specialize in mutually supportive tasks is team production. Sport provides the best example of team activity. In baseball, some team members specialize in pitching and some in batting. In basketball, some team members specialize in defense and some in offense. The production of goods and services offers many examples of team activity. For example, production lines in automobile and TV manufacturing plants work most efficiently when individual activity is organized in teams, each specializing in a small task. You can also think of an entire firm as being a team. The team has buyers of raw material and other inputs, production workers, and salespeople. Each individual member of the team specializes, but the value of the output of the team and the profit that it earns depend on the coordinated activities of all the team's members. The idea that firms arise as a consequence of the economies of team production was first suggested by Armen Alchian and Harold Demsetz of the University of California at Los Angeles.

Because firms can economize on transactions costs, reap economies of scale and economies of scope, and organize efficient team production, it is firms rather than markets that coordinate most of our economic activity. But there are limits to the economic efficiency of firms. If a firm becomes too big or too diversified in the things that it seeks to do, the cost of management and monitoring per unit of output begins to rise, and at some point, the market becomes more efficient at coordinating the use of resources. IBM is an example of a firm that became too big to be efficient. In an attempt to restore efficient operations, IBM split up its large organization into a number of "Baby Blues," each of which specializes in a segment of the computer market.

Sometimes firms enter into long-term relationships with each other that make it difficult to see where one firm ends and another begins. For example, GM has long-term relationships with suppliers of windows, tires, and other parts. Wal-Mart has long-term relationships with suppliers of the goods it sells. Such relationships make transactions costs lower than they would be if GM or Wal-Mart went shopping on the open market each time it wanted new supplies.

Reading Between the Lines on pp. 122–124 explores the internet search business. We continue to study firms and their decisions in the next four readings. In the reading on output and costs, we learn about the relationships between cost and output at different output levels. These cost-output relationships are common to all types of firms in all types of markets. We then turn to problems that are specific to firms in different types of markets.

7 ▸ READING BETWEEN THE LINES

Battling for Markets in Internet Search

HTTP://MONEY.CNN.COM, OCTOBER 13, 2006

Yawns for Yahoo, Ga-Ga for Google

Earnings from the two search leaders are coming and guess what? Google's eating Yahoo's lunch.

. . . Yahoo stunned Wall Street last month when chief financial officer Sue Decker somewhat casually said at a Goldman Sachs' conference in New York that sales for the quarter would be at the low end of the company's forecast due to softness in auto and financial services advertising. . . .

Google, on the other hand, keeps wowing the Street. It bested sales and profit forecasts for the second quarter back in July.

And on Monday, Google unveiled a deal to buy YouTube, the popular online video sharing site, for $1.6 billion, a marriage uniting the top search engine and No. 1 video site. Analysts were raving about Google's chances to get a big piece of the potentially lucrative online video advertising market. . . .

Yahoo is playing catch-up with Google in the hot market for paid search, ads tied to specific keyword queries. According to the most recent numbers from Web tracking firm comScore Networks, Google widened its lead in search over Yahoo in August. . . .

And looking ahead to next year, Yahoo could face a much tougher challenge from Google in so-called display advertising, sales of video ads, banners and other ads not tied to search results, thanks to Google's pending deal for YouTube.

Yahoo has so far maintained an edge over Google in display advertising, which tends to be more attractive to big brand-name companies than search ads. But it is a big market opportunity for Google.

Essence of the Story

▶ Yahoo! lags behind Google in the market for advertising tied to keyword queries—known as paid search.

▶ Yahoo! leads Google in sales of video ads, banners, and other ads not tied to search results—known as display advertising.

▶ By buying YouTube (for $1.6 billion), Google has created a marriage of the top search engine and the top video sharing site.

▶ Google is expected to gain a large share of the profitable online video advertising market, which big brand-name companies use.

Economic Analysis

► Like all firms, Yahoo! and Google aim to maximize profit.

► Also, like all firms, Yahoo! and Google face constraints imposed by technology and the market.

► These firms provide search engines to access information on the internet.

► People who use a search engine demand information, and Yahoo! and Google (and other firms) supply information.

► The equilibrium price of search engine services to their users is zero!

► To generate revenue and profit, search engine providers offer advertising services.

► Two types of advertising are offered: paid search and display.

► Google's focus is on paid search—see Figs. 4 and 5. Yahoo!'s focus is on display—see Fig. 6.

FIGURE 4   Paid Search Advertising

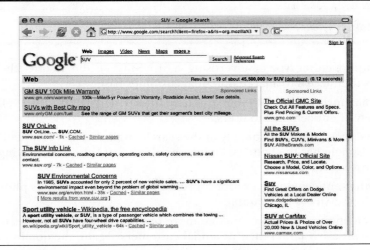

Source: © 2006 Google.

FIGURE 5   Google's Focus Is Search

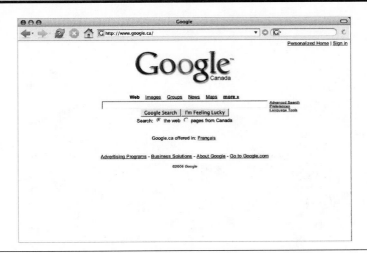

Source: © 2006 Google.

FIGURE 6   Yahoo! Features Display Advertising

Source: Copyright © 2007 Yahoo! Inc. All rights reserved.

► To attract either type of advertising, a firm must be able to offer the advertiser access to a large potential customer base.

► To maximize the use of their search engines, Google and Yahoo! offer a variety of enticements to users.

► One enticement is the quality of the search engine itself. Most people think that Google has the better search technology. But Yahoo! is working on improved search.

► Another enticement is a variety of related attractions. Yahoo!'s photo-sharing service is an example.

► Search engines can also generate more revenue by enabling advertisers to more precisely target their potential customers. Again, the quality of the search technology is the key ingredient. And again, Google is reckoned by many to have the edge.

► Google hopes to attract even more users and to increase its ability to use video and other display technologies through its acquisition of YouTube.

SUMMARY

► Firms hire and organize factors of production to produce and sell goods and services.

► Firms seek to maximize economic profit, which is total revenue minus opportunity cost.

► A firm's opportunity cost of production is the sum of explicit costs and the implicit costs of using the firm's capital and the owner's resources.

► Normal profit is the opportunity cost of entrepreneurship and is part of the firm's implicit costs.

► Technology, information, and markets limit a firm's profit.

► A method of production is technologically efficient when a firm produces a given output by using the least amount of inputs.

► A method of production is economically efficient when the cost of producing a given output is as low as possible.

► Firms use a combination of command systems and incentive systems to organize production.

► Faced with incomplete information and uncertainty, firms induce managers and workers to perform in ways that are consistent with the firm's goals.

► Proprietorships, partnerships, and corporations use ownership, incentive pay, and long-term contracts to cope with the principal-agent problem.

► In perfect competition, many sellers offer an identical product to many buyers and entry is free.

► In monopolistic competition, many sellers offer slightly different products to many buyers and entry is free.

► In oligopoly, a small number of sellers compete.

► In monopoly, one firm produces an item that has no close substitutes and the firm is protected by a barrier to entry that prevents the entry of competitors.

► Firms coordinate economic activities when they can perform a task more efficiently—at lower cost—than markets can.

► Firms economize on transactions costs and achieve the benefits of economies of scale, economies of scope, and economies of team production.

PRACTICE PROBLEMS FOR READING 16

1. With regard to organizational structure and the calculation of costs and profits, which of the following statements is *most* accurate? Compared to accounting costs, economic costs tend to be:

   A. lower, especially for large firms organized as corporations.

   B. higher, especially for large firms organized as corporations.

   C. higher, especially for small firms organized as proprietorships.

2. Four years ago a company purchased a $500,000 machine with an estimated useful life of 10 years. For accounting purposes, the machine is being depreciated in the amount of $50,000 annually. The machine is used to manufacture a particular product and has no alternative use or scrap value. The annual revenue generated from operating the machine is $650,000 and the annual cost of the factors of production, other than depreciation, employed to generate that revenue is $600,000. Should the company continue to operate the machine?

   A. Yes.

   B. No, because operating costs are equal to operating revenues.

   C. No, because the opportunity cost of operating the machine is zero.

3. Four years ago a company purchased a $1 million machine with an estimated useful life of 10 years. For accounting purposes, the machine is being depreciated in the amount of $100,000 annually. The machine is used to manufacture a particular product and has no alternative use or scrap value. The annual revenue generated from operating the machine is $650,000 and the annual cost of the factors of production, other than deprecation, employed to generate that revenue is $600,000. Should the company continue to operate the machine?

   A. Yes.

   B. No, because the machine is being operated at a net loss.

   C. No, because the opportunity cost of operating the machine is zero.

4. Using the following information, calculate the firm's economic profit.

Revenues	200,000
Cash Expenses	100,000
Economic depreciation	15,000
Accounting depreciation	20,000
Normal profit	30,000
Forgone interest	12,000

   A. 38,000.

   B. 43,000.

   C. 73,000.

5. Which of the following is not a type of opportunity cost?

   A. Normal profit.

   B. Economic profit.

   C. Implicit rental rate of capital.

6. Using the following information, calculate which method is the most economically efficient to produce 8 units per day if one unit of labor costs $50 and each unit of capital costs $700.

	Quantity of Inputs	
	Labor	**Capital**
Manual process	100	5
Automated process	10	20

   A. Manual, with per unit cost of $840.00.

   B. Manual, with per unit cost of $1,062.50.

   C. Automated, with per unit cost of $1,812.50.

7. Which of the following *best* defines the described production efficiency?

	Technological	Economic
A.	Least inputs	Least cost
B.	Least cost	Least inputs
C.	Most outputs	Least cost

8. Which of the following is the *least likely* effective means of addressing the principal-agent problem?

   A. Ownership.

   B. Commands.

   C. Multi-year contracts.

9. Which of the following is not an advantage of a partnership?

   A. Perpetual life.

   B. Easy to set up.

   C. Profits only taxed once as owners' incomes.

10. A market structure in which a small number of firms compete is *best* termed:

   A. oligopoly.

   B. perfect competition.

   C. monopolistic competition.

11. Which of the following four-firm concentration ratios *most likely* would indicate an oligopolistic market structure?

   A. 25%.

   B. 55%.

   C. 75%.

12. An industry ascertained to have many firms producing differentiated products, no barriers to entry, and a low concentration ratio has a market structure *best* described as:

    A. oligopoly.

    B. perfect competition.

    C. monopolistic competition.

13. Which of the following is *least likely* to be classified as an explicit opportunity cost?

    A. Employee payroll.

    B. Economic depreciation.

    C. Salary paid to the owner.

14. An analyst gathered the following market share data for an industry comprised of six firms:

Firm	Market Share
A	30%
B	20%
C	15%
D	15%
E	10%
F	10%

The industry's four-firm concentration ratio and Herfindahl-Hirschman Index are closest to

	Four-Firm Concentration Ratio	Herfindahl-Hirschman Index
A.	50%	1750
B.	80%	1750
C.	80%	1950

SOLUTIONS FOR READING 16

1. **C is correct.** Accounting costs do not include implicit costs (opportunity costs); small proprietorships would have a higher proportion of implicit costs than would corporations, because the opportunity cost of the owner's time and capital is not included in the accounting costs.

2. **A is correct.** The company should continue to operate the machine. The opportunity cost of operating the machine is zero. The machine generates net economic profit of $50,000.

3. **A is correct.** The company should continue to operate the machine. The opportunity cost of operating the machine is zero. The machine generates net economic profit of $50,000.

4. **B is correct.** $200,000 - 100,000 - 15,000 - 30,000 - 12,000 = 43,000$. Economic depreciation is the change in market value of an asset over a period, and is the implicit cost of using the asset. Normal profit, the return that an entrepreneur can expect to receive on average, is part of a firm's opportunity cost because it is the cost of a forgone alternative. The forgone interest is the opportunity cost of using funds to purchase capital rather than an asset such as government bonds.

5. **B is correct.** Economic profit = Total revenue − Opportunity cost. The other choices are varieties of opportunity costs.

6. **B is correct.** Cost using the manual process is [(100 units of labor at $50) + (5 units of capital at $700)]/8 units = $1,062.50 per unit. Cost using the automated process is [(10 units of labor at $50) + (20 units of capital at $700)]/8 units = $1,812.50 per unit. The manual process has a lower cost per unit.

7. **A is correct.** This is a definitional question: technological efficiency is defined as that process which requires the least inputs for a given output, while economic efficiency is defined as that process which is accomplished with the least cost for a given output.

8. **B is correct.** The remaining choices are all means advocated to alleviate the principal-agent problem.

9. **A is correct.** A partnership can survive the withdrawal of a partner, but only a corporation has the opportunity of perpetual life.

10. **A is correct.** An oligopoly is defined as a market in which a small number of firms compete.

11. **C is correct.** A four-firm concentration ratio that exceeds 60% is regarded as indicative of an oligopoly.

12. **C is correct.** Monopolistic competition is a market structure in which a large number of firms compete by making similar but differentiated products. There are no barriers to entry and a low concentration ratio.

13. **B is correct.** Economic depreciation is classified as an implicit opportunity cost. The salary was paid to the owner not forgone and thus is an explicit cost.

14. **C is correct.** The four-firm concentration ratio = 30% + 20% + 15% + 15% = 80%. The Herfindahl-Hirschman Index = $30^2 + 20^2 + 15^2 + 15^2 + 10^2 + 10^2 = 1950$.

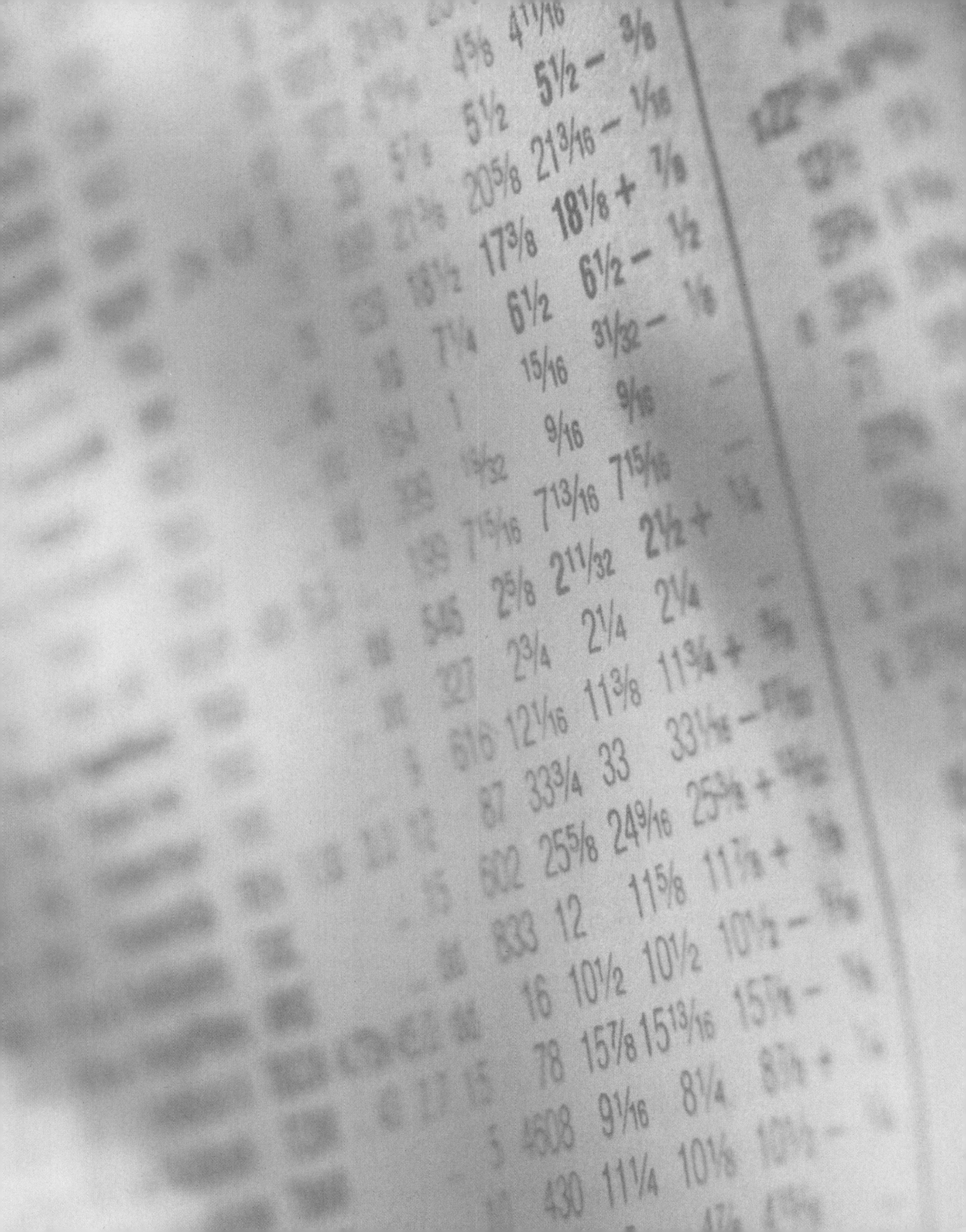

4⅝	4¹¹/₁₆		
5½	5½	−	⅜
20⅝	21³/₁₆	−	⅛
17⅜	18⅛	+	⅜
6½	6½	−	½
15/₁₆	3¹/₃₂	−	⅛
9/₁₆	9/₁₆		
7¹⁵/₁₆	7¹³/₁₆	7¹⁵/₁₆	
2⅝	2¹¹/₃₂	2½	+
2¾	2¼	2¼	
12¹/₁₆	11³/₈	11¾	+
33¾	33	33¹/₈	−
25⅝	24⁹/₁₆	25⅜	+
12	11⅝	11⅞	+
10½	10½	10½	−
15⅞	15¹³/₁₆	15⅞	−
9¹/₁₆	8¼		
11¼	10⅛		

OUTPUT AND COSTS
by Michael Parkin

LEARNING OUTCOMES

The candidate should be able to:	Mastery
a. differentiate between short-run and long-run decision time frames;	☐
b. describe and explain the relations among total product of labor, marginal product of labor, and average product of labor, and describe increasing and decreasing marginal returns;	☐
c. distinguish among total cost (including both fixed cost and variable cost), marginal cost, and average cost, and explain the relations among the various cost curves;	☐
d. explain the firm's production function, its properties of diminishing returns and diminishing marginal product of capital, the relation between short-run and long-run costs, and how economies and diseconomies of scale affect long-run costs.	☐

SURVIVAL OF THE FITTEST 1

Size does not guarantee survival in business. Even large firms disappear or get eaten up by other firms. But remaining small does not guarantee survival either. Every year, millions of small businesses close down. Call a random selection of restaurants and fashion boutiques from the 1995 yellow pages and see how many have vanished. What does a firm have to do to be a survivor?

Firms differ in lots of ways—from mom-and-pop convenience stores to multinational giants producing high-tech goods. But regardless of their size or what they produce, all firms must decide how much to produce and how to produce it. How do firms make these decisions?

Most automakers in the United States could produce more cars than they can sell. Why do automakers have expensive equipment lying around that isn't fully used? Many electric utilities in the United States don't have enough production equipment on hand to meet demand on the coldest and hottest days and must buy power from other producers. Why don't these firms install more equipment so that they can supply the market themselves?

We are going to answer these questions in this reading. To do so, we are going to study the economic decisions of a small, imaginary firm: Cindy's Sweaters, Inc., a producer of knitted sweaters. By studying the way Cindy copes with her firm's economic problems, we will be able to get a clear view of the problems that face all firms—small ones like a mom-and-pop convenience store as well as big firms such as automakers and electric utilities. We're going to begin by describing the time frames in which firms make decisions. At the end of the reading, in *Reading Between the Lines*, we'll look at the reasons why a speculated merger between Ford and GM didn't happen and would not have been a good idea.

2   DECISION TIME FRAMES

People who operate firms make many decisions. And all of the decisions are aimed at one overriding objective: maximum attainable profit. But the decisions are not all equally critical. Some of the decisions are big ones. Once made, they are costly (or impossible) to reverse. If such a decision turns out to be incorrect, it might lead to the failure of the firm. Some of the decisions are small ones. They are easily changed. If one of these decisions turns out to be incorrect, the firm can change its actions and survive.

The biggest decision that any firm makes is what industry to enter. For most entrepreneurs, their background knowledge and interests drive this decision. But the decision also depends on profit prospects—on the expectation that total revenue will exceed total cost.

The firm that we study has already chosen the industry in which to operate. It has also chosen its most effective method of organization. But it has not decided the quantity to produce, the quantities of factors of production to hire, or the price at which to sell its output.

Decisions about the quantity to produce and the price to charge depend on the type of market in which the firm operates. Perfect competition, monopolistic competition, oligopoly, and monopoly all confront the firm with their own special problems.

But decisions about *how* to produce a given output do not depend on the type of market in which the firm operates. These decisions are similar for *all* types of firms in *all* types of markets.

The actions that a firm can take to influence the relationship between output and cost depend on how soon the firm wants to act. A firm that plans to change its output rate tomorrow has fewer options than one that plans to change its output rate six months or six years from now.

To study the relationship between a firm's output decision and its costs, we distinguish between two decision time frames:

► The short run
► The long run

The Short Run

The **short run** is a time frame in which the quantity of at least one factor of production is fixed. For most firms, capital, land, and entrepreneurship are fixed factors of production and labor is the variable factor of production. We call the fixed factors of production the firm's *plant*: In the short run, a firm's plant is fixed.

For Cindy's Sweaters, the fixed plant is its factory building and its knitting machines. For an electric power utility, the fixed plant is its buildings, generators, computers, and control systems.

To increase output in the short run, a firm must increase the quantity of a variable factor of production, which is usually labor. So to produce more output, Cindy's Sweaters must hire more labor and operate its knitting machines for more hours per day. Similarly, an electric power utility must hire more labor and operate its generators for more hours per day.

Short-run decisions are easily reversed. The firm can increase or decrease its output in the short run by increasing or decreasing the amount of labor it hires.

The Long Run

The **long run** is a time frame in which the quantities of *all* factors of production can be varied. That is, the long run is a period in which the firm can change its *plant*.

To increase output in the long run, a firm is able to choose whether to change its plant as well as the quantity of labor it hires. Cindy's Sweaters can decide whether to install more knitting machines, use a new type of machine, reorganize its management, or hire more labor. Long-run decisions are *not* easily reversed. Once a plant decision is made, the firm usually must live with it for some time. To emphasize this fact, we call the past expenditure on a plant that has no resale value a **sunk cost**. A sunk cost is irrelevant to the firm's current decisions. The only costs that influence its current decisions are the short-run cost of changing its labor inputs and the long-run cost of changing its plant.

We're going to study costs in the short run and the long run. We begin with the short run and describe the technology constraint the firm faces.

SHORT-RUN TECHNOLOGY CONSTRAINT   3

To increase output in the short run, a firm must increase the quantity of labor employed. We describe the relationship between output and the quantity of labor employed by using three related concepts:

1. Total product
2. Marginal product
3. Average product

These product concepts can be illustrated either by product schedules or by product curves. Let's look first at the product schedules.

Product Schedules

Table 1 shows some data that describe Cindy's Sweaters' total product, marginal product, and average product. The numbers tell us how Cindy's Sweaters' production increases as more workers are employed. They also tell us about the productivity of Cindy's Sweaters' labor force.

TABLE 1   Total Product, Marginal Product, and Average Product

	Labor (Workers per Day)	Total Product (Sweaters per Day)	Marginal Product (Sweaters per Additional Worker)	Average Product (Sweaters per Worker)
A	0	0		
			 4	
B	1	4		4.00
			 6	
C	2	10		5.00
			 3	
D	3	13		**4.33**
			 2	
E	4	15		3.75
			 1	
F	5	16		3.20

Total product is the total amount produced. Marginal product is the change in total product that results from a one-unit increase in labor. For example, when labor increases from 2 to 3 workers a day (row C to row D), total product increases from 10 to 13 sweaters a day. The marginal product of going from 2 to 3 workers is 3 sweaters. Average product is total product divided by the quantity of labor employed. For example, the average product of 3 workers is 4.33 sweaters per worker (13 sweaters a day divided by 3 workers).

Focus first on the columns headed "Labor" and "Total product." **Total product** is the maximum output that a given quantity of labor can produce. You can see from the numbers in these columns that as Cindy's employs more labor, total product increases. For example, when Cindy's employs 1 worker, total product is 4 sweaters a day, and when Cindy's employs 2 workers, total product is 10 sweaters a day. Each increase in employment increases total product.

The **marginal product** of labor is the increase in total product that results from a one-unit increase in the quantity of labor employed with all other inputs remaining the same. For example, in Table 1, when Cindy's increases employment from 2 to 3 workers and does not change its capital, the marginal product of the third worker is 3 sweaters—total product increases from 10 to 13 sweaters.

Average product tells how productive workers are on the average. The **average product** of labor is equal to total product divided by the quantity of labor employed. For example, in Table 1, the average product of 3 workers is 4.33 sweaters per worker—13 sweaters a day divided by 3 workers.

If you look closely at the numbers in Table 1, you can see some patterns. As Cindy's hires more labor, marginal product at first increases and then begins to decrease. For example, marginal product increases from 4 sweaters a day for the first worker to 6 sweaters a day for the second worker and then decreases to 3 sweaters a day for the third worker. Also average product at first increases and then decreases. You can see the relationships between the quantity of labor hired and the three product concepts more clearly by looking at the product curves.

Product Curves

The product curves are graphs of the relationships between employment and the three product concepts you've just studied. They show how total product, marginal product, and average product change as employment changes. They also show the relationships among the three concepts. Let's look at the product curves.

Total Product Curve

Figure 1 shows Cindy's Sweaters' total product curve, *TP*. As employment increases, so does the number of sweaters knitted. Points *A* through *F* in the figure correspond to the same rows in Table 1. These points show total product as the quantity of labor changes by one day of labor. But labor is divisible into hours and even minutes. By varying the amount of labor in the smallest units possible, we can draw the total product curve shown in Fig. 1.

Notice the shape of the total product curve. As employment increases from zero to 1 worker a day, the curve becomes steeper. Then, as employment increases to 3, 4, and 5 workers a day, the curve becomes less steep.

The total product curve is similar to the *production possibilities frontier*. It separates the attainable output levels from those that are unattainable. All the points that lie above the curve are unattainable. Points that lie below the curve, in the gray area, are attainable. But they are inefficient—they use more labor than is necessary to produce a given output. Only the points *on* the total product curve are technologically efficient.

FIGURE 1   Total Product Curve

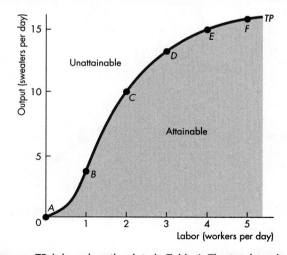

The total product curve, *TP*, is based on the data in Table 1. The total product curve shows how the quantity of sweaters changes as the quantity of labor employed changes. For example, 2 workers can produce 10 sweaters a day (point *C*). Points *A* through *F* on the curve correspond to the rows of Table 1. The total product curve separates attainable outputs from unattainable outputs. Points below the *TP* curve are inefficient.

Marginal Product Curve

Figure 2 shows Cindy's Sweaters' marginal product of labor. Part (a) reproduces the total product curve from Fig. 1. Part (b) shows the marginal product curve, *MP*.

In part (a), the gray bars illustrate the marginal product of labor. The height of each bar measures marginal product. Marginal product is also measured by the slope of the total product curve. Recall that the slope of a curve is the change

FIGURE 2   Total Product and Marginal Product

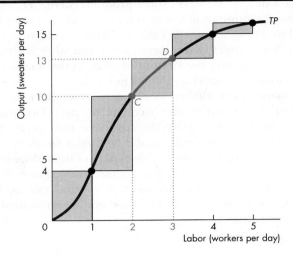

(a) Total product

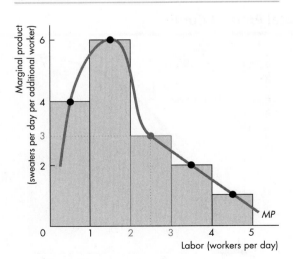

(b) Marginal product

Marginal product is illustrated by the gray bars. For example, when labor increases from 2 to 3 workers a day, marginal product is the gray bar whose height is 3 sweaters. (Marginal product is shown midway between the quantities of labor to emphasize that it is the result of *changing* the quantity of labor.) The steeper the slope of the total product curve (*TP*) in part (a), the larger is marginal product (*MP*) in part (b). Marginal product increases to a maximum (in this example when the second worker is employed) and then declines—diminishing marginal product.

in the value of the variable measured on the y-axis—output—divided by the change in the variable measured on the x-axis—labor—as we move along the curve. A one-unit increase in labor, from 2 to 3 workers, increases output from 10 to 13 sweaters, so the slope from point C to point D is 3 sweaters per worker, the same as the marginal product that we've just calculated.

Again varying the amount of labor in the smallest units possible, we can draw the marginal product curve shown in Fig. 2(b). The *height* of this curve measures the *slope* of the total product curve at a point. Part (a) shows that an increase in employment from 2 to 3 workers increases output from 10 to 13 sweaters (an increase of 3). The increase in output of 3 sweaters appears on the vertical axis of part (b) as the marginal product of going from 2 to 3 workers. We plot that marginal product at the midpoint between 2 and 3 workers. Notice that marginal product shown in Fig. 2(b) reaches a peak at 1.5 workers, and at that point, marginal product is 6 sweaters per worker. The peak occurs at 1.5 workers because the total product curve is steepest when employment increases from 1 worker to 2 workers.

The total product and marginal product curves differ across firms and types of goods. Ford Motor Company's product curves are different from those of Jim's Burger Stand, which in turn are different from those of Cindy's Sweaters. But the shapes of the product curves are similar because almost every production process has two features:

► Increasing marginal returns initially
► Diminishing marginal returns eventually

Increasing Marginal Returns

Increasing marginal returns occur when the marginal product of an additional worker exceeds the marginal product of the previous worker. Increasing marginal returns arise from increased specialization and division of labor in the production process.

For example, if Cindy's employs just one worker, that person must learn all the aspects of sweater production: running the knitting machines, fixing breakdowns, packaging and mailing sweaters, buying and checking the type and color of the wool. All these tasks must be performed by that one person.

If Cindy's hires a second person, the two workers can specialize in different parts of the production process. As a result, two workers produce more than twice as much as one. The marginal product of the second worker is greater than the marginal product of the first worker. Marginal returns are increasing.

Diminishing Marginal Returns

Most production processes experience increasing marginal returns initially. But all production processes eventually reach a point of *diminishing* marginal returns. **Diminishing marginal returns** occur when the marginal product of an additional worker is less than the marginal product of the previous worker.

Diminishing marginal returns arise from the fact that more and more workers are using the same capital and working in the same space. As more workers are added, there is less and less for the additional workers to do that is productive. For example, if Cindy's hires a third worker, output increases but not by as much as it did when it hired the second worker. In this case, after two workers are hired, all the gains from specialization and the division of labor have been exhausted. By hiring a third worker, the factory produces more sweaters, but the equipment is being operated closer to its limits. There are even times when the third worker has nothing to do because the machines are running without the need for further attention. Hiring more and more workers continues to increase output but by successively smaller amounts. Marginal returns are diminishing. This phenomenon is such a pervasive one that it is called a "law"—the law of diminishing returns. The **law of diminishing returns** states that

> As a firm uses more of a variable factor of production, with a given quantity of the fixed factor of production, the marginal product of the variable factor eventually diminishes.

You are going to return to the law of diminishing returns when we study a firm's costs. But before we do that, let's look at the average product of labor and the average product curve.

Average Product Curve

Figure 3 illustrates Cindy's Sweaters' average product of labor and shows the relationship between average product and marginal product. Points *B* through *F* on the average product curve *AP* correspond to those same rows in Table 1. Average product increases from 1 to 2 workers (its maximum value at point *C*) but then decreases as yet more workers are employed. Notice also that average product is largest when average product and marginal product are equal. That is, the marginal product curve cuts the average product curve at the point of maximum average product. For the number of workers at which marginal product exceeds average product, average product is increasing. For the number of workers at which marginal product is less than average product, average product is decreasing.

The relationship between the average and marginal product curves is a general feature of the relationship between the average and marginal values of any variable. Let's look at a familiar example.

FIGURE 3   Average Product

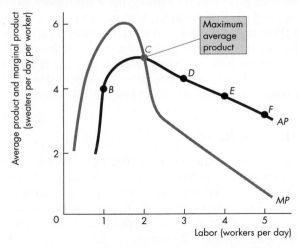

The figure shows the average product of labor and the connection between the average product and marginal product. With 1 worker per day, marginal product exceeds average product, so average product is increasing. With 2 workers per day, marginal product equals average product, so average product is at its maximum. With more than 2 workers per day, marginal product is less than average product, so average product is decreasing.

Marginal Grade and Grade Point Average

To see the relationship between average product and marginal product, think about the similar relationship between Cindy's marginal grade and average grade over five semesters. (Suppose Cindy is a part-time student who takes just one course each semester.) In the first semester, Cindy takes calculus and her grade is a C (2.0). This grade is her marginal grade. It is also her average grade— her GPA. In the next semester, Cindy takes French and gets a B (3.0). French is Cindy's marginal course, and her marginal grade is 3.0. Her GPA rises to 2.5. Because her marginal grade exceeds her average grade, it pulls her average up. In the third semester, Cindy takes economics and gets an A (4.0)—her new marginal grade. Because her marginal grade exceeds her GPA, it again pulls her average up. Cindy's GPA is now 3.0, the average of 2.0, 3.0, and 4.0. The fourth semester, she takes history and gets a B (3.0). Because her marginal grade is equal to her average, her GPA does not change. In the fifth semester, Cindy takes English and gets a D (1.0). Because her marginal grade, a 1.0, is below her GPA of 3.0, her GPA falls.

Cindy's GPA increases when her marginal grade exceeds her GPA. Her GPA falls when her marginal grade is below her GPA. And her GPA is constant when her marginal grade equals her GPA. The relationship between Cindy's marginal and average grades is exactly the same as that between marginal product and average product.

Cindy's cares about its product curves because they influence its costs. Let's look at Cindy's costs.

SHORT-RUN COST 4

To produce more output in the short run, a firm must employ more labor, which means that it must increase its costs. We describe the relationship between output and cost by using three cost concepts:

► Total cost
► Marginal cost
► Average cost

Total Cost

A firm's **total cost** (*TC*) is the cost of *all* the factors of production it uses. We separate total cost into total *fixed* cost and total *variable* cost.

Total fixed cost (*TFC*) is the cost of the firm's fixed factors. For Cindy's Sweaters, total fixed cost includes the cost of renting knitting machines and *normal profit*, which is the opportunity cost of Cindy's entrepreneurship (see the reading on organizing production). The quantities of fixed factors don't change as output changes, so total fixed cost is the same at all outputs.

Total variable cost (*TVC*) is the cost of the firm's variable factors. For Cindy's, labor is the variable factor, so this component of cost is its wage bill. Total variable cost changes as total product changes.

Total cost is the sum of total fixed cost and total variable cost. That is,

$$TC = TFC + TVC.$$

FIGURE 4   Total Cost Curves

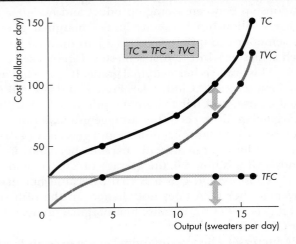

	Labor (Workers per Day)	Output (Sweaters per Day)	Total Fixed Cost (*TFC*)	Total Variable Cost (*TVC*)	Total Cost (*TC*)
			(Dollars per Day)		
A	0	0	25	0	25
B	1	4	25	25	50
C	2	10	25	50	75
D	3	13	25	75	100
E	4	15	25	100	125
F	5	16	25	125	150

Cindy's rents a knitting machine for $25 a day. This amount is Cindy's total fixed cost. Cindy's hires workers at a wage rate of $25 a day, and this cost is Cindy's total variable cost. For example, if Cindy's employs 3 workers, total variable cost is 3 × $25, which equals $75. Total cost is the sum of total fixed cost and total variable cost. For example, when Cindy's employs 3 workers, total cost is $100—total fixed cost of $25 plus total variable cost of $75. The graph shows Cindy's Sweaters' total cost curves. Total fixed cost (*TFC*) is constant—it graphs as a horizontal line—and total variable cost (*TVC*) increases as output increases. Total cost (*TC*) increases as output increases. The vertical distance between the total cost curve and the total variable cost curve is total fixed cost, as illustrated by the two arrows.

The table in Fig. 4 shows Cindy's total costs. With one knitting machine that Cindy's rents for $25 a day, *TFC* is $25. To produce sweaters, Cindy's hires labor, which costs $25 a day. *TVC* is the number of workers multiplied by $25. For example, to produce 13 sweaters a day, Cindy's hires 3 workers and *TVC* is $75. *TC* is the sum of *TFC* and *TVC*, so to produce 13 sweaters a day, Cindy's total cost, *TC*, is $100. Check the calculation in each row of the table.

Figure 4 shows Cindy's total cost curves, which graph total cost against output. The light blue total fixed cost curve (*TFC*) is horizontal because total fixed cost is a constant at $25. It does not change when output changes. The gray total variable cost curve (*TVC*) and the dark blue total cost curve (*TC*) both slope upward because total variable cost increases as output increases. The arrows highlight total fixed cost as the vertical distance between the *TVC* and *TC* curves.

Let's now look at Cindy's marginal cost.

Marginal Cost

In Fig. 4, total variable cost and total cost increase at a decreasing rate at small levels of output and then begin to increase at an increasing rate as output increases. To understand this pattern in the change in total cost as output increases, we need to use the concept of *marginal cost*.

A firm's **marginal cost** is the increase in total cost that results from a one-unit increase in output. We calculate marginal cost as the increase in total cost divided by the increase in output. The table in Fig. 5 shows this calculation. When, for example, output increases from 10 sweaters to 13 sweaters, total cost increases from $75 to $100. The change in output is 3 sweaters, and the change in total cost is $25. The marginal cost of one of those 3 sweaters is ($25 ÷ 3), which equals $8.33.

Figure 5 graphs the marginal cost data in the table as the light gray marginal cost curve, *MC*. This curve is U-shaped because when Cindy's Sweaters hires a second worker, marginal cost decreases, but when it hires a third, a fourth, and a fifth worker, marginal cost successively increases.

Marginal cost decreases at low outputs because of economies from greater specialization. It eventually increases because of the *law of diminishing returns.* The law of diminishing returns means that each additional worker produces a successively smaller addition to output. So to get an additional unit of output, ever more workers are required. Because more workers are required to produce one additional unit of output, the cost of the additional unit of output—marginal cost—must eventually increase.

Marginal cost tells us how total cost changes as output changes. The final cost concept tells us what it costs, on the average, to produce a unit of output. Let's now look at Cindy's Sweaters' average costs.

Average Cost

There are three average costs:

1. Average fixed cost

2. Average variable cost

3. Average total cost

Average fixed cost (*AFC*) is total fixed cost per unit of output. **Average variable cost** (*AVC*) is total variable cost per unit of output. **Average total cost** (*ATC*) is total cost per unit of output. The average cost concepts are calculated from the total cost concepts as follows:

$$TC = TFC + TVC.$$

Divide each total cost term by the quantity produced, Q, to get

$$\frac{TC}{Q} = \frac{TFC}{Q} + \frac{TVC}{Q},$$

or

$$ATC = AFC + AVC.$$

The table in Fig. 5 shows the calculation of average total cost. For example, in row C output is 10 sweaters. Average fixed cost is ($25 ÷ 10), which equals

FIGURE 5   Marginal Cost and Average Costs

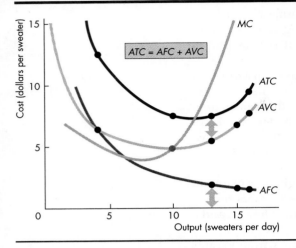

ATC = AFC + AVC

Marginal cost is calculated as the change in total cost divided by the change in output. When output increases from 4 to 10 sweaters, an increase of 6 sweaters, total cost increases by $25 and marginal cost is $25 ÷ 6, which equals $4.17. Each average cost concept is calculated by dividing the related total cost by output. When 10 sweaters are produced, AFC is $2.50 ($25 ÷ 10), AVC is $5 ($50 ÷ 10), and ATC is $7.50 ($75 ÷ 10).

The graph shows that the marginal cost curve (MC) is U-shaped and intersects the average variable cost curve and the average total cost curve at their minimum points. Average fixed cost (AFC) decreases as output increases. The average total cost curve (ATC) and average variable cost curve (AVC) are U-shaped. The vertical distance between these two curves is equal to average fixed cost, as illustrated by the two arrows.

	Labor (Workers per Day)	Output (Sweaters per Day)	Total Fixed Cost (TFC)	Total Variable Cost (TVC)	Total Cost (TC)	Marginal Cost (MC) (Dollars per Additional Sweater)	Average Fixed Cost (AFC)	Average Variable Cost (AVC)	Average Total Cost (ATC)
			(Dollars per Day)				(Dollars per Sweater)		
A	0	0	25	0	25		—	—	—
						...... 6.25			
B	1	4	25	25	50		6.25	6.25	12.50
						...... 4.17			
C	2	10	25	50	75		2.50	5.00	7.50
						...... 8.33			
D	3	13	25	75	100		1.92	5.77	7.69
						...... 12.50			
E	4	15	25	100	125		1.67	6.67	8.33
						...... 25.00			
F	5	16	25	125	150		1.56	7.81	9.38

$2.50, average variable cost is ($50 ÷ 10), which equals $5.00, and average total cost is ($75 ÷ 10), which equals $7.50. Note that average total cost is equal to average fixed cost ($2.50) plus average variable cost ($5.00).

Figure 5 shows the average cost curves. The dark gray average fixed cost curve (AFC) slopes downward. As output increases, the same constant total fixed cost is spread over a larger output. The dark blue average total cost curve (ATC) and the light blue average variable cost curve (AVC) are U-shaped. The vertical distance between the average total cost and average variable cost curves is equal to average fixed cost—as indicated by the two arrows. That distance shrinks as output increases because average fixed cost declines with increasing output.

The marginal cost curve (MC) intersects the average variable cost curve and the average total cost curve at their minimum points. That is, when marginal cost is less than average cost, average cost is decreasing, and when marginal cost exceeds average cost, average cost is increasing. This relationship holds for both the *ATC* curve and the *AVC* curve and is another example of the relationship you saw in Fig. 3 for average product and marginal product and in Cindy's course grades.

Why the Average Total Cost Curve Is U-Shaped

Average total cost, *ATC*, is the sum of average fixed cost, *AFC*, and average variable cost, *AVC*. So the shape of the *ATC* curve combines the shapes of the *AFC* and *AVC* curves. The U shape of the average total cost curve arises from the influence of two opposing forces:

1. Spreading total fixed cost over a larger output
2. Eventually diminishing returns

When output increases, the firm spreads its total fixed cost over a larger output and so its average fixed cost decreases—its average fixed cost curve slopes downward.

Diminishing returns means that as output increases, ever-larger amounts of labor are needed to produce an additional unit of output. So average variable cost eventually increases, and the *AVC* curve eventually slopes upward.

The shape of the average total cost curve combines these two effects. Initially, as output increases, both average fixed cost and average variable cost decrease, so average total cost decreases and the *ATC* curve slopes downward. But as output increases further and diminishing returns set in, average variable cost begins to increase. Eventually, average variable cost increases more quickly than average fixed cost decreases, so average total cost increases and the *ATC* curve slopes upward.

Cost Curves and Product Curves

The technology that a firm uses determines its costs. Figure 6 shows the links between the firm's technology constraint (its product curves) and its cost curves. The upper part of the figure shows the average product curve and the marginal product curve—like those in Fig. 3. The lower part of the figure shows the average variable cost curve and the marginal cost curve—like those in Fig. 5.

The figure highlights the links between technology and costs. As labor increases initially, marginal product and average product rise and marginal cost and average variable cost fall. Then, at the point of maximum marginal product, marginal cost is a minimum. As labor increases further, marginal product diminishes and marginal cost increases. But average product continues to rise, and average variable cost continues to fall. Then, at the point of maximum average product, average variable cost is a minimum. As labor increases further, average product diminishes and average variable cost increases.

Shifts in the Cost Curves

The position of a firm's short-run cost curves depends on two factors:

▶ Technology
▶ Prices of factors of production

FIGURE 6   Product Curves and Cost Curves

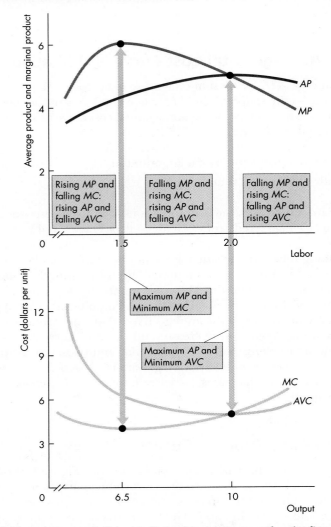

A firm's marginal product curve is linked to its marginal cost curve. If as the firm hires more labor its marginal product rises, its marginal cost falls. If marginal product is a maximum, marginal cost is a minimum. If as the firm hires more labor its marginal product diminishes, its marginal cost rises.

A firm's average product curve is linked to its average variable cost curve. If as the firm hires more labor its average product rises, its average variable cost falls. If average product is a maximum, average variable cost is a minimum. If as the firm hires more labor its average product diminishes, its average variable cost rises.

Technology

A technological change that increases productivity shifts the total product curve upward. It also shifts the marginal product curve and the average product curve upward. With a better technology, the same factors of production can produce more output, so technological change lowers costs and shifts the cost curves downward.

For example, advances in robot production techniques have increased productivity in the automobile industry. As a result, the product curves of Chrysler,

Ford, and GM have shifted upward, and their cost curves have shifted downward. But the relationships between their product curves and cost curves have not changed. The curves are still linked in the way shown in Fig. 6.

Often, a technological advance results in a firm using more capital, a fixed factor, and less labor, a variable factor. For example, today the telephone companies use computers to provide directory assistance in place of the human operators they used in the 1980s. When such a technological change occurs, total cost decreases, but fixed costs increase and variable costs decrease. This change in the mix of fixed cost and variable cost means that at low output levels, average total cost might increase, while at high output levels, average total cost decreases.

Prices of Factors of Production

An increase in the price of a factor of production increases costs and shifts the cost curves. But how the curves shift depends on which factor price changes. An increase in rent or some other component of *fixed* cost shifts the fixed cost curves (*TFC* and *AFC*) upward and shifts the total cost curve (*TC*) upward but leaves the variable cost curves (*AVC* and *TVC*) and the marginal cost curve (*MC*) unchanged. An increase in wages or another component of *variable* cost shifts the variable cost curves (*TVC* and *AVC*) upward and shifts the marginal cost curve (*MC*) upward but leaves the fixed cost curves (*AFC* and *TFC*) unchanged. So, for example, if truck drivers' wages increase, the variable cost and marginal cost of transportation services increase. If the interest expense paid by a trucking company increases, the fixed cost of transportation services increases.

You've now completed your study of short-run costs. All the concepts that you've met are summarized in a compact glossary in Table 2.

TABLE 2   A Compact Glossary of Costs

Term	Symbol	Definition	Equation
Fixed cost		Cost that is independent of the output level; cost of a fixed input	
Variable cost		Cost that varies with the output level; cost of a variable input	
Total fixed cost	*TFC*	Cost of the fixed inputs	
Total variable cost	*TVC*	Cost of the variable inputs	
Total cost	*TC*	Cost of all inputs	$TC = TFC + TVC$
Output (total product)	*TP*	Total quantity produced (output Q)	
Marginal cost	*MC*	Change in total cost resulting from a one-unit increase in total product	$MC = \Delta TC \div \Delta Q$
Average fixed cost	*AFC*	Total fixed cost per unit of output	$AFC = TFC \div Q$
Average variable cost	*AVC*	Total variable cost per unit of output	$AVC = TVC \div Q$
Average total cost	*ATC*	Total cost per unit of output	$ATC = AFC + AVC$

5

LONG-RUN COST

In the short run, a firm can vary the quantity of labor but the quantity of capital is fixed. So the firm has variable costs of labor and fixed costs of capital. In the long run, a firm can vary both the quantity of labor and the quantity of capital. So in the long run, all the firm's costs are variable. We are now going to study the firm's costs in the long run, when *all* costs are variable costs and when the quantities of labor and capital vary.

The behavior of long-run cost depends on the firm's *production function*, which is the relationship between the maximum output attainable and the quantities of both labor and capital.

The Production Function

Table 3 shows Cindy's Sweaters' production function. The table lists total product schedules for four different quantities of capital. We identify the quantity of capital by the plant size. The numbers for Plant 1 are for a factory with 1 knitting machine—the case we've just studied. The other three plants have 2, 3, and 4 machines. If Cindy's Sweaters doubles its capital from 1 to 2 knitting machines, the various amounts of labor can produce the outputs shown in the second column of the table. The other two columns show the outputs of yet larger quantities of capital. Each column of the table could be graphed as a total product curve for each plant.

Diminishing Returns

Diminishing returns occur at all four quantities of capital as the quantity of labor increases. You can check that fact by calculating the marginal product of labor in plants with 2, 3, and 4 machines. At each plant size, as the quantity of labor increases, the marginal product of labor (eventually) diminishes.

TABLE 3   The Production Function

Labor (Workers per Day)	Output (Sweaters per Day)			
	Plant 1	Plant 2	Plant 3	Plant 4
1	4	10	13	15
2	10	15	18	20
3	13	18	22	24
4	15	20	24	26
5	16	21	25	27
Knitting machines (number)	1	2	3	4

The table shows the total product data for four quantities of capital. The greater the plant size, the larger is the total product for any given quantity of labor. But for a given plant size, the marginal product of labor diminishes. And for a given quantity of labor, the marginal product of capital diminishes.

Diminishing Marginal Product of Capital

Diminishing returns also occur as the quantity of capital increases. You can check that fact by calculating the marginal product of capital at a given quantity of labor. The *marginal product of capital* is the change in total product divided by the change in capital when the quantity of labor is constant—equivalently, the change in output resulting from a one-unit increase in the quantity of capital. For example, if Cindy's has 3 workers and increases its capital from 1 machine to 2 machines, output increases from 13 to 18 sweaters a day. The marginal product of capital is 5 sweaters per day. If Cindy increases the number of machines from 2 to 3, output increases from 18 to 22 sweaters per day. The marginal product of the third machine is 4 sweaters per day, down from 5 sweaters per day for the second machine.

Let's now see what the production function implies for long-run costs.

Short-Run Cost and Long-Run Cost

Continue to assume that Cindy can hire workers for $25 per day and rent knitting machines for $25 per machine per day. Using these factor prices and the data in Table 3, we can calculate and graph the average total cost curves for factories with 1, 2, 3, and 4 knitting machines. We've already studied the costs of a factory with 1 machine in Figs. 4 and 5. In Fig. 7, the average total cost curve for that case is ATC_1. Figure 7 also shows the average total cost curve for a factory with 2 machines, ATC_2, with 3 machines, ATC_3, and with 4 machines, ATC_4.

You can see, in Fig. 7, that plant size has a big effect on the firm's average total cost. Two things stand out:

1. Each short-run ATC curve is U-shaped.
2. For each short-run ATC curve, the larger the plant, the greater is the output at which average total cost is a minimum.

FIGURE 7   Short-Run Costs of Four Different Plants

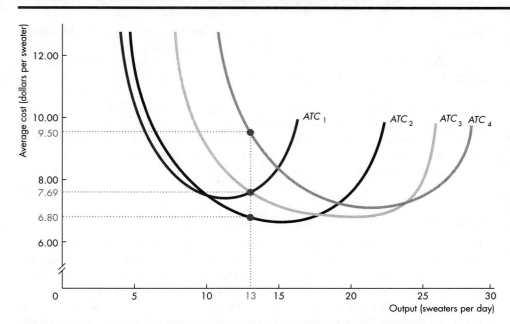

The figure shows short-run average total cost curves for four different quantities of capital. Cindy's can produce 13 sweaters a day with 1 knitting machine on ATC_1 or with 3 knitting machines on ATC_3 for an average cost of $7.69 per sweater. Cindy's can produce the same number of sweaters by using 2 machines on ATC_2 for $6.80 per sweater or by using 4 machines on ATC_4 for $9.50 per sweater. If Cindy's produces 13 sweaters a day, the least-cost method of production—the long-run method—is with 2 machines on ATC_2.

Each short-run average total cost curve is U-shaped because, as the quantity of labor increases, its marginal product at first increases and then diminishes. And this pattern in the marginal product of labor, which we examined in some detail earlier for the plant with 1 knitting machine, occurs at all plant sizes.

The minimum average total cost for a larger plant occurs at a greater output than it does for a smaller plant because the larger plant has a higher total fixed cost and therefore, for any given output, a higher average fixed cost.

Which short-run average cost curve Cindy's operates on depends on its plant size. But in the long run, Cindy's chooses its plant size. And which plant size it chooses depends on the output it plans to produce. The reason is that the average total cost of producing a given output depends on the plant size.

To see why, suppose that Cindy plans to produce 13 sweaters a day. With 1 machine, the average total cost curve is ATC_1 (in Fig. 7) and the average total cost of 13 sweaters a day is $7.69 per sweater. With 2 machines, on ATC_2, average total cost is $6.80 per sweater. With 3 machines, on ATC_3, average total cost is $7.69 per sweater, the same as with 1 machine. Finally, with 4 machines, on ATC_4, average total cost is $9.50 per sweater.

The economically efficient plant size for producing a given output is the one that has the lowest average total cost. For Cindy's, the economically efficient plant to use to produce 13 sweaters a day is the one with 2 machines.

In the long run, Cindy's chooses the plant size that minimizes average total cost. When a firm is producing a given output at the least possible cost, it is operating on its *long-run average cost curve.*

The **long-run average cost curve** is the relationship between the lowest attainable average total cost and output when both the plant size and labor are varied.

The long-run average cost curve is a planning curve. It tells the firm the plant size and the quantity of labor to use at each output to minimize cost. Once the plant size is chosen, the firm operates on the short-run cost curves that apply to that plant size.

The Long-Run Average Cost Curve

Figure 8 shows Cindy's Sweaters' long-run average cost curve, *LRAC*. This long-run average cost curve is derived from the short-run average total cost curves in Fig. 7. For output rates up to 10 sweaters a day, average total cost is the lowest on ATC_1. For output rates between 10 and 18 sweaters a day, average total cost is the lowest on ATC_2. For output rates between 18 and 24 sweaters a day, average total cost is the lowest on ATC_3. And for output rates in excess of 24 sweaters a day, average total cost is the lowest on ATC_4. The segment of each average total cost curve with the lowest average total cost is highlighted in dark blue in Fig. 8. This dark blue scallop-shaped curve made up of the four segments of average total cost curves is the *LRAC* curve.

Economies and Diseconomies of Scale

Economies of scale are features of a firm's technology that lead to falling long-run average cost as output increases. When economies of scale are present, the *LRAC* curve slopes downward. The *LRAC* curve in Fig. 8 shows that Cindy's Sweaters experiences economies of scale for outputs up to 15 sweaters a day.

With given factor prices, economies of scale occur if the percentage increase in output exceeds the percentage increase in all factors of production. For exam-

FIGURE 8   Long-Run Average Cost Curve

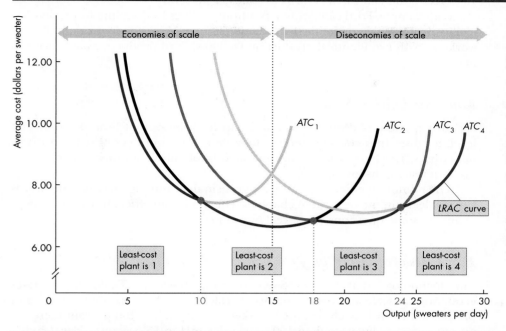

In the long run, Cindy's Sweaters can vary both its capital and labor. The long-run average cost curve traces the lowest attainable average total cost of production. Cindy's Sweaters produces on its long-run average cost curve if it uses 1 machine to produce up to 10 sweaters a day, 2 machines to produce between 10 and 18 sweaters a day, 3 machines to produce between 18 and 24 sweaters a day, and 4 machines to produce more than 24 sweaters a day. Within these ranges, Cindy's Sweaters varies its output by varying its labor.

ple, if output increases by more than 10 percent when a firm increases its labor and capital by 10 percent, its average total cost falls. Economies of scale are present.

The main source of economies of scale is greater specialization of both labor and capital. For example, if GM produces 100 cars a week, each worker must perform many different tasks and the capital must be general-purpose machines and tools. But if GM produces 10,000 cars a week, each worker specializes and becomes highly proficient in a small number of tasks.

Diseconomies of scale are features of a firm's technology that lead to rising long-run average cost as output increases. When diseconomies of scale are present, the *LRAC* curve slopes upward. In Fig. 8, Cindy's Sweaters experiences diseconomies of scale at outputs greater than 15 sweaters a day.

With given factor prices, diseconomies of scale occur if the percentage increase in output is less than the percentage increase in all factors of production. For example, if output increases by less than 10 percent when a firm increases its labor and capital by 10 percent, its average total cost rises. Diseconomies of scale are present.

The main source of diseconomies of scale is the difficulty of managing a very large enterprise. The larger the firm, the greater is the challenge of organizing it and the greater is the cost of communicating both up and down the management hierarchy and among managers. Eventually, management complexity brings rising average cost.

Diseconomies of scale occur in all production processes but perhaps only at a very large output rate.

Constant returns to scale are features of a firm's technology that lead to constant long-run average cost as output increases. When constant returns to scale are present, the *LRAC* curve is horizontal.

Constant returns to scale occur if the percentage increase in output equals the percentage increase in all factors of production. For example, if output increases by exactly 10 percent when a firm increases its labor and capital by 10 percent, then constant returns to scale are present.

For example, Ford can double its output of ZX2s by doubling its production facility. It can build an identical production line and hire an identical number of workers. With two identical production facilities, Ford produces exactly twice as many cars.

Minimum Efficient Scale

A firm experiences economies of scale up to some output level. Beyond that level, it moves into constant returns to scale or diseconomies of scale. A firm's **minimum efficient scale** is the smallest quantity of output at which long-run average cost reaches its lowest level.

The minimum efficient scale plays a role in determining market structure, as you will learn in the next three chapters. The minimum efficient scale also helps to answer some questions about real businesses.

Economies of Scale at Cindy's Sweaters

The technology that Cindy's Sweaters uses, shown in Table 3, illustrates economies of scale and diseconomies of scale. If Cindy's increases its factors of production from 1 machine and 1 worker to 2 of each, a 100 percent increase, output increases by more than 100 percent from 4 to 15 sweaters a day. Cindy's experiences economies of scale, and its long-run average cost decreases. But if Cindy's increases its factor of production to 3 machines and 3 workers, a 50 percent increase, output increases by less than 50 percent, from 15 to 22 sweaters a day. Now Cindy's experiences diseconomies of scale, and its long-run average cost increases. Its minimum efficient scale is at 15 sweaters a day.

Producing Cars and Generating Electric Power

Why do automakers have expensive equipment lying around that isn't fully used? You can now answer this question. An automaker uses the plant that minimizes the average total cost of producing the output that it can sell. But it operates below the minimum efficient scale. Its short-run average total cost curve looks like ATC_1. If it could sell more cars, it would produce more cars and its average total cost would fall.

Why do many electric utilities have too little production equipment to meet demand on the coldest and hottest days and so have to buy power from other producers? You can now see why this happens and why an electric utility doesn't build more generating capacity. A power producer uses the plant size that minimizes the average total cost of producing the output that it can sell on a normal day. But it produces above the minimum efficient scale and experiences diseconomies of scale. Its short-run average total cost curve looks like ATC_3. With a larger plant size, its average total costs of producing its normal output would be higher.

Reading Between the Lines applies what you've learned about a firm's short-run and long-run cost curves. It looks at the cost curves of Ford and GM and explains why a merger of these two firms wouldn't be a smart move.

READING BETWEEN THE LINES   6

Mergers and Costs

THE NEW YORK TIMES, SEPTEMBER 19, 2006

G.M. Talked with Ford About Merger, Report Says

As Detroit waits to learn whether General Motors will pursue a tricontinental alliance with Nissan and Renault, word has emerged that the company briefly pondered a linkup with an archrival in its own backyard.

Executives at G.M. and Ford Motor, according to a report on Monday in Automotive News, a trade journal, held discussions about a partnership or merger this year. But industry analysts quickly dismissed the notion of the two struggling automakers possibly joining forces.

"While no longer quite as unthinkable as it once was," Efraim Levy, a Standard & Poor's automotive analyst, wrote in a note to clients, "we consider it highly doubtful that a merger would take place and do not see the benefits for either company as they attempt to restructure." . . .

News that the two automakers would even consider a broad partnership comes as Detroit is reeling from both companies' plans to cut thousands of jobs and close dozens of plants as part of their turnaround efforts. Profits have been elusive for Detroit's automakers, most recently because high gasoline prices have cut into sales of their lucrative sport utility vehicles and pickup trucks. . . .

Essence of the Story

► It has been reported that General Motors, Nissan, and Renault might consider trying to form an alliance.

► Another report says that General Motors and Ford Motor Company might seek a merger.

► An auto analyst, Efraim Levy, says that it is hard to see any benefits for either company from a merger.

► Both companies plan to cut thousands of jobs and close dozens of plants.

Economic Analysis

► The big three U.S. automakers are having a hard time competing with Japanese and European automakers.

► It has been speculated that two of the big three, Ford and GM, might attempt a merger.

► Mergers occur when two firms can eliminate duplicate production facilities while maintaining or increasing total product.

► The big U.S. automakers are unusual in that most of their costs are fixed.

▶ Even much of the cost of labor is fixed because unions have negotiated retirement and redundancy packages that pay workers after they leave the firms.

▶ Both companies are trying to lower their costs by closing plants and laying off thousands of workers.

▶ A merger between these two firms is unlikely to achieve any cost saving for either firm beyond what they can accomplish separately. The figures illustrate why.

▶ Figure 9 shows how an automaker might lower its average variable cost by increasing total product.

▶ In this example, if the firm produces 8 million vehicles a year (a rough average of what Ford and GM produce), the average total cost is $25,000 per vehicle (again, a rough average of Ford's and GM's average total cost).

▶ If the firm could increase production, average total cost would fall along the ATC curve.

▶ Figure 10 illustrates the likely effects of a merger.

▶ Separately, each firm has an average total cost curve ATC_0.

▶ If the firms merged, there would be no major cost saving. So the new firm would have fixed costs roughly equal to double those of one of the firms.

▶ The average total cost curve of the new bigger firm would be ATC_1.

▶ Total product of the new firm would be (roughly) double that of each firm before the merger, and the average total cost would be unchanged.

FIGURE 9   An Automaker Like GM or Ford

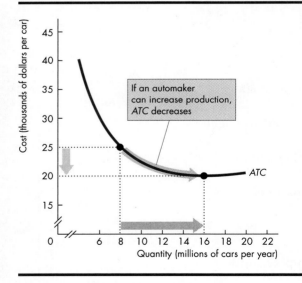

FIGURE 10   An Automaker Like a Merged GM and Ford

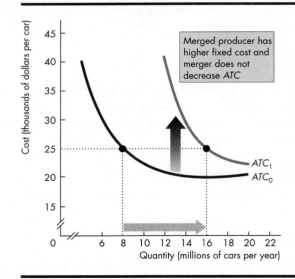

SUMMARY

▶ In the short run, the quantity of at least one factor of production is fixed and the quantities of the other factors of production can be varied.

▶ In the long run, the quantities of all factors of production can be varied.

▶ A total product curve shows the quantity a firm can produce with a given quantity of capital and different quantities of labor.

▶ Initially, the marginal product of labor increases as the quantity of labor increases, but eventually, marginal product diminishes—the law of diminishing returns.

▶ Average product increases initially and eventually diminishes.

▶ As output increases, total fixed cost is constant, and total variable cost and total cost increase.

▶ As output increases, average fixed cost decreases and average variable cost, average total cost, and marginal cost decrease at low outputs and increase at high outputs. These cost curves are U-shaped.

▶ There is a set of short-run cost curves for each different plant size. There is one least-cost plant size for each output. The larger the output, the larger is the plant size that will minimize average total cost.

▶ The long-run average cost curve traces out the lowest attainable average total cost at each output when both capital and labor inputs can be varied.

▶ With economies of scale, the long-run average cost curve slopes downward. With diseconomies of scale, the long-run average cost curve slopes upward.

PRACTICE PROBLEMS FOR READING 17

1. Which of the following is generally not considered a long-run resource?
   A. Labor.
   B. Buildings.
   C. Technology.

2. Using the following information, determine which of the answers most accurately describes the marginal and average production at Bronze Star Manufacturing when labor increases from 7 to 8 workers per day.

Labor (Workers/Day)	Total Production (Bronze Stars/Day)
5	100
6	120
7	135
8	148

	Marginal Production	Average Production
A.	13 stars	18.5 stars
B.	13 stars	21.1 stars
C.	48 stars	18.5 stars

3. If adding one additional unit of labor results in a positive but declining marginal product of labor, then total product *most likely* is:
   A. constant.
   B. decreasing.
   C. increasing at a decreasing rate.

4. If marginal cost per unit is greater than average total cost per unit, increasing output will *most likely* cause:
   A. marginal cost to decrease.
   B. average fixed cost to increase.
   C. average variable cost to increase.

5. In the long run, if increasing output causes total production costs to increase at a decreasing rate, then the firm *most likely* is experiencing:
   A. lower fixed costs.
   B. economies of scale.
   C. constant returns to scale.

6. Increasing marginal returns *most likely* occur when:
   A. specialization and division of labor increase.
   B. more and more workers use the same capital.
   C. addition of workers increases output by successively smaller amounts.

SOLUTIONS FOR READING 17

1. A is correct. Labor is considered a flexible resource in the short term, while technology, buildings, and equipment are considered fixed in the short term, and therefore are long-run resources.

2. A is correct. Marginal product is the increase in total product from one additional unit of labor. For Bronze Star, total product increases by 13 units, from 135 to 148. Average product equals total product divided by the quantity of labor employed, which in this case is $148/8 = 18.5$.

3. C is correct. As long as marginal product is positive, total product is increasing. If the marginal product declines as additional units of labor are added, then the rate of increase in total product is declining, i.e., increasing at a decreasing rate.

4. C is correct. If marginal cost is greater than average total cost, then increasing output will cause marginal, average variable, and average total costs to increase. Average fixed cost will continue to decrease as output increases.

5. B is correct. If total production costs are increasing at a decreasing rate as output increases, then average total costs are decreasing and the firm is experiencing economies of scale.

6. A is correct. As specialization and division of labor increase, a firm will enjoy increasing marginal returns. A firm will likely face decreasing marginal returns when the labor force increases (without any further specialization) using the same capital and work space (plant and machinery).

4⅝ 4¹¹⁄₁₆ — 3⅝
5½ 5½ — 3⅛
5½ 21³⁄₁₆ — ¹⁄₁₆
20⅝
17⅜ 18⅛ + ⅞
15½ 6½ 6½ — ½
7¼ 6½ 3¹⁄₃₂ — ⅛
15⁄₁₆
9⁄₁₆ 9⁄₁₆
¹³⁄₃₂ 7¹³⁄₁₆ 7¹⁵⁄₁₆
7¹⁵⁄₁₆ 2½ +
2⅝ 2¹¹⁄₃₂ 2¼
27 2¾ 2¼
6⅛ 12¹⁄₁₆ 11⅜ 11¾ +
87 33¾ 33 33⅛ —
6½ 25⅝ 24⁹⁄₁₆ 25⅜ +
833 12 11⅝ 11⅞ +
16 10½ 10½ 10⅛ —
78 15⅞ 15¹³⁄₁₆ 15⅞ —
4508 9¹⁄₁₆ 8¼ 8⅜ +
430 11¼ 10⅛

STUDY SESSION 5
ECONOMICS:
Market Structure and Macroeconomic Analysis

This study session first compares and contrasts the different market structures in which firms operate. The market environment influences the price a firm can demand for its goods or services. The most important of these market forms are monopoly and perfect competition, although monopolistic competition and oligopoly are also covered.

The study session then introduces the macroeconomic concepts that have an effect on all firms in the same environment, be it a country, a group of related countries, or a particular industry. The study session concludes by describing how an economy's aggregate supply and aggregate demand are determined and the macroeconomic schools of thought that explain short-term fluctuations.

READING ASSIGNMENTS

Reading 18   Perfect Competition
              Economics, Eighth Edition, by Michael Parkin

Reading 19   Monopoly
              Economics, Eighth Edition, by Michael Parkin

Reading 20   Monopolistic Competition and Oligopoly
              Economics, Eighth Edition, by Michael Parkin

Reading 21   Markets for Factors of Production
              Economics, Eighth Edition, by Michael Parkin

Reading 22   Monitoring Jobs and the Price Level
              Economics, Eighth Edition, by Michael Parkin

Reading 23   Aggregate Supply and Aggregate Demand
              Economics, Eighth Edition, by Michael Parkin

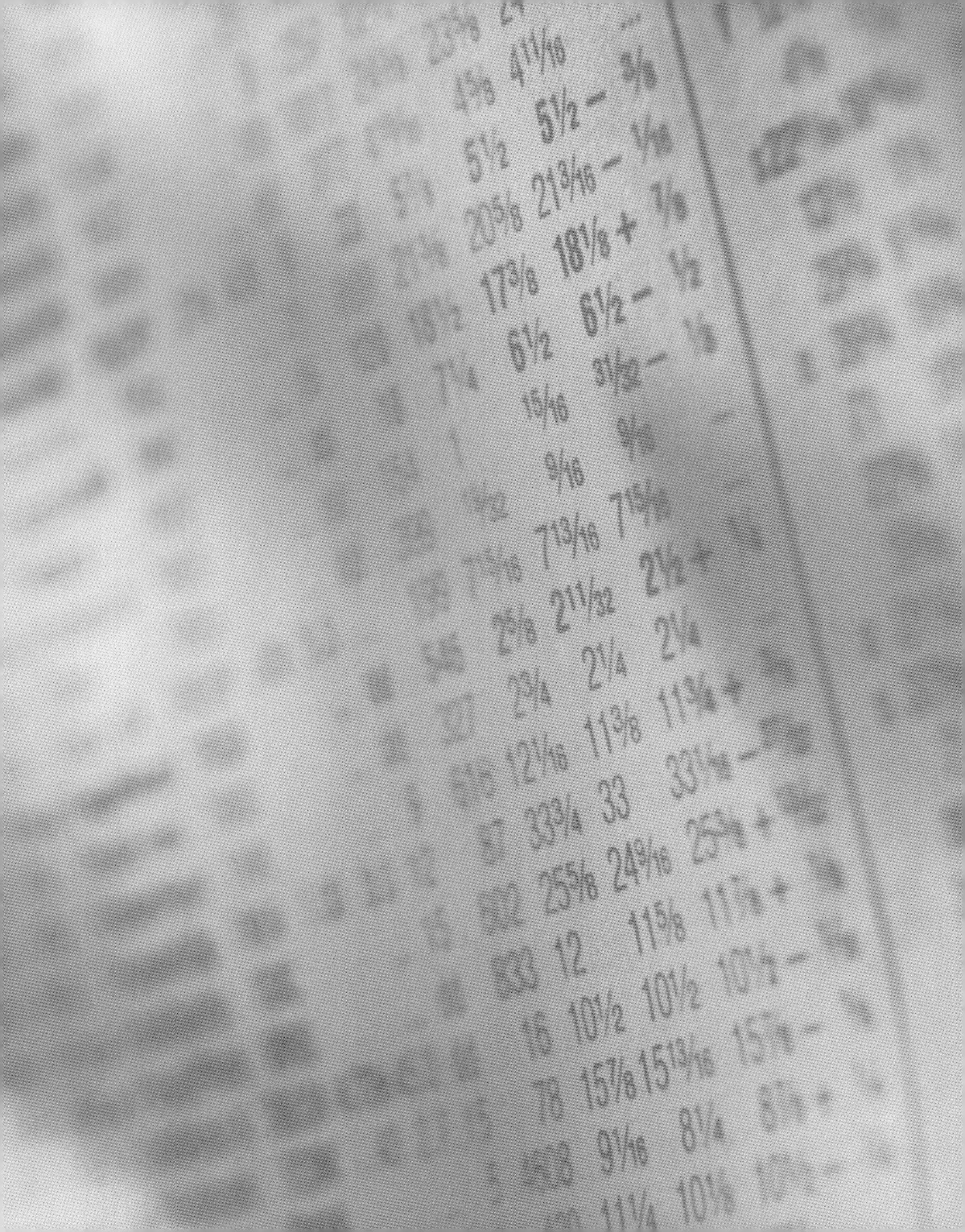

PERFECT COMPETITION

by Michael Parkin

LEARNING OUTCOMES

The candidate should be able to:	Mastery
a. describe the characteristics of perfect competition, explain why firms in a perfectly competitive market are price takers, and differentiate between market and firm demand curves;	☐
b. determine the profit maximizing (loss minimizing) output for a perfectly competitive firm, and explain marginal cost, marginal revenue, and economic profit and loss;	☐
c. describe a perfectly competitive firm's short-run supply curve and explain the impact of changes in demand, entry and exit of firms, and changes in plant size on the long-run equilibrium;	☐
d. discuss how a permanent change in demand or changes in technology affect price, output, and economic profit.	☐

THE BUSY BEE   1

The next time you eat a nut or a piece of fruit, think about the busy bee that pollinated the tree on which it grew and the beekeepers who rented their hives to the farmers. Across the United States, from Vermont to California, beekeepers are struggling under the strain of a parasite that is killing their bees. But the prices that those who still have bees can get for renting out hives to pollinate fruit and nut trees have more than doubled.

How does competition in beekeeping and other industries affect prices and profits? What causes some firms to enter an industry and others to leave it? What are the effects on profits and prices of new firms entering and old firms leaving an industry?

Economics, Eighth Edition, by Michael Parkin. Copyright © 2008 by Pearson Education. Reprinted with permission of Pearson Education, publishing as Pearson Addison Wesley.

In October 2006, more than 3 million people were unemployed because they had been laid off by the firms that previously employed them. Why do firms lay off workers? Why do firms temporarily shut down?

Over the past few years, the prices of personal computers have fallen sharply. For example, a slow computer cost almost $4,000 a few years ago, and a fast one costs only $500 today. What goes on in an industry when the price of its output falls sharply? What happens to the profits of the firms producing such goods? The pollination services of bees, computers, and most other goods are produced by more than one firm, and these firms compete for sales.

To study competitive markets, we are going to build a model of a market in which competition is as fierce and extreme as possible—more extreme than in the examples we've just considered. We call this situation "perfect competition." In *Reading Between the Lines* at the end of the reading, we'll return to the market for pollination services and see how it copes with a drastic decrease in the quantity of bees.

2   WHAT IS PERFECT COMPETITION?

The firms that you study in this reading face the force of raw competition. We call this extreme form of competition perfect competition. **Perfect competition** is an industry in which

- ▶ Many firms sell identical products to many buyers.
- ▶ There are no restrictions on entry into the industry.
- ▶ Established firms have no advantage over new ones.
- ▶ Sellers and buyers are well informed about prices.

Farming, fishing, wood pulping and paper milling, the manufacture of paper cups and plastic shopping bags, grocery retailing, photo finishing, lawn service, plumbing, painting, dry cleaning, and the provision of laundry services are all examples of highly competitive industries.

How Perfect Competition Arises

Perfect competition arises if the minimum efficient scale of a single producer is small relative to the demand for the good or service. A firm's *minimum efficient scale* is the smallest quantity of output at which long-run average cost reaches its lowest level. (See the reading on output and costs.) Where the minimum efficient scale of a firm is small relative to market demand, there is room for many firms in an industry.

Second, perfect competition arises if each firm is perceived to produce a good or service that has no unique characteristics so that consumers don't care which firm they buy from.

Price Takers

Firms in perfect competition are price takers. A **price taker** is a firm that cannot influence the market price and that sets its own price at the market price.

The key reason why a perfectly competitive firm is a price taker is that it produces a tiny proportion of the total output of a particular good and buyers are well informed about the prices of other firms.

Imagine that you are a wheat farmer in Kansas. You have a thousand acres under cultivation—which sounds like a lot. But compared to the millions of acres in Colorado, Oklahoma, Texas, Nebraska, and the Dakotas, as well as the millions more in Canada, Argentina, Australia, and Ukraine, your thousand acres is a drop in the ocean. Nothing makes your wheat any better than any other farmer's, and all the buyers of wheat know the price at which they can do business.

If the market price of wheat is $4 a bushel and you ask for $4.10, no one will buy from you. People can go to the next farmer and the next and the one after that and buy all they need for $4 a bushel. If you set your price at $3.90, you'll have lots of buyers. But you can sell all your output for $4 a bushel, so you're just giving away 10¢ a bushel. You can do no better than sell for the market price— you are a *price taker*.

Economic Profit and Revenue

A firm's goal is to maximize *economic profit*, which is equal to total revenue minus total cost. Total cost is the *opportunity cost* of production, which includes *normal profit*, the return that the entrepreneur can expect to receive on the average in an alternative business.

A firm's **total revenue** equals the price of its output multiplied by the number of units of output sold (price × quantity). **Marginal revenue** is the change in total revenue that results from a one-unit increase in the quantity sold. Marginal revenue is calculated by dividing the change in total revenue by the change in the quantity sold.

Figure 1 illustrates these revenue concepts. In part (a), the market demand curve, *D*, and market supply curve, *S*, determine the market price. The market price remains at $25 a sweater regardless of the quantity of sweaters that Cindy's produces. The best Cindy's can do is to sell its sweaters at this price.

Total Revenue

Total revenue is equal to the price multiplied by the quantity sold. In the table in Fig. 1, if Cindy's sells 9 sweaters, the firm's total revenue is 9 × $25, which equals $225.

Figure 1(b) shows the firm's total revenue curve (*TR*), which graphs the relationship between total revenue and the quantity sold. At point *A* on the *TR* curve, Cindy's sells 9 sweaters and has a total revenue of $225. Because each additional sweater sold brings in a constant amount—$25—the total revenue curve is an upward-sloping straight line.

Marginal Revenue

Marginal revenue is the change in total revenue that results from a one-unit increase in quantity. In the table in Fig. 1, when the quantity sold increases from 8 to 9 sweaters, total revenue increases from $200 to $225. Marginal revenue is $25 a sweater. Because the price remains constant when the quantity

FIGURE 1   Demand, Price, and Revenue in Perfect Competition

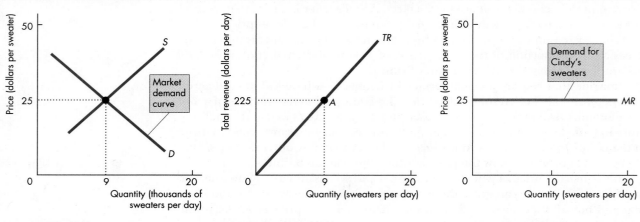

(a) Sweater market   **(b) Cindy's total revenue**   **(c) Cindy's marginal revenue**

Quantity Sold (Q) (Sweaters per Day)	Price (P) (Dollars per Sweater)	Total Revenue (TR = P × Q) (Dollars)	Marginal Revenue (MR = ΔTR/ΔQ) (Dollars per Additional Sweater)
8	25	200	
			 25
9	25	225	
			 25
10	25	250	

In part (a), market demand and market supply determine the market price (and quantity). Part (b) shows Cindy's total revenue curve (*TR*). Point *A* corresponds to the second row of the table—Cindy's sells 9 sweaters at $25 a sweater, so total revenue is $225. Part (c) shows Cindy's marginal revenue curve (*MR*). This curve is also the demand curve for Cindy's sweaters. Cindy's Sweaters faces a perfectly elastic demand for its sweaters at the market price of $25 a sweater.

sold changes, the change in total revenue that results from a one-unit increase in the quantity sold equals price—in perfect competition, marginal revenue equals price.

Figure 1(c) shows Cindy's marginal revenue curve (*MR*) which is a horizontal line at the going market price.

The firm can sell any quantity it chooses at the market price. So the demand curve for the firm's product is a horizontal line at the market price, the same as the firm's marginal revenue curve.

Demand for Firm's Product and Market Demand

A horizontal demand curve is perfectly elastic. So the firm faces a perfectly elastic demand for its output. One of Cindy's sweaters is a *perfect substitute* for sweaters from the factory next door or from any other factory. Notice, though, that the *market* demand for sweaters in Fig. 1(a) is not perfectly elastic. The market demand curve is downward-sloping, and its elasticity depends on the substitutability of sweaters for other goods and services.

THE FIRM'S DECISIONS IN PERFECT COMPETITION

Firms in a perfectly competitive industry face a given market price and have the revenue curves that you've studied. These revenue curves summarize the market constraint faced by a perfectly competitive firm.

Firms also face a technology constraint, which is described by the product curves (total product, average product, and marginal product) that you studied in the reading on output and costs. The technology available to the firm determines its costs, which are described by the cost curves (total cost, average cost, and marginal cost) that you also studied in the reading on output and costs.

The goal of the competitive firm is to make the maximum economic profit possible, given the constraints it faces. To achieve this objective, a firm must make four key decisions: two in the short run and two in the long run.

Short-Run Decisions

The short run is a time frame in which each firm has a given plant and the number of firms in the industry is fixed. But many things can change in the short run, and the firm must react to these changes. For example, the price for which the firm can sell its output might fluctuate with the season or general business conditions. The firm must react to such short-run price fluctuations and decide

1. Whether to produce or to shut down temporarily

2. If the decision is to produce, what quantity to produce

Long-Run Decisions

The long run is a time frame in which each firm can change the size of its plant and decide whether to leave the industry. Other firms can decide whether to enter the industry. So in the long run, both the plant size of each firm and the number of firms in the industry can change. Also in the long run, the constraints that firms face can change. For example, the demand for the good can permanently fall, or a technological advance can change the industry's costs. The firm must react to such long-run changes and decide

1. Whether to increase or decrease its plant size

2. Whether to stay in an industry or leave it

The Firm and the Industry in the Short Run and the Long Run

To study a competitive industry, we begin by looking at an individual firm's short-run decisions. We then see how the short-run decisions of all firms in a competitive industry combine to determine the industry price, output, and economic profit. We then turn to the long run and study the effects of long-run decisions on the industry price, output, and economic profit. All the decisions we study are driven by the pursuit of a single objective: maximization of economic profit.

Profit-Maximizing Output

A perfectly competitive firm maximizes economic profit by choosing its output level. One way of finding the profit-maximizing output is to study a firm's total revenue and total cost curves and find the output level at which total revenue exceeds total cost by the largest amount. Figure 2 shows how to do this for

FIGURE 2   Total Revenue, Total Cost, and Economic Profit

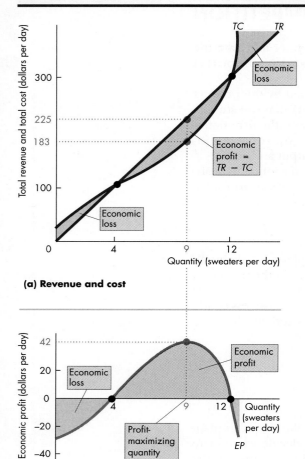

(a) Revenue and cost

(b) Economic profit and loss

Quantity (Q) (Sweaters per Day)	Total Revenue (TR) (Dollars)	Total Cost (TC) (Dollars)	Economic Profit (TR − TC) (Dollars)
0	0	22	−22
1	25	45	−20
2	50	66	−16
3	75	85	−10
4	100	100	0
5	125	114	11
6	150	126	24
7	175	141	34
8	200	160	40
9	**225**	**183**	**42**
10	250	210	40
11	275	245	30
12	300	300	0
13	325	360	−35

The table lists Cindy's total revenue, total cost, and economic profit. Part (a) graphs the total revenue and total cost curves. Economic profit, in part (a), is the height of the blue area between the total cost and total revenue curves. Cindy's makes maximum economic profit, $42 a day ($225 − $183), when it produces 9 sweaters—the output at which the vertical distance between the total revenue and total cost curves is at its largest. At outputs of 4 sweaters a day and 12 sweaters a day, Cindy's makes zero economic profit—these are break-even points. At outputs less than 4 and greater than 12 sweaters a day, Cindy's incurs an economic loss. Part (b) of the figure shows Cindy's profit curve. The profit curve is at its highest when economic profit is at a maximum and cuts the horizontal axis at the break-even points.

Cindy's Sweaters. The table lists Cindy's total revenue and total cost at different outputs, and part (a) of the figure shows Cindy's total revenue and total cost curves. These curves are graphs of the numbers shown in the first three columns of the table. The total revenue curve (*TR*) is the same as that in Fig. 1(b). The total cost curve (*TC*) is similar to the one that you met in the reading on output and costs. As output increases, so does total cost.

Economic profit equals total revenue minus total cost. The fourth column of the table in Fig. 2 shows Cindy's economic profit, and part (b) of the figure illustrates these numbers as Cindy's profit curve *EP*. This curve shows that Cindy's makes an economic profit at outputs between 4 and 12 sweaters a day. At outputs less than 4 sweaters a day, Cindy's incurs an economic loss. It also incurs an economic loss if output exceeds 12 sweaters a day. At outputs of 4 sweaters and 12 sweaters a day, total cost equals total revenue and Cindy's economic profit is zero. An output at which total cost equals total revenue is called a *break-even point*. The firm's economic profit is zero. Normal profit is part of the firm's costs, so at the break-even point, the entrepreneur makes normal profit.

Notice the relationship between the total revenue, total cost, and profit curves. Economic profit is measured by the vertical distance between the total revenue and total cost curves. When the total revenue curve in Fig. 2(a) is above the total cost curve, between 4 and 12 sweaters, the firm is making an economic profit and the profit curve in Fig. 2(b) is above the horizontal axis. At the break-even point, where the total cost and total revenue curves intersect, the profit curve intersects the horizontal axis. The profit curve is at its highest when the distance between *TR* and *TC* is greatest. In this example, profit maximization occurs at an output of 9 sweaters a day. At this output, Cindy's Sweaters makes an economic profit of $42 a day.

Marginal Analysis

Another way of finding the profit-maximizing output is to use *marginal analysis* and compare marginal revenue, *MR*, with marginal cost, *MC*. As output increases, marginal revenue remains constant but marginal cost changes. At low output levels, marginal cost decreases, but it eventually increases. So where the marginal cost curve intersects the marginal revenue curve, marginal cost is rising.

If marginal revenue exceeds marginal cost (if *MR* > *MC*), then the extra revenue from selling one more unit exceeds the extra cost incurred to produce it. The firm makes an economic profit on the marginal unit, so its economic profit increases if output *increases*.

If marginal revenue is less than marginal cost (if *MR* < *MC*), then the extra revenue from selling one more unit is less than the extra cost incurred to produce it. The firm incurs an economic loss on the marginal unit, so its economic profit decreases if output increases and its economic profit increases if output *decreases*.

If marginal revenue equals marginal cost (if *MR* = *MC*), economic profit is maximized. The rule *MR* = *MC* is an example of marginal analysis. Let's check that this rule for finding the profit-maximizing output works by returning to Cindy's Sweaters.

Look at Fig. 3. The table records Cindy's marginal revenue and marginal cost. Marginal revenue is a constant $25 a sweater. Over the range of outputs shown in the table, marginal cost increases from $19 a sweater to $35 a sweater.

Focus on the highlighted rows of the table. If Cindy increases output from 8 sweaters to 9 sweaters, marginal revenue is $25 and marginal cost is $23. Because marginal revenue exceeds marginal cost, economic profit increases. The last column of the table shows that economic profit increases from $40 to $42, an increase of $2. This economic profit from the ninth sweater is shown as the blue area in the figure.

If Cindy increases output from 9 sweaters to 10 sweaters, marginal revenue is still $25 but marginal cost is $27. Because marginal revenue is less than marginal cost, economic profit decreases. The last column of the table shows that economic profit decreases from $42 to $40. This loss from the tenth sweater is shown as the gray area in the figure.

Cindy maximizes economic profit by producing 9 sweaters a day, the quantity at which marginal revenue equals marginal cost.

Profits and Losses in the Short Run

In short-run equilibrium, although the firm produces the profit-maximizing output, it does not necessarily end up making an economic profit. It might do so, but it might alternatively break even or incur an economic loss. Economic profit (or

FIGURE 3   Profit-Maximizing Output

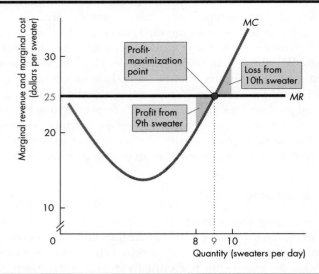

Quantity (Q) (Sweaters per Day)	Total Revenue (TR) (Dollars)	Marginal Revenue (MR) (Dollars per Additional Sweater)	Total Cost (TC) (Dollars)	Marginal Cost (MC) (Dollars per Additional Sweater)	Economic Profit (TR – TC) (Dollars)
7	175		141		34
		 25		 19	
8	200		160		40
		 25		 23	
9	**225**		**183**		**42**
		 25		 27	
10	250		210		40
		 25		 35	
11	275		245		30

Another way of finding the profit-maximizing output is to determine the output at which marginal revenue equals marginal cost. The table shows that if output increases from 8 to 9 sweaters, marginal cost is $23, which is less than the marginal revenue of $25. If output increases from 9 to 10 sweaters, marginal cost is $27, which exceeds the marginal revenue of $25. The figure shows that marginal cost and marginal revenue are equal when Cindy's produces 9 sweaters a day. If marginal revenue exceeds marginal cost, an increase in output increases economic profit. If marginal revenue is less than marginal cost, an increase in output decreases economic profit. If marginal revenue equals marginal cost, economic profit is maximized.

loss) per sweater is price, P, minus average total cost, ATC. So economic profit (or loss) is $(P - ATC) \times Q$. If price equals average total cost, a firm breaks even—the entrepreneur makes normal profit. If price exceeds average total cost, a firm makes an economic profit. If price is less than average total cost, a firm incurs an economic loss. Figure 4 shows these three possible short-run profit outcomes.

FIGURE 4   Three Possible Profit Outcomes in the Short Run

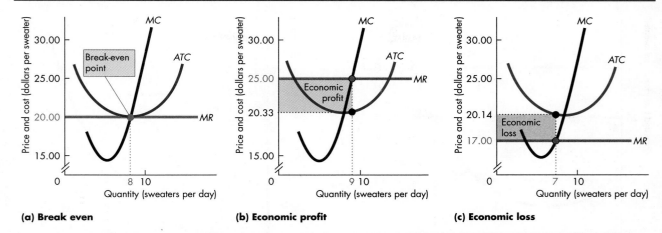

(a) Break even   **(b) Economic profit**   **(c) Economic loss**

In the short run, the firm might break even (make zero economic profit), make an economic profit, or incur an economic loss. If the price equals minimum average total cost, the firm breaks even and makes zero economic profit (part a). If the price exceeds the average total cost of producing the profit-maximizing output, the firm makes an economic profit equal to the area of the blue rectangle in part (b). If the price is below minimum average total cost, the firm incurs an economic loss equal to the area of the gray rectangle in part (c).

Three Possible Profit Outcomes

In Fig. 4(a), the price of a sweater is $20. Cindy's produces 8 sweaters a day. Average total cost is $20 a sweater. Price equals average total cost (*ATC*), so Cindy's Sweaters breaks even (zero economic profit) and Cindy makes normal profit.

In Fig. 4(b), the price of a sweater is $25. Profit is maximized when output is 9 sweaters a day. Here, price exceeds average total cost, so Cindy's makes an economic profit. This economic profit is $42 a day. It is made up of $4.67 per sweater ($25.00 – $20.33) multiplied by the number of sweaters ($4.67 × 9 = $42). The blue rectangle shows this economic profit. The height of that rectangle is profit per sweater, $4.67, and the length is the quantity of sweaters produced, 9 a day, so the area of the rectangle is Cindy's economic profit of $42 a day.

In Fig. 4(c), the price of a sweater is $17. Here, price is less than average total cost and Cindy's incurs an economic loss. Price and marginal revenue are $17 a sweater, and the profit-maximizing (in this case, loss-minimizing) output is 7 sweaters a day. Cindy's total revenue is $119 a day (7 × $17). Average total cost is $20.14 a sweater, so the economic loss is $3.14 per sweater ($20.14 – $17.00). This loss per sweater multiplied by the number of sweaters is $22 ($3.14 × 7 = $22). The gray rectangle shows this economic loss. The height of that rectangle is economic loss per sweater, $3.14, and the length is the quantity of sweaters produced, 7 a day, so the area of the rectangle is Cindy's economic loss of $22 a day.

The Firm's Short-Run Supply Curve

A perfectly competitive firm's short-run supply curve shows how the firm's profit-maximizing output varies as the market price varies, other things remaining the same. Figure 5 shows how to derive Cindy's supply curve. Part (a) shows Cindy's marginal cost and average variable cost curves, and part (b) shows its supply curve. There is a direct link between the marginal cost and average variable cost curves and the supply curve. Let's see what that link is.

FIGURE 5   A Firm's Supply Curve

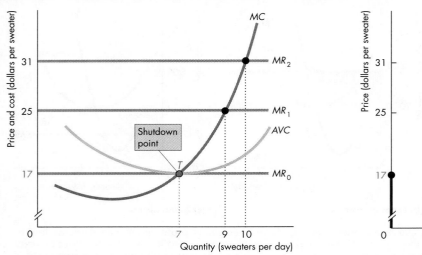

(a) Marginal cost and average variable cost

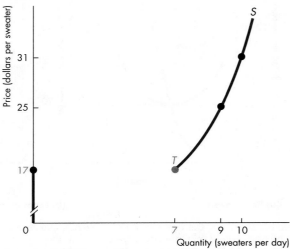

(b) Cindy's short-run supply curve

Part (a) shows Cindy's profit-maximizing output at various market prices. At $25 a sweater, Cindy produces 9 sweaters. At $17 a sweater, Cindy produces 7 sweaters. At any price below $17 a sweater, Cindy produces nothing. Cindy's shutdown point is *T*. Part (b) shows Cindy's supply curve—the number of sweaters Cindy will produce at each price. It is made up of the marginal cost curve (part a) at all points above minimum average variable cost and the vertical axis at all prices below minimum average variable cost.

Temporary Plant Shutdown

In the short run, a firm cannot avoid incurring its fixed cost. But the firm can avoid variable costs by temporarily laying off its workers and shutting down. If a firm shuts down, it produces no output and it incurs a loss equal to total fixed cost. This loss is the largest that a firm need incur. A firm shuts down if price falls below the minimum of average variable cost. The **shutdown point** is the output and price at which the firm just covers its total variable cost—point *T* in Fig. 5(a). If the price is $17, the marginal revenue curve is MR_0 and the profit-maximizing output is 7 sweaters a day at point *T*. But both price and average variable cost equal $17, so Cindy's total revenue equals total variable cost. Cindy's incurs an economic loss equal to total fixed cost. At a price below $17, no matter what quantity Cindy produces, average *variable* cost exceeds price and the firm's loss exceeds total fixed cost. At a price below $17, the firm shuts down temporarily.

The Short-Run Supply Curve

If the price is above minimum average variable cost, Cindy maximizes profit by producing the output at which marginal cost equals price. At a price of $25, the marginal revenue curve is MR_1 and Cindy maximizes profit by producing 9 sweaters. At a price of $31, the marginal revenue curve is MR_2 and Cindy produces 10 sweaters.

Cindy's short-run supply curve, shown in Fig. 5(b), has two separate parts: First, at prices that exceed minimum average variable cost, the supply curve is the same as the marginal cost curve above the shutdown point (*T*). Second, at prices below minimum average variable cost, Cindy shuts down and produces nothing. The supply curve runs along the *y*-axis. At a price of $17, Cindy is indifferent between shutting down and producing 7 sweaters a day. Either way, Cindy's incurs an economic loss equal to total fixed cost.

FIGURE 6   Industry Supply Curve

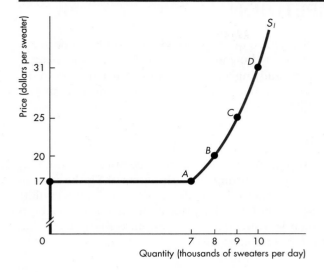

	Price (Dollars per Sweater)	Quantity Supplied by Cindy's Sweaters (Sweaters per Day)	Quantity Supplied by Industry (Sweaters per Day)
A	17	0 or 7	0 to 7,000
B	20	8	8,000
C	25	9	9,000
D	31	10	10,000

The industry supply schedule is the sum of the supply schedules of all individual firms. An industry that consists of 1,000 identical firms has a supply schedule similar to that of the individual firm, but the quantity supplied by the industry is 1,000 times as large as that of the individual firm (see the table). The industry supply curve is S_I. Points *A*, *B*, *C*, and *D* correspond to the rows of the table. At the shutdown price of $17, each firm produces either 0 or 7 sweaters per day. The industry supply is perfectly elastic at the shutdown price.

Short-Run Industry Supply Curve

The **short-run industry supply curve** shows the quantity supplied by the industry at each price when the plant size of each firm and the number of firms remain constant. The quantity supplied by the industry at a given price is the sum of the quantities supplied by all firms in the industry at that price.

Figure 6 shows the supply curve for the competitive sweater industry. In this example, the industry consists of 1,000 firms exactly like Cindy's Sweaters. At each price, the quantity supplied by the industry is 1,000 times the quantity supplied by a single firm.

The table in Fig. 6 shows the firm's and the industry's supply schedule and how the industry supply curve is constructed. At prices below $17, every firm in the industry shuts down; the quantity supplied by the industry is zero. At a price of $17, each firm is indifferent between shutting down and producing nothing or operating and producing 7 sweaters a day. Some firms will shut down, and others will supply 7 sweaters a day. The quantity supplied by each firm is *either* 0 or 7 sweaters, but the quantity supplied by the industry is *between* 0 (all firms shut down) and 7,000 (all firms produce 7 sweaters a day each).

To construct the industry supply curve, we sum the quantities supplied by the individual firms. Each of the 1,000 firms in the industry has a supply schedule like Cindy's. At prices below $17, the industry supply curve runs along the *y*-axis. At a price of $17, the industry supply curve is horizontal—supply is perfectly elastic. As the price rises above $17, each firm increases its quantity supplied and the quantity supplied by the industry increases by 1,000 times that of one firm.

So far, we have studied a single firm in isolation. We have seen that the firm's profit-maximizing actions depend on the market price, which the firm takes as given. But how is the market price determined? Let's find out.

4

OUTPUT, PRICE, AND PROFIT IN PERFECT COMPETITION

To determine the market price and the quantity bought and sold in a perfectly competitive market, we need to study how market demand and market supply interact. We begin this process by studying a perfectly competitive market in the short run when the number of firms is fixed and each firm has a given plant size.

Short-Run Equilibrium

Market demand and market supply determine the market price and industry output. Figure 7 shows a short-run equilibrium. The supply curve S is the same as S_I in Fig. 6. If the market demand is shown by the demand curve D_1, the equilibrium price is $20 a sweater. Each firm takes this price as given and produces its profit-maximizing output, which is 8 sweaters a day. Because the industry has 1,000 firms, industry output is 8,000 sweaters a day.

FIGURE 7   Short-Run Equilibrium

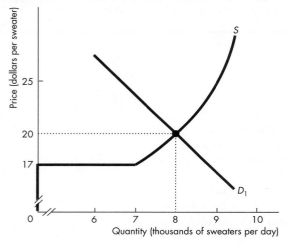

(a) Equilibrium

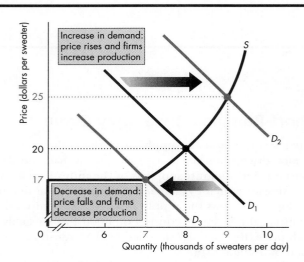

(b) Change in equilibrium

In part (a), the industry supply curve is S. Demand is D_1, and the price is $20. At this price, each firm produces 8 sweaters a day and the industry produces 8,000 sweaters a day. In part (b), when demand increases to D_2, the price rises to $25 and each firm increases its output to 9 sweaters a day. Industry output is 9,000 sweaters a day. When demand decreases to D_3, the price falls to $17 and each firm decreases its output to 7 sweaters a day. Industry output is 7,000 sweaters a day.

A Change in Demand

Changes in demand bring changes to short-run industry equilibrium. Figure 7 shows these changes.

If demand increases, the demand curve shifts rightward to D_2. The price rises to $25. At this price, each firm maximizes profit by increasing output. The new output is 9 sweaters a day for each firm and 9,000 sweaters a day for the industry.

If demand decreases, the demand curve shifts leftward to D_3. The price now falls to $17. At this price, each firm maximizes profit by decreasing its output. The new output is 7 sweaters a day for each firm and 7,000 sweaters a day for the industry.

If the demand curve shifts farther leftward than D_3, the price remains constant at $17 because the industry supply curve is horizontal at that price. Some firms continue to produce 7 sweaters a day, and others temporarily shut down. Firms are indifferent between these two activities, and whichever they choose, they incur an economic loss equal to total fixed cost. The number of firms continuing to produce is just enough to satisfy the market demand at a price of $17 a sweater.

Long-Run Adjustments

In short-run equilibrium, a firm might make an economic profit, incur an economic loss, or break even. Although each of these three situations is a short-run equilibrium, only one of them is a long-run equilibrium. To see why, we need to examine the forces at work in a competitive industry in the long run.

In the long run, an industry adjusts in two ways:

► Entry and exit

► Changes in plant size

Let's look at entry and exit.

Entry and Exit

In the long run, firms respond to economic profit and economic loss by either entering or exiting an industry. Firms enter an industry in which firms are making an economic profit, and firms exit an industry in which firms are incurring an economic loss. Temporary economic profit and temporary economic loss do not trigger entry and exit. But the prospect of persistent economic profit or loss does.

Entry and exit influence price, the quantity produced, and economic profit. The immediate effect of these decisions is to shift the industry supply curve. If more firms enter an industry, supply increases and the industry supply curve shifts rightward. If firms exit an industry, supply decreases and the industry supply curve shifts leftward.

Let's see what happens when new firms enter an industry.

The Effects of Entry

Figure 8 shows the effects of entry. Suppose that all the firms in this industry have cost curves like those in Fig. 4. At any price greater than $20 a sweater, firms make an economic profit. At any price less than $20 a sweater, firms incur an economic loss. And at a price of $20 a sweater, firms make zero economic profit. Also suppose that the demand curve for sweaters is D. If the industry supply curve is S_1, sweaters sell for $23, and 7,000 sweaters a day are produced. Firms in the industry make an economic profit.

This economic profit is a signal for new firms to enter the industry. As these events unfold, supply increases and the industry supply curve shifts rightward to S_0. With the greater supply and unchanged demand, the market price falls from $23 to $20 a sweater and the quantity produced by the industry increases from 7,000 to 8,000 sweaters a day.

Industry output increases, but Cindy's Sweaters, like each other firm in the industry, *decreases* output! Because the price falls, each firm moves down its supply curve and produces less. But because the number of firms in the industry increases, the industry as a whole produces more.

Because price falls, each firm's economic profit decreases. When the price falls to $20 a sweater, economic profit disappears and each firm makes a zero economic profit.

FIGURE 8   Entry and Exit

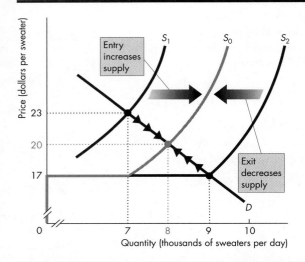

When new firms enter the sweater industry, the industry supply curve shifts rightward, from S_1 to S_0. The equilibrium price falls from \$23 to \$20, and the quantity produced increases from 7,000 to 8,000 sweaters.

When firms exit the sweater industry, the industry supply curve shifts leftward, from S_2 to S_0. The equilibrium price rises from \$17 to \$20, and the quantity produced decreases from 9,000 to 8,000 sweaters.

You have just discovered a key proposition:

As new firms enter an industry, the price falls and the economic profit of each existing firm decreases.

An example of this process occurred during the 1980s in the personal computer industry. When IBM introduced its first PC, there was little competition and the price of a PC gave IBM a big profit. But new firms such as Compaq, NEC, Dell, and a host of others entered the industry with machines that were technologically identical to IBM's. In fact, they were so similar that they came to be called "clones." The massive wave of entry into the personal computer industry shifted the industry supply curve rightward and lowered the price and the economic profit.

Let's now look at the effects of exit.

The Effects of Exit

Figure 8 also shows the effects of exit. Suppose that firms' costs and the market demand are the same as before. But now suppose the supply curve is S_2. The market price is \$17, and 9,000 sweaters a day are produced. Firms in the industry now incur an economic loss. This economic loss is a signal for some firms to exit the industry. As firms exit, the industry supply curve shifts leftward to S_0. With the decrease in supply, industry output decreases from 9,000 to 8,000 sweaters and the price rises from \$17 to \$20 a sweater.

As the price rises, Cindy's Sweaters, like each other firm in the industry, moves up along its supply curve and increases output. That is, for each firm that remains in the industry, the profit-maximizing output increases. Because the price rises and each firm sells more, economic loss decreases. When the price rises to \$20, each firm makes a zero economic profit.

You've now discovered a second key proposition:

As firms leave an industry, the price rises and the economic loss of each remaining firm decreases.

The same PC industry that saw a large amount of entry during the 1980s and 1990s has seen some exit. For example, in 2001, IBM, the firm that first launched the PC, announced that it would no longer produce PCs. The intense competition from Compaq, NEC, Dell, and others that entered the industry following IBM's lead has lowered the price and eliminated the economic profit. So IBM now concentrates on servers and other parts of the computer market.

IBM exited the PC market because it was incurring economic losses. Its exit decreased supply and made it possible for the remaining firms in the industry to make zero economic profit.

You've now seen how economic profits induce entry, which in turn lowers profits. And you've seen how economic losses induce exit, which in turn eliminate losses. Let's now look at changes in plant size.

Changes in Plant Size

A firm changes its plant size if, by doing so, it can lower its costs and increase its economic profit. You can probably think of lots of examples of firms that have changed their plant size.

One example that has almost certainly happened near your campus in recent years is a change in the plant size of Kinko's or similar copy shops. Another is the number of FedEx vans that you see on the streets and highways. And another is the number of square feet of retail space devoted to selling computers and video games. These are examples of firms increasing their plant size to seek larger profits.

There are also many examples of firms that have decreased their plant size to avoid economic losses. One of these is Schwinn, the Chicago-based maker of bicycles. As competition from Asian bicycle makers became tougher, Schwinn cut back. Many firms have scaled back their operations—a process called *downsizing*—in recent years.

Figure 9 shows a situation in which Cindy's Sweaters has an incentive to increase its plant size. Suppose with its current plant, Cindy's marginal cost curve

FIGURE 9   Plant Size and Long-Run Equilibrium

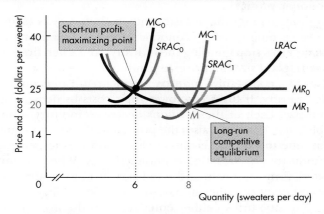

Initially, Cindy's plant has marginal cost curve MC_0 and short-run average total cost curve $SRAC_0$. The market price is $25 a sweater, and Cindy's marginal revenue is MR_0. The short-run profit-maximizing quantity is 6 sweaters a day. Cindy's Sweaters can increase profit by increasing the plant size. If all firms in the sweater industry increase their plant sizes, the short-run industry supply increases and the market price falls. In long-run equilibrium, a firm operates with the plant size that minimizes its average total cost. Here, Cindy's Sweaters operates the plant with short-run marginal cost MC_1 and short-run average cost $SRAC_1$. Cindy's Sweaters is also on its long-run average cost curve $LRAC$ and produces at point M. Its output is 8 sweaters a day, and its average total cost equals the price of a sweater: $20.

is MC_0, and its short-run average total cost curve is $SRAC_0$. The market price is $25 a sweater, so Cindy's marginal revenue curve is MR_0. Cindy's maximizes profit by producing 6 sweaters a day.

Cindy's Sweaters' long-run average cost curve is $LRAC$. By increasing its plant size—installing more knitting machines—Cindy's Sweaters can move along its long-run average cost curve. As Cindy's Sweaters increases its plant size, its short-run marginal cost curve shifts rightward.

Recall that a firm's short-run supply curve is linked to its marginal cost curve. As Cindy's marginal cost curve shifts rightward, so does its supply curve. If Cindy's Sweaters and the other firms in the industry increase their plants, the short-run industry supply curve shifts rightward and the market price falls. The fall in the market price limits the extent to which Cindy's can profit from increasing its plant size.

Figure 9 also shows Cindy's Sweaters in a long-run competitive equilibrium. This situation arises when the market price has fallen to $20 a sweater. Marginal revenue is MR_1, and Cindy's maximizes profit by producing 8 sweaters a day. In this situation, Cindy's cannot increase profit by changing the plant size. Cindy's is producing at minimum long-run average cost (point M on $LRAC$).

Because Cindy's Sweaters is producing at minimum long-run average cost, it has no incentive to change its plant size. A bigger plant or a smaller plant has a higher long-run average cost. If Fig. 9 describes the situation of all firms in the sweater industry, the industry is in long-run equilibrium. No firm has an incentive to change its plant size. Also, because each firm is making zero economic profit, no firm has an incentive to enter or to leave the industry.

Long-Run Equilibrium

Long-run equilibrium occurs in a competitive industry when economic profit is zero (when firms earn normal profit). If the firms in a competitive industry are making an economic profit, new firms enter the industry. If firms can lower their costs by increasing their plant size, they expand. Each of these actions increases industry supply, shifts the industry supply curve rightward, lowers the price, and decreases economic profit.

Firms continue to enter the industry and profit decreases as long as firms in the industry are earning positive economic profits. When economic profit has been eliminated, firms stop entering the industry. And when firms are operating with the least-cost plant size, they stop expanding.

If the firms in a competitive industry are incurring an economic loss, some firms exit the industry. If firms can lower their costs by decreasing their plant size, they downsize. Each of these actions decreases industry supply, shifts the industry supply curve leftward, raises the price, and decreases economic loss.

Firms continue to exit and economic loss continues to decrease as long as firms in the industry are incurring economic losses. When economic loss has been eliminated, firms stop exiting the industry. And when firms are operating with the least-cost plant size, they stop downsizing. So in long-run equilibrium in a competitive industry, firms neither enter nor exit the industry and old firms neither expand nor downsize. Each firm makes zero economic profit.

You've seen how a competitive industry adjusts toward its long-run equilibrium. But a competitive industry is rarely *in* a state of long-run equilibrium. A competitive industry is constantly and restlessly evolving toward such an equilibrium. But the constraints that firms in the industry face are constantly changing. The two most persistent sources of change are in tastes and technology. Let's see how a competitive industry reacts to such changes.

CHANGING TASTES
AND ADVANCING TECHNOLOGY

5

Increased awareness of the health hazards of smoking has caused a decrease in the demand for tobacco and cigarettes. The development of inexpensive car and air transportation has caused a huge decrease in the demand for long-distance trains and buses. Solid-state electronics have caused a large decrease in the demand for TV and radio repair. The development of good-quality inexpensive clothing has decreased the demand for sewing machines. What happens in a competitive industry when there is a permanent decrease in the demand for its product?

The development of the microwave oven has produced an enormous increase in demand for paper, glass, and plastic cooking utensils and for plastic wrap. The widespread use of the personal computer has brought a huge increase in the demand for CD-Rs. What happens in a competitive industry when the demand for its output increases?

Advances in technology are constantly lowering the costs of production. New biotechnologies have dramatically lowered the costs of producing many food and pharmaceutical products. New electronic technologies have lowered the cost of producing just about every good and service. What happens in a competitive industry when technological change lowers its production costs?

Let's use the theory of perfect competition to answer these questions.

A Permanent Change in Demand

Figure 10(a) shows a competitive industry that initially is in long-run equilibrium. The demand curve is D_0, the supply curve is S_0, the market price is P_0, and industry output is Q_0. Figure 10(b) shows a single firm in this initial long-run equilibrium. The firm produces q_0 and makes zero economic profit.

Now suppose that demand decreases and the demand curve shifts leftward to D_1, as shown in Fig. 10(a). The price falls to P_1, and the quantity supplied by the industry decreases from Q_0 to Q_1 as the industry slides down its short-run supply curve S_0. Figure 10(b) shows the situation facing a firm. Price is now below the firm's minimum average total cost, so the firm incurs an economic loss. But to keep its loss to a minimum, the firm adjusts its output to keep marginal cost equal to price. At a price of P_1, each firm produces an output of q_1.

The industry is now in short-run equilibrium but not long-run equilibrium. It is in short-run equilibrium because each firm is maximizing profit. But it is not in long-run equilibrium because each firm is incurring an economic loss—its average total cost exceeds the price.

The economic loss is a signal for some firms to leave the industry. As they do so, short-run industry supply decreases and the supply curve gradually shifts leftward. As industry supply decreases, the price rises. At each higher price, a firm's profit-maximizing output is greater, so the firms remaining in the industry increase their output as the price rises. Each firm slides up its marginal cost or supply curve in Fig. 10(b). That is, as firms exit the industry, industry output decreases but the output of the firms that remain in the industry increases.

Eventually, enough firms leave the industry for the industry supply curve to have shifted to S_1 in Fig. 10(a). At this time, the price has returned to its original level, P_0. At this price, the firms remaining in the industry produce q_0, the same

FIGURE 10   A Decrease in Demand

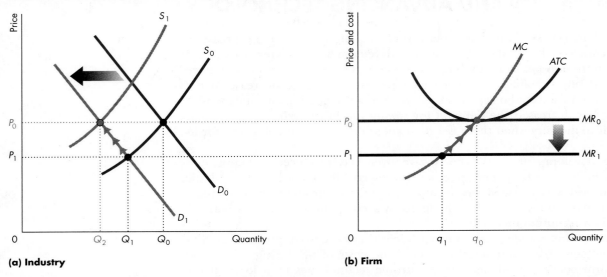

(a) Industry   **(b) Firm**

An industry starts out in long-run competitive equilibrium. Part (a) shows the industry demand curve D_0, the industry supply curve S_0, the equilibrium quantity Q_0, and the market price P_0. Each firm sells its output at price P_0, so its marginal revenue curve is MR_0 in part (b). Each firm produces q_0 and makes zero economic profit.

Demand decreases permanently from D_0 to D_1 (part a). The market price falls to P_1, each firm decreases its output to q_1 (part b), and industry output decreases to Q_1 (part a).

In this new situation, firms incur economic losses and some firms leave the industry. As they do so, the industry supply curve gradually shifts leftward, from S_0 to S_1. This shift gradually raises the market price from P_1 back to P_0. While the price is below P_0, firms incur economic losses and some firms leave the industry. Once the price has returned to P_0, each firm makes zero economic profit. Firms have no further incentive to leave the industry. Each firm produces q_0, and industry output is Q_2.

quantity that they produced before the decrease in demand. Because firms are now making zero economic profit, no firm wants to enter or exit the industry. The industry supply curve remains at S_1, and industry output is Q_2. The industry is again in long-run equilibrium.

The difference between the initial long-run equilibrium and the final long-run equilibrium is the number of firms in the industry. A permanent decrease in demand has decreased the number of firms. Each remaining firm produces the same output in the new long-run equilibrium as it did initially and earns zero economic profit. In the process of moving from the initial equilibrium to the new one, firms incur economic losses.

We've just worked out how a competitive industry responds to a permanent *decrease* in demand. A permanent increase in demand triggers a similar response, except in the opposite direction. The increase in demand brings a higher price, economic profit, and entry. Entry increases industry supply and eventually lowers the price to its original level and economic profit to zero.

The demand for internet service increased permanently during the 1990s and huge profit opportunities arose in this industry. The result was a massive rate of entry of internet service providers. The process of competition and change in the internet service industry is similar to what we have just studied but with an increase in demand rather than a decrease in demand.

We've now studied the effects of a permanent change in demand for a good. In doing so, we began and ended in a long-run equilibrium and examined the process that takes a market from one equilibrium to another. It is this process, not the equilibrium points, that describes the real world.

One feature of the predictions that we have just generated seems odd: In the long run, regardless of whether demand increases or decreases, the market price returns to its original level. Is this outcome inevitable? In fact, it is not. It is possible for the equilibrium market price in the long run to remain the same, rise, or fall.

External Economies and Diseconomies

The change in the long-run equilibrium price depends on external economies and external diseconomies. **External economies** are factors beyond the control of an individual firm that lower the firm's costs as the *industry* output increases. **External diseconomies** are factors outside the control of a firm that raise the firm's costs as the *industry* output increases. With no external economies or external diseconomies, a firm's costs remain constant as the industry output changes.

Figure 11 illustrates these three cases and introduces a new supply concept: the long-run industry supply curve.

A **long-run industry supply curve** shows how the quantity supplied by an industry varies as the market price varies after all the possible adjustments have been made, including changes in plant size and the number of firms in the industry.

Figure 11(a) shows the case we have just studied—no external economies or diseconomies. The long-run industry supply curve (LS_A) is perfectly elastic. In this case, a permanent increase in demand from D_0 to D_1 has no effect on the price in the long run. The increase in demand brings a temporary increase in price to P_S and a short-run quantity increase from Q_0 to Q_S. Entry increases short-run supply from S_0 to S_1, which lowers the price from P_S back to P_0, and increases the quantity to Q_1.

FIGURE 11   Long-Run Changes in Price and Quantity

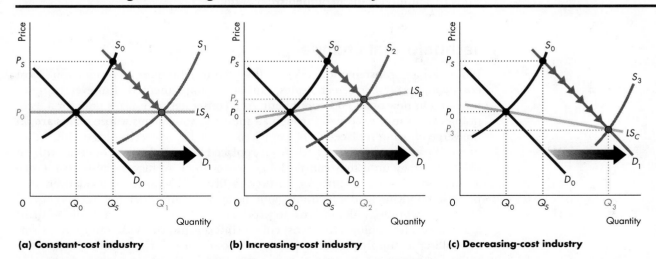

(a) Constant-cost industry   **(b) Increasing-cost industry**   **(c) Decreasing-cost industry**

Three possible changes in price and quantity occur in the long run. When demand increases from D_0 to D_1, entry occurs and the industry supply curve shifts rightward from S_0 to S_1. In part (a), the long-run industry supply curve, LS_A, is horizontal. The quantity increases from Q_0 to Q_1, and the price remains constant at P_0.

In part (b), the long-run industry supply curve is LS_B; the price rises to P_2, and the quantity increases to Q_2. This case occurs in industries with external diseconomies. In part (c), the long-run industry supply curve is LS_C; the price falls to P_3, and the quantity increases to Q_3. This case occurs in an industry with external economies.

Figure 11(b) shows the case of external diseconomies. The long-run industry supply curve (LS_B) slopes upward. A permanent increase in demand from D_0 to D_1 increases the price in both the short run and the long run. The increase in demand brings a temporary increase in price to P_S and a short-run quantity increase from Q_0 to Q_S. Entry increases short-run supply from S_0 to S_2, which lowers the price from P_S to P_2 and increases the quantity to Q_2.

One source of external diseconomies is congestion. The airline industry provides a good example. With bigger airline industry output, congestion at airports and airspace increase and results in longer delays and extra waiting time for passengers and airplanes. These external diseconomies mean that as the output of air transportation services increases (in the absence of technological advances), average cost increases. As a result, the long-run industry supply curve is upward sloping. So a permanent increase in demand brings an increase in quantity and a rise in the price. (Industries with external diseconomies might nonetheless have a falling price because technological advances shift the long-run supply curve downward.)

Figure 11(c) shows the case of external economies. In this case, the long-run industry supply curve (LS_C) slopes downward. A permanent increase in demand from D_0 to D_1 increases the price in the short run and lowers it in the long run. Again, the increase in demand brings a temporary increase in price to P_S, and a short-run quantity increase from Q_0 to Q_S. Entry increases short-run supply from S_0 to S_3, which lowers the price to P_3 and increases the quantity to Q_3.

An example of external economies is the growth of specialist support services for an industry as it expands. As farm output increased in the nineteenth and early twentieth centuries, the services available to farmers expanded. New firms specialized in the development and marketing of farm machinery and fertilizers. As a result, average farm costs decreased. Farms enjoyed the benefits of external economies. As a consequence, as the demand for farm products increased, the output increased but the price fell.

Over the long term, the prices of many goods and services have fallen, not because of external economies but because of technological change. Let's now study this influence on a competitive market.

Technological Change

Industries are constantly discovering lower-cost techniques of production. Most cost-saving production techniques cannot be implemented, however, without investing in new plant and equipment. As a consequence, it takes time for a technological advance to spread through an industry. Some firms whose plants are on the verge of being replaced will be quick to adopt the new technology, while other firms whose plants have recently been replaced will continue to operate with an old technology until they can no longer cover their average variable cost. Once average variable cost cannot be covered, a firm will scrap even a relatively new plant (embodying an old technology) in favor of a plant with a new technology.

New technology allows firms to produce at a lower cost. As a result, as firms adopt a new technology, their cost curves shift downward. With lower costs, firms are willing to supply a given quantity at a lower price or, equivalently, they are willing to supply a larger quantity at a given price. In other words, industry supply increases, and the industry supply curve shifts rightward. With a given demand, the quantity produced increases and the price falls.

Two forces are at work in an industry undergoing technological change. Firms that adopt the new technology make an economic profit. So there is entry by new-technology firms. Firms that stick with the old technology incur economic losses. They either exit the industry or switch to the new technology.

As old-technology firms disappear and new-technology firms enter, the price falls and the quantity produced increases. Eventually, the industry arrives at a long-run equilibrium in which all the firms use the new technology and make a zero economic profit. Because in the long run competition eliminates economic profit, technological change brings only temporary gains to producers. But the lower prices and better products that technological advances bring are permanent gains for consumers.

The process that we've just described is one in which some firms experience economic profits and others experience economic losses. It is a period of dynamic change for an industry. Some firms do well, and others do badly. Often, the process has a geographical dimension—the expanding new technology firms bring prosperity to what was once the boondocks, and traditional industrial regions decline. Sometimes, the new-technology firms are in a foreign country, while the old-technology firms are in the domestic economy. The information revolution of the 1990s produced many examples of changes like these. Commercial banking, which was traditionally concentrated in New York, San Francisco, and other large cities now flourishes in Charlotte, North Carolina, which has become the nation's number three commercial banking city. Television shows and movies, traditionally made in Los Angeles and New York, are now made in large numbers in Orlando.

Technological advances are not confined to the information and entertainment industries. Even food production is undergoing a major technological change because of genetic engineering.

We've seen how a competitive industry operates in the short run and the long run. But is a competitive industry efficient?

COMPETITION AND EFFICIENCY　　　　6

A competitive industry can achieve an efficient use of resources. In the reading on efficiency and equity, using only the concepts of demand, supply, consumer surplus, and producer surplus, you saw how a competitive market achieves efficiency. Now that you have learned what lies behind the demand and supply curves of a competitive market, you can gain a deeper understanding of the efficiency of a competitive market.

Efficient Use of Resources

Recall that resource use is efficient when we produce the goods and services that people value most highly (see the reading on efficiency and equity). If someone can become better off without anyone else becoming worse off, resources are *not* being used efficiently. For example, suppose we produce a computer that no one wants and no one will ever use and, at the same time, some people are clamoring for more video games. If we produce one less computer and reallocate the unused resources to produce more video games, some people will become better off and no one will be worse off. So the initial resource allocation was inefficient.

In the more technical language that you have learned, resource use is efficient when marginal social benefit equals marginal social cost. In the computer and video games example, the marginal social benefit of a video game exceeds its marginal social cost. And the marginal social cost of a computer exceeds its marginal social benefit. So by producing fewer computers and more video games, we move resources toward a higher-valued use.

Choices, Equilibrium, and Efficiency

We can use what you have learned about the decisions made by consumers and competitive firms and market equilibrium to describe an efficient use of resources.

Choices

Consumers allocate their budgets to get the most value possible out of them. And we derive a consumer's demand curve by finding how the best budget allocation changes as the price of a good changes. So consumers get the most value out of their resources at all points along their demand curves. If the people who consume a good or service are the only ones who benefit from it, there are no external benefits and the market demand curve is the marginal social benefit curve.

Competitive firms produce the quantity that maximizes profit. And we derive the firm's supply curve by finding the profit-maximizing quantity at each price. So firms get the most value out of their resources at all points along their supply curves. If the firms that produce a good or service bear all the costs of producing it, there are no external costs and the market supply curve is the marginal social cost curve.

Equilibrium and Efficiency

Resources are used efficiently when marginal social benefit equals marginal social cost. And competitive equilibrium achieves this efficient outcome because for consumers, price equals marginal social benefit and for producers, price equals marginal social cost.

The gains from trade are the consumer surplus plus the producer surplus. The gains from trade for consumers are measured by *consumer surplus*, which is the area below the demand curve and above the price paid. (See the reading on efficiency and equity.) The gains from trade for producers are measured by *producer surplus*, which is the area above the supply curve and below the price received. (See again the reading on efficiency and equity.) The total gains from trade are the sum of consumer surplus and producer surplus. When the market for a good or service is in equilibrium, the gains from trade are maximized.

Illustrating an Efficient Allocation

Figure 12 illustrates an efficient allocation in perfect competition in long-run equilibrium. Part (a) shows the situation of an individual firm, and part (b) shows the market. The equilibrium market price is P^*. At that price, each firm makes zero economic profit. Each firm has a plant size that enables it to produce at the lowest possible average total cost. In this situation, consumers are as well off as possible because the good cannot be produced at a lower cost and the price equals that least possible cost.

In part (b), consumers are efficient at all points on the market demand curve, $D = MSB$. Producers are efficient at all points on the market supply curve, $S = MSC$. Resources are used efficiently at the quantity Q^* and price P^*. At this point, marginal social benefit equals marginal social cost, and the sum of producer surplus (blue area) and consumer surplus (gray area) is maximized.

When firms in perfect competition are away from long-run equilibrium, either entry or exit is taking place and the market is moving toward the situation

FIGURE 12   Efficiency of Perfect Competition

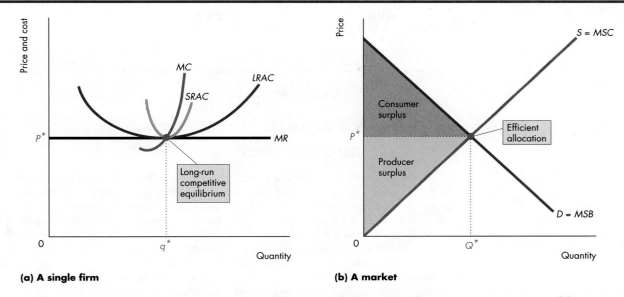

(a) A single firm

(b) A market

In part (a), a firm in perfect competition produces at the lowest possible long-run average total cost at q^*. In part (b), consumers have made the best available choices and are on the market demand curve and firms are producing at least cost and are on the market supply curve. With no external benefits or external costs, resources are used efficiently at the quantity Q^* and the price P^*. Perfect competition achieves an efficient use of resources.

depicted in Figure 12. But the market is still efficient. As long as marginal social benefit (on the market demand curve) equals marginal social cost (on the market supply curve), the market is efficient. But it is only in long-run equilibrium that consumers pay the lowest possible price.

You've now completed your study of perfect competition. And *Reading Between the Lines* gives you an opportunity to use what you have learned to understand recent events in the competitive market for the pollination services of bees.

Although many markets approximate the model of perfect competition, many do not. In the reading on monopoly, we study markets at the opposite extreme of market power: monopoly. Then, in the reading on monopolistic competition and oligopoly, we'll study markets that lie between perfect competition and monopoly: monopolistic competition (competition with monopoly elements) and oligopoly (competition among a few producers). When you have completed this study, you'll have a tool kit that will enable you to understand the variety of real-world markets.

7   READING BETWEEN THE LINES

Competition in the Orchard

THE NEW YORK TIMES, MAY 2, 2005

A Parasite Devastates Bees, and Farmers Are Worried

"Do you want to see a ghost town?" Joe Linelho asked. He pulled the lid off one of his beehives and worked one of the honey frames loose with a small blade. Not a bee responded to the intrusion. The hundreds of little hexagonal cells, where young bees should be incubating, were empty, and at the center hung a cluster of bees, all dead. . . .

"This is a national problem," said Kevin Hackett, national program leader for bees and pollination at the Agriculture Department's Research Service. "We've lost at least half of our hives, and 70 percent in some areas. With a couple of million hives in the U.S., and you reduce that population by half, that's very serious."

The problem is not just about honey. Bees are needed to pollinate $15 billion worth of agricultural prod-

ucts a year. Growers report increasing competition, and rising prices, for the hives that are moved around the country in the spring, from the almonds in California in February to the apples, blueberries and other fruits elsewhere later in the season. . . .

. . . most of the losses are being attributed to the Varroa mite, which came into the country in the early 1980s, Mr. Raybold said, and began by devastating the country's wild honeybee population. . . .

Fruit growers usually pay $30 to $40 to have a hive placed among their plants in the spring, with the hive's owner keeping the honey. But Chris Heintz, director of research for the Almond Board of California, said she had heard reports of growers paying more than $100 per hive. . . .

Essence of the Story

▶ The Varroa mite, which has been in the United States since the early 1980s, has devastated the honeybee population.

▶ The number of active beehives has decreased by 50 percent and in some areas by 70 percent.

▶ Both honey production and pollination have decreased.

▶ Fruit growers usually pay $30 to $40 per hive with the hive's owner keeping the honey in return for pollination services.

▶ The price per hive has increased to more than $100.

Economic Analysis

► Beekeepers produce two goods: honey and pollination services.

► Here, we focus on the competitive market for pollination services.

► Orchard farmers rent hives of bees from beekeepers and pay a fee for the service.

► Figure 13 shows the market for pollination services.

► The demand curve D is the demand by orchard farmers.

► The supply curve S_0 is the supply by beekeepers before the Varroa mite devastated the honeybee population.

► The market was in equilibrium at a price of $40 per hive and a quantity Q_0.

► Figure 14 shows the cost and revenue curves for an individual beekeeper.

FIGURE 13   The Market for Pollination Services

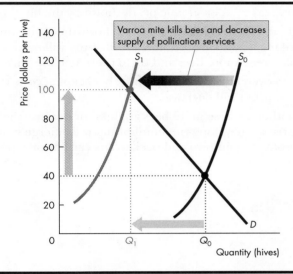

FIGURE 14   One Beekeeper

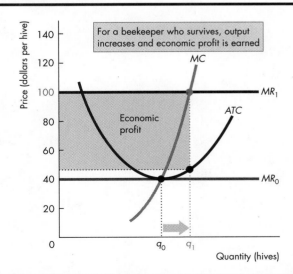

► Before the mite attack, the marginal revenue curve is MR_0, the marginal cost curve is MC, and the average total cost curve is ATC.

► The beekeeper maximizes profit by producing q_0 and the firm is assumed to be in long-run equilibrium.

► As the Varroa mite attacks, many beekeepers lose their honeybees and go out of business.

► Supply decreases, and in Fig. 13, the supply curve shifts leftward to S_1.

► The price for renting a hive rises to $100 and the equilibrium quantity decreases to Q_1.

► Figure 14 shows what happens to a beekeeper who remains in business and escapes the Varroa mite.

► The rise in price shifts the marginal revenue curve upward to MR_1.

► To maximize profit, the beekeeper increases the number of hives rented to orchard farmers to q_1.

► The firm now makes an economic profit shown by the blue rectangle.

► The situation shown in Fig. 13 and 14 is a short-run equilibrium. Because firms are making a positive economic profit, entry will occur in the long run as people breed more bees and try to overcome the Varroa mite.

► If it is costly to overcome the Varroa mite, beekeeping costs will increase and economic profit will decrease.

► Eventually, either because more bees are bred or because the cost of beekeeping rises, a new long-run equilibrium will emerge in which economic profit is again zero and beekeepers earn normal profit.

SUMMARY

- ▶ A perfectly competitive firm is a price taker.
- ▶ The firm produces the output at which marginal revenue (price) equals marginal cost.
- ▶ In short-run equilibrium, a firm can make an economic profit, incur an economic loss, or break even.
- ▶ If price is less than minimum average variable cost, the firm temporarily shuts down.
- ▶ A firm's supply curve is the upward-sloping part of its marginal cost curve above minimum average variable cost.
- ▶ An industry supply curve shows the sum of the quantities supplied by each firm at each price.
- ▶ Market demand and market supply determine price.
- ▶ Persistent economic profit induces entry. Persistent economic loss induces exit.
- ▶ Entry and plant expansion increase supply and lower price and profit. Exit and downsizing decrease supply and raise price and profit.
- ▶ In long-run equilibrium, economic profit is zero (the entrepreneur makes normal profit). There is no entry, exit, plant expansion, or downsizing.
- ▶ A permanent decrease in demand leads to a smaller industry output and a smaller number of firms.
- ▶ A permanent increase in demand leads to a larger industry output and a larger number of firms.
- ▶ The long-run effect of a change in demand on price depends on whether there are external economies (the price falls) or external diseconomies (the price rises) or neither (the price remains constant).
- ▶ New technologies increase supply and in the long run lower the price and increase the quantity.
- ▶ Resources are used efficiently when we produce goods and services in the quantities that people value most highly.
- ▶ When there are no external benefits and external costs, perfect competition achieves an efficient allocation. In long-run equilibrium, consumers pay the lowest possible price, marginal social benefit equals marginal social cost, and the sum of consumer surplus and producer surplus is maximized.

PRACTICE PROBLEMS FOR READING 18

1. Which of the following *best* describes the elasticity of demand in a perfectly competitive market?
   A. The firm elasticity is zero and the market elasticity is infinite.
   B. The firm elasticity is infinite and the market elasticity is zero.
   C. The firm elasticity is infinite and the market elasticity is some finite number.

2. In a perfectly competitive market that is operating with economic loss, what is the effect on the quantity supplied when firms exit the industry?
   A. The output of the industry and the output of the remaining firms both decline.
   B. The output of the industry declines, but the output of the remaining firms increases.
   C. The output of the industry increases, but the output of the remaining firms declines.

3. Which of the following is *least likely* a characteristic of perfect competition?
   A. A large number of buyers and sellers.
   B. Firms produce differentiated products.
   C. Ease of entry into and exit from the market.

4. In a perfectly competitive market, the individual firm's demand curve is *most likely*:
   A. vertical.
   B. horizontal.
   C. upward sloping.

SOLUTIONS FOR READING 18

1. C is correct. Infinite elasticity reflects perfect elasticity of demand. This characterizes the elasticity of demand for the products of a firm operating in a perfectly competitive market. If the firm increases prices, customers will go to another firm. However, the market demand is not perfectly elastic as it depends on substitutability with other products. Market elasticity will be greater than zero but less than infinite.

2. B is correct. As firms leave the industry, industry output declines, which raises the unit price and the profit-maximizing output for the remaining firms.

3. B is correct. In perfect competition, firms produce identical products.

4. B is correct. In perfect competition, the individual firm faces a horizontal demand curve, i.e., the individual firm's output has no effect on market price. Each firm is a price taker.

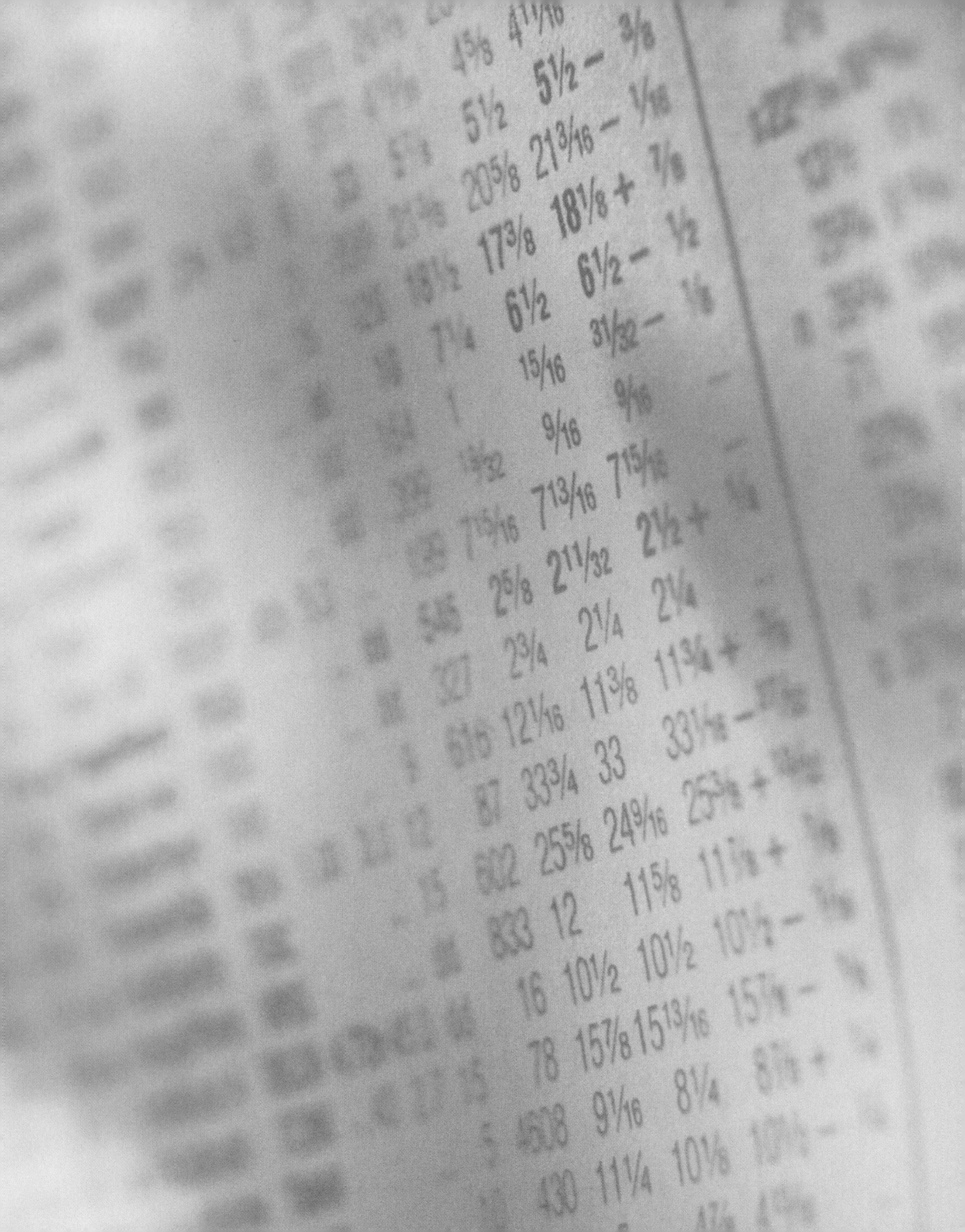

MONOPOLY
by Michael Parkin

LEARNING OUTCOMES

The candidate should be able to:

		Mastery
a.	describe the characteristics of a monopoly, including factors that allow a monopoly to arise, and monopoly price-setting strategies;	☐
b.	explain the relation between price, marginal revenue, and elasticity for a monopoly, and determine a monopoly's profit-maximizing price and quantity;	☐
c.	explain price discrimination and why perfect price discrimination is efficient;	☐
d.	explain how consumer and producer surplus are redistributed in a monopoly, including the occurrence of deadweight loss and rent seeking;	☐
e.	explain the potential gains from monopoly and the regulation of a natural monopoly.	☐

DOMINATING THE INTERNET 1

eBay and Google are dominant players in the markets they serve. Because most buyers use eBay, most sellers do too. And because most sellers use eBay, so do most buyers. This phenomenon, called a network externality, makes it hard for any other firm to break into the internet auction business. Because Google is such a good search engine, most people use it to find what they're seeking on the internet. And because most people use it, most website operators who want hits advertise with Google.

eBay and Google are obviously not like firms in perfect competition. They don't face a market-determined price. They can choose their own prices. How do firms like these choose the quantity to produce and the price at which to sell it?

How does their behavior compare with that of firms in perfectly competitive industries? Do they charge prices that are too high and that damage the interests of consumers? What benefits do they bring?

As a student, you get lots of discounts: when you get your hair cut, go to a museum, or go to a movie. When you take a trip by air, you almost never pay the full fare. Instead, you buy a discounted ticket. Are the people who operate barbershops, museums, movie theaters, and airlines simply generous folks who don't maximize profit? Aren't they throwing profit away by offering discounts?

In this reading, we study markets in which the firm can influence the price. We also compare the performance of the firm in such a market with that in a competitive market and examine whether monopoly is as efficient as competition. In *Reading Between the Lines* at the end of the reading, we'll take a look at what's been happening to airfares as low-cost airlines have put a squeeze on the traditional airlines.

2   MARKET POWER

Market power and competition are the two forces that operate in most markets. **Market power** is the ability to influence the market, and in particular the market price, by influencing the total quantity offered for sale.

The firms in perfect competition that you studied in the reading on perfect competition have no market power. They face the force of raw competition and are price takers. The firms that we study in this reading operate at the opposite extreme. They face no competition and exercise raw market power. We call this extreme monopoly. A **monopoly** is a firm that produces a good or service for which no close substitute exists and that is protected by a barrier that prevents other firms from selling that good or service. In monopoly, the firm is the industry.

Examples of monopoly include the firms that operate the pipelines and cables that bring gas, water, and electricity to your home. Microsoft Corporation, the software firm that created the Windows operating system, is close to being a monopoly.

How Monopoly Arises

Monopoly has two key features:

▶ No close substitutes
▶ Barriers to entry

No Close Substitutes

If a good has a close substitute, even though only one firm produces it, that firm effectively faces competition from the producers of substitutes. Water supplied by a local public utility is an example of a good that does not have close substitutes. While it does have a close substitute for drinking—bottled spring water—it has no effective substitutes for showering or washing a car.

Monopolies are constantly under attack from new products and ideas that substitute for products produced by monopolies. For example, FedEx, UPS, the fax machine, and e-mail have weakened the monopoly of the U.S. Postal Service. Similarly, the satellite dish has weakened the monopoly of cable television companies.

But new products also are constantly creating monopolies. An example is Microsoft's monopoly in the DOS operating system during the 1980s and in the Windows operating system today.

Barriers to Entry

Legal or natural constraints that protect a firm from potential competitors are called **barriers to entry**. A firm can sometimes create its own barrier to entry by acquiring a significant portion of a key resource. For example, De Beers controls more than 80 percent of the world's supply of natural diamonds. But most monopolies arise from two other types of barrier: legal barriers and natural barriers.

Legal Barriers to Entry   Legal barriers to entry create legal monopoly. A **legal monopoly** is a market in which competition and entry are restricted by the granting of a public franchise, government license, patent, or copyright.

A *public franchise* is an exclusive right granted to a firm to supply a good or service. Examples are the U.S. Postal Service, which has the exclusive right to carry first-class mail. A *government license* controls entry into particular occupations, professions, and industries. Examples of this type of barrier to entry occur in medicine, law, dentistry, schoolteaching, architecture, and many other professional services. Licensing does not always create a monopoly, but it does restrict competition.

A *patent* is an exclusive right granted to the inventor of a product or service. A *copyright* is an exclusive right granted to the author or composer of a literary, musical, dramatic, or artistic work. Patents and copyrights are valid for a limited time period that varies from country to country. In the United States, a patent is valid for 20 years. Patents encourage the *invention* of new products and production methods. They also stimulate *innovation*—the use of new inventions—by encouraging inventors to publicize their discoveries and offer them for use under license. Patents have stimulated innovations in areas as diverse as soybean seeds, pharmaceuticals, memory chips, and video games.

Natural Barriers to Entry   Natural barriers to entry create a **natural monopoly**: an industry in which economies of scale enable one firm to supply the entire market at the lowest possible cost.

Figure 1 shows a natural monopoly in the distribution of electric power. Here, the market demand curve for electric power is *D*, and the long-run average cost curve is *LRAC*. Because long-run average cost decreases as output increases, economies of scale prevail over the entire length of the *LRAC* curve. One firm can produce 4 million kilowatt-hours at 5 cents a kilowatt-hour. At this price, the quantity demanded is 4 million kilowatt-hours. So if the price was 5 cents, one firm could supply the entire market. If two firms shared the market equally, it would cost each of them 10 cents a kilowatt-hour to produce a total of 4 million kilowatt-hours. If four firms shared the market equally, it would cost each of them 15 cents a kilowatt-hour to produce a total of 4 million kilowatt-hours. So in conditions like those shown in Fig. 1, one firm can supply the entire market at a lower cost than two or more firms can. The distribution of electric power is an example of natural monopoly.

Most monopolies are regulated in some way by government agencies. We will study such regulation at the end of this reading. But for two reasons, we'll begin by studying unregulated monopoly. First, we can better understand why

FIGURE 1   Natural Monopoly

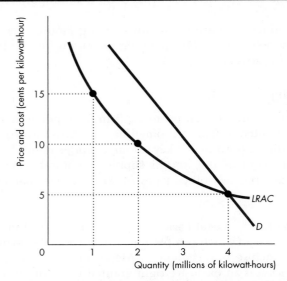

The market demand curve for electric power is *D*, and the long-run average cost curve is *LRAC*. Economies of scale exist over the entire *LRAC* curve. One firm can distribute 4 million kilowatt-hours at a cost of 5 cents a kilowatt-hour. This same total output costs 10 cents a kilowatt-hour with two firms and 15 cents a kilowatt-hour with four firms. So one firm can meet the market demand at a lower cost than two or more firms can, and the market is a natural monopoly.

governments regulate monopolies and the effects of regulation if we also know how an unregulated monopoly behaves. Second, even in industries with more than one producer, firms often have a degree of monopoly power, and the theory of monopoly sheds light on the behavior of such firms and industries.

A major difference between monopoly and competition is that a monopoly sets its own price. But in doing so, it faces a market constraint. Let's see how the market limits a monopoly's pricing choices.

Monopoly Price-Setting Strategies

All monopolies face a tradeoff between price and the quantity sold. To sell a larger quantity, the monopoly must charge a lower price. But there are two broad monopoly situations that create different tradeoffs. They are

► Single price
► Price discrimination

Single Price

De Beers sells diamonds (of a given size and quality) for the same price to all its customers. If it tried to sell at a low price to some customers and at a higher price to others, only the low-price customers would buy from De Beers. Others would buy from De Beers' low-price customers. De Beers is a *single-price* monopoly. A **single-price monopoly** is a firm that must sell each unit of its output for the same price to all its customers.

Price Discrimination

Airlines offer a dizzying array of different prices for the same trip. Pizza producers charge one price for a single pizza and almost give away a second pizza. These are examples of *price discrimination*. **Price discrimination** is the practice of selling different units of a good or service for different prices.

When a firm price discriminates, it looks as though it is doing its customers a favor. In fact, it is charging the highest possible price for each unit sold and making the largest possible profit.

A SINGLE-PRICE MONOPOLY'S OUTPUT AND PRICE DECISION

3

To understand how a single-price monopoly makes its output and price decision, we must first study the link between price and marginal revenue.

Price and Marginal Revenue

Because in a monopoly there is only one firm, the demand curve facing the firm is the market demand curve. Let's look at Bobbie's Barbershop, the sole supplier of haircuts in Cairo, Nebraska. The table in Fig. 2 shows the market demand schedule. At a price of $20, she sells no haircuts. The lower the price, the more

FIGURE 2 Demand and Marginal Revenue

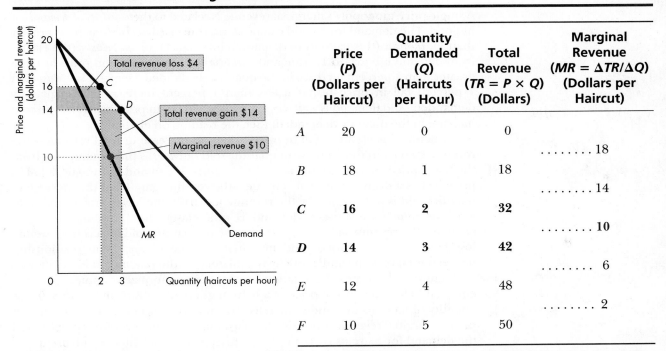

	Price (P) (Dollars per Haircut)	Quantity Demanded (Q) (Haircuts per Hour)	Total Revenue (TR = P × Q) (Dollars)	Marginal Revenue (MR = ΔTR/ΔQ) (Dollars per Haircut)
A	20	0	0	
				 18
B	18	1	18	
				 14
C	**16**	**2**	**32**	
				 10
D	**14**	**3**	**42**	
				 6
E	12	4	48	
				 2
F	10	5	50	

The table shows the demand schedule. Total revenue (*TR*) is price multiplied by quantity sold. For example, in row *C*, the price is $16 a haircut, Bobbie sells 2 haircuts, and total revenue is $32. Marginal revenue (*MR*) is the change in total revenue that results from a one-unit increase in the quantity sold. For example, when the price falls from $16 to $14 a haircut, the quantity sold increases by 1 haircut and total revenue increases by $10. Marginal revenue is $10. The demand curve and the marginal revenue curve, *MR*, are based on the numbers in the table and illustrate the calculation of marginal revenue when the price falls from $16 to $14 a haircut.

haircuts per hour Bobbie can sell. For example, at $12, consumers demand 4 haircuts per hour (row E).

Total revenue (*TR*) is the price (*P*) multiplied by the quantity sold (*Q*). For example, in row D, Bobbie sells 3 haircuts at $14 each, so total revenue is $42. *Marginal revenue* (*MR*) is the change in total revenue (ΔTR) resulting from a one-unit increase in the quantity sold. For example, if the price falls from $16 (row C) to $14 (row D), the quantity sold increases from 2 to 3 haircuts. Total revenue rises from $32 to $42, so the change in total revenue is $10. Because the quantity sold increases by 1 haircut, marginal revenue equals the change in total revenue and is $10. Marginal revenue is placed between the two rows to emphasize that marginal revenue relates to the *change* in the quantity sold.

Figure 2 shows the market demand curve and marginal revenue curve (*MR*) and also illustrates the calculation we've just made. Notice that at each level of output, marginal revenue is less than price—the marginal revenue curve lies below the demand curve. Why is marginal revenue *less* than price? It is because when the price is lowered to sell one more unit, two opposing forces affect total revenue. The lower price results in a revenue loss, and the increased quantity sold results in a revenue gain. For example, at a price of $16, Bobbie sells 2 haircuts (point C). If she lowers the price to $14, she sells 3 haircuts and has a revenue gain of $14 on the third haircut. But she now receives only $14 on the first two—$2 less than before. As a result, she loses $4 of revenue on the first 2 haircuts. To calculate marginal revenue, she must deduct this amount from the revenue gain of $14. So her marginal revenue is $10, which is less than the price.

Marginal Revenue and Elasticity

A single-price monopoly's marginal revenue is related to the *elasticity of demand* for its good. The demand for a good can be *elastic* (the elasticity of demand is greater than 1), *inelastic* (the elasticity of demand is less than 1), or *unit elastic* (the elasticity of demand is equal to 1). Demand is *elastic* if a 1 percent fall in price brings a greater than 1 percent increase in the quantity demanded. Demand is *inelastic* if a 1 percent fall in price brings a less than 1 percent increase in the quantity demanded. And demand is *unit elastic* if a 1 percent fall in price brings a 1 percent increase in the quantity demanded. (See the reading on elasticity.)

If demand is elastic, a fall in price brings an increase in total revenue—the revenue gain from the increase in quantity sold outweighs the revenue loss from the lower price—and marginal revenue is *positive*. If demand is inelastic, a fall in price brings a decrease in total revenue—the revenue gain from the increase in quantity sold is outweighed by the revenue loss from the lower price—and marginal revenue is *negative*. If demand is unit elastic, total revenue does not change—the revenue gain from the increase in quantity sold offsets the revenue loss from the lower price—and marginal revenue is *zero*. (The relationship between total revenue and elasticity is explained in the reading on elasticity.)

Figure 3 illustrates the relationship between marginal revenue, total revenue, and elasticity. As the price of a haircut gradually falls from $20 to $10, the quantity of haircuts demanded increases from 0 to 5 an hour. Over this output range, marginal revenue is positive (part a), total revenue increases (part b), and the demand for haircuts is elastic. As the price falls from $10 to $0 a haircut, the quantity of haircuts demanded increases from 5 to 10 an hour. Over this output range, marginal revenue is negative (part a), total revenue decreases (part b), and the demand for haircuts is inelastic. When the price is $10 a haircut, marginal revenue is zero (part a), total revenue is a maximum (part b), and the demand for haircuts is unit elastic.

FIGURE 3   Marginal Revenue and Elasticity

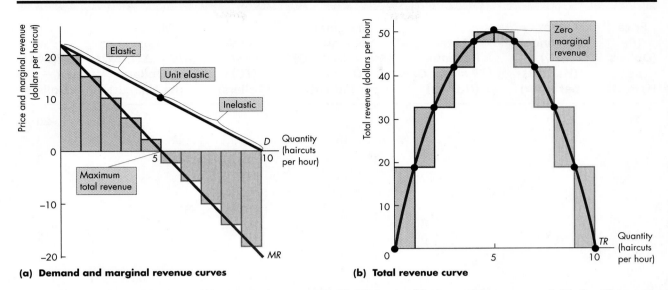

(a) Demand and marginal revenue curves

(b) Total revenue curve

In part (a), the demand curve is *D* and the marginal revenue curve is *MR*. In part (b), the total revenue curve is *TR*. Over the range from 0 to 5 haircuts an hour, a price cut increases total revenue, so marginal revenue is positive—as shown by the blue bars. Demand is elastic. Over the range from 5 to 10 haircuts an hour, a price cut decreases total revenue, so marginal revenue is negative—as shown by the gray bars. Demand is inelastic. At 5 haircuts an hour, total revenue is maximized and marginal revenue is zero. Demand is unit elastic.

In Monopoly, Demand Is Always Elastic

The relationship between marginal revenue and elasticity of demand that you've just discovered implies that a profit-maximizing monopoly never produces an output in the inelastic range of the market demand curve. If it did so, it could charge a higher price, produce a smaller quantity, and increase its profit. Let's now look at a monopoly's price and output decision.

Price and Output Decision

A monopoly sets its price and output at the levels that maximize economic profit. To determine this price and output level, we need to study the behavior of both cost and revenue as output varies. A monopoly faces the same types of technology and cost constraints as a competitive firm. So its costs (total cost, average cost, and marginal cost) behave just like those of a firm in perfect competition. And its revenues (total revenue, price, and marginal revenue) behave in the way we've just described.

Table 1 provides information about Bobbie's costs, revenues, and economic profit and Figure 4 shows the same information graphically.

Maximizing Economic Profit

You can see in Table 1 and Fig. 4(a) that total cost (*TC*) and total revenue (*TR*) both rise as output increases, but *TC* rises at an increasing rate and *TR* rises at a decreasing rate. Economic profit, which equals *TR* minus *TC*, increases at small output levels, reaches a maximum, and then decreases. The maximum profit ($12) occurs when Bobbie sells 3 haircuts for $14 each. If she sells 2 haircuts for $16 each or 4 haircuts for $12 each, her economic profit will be only $8.

TABLE 1 A Monopoly's Output and Price Decision

Price (P) (Dollars per Haircut)	Quantity Demanded (Q) (Haircuts per Hour)	Total Revenue (TR = P × Q) (Dollars)	Marginal Revenue (MR = ΔTR/ΔQ) (Dollars per Haircut)	Total Cost (TC) (Dollars)	Marginal Cost (MC = ΔTC/ΔQ) (Dollars per Haircut)	Profit (TR − TC) (Dollars)
20	0	0		20		−20
			18		1	
18	1	18		21		−3
			14		3	
16	2	32		24		+8
			10		6	
14	3	42		30		+12
			6		10	
12	4	48		40		+8
			2		15	
10	5	50		55		−5

This table gives the information needed to find the profit-maximizing output and price. Total revenue (TR) equals price multiplied by the quantity sold. Profit equals total revenue minus total cost (TC). Profit is maximized when 3 haircuts are sold at a price of $14 each. Total revenue is $42, total cost is $30, and economic profit is $12 ($42 − $30).

Marginal Revenue Equals Marginal Cost

You can see in Table 1 and Fig. 4(b) Bobbie's marginal revenue (MR) and marginal cost (MC).

When Bobbie increases output from 2 to 3 haircuts, MR is $10 and MC is $6. MR exceeds MC by $4 and Bobbie's profit increases by that amount. If Bobbie increases output yet further, from 3 to 4 haircuts, MR is $6 and MC is $10. In this case, MC exceeds MR by $4, so profit decreases by that amount. When MR exceeds MC, profit increases if output increases. When MC exceeds MR, profit increases if output *decreases*. When MC equals MR, profit is maximized.

Figure 4(b) shows the maximum profit as price (on the demand curve D) minus average total cost (on the ATC curve) multiplied by the quantity produced—the blue rectangle.

Maximum Price the Market Will Bear

Unlike a firm in perfect competition, a monopoly influences the price of what it sells. But a monopoly doesn't set the price at the maximum *possible* price. At the maximum possible price, the firm would be able to sell only one unit of output, which in general is less than the profit-maximizing quantity. Rather, a monopoly produces the profit-maximizing quantity and sells that quantity for the highest price it can get.

All firms maximize profit by producing the output at which marginal revenue equals marginal cost. For a competitive firm, price equals marginal revenue, so price also equals marginal cost. For a monopoly, price exceeds marginal revenue, so price also exceeds marginal cost.

FIGURE 4   A Monopoly's Output and Price

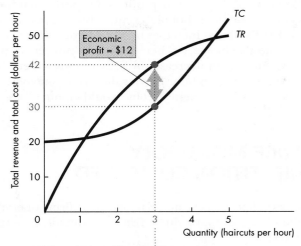

(a) Total revenue and total cost curves

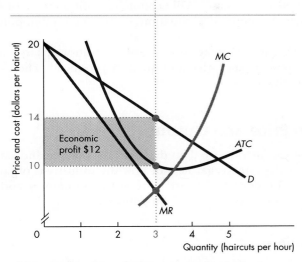

(b) Demand and marginal revenue and cost curves

In part (a), economic profit is the vertical distance equal to total revenue (*TR*) minus total cost (*TC*) and it is maximized at 3 haircuts an hour. In part (b), economic profit is maximized when marginal cost (*MC*) equals marginal revenue (*MR*). The profit-maximizing output is 3 haircuts an hour. The price is determined by the demand curve (*D*) and is $14 a haircut. The average total cost of a haircut is $10, so economic profit, the blue rectangle, is $12—the profit per haircut ($4) multiplied by 3 haircuts.

A monopoly charges a price that exceeds marginal cost, but does it always make an economic profit? In Fig. 4(b), Bobbie produces 3 haircuts an hour. Her average total cost is $10 (on the *ATC* curve) and her price is $14 (on the *D* curve), so her profit per haircut is $4 ($14 minus $10). Bobbie's economic profit is shown by the blue rectangle, which equals the profit per haircut ($4) multiplied by the number of haircuts (3), for a total of $12.

If firms in a perfectly competitive industry make a positive economic profit, new firms enter. That does *not* happen in monopoly. Barriers to entry prevent new firms from entering an industry which is a monopoly. So a monopoly can make a positive economic profit and might continue to do so indefinitely. Sometimes that profit is large, as in the international diamond business.

Bobbie makes a positive economic profit. But suppose that the owner of the shop that Bobbie rents increases Bobbie's rent. If Bobbie pays an additional $12 an hour for rent, her fixed cost increases by $12 an hour. Her marginal cost and marginal revenue don't change, so her profit-maximizing output remains at 3 haircuts an hour. Her profit decreases by $12 an hour to zero. If Bobbie pays more than an additional $12 an hour for her shop rent, she incurs an economic loss. If this situation were permanent, Bobbie would go out of business.

4   SINGLE-PRICE MONOPOLY AND COMPETITION COMPARED

Imagine an industry that is made up of many small firms operating in perfect competition. Then imagine that a single firm buys out all these small firms and creates a monopoly.

What will happen in this industry? Will the price rise or fall? Will the quantity produced increase or decrease? Will economic profit increase or decrease? Will either the original competitive situation or the new monopoly situation be efficient?

These are the questions we're now going to answer. First, we look at the effects of monopoly on the price and quantity produced. Then we turn to the questions about efficiency.

Comparing Price and Output

Figure 5 shows the market we'll study. The market demand curve is *D*. The demand curve is the same regardless of how the industry is organized. But the supply side and the equilibrium are different in monopoly and competition. First, let's look at the case of perfect competition.

Perfect Competition

Initially, with many small perfectly competitive firms in the market, the market supply curve is *S*. This supply curve is obtained by summing the supply curves of all the individual firms in the market.

In perfect competition, equilibrium occurs where the supply curve and the demand curve intersect. The price is P_C, and the quantity produced by the industry is Q_C. Each firm takes the price P_C and maximizes its profit by producing the output at which its own marginal cost equals the price. Because each firm is a small part of the total industry, there is no incentive for any firm to try to manipulate the price by varying its output.

Monopoly

Now suppose that this industry is taken over by a single firm. Consumers do not change, so the market demand curve remains the same as in the case of perfect competition. But now the monopoly recognizes this demand curve as a constraint on the price at which it can sell its output. The monopoly's marginal revenue curve is *MR*.

FIGURE 5   Monopoly's Smaller Output and Higher Price

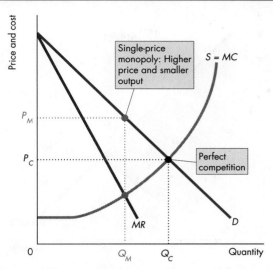

A competitive industry produces the quantity Q_C at price P_C. A single-price monopoly produces the quantity Q_M at which marginal revenue equals marginal cost and sells that quantity for the price P_M. Compared to perfect competition, a single-price monopoly produces a smaller output and charges a higher price.

The monopoly maximizes profit by producing the quantity at which marginal revenue equals marginal cost. To find the monopoly's marginal cost curve, first recall that in perfect competition, the industry supply curve is the sum of the supply curves of the firms in the industry. Also recall that each firm's supply curve is its marginal cost curve (see the reading on perfect competition). So when the industry is taken over by a single firm, the competitive industry's supply curve becomes the monopoly's marginal cost curve. To remind you of this fact, the supply curve is also labeled *MC*.

The output at which marginal revenue equals marginal cost is Q_M. This output is smaller than the competitive output Q_C. And the monopoly charges the price P_M, which is higher than P_C. We have established that

> Compared to a perfectly competitive industry, a single-price monopoly produces a smaller output and charges a higher price.

We've seen how the output and price of a monopoly compare with those in a competitive industry. Let's now compare the efficiency of the two types of market.

Efficiency Comparison

You saw in the reading on perfect competition that perfect competition (with no external costs and benefits) is efficient. Figure 6(a) illustrates the efficiency of perfect competition and serves as a benchmark against which to measure the inefficiency of monopoly.

Along the demand curve and marginal social benefit curve ($D = MSB$), consumers are efficient. Along the supply curve and marginal social cost curve ($S = MSC$), producers are efficient. In competitive equilibrium, the price is P_C, the quantity is Q_C, and marginal social benefit equals marginal social cost.

FIGURE 6   Inefficiency of Monopoly

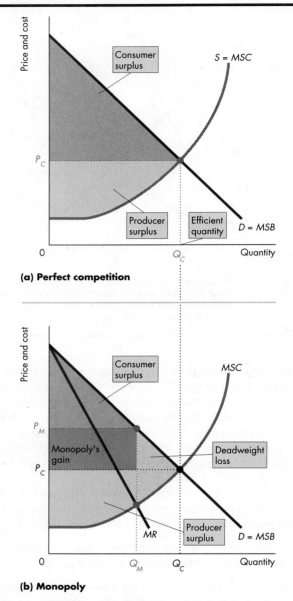

(a) Perfect competition

(b) Monopoly

In perfect competition (part a), output is Q_C and the price is P_C. Marginal social benefit (*MSB*) equals marginal social cost (*MSC*); consumer surplus (the dark gray triangle) plus producer surplus (the light blue area) is maximized; and in the long-run, firms produce at the lowest possible average cost. Monopoly (part b) restricts output to Q_M and raises the price to P_M. Consumer surplus shrinks, the monopoly gains, and a deadweight loss (the light gray triangle) arises.

Consumer surplus is the dark gray triangle under the demand curve and above the equilibrium price (see the reading on perfect competition). *Producer surplus* is the light blue area above the supply curve and below the equilibrium price (see the reading on perfect competition). The sum of the consumer surplus and producer surplus is maximized.

Also, in long-run competitive equilibrium, entry and exit ensure that each firm produces its output at the minimum possible long-run average cost.

To summarize: At the competitive equilibrium, marginal social benefit equals marginal social cost; the sum of consumer surplus and producer surplus is maximized; firms produce at the lowest possible long-run average cost; and resource use is efficient.

Figure 6(b) illustrates the inefficiency of monopoly and the sources of that inefficiency. A monopoly produces Q_M and sells its output for P_M. The smaller output and higher price drive a wedge between marginal social benefit and marginal social cost and create a *deadweight loss*. The light gray triangle shows the deadweight loss and its magnitude is a measure of the inefficiency of monopoly.

Consumer surplus shrinks for two reasons. First, consumers lose by having to pay more for the good. This loss to consumers is a gain for the producer and increases the producer surplus. Second, consumers lose by getting less of the good, and this loss is part of the deadweight loss.

Although the monopoly gains from a higher price, it loses some of the original producer surplus because of the smaller monopoly output. That loss is another part of the deadweight loss.

Because a monopoly restricts output below the level in perfect competition and faces no competitive threat, it does not produce at the minimum possible long-run average cost. As a result, monopoly damages the consumer interest in three ways: It produces less, it increases the cost of production, and it increases the price to above the increased cost of production.

Redistribution of Surpluses

You've seen that monopoly is inefficient because marginal social benefit exceeds marginal social cost and there is deadweight loss—a social loss. But monopoly also brings a *redistribution* of surpluses.

Some of the lost consumer surplus goes to the monopoly. In Fig. 6, the monopoly takes the difference between the higher price, P_M, and the competitive price, P_C, on the quantity sold, Q_M. So the monopoly takes the part of the consumer surplus shown by the darker blue rectangle. This portion of the loss of consumer surplus is not a loss to society. It is redistribution from consumers to the monopoly producer.

Rent Seeking

You've seen that monopoly creates a deadweight loss and is inefficient. But the social cost of monopoly can exceed the deadweight loss because of an activity called rent seeking. Any surplus—consumer surplus, producer surplus, or economic profit—is called **economic rent**. And **rent seeking** is the pursuit of wealth by capturing economic rent.

You've seen that a monopoly makes its economic profit by diverting part of consumer surplus to itself—by converting consumer surplus into economic profit. So the pursuit of economic profit by a monopoly is rent seeking. It is the attempt to capture consumer surplus.

Rent seekers pursue their goals in two main ways. They might

▶ Buy a monopoly
▶ Create a monopoly

Buy a Monopoly

To rent seek by buying a monopoly, a person searches for a monopoly that is for sale at a lower price than the monopoly's economic profit. Trading of taxicab licenses is an example of this type of rent seeking. In some cities, taxicabs are regulated. The city restricts both the fares and the number of taxis that can operate so that operating a taxi results in economic profit. A person who wants to operate a taxi must buy a license from someone who already has one. People rationally devote time and effort to seeking out profitable monopoly businesses to buy. In the process, they use up scarce resources that could otherwise have been used to produce goods and services. The value of this lost production is part of the social cost of monopoly. The amount paid for a monopoly is not a social cost because the payment is just a transfer of an existing producer surplus from the buyer to the seller.

Create a Monopoly

Rent seeking by creating monopoly is mainly a political activity. It takes the form of lobbying and trying to influence the political process. Such influence might be sought by making campaign contributions in exchange for legislative support or by indirectly seeking to influence political outcomes through publicity in the media or more direct contacts with politicians and bureaucrats. An example of a monopoly created in this way is the government-imposed restrictions on the quantities of textiles that may be imported into the United States. Another is a regulation that limits the number of oranges that may be sold in the United States. These are regulations that restrict output and increase price.

This type of rent seeking is a costly activity that uses up scarce resources. Taken together, firms spend billions of dollars lobbying Congress, state legislators, and local officials in the pursuit of licenses and laws that create barriers to entry and establish a monopoly. Everyone has an incentive to rent seek, and because there are no barriers to entry into rent seeking, there is a great deal of competition in this activity. The winners of the competition become monopolists.

Rent-Seeking Equilibrium

Barriers to entry create monopoly. But there is no barrier to entry into rent seeking. Rent seeking is like perfect competition. If an economic profit is available, a new rent seeker will try to get some of it. And competition among rent seekers pushes up the price that must be paid for a monopoly to the point at which the rent seeker makes zero economic profit by operating the monopoly. For example, competition for the right to operate a taxi in New York City leads to a price of more than $100,000 for a taxi license, which is sufficiently high to eliminate the economic profit made by taxi operators.

Figure 7 shows a rent-seeking equilibrium. The cost of rent seeking is a fixed cost that must be added to a monopoly's other costs. Rent seeking and rent-seeking costs increase to the point at which no economic profit is made. The average total cost curve, which includes the fixed cost of rent seeking, shifts upward until it just touches the demand curve. Economic profit is zero. It has been lost in rent seeking. Consumer surplus is unaffected. But the deadweight loss of monopoly now includes the original deadweight loss triangle plus the lost producer surplus, shown by the enlarged light gray area in the figure.

So far, we've considered only a single-price monopoly. But many monopolies do not operate with a single price. Instead, they price discriminate. Let's now see how price-discriminating monopoly works.

FIGURE 7   Rent-Seeking Equilibrium

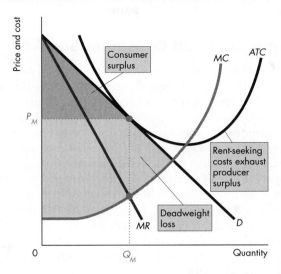

With competitive rent seeking, a monopoly uses all its economic profit to maintain its monopoly. The firm's rent-seeking costs are fixed costs. They add to total fixed cost and to average total cost. The *ATC* curve shifts upward until, at the profit-maximizing price, the firm breaks even.

PRICE DISCRIMINATION   5

Price discrimination—selling a good or service at a number of different prices—is widespread. You encounter it when you travel, go to the movies, get your hair cut, buy pizza, or visit an art museum. Most price discriminators are not monopolies, but monopolies price discriminate when they can do so.

To be able to price discriminate, a monopoly must

1. Identify and separate different buyer types.
2. Sell a product that cannot be resold.

Price discrimination is charging different prices for a single good or service because of differences in buyers' willingness to pay and not because of differences in production costs. So not all price *differences* are price *discrimination*. Some goods that are similar but not identical have different prices because they have different production costs. For example, the cost of producing electricity depends on time of day. If an electric power company charges a higher price during the peak consumption periods from 7:00 to 9:00 in the morning and from 4:00 to 7:00 in the evening than it does at other times of the day, the electric power company is not price discriminating.

At first sight, it appears that price discrimination contradicts the assumption of profit maximization. Why would a movie theater allow children to see movies at half price? Why would a hairdresser charge students and senior citizens less? Aren't these firms losing profit by being nice to their customers?

Deeper investigation shows that far from losing profit, firms that price discriminate make bigger profits than they would otherwise. So a monopoly has an incentive to find ways of discriminating and charging each buyer the highest possible price. Some people pay less with price discrimination, but others pay more.

Price Discrimination and Consumer Surplus

The key idea behind price discrimination is to convert consumer surplus into economic profit. Demand curves slope downward because the value that people place on any good decreases as the quantity of that good increases. When all the units of the good are sold for a single price, consumers benefit. The benefit is the value the consumers get from each unit of the good minus the price actually paid for it. This benefit is *consumer surplus*. Price discrimination is an attempt by a monopoly to capture as much of the consumer surplus as possible for itself.

To extract every dollar of consumer surplus from every buyer, the monopoly would have to offer each individual customer a separate price schedule based on that customer's own willingness to pay. Clearly, such price discrimination cannot be carried out in practice because a firm does not have enough information about each consumer's demand curve.

But firms try to extract as much consumer surplus as possible, and to do so, they discriminate in two broad ways:

▶ Among units of a good
▶ Among groups of buyers

Discriminating among Units of a Good

One method of price discrimination charges each buyer a different price on each unit of a good bought. A discount for bulk buying is an example of this type of discrimination. The larger the quantity bought, the larger is the discount— and the lower is the price. (Note that some discounts for bulk arise from lower costs of production for greater bulk. In these cases, such discounts are not price discrimination.)

Discriminating among Groups of Buyers

Price discrimination often takes the form of discriminating among different groups of consumers on the basis of age, employment status, or some other easily distinguished characteristic. This type of price discrimination works when each group has a different average willingness to pay for the good or service.

For example, a face-to-face sales meeting with a customer might bring a large and profitable order. For salespeople and other business travelers, the marginal benefit from a trip is large and the price that such a traveler will pay for a trip is high. In contrast, for a vacation traveler, any of several different trips and even no vacation trip are options. So for vacation travelers, the marginal benefit of a trip is small and the price that such a traveler will pay for a trip is low. Because business travelers are willing to pay more than vacation travelers are, it is possible for an airline to profit by price discriminating between these two groups. Similarly, because students have a lower willingness to pay for a haircut than do working people, it is possible for a hairdresser to profit by price discriminating between these two groups.

Let's see how an airline exploits the differences in demand by business and vacation travelers and increases its profit by price discriminating.

FIGURE 8   A Single Price of Air Travel

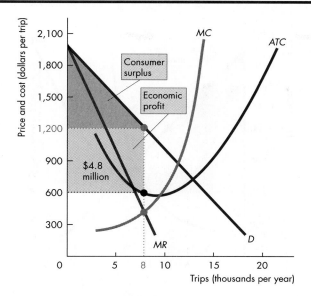

Global Airlines has a monopoly on an air route. The market demand curve is *D*. Global Airline's marginal revenue curve is *MR*, marginal cost curve is *MC*, and its average total cost curve is *ATC*. As a single-price monopoly, Global maximizes profit by selling 8,000 trips a year at $1,200 a trip. Its profit is $4.8 million a year—the blue rectangle. Global's customers enjoy a consumer surplus—the gray triangle.

Profiting by Price Discriminating

Global Airlines has a monopoly on an exotic route. Figure 8 shows the market demand curve (*D*) for travel on this route. It also shows Global Airline's marginal revenue curve (*MR*), marginal cost curve (*MC*), and average total cost curve (*ATC*).

Initially, Global is a single-price monopoly and maximizes its profit by producing 8,000 trips a year (the quantity at which *MR* equals *MC*). The price is $1,200 per trip. The average total cost of producing a trip is $600, so economic profit is $600 a trip. On 8,000 trips, Global's economic profit is $4.8 million a year, shown by the blue rectangle. Global's customers enjoy a consumer surplus shown by the gray triangle.

Global is struck by the fact that many of its customers are business travelers, and it suspects they are willing to pay more than $1,200 a trip. So Global does some market research, which reveals that some business travelers are willing to pay as much as $1,800 a trip. Also, these customers frequently change their travel plans at the last moment. Another group of business travelers is willing to pay $1,600. These customers know a week ahead when they will travel, and they never want to stay over a weekend. Yet another group would pay up to $1,400. These travelers know two weeks ahead when they will travel and also don't want to stay away over a weekend.

So Global announces a new fare schedule. No restrictions, $1,800; 7-day advance purchase, nonrefundable, $1,600; 14-day advance purchase, nonrefundable, $1,400; 14-day advance purchase, must stay over a weekend, $1,200.

FIGURE 9   Price Discrimination

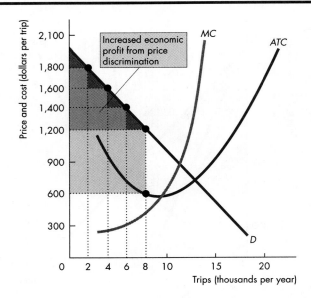

Global revises its fare structure: no restrictions at $1,800, 7-day advance purchase at $1,600, 14-day advance purchase at $1,400, and must stay over a weekend at $1,200. Global sells 2,000 trips at each of its four new fares. Its economic profit increases by $2.4 million a year to $7.2 million a year, which is shown by the original blue rectangle plus the dark blue steps. Global's customers' consumer surplus shrinks.

Figure 9 shows the outcome with this new fare structure and also shows why Global is pleased with its new fares. It sells 2,000 seats at each of its four prices. Global's economic profit increases by the dark blue steps. Its economic profit is now its original $4.8 million a year plus an additional $2.4 million from its new higher fares. Consumer surplus has shrunk to the sum of the smaller gray area.

Perfect Price Discrimination

Perfect price discrimination occurs if a firm is able to sell each unit of output for the highest price anyone is willing to pay for it. In such a case, the entire consumer surplus is eliminated and captured by the producer. To practice perfect price discrimination, a firm must be creative and come up with a host of prices and special conditions each one of which appeals to a tiny segment of the market.

With perfect price discrimination, something special happens to marginal revenue. For the perfect price discriminator, the market demand curve becomes the marginal revenue curve. The reason is that when the price is cut to sell a larger quantity, the firm sells only the marginal unit at the lower price. All the other units continue to be sold for the highest price that each buyer is willing to pay. So for the perfect price discriminator, marginal revenue *equals* price and the demand curve becomes the marginal revenue curve.

With marginal revenue equal to price, Global can obtain even greater profit by increasing output up to the point at which price (and marginal revenue) is equal to marginal cost.

So Global now seeks additional travelers who will not pay as much as $1,200 a trip but who will pay more than marginal cost. Global gets more creative and comes up with vacation specials and other fares that have combinations of

FIGURE 10   Perfect Price Discrimination

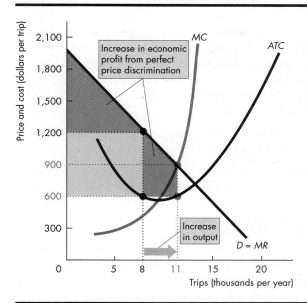

Dozens of fares discriminate among many different types of business traveler, and many new low fares with restrictions appeal to vacation travelers. With perfect price discrimination, the market demand curve becomes Global's marginal revenue curve. Economic profit is maximized when the lowest price equals marginal cost. Global sells 11,000 trips and makes an economic profit of $9.35 million a year.

advance reservation, minimum stay, and other restrictions that make these fares unattractive to its existing customers but attractive to a different group of travelers. With all these fares and specials, Global increases sales, extracts the entire consumer surplus, and maximizes economic profit.

Figure 10 shows the outcome with perfect price discrimination. The dozens of fares paid by the original travelers who are willing to pay between $1,200 and $2,000 have extracted the entire consumer surplus from this group and converted it into economic profit for Global.

The new fares between $900 and $1,200 have attracted 3,000 additional travelers but taken their entire consumer surplus also. Global now makes an economic profit of more than $9 million.

Real-world airlines are just as creative as Global, as you can see in the cartoon!

Would it bother you to hear how little I paid for this flight?

From William Hamilton, "Voodoo Economics," © 1992 by The Chronicle Publishing Company, p. 3. Reprinted with permission of Chronicle Books.

Efficiency and Rent Seeking with Price Discrimination

With perfect price discrimination, output increases to the point at which price equals marginal cost—where the marginal cost curve intersects the demand curve. This output is identical to that of perfect competition. Perfect price discrimination pushes consumer surplus to zero but increases the monopoly's producer surplus to equal the sum of consumer surplus and producer surplus in perfect competition. Deadweight loss with perfect price discrimination is zero. So perfect price discrimination achieves efficiency.

The more perfectly the monopoly can price discriminate, the closer its output is to the competitive output and the more efficient is the outcome.

But there are two differences between perfect competition and perfect price discrimination. First, the distribution of the total surplus is different. It is shared by consumers and producers in perfect competition, while the producer gets it all with perfect price discrimination. Second, because the producer grabs all the surplus, rent seeking becomes profitable.

People use resources in pursuit of economic rent, and the bigger the rents, the more resources get used in pursuing them. With free entry into rent seeking, the long-run equilibrium outcome is that rent seekers use up the entire producer surplus.

You've seen that monopoly is profitable for the monopoly but costly for consumers. It results in inefficiency. Because of these features of monopoly, it is subject to policy debate and regulation. We'll now study the key monopoly policy issues.

6   MONOPOLY POLICY ISSUES

Monopoly looks bad when we compare it with competition. Monopoly is inefficient, and it captures consumer surplus and converts it into producer surplus or pure waste in the form of rent-seeking costs. If monopoly is so bad, why do we put up with it? Why don't we have laws that crack down on monopoly so hard that it never rears its head? We do indeed have laws that limit monopoly power and regulate the prices that monopolies are permitted to charge. But monopoly also brings some benefits. We begin this review of monopoly policy issues by looking at the benefits of monopoly. We then look at monopoly regulation.

Gains from Monopoly

The main reason why monopoly exists is that it has potential advantages over a competitive alternative. These advantages arise from

▶ Incentives to innovation
▶ Economies of scale and economies of scope

Incentives to Innovation

Invention leads to a wave of innovation as new knowledge is applied to the production process. Innovation may take the form of developing a new product or a lower-cost way of making an existing product. Controversy has raged over whether large firms with market power or small competitive firms lacking such market power are the most innovative. It is clear that some temporary market power arises from innovation. A firm that develops a new product or process and patents it obtains an exclusive right to that product or process for the term of the patent.

But does the granting of a monopoly, even a temporary one, to an innovator increase the pace of innovation? One line of reasoning suggests that it does. Without protection, an innovator is not able to enjoy the profits from innovation for very long. Thus the incentive to innovate is weakened. A contrary argument is that a monopoly can afford to be lazy while competitive firms cannot. Competitive firms must strive to innovate and cut costs even though they know that they cannot hang on to the benefits of their innovation for long. But that knowledge spurs them on to greater and faster innovation.

The evidence on whether monopoly leads to greater innovation than competition is mixed. Large firms do more research and development than do small firms. But research and development are inputs into the process of innovation. What matters is not input but output. Two measures of the output of research and development are the number of patents and the rate of productivity growth. On these measures, it is not clear that bigger is better. But as a new process or product spreads through an industry, the large firms adopt the new process or product more quickly than do small firms. So large firms help to speed the process of diffusion of technological change.

Economies of Scale and Scope

Economies of scale and economies of scope can lead to natural monopoly. And as you saw at the beginning of this reading, in a natural monopoly, a single firm can produce at a lower average cost than a number of firms can.

A firm experiences *economies of scale* when an increase in its output of a good or service brings a decrease in the average total cost of producing it (see the reading on outputs and costs). A firm experiences *economies of scope* when an increase in the *range of goods produced* brings a decrease in average total cost (see the reading on organizing production). Economies of scope occur when different goods can share specialized (and usually costly) capital resources. For example, McDonald's can produce both hamburgers and french fries at a lower average total cost than can two separate firms—a burger firm and a french fries firm—because at McDonald's, hamburgers and french fries share the use of specialized food storage and preparation facilities. A firm that produces a wide range of products can hire specialist computer programmers, designers, and marketing experts whose skills can be used across the product range, thereby spreading their costs and lowering the average total cost of production of each of the goods.

There are many examples in which a combination of economies of scale and economies of scope arise, but not all of them lead to monopoly. Some examples are the brewing of beer, the manufacture of refrigerators and other household appliances, the manufacture of pharmaceuticals, and the refining of petroleum.

Examples of industries in which economies of scale are so significant that they lead to a natural monopoly are becoming rare. Public utilities such as gas, electric power, local telephone service, and garbage collection once were natural monopolies. But technological advances now enable us to separate the *production* of electric power or natural gas from its *distribution*. The provision of water, though, remains a natural monopoly.

A large-scale firm that has control over supply and can influence price—and therefore behaves like the monopoly firm that you've studied in this reading— can reap these economies of scale and scope. Small, competitive firms cannot.

Consequently, there are situations in which the comparison of monopoly and competition that we made earlier in this reading is not valid. Recall that we imagined the takeover of a large number of competitive firms by a monopoly firm. But we also assumed that the monopoly would use exactly the same technology as the small firms and have the same costs. If one large firm can reap economies of scale and scope, its marginal cost curve will lie below the supply curve of a competitive industry made up of many small firms. It is possible for such economies of scale and scope to be so large as to result in a larger output and lower price under monopoly than a competitive industry would achieve.

Where significant economies of scale and scope exist, it is usually worth putting up with monopoly and regulating its price.

Regulating Natural Monopoly

Where demand and cost conditions create a natural monopoly, a federal, state, or local government agency usually steps in to regulate the price of the monopoly. By regulating a monopoly, some of the worst aspects of monopoly can be avoided or at least moderated. Let's look at monopoly price regulation.

Figure 11 shows the demand curve *D*, the marginal revenue curve *MR*, the long-run average cost curve *LRAC*, and the marginal cost curve *MC* for a natural gas distribution company that is a natural monopoly.

FIGURE 11   Regulating a Natural Monopoly

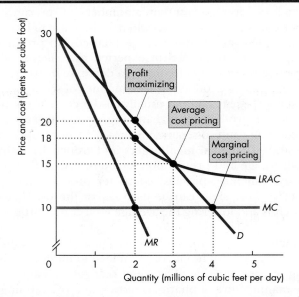

A natural monopoly is an industry in which average cost is falling even when the entire market demand is satisfied. A natural gas producer faces the demand curve *D*. The firm's marginal cost is constant at 10 cents per cubic foot, as shown by the curve labeled *MC*. The long-run average cost curve is *LRAC*.

A profit-maximizing monopoly produces 2 million cubic feet a day and charges a price of 20 cents per cubic foot. An average cost pricing rule sets the price at 15 cents per cubic foot. The monopoly produces 3 million cubic feet per day and makes zero economic profit. A marginal cost pricing rule sets the price at 10 cents per cubic foot. The monopoly produces 4 million cubic feet per day and incurs an economic loss.

The firm's marginal cost is constant at 10 cents per cubic foot. But average cost decreases as output increases. The reason is that the natural gas company has a large investment in pipelines and has economies of scale. At low output levels, average cost is extremely high. The long-run average cost curve slopes downward because as the number of cubic feet sold increases, the high cost of the distribution system is spread over a larger number of units.

This one firm can supply the entire market at the lowest possible cost because long-run average cost is falling even when the entire market is supplied.

Profit Maximization

First, suppose the natural gas company is not regulated and instead maximizes profit. Figure 11 shows the outcome. The company produces 2 million cubic feet a day, the quantity at which marginal cost equals marginal revenue. It prices the gas at 20 cents a cubic foot and makes an economic profit of 2 cents a cubic foot, or $40,000 a day.

This outcome is fine for the gas company, but it is inefficient. The price of gas is 20 cents a cubic foot when its marginal cost is only 10 cents a cubic foot. Also, the gas company is making a big profit. What can regulation do to improve this outcome?

The Efficient Regulation

If the monopoly regulator wants to achieve an efficient use of resources, it must require the gas monopoly to produce the quantity of gas that brings marginal social benefit into equality with marginal social cost. With no external benefits, marginal social benefit is what the consumer is willing to pay and is shown by the demand curve. With no external costs, marginal social cost is shown by the firm's marginal cost curve. You can see in Fig. 11 that this outcome occurs if the price is regulated at 10 cents per cubic foot and if 4 million cubic feet per day are produced.

The regulation that produces this outcome is called a marginal cost pricing rule. A **marginal cost pricing rule** sets price equal to marginal cost. It maximizes total surplus in the regulated industry. In this example, that surplus is all consumer surplus and it equals the area of the triangle beneath the demand curve and above the marginal cost curve.

The marginal cost pricing rule is efficient. But it leaves the natural monopoly incurring an economic loss. Because average cost is falling as output increases, marginal cost is below average cost. And because price equals marginal cost, price is below average cost. Average cost minus price is the loss per unit produced. It's obvious that a natural gas company that is required to use a marginal cost pricing rule will not stay in business for long. How can a company cover its costs and, at the same time, obey a marginal cost pricing rule?

One possibility is price discrimination. The company might charge a higher price to some customers but marginal cost to the customers who pay least. Another possibility is to use a two-part price (called a two-part tariff). For example, the gas company might charge a monthly fixed fee that covers its fixed cost and then charge for gas consumed at marginal cost.

But a natural monopoly cannot always cover its costs in these ways. If a natural monopoly cannot cover its total cost from its customers, and if the government wants it to follow a marginal cost pricing rule, the government must give the firm a subsidy. In such a case, the government raises the revenue for the subsidy by taxing some other activity. But as we saw in the reading on markets in action, taxes themselves generate deadweight loss. Thus the deadweight loss resulting from additional taxes must be subtracted from the efficiency gained by forcing the natural monopoly to adopt a marginal cost pricing rule.

Average Cost Pricing

Regulators almost never impose efficient pricing because of its consequences for the firm's economic profit. Instead, they compromise by permitting the firm to cover its costs and to break even (make zero economic profit). So pricing to cover total cost means setting price equal to average cost—called an **average cost pricing rule**.

Figure 11 shows the average cost pricing outcome. The natural gas company charges 15 cents a cubic foot and sells 3 million cubic feet per day. This outcome is better for consumers than the unregulated profit-maximizing outcome. The price is 5 cents a cubic foot lower, and the quantity consumed is 1 million cubic feet per day more. And the outcome is better for the producer than the marginal cost pricing rule outcome. The firm breaks even (makes zero economic profit). The outcome is inefficient but less so than the unregulated profit-maximizing outcome.

You've now studied perfect competition and monopoly. *Reading Between the Lines* looks at airfares in the United States as low-cost airlines have cut the market power of traditional airlines. In the next reading, we study markets that lie between the extremes of perfect competition and monopoly and that blend elements of the two.

READING BETWEEN THE LINES

7

Airline Monopolies Fade

THE NEW YORK TIMES, JANUARY 14, 2006

Commercial Travelers Feel Less Gouged . . .

Clients of his educational software firm, the Critical Skills Group, reimburse him for his travel costs, but Charles C. Jett said it still offended him to be charged $1,900 to fly round trip to Los Angeles. "I wouldn't charge anyone that," Mr. Jett said.

Increasingly, neither would airlines, which are becoming less inclined to try to charge very high fares, a trend that has pleased Mr. Jett. He paid just $400 recently to fly to and from San Francisco. "The price was a lot lower than I thought it was going to be."

Business travelers have long been irritated to know that the casually dressed person in the next seat—a vacationer or a student headed back to college—paid a lot less to be on the same flight.

A substantial gap still remains between business and leisure fares. But . . . the ratio of domestic business fares to leisure fares, tracked by Harrell Associates, an airline consulting firm in New York, has fallen to about four to one today from about six to one as recently as a year ago. Average one-way business fares fell to $400 from $600 and leisure fares held steady at about $100.

The expansion of low-cost carriers like Southwest Airlines into more markets has forced traditional carriers, including American Airlines and United Airlines, to reduce fares, including those of business travelers. The Internet, which allows travelers to comparison shop far more effectively than in the past, helps, too. . . .

Essence of the Story

► Business travelers pay higher airfares than leisure travelers do, on the average.

► A New York airline consulting firm reports that the ratio of domestic business fares to leisure fares fell from about six to one in 2005 to about four to one in 2006.

► The average one-way business fare fell from $600 to $400, and the average leisure fare remained at about $100.

► The entry of low-cost carriers into more markets has forced traditional carriers to cut all their fares.

► The internet has made it easy to compare fares and get the best deal.

Economic Analysis

▶ To study monopoly in the market for air travel, we must consider each route as a market.

▶ If only one airline has the right to fly a given route, that airline acts as a monopoly on that route.

▶ Before the expansion of the role of low-cost budget airlines, the traditional airlines such as American Airlines and United Airlines had a monopoly on some routes.

▶ On most of these routes, the airlines carry both business travelers and leisure travelers.

▶ The two types of traveler have different demand curves. The business traveler is willing to pay a higher price, if necessary, and has a less elastic demand than does the leisure traveler.

▶ Figure 12 shows the demand for business travel on a route for which a traditional airline has a monopoly.

FIGURE 12   United and American Airlines before Entry

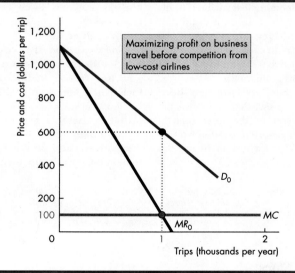

▶ The airline maximizes profit by carrying the number of business travelers at which marginal revenue equals marginal cost and charging the highest price that travelers will pay for that quantity.

▶ The profit-maximizing outcome in Fig. 12 is a quantity of 1,000 trips per month at a price of $600 per trip.

▶ Because marginal cost, in this example, is constant at $100 a trip, the monopoly would maximize profit by offering trips to leisure travelers for $100 a trip.

▶ Because the low-cost airlines are now flying routes that were previously flown only by the traditional airlines, business travelers have a choice. And some choose the low-price, no-frills option.

▶ This competition from low-price airlines decreases the demand for business travel and willingness to pay by business travelers.

FIGURE 13   The Effect of Entry of Low-Cost Airlines

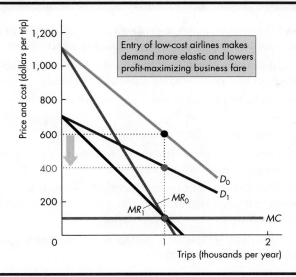

- ▶ Figure 13 shows these effects on the traditional airline.
- ▶ Demand becomes more elastic, and the demand curve shifts from D_0 to D_1.
- ▶ This example has been set up to leave the profit-maximizing quantity unchanged at 1,000 trips per month, but the price falls to $400 per trip.
- ▶ Because marginal cost is constant at $100 per trip, the price for leisure travel remains at $100 per trip.

You're the Voter

- ▶ Do you think the airlines are efficient?
- ▶ Do you think that the suppliers of air travel services operate in a competitive market or a monopoly market?
- ▶ What changes in the regulation or deregulation of airlines would you vote for to make the industry more efficient?

SUMMARY

▶ A monopoly is an industry with a single supplier of a good or service that has no close substitutes and in which barriers to entry prevent competition.

▶ Barriers to entry may be legal (public franchise, license, patent, copyright, firm owns control of a resource) or natural (created by economies of scale).

▶ A monopoly might be able to price discriminate when there is no resale possibility.

▶ Where resale is possible, a firm charges one price.

▶ A monopoly's demand curve is the market demand curve and a single-price monopoly's marginal revenue is less than price.

▶ A monopoly maximizes profit by producing the output at which marginal revenue equals marginal cost and by charging the maximum price that consumers are willing to pay for that output.

▶ A single-price monopoly charges a higher price and produces a smaller quantity than a perfectly competitive industry.

▶ A single-price monopoly restricts output and creates a deadweight loss.

▶ The total loss that arises from monopoly equals the deadweight loss plus the cost of the resources devoted to rent seeking.

▶ Price discrimination is an attempt by the monopoly to convert consumer surplus into economic profit.

▶ Perfect price discrimination extracts the entire consumer surplus. Such a monopoly charges a different price for each unit sold and obtains the maximum price that each consumer is willing to pay for each unit bought.

▶ With perfect price discrimination, the monopoly produces the same output as would a perfectly competitive industry.

▶ Rent seeking with perfect price discrimination might eliminate the entire consumer surplus and producer surplus.

▶ A monopoly with large economies of scale and economies of scope can produce a larger quantity at a lower price than a competitive industry can achieve, and monopoly might be more innovative than small competitive firms.

▶ Efficient regulation requires a monopoly to charge a price equal to marginal cost, but for a natural monopoly, such a price is less than average cost.

▶ Average cost pricing is a compromise pricing rule that covers a firm's costs and allows the firm to break even but it is not efficient.

PRACTICE PROBLEMS FOR READING 19

1. Which of the following is not a constraint that helps to create a monopoly?
   A. Public franchise.
   B. Innovative culture.
   C. Economies of scale along the entire long-run average cost curve.

2. Use the information in the following table to determine a monopolist's profit-maximizing output and price.

	Price/Unit	Cost/Unit	Quantity Demanded
A.	50	40	175
B.	60	45	150
C.	70	50	125

3. Which of the following is the *best* reason for price discrimination?
   A. Differences in applicable tariffs.
   B. Differences in consumers' willingness to pay.
   C. Differences in production and/or transportation costs.

4. A monopoly's equilibrium level of output is *least likely* to occur where:
   A. demand is elastic.
   B. demand is inelastic.
   C. marginal revenue equals marginal cost.

5. Compared to perfect competition, a natural monopoly will *most likely* be associated with a decrease in:
   A. deadweight loss.
   B. producer surplus.
   C. consumer surplus.

6. Which of the following statements is *most* accurate? Price discrimination:
   A. increases consumer surplus.
   B. reduces the monopolist's economic profits.
   C. allows different prices to be charged to different buyers.

7. When rent-seeking equilibrium is reached, a monopoly's economic profit will *most likely* be:
   A. zero.
   B. positive.
   C. negative.

SOLUTIONS FOR READING 19

1. B is correct. An innovative culture may allow development of an invention which may, with successful commercialization, lead to monopolizing a market, but an innovative culture does not necessarily lead to a monopoly and so cannot be considered a constraint. A public franchise, by definition as an exclusive right, is a monopoly. The effects of having economics of scale along the entire *LRAC*, a natural barrier to entry, is that "one firm can supply the entire market at a lower cost than two or more firms can."

2. C is correct. $(70 - 50) \times 125 = \$2500$. The other alternatives generate total profit less than \$2500.

3. B is correct. Price discrimination is charging different prices for a single good or service because of differences in buyers' willingness to pay and not because of differences in production costs.

4. B is correct. A monopoly will never choose to operate where demand is inelastic because marginal revenue is negative in the inelastic portion of the demand curve.

5. C is correct. The consumer surplus under a monopoly will be less than if the same market were perfectly competitive.

6. C is correct. Price discrimination allows different buyers to be charged different prices depending on how much they are willing to pay.

7. A is correct. With competitive rent seeking, a monopoly uses all its economic profit to maintain its monopoly. The firm's rent-seeking costs add to total fixed costs and to average total costs (*ATC*). The *ATC* curve shifts upward until, at the profit-maximizing price, the monopolistic firm breaks even.

MONOPOLISTIC COMPETITION AND OLIGOPOLY

by Michael Parkin

LEARNING OUTCOMES

The candidate should be able to:	Mastery
a. describe the characteristics of monopolistic competition and an oligopoly;	☐
b. determine the profit-maximizing (loss-minimizing) output under monopolistic competition, explain why long-run economic profit under monopolistic competition is zero, and determine if monopolistic competition is efficient;	☐
c. compare and contrast monopolistic competition and perfect competition;	☐
d. explain the importance of innovation, product development, advertising, and branding under monopolistic competition;	☐
e. explain the kinked demand curve model and the dominant firm model, and determine the profit-maximizing (loss-minimizing) output under each model;	☐
f. describe oligopoly games including the Prisoners' Dilemma.	☐

PC WAR GAMES　　　1

The PC price war has been raging for some time. But during 2006, the war became very hot. The age of the $1,000 laptop and $500 desktop had arrived. Dell was one of the most aggressive price cutters. But despite slashing its prices by up to $700 per machine, Dell lost its position as market leader to Hewlett-Packard. These two firms, along with Lenovo, Acer, and Toshiba, accounted for one half of the global market of 60 billion PCs in 2006.

In the market for PCs, the two big firms, Dell and Hewlett-Packard, must pay close attention to what the other firm is doing. But these two firms also compete with the other firms in the market.

In some markets, there are only two firms. Computer chips are an example. The chips that drive most PCs are made by Intel and Advanced Micro Devices. How does competition between just two chip makers work?

When a small number of firms compete in a market, do they operate in the social interest, like firms in perfect competition? Or do they restrict output to increase profit, like a monopoly?

The theories of perfect competition and monopoly don't predict the behavior of the firms we've just described. To understand how markets work when only a handful of firms compete, we need the richer models that are explained in this reading. In *Reading Between the Lines* at the end of this reading, we'll return to the market for personal computers and see how Dell and Hewlett-Packard slugged it out for dominance in 2006.

2   WHAT IS MONOPOLISTIC COMPETITION?

You have studied perfect competition, in which a large number of firms produce at the lowest possible cost, make zero economic profit, and are efficient. And you've studied monopoly, in which a single firm restricts output, produces at a higher cost and price than in perfect competition, and is inefficient.

Most real-world markets are competitive but not perfectly competitive because firms in these markets possess some power to set their prices as monopolies do. We call this type of market *monopolistic competition.*

Monopolistic competition is a market structure in which

► A large number of firms compete.
► Each firm produces a differentiated product.
► Firms compete on product quality, price, and marketing.
► Firms are free to enter and exit.

Large Number of Firms

In monopolistic competition, as in perfect competition, the industry consists of a large number of firms. The presence of a large number of firms has three implications for the firms in the industry.

Small Market Share

In monopolistic competition, each firm supplies a small part of the total industry output. Consequently, each firm has only limited power to influence the price of its product. Each firm's price can deviate from the average price of other firms by a relatively small amount.

Ignore Other Firms

A firm in monopolistic competition must be sensitive to the average market price of the product. But the firm does not pay attention to any one individual competitor. Because all the firms are relatively small, no one firm can dictate market conditions, and so no one firm's actions directly affect the actions of the other firms.

Collusion Impossible

Firms in monopolistic competition would like to be able to conspire to fix a higher price—called *collusion*. But because there are many firms, collusion is not possible.

Product Differentiation

A firm practices **product differentiation** if it makes a product that is slightly different from the products of competing firms. A differentiated product is one that is a close substitute but not a perfect substitute for the products of the other firms. Some people will pay more for one variety of the product, so when its price rises, the quantity demanded falls, but it does not (necessarily) fall to zero. For example, Adidas, Asics, Diadora, Etonic, Fila, New Balance, Nike, Puma, and Reebok all make differentiated running shoes. Other things remaining the same, if the price of Adidas running shoes rises and the prices of the other shoes remain constant, Adidas sells fewer shoes and the other producers sell more. But Adidas shoes don't disappear unless the price rises by a large enough amount.

Competing on Quality, Price, and Marketing

Product differentiation enables a firm to compete with other firms in three areas: product quality, price, and marketing.

Quality

The quality of a product is the physical attributes that make it different from the products of other firms. Quality includes design, reliability, the service provided to the buyer, and the buyer's ease of access to the product. Quality lies on a spectrum that runs from high to low. Some firms—such as Dell Computer Corp.—offer high-quality products. They are well designed and reliable, and the customer receives quick and efficient service. Other firms offer a lower-quality product that is less well designed, that might not work perfectly, and that the buyer must travel some distance to obtain.

Price

Because of product differentiation, a firm in monopolistic competition faces a downward-sloping demand curve. So, like a monopoly, the firm can set both its price and its output. But there is a tradeoff between the product's quality and price. A firm that makes a high-quality product can charge a higher price than a firm that makes a low-quality product can.

Marketing

Because of product differentiation, a firm in monopolistic competition must market its product. Marketing takes two main forms: advertising and packaging. A firm that produces a high-quality product wants to sell it for a suitably high price. To be able to do so, it must advertise and package its product in a way that convinces buyers that they are getting the higher quality for which they are paying a higher price. For example, pharmaceutical companies advertise and package their brand-name drugs to persuade buyers that these items are superior to the lower-priced generic alternatives. Similarly, a low-quality producer uses advertising and packaging to persuade buyers that although the quality is low, the low price more than compensates for this fact.

Entry and Exit

In monopolistic competition, firms can enter and exit. Consequently, a firm cannot make an economic profit in the long run. When firms make an economic profit, new firms enter the industry. This entry lowers prices and eventually eliminates economic profit. When firms incur economic losses, some firms leave the industry. This exit increases prices and profits and eventually eliminates the economic loss. In long-run equilibrium, firms neither enter nor leave the industry and the firms in the industry make zero economic profit.

Examples of Monopolistic Competition

Figure 1 shows 10 industries that are good examples of monopolistic competition. These industries have a large number of firms (shown in parentheses after the name of the industry). In the most concentrated of these industries, audio and video equipment, the largest 4 firms produce only 30 percent of the industry's total sales and the largest 20 firms produce 75 percent of total sales. The number on the right is the Herfindahl-Hirschman Index. Producers of clothing, jewelry, computers, and sporting goods operate in monopolistic competition.

FIGURE 1   Examples of Monopolistic Competition

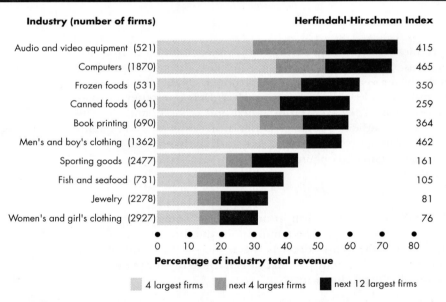

These industries operate in monopolistic competition. The number of firms in the industry is shown in parentheses after the name of the industry. The light blue bars show the percentage of industry sales by the largest 4 firms. The gray bars show the percentage of industry sales by the next 4 largest firms, and the dark blue bars show the percentage of industry sales by the next 12 largest firms. So the entire length of the combined light blue, gray, and dark blue bars show the percentage of industry sales by the largest 20 firms. The Herfindahl-Hirschman Index is shown on the right.

Source: U.S. Census Bureau.

PRICE AND OUTPUT IN MONOPOLISTIC COMPETITION

Suppose you've been hired by VF Corporation, the firm that owns Nautica Clothing Corporation, to manage the production and marketing of Nautica jackets. Think about the decisions that you must make at Nautica. First, you must decide on the design and quality of jackets and on your marketing program. Second, you must decide on the quantity of jackets to produce and the price at which to sell them.

We'll suppose that Nautica has already made its decisions about design, quality, and marketing and now we'll concentrate on the output and pricing decision. We'll study quality and marketing decisions in the next section.

For a given quality of jackets and marketing activity, Nautica faces given costs and market conditions. How, given its costs and the demand for its jackets, does Nautica decide the quantity of jackets to produce and the price at which to sell them?

The Firm's Short-Run Output and Price Decision

In the short run, a firm in monopolistic competition makes its output and price decision just like a monopoly firm does. Figure 2 illustrates this decision for Nautica jackets.

FIGURE 2   Economic Profit in the Short Run

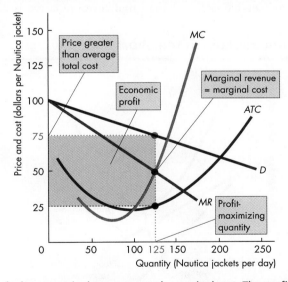

Profit is maximized where marginal revenue equals marginal cost. The profit-maximizing quantity is 125 jackets a day. The price of $75 a jacket exceeds the average total cost of $25 a jacket, so the firm makes an economic profit of $50 a jacket. The blue rectangle illustrates economic profit, which equals $6,250 a day ($50 a jacket multiplied by 125 jackets a day).

The demand curve for Nautica jackets is *D*. This demand curve tells us the quantity of Nautica jackets demanded at each price, given the prices of other jackets. It is not the demand curve for jackets in general.

The *MR* curve shows the marginal revenue curve associated with the demand curve for Nautica jackets. It is derived just like the marginal revenue curve of a single-price monopoly that you studied in the reading on monopoly.

The *ATC* curve and the *MC* curve show the average total cost and the marginal cost of producing Nautica jackets.

Nautica's goal is to maximize its economic profit. To do so, it produces the output at which marginal revenue equals marginal cost. In Fig. 2, this output is 125 jackets a day. Nautica charges the price that buyers are willing to pay for this quantity, which is determined by the demand curve. This price is $75 per jacket. When Nautica produces 125 jackets a day, its average total cost is $25 per jacket and it makes an economic profit of $6,250 a day ($50 per jacket multiplied by 125 jackets a day). The blue rectangle shows Nautica's economic profit.

Profit Maximizing Might Be Loss Minimizing

Figure 2 shows that Nautica is earning a large economic profit. But such an outcome is not inevitable. A firm might face a level of demand for its product that is too low for it to make an economic profit.

Excite@Home was such a firm. Offering high-speed internet service over the same cable that provides television, Excite@Home hoped to capture a large share of the internet portal market in competition with AOL, MSN, and a host of other providers.

Figure 3 illustrates the situation facing Excite@Home in 2001. The demand curve for its portal service is *D*, the marginal revenue curve is *MR*, the average

FIGURE 3   Economic Loss in the Short Run

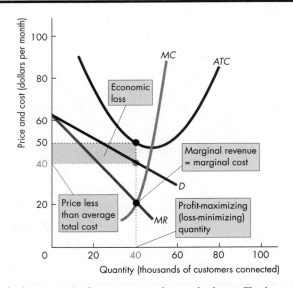

Profit is maximized where marginal revenue equals marginal cost. The loss-minimizing quantity is 40,000 customers. The price of $40 a month is less than the average total cost of $50 a month, so the firm incurs an economic loss of $10 a customer. The gray rectangle illustrates economic loss, which equals $400,000 a month ($10 a customer multiplied by 40,000 customers).

total cost curve is *ATC*, and the marginal cost curve is *MC*. Excite@Home maximized profit—equivalently, it minimized its loss—by producing the output at which marginal revenue equals marginal cost. In Fig. 3, this output is 40,000 customers. Excite@Home charged the price that buyers were willing to pay for this quantity, which was determined by the demand curve and which was $40 a month. With 40,000 customers, Excite@Home's average total cost was $50 per customer, so it incurred an economic loss of $400,000 a month ($10 a customer multiplied by 40,000 customers). The gray rectangle shows Excite@Home's economic loss.

So far, the firm in monopolistic competition looks like a single-price monopoly. It produces the quantity at which marginal revenue equals marginal cost and then charges the price that buyers are willing to pay for that quantity, determined by the demand curve. The key difference between monopoly and monopolistic competition lies in what happens next when firms either make an economic profit or incur an economic loss.

Long Run: Zero Economic Profit

A firm like Excite@Home is not going to incur an economic loss for long. Eventually, it goes out of business. Also, there is no restriction on entry into monopolistic competition, so if firms in an industry are making economic profit, other firms have an incentive to enter that industry.

As the Gap and other firms start to make jackets similar to those made by Nautica, the demand for Nautica jackets decreases. The demand curve for Nautica jackets and the marginal revenue curve shift leftward. And as these curves shift leftward, the profit-maximizing quantity and price fall.

Figure 4 shows the long-run equilibrium. The demand curve for Nautica jackets and the marginal revenue curve have shifted leftward. The firm produces

FIGURE 4   Output and Price in the Long Run

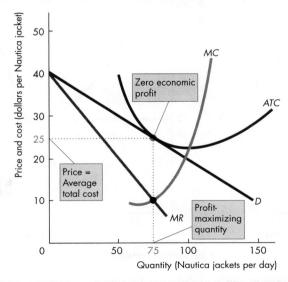

Economic profit encourages entry, which decreases the demand for each firm's product. When the demand curve touches the *ATC* curve at the quantity at which *MR* equals *MC*, the market is in long-run equilibrium. The output that maximizes profit is 75 jackets a day, and the price is $25 per jacket. Average total cost is also $25 per jacket, so economic profit is zero.

75 jackets a day and sells them for $25 each. At this output level, average total cost is also $25 per jacket.

So Nautica is making zero economic profit on its jackets. When all the firms in the industry are making zero economic profit, there is no incentive for new firms to enter.

If demand is so low relative to costs that firms incur economic losses, exit will occur. As firms leave an industry, the demand for the products of the remaining firms increases and their demand curves shift rightward. The exit process ends when all the firms in the industry are making zero economic profit.

Monopolistic Competition and Perfect Competition

Figure 5 compares monopolistic competition and perfect competition and highlights two key differences between them:

► Excess capacity
► Markup

Excess Capacity

A firm has excess capacity if it produces below its efficient scale, which is the quantity at which average total cost is a minimum—the quantity at the bottom of the U-shaped *ATC* curve. In Fig. 5, the efficient scale is 100 jackets a day. Nautica (part a) produces 75 Nautica jackets a day and has *excess capacity* of 25 jackets a day. But if all jackets are alike and are produced by firms in perfect competition

FIGURE 5   Excess Capacity and Markup

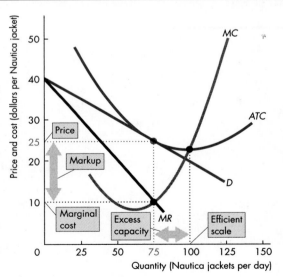

(a) Monopolistic competition

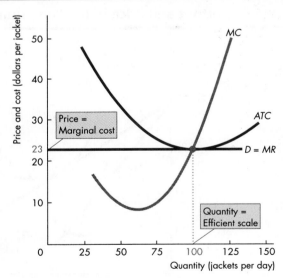

(b) Perfect competition

The efficient scale is 100 jackets a day. In monopolistic competition in the long run, because the firm faces a downward-sloping demand curve for its product, the quantity produced is less than the efficient scale and the firm has excess capacity. Price exceeds marginal cost by the amount of the markup.

In contrast, because in perfect competition the demand for each firm's product is perfectly elastic, the quantity produced equals the efficient scale and price equals marginal cost. The firm produces at the least possible cost and there is no markup.

(part b) each firm produces 100 jackets a day, which is the efficient scale. Average total cost is the lowest possible only in *perfect* competition.

You can see the excess capacity in monopolistic competition all around you. Family restaurants (except for the truly outstanding ones) almost always have some empty tables. You can always get a pizza delivered in less than 30 minutes. It is rare that every pump at a gas station is in use with customers waiting in line. There is always an abundance of realtors ready to help find or sell a home. These industries are examples of monopolistic competition. The firms have excess capacity. They could sell more by cutting their prices, but they would then incur losses.

Markup

A firm's markup is the amount by which price exceeds marginal cost. Figure 5(a) shows Nautica's markup. In perfect competition, price always equals marginal cost and there is no markup. Figure 5(b) shows this case. In monopolistic competition, buyers pay a higher price than in perfect competition and also pay more than marginal cost.

Is Monopolistic Competition Efficient?

Resources are used efficiently when marginal social benefit equals marginal social cost. Price equals marginal social benefit and the firm's marginal cost equals marginal social cost (assuming there are no external benefits or costs). So if the price of a Nautica jacket exceeds the marginal cost of producing it, the quantity of Nautica jackets produced is less than the efficient quantity. And you've just seen that in long-run equilibrium in monopolistic competition, price *does* exceed marginal cost. So is the quantity produced in monopolistic competition less than the efficient quantity?

Making the Relevant Comparison

Two economists meet in the street, and one asks the other how her husband is. "Compared to what?" is the quick reply. This bit of economic wit illustrates a key point: Before we can conclude that something needs fixing, we must check out the available alternatives.

The markup that drives a gap between price and marginal cost in monopolistic competition arises from product differentiation. It is because Nautica jackets are not quite the same as jackets from Banana Republic, CK, Diesel, DKNY, Earl Jackets, Gap, Levi, Ralph Lauren, or any of the other dozens of producers of jackets that the demand for Nautica jackets is not perfectly elastic. The only way in which the demand for jackets from Nautica might be perfectly elastic is if there is only one kind of jacket and all firms make it. In this situation, Nautica jackets are indistinguishable from all other jackets. They don't even have identifying labels.

If there was only one kind of jacket, the total benefit of jackets would almost certainly be less than it is with variety. People value variety. And people value variety not only because it enables each person to select what he or she likes best but also because it provides an external benefit. Most of us enjoy seeing variety in the choices of others. Contrast a scene from the China of the 1960s, when everyone wore a Mao tunic, with the China of today, where everyone wears the clothes of their own choosing. Or contrast a scene from the Germany of the 1930s, when almost everyone who could afford a car owned a first-generation Volkswagen

Beetle, with the world of today with its enormous variety of styles and types of automobiles.

If people value variety, why don't we see infinite variety? The answer is that variety is costly. Each different variety of any product must be designed, and then customers must be informed about it. These initial costs of design and marketing—called setup costs—mean that some varieties that are too close to others already available are just not worth creating.

The Bottom Line

Product variety is both valued and costly. The efficient degree of product variety is the one for which the marginal social benefit of product variety equals its marginal social cost. The loss that arises because the quantity produced is less than the efficient quantity is offset by the gain that arises from having a greater degree of product variety. So compared to the alternative—product uniformity—monopolistic competition might be efficient.

You've seen how the firm in monopolistic competition determines its output and price in both the short run and the long run when it produces a given product and undertakes a *given* marketing effort. But how does the firm choose its product quality and marketing effort? We'll now study these decisions.

4   PRODUCT DEVELOPMENT AND MARKETING

When we studied Nautica's price and output decision, we assumed that it had already made its product quality and marketing decisions. We're now going to study these decisions and the impact they have on the firm's output, price, and economic profit.

Innovation and Product Development

The prospect of new firms entering the industry keeps firms in monopolistic competition on their toes!

To enjoy economic profits, firms in monopolistic competition must be continually seeking ways of keeping one step ahead of imitators—other firms who imitate the success of the economically profitable firms.

One major way of trying to maintain economic profit is for a firm to seek out new products that will provide it with a competitive edge, even if only temporarily. A firm that introduces a new and differentiated product faces a demand that is less elastic and is able to increase its price and make an economic profit. Eventually, imitators will make close substitutes for the innovative product and compete away the economic profit arising from an initial advantage. So to restore economic profit, the firm must again innovate.

Profit-Maximizing Product Innovation

The decision to innovate and develop a new or improved product is based on the same type of profit-maximizing calculation that you've already studied.

Innovation and product development are costly activities, but they also bring in additional revenues. The firm must balance the cost and revenue at the margin. The marginal dollar spent on developing a new or improved product is the marginal cost of product development. The marginal dollar that the new or improved product earns for the firm is the marginal revenue of product development. At a low level of product development, the marginal revenue from a better product exceeds the marginal cost. At a high level of product development, the marginal cost of a better product exceeds the marginal revenue. When the marginal cost and marginal revenue of product development are equal, the firm is undertaking the profit-maximizing amount of product development.

Efficiency and Product Innovation

Is the profit-maximizing amount of product innovation also the efficient amount? Efficiency is achieved if the marginal social benefit of a new and improved product equals its marginal social cost.

The marginal social benefit of an innovation is the increase in price that consumers are willing to pay for it. The marginal social cost is the amount that the firm must pay to make the innovation. Profit is maximized when marginal *revenue* equals marginal cost. But in monopolistic competition, marginal revenue is less than price, so product innovation is probably not pushed to its efficient level.

Monopolistic competition brings many product innovations that cost little to implement and are purely cosmetic such as new and improved packaging or a new scent in laundry powder. And even when there is a genuine improved product, it is never as good as what the consumer is willing to pay for. For example, "The Legend of Zelda: Twilight Princess," is regarded as an almost perfect and very cool game, but reviewers complain that it isn't quite perfect. It is a game with features whose marginal revenue equal the marginal cost of creating them.

Advertising

Designing and developing products that are actually different from those of its competitors helps a firm achieve some product differentiation. But firms also attempt to create a consumer perception of product differentiation even when actual differences are small. Advertising and packaging are the principal means firms use to achieve this end. A Canon PowerShot camera is a different product from a Kodak EasyShare. But the actual differences are not the main ones that Canon emphasizes in its marketing. The deeper message is that if you use a Canon, you can be like Maria Sharapova (or some other high-profile successful person).

Advertising Expenditures

Firms in monopolistic competition incur huge costs to ensure that buyers appreciate and value the differences between their own products and those of their competitors. So a large proportion of the prices that we pay cover the cost of selling a good. And this proportion is increasing. Advertising in newspapers and magazines and on radio, television, and the internet is the main selling cost. But it is not the only one. Selling costs include the cost of shopping malls that look like movie sets, glossy catalogs and brochures, and the salaries, airfare, and hotel bills of salespeople.

The total scale of advertising costs is hard to estimate, but some components can be measured. A survey conducted by a commercial agency suggests that for cleaning supplies and toys, around 15 percent of the price of an item is spent on advertising. Figure 6 shows estimates for some industries.

FIGURE 6   Advertising Expenditures

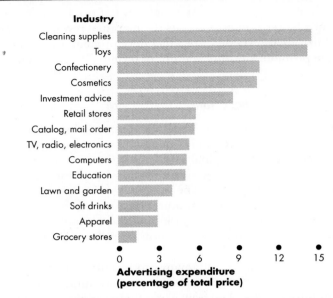

Advertising expenditures are a large part of total revenue received by producers of cleaning supplies, toys, confectionery, and cosmetics.

Source: From Schoenfeld & Associates, Lincolnwood, IL. Reported at www.toolkit.cch.com/text/p03_7006.asp.

For the U.S. economy as a whole, there are some 20,000 advertising agencies, which employ more than 200,000 people and have sales of $45 billion. But these numbers are only part of the total cost of advertising because firms have their own internal advertising departments, the costs of which we can only guess.

Advertising expenditures and other selling costs affect the profits of firms in two ways: They increase costs, and they change demand. Let's look at these effects.

Selling Costs and Total Costs

Selling costs such as advertising expenditures increase the costs of a monopolistically competitive firm above those of a perfectly competitive firm or a monopoly. Advertising costs and other selling costs are fixed costs. They do not vary as total output varies. So, just like fixed production costs, advertising costs per unit decrease as production increases.

Figure 7 shows how selling costs and advertising expenditures change a firm's average total cost. The blue curve shows the average total cost of production. The gray curve shows the firm's average total cost of production plus advertising. The height of the gray area between the two curves shows the average fixed cost of advertising. The *total* cost of advertising is fixed. But the *average* cost of advertising decreases as output increases.

Figure 7 shows that if advertising increases the quantity sold by a large enough amount, it can lower average total cost. For example, if the quantity sold increases from 25 jackets a day with no advertising to 100 jackets a day with advertising, average total cost falls from $60 to $40 a jacket. The reason is that although the *total* fixed cost has increased, the greater fixed cost is spread over a greater output, so average total cost decreases.

FIGURE 7   Selling Costs and Total Cost

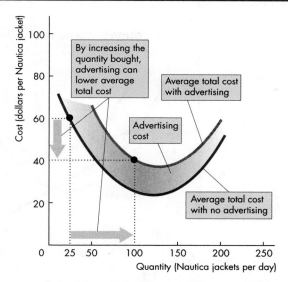

Selling costs such as the cost of advertising are fixed costs. When added to the average total cost of production, selling costs increase average total cost by a greater amount at small outputs than at large outputs. If advertising enables sales to increase from 25 jackets a day to 100 jackets a day, average total cost *falls* from $60 to $40 a jacket.

Selling Costs and Demand

Advertising and other selling efforts change the demand for a firm's product. But how? Does demand increase or does it decrease? The most natural answer is that advertising increases demand. By informing people about the quality of its products or by persuading people to switch from the products of other firms, a firm might expect to increase the demand for its own products.

But all firms in monopolistic competition advertise. And all seek to persuade customers that they have the best deal. If advertising enables a firm to survive, the number of firms in the market might increase. And to the extent that the number of firms does increase, advertising *decreases* the demand faced by any one firm. It also makes the demand for any one firm's product more elastic. So advertising can end up not only lowering average total cost but also lowering the markup and the price.

Figure 8 illustrates this possible effect of advertising. In part (a), with no advertising, the demand for Nautica jackets is not very elastic. Profit is maximized at 75 jackets per day, and the markup is large. In part (b), advertising, which is a fixed cost, increases average total cost from ATC_0 to ATC_1 but leaves marginal cost unchanged at MC. Demand becomes much more elastic, the profit-maximizing quantity increases, and the markup shrinks.

Using Advertising to Signal Quality

Some advertising, like the Maria Sharapova Canon camera ads on television and in glossy magazines or the huge number of dollars that Coke and Pepsi spend, seems hard to understand. There doesn't seem to be any concrete information about a camera in the glistening smile of a tennis player. And surely everyone knows about Coke and Pepsi. What is the gain from pouring millions of dollars a month into advertising these well-known colas?

FIGURE 8   Advertising and the Markup

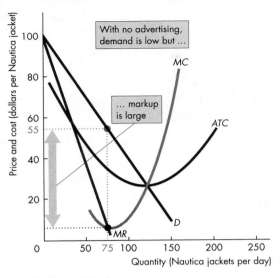

(a) No firms advertise

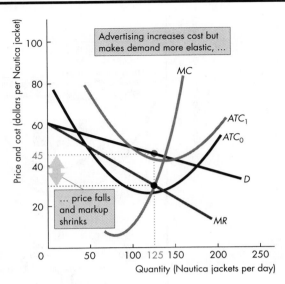

(b) All firms advertise

If no firms advertise, demand for each firm's product is low and not very elastic. The profit-maximizing output is small, the markup is large, and the price is high.

Advertising increases average total cost and shifts the ATC curve upward from ATC_0 to ATC_1. If all firms advertise, the demand for each firm's product becomes more elastic. Output increases, the price falls, and the markup shrinks.

One answer is that advertising is a signal to the consumer of a high-quality product. A **signal** is an action taken by an informed person (or firm) to send a message to uninformed people. Think about two colas: Coke and Oke. Oke knows that its cola is not very good and that its taste varies a lot depending on which cheap batch of unsold cola it happens to buy each week. So Oke knows that while it could get a lot of people to try Oke by advertising, they would all quickly discover what a poor product it is and switch back to the cola they bought before. Coke, in contrast, knows that its product has a high-quality consistent taste and that once consumers have tried it, there is a good chance they'll never drink anything else. On the basis of this reasoning, Oke doesn't advertise but Coke does. And Coke spends a lot of money to make a big splash.

Cola drinkers who see Coke's splashy ads know that the firm would not spend so much money advertising if its product were not truly good. So consumers reason that Coke is indeed a really good product. The flashy expensive ad has signaled that Coke is really good without saying anything about Coke.

Notice that if advertising is a signal, it doesn't need any specific product information. It just needs to be expensive and hard to miss. That's what a lot of advertising looks like. So the signaling theory of advertising predicts much of the advertising that we see.

Brand Names

Many firms create and spend a lot of money promoting a brand name. Why? What benefit does a brand name bring to justify the sometimes high cost of establishing it?

The basic answer is that a brand name provides information about the quality of a product to consumers and an incentive to the producer to achieve a high and consistent quality standard.

To see how a brand name helps the consumer, think about how you use brand names to get information about quality. You're on a road trip, and it is time to find a place to spend the night. You see roadside advertisements for Holiday Inn and Embassy Suites and for Joe's Motel and Annie's Driver's Stop. You know about Holiday Inn and Embassy Suites because you've stayed in them before. And you've seen their advertisements. You know what to expect from them. You have no information at all about Joe's and Annie's. They might be better than the lodging you do know about, but without that knowledge, you're not going to chance them. You use the brand name as information and stay at Holiday Inn.

This same story explains why a brand name provides an incentive to achieve high and consistent quality. Because no one would know whether Joe's and Annie's were offering a high standard of service, they have no incentive to do so. But equally, because everyone expects a given standard of service from Holiday Inn, a failure to meet a customer's expectation would almost surely lose that customer to a competitor. So Holiday Inn has a strong incentive to deliver what it promises in the advertising that creates its brand name.

Efficiency of Advertising and Brand Names

To the extent that advertising and brand names provide consumers with information about the precise nature of product differences and about product quality, they benefit the consumer and enable a better product choice to be made. But the opportunity cost of the additional information must be weighed against the gain to the consumer.

The final verdict on the efficiency of monopolistic competition is ambiguous. In some cases, the gains from extra product variety unquestionably off-set the selling costs and the extra cost arising from excess capacity. The tremendous varieties of books and magazines, clothing, food, and drinks are examples of such gains. It is less easy to see the gains from being able to buy a brand-name drug that has a chemical composition identical to that of a generic alternative. But many people do willingly pay more for the brand-name alternative.

WHAT IS OLIGOPOLY?   5

Oligopoly, like monopolistic competition, lies between perfect competition and monopoly. The firms in oligopoly might produce an identical product and compete only on price, or they might produce a differentiated product and compete on price, product quality, and marketing. **Oligopoly** is a market structure in which

- ▶ Natural or legal barriers prevent the entry of new firms.
- ▶ A small number of firms compete.

Barriers to Entry

Natural or legal barriers to entry can create oligopoly. You saw in the reading on monopoly how economies of scale and demand form a natural barrier to entry that can create a *natural monopoly*. These same factors can create a *natural oligopoly*.

FIGURE 9   Natural Oligopoly

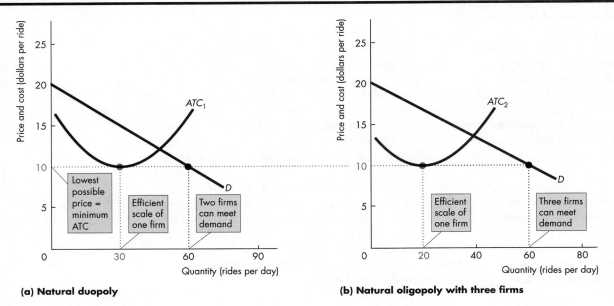

(a) Natural duopoly   **(b) Natural oligopoly with three firms**

The lowest possible price is $10 a ride, which is the minimum average total cost. When a firm produces 30 rides a day, the efficient scale, two firms can satisfy the market demand. This natural oligopoly has two firms—a natural duopoly.
   When the efficient scale of one firm is 20 rides per day, three firms can satisfy the market demand at the lowest possible price. This natural oligopoly has three firms.

Figure 9 illustrates two natural oligopolies. The demand curve, D (in both parts of the figure), shows the demand for taxi rides in a town. If the average total cost curve of a taxi company is ATC_1 in part (a), the market is a natural **duopoly**—an oligopoly market with two firms. You can probably see some examples of duopoly where you live. Some cities have only two taxi companies, two car rental firms, two copy centers, or two college bookstores.

The lowest price at which the firm would remain in business is $10 a ride. At that price, the quantity of rides demanded is 60 a day, the quantity that can be provided by just two firms. There is no room in this market for three firms. But if there were only one firm, it would make an economic profit and a second firm would enter to take some of the business and economic profit.

If the average total cost curve of a taxi company is ATC_2 in part (b), the efficient scale of one firm is 20 rides a day. This market is large enough for three firms.

A legal oligopoly arises when a legal barrier to entry protects the small number of firms in a market. A city might license two taxi firms or two bus companies, for example, even though the combination of demand and economies of scale leaves room for more than two firms.

Small Number of Firms

Because barriers to entry exist, oligopoly consists of a small number of firms, each of which has a large share of the market. Such firms are interdependent, and they face a temptation to cooperate to increase their joint economic profit.

FIGURE 10   Examples of Oligopoly

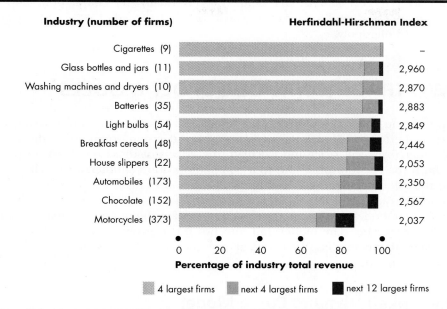

These industries operate in oligopoly. The number of firms in the industry is shown in parentheses after the name of the industry. The light blue bars show the percentage of industry sales by the largest 4 firms. The gray bars show the percentage of industry sales by the next 4 largest firms, and the dark blue bars show the percentage of industry sales by the next 12 largest firms. So the entire length of the combined light blue, gray and dark blue bars shows the percentage of industry sales by the largest 20 firms. The Herfindahl-Hirschman Index is shown on the right.

Source: U.S. Census Bureau.

Interdependence

With a small number of firms in a market, each firm's actions influence the profits of all the other firms. When Penny Stafford opened her coffee shop in Bellevue, Washington, a nearby Starbucks coffee shop took a hit. Within days, Starbucks began to attract Penny's customers with enticing offers and lower prices. Starbucks survived but Penny eventually went out of business. Penny Stafford and Starbucks were interdependent.

Temptation to Cooperate

When a small number of firms share a market, they can increase their profits by forming a cartel and acting like a monopoly. A **cartel** is a group of firms acting together—colluding—to limit output, raise price, and increase economic profit. Cartels are illegal, but they do operate in some markets. But for reasons that you'll discover in this chapter, cartels tend to break down.

Examples of Oligopoly

Figure 10 shows some examples of oligopoly. The dividing line between oligopoly and monopolistic competition is hard to pin down. As a practical matter, we identify oligopoly by looking at concentration ratios, the Herfindahl-Hirschman Index, and information about the geographical scope of the market and barriers to entry. The HHI that divides oligopoly from monopolistic competition is generally taken to be 1,000. An HHI below 1,000 is usually an example of monopolistic competition, and a market in which the HHI exceeds 1,000 is usually an example of oligopoly.

6   TWO TRADITIONAL OLIGOPOLY MODELS

Suppose you run one of three gas stations in a small town. You're trying to decide whether to cut your price. To make your decision, you must predict how the other firms will react and calculate the effects of those reactions on your profit. If you cut your price and your competitors don't cut theirs, you sell more and the other two firms sell less. But won't the other firms cut their prices too and make your profits fall. So what will you do?

Several models have been developed to explain the prices and quantities in oligopoly markets. The models fall into two broad groups: traditional models and game theory models. We'll look at examples of both types, starting with two traditional models.

The Kinked Demand Curve Model

The kinked demand curve model of oligopoly is based on the assumption that each firm believes that if it raises its price, others will not follow, but if it cuts its price, other firms will cut theirs.

Figure 11 shows the demand curve (D) that a firm believes it faces. The demand curve has a kink at the current price, P, and quantity, Q. At prices above P, a small price rise brings a big decrease in the quantity sold. The other firms hold their current price and the firm has the highest price for the good, so it loses market share. At prices below P, even a large price cut brings only a small increase in the quantity sold. In this case, other firms match the price cut, so the firm gets no price advantage over its competitors.

The kink in the demand curve creates a break in the marginal revenue curve (MR). To maximize profit, the firm produces the quantity at which marginal cost equals marginal revenue. That quantity, Q, is where the marginal cost curve passes through the gap AB in the marginal revenue curve. If marginal cost fluctuates between A and B, like the marginal cost curves MC_0 and MC_1, the firm does not change its price or its output. Only if marginal cost fluctuates outside the range AB does the firm change its price and output. So the kinked demand curve model predicts that price and quantity are insensitive to small cost changes.

But this model has a problem. If marginal cost increases by enough to cause the firm to increase its price and if all firms experience the same increase in marginal cost, they all increase their prices together. The firm's belief that others will not join it in a price rise is incorrect. A firm that bases its actions on beliefs that are wrong does not maximize profit and might even end up incurring an economic loss.

Dominant Firm Oligopoly

A second traditional model explains a dominant firm oligopoly, which arises when one firm—the dominant firm—has a big cost advantage over the other firms and produces a large part of the industry output. The dominant firm sets

FIGURE 11   The Kinked Demand Curve Model

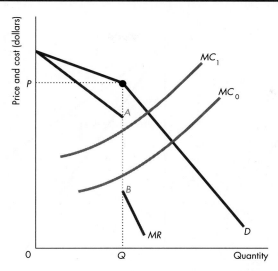

The price in an oligopoly market is *P*. Each firm believes it faces the demand curve *D*. At prices above *P*, a small price rise brings a big decrease in the quantity sold because other firms do not raise their prices. At prices below *P*, even a big price cut brings only a small increase in the quantity sold because other firms also cut their prices. Because the demand curve is kinked, the marginal revenue curve, *MR*, has a break *AB*. Profit is maximized by producing *Q*. The marginal cost curve passes through the break in the marginal revenue curve. Marginal cost changes inside the range *AB* leave the price and quantity unchanged.

the market price and the other firms are price takers. Examples of dominant firm oligopoly are a large gasoline retailer or a big video rental store that dominates its local market.

To see how a dominant firm oligopoly works, suppose that 11 firms operate gas stations in a city. Big-G is the dominant firm. Figure 12 shows the market for gas in this city. In part (a), the demand curve *D* tells us the total quantity of gas demanded in the city at each price. The supply curve S_{10} is the supply curve of the 10 small firms. Part (b) shows the situation facing Big-G. Its marginal cost curve is *MC*. Big-G faces the demand curve *XD*, and its marginal revenue curve is *MR*. The demand curve *XD* shows the excess demand not met by the 10 small firms. For example, at a price of $1 a gallon, the quantity demanded is 20,000 gallons, the quantity supplied by the 10 small firms is 10,000 gallons, and the excess quantity demanded is 10,000 gallons, measured by the distance *AB* in both parts of the figure.

To maximize profit, Big-G operates like a monopoly. It sells 10,000 gallons a week, where its marginal revenue equals its marginal cost, for a price of $1 a gallon. The 10 small firms take the price of $1 a gallon. They behave just like firms in perfect competition. The quantity of gas demanded in the entire city at $1 a gallon is 20,000 gallons, as shown in part (a). Of this amount, Big-G sells 10,000 gallons and the 10 small firms each sell 1,000 gallons.

The traditional models don't enable us to understand all oligopoly markets and we're now going to study some newer models based on game theory.

FIGURE 12   A Dominant Firm Oligopoly

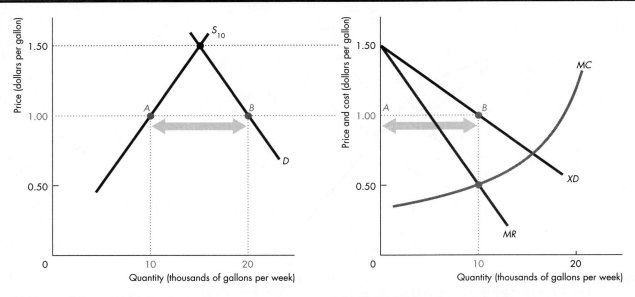

(a) Ten small firms and market demand   **(b) Big-G's price and output decision**

The demand curve for gas in a city is *D* in part (a). There are 10 small competitive firms that together have a supply curve of S_{10}. In addition, there is 1 large firm, Big-G, shown in part (b). Big-G faces the demand curve *XD*, determined as the market demand *D* minus the supply of the 10 small firms S_{10}—the demand that is not satisfied by the small firms.

Big-G's marginal revenue curve is *MR,* and marginal cost curve is *MC.* Big-G sets its output to maximize profit by equating marginal cost and marginal revenue. This output is 10,000 gallons per week. The price at which Big-G can sell this quantity is $1 a gallon. The 10 small firms take this price, and each firm sells 1,000 gallons per week, point *A* in part (a).

---

7   OLIGOPOLY GAMES

Economists think about oligopoly as a game, and to study oligopoly markets they use a set of tools called game theory. **Game theory** is a tool for studying *strategic behavior*—behavior that takes into account the expected behavior of others and the recognition of mutual interdependence. Game theory was invented by John von Neumann in 1937 and extended by von Neumann and Oskar Morgenstern in 1944. Today, it is one of the major research fields in economics.

Game theory seeks to understand oligopoly as well as other forms of economic, political, social, and even biological rivalries by using a method of analysis specifically designed to understand games of all types, including the familiar games of everyday life. We will begin our study of game theory and its application to the behavior of firms by thinking about familiar games.

What Is a Game?

What is a game? At first thought, the question seems silly. After all, there are many different games. There are ball games and parlor games, games of chance and games of skill. But what is it about all these different activities that make them games? What do all these games have in common? We're going to answer these questions by looking at a game called "the prisoners' dilemma." This game captures the essential features of many games, including oligopoly, and it gives a good illustration of how game theory works and how it generates predictions.

The Prisoners' Dilemma

Art and Bob have been caught red-handed, stealing a car. Facing airtight cases, they will receive a sentence of two years each for their crime. During his interviews with the two prisoners, the district attorney begins to suspect that he has stumbled on the two people who were responsible for a multimillion-dollar bank robbery some months earlier. But this is just a suspicion. He has no evidence on which he can convict them of the greater crime unless he can get them to confess. But how can he extract a confession? The answer is by making the prisoners play a game. So the district attorney makes the prisoners play the game that we will now describe.

All games share four common features:

► Rules
► Strategies
► Payoffs
► Outcome

Rules

Each prisoner (player) is placed in a separate room and cannot communicate with the other prisoner. Each is told that he is suspected of having carried out the bank robbery and that

> If both of them confess to the larger crime, each will receive a sentence of 3 years for both crimes.

> If he alone confesses and his accomplice does not, he will receive only a 1-year sentence while his accomplice will receive a 10-year sentence.

Strategies

In game theory, **strategies** are all the possible actions of each player. Art and Bob each have two possible actions:

1. Confess to the bank robbery.
2. Deny having committed the bank robbery.

Because there are two players, each with two strategies, there are four possible outcomes:

1. Both confess.
2. Both deny.
3. Art confesses and Bob denies.
4. Bob confesses and Art denies.

Payoffs

Each prisoner can work out his *payoff* in each of these situations, and we can tabulate the four possible payoffs for each of the prisoners in what is called a payoff matrix for the game. A **payoff matrix** is a table that shows the payoffs for every possible action by each player for every possible action by each other player.

TABLE 1   Prisoners' Dilemma Payoff Matrix

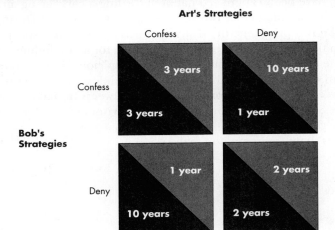

Each square shows the payoffs for the two players, Art and Bob, for each possible pair of actions. In each square, the gray triangle shows Art's payoff and the blue triangle shows Bob's. For example, if both confess, the payoffs are in the top left square. The equilibrium of the game is for both players to confess and each gets a 3-year sentence.

Table 1 shows a payoff matrix for Art and Bob. The squares show the payoffs for each prisoner—the gray triangle in each square shows Art's and the blue triangle shows Bob's. If both prisoners confess (top left), each gets a prison term of 3 years. If Bob confesses but Art denies (top right), Art gets a 10-year sentence and Bob gets a 1-year sentence. If Art confesses and Bob denies (bottom left), Art gets a 1-year sentence and Bob gets a 10-year sentence. Finally, if both of them deny (bottom right), neither can be convicted of the bank robbery charge but both are sentenced for the car theft—a 2-year sentence.

Outcome

The choices of both players determine the outcome of the game. To predict that outcome, we use an equilibrium idea proposed by John Nash of Princeton University (who received the Nobel Prize for Economic Science in 1994 and was the subject of the 2001 movie *A Beautiful Mind*). In **Nash equilibrium**, player *A* takes the best possible action given the action of player *B* and player *B* takes the best possible action given the action of player *A*.

In the case of the prisoners' dilemma, the Nash equilibrium occurs when Art makes his best choice given Bob's choice and when Bob makes his best choice given Art's choice.

To find the Nash equilibrium, we compare all the possible outcomes associated with each choice and eliminate those that are dominated—that are not as good as some other choice. Let's find the Nash equilibrium for the prisoners' dilemma game.

Finding the Nash Equilibrium

Look at the situation from Art's point of view. If Bob confesses (top row), Art's best action is to confess because in that case, he is sentenced to 3 years rather than 10 years. If Bob denies (bottom row), Art's best action is still to confess because in that case he receives 1 year rather than 2 years. So Art's best action is to confess.

Now look at the situation from Bob's point of view. If Art confesses (left column), Bob's best action is to confess because in that case, he is sentenced to 3 years rather than 10 years. If Art denies (right column), Bob's best action is still to confess because in that case, he receives 1 year rather than 2 years. So Bob's best action is to confess.

Because each player's best action is to confess, each does confess, each goes to jail for 3 years, and the district attorney has solved the bank robbery. This is the Nash equilibrium of the game.

The Dilemma

Now that you have found the outcome to the prisoners' dilemma, you can better see the dilemma. The dilemma arises as each prisoner contemplates the consequences of denying. Each prisoner knows that if both of them deny, they will receive only a 2-year sentence for stealing the car. But neither has any way of knowing that his accomplice will deny. Each poses the following questions: Should I deny and rely on my accomplice to deny so that we will both get only 2 years? Or should I confess in the hope of getting just 1 year (provided that my accomplice denies) knowing that if my accomplice does confess, we will both get 3 years in prison? The dilemma leads to the equilibrium of the game.

A Bad Outcome

For the prisoners, the equilibrium of the game, with each confessing, is not the best outcome. If neither of them confesses, each gets only 2 years for the lesser crime. Isn't there some way in which this better outcome can be achieved? It seems that there is not, because the players cannot communicate with each other. Each player can put himself in the other player's place, and so each player can figure out that there is a best strategy for each of them. The prisoners are indeed in a dilemma. Each knows that he can serve 2 years only if he can trust the other to deny. But each prisoner also knows that it is not in the best interest of the other to deny. So each prisoner knows that he must confess, thereby delivering a bad outcome for both.

The firms in an oligopoly are in a similar situation to Art and Bob in the prisoners' dilemma game. Let's see how we can use this game to understand oligopoly.

An Oligopoly Price-Fixing Game

We can use game theory and a game like the prisoners' dilemma to understand price fixing, price wars, and other aspects of the behavior of firms in oligopoly. We'll begin with a price-fixing game.

To understand price fixing, we're going to study the special case of duopoly—an oligopoly with two firms. Duopoly is easier to study than oligopoly with three or more firms, and it captures the essence of all oligopoly situations. Somehow, the two firms must share the market. And how they share it depends on the actions of each. We're going to describe the costs of the two firms and the market demand for the item they produce. We're then going to see how game theory helps us to predict the prices charged and the quantities produced by the two firms in a duopoly.

FIGURE 13   Costs and Demand

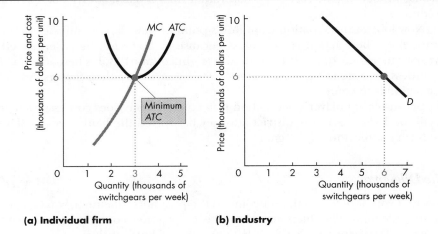

(a) Individual firm

(b) Industry

The average total cost curve for each firm is *ATC,* and the marginal cost curve is *MC* (part a). Minimum average total cost is $6,000 a unit, and it occurs at a production of 3,000 units a week.

Part (b) shows the market demand curve. At a price of $6,000, the quantity demanded is 6,000 units per week. The two firms can produce this output at the lowest possible average cost. If the market had one firm, it would be profitable for another to enter. If the market had three firms, one would exit. There is room for only two firms in this industry. It is a natural duopoly.

Cost and Demand Conditions

Two firms, Trick and Gear, produce switchgears. They have identical costs. Figure 13(a) shows their average total cost curve (*ATC*) and marginal cost curve (*MC*). Figure 13(b) shows the market demand curve for switchgears (*D*). The two firms produce identical switchgears, so one firm's switchgear is a perfect substitute for the other's. So the market price of each firm's product is identical. The quantity demanded depends on that price—the higher the price, the smaller is the quantity demanded.

This industry is a natural duopoly. Two firms can produce this good at a lower cost than either one firm or three firms can. For each firm, average total cost is at its minimum when production is 3,000 units a week. And when price equals minimum average total cost, the total quantity demanded is 6,000 units a week. So two firms can just produce that quantity.

Collusion

We'll suppose that Trick and Gear enter into a collusive agreement. A **collusive agreement** is an agreement between two (or more) producers to form a cartel to restrict output, raise the price, and increase profits. Such an agreement is illegal in the United States and is undertaken in secret. The strategies that firms in a cartel can pursue are to

► Comply
► Cheat

A firm that complies carries out the agreement. A firm that cheats breaks the agreement to its own benefit and to the cost of the other firm.

Because each firm has two strategies, there are four possible combinations of actions for the firms:

1. Both firms comply.

2. Both firms cheat.

3. Trick complies and Gear cheats.

4. Gear complies and Trick cheats.

Colluding to Maximize Profits

Let's work out the payoffs to the two firms if they collude to make the maximum profit for the cartel by acting like a monopoly. The calculations that the two firms perform are the same calculations that a monopoly performs. (You can refresh your memory of these calculations by looking at the reading on monopoly.) The only thing that the firms in duopoly must do beyond what a monopoly does is to agree on how much of the total output each of them will produce.

Figure 14 shows the price and quantity that maximize industry profit for the duopoly. Part (a) shows the situation for each firm, and part (b) shows the situation for the industry as a whole. The curve labeled MR is the industry marginal revenue curve. This marginal revenue curve is like that of a single-price monopoly (see the reading on monopoly). The curve labeled MC_I is the industry marginal cost curve if each firm produces the same quantity of output. That curve is constructed by adding together the outputs of the two firms at each level of marginal cost. That is, at each level of marginal cost, industry output is twice the output of each individual firm. So the curve MC_I in part (b) is twice as far to the right as the curve MC in part (a).

To maximize industry profit, the firms in the duopoly agree to restrict output to the rate that makes the industry marginal cost and marginal revenue equal. That output rate, as shown in part (b), is 4,000 units a week. The demand

FIGURE 14   Colluding to Make Monopoly Profits

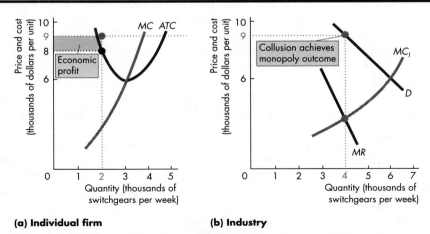

(a) Individual firm   **(b) Industry**

The industry marginal cost curve, MC_I in part (b), is the horizontal sum of the two firms' marginal cost curves, MC in part (a). The industry marginal revenue curve is MR. To maximize profit, the firms produce 4,000 units a week (the quantity at which marginal revenue equals marginal cost). They sell that output for $9,000 a unit. Each firm produces 2,000 units a week. Average total cost is $8,000 a unit, so each firm makes an economic profit of $2 million (blue rectangle)—2,000 units multiplied by $1,000 profit a unit.

curve shows that the highest price for which the 4,000 switchgears can be sold is $9,000 each. Trick and Gear agree to charge this price.

To hold the price at $9,000 a unit, production must be 4,000 units a week. So Trick and Gear must agree on output rates for each of them that total 4,000 units a week. Let's suppose that they agree to split the market equally so that each firm produces 2,000 switchgears a week. Because the firms are identical, this division is the most likely.

The average total cost (ATC) of producing 2,000 switchgears a week is $8,000, so the profit per unit is $1,000 and economic profit is $2 million (2,000 units × $1,000 per unit). The economic profit of each firm is represented by the blue rectangle in Fig. 14(a).

We have just described one possible outcome for a duopoly game: The two firms collude to produce the monopoly profit-maximizing output and divide that output equally between themselves. From the industry point of view, this solution is identical to a monopoly. A duopoly that operates in this way is indistinguishable from a monopoly. The economic profit that is made by a monopoly is the maximum total profit that can be made by the duopoly when the firms collude.

But with price greater than marginal cost, either firm might think of trying to increase profit by cheating on the agreement and producing more than the agreed amount. Let's see what happens if one of the firms does cheat in this way.

One Firm Cheats on a Collusive Agreement

To set the stage for cheating on their agreement, Trick convinces Gear that demand has decreased and that it cannot sell 2,000 units a week. Trick tells Gear that it plans to cut its price so that it can sell the agreed 2,000 units each week. Because the two firms produce an identical product, Gear matches Trick's price cut but still produces only 2,000 units a week.

In fact, there has been no decrease in demand. Trick plans to increase output, which it knows will lower the price, and Trick wants to ensure that Gear's output remains at the agreed level.

Figure 15 illustrates the consequences of Trick's cheating. Part (a) shows Gear (the complier); part (b) shows Trick (the cheat); and part (c) shows the industry as a whole. Suppose that Trick increases output to 3,000 units a week. If Gear sticks to the agreement to produce only 2,000 units a week, total output is 5,000 a week, and given demand in part (c), the price falls to $7,500 a unit.

Gear continues to produce 2,000 units a week at a cost of $8,000 a unit and incurs a loss of $500 a unit, or $1 million a week. This economic loss is shown by the gray rectangle in part(a). Trick produces 3,000 units a week at an average total cost of $6,000 each. With a price of $7,500, Trick makes a profit of $1,500 a unit and therefore an economic profit of $4.5 million. This economic profit is the blue rectangle in part (b).

We've now described a second possible outcome for the duopoly game: One of the firms cheats on the collusive agreement. In this case, the industry output is larger than the monopoly output and the industry price is lower than the monopoly price. The total economic profit made by the industry is also smaller than the monopoly's economic profit. Trick (the cheat) makes an economic profit of $4.5 million, and Gear (the complier) incurs an economic loss of $1 million. The industry makes an economic profit of $3.5 million. This industry profit is $0.5 million less than the economic profit that a monopoly would make. But the profit is distributed unevenly. Trick makes a bigger economic profit than it would under the collusive agreement, while Gear incurs an economic loss.

A similar outcome would arise if Gear cheated and Trick complied with the agreement. The industry profit and price would be the same, but in this case,

FIGURE 15   One Firm Cheats

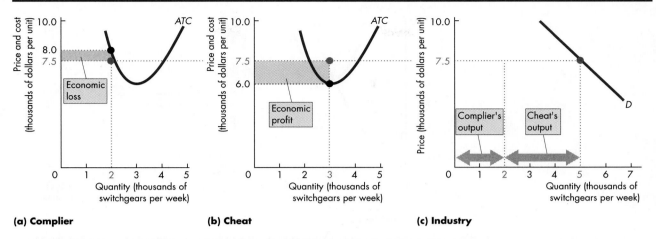

(a) Complier   **(b) Cheat**   **(c) Industry**

One firm, shown in part (a), complies with the agreement and produces 2,000 units. The other firm, shown in part (b), cheats on the agreement and increases its output to 3,000 units a week. Given the market demand curve, shown in part (c), and with a total production of 5,000 units a week, the price falls to $7,500 a unit. At this price, the complier in part (a) incurs an economic loss of $1 million ($500 per unit × 2,000 units), shown by the gray rectangle. In part (b), the cheat makes an economic profit of $4.5 million ($1,500 per unit × 3,000 units), shown by the blue rectangle.

Gear (the cheat) would make an economic profit of $4.5 million and Trick (the complier) would incur an economic loss of $1 million.

Let's next see what happens if both firms cheat.

Both Firms Cheat

Suppose that both firms cheat and that each firm behaves like the cheating firm that we have just analyzed. Each tells the other that it is unable to sell its output at the going price and that it plans to cut its price. But because both firms cheat, each will propose a successively lower price. As long as price exceeds marginal cost, each firm has an incentive to increase its production—to cheat. Only when price equals marginal cost is there no further incentive to cheat. This situation arises when the price has reached $6,000. At this price, marginal cost equals price. Also, price equals minimum average total cost. At a price less than $6,000, each firm incurs an economic loss. At a price of $6,000, each firm covers all its costs and makes zero economic profit. Also, at a price of $6,000, each firm wants to produce 3,000 units a week, so the industry output is 6,000 units a week. Given the demand conditions, 6,000 units can be sold at a price of $6,000 each.

Figure 16 illustrates the situation just described. Each firm, in part (a), produces 3,000 units a week, and its average total cost is a minimum ($6,000 per unit). The market as a whole, in part (b), operates at the point at which the market demand curve *(D)* intersects the industry marginal cost curve *(MC$_I$)*. Each firm has lowered its price and increased its output to try to gain an advantage over the other firm. Each has pushed this process as far as it can without incurring an economic loss.

We have now described a third possible outcome of this duopoly game: Both firms cheat. If both firms cheat on the collusive agreement, the output of each firm is 3,000 units a week and the price is $6,000 a unit. Each firm makes zero economic profit.

FIGURE 16   Both Firms Cheat

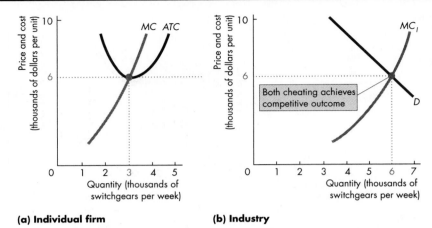

(a) Individual firm   **(b) Industry**

If both firms cheat by increasing production, the collusive agreement collapses. The limit to the collapse is the competitive equilibrium. Neither firm will cut price below $6,000 (minimum average total cost) because to do so will result in losses. In part (a), each firm produces 3,000 units a week at an average total cost of $6,000. In part (b), with a total production of 6,000 units, the price falls to $6,000. Each firm now makes zero economic profit. This output and price are the ones that would prevail in a competitive industry.

The Payoff Matrix

Now that we have described the strategies and payoffs in the duopoly game, we can summarize the strategies and the payoffs in the form of the game's payoff matrix. Then we can find the Nash equilibrium.

Table 2 sets out the payoff matrix for this game. It is constructed in the same way as the payoff matrix for the prisoners' dilemma in Table 1. The squares show the payoffs for the two firms—Gear and Trick. In this case, the payoffs are profits. (For the prisoners' dilemma, the payoffs were losses.)

The table shows that if both firms cheat (top left), they achieve the perfectly competitive outcome—each firm makes zero economic profit. If both firms comply (bottom right), the industry makes the monopoly profit and each firm makes an economic profit of $2 million. The top right and bottom left squares show the payoff if one firm cheats while the other complies. The firm that cheats makes an economic profit of $4.5 million, and the one that complies incurs a loss of $1 million.

Nash Equilibrium in the Duopolists' Dilemma

The duopolists have a dilemma like the prisoners' dilemma. Do they comply or cheat? To answer this question, we must find the Nash equilibrium.

Look at things from Gear's point of view. Gear reasons as follows: Suppose that Trick cheats. If I comply, I will incur an economic loss of $1 million. If I also cheat, I will make zero economic profit. Zero is better than *minus* $1 million, so I'm better off if I cheat. Now suppose Trick complies. If I cheat, I will make an economic profit of $4.5 million, and if I comply, I will make an economic profit of $2 million. A $4.5 million profit is better than a $2 million profit, so I'm better off if I cheat. So regardless of whether Trick cheats or complies, it pays Gear to cheat. Cheating is Gear's best strategy.

TABLE 2   Duopoly Payoff Matrix

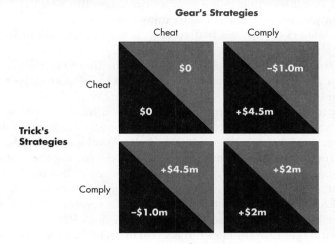

Each square shows the payoffs from a pair of actions. For example, if both firms comply with the collusive agreement, the payoffs are recorded in the bottom right square. The gray triangle shows Gear's payoff, and the blue triangle shows Trick's. In Nash equilibrium, both firms cheat.

Trick comes to the same conclusion as Gear because the two firms face an identical situation. So both firms cheat. The Nash equilibrium of the duopoly game is that both firms cheat. And although the industry has only two firms, they charge the same price and produce the same quantity as those in a competitive industry. Also, as in perfect competition, each firm makes zero economic profit.

This conclusion is not general and will not always arise. We'll see why not first by looking at some other games that are like the prisoners' dilemma. Then we'll broaden the types of games we consider.

Other Oligopoly Games

Firms in oligopoly must decide whether to mount expensive advertising campaigns; whether to modify their product; whether to make their product more reliable and more durable; whether to price discriminate and, if so, among which groups of customers and to what degree; whether to undertake a large research and development (R&D) effort aimed at lowering production costs; and whether to enter or leave an industry.

All of these choices can be analyzed as games that are similar to the one that we've just studied. Let's look at one example: an R&D game.

An R&D Game

Disposable diapers were first marketed in 1966. The two market leaders from the start of this industry have been Procter & Gamble (the maker of Pampers) and Kimberly-Clark (the maker of Huggies). Procter & Gamble has about 40 percent of the total market, and Kimberly-Clark has about 33 percent. When the disposable diaper was first introduced, it had to be cost-effective in competition with reusable, laundered diapers. A costly research and development effort resulted in the development of machines that could make disposable diapers at a low enough cost to achieve that initial competitive edge. But new firms tried to get into the business and take market share away from the two industry leaders, and the industry leaders themselves battled each other to maintain or increase their own market share.

During the early 1990s, Kimberly-Clark was the first to introduce Velcro closures. And in 1996, Procter & Gamble was the first to introduce "breathable" diapers into the U.S. market.

The key to success in this industry (as in any other) is to design a product that people value highly relative to the cost of producing them. The firm that creates the most highly valued product and also develops the least-cost technology for producing it gains a competitive edge, undercutting the rest of the market, increasing its market share, and increasing its profit. But the R&D that must be undertaken to achieve product improvements and cost reductions is costly. So the cost of R&D must be deducted from the profit resulting from the increased market share that lower costs achieve. If no firm does R&D, every firm can be better off, but if one firm initiates the R&D activity, all must follow.

Table 3 illustrates the dilemma (with hypothetical numbers) for the R&D game that Kimberly-Clark and Procter & Gamble play. Each firm has two strategies: Spend $25 million a year on R&D or spend nothing on R&D. If neither firm spends on R&D, they make a joint profit of $100 million: $30 million for Kimberly-Clark and $70 million for Procter & Gamble (bottom right of the payoff matrix). If each firm conducts R&D, market shares are maintained but each firm's profit is lower by the amount spent on R&D (top left square of the payoff matrix). If Kimberly-Clark pays for R&D but Procter & Gamble does not, Kimberly-Clark gains a large part of Procter & Gamble's market. Kimberly-Clark

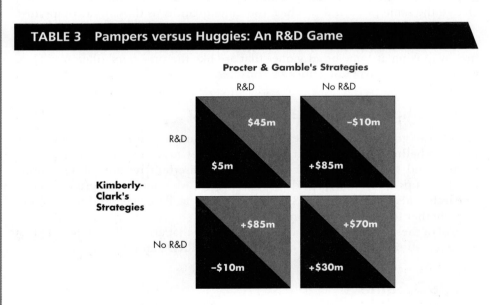

TABLE 3   Pampers versus Huggies: An R&D Game

If both firms undertake R&D, their payoffs are those shown in the top left square. If neither firm undertakes R&D, their payoffs are in the bottom right square. When one firm undertakes R&D and the other one does not, their payoffs are in the top right and bottom left squares. The gray triangle shows Procter & Gamble's payoff, and the blue triangle shows Kimberly-Clark's. The Nash equilibrium for this game is for both firms to undertake R&D. The structure of this game is the same as that of the prisoners' dilemma.

profits, and Procter & Gamble loses (top right square of the payoff matrix). Finally, if Procter & Gamble conducts R&D and Kimberly-Clark does not, Procter & Gamble gains market share from Kimberly-Clark, increasing its profit, while Kimberly-Clark incurs a loss (bottom left square).

Confronted with the payoff matrix in Table 3, the two firms calculate their best strategies. Kimberly-Clark reasons as follows: If Procter & Gamble does not undertake R&D, we will make $85 million if we do and $30 million if we do not; so it pays us to conduct R&D. If Procter & Gamble conducts R&D, we will lose $10 million if we don't and make $5 million if we do. Again, R&D pays off. So conducting R&D is the best strategy for Kimberly-Clark. It pays, regardless of Procter & Gamble's decision.

Procter & Gamble reasons similarly: If Kimberly-Clark does not undertake R&D, we will make $70 million if we follow suit and $85 million if we conduct R&D. It therefore pays to conduct R&D. If Kimberly-Clark does undertake R&D, we will make $45 million by doing the same and lose $10 million by not doing R&D. Again, it pays us to conduct R&D. So for Procter & Gamble, R&D is also the best strategy.

Because R&D is the best strategy for both players, it is the Nash equilibrium. The outcome of this game is that both firms conduct R&D. They make less profit than they would if they could collude to achieve the cooperative outcome of no R&D.

The real-world situation has more players than Kimberly-Clark and Procter & Gamble. A large number of other firms share a small portion of the market, all of them ready to eat into the market share of Procter & Gamble and Kimberly-Clark. So the R&D effort by these two firms not only serves the purpose of maintaining shares in their own battle, but also helps to keep barriers to entry high enough to preserve their joint market share.

The Disappearing Invisible Hand

All the games that we've studied are versions of the prisoners' dilemma. The essence of that game lies in the structure of its payoffs. The worst possible outcome for each player arises from cooperating when the other player cheats. The best possible outcome, for each player to cooperate, is not a Nash equilibrium because it is in neither player's *self-interest* to cooperate if the other one cooperates. It is this failure to achieve the best outcome for both players—the best social outcome if the two players are the entire economy—that led John Nash to claim (as he was portrayed as doing in the movie *A Beautiful Mind*) that he had challenged Adam Smith's idea that we are always guided, as if by an invisible hand, to promote the social interest when we are pursuing our self-interest.

A Game of Chicken

The Nash equilibrium for the prisoners' dilemma is called a **dominant strategy equilibrium**, which is an equilibrium in which the best strategy of each player is to cheat (confess) *regardless of the strategy of the other player*. Not all games have such an equilibrium, and one that doesn't is a game called "chicken."

In a graphic, if disturbing, version of this game, two cars race toward each other. The first driver to swerve and avoid a crash is "chicken." The payoffs are a big loss for both if no one "chickens," zero for the chicken, and a gain for the player who hangs tough.

If player 1 chickens, player 2's best strategy is to hang tough. And if player 1 hangs tough, player 2's best strategy is to chicken.

For an economic form of this game, suppose the R&D that creates a new diaper technology results in information that cannot be kept secret or patented, so both firms benefit from the R&D of either firm. The chicken in this case is the firm that does the R&D.

Table 4 illustrates a payoff matrix for an R&D game of chicken between Kimberly-Clark and Procter & Gamble. Each firm has two strategies: Do the R&D (and "chicken") or do not do the R&D (and hang tough).

TABLE 4   An R&D Game of Chicken

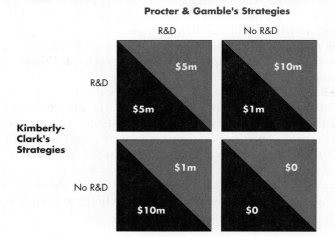

If both firms undertake R&D, their payoffs are those shown in the top left square. If neither firm undertakes R&D, their payoffs are in the bottom right square. When one firm undertakes R&D and the other one does not, their payoffs are in the top right and bottom left squares. The gray triangle shows Procter & Gamble's payoff, and the blue triangle shows Kimberly-Clark's. The equilibrium for this R&D game of chicken is for only one firm to undertake R&D. We cannot tell which firm will do the R&D and which will not.

If neither "chickens," there is no R&D and each firm makes zero additional profit. If each firm conducts R&D—each "chickens"—each firm makes $5 million (the profit from the new technology minus the cost of the research). If one of the firms does the R&D, the payoffs are $1 million for the chicken and $10 million for the one who hangs tough.

Confronted with the payoff matrix in Table 4, the two firms calculate their best strategies. Kimberly-Clark is better off doing R&D if Procter & Gamble does not undertake it. Procter & Gamble is better off doing R&D if Kimberly-Clark doesn't do it. There are two equilibrium outcomes: One firm does the R&D, but we can't predict which firm it will be.

You can see that it isn't a Nash equilibrium if no firm does the R&D because one firm would then be better off doing it. And you can see that it isn't a Nash equilibrium if both firms do the R&D because then one firm would be better off not doing it.

The firms could toss a coin or use some other random device to make a decision in this game. In some circumstances, such a strategy—called a mixed strategy—is actually better for both firms than choosing any of the strategies we've considered.

REPEATED GAMES AND SEQUENTIAL GAMES

8

The games that we've studied are played just once. In contrast, many real-world games are played repeatedly. This feature of games turns out to enable real-world duopolists to cooperate, collude, and make a monopoly profit.

Another feature of the games that we've studied is that the players move simultaneously. But in many real-world situations, one player moves first and then the other moves—the play is sequential rather than simultaneous. This feature of real-world games creates a large number of possible outcomes.

We're now going to examine these two aspects of strategic decision-making.

A Repeated Duopoly Game

If two firms play a game repeatedly, one firm has the opportunity to penalize the other for previous "bad" behavior. If Gear cheats this week, perhaps Trick will cheat next week. Before Gear cheats this week, won't it consider the possibility that Trick will cheat next week? What is the equilibrium of this game?

Actually, there is more than one possibility. One is the Nash equilibrium that we have just analyzed. Both players cheat, and each makes zero economic profit forever. In such a situation, it will never pay one of the players to start complying unilaterally because to do so would result in a loss for that player and a profit for the other. But a **cooperative equilibrium** in which the players make and share the monopoly profit is possible.

A cooperative equilibrium might occur if cheating is punished. There are two extremes of punishment. The smallest penalty is called "tit for tat." A *tit-for-tat strategy* is one in which a player cooperates in the current period if the other player cooperated in the previous period but cheats in the current period if the other player cheated in the previous period. The most severe form of punishment is called a trigger strategy. A *trigger strategy* is one in which a player cooperates if the other player cooperates but plays the Nash equilibrium strategy forever thereafter if the other player cheats.

In the duopoly game between Gear and Trick, a tit-for-tat strategy keeps both players cooperating and making monopoly profits. Let's see why with an example.

Table 5 shows the economic profit that Trick and Gear will make over a number of periods under two alternative sequences of events: colluding and cheating with a tit-for-tat response by the other firm.

If both firms stick to the collusive agreement in period 1, each makes an economic profit of $2 million. Suppose that Trick contemplates cheating in period 1. The cheating produces a quick $4.5 million economic profit and inflicts a $1 million economic loss on Gear. But a cheat in period 1 produces a response from Gear in period 2. If Trick wants to get back into a profit-making situation, it must return to the agreement in period 2 even though it knows that Gear will punish it for cheating in period 1. So in period 2, Gear punishes Trick and Trick cooperates. Gear now makes an economic profit of $4.5 million, and Trick incurs an economic loss of $1 million. Adding up the profits over two periods of play, Trick would have made more profit by cooperating—$4 million compared with $3.5 million.

What is true for Trick is also true for Gear. Because each firm makes a larger profit by sticking with the collusive agreement, both firms do so and the monopoly price, quantity, and profit prevail.

Period of Play	Collude		Cheat with Tit-for-Tat	
	Trick's Profit	Gear's Profit	Trick's Profit	Gear's Profit
	(Millions of Dollars)		(Millions of Dollars)	
1	2	2	4.5	−1.0
2	2	2	−1.0	4.5
3	2	2	2.0	2.0
4	•	•	•	•

TABLE 5   Cheating with Punishment

If duopolists repeatedly collude, each makes a profit of $2 million per period of play. If one player cheats in period 1, the other player plays a tit-for-tat strategy and cheats in period 2. The profit from cheating can be made for only one period and must be paid for in the next period by incurring a loss. Over two periods of play, the best that a duopolist can achieve by cheating is a profit of $3.5 million, compared to an economic profit of $4 million by colluding.

In reality, whether a cartel works like a one-play game or a repeated game depends primarily on the number of players and the ease of detecting and punishing cheating. The larger the number of players, the harder it is to maintain a cartel.

Games and Price Wars

A repeated duopoly game can help us understand real-world behavior and, in particular, price wars. Some price wars can be interpreted as the implementation of a tit-for-tat strategy. But the game is a bit more complicated than the one we've looked at because the players are uncertain about the demand for the product.

Playing a tit-for-tat strategy, firms have an incentive to stick to the monopoly price. But fluctuations in demand lead to fluctuations in the monopoly price, and sometimes, when the price changes, it might seem to one of the firms that the price has fallen because the other has cheated. In this case, a price war will break out. The price war will end only when each firm is satisfied that the other is ready to cooperate again. There will be cycles of price wars and the restoration of collusive agreements. Fluctuations in the world price of oil might be interpreted in this way.

Some price wars arise from the entry of a small number of firms into an industry that had previously been a monopoly. Although the industry has a small number of firms, the firms are in a prisoners' dilemma and they cannot impose effective penalties for price cutting. The behavior of prices and outputs in the computer chip industry during 1995 and 1996 can be explained in this way. Until 1995, the market for Pentium chips for IBM-compatible computers was dominated by one firm, Intel Corporation, which was able to make maximum economic profit by producing the quantity of chips at which marginal cost equaled marginal revenue. The price of Intel's chips was set to ensure that the quantity demanded equaled the quantity produced. Then in 1995 and 1996, with the entry of a small number of new firms, the industry became an oligopoly. If the firms had maintained Intel's price and shared the market, together they could have made economic profits equal to Intel's profit. But the firms were in a prisoners' dilemma. So prices fell toward the competitive level.

Let's now study a sequential game. There are many such games, and the one we'll examine is among the simplest. It has an interesting implication and it will give you the flavor of this type of game. The sequential game that we'll study is an entry game in a contestable market.

A Sequential Entry Game in a Contestable Market

If two firms play a sequential game, one firm makes a decision at the first stage of the game and the other makes a decision at the second stage.

We're going to study a sequential game in a **contestable market**—a market in which firms can enter and leave so easily that firms in the market face competition from *potential* entrants. Examples of contestable markets are routes served by airlines and by barge companies that operate on the major waterways. These markets are contestable because firms could enter if an opportunity for economic profit arose and could exit with no penalty if the opportunity for economic profit disappeared.

If the Herfindahl-Hirschman Index is used to determine the degree of competition, a contestable market appears to be uncompetitive. But a contestable market can behave as if it were perfectly competitive. To see why, let's look at an entry game for a contestable air route.

A Contestable Air Route

Agile Air is the only firm operating on a particular route. Demand and cost conditions are such that there is room for only one airline to operate. Wanabe, Inc., is another airline that could offer services on the route.

We describe the structure of a sequential game by using a *game tree* like that in Fig. 17. At the first stage, Agile Air must set a price. Once the price is set and advertised, Agile can't change it. That is, once set, Agile's price is fixed and Agile can't react to Wanabe's entry decision. Agile can set its price at either the monopoly level or the competitive level.

FIGURE 17   Agile versus Wanabe: A Sequential Entry Game in a Contestable Market

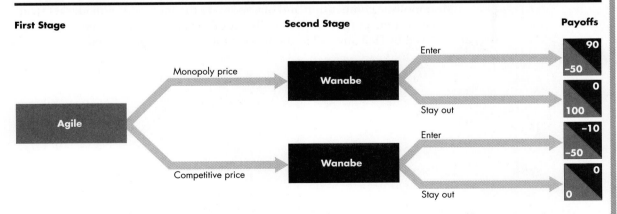

If Agile sets the monopoly price, Wanabe makes 90 (thousand dollars) by entering and earns nothing by staying out. So if Agile sets the monopoly price, Wanabe enters.

If Agile sets the competitive price, Wanabe earns nothing if it stays out and incurs a loss if it enters. So if Agile sets the competitive price, Wanabe stays out.

At the second stage, Wanabe must decide whether to enter or to stay out. Customers have no loyalty (there are no frequent flyer programs) and they buy from the lowest-price firm. So if Wanabe enters, it sets a price just below Agile's and takes all the business.

Figure 17 shows the payoffs from the various decisions (Agile's in the gray triangles and Wanabe's in the blue triangles).

To decide on its price, Agile's CEO reasons as follows: Suppose that Agile sets the monopoly price. If Wanabe enters, it earns 90 (think of all payoff numbers as thousands of dollars). If Wanabe stays out, it earns nothing. So Wanabe will enter. In this case Agile will lose 50.

Now suppose that Agile sets the competitive price. If Wanabe stays out, it earns nothing and if it enters, it loses 10, so Wanabe will stay out. In this case, Agile will make zero economic profit.

Agile's best strategy is to set its price at the competitive level and make zero economic profit. The option of earning 100 by setting the monopoly price with Wanabe staying out is not available to Agile. If Agile sets the monopoly price, Wanabe enters, undercuts Agile, and takes all the business.

In this example, Agile sets its price at the competitive level and makes zero economic profit. A less costly strategy, called **limit pricing**, sets the price at the highest level that inflicts a loss on the entrant. Any loss is big enough to deter entry, so it is not always necessary to set the price as low as the competitive price. In the example of Agile and Wanabe, at the competitive price, Wanabe incurs a loss of 10 if it enters. A smaller loss would still keep Wanabe out.

This game is interesting because it points to the possibility of a monopoly behaving like a competitive industry and serving the social interest without regulation. But the result is not general and depends on one crucial feature of the setup of the game: At the second stage, Agile is locked into the price set at the first stage.

If Agile could change its price in the second stage, it would want to set the monopoly price if Wanabe stayed out—100 with the monopoly price beats zero with the competitive price. But Wanabe can figure out what Agile would do, so the price set at the first stage has no effect on Wanabe. Agile sets the monopoly price and Wanabe might either stay out or enter.

We've looked at two of the many possible repeated and sequential games, and you've seen how these types of game can provide insights into the complex forces that determine prices and profits.

Monopolistic competition and oligopoly are the most common market structures that you encounter in your daily life. *Reading Between the Lines* looks at a game played by Dell and HP in the market for personal computers.

READING BETWEEN THE LINES

9

Dell and HP in a Market Share Game

THE NEW YORK TIMES, May 13, 2006

The Old Price-War Tactic May Not Faze Rivals Now

Dell is sharply reducing prices on its computers.

The tactic is classic, straight out of the playbook that made the company the world's largest computer maker. As overall demand for personal computers slows, lower your prices. Profit margins will take a temporary hit, but the move would hurt competitors worse as you take market share and enjoy revenue growth for years to come.

Dell did it in 2000 and it worked beautifully. But after Dell rolled out the plan last month, knocking as much as $700 off a $1,200 Inspiron and $500 off a $1,079 Dimension desktop, many of the securities analysts who follow the company, based in Round Rock, Tex., said that this time around it could be folly. . . .

What changed? . . . More than anything else, Dell's competitors have changed. In particular, Hewlett-Packard is no longer the bloated and slow-moving company it was six years ago. . . .

The most telling evidence of the new landscape for PCs was seen in statistics on worldwide shipments. While the industry grew 12.9 percent in the first three months of the year, . . . Dell's shipments grew 10.2 percent. It was the first time since analysts began tracking Dell that its shipments grew more slowly than the industry's. Hewlett's shipments, meanwhile, grew 22.2 percent. . . .

Inside Hewlett, however, there is a feeling that it can beat Dell without resorting to price wars. . . . The company has started an ambitious marketing campaign to make that point with ads that proclaim, "the computer is personal again." . . .

The campaign . . . will feature celebrities and how they individualize their computers . . . [HP] has added technology like QuickPlay, which lets a user view a DVD or listen to a CD without waiting for the laptop's operating system to boot up. The ads will say, "Don't boot. Play." . . .

Essence of the Story

► In April 2006, Dell slashed its prices.

► Dell cut its prices in 2000 and increased its market share and revenue in the years that followed.

► But experts say the price cut will not work as well today.

► Hewlett-Packard (HP) is much stronger than it was six years ago.

► Total PC shipments increased by 12.9 percent in the first quarter of 2006: Dell's shipments increased by 10.2 percent, and HP's increased by 22.2 percent.

▶ HP says that it can beat Dell without a price cut. Instead it will launch a campaign to market PCs with new and improved features that play DVDs and CDs without booting the operating system.

Economic Analysis

▶ The global PC market has many firms, but two firms dominate the market: Dell and Hewlett-Packard (HP).

▶ Figure 18 shows the market shares in the global PC market. You can see that Dell and HP are the two biggest players but that almost 50 percent of the market is served by small firms.

▶ Table 6 shows the payoff matrix (millions of dollars of profit) for the game played by Dell and HP in 2000. (The numbers are hypothetical.)

FIGURE 18   Market Shares in the PC Market in 2006

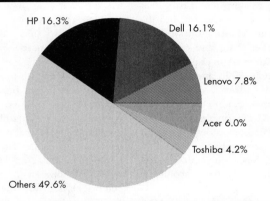

TABLE 6   The Strategies and Equilibrium in 2000

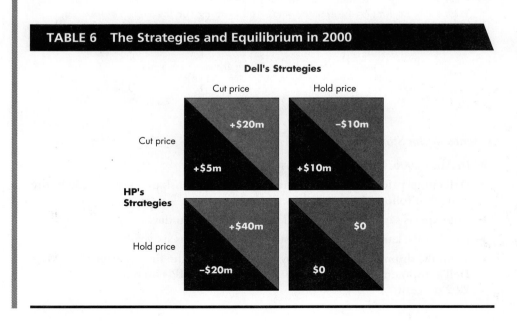

► This game has a dominant strategy equilibrium similar to that for the duopoly game on p. 247.

► If HP cuts its price, Dell makes a larger profit by cutting its price (+$20m versus −$10m), and if HP holds its price constant, Dell again makes a larger profit by cutting its price (+$40m versus zero).

► So Dell's best strategy is to cut its price.

► If Dell cuts its price, HP makes a larger profit by cutting its price (+$5m versus −$20m), and if Dell holds its price constant, HP again makes a larger profit by cutting its price (+$10m versus zero).

► So HP's best strategy is to cut its price.

► Table 7 shows the payoffs from the game between Dell and HP in 2006.

TABLE 7   The Strategies and Equilibrium in 2006

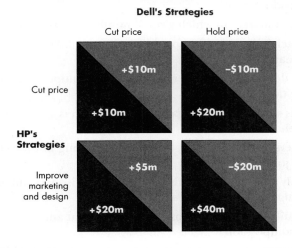

► This game, too, has a dominant strategy equilibrium.

► If HP cuts its price, Dell makes a larger profit by cutting its price (+$10m versus −$10m), and if HP improves its marketing and design, Dell again makes a larger profit by cutting its price (+$5m versus −$20m).

► So Dell's best strategy is to cut its price.

► If Dell cuts its price, HP makes a larger profit by improving its marketing and design (+$20m versus +$10m), and if Dell holds its price constant, HP again makes a larger profit by improving its marketing and design (+$40m versus +$20m).

► So HP's best strategy is to improve its marketing and design.

SUMMARY

► Monopolistic competition occurs when a large number of firms compete with each other on product quality, price, and marketing.

► Each firm in monopolistic competition faces a downward-sloping demand curve and produces the profit-maximizing quantity.

► Entry and exit result in zero economic profit and excess capacity in long-run equilibrium.

► Firms in monopolistic competition innovate and develop new products.

► Advertising expenditures increase total cost, but average total cost might fall if the quantity sold increases by enough.

► Advertising expenditures might increase demand, but demand might decrease if competition increases.

► Whether monopolistic competition is inefficient depends on the value we place on product variety.

► Oligopoly is a market in which a small number of firms compete.

► If rivals match price cuts but do not match price hikes, each firm faces a kinked demand curve.

► If one firm dominates a market, it acts like a monopoly and the small firms act as price takers.

► Oligopoly is studied by using game theory, which is a method of analyzing strategic behavior.

► In a prisoners' dilemma game, two prisoners acting in their own interest harm their joint interest.

► An oligopoly (duopoly) price-fixing game is a prisoners' dilemma in which the firms might collude or cheat.

► In Nash equilibrium, both firms cheat and output and price are the same as in perfect competition.

► Firms' decisions about advertising and R&D can be studied by using game theory.

► In a repeated game, a punishment strategy can produce a cooperative equilibrium in which price and output are the same as in a monopoly.

► In a sequential contestable market game, a small number of firms can behave like firms in perfect competition.

PRACTICE PROBLEMS FOR READING 20

1. Compared with outcomes that result from collusion, independent action by companies operating in an oligopolistic industry would tend to increase:
   A. output but not prices.
   B. prices but not output.
   C. both output and prices.

2. All else being equal, will the joint profit of an oligopolistic industry *most likely* be maximized if the:

	barriers to entry in the industry are low?	demand for the industry's products is stable?
A.	No	No
B.	No	Yes
C.	Yes	No

3. The lowest possible average total cost is found only in which market structure?
   A. Oligopoly.
   B. Monopoly.
   C. Perfect competition.

4. Branding is *most* important in which of the following market structures?
   A. Monopoly.
   B. Perfect competition.
   C. Monopolistic competition.

5. A cartel is *most likely* in which of the following market structures?
   A. Oligopoly.
   B. Monopoly.
   C. Perfect competition.

6. The *most likely* difference between monopolistic competition and perfect competition is that in monopolistically competitive markets:
   A. firms offer differentiated products.
   B. firms are free to enter and exit the market.
   C. firms produce the output where marginal cost equals marginal revenue.

7. An oligopoly market structure is *best* characterized by a small number of firms that:
   A. are free to enter or exit the market.
   B. compete with each other on the basis of price.
   C. consider the reaction of other market participants.

8. In the long run, firms in a monopolistically competitive market are *least likely* to:
   A. earn an economic profit.
   B. have excess productive capacity.
   C. produce the quantity where price equals average total cost.

9. Under monopolistic competition, a firm that introduces a new and differentiated product is *least likely* to:

    A. increase its price.

    B. make an economic profit.

    C. face a demand that is more elastic.

10. The Nash equilibrium of the duopoly game *most* accurately dictates that:

    A. both firms cheat.

    B. both firms comply.

    C. one firm complies and the other cheats.

SOLUTIONS FOR READING 20

1. A is correct. Collusion among oligopolistic firms tends to restrict output and increase prices; independent action by the same firms would increase competition, thus reducing prices and increasing output.

2. B is correct. Joint profits in an oligopolistic industry are maximized when collusion is effective. The lower the number of firms in the industry (higher barriers to entry), the more effective collusion will be. Successful collusion is more likely when demand is stable because most firms will have similar expectations for the future of the industry.

3. C is correct. Monopolies and oligopolies set prices above the efficient point, which reduces the quantity sold and increases average costs. (In monopolistic competition firms produce below the efficient scale, which increases average total costs.)

4. C is correct. Due to the large number of firms, but differentiated products, branding is most important in a market with monopolistic competition.

5. A is correct. Firms in an oligopoly are frequently tempted to cooperate and form a cartel to experience monopolistic profits.

6. A is correct. A monopolistically competitive market differs from a perfectly competitive market in that firms differentiate and market their products to gain market share.

7. C is correct. A firm operating in an oligopoly must always consider the reaction of the other firms in the market to a price or marketing decision.

8. A is correct. In the long run, monopolistically competitive firms will earn zero economic profit. They should earn a normal profit.

9. C is correct. A firm in a monopolistic competition that introduces a new and differentiated product is able to better differentiate its products, and thus demand would be less elastic as close substitutes would be less readily available. Thus the firm would be able to increase price and enjoy economic profit in the short run.

10. A is correct. Both firms believe they are better off cheating, as the payoffs from each scenario dictates they are better off cheating.

$4\frac{5}{8}$ $4\frac{11}{16}$

$5\frac{1}{8}$ $5\frac{1}{2}$ $5\frac{1}{2}$ $-$ $\frac{3}{8}$

$5\frac{1}{2}$ $5\frac{1}{2}$ $-$

$20\frac{5}{8}$ $21\frac{3}{16}$ $-$ $\frac{1}{8}$

$17\frac{3}{8}$ $18\frac{1}{8}$ $+$ $\frac{7}{8}$

$18\frac{1}{2}$ $6\frac{1}{2}$ $6\frac{1}{2}$ $-$ $\frac{1}{2}$

$7\frac{1}{4}$ $6\frac{1}{2}$ $\frac{31}{32}$ $-$ $\frac{1}{8}$

$\frac{15}{16}$

$\frac{9}{16}$ $\frac{9}{16}$

$\frac{7}{32}$

$7\frac{1}{16}$ $7\frac{13}{16}$ $7\frac{15}{16}$

$2\frac{5}{8}$ $2\frac{11}{32}$ $2\frac{1}{2}$ $+$

$2\frac{3}{4}$ $2\frac{1}{4}$ $2\frac{1}{4}$

$6\frac{1}{8}$ $12\frac{1}{16}$ $11\frac{3}{8}$ $11\frac{3}{4}$ $+$

$333\frac{3}{4}$ 33 $33\frac{1}{8}$ $-$

$25\frac{5}{8}$ $24\frac{9}{16}$ $25\frac{5}{8}$ $+$

333 12 $11\frac{5}{8}$ $11\frac{5}{8}$ $+$

16 $10\frac{1}{2}$ $10\frac{1}{2}$ $10\frac{1}{2}$ $-$

78 $15\frac{7}{8}$ $15\frac{13}{16}$ $15\frac{7}{8}$ $-$

$9\frac{1}{16}$ $8\frac{1}{4}$ $8\frac{3}{8}$ $+$

430 $11\frac{1}{4}$ $10\frac{1}{8}$ $10\frac{3}{4}$

MARKETS FOR FACTORS OF PRODUCTION
by Michael Parkin

LEARNING OUTCOMES

The candidate should be able to:	Mastery
a. explain why demand for the factors of production is called derived demand, differentiate between marginal revenue and marginal revenue product (MRP), and describe how the MRP determines the demand for labor and the wage rate;	☐
b. describe the factors that cause changes in the demand for labor and the factors that determine the elasticity of the demand for labor;	☐
c. describe the factors determining the supply of labor, including the substitution and income effects, and discuss the factors related to changes in the supply of labor, including capital accumulation;	☐
d. describe the effects on wages of labor unions and of a monopsony and explain the possible consequences for a market that offers an efficient wage;	☐
e. differentiate between physical capital and financial capital and explain the relation between the demand for physical capital and the demand for financial capital;	☐
f. explain the factors that influence the demand and supply of capital;	☐
g. differentiate between renewable and nonrenewable natural resources and describe the supply curve for each;	☐
h. differentiate between economic rent and opportunity costs.	☐

MANY HAPPY RETURNS   1

It may not be your birthday, and even if it is, chances are you are spending most of it working. But at the end of the week or month (or, if you're devoting all your time to college, when you graduate), you will receive the *returns* from your labor. Those returns vary a lot. Demetrio Luna, who spends his days in a small container suspended from the top of Houston's high-rise buildings cleaning windows, makes a happy return of $12 an hour. Katie Couric, who anchors the CBS evening news show each weekday, makes a very happy return of $15 million a year. Some differences in earnings might seem surprising. For example, your college football coach might earn much more than your economics professor. Why aren't *all* jobs well paid?

Most of us have little trouble spending our paycheck. But most of us do manage to save some of what we earn. What determines the amount of saving that people do and the returns they make on that saving?

Some people earn their income by supplying natural resources such as oil. What determines the price of a natural resource such as oil? And what determines when we will run out of oil and other nonrenewable resources?

What happens if we tax big incomes? Do the people who earn those incomes just shrug and put up with the tax but continue to supply the same quantity of resources? Or do taxes shrink the quantities of resources supplied?

In this reading, we study the markets for factors of production—labor, capital, natural resources—and learn how their prices and people's incomes are determined. We'll see that some, but not all, high incomes can be taxed without adverse effect. And we'll see in *Reading Between the Lines* at the end of the reading why universities often pay their football coaches more than they pay professors.

2   FACTOR PRICES AND INCOMES

Goods and services are produced using the *four factors of production—labor, capital, land,* and *entrepreneurship.* Incomes are determined by the quantities of the factors used and by factor prices. The factor prices are the *wage* rate earned by labor, the *interest* rate earned by capital, the *rental* rate earned by land, and the *normal profit* rate earned by entrepreneurship. In addition, a residual income, *economic profit* (or *economic loss*), is earned (or borne) by the firm's owners, who might be the entrepreneur or the stockholders.

Factors of production, like goods and services, are traded in markets. Some factor markets are competitive and behave similarly to competitive markets for goods and services. Some labor markets have noncompetitive elements.

Demand and supply is the main tool used to understand a competitive factor market. Firms demand factors of production and households supply them.

The demand for a factor of production is called a **derived demand** because it is *derived* from the demand for the goods and services produced by the factor. The quantity demanded of a factor of production is the quantity that firms plan to hire during a given time period and at a given factor price. The law of demand applies to factors of production just as it does to goods and services. The lower the factor price, other things remaining the same, the greater is the quantity demanded of that factor.

The quantity supplied of a factor of production also depends on its price. With a possible exception that you'll see later in this reading, the law of supply

FIGURE 1   Demand and Supply in a Factor Market

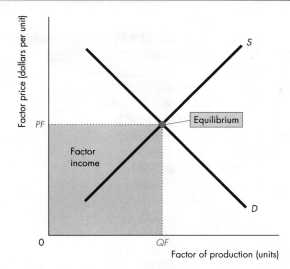

The demand curve for a factor of production, *D*, slopes downward, and the supply curve, *S*, slopes upward.Where the demand and supply curves intersect, the factor price, *PF*, and the quantity of the factor used, *QF*, are determined. The factor income is the product of the factor price and the quantity of the factor, as represented by the blue rectangle.

applies to factors of production. The higher the price of a factor, other things remaining the same, the greater is the quantity supplied of that factor.

Figure 1 shows a factor market. The demand curve for the factor is *D*, and the supply curve of the factor is *S*. The equilibrium factor price is *PF*, and the equilibrium quantity is *QF*. The income earned by the factor is its price multiplied by the quantity used. In Fig. 1, the factor income equals the area of the blue rectangle.

A change in demand or supply changes the equilibrium price, quantity, and income. An increase in demand shifts the demand curve rightward and increases income. An increase in supply shifts the supply curve rightward and income might increase, decrease, or remain constant depending on the elasticity of demand for the factor. If demand is elastic, income rises; if demand is inelastic, income falls; and if demand is unit elastic, income remains constant (see the reading on elasticity).

The rest of this reading explores the influences on the demand for and supply of factors of production. We begin with the market for labor.

LABOR MARKETS   3

For most people, the labor market is the major source of income. And for many people, it is the only source of income. In 2002, labor income represented 72 percent of total income. And in that year, the average amount earned per hour of work—the economy-wide average hourly wage rate—was close to $25 (of which $21 was paid out as a wage or salary and $4 was paid in supplementary benefits).

The average wage rate hides a lot of diversity across individual wage rates. You can see some of that diversity in Fig. 2, which shows a sample of wage rates for twenty jobs. (These numbers are for 2001, which is the most recent year for which this detail of information was available at the time of writing.)

The Bureau of Labor Statistics publishes wage data for 711 job categories, and of these, 78 percent pay below the average and 22 percent pay above the

FIGURE 2   Wage Rates in Twenty Jobs

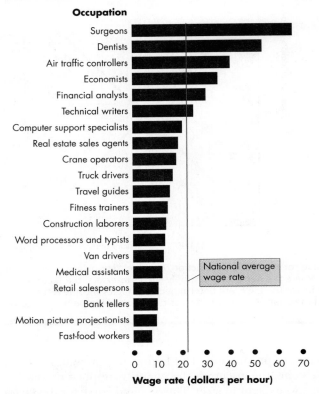

The national (economy-wide) wage rate is $21 an hour. Twenty jobs selected from the 711 jobs for which the BLS reports wage rate data show a sample of the distribution of wage rates around the national average. Most jobs pay wage rates below the national average. And some of the jobs that pay above the average exceed it by a large amount.

Source: Bureau of Labor Statistics.

average. This distribution around the average means that a small number of people earn more than the average but their wage rates exceed the average by a large amount.

The range of average hourly wage rates in Fig. 2 is from $7 to almost $70. At the low end of the wage distribution are fast-food workers, motion picture projectionists, bank tellers, and retail salespersons. Computer support specialists (such as the people who answer your tech support calls) earn just about the average wage rate. Technical writers (such as the people who write the manuals that tell you how to use all the features on your cell phone) earn a bit more than the average. A sampling of the jobs that pay wage rates that exceed the average includes financial analysts and economists. But economists earn less than air traffic controllers, dentists, and surgeons. (John Maynard Keynes said that he hoped economists would one day become as useful as dentists. Maybe the wage rates are telling us that they are not yet there!)

To understand these wage rates, we must probe the forces that influence the demand for labor and the supply of labor. We'll begin on the demand side of the labor market.

The Demand for Labor

There is a link between the quantity of labor that a firm employs and the quantity of output that it plans to produce. The *total product curve* shows that link (see the reading on output and costs).

A firm's demand for labor is the flip side of its supply of output. A firm produces the quantity that maximizes profit. And the profit-maximizing quantity is that at which marginal revenue equals marginal cost. To produce the profit-maximizing quantity, a firm hires the profit-maximizing quantity of labor.

What is the profit-maximizing quantity of labor? And how does it change as the wage rate changes? We can answer these questions by comparing the marginal revenue earned by hiring one more worker with the marginal cost of that worker. Let's look first at the marginal revenue side of this comparison.

Marginal Revenue Product

The **marginal revenue product** of labor is the change in total revenue that results from employing one more unit of labor. Table 1 shows you how to calculate marginal revenue product.

The first two columns show the total product schedule for Max's Wash 'n' Wax car wash service. The numbers tell us how the number of car washes per hour varies as the quantity of labor varies. The third column shows the *marginal product of labor*—the change in total product that results from a one-unit increase in the quantity of labor employed (see the reading on output and costs to review this concept).

TABLE 1   Marginal Revenue Product at Max's Wash 'n' Wax

	Quantity of Labor (L) (Workers)	Total Product (TP) (Car Washes per Hour)	Marginal Product (MP = ΔTP/ΔL) (Washes per Worker)	Marginal Revenue Product (MRP = MR × MP) (Dollars per Worker)	Total Revenue (TR = P × TP) (Dollars)	Marginal Revenue Product (MRP = ΔTR/ΔL) (Dollars per Worker)
A	0	0			0	
			5	20		20
B	1	5			20	
			4	16		16
C	2	9			36	
			3	12		12
D	3	12			48	
			2	8		8
E	4	14			56	
			1	4		4
F	5	15			60	

The car wash market is perfectly competitive and the price is $4 a wash, so marginal revenue is $4 a wash. Marginal revenue product equals marginal product (column 3) multiplied by marginal revenue. For example, the marginal product of the second worker is 4 washes and marginal revenue is $4 a wash, so the marginal revenue product of the second worker (in column 4) is $16. Alternatively, if Max hires 1 worker (row *B*), total product is 5 washes an hour and total revenue is $20 (column 5). If he hires 2 workers (row *C*), total product is 9 washes an hour and total revenue is $36. By hiring the second worker, total revenue rises by $16—the marginal revenue product of the second worker is $16.

The car wash market is perfectly competitive, and Max can sell as many washes as he chooses at $4 a wash, the assumed market price. So Max's *marginal revenue* is $4 a wash.

Given this information, we can calculate *marginal revenue product* (the fourth column). It equals marginal product multiplied by marginal revenue. For example, the marginal product of the second worker is 4 car washes an hour, and because marginal revenue is $4 a wash, the marginal revenue product of the second worker is $16 (4 washes at $4 each).

The last two columns of Table 1 show an alternative way of calculating the marginal revenue product of labor. Total revenue is equal to total product multiplied by price. For example, two workers produce 9 washes per hour and generate a total revenue of $36 (9 washes at $4 each). One worker produces 5 washes per hour and generates a total revenue of $20 (5 washes at $4 each). Marginal revenue product, in the sixth column, is the change in total revenue from hiring one more worker. When the second worker is hired, total revenue increases from $20 to $36, an increase of $16. So the marginal revenue product of the second worker is $16, which agrees with our previous calculation.

Diminishing Marginal Revenue Product

As the quantity of labor increases, marginal revenue product diminishes. For a firm in perfect competition, marginal revenue product diminishes because marginal product diminishes. For a monopoly (or in monopolistic competition or oligopoly), marginal revenue product diminishes for a second reason. When more labor is hired and total product increases, the firm must cut its price to sell the extra product. So marginal product *and* marginal revenue decrease, both of which bring decreasing marginal revenue product.

The Labor Demand Curve

Figure 3 shows how the labor demand curve is derived. The *marginal revenue product curve* graphs the marginal revenue product of labor at each quantity hired. Figure 3(a) is Max's marginal revenue product curve. The *x*-axis measures the number of workers that Max hires, and the *y*-axis measures the marginal revenue product of labor. The blue bars show the marginal revenue product of labor as Max employs more workers. These bars correspond to the numbers in Table 1. The curve labeled *MRP* is Max's marginal revenue product curve.

A firm's marginal revenue product curve is also its demand for labor curve. Figure 3(b) shows Max's demand for labor curve, *D*. The horizontal axis measures the number of workers hired—the same as in part (a). The vertical axis measures the wage rate in dollars per hour. In Fig. 3(a), when Max increases the quantity of labor employed from 2 workers an hour to 3 workers an hour, marginal revenue product is $12 an hour. In Fig. 3(b), at a wage rate of $12 an hour, Max hires 3 workers.

The marginal revenue product curve is also the demand for labor curve because the firm hires the profit-maximizing quantity of labor. If the wage rate is *less* than marginal revenue product, the firm can increase its profit by employing one more worker. Conversely, if the wage rate is *greater* than marginal revenue product, the firm can increase its profit by employing one fewer worker.

But if the wage rate *equals* marginal revenue product, then the firm cannot increase its profit by changing the number of workers it employs. The firm is making the maximum possible profit. So the quantity of labor demanded by the firm is such that the wage rate equals the marginal revenue product of labor.

FIGURE 3   The Demand for Labor at Max's Wash 'n' Wax

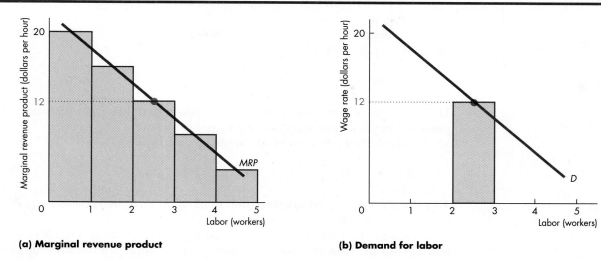

(a) Marginal revenue product

(b) Demand for labor

Max's Wash 'n' Wax operates in a perfectly competitive car wash market and can sell any quantity of washes at $4 a wash. The blue bars in part (a) represent the firm's marginal revenue product of labor. They are based on the numbers in Table 1. The gray line is the firm's marginal revenue product of labor curve. Part (b) shows Max's demand for labor curve. This curve is identical to Max's marginal revenue product curve. Max demands the quantity of labor that makes the wage rate equal to the marginal revenue product of labor. The demand for labor curve slopes downward because marginal revenue product diminishes as the quantity of labor employed increases.

Because the marginal revenue product curve is also the demand curve, and because marginal revenue product diminishes as the quantity of labor employed increases, the demand for labor curve slopes downward. The lower the wage rate, other things remaining the same, the more workers a firm hires.

When we studied the firm's output decision, we discovered that a condition for maximum profit is that marginal revenue equals marginal cost. We've now discovered another condition for maximum profit: Marginal revenue product of labor equals the wage rate. Let's study the connection between these two conditions.

Equivalence of Two Conditions for Profit Maximization

Profit is maximized when, at the quantity of labor hired, *marginal revenue product* equals the wage rate and when, at the output produced, *marginal revenue* equals *marginal cost.*

These two conditions for maximum profit are equivalent. The quantity of labor that maximizes profit produces the output that maximizes profit.

To see the equivalence of the two conditions for maximum profit, first recall that

Marginal revenue product = Marginal revenue × Marginal product.

If we call marginal revenue product *MRP*, marginal revenue *MR*, and marginal product *MP*, we have

$$MRP = MR \times MP.$$

If we call the wage rate W, the first condition for profit to be maximized is

$$MRP = W.$$

But $MRP = MR \times MP$, so

$$MR \times MP = W.$$

This equation tells us that when profit is maximized, marginal revenue multiplied by marginal product equals the wage rate.

Divide the last equation by MP to obtain

$$MR = W \div MP.$$

This equation states that when profit is maximized, marginal revenue equals the wage rate divided by the marginal product of labor.

The wage rate divided by the marginal product of labor equals marginal cost. It costs the firm W to hire one more hour of labor. But the labor produces MP units of output. So the cost of producing one of those units of output, which is marginal cost, is W divided by MP.

If we call marginal cost MC, then

$$MR = MC,$$

which is the second condition for maximum profit.

Because the first condition for maximum profit implies the second condition, these two conditions are equivalent. Table 2 summarizes the calculations you've just done and shows the equivalence of the two conditions for maximum profit.

Max's Numbers

Check the numbers for Max's Wash 'n' Wax and confirm that the conditions you've just examined work. Max's profit-maximizing labor decision is to hire 3 workers if the total wage rate is $12 an hour. When Max hires 3 workers, marginal product is 3 washes an hour. Max sells the 3 washes for a marginal revenue of $4 a wash. So marginal revenue product is 3 washes multiplied by $4 a wash, which equals $12 an hour. At a wage rate of $12 an hour, Max is maximizing profit.

Equivalently, Max's marginal cost is $12 an hour divided by 3 washes an hour, which equals $4 a wash. At a marginal revenue of $4 a wash, Max is maximizing profit.

You've discovered that the law of demand applies for labor just as it does for goods and services. Other things remaining the same, the lower the wage rate (the price of labor), the greater is the quantity of labor demanded.

Let's now study the influences that change the demand for labor and shift the demand for labor curve.

Changes in the Demand for Labor

The demand for labor depends on three factors:

1. The price of the firm's output
2. Other factor prices
3. Technology and capital

TABLE 2   Two Conditions for Maximum Profit

Symbols

Marginal product	*MP*
Marginal revenue	*MR*
Marginal cost	*MC*
Marginal revenue product	*MRP*
Wage rate	*W*

Two Conditions for Maximum Profit

1. **$MR = MC$**   2. **$MRP = W$**

Equivalence of Conditions

1. $MRP/MP =$ **MR** $=$ **MC** $= W/MP$

Multiply by
MP
to give
$MRP = MR \times MP$

Multiply by
MP
to give
$MC \times MP = W$

Flipping the
equation over

Flipping the
equation over

2. $MR \times MP =$ **MRP** $=$ **W** $= MC \times MP$

The two conditions for maximum profit are that marginal revenue (*MR*) equals marginal cost (*MC*) and that marginal revenue product (*MRP*) equals the wage rate (*W*). These two conditions are equivalent because marginal revenue product (*MRP*) equals marginal revenue (*MR*) multiplied by marginal product (*MP*) and the wage rate (*W*) equals marginal cost (*MC*) multiplied by marginal product (*MP*).

The Price of the Firm's Output

The higher the price of the firm's output, the greater is the firm's demand for labor. The price of output affects the demand for labor through its influence on marginal revenue product. A higher price for the firm's output increases marginal revenue, which, in turn, increases the marginal revenue product of labor. A change in the price of a firm's output leads to a shift in the firm's demand for labor curve. If the price of the firm's output increases, the demand for labor increases and the demand for labor curve shifts rightward.

Other Factor Prices

If the price of some other factor of production changes, the demand for labor changes, but only in the *long run* when all factors of production can be varied. The effect of a change in some other factor price depends on whether that factor is a *substitute* for or a *complement* of labor. Computers are substitutes for telephone operators but complements of word processor operators. So if computers become less costly to use, the demand for telephone operators decreases but the demand for word processor operators increases.

Technology and Capital

An advance in technology or an increase in capital that changes the marginal product of labor changes the demand for labor. There is a general belief that advances in technology and capital accumulation destroy jobs and therefore decrease the demand for labor. But while new technologies and capital are substitutes for some types of labor and decrease the demand for labor, they are complements of other kinds and increase the demand for labor. For example, the electronic telephone exchange is a substitute for telephone operators, so the arrival of this new technology has decreased the demand for telephone operators. This same new technology is a complement of systems managers, programmers, and electronic engineers. So its arrival has increased the demand for these types of labor.

Again, these effects on the demand for labor are long-run effects that occur when a firm adjusts all its resources and incorporates new technologies into its production process.

Table 3 summarizes the influences on a firm's demand for labor.

TABLE 3   A Firm's Demand for Labor

**The Law of Demand
(Movements along the Demand Curve for Labor)**

The quantity of labor demanded by a firm

Decreases if:	*Increases if:*
► The wage rate increases	► The wage rate decreases

**Changes in Demand
(Shifts in the Demand Curve for Labor)**

A firm's demand for labor

Decreases if:	*Increases if:*
► The price of the firm's output decreases	► The price of the firm's output increases
► The price of a substitute for labor falls	► The price of a substitute for labor rises
► The price of a complement of labor rises	► The price of a complement of labor falls
► A new technology or new capital decreases the marginal product of labor	► A new technology or new capital increases the marginal product of labor

---

Market Demand

So far, we've studied the demand for labor by an individual firm. The market demand for labor is the total demand by all firms. The market demand for labor is derived (similarly to the market demand for any good or service) by adding together the quantities demanded by all firms at each wage rate. Because each firm's demand for labor curve slopes downward, so does the market demand for labor curve.

Elasticity of Demand for Labor

The elasticity of demand for labor measures the responsiveness of the quantity of labor demanded to the wage rate. This elasticity is important because it tells us how labor income changes when the supply of labor changes. An increase in supply (other things remaining the same) lowers the wage rate. If demand is inelastic, an increase in supply also lowers labor income. But if demand is elastic, an increase in supply lowers the wage rate and increases labor income. And if the demand for labor is unit elastic, a change in supply leaves labor income unchanged.

The demand for labor is less elastic in the short run, when only the quantity of labor can be varied, than in the long run, when the quantities of labor and other factors of production can be varied. The elasticity of demand for labor depends on the

▶ Labor intensity of the production process
▶ Elasticity of demand for the good produced
▶ Substitutability of capital for labor

Labor Intensity

A labor-intensive production process is one that uses a lot of labor and little capital. Home building is an example. The greater the degree of labor intensity, the more elastic is the demand for labor. To see why, first suppose that wages are 90 percent of total cost. A 10 percent increase in the wage rate increases total cost by 9 percent. Firms will be sensitive to such a large change in total cost, so if the wage rate increases, firms will decrease the quantity of labor demanded by a relatively large amount. But if wages are 10 percent of total cost, a 10 percent increase in the wage rate increases total cost by only 1 percent. Firms will be less sensitive to this increase in total cost, so if the wage rate increases, firms will decrease the quantity of labor demanded by a relatively small amount.

Elasticity of Demand for the Good Produced

The greater the elasticity of demand for the good, the larger is the elasticity of demand for the labor used to produce it. An increase in the wage rate increases the marginal cost of producing the good and decreases the supply of it. The decrease in the supply of the good increases the price of the good and decreases the quantity demanded of the good and the quantities of the factors of production used to produce it. The greater the elasticity of demand for the good, the larger is the decrease in the quantity demanded of the good and so the larger is the decrease in the quantities of the factors of production used to produce it.

Substitutability of Capital for Labor

The more easily capital can be used instead of labor in production, the more elastic is the long-run demand for labor. For example, it is easy to use robots rather than assembly-line workers in car factories and grape-picking machines rather than labor in vineyards. So the demand for these types of labor is elastic. At the other extreme, it is difficult (though possible) to substitute computers for newspaper reporters, bank loan officers, and teachers. So the demand for these types of labor is inelastic.

Let's now turn from the demand side of the labor market to the supply side and examine the decisions that people make about how to allocate time between working and other activities.

The Supply of Labor

People can allocate their time to two broad activities: labor supply and leisure. (Leisure is a catch-all term. It includes all activities other than supplying labor.) For most people, leisure is more enjoyable than supplying labor. We'll look at the labor supply decision of Jill, who is like most people. She enjoys her leisure time, and she would be pleased if she didn't have to spend her weekends working a supermarket checkout line.

But Jill has chosen to work weekends. The reason is that she is offered a wage rate that exceeds her *reservation wage*. Jill's reservation wage is the lowest wage at which she is willing to supply labor. If the wage rate exceeds her reservation wage, she supplies some labor. But how much labor does she supply? The quantity of labor that Jill supplies depends on the wage rate.

Substitution Effect

Other things remaining the same, the higher the wage rate Jill is offered, at least over a range, the greater is the quantity of labor that she supplies. The reason is that Jill's wage rate is her *opportunity cost of leisure*. If she quits work an hour early to catch a movie, the cost of that extra hour of leisure is the wage rate that Jill forgoes. The higher the wage rate, the less willing Jill is to forgo the income and take the extra leisure time. This tendency for a higher wage rate to induce Jill to work longer hours is a *substitution effect*.

But there is also an *income effect* that works in the opposite direction to the substitution effect.

Income Effect

The higher Jill's wage rate, the higher is her income. A higher income, other things remaining the same, induces Jill to increase her demand for most goods. Leisure is one of those goods. Because an increase in income creates an increase in the demand for leisure, it also creates a decrease in the quantity of labor supplied.

Backward-Bending Supply of Labor Curve

As the wage rate rises, the substitution effect brings an increase in the quantity of labor supplied while the income effect brings a decrease in the quantity of labor supplied. At low wage rates, the substitution effect is larger than the income effect, so as the wage rate rises, people supply more labor. But as the wage rate continues to rise, the income effect eventually becomes larger than the substitution effect and the quantity of labor supplied decreases. The labor supply curve is *backward bending*.

Figure 4(a) shows the labor supply curves for Jill, Jack, and Kelly. Each labor supply curve is backward bending, but the three people have different reservation wage rates.

FIGURE 4   The Supply of Labor

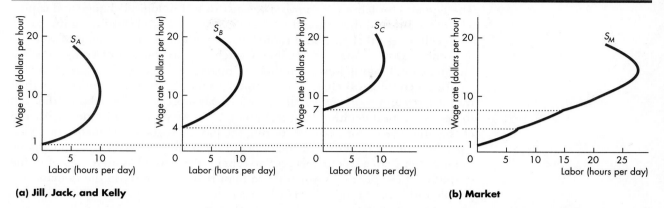

(a) Jill, Jack, and Kelly   **(b) Market**

Part (a) shows the labor supply curves of Jill, Jack, and Kelly (S_A, S_B, and S_C, respectively). Each person has a reservation wage below which she or he will supply no labor. As the wage rate rises, the quantity of labor supplied increases to a maximum and then begins to decrease as the wage rate rises further. Each person's supply curve eventually bends backward. Part (b) shows how, by adding the quantities of labor supplied by each person at each wage rate, we derive the market supply curve of labor, S_M. The market supply curve has a long upward-sloping section before it bends backward.

Market Supply

The market supply of labor curve is the sum of the individual supply curves. Figure 4(b) shows the market supply curve, S_M, derived from the supply curves of Jill, Jack, and Kelly (S_A, S_B, and S_C, respectively) in Fig. 4(a). At a wage rate of less than $1 an hour, no one supplies labor. At a wage rate of $1 an hour, Jill works but Jack and Kelly don't. As the wage rate increases and reaches $7 an hour, all three of them are working. The market supply curve S_M eventually bends backward, but it has a long upward-sloping section.

Changes in the Supply of Labor

The supply of labor changes when influences other than the wage rate change. The key factors that change the supply of labor and that over the years have increased it are

1. Increases in adult population
2. Technological change and capital accumulation in home production

As the adult population has increased and as technological change and capital accumulation in the home have decreased the time needed to produce meals, laundry services, and cleaning services, the supply of labor has increased.

Let's now build on what we've learned about the demand for labor and the supply of labor and study labor market equilibrium and the trends in wage rates and employment.

Labor Market Equilibrium

Wages and employment are determined by equilibrium in the labor market as you saw in Fig. 1. Over the years, the equilibrium wage rate and employment level have both increased. You can now explain why.

Trends in the Demand for Labor

The demand for labor has *increased* because of technological change and capital accumulation, and the demand for labor curve has shifted steadily rightward.

Technological change and capital accumulation destroy some jobs and create others. Downsizing has become a catchword as the use of computers has eliminated millions of jobs, even those of managers.

But technological change and capital accumulation create more jobs than they destroy and *on the average*, the new jobs pay more than the old ones did. But to benefit from the advances in technology, people must acquire new skills and change their jobs. For example, during the past 20 years, the demand for typists has fallen almost to zero. But the demand for people who can type (on a computer rather than a typewriter) and do other tasks as well has increased. And the output of these people is worth more than that of a typist. So the demand for people with typing (and other) skills has increased.

Trends in the Supply of Labor

The supply of labor has increased because of population growth and technological change as well as capital accumulation in the home. The mechanization of home production of fast-food preparation services (the freezer and the microwave oven) and laundry services (the automatic washer and dryer and wrinkle-free fabrics) has decreased the time spent on activities that once were full-time jobs and have led to a large increase in the supply of labor. As a result, the supply of labor curve has shifted steadily rightward, but at a slower pace than the shift in the demand curve.

Trends in Equilibrium

Because technological advances and capital accumulation have increased demand by more than population growth and technological change in home production have increased supply, both wage rates and employment have increased. But not everyone has shared in the increased prosperity that comes from higher wage rates. Some groups have been left behind, and some have even seen their wage rates fall. Why?

Two key reasons can be identified. First, technological change affects the marginal product of different groups in different ways. High-skilled computer-literate workers have benefited from the information revolution while low-skilled workers have suffered. The demand for the services of the first group has increased, and the demand for the services of the second group has decreased. (Draw a supply and demand figure, and you will see that these changes widen the wage difference between the two groups.) Second, international competition has lowered the marginal revenue product of low-skilled workers and so has decreased the demand for their labor.

4   LABOR MARKET POWER

In some labor markets, workers organized by labor unions possess market power and are able to raise the wage rate above the competitive level. In some other labor markets, a large employer dominates the demand side of the market and can exert market power that lowers the wage rate below its competitive level. But an employer might also decide to pay more than the competitive wage rate to attract the best workers. Let's look at these cases.

Labor Unions

A **labor union** is an organized group of workers that aims to increase wages and influence other job conditions. The two types of unions are craft unions and industrial unions. A *craft union* is a group of workers who have a similar range of skills but work in many different industries. Examples are the carpenters' union (UBC) and the electrical workers union (IBEW). An *industrial union* is a group of workers who have a variety of skills and job types but work in the same industry. The United Auto Workers (UAW) and the Steelworkers Union (USWA) are examples of industrial unions.

Most unions are members of the AFL-CIO, which was created in 1955 when the American Federation of Labor (AFL) and the Congress of Industrial Organizations (CIO) combined.

Unions vary enormously in size. Craft unions are the smallest, and industrial unions are the biggest. Union strength peaked in the 1950s, when 35 percent of the labor force belonged to unions. That percentage has declined steadily and is now 12 percent.

Unions negotiate with employers in a process called *collective bargaining*. A *strike*, a group decision to refuse to work under prevailing conditions, is the main weapon available to the union. A *lockout*, a firm's refusal to operate its plant and employ its workers, is the main weapon available to the employer. Each party uses the threat of a strike or a lockout to try to get an agreement in its own favor. Sometimes, when the two parties in the collective bargaining process cannot agree on the wage rate or other conditions of employment, they agree to submit their disagreement to binding arbitration. *Binding arbitration* is a process in which a third party—an arbitrator—determines wages and other employment conditions on behalf of the negotiating parties.

Unions' Objectives and Constraints

A union has three broad objectives: It seeks to

1. Increase compensation
2. Improve working conditions
3. Expand job opportunities

A union's ability to pursue its objectives is restricted by two sets of constraints—one on the supply side of the labor market and the other on the demand side. On the supply side, the union's activities are limited by how well it can restrict nonunion workers from offering their labor in the same market as union labor. The larger the fraction of the work force controlled by the union, the more effective the union can be in this regard. It is difficult for unions to operate in markets where there is an abundant supply of willing nonunion labor. For example, the market for farm labor in southern California is very tough for a union to organize because of the ready flow of nonunion, often illegal, labor from Mexico. At the other extreme, unions in the construction industry can better pursue their goals because they can influence the number of people who can obtain skills as electricians, plasterers, and carpenters. The professional associations of dentists and physicians are best able to restrict the supply of dentists and physicians. These groups control the number of qualified workers by controlling either the examinations that new entrants must pass or entrance into professional degree programs.

On the demand side of the labor market, the union faces a tradeoff that arises from firms' profit-maximizing decisions. Because labor demand curves slope downward, anything a union does that increases the wage rate or other employment costs decreases the quantity of labor demanded.

Let's see how unions operate in an otherwise competitive labor market.

A Union Enters a Competitive Labor Market

When a union enters a competitive labor market, it seeks to increase the wage rate and to increase the demand for the labor of its members. That is, the union tries to take actions that shift the demand curve for its members' labor rightward.

Figure 5 illustrates a labor market. The demand curve is D_C, and the supply curve is S_C. Before the union enters the market, the wage rate is \$7 an hour and 100 hours of labor are employed.

Now suppose that a union is formed to organize the workers in this market. The union can attempt to increase the wage rate in this market in two ways. It can try to restrict the supply of labor, or it can try to stimulate the demand for labor. First, look at what happens if the union has sufficient control over the supply of labor to be able to artificially restrict that supply below its competitive level—to S_U. If that is all the union is able to do, employment falls to 85 hours of labor and the wage rate rises to \$8 an hour. The union simply picks its preferred position along the demand curve that defines the tradeoff it faces between employment and the wage rate.

You can see that if the union can only restrict the supply of labor, it raises the wage rate but decreases the number of jobs available. Because of this outcome,

FIGURE 5   A Union Enters a Competitive Labor Market

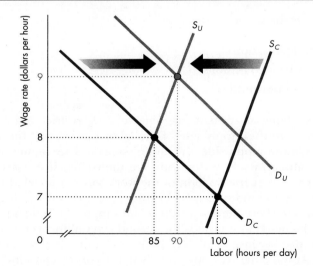

In a competitive labor market, the demand curve is D_C and the supply curve is S_C. Competitive equilibrium occurs at a wage rate of \$7 an hour with 100 hours a day employed. By restricting employment below the competitive level, the union shifts the supply of labor to S_U. If the union can do no more than that, the wage rate will increase to \$8 an hour but employment will fall to 85 hours a day. If the union can increase the demand for labor (by increasing the demand for the good produced by union members or by raising the price of substitute labor) and shift the demand curve to D_U, then it can increase the wage rate still higher, to \$9 an hour, and achieve employment of 90 hours a day.

unions try to increase the demand for labor and shift the demand curve rightward. Let's see what they might do to achieve this outcome.

How Unions Try to Change the Demand for Labor

The union tries to change the demand for labor in two ways. First, it tries to make the demand for union labor less elastic. Second, it tries to increase the demand for union labor. Making the demand for labor less elastic does not eliminate the tradeoff between employment and the wage rate. But it does make the tradeoff less unfavorable. If a union can make the demand for labor less elastic, it can increase the wage rate at a lower cost in terms of lost employment opportunities. But if the union can increase the demand for labor, it might even be able to increase both the wage rate and the employment opportunities of its members. Some of the methods used by the unions to change the demand for the labor of its members are to

▶ Increase the marginal product of union members

▶ Encourage import restrictions

▶ Support minimum wage laws

▶ Support immigration restrictions

▶ Increase demand for the good produced

Unions try to increase the marginal product of their members, which in turn increases the demand for their labor, by organizing and sponsoring training schemes, by encouraging apprenticeship and other on-the-job training activities, and by professional certification.

Unions lobby to restrict imports and encourage people to buy goods made by unionized workers in the United States.

Unions support minimum wage laws to increase the cost of employing low-skilled labor. An increase in the wage rate of low-skilled labor leads to a decrease in the quantity demanded of low-skilled labor and to an increase in demand for high-skilled union labor, a substitute for low-skilled labor.

Restrictive immigration laws decrease the supply of foreign workers. As a result, the demand for union labor in the United States increases.

Because the demand for labor is a derived demand, an increase in the demand for the good produced by union labor increases the demand for union labor. The garment workers' union urging us to buy union-made clothes and the UAW asking us to buy only American cars made by union workers are examples of attempts by unions to increase the demand for union labor.

Figure 5 illustrates the effects of an increase in the demand for the labor of a union's members. If the union can also take steps that increase the demand for labor to D_U, it can achieve an even bigger increase in the wage rate with a smaller fall in employment. By maintaining the restricted labor supply at S_U, the union increases the wage rate to $9 an hour and achieves an employment level of 90 hours a day.

Because a union restricts the supply of labor in the market in which it operates, the union's actions increase the supply of labor in nonunion markets. Workers who can't get union jobs must look elsewhere for work. This increase in the supply of labor in nonunion markets lowers the wage rate in those markets and further widens the gap between union and nonunion wages.

The Scale of Union-Nonunion Wage Gap

How much of a difference to wage rates do unions make? To answer this question, we must look at the wages of unionized and nonunionized workers who do similar work. The evidence suggests that after allowing for skill differences, the union-nonunion wage gap lies between 10 percent and 25 percent. For example, unionized airline pilots earn about 25 percent more than nonunion pilots with the same level of skill.

Let's now look at a labor market in which the employer possesses market power.

Monopsony in the Labor Market

A market in which there is a single buyer is called **monopsony**. In a monopsony labor market, there is one employer and the wage rate is the lowest at which the firm can attract the labor it plans to hire.

With the growth of large-scale production over the last century, large manufacturing plants such as coal mines, steel and textile mills, and car manufacturers became the major employer in some regions, and in some places a single firm employed almost all the labor. Today, in some parts of the country, managed health care organizations are the major employer of health care professionals. In some communities, Wal-Mart is the main employer of sales clerks. These firms have market power.

Let's see how a monopsony uses its power to lower the wage rate below the level paid by firms that must compete for their labor.

Like all firms, a monopsony has a downward-sloping marginal revenue product curve, which is *MRP* in Fig. 6. This curve tells us the extra revenue the monopsony receives by selling the output produced by an extra hour of labor. The supply of labor curve is *S*. This curve tells us how many hours are supplied at each wage rate. It also tells us the minimum wage for which a given quantity of labor is willing to work.

A monopsony recognizes that to hire more labor, it must pay a higher wage; equivalently, by hiring less labor, it can pay a lower wage. Because a monopsony

FIGURE 6   A Monopsony Labor Market

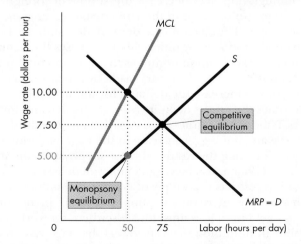

A monopsony is a market structure in which there is a single buyer. A monopsony in the labor market has a marginal revenue product curve *MRP* and faces a labor supply curve *S*. The marginal cost of labor curve is *MCL*. Making the marginal cost of labor equal to marginal revenue product maximizes profit. The monopsony hires 50 hours of labor a day and pays the lowest wage rate for which that quantity of labor will work, which is $5 an hour.

controls the wage rate, the marginal cost of labor exceeds the wage rate. The marginal cost of labor is shown by the curve *MCL*. The relationship between the marginal cost of labor curve and the supply curve is similar to the relationship between the marginal cost and average cost curves that you studied in the reading on output and costs. The supply curve is like the average cost of labor curve. In Fig. 6, the firm can hire 49 hours of labor for a wage rate of just below $4.90 an hour. The firm's total labor cost is $240. But suppose that the firm hires 50 hours of labor. It can hire the 50th hour of labor for $5 an hour. The total cost of labor is now $250 an hour. So hiring the 50th hour of labor increases the cost of labor from $240 to $250, which is a $10 increase. The marginal cost of labor is $10 an hour. The curve *MCL* shows the $10 marginal cost of hiring the 50th hour of labor.

To calculate the profit-maximizing quantity of labor to hire, the firm sets the marginal cost of labor equal to the marginal revenue product of labor. That is, the firm wants the cost of the last worker hired to equal the extra total revenue brought in. In Fig. 6, this outcome occurs when the monopsony employs 50 hours of labor. What is the wage rate that the monopsony pays? To hire 50 hours of labor, the firm must pay $5 an hour, as shown by the supply of labor curve. So each worker is paid $5 an hour. But the marginal revenue product of labor is $10 an hour, which means that the firm makes an economic profit of $5 on the last hour of labor that it hires.

Compare this outcome with that in a competitive labor market. If the labor market shown in Fig. 6 were competitive, equilibrium would occur at the point of intersection of the demand curve and the supply curve. The wage rate would be $7.50 an hour, and 75 hours of labor a day would be employed. So compared with a competitive labor market, a monopsony decreases both the wage rate and employment.

The ability of a monopsony to cut the wage rate and employment and make an economic profit depends on the elasticity of labor supply. If the supply of labor is highly elastic, a monopsony has little power to cut the wage rate and employment to boost its profit.

A Union and a Monopsony

In the reading on monopoly, we discovered that in monopoly, the seller determines the market price. We've now seen that in monopsony—a market with a single buyer—the buyer determines the price. Suppose that a union operates in a monopsony labor market. A union is like a monopoly. If the union (monopoly seller) faces a monopsony buyer, the situation is called **bilateral monopoly**. In bilateral monopoly, the wage rate is determined by bargaining.

In Fig. 6, if the monopsony is free to determine the wage rate and the level of employment, it hires 50 hours of labor for a wage rate of $5 an hour. But suppose that a union represents the workers. The union agrees to maintain employment at 50 hours but seeks the highest wage rate the employer can be forced to pay. That wage rate is $10 an hour—the wage rate that equals the marginal revenue product of labor. The union might not be able to get the wage rate up to $10 an hour, but it won't accept $5 an hour. The monopsony firm and the union bargain over the wage rate, and the result is an outcome between $10 an hour and $5 an hour.

The outcome of the bargaining depends on the costs that each party can inflict on the other as a result of a failure to agree on the wage rate. The firm can shut down the plant and lock out its workers, and the workers can shut down the plant by striking. Each party knows the other's strength and knows what it will lose if it does not agree to the other's demands.

If the two parties are equally strong and they realize it, they will split the gap between $5 and $10 and agree to a wage rate of $7.50 an hour. If one party is stronger than the other—and both parties know that—the agreed wage will favor the stronger party. Usually, an agreement is reached without a strike or a lock-out. The threat is usually enough to bring the bargaining parties to an agreement. When a strike or lockout does occur, it is usually because one party has misjudged the costs each party can inflict on the other.

Minimum wage laws have interesting effects in monopsony labor markets. Let's study these effects.

Monopsony and the Minimum Wage

In a competitive labor market, a minimum wage that exceeds the equilibrium wage decreases employment (see the reading on markets in action). In a monopsony labor market, a minimum wage can increase both the wage rate and employment. Let's see how.

Figure 7 shows a monopsony labor market in which the wage rate is $5 an hour and 50 hours of labor are employed. A minimum wage law is passed that requires employers to pay at least $7.50 an hour. The monopsony now faces a perfectly elastic supply of labor at $7.50 an hour up to 75 hours. Above 75 hours, a wage above $7.50 an hour must be paid to hire additional hours of labor. Because the wage rate is a fixed $7.50 an hour up to 75 hours, the marginal cost of labor is also constant at $7.50 up to 75 hours. Beyond 75 hours, the marginal cost of labor rises above $7.50 an hour. To maximize profit, the monopsony sets the marginal cost of labor equal to the marginal revenue product of labor. That is, the monopsony hires 75 hours of labor at $7.50 an hour.

The minimum wage law has made the supply of labor perfectly elastic and made the marginal cost of labor the same as the wage rate up to 75 hours. The law has not affected the supply of labor or the marginal cost of labor at employment levels above 75 hours. The minimum wage law has succeeded in raising the wage rate by $2.50 an hour and increasing the amount of labor employed by 25 hours.

FIGURE 7   Minimum Wage Law in Monopsony

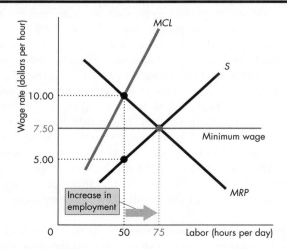

In a monopsony labor market, the wage rate is $5 an hour and 50 hours a day are hired. If a minimum wage law increases the wage rate to $7.50 an hour, employment increases to 75 hours a day.

Efficiency Wages

An **efficiency wage** is a wage rate that a firm pays above the competitive equilibrium wage rate with the aim of attracting the most productive workers.

In a perfectly competitive labor market, firms and workers are well informed. Workers know exactly what they are being hired to do and firms can observe the marginal product of each worker. In this state of complete knowledge of all the relevant factors, a firm would never pay more than the going competitive market wage rate.

In some labor markets, the employer is not able to observe a worker's marginal product. It is costly to monitor all the actions of every worker. For example, if McDonald's employed enough managers to keep a close watch on the activities of all the servers, its costs would be very high. And who would monitor all those managers? Because it is costly to monitor everything that a worker does, workers have some power. They might work hard or shirk.

If every firm pays its workers the going competitive wage rate, some workers will choose to work hard and some will choose to shirk. And threatening to fire a shirker won't help much because the shirker knows another job can be found at the going wage and the firm doesn't know if it will replace one shirker with a hard worker or another shirker.

If a firm pays a wage rate above the competitive level—an efficiency wage—the threat of being fired for shirking has some force. A fired worker can expect to find another job but only at the lower market equilibrium wage rate. So the worker now has an incentive not to shirk. Also, hard workers will be more likely to want to work for the firm, so if a shirking worker is fired, most likely the firm will attract a hard worker as the replacement.

So a firm that pays an efficiency wage attracts more productive workers but at the cost of a higher wage bill. So the firm must decide just how much more than the competitive wage to pay. The firm makes this decision by making the marginal improvement in productivity equal the marginal cost of the higher wage rate. If most firms pay an efficiency wage, the quantity of labor supplied will exceed the quantity demanded and unemployment will arise that strengthens the incentive that workers face and further discourages shirking.

CAPITAL MARKETS   5

Capital markets are the channels through which firms obtain *financial* resources to buy *physical* capital resources. *Physical capital* is the *stock* of tools, instruments, machines, buildings, and other constructions that firms use to produce goods and services. Physical capital also includes the inventories of raw material and semi-finished and finished goods that firms hold. These capital resources are called *physical capital* to emphasize that they are real physical objects. They are goods that have been produced by some firms and bought by other firms. Physical capital is a *stock*—a quantity of objects that exists at a given time. But each year, that stock changes. It is depleted as old capital wears out and it is replenished and added to as firms buy new items of capital.

The markets in which each item of physical capital is traded are not the capital markets. They are goods markets just like the ones that you've studied in the readings on perfect competition, monopoly, and monopolistic competition and oligopoly. For example, the prices and quantities of tower cranes and earth movers are determined in the markets for those items.

A firm buys many different items of capital during a given time period. The dollar value of those capital goods is called the firm's *investment*. But it

FIGURE 8   The Rate of Return to Capital: 1960–2005

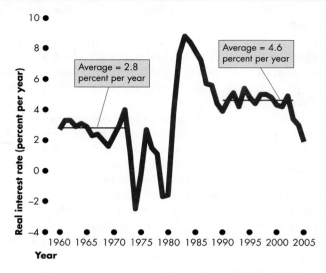

The real interest rate (the interest rate adjusted for inflation) fluctuated between a negative return in 1974 and 1975 and a high of 9 percent in 1984. It was steady at 2.8 percent during the 1960s and at 4.6 percent during the 1990s and early 2000s. It fell to 2 percent in 2005.

Source: *Economic Report of the President*, 2006.

is the objects themselves that are the capital, not the dollars of value that they represent.

The financial resources used to buy physical capital are called *financial capital*. These resources come from saving. The interest rate is the "price of capital," which adjusts to make the quantity of financial capital supplied equal to the quantity demanded.

For most of us, capital markets are where we make our biggest-ticket transactions. We borrow in a capital market to buy a home. And we lend in capital markets to build up a fund on which to live when we retire.

Do the rates of return in capital markets increase over time as wage rates do? Figure 8 answers this question by showing the record from 1960 to 2005. Measuring the interest rate as a *real* interest rate, which means that we subtract the loss in the value of money from inflation, the rate of return to capital has fluctuated. It averaged 2.8 percent a year during the 1960s, became negative during the 1970s, climbed to 9 percent a year during the 1980s, steadied to average 4.6 percent a year during the 1990s and early 2000s, and then fell to 2 percent in 2005.

The ideas you've already met in your study of demand and supply in the labor market apply to the capital market as well. But there is a special feature of capital: People must compare the *present* expenditure on capital with the *future* income it will earn.

Let's look at the demand for capital.

The Demand for Capital

A firm's demand for *financial* capital stems from its demand for *physical* capital, and the amount that a firm plans to borrow in a given time period is determined by its *planned investment*—its planned purchases of new capital. This decision is driven by the firm's attempt to maximize profit. The factors that determine investment and borrowing plans are the

▶ Marginal revenue product of capital
▶ Interest rate

Let's see how these factors influence Tina's investment and borrowing decisions.

Marginal Revenue Product of Capital

The *marginal revenue product of capital* is the change in total revenue that results from employing one more unit of capital. Suppose, for example, that Tina, an accountant who operates Taxfile, Inc., buys a new computer and software, which increases Taxfile's revenue by $1,150 a year for the next two years. Then the marginal revenue product of this computer is $1,150 a year.

The marginal revenue product of capital diminishes as the quantity of capital increases. Capital is just like labor in this respect. If Tina buys a second computer, Taxfile's total revenue will increase by less than the $1,150 generated by the first computer.

Interest Rate

The interest rate is the opportunity cost of the funds borrowed to finance investment. The interest rate is also the opportunity cost of a firm using its own funds because it could lend those funds to another firm and earn the going interest rate on the loan. The higher the interest rate, the smaller is the quantity of planned investment and borrowing in the capital market.

Firms demand the quantity of capital that makes the marginal revenue product of capital equal to the expenditure on capital. But the expenditure on capital is a *present* outlay and the marginal revenue product is a *future* return. The higher the interest rate, the smaller is the *present value* of future returns, and so the smaller is the quantity of planned investment.

Demand Curve for Capital

A firm's demand curve for capital shows the relationship between the quantity of financial capital demanded by the firm and the interest rate, other things remaining the same. Figure 9(a) shows Tina's demand curve for capital. Tina demands no capital at an interest rate of 12 percent a year; but at an interest rate of 8 percent a year, she spends $2,000 on a new computer; and at an interest rate of 4 percent a year, she spends $4,000 on two new computers.

Figure 9(b) shows the market demand curve for capital, *KD*, which is the horizontal sum of the demand curves of all firms. In the figure, the quantity of capital demanded in the entire capital market is $1,500 billion when the interest rate is 6 percent a year.

You've seen how the demand for capital is determined. Let's now look at the supply side of the capital market.

FIGURE 9   A Firm's Demand and the Market Demand for Capital

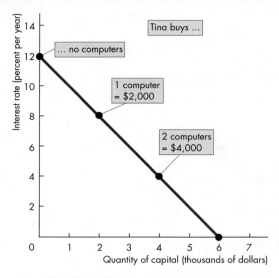

(a) Taxfile's demand curve for capital

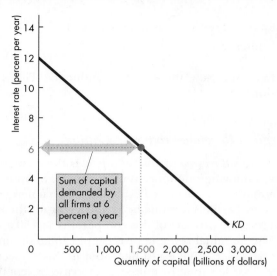

(b) Market demand curve for capital

For each firm, the lower the interest rate, the greater is the quantity of capital demanded. The market demand curve is the (horizontal) sum of the firms' demand curves.

The Supply of Capital

The quantity of capital supplied results from people's saving decisions. The main factors that determine saving are

► Income

► Expected future income

► Interest rate

Let's see how these factors influence Aaron's saving decisions.

Income

Saving is the act of converting *current* income into *future* consumption. When Aaron's income increases, he plans to consume more both now and in the future. But to increase *future* consumption, Aaron must save today. So, other things remaining the same, the higher Aaron's income, the more he saves.

Expected Future Income

If Aaron's current income is high and his expected future income is low, he will have a high level of saving. But if Aaron's current income is low and his expected future income is high, he will have a low (perhaps even negative) level of saving.

Students have low current incomes compared with expected future incomes so they tend to consume more than they earn. In middle age, most people are earning more than they expect to earn when they retire. So they save for their retirement years.

Interest Rate

A dollar saved today grows into a dollar plus interest tomorrow. The higher the interest rate, the greater is the amount that a dollar saved today becomes in the future. So the higher the interest rate, the greater is the opportunity cost of current consumption. With a higher opportunity cost of current consumption, Aaron cuts his current consumption and increases his saving.

Supply Curve of Capital

The supply curve of capital shows the relationship between the quantity of capital supplied and the interest rate, other things remaining the same. The curve KS_0 in Fig. 10 is a supply curve of capital. An increase in the interest rate brings an increase in the quantity of capital supplied and a movement along the supply curve.

Let's now use what we've learned about the demand for and supply of capital and see how the interest rate is determined.

Capital Market Equilibrium

Saving plans and investment plans are coordinated through capital markets, and the interest rate adjusts to make these plans compatible.

Figure 10 shows the capital market. The demand for capital is KD_0, and the supply of capital is KS_0. The equilibrium interest rate is 6 percent a year, and the quantity of capital—the amount of investment by firms and saving by households—is $1,500 billion.

FIGURE 10 Capital Market Equilibrium

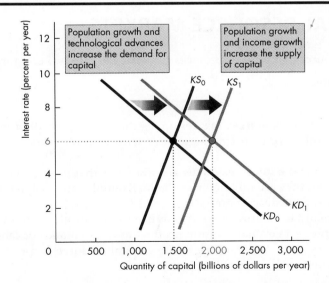

Initially, the demand for capital is KD_0 and the supply of capital is KS_0. The equilibrium interest rate is 6 percent a year, and the quantity of capital is $1,500 billion. Over time, both the demand and supply of capital increase to KD_1 and KS_1. The quantity of capital increases, but the interest rate is constant. The demand and supply of capital are influenced by common and related factors.

If the interest rate exceeded 6 percent a year, the quantity of capital supplied would exceed the quantity of capital demanded and the interest rate would fall. The interest rate would keep falling until the surplus of capital was eliminated.

If the interest rate were less than 6 percent a year, the quantity of capital demanded would exceed the quantity of capital supplied and the interest rate would rise. The interest rate would keep rising until the shortage of capital was eliminated.

Changes in Demand and Supply

Over time, both the demand for capital and the supply of capital increase. The demand curve shifts rightward to KD_1, and the supply curve shifts to KS_1. Both curves shift because the same or related forces influence them. Population growth increases both demand and supply. Technological advances increase demand and bring higher incomes, which in turn increase supply. Because both demand and supply increase over time, the quantity of capital increases but the interest rate remains constant.

In reality, the real interest rate fluctuates, as you can see in Fig. 8. The reason is that the demand for capital and the supply of capital do not change in lock-step. Sometimes rapid technological change brings an increase in the demand for capital *before* it brings the higher incomes that increase the supply of capital. When this sequence of events occurs, the real interest rate rises. The first half of the 1980s was such a time, as you can see in Fig. 8.

At other times, the demand for capital grows slowly or even decreases temporarily. In this situation, supply outgrows demand and the real interest rate falls. Figure 8 shows that the mid-1970s and the period from 1984 through 1991 were two such periods.

The lessons that we've just learned about capital markets can be used to understand the prices of nonrenewable natural resources. Let's see how.

6   NATURAL RESOURCE MARKETS

Natural resources, or what economists call *land*, fall into two categories:

► Renewable
► Nonrenewable

Renewable natural resources are resources that are repeatedly replenished by nature. Examples are land (in its everyday sense), rivers, lakes, rain, wind, and sunshine.

Nonrenewable natural resources are resources that nature does not replenish. Once used, they are no longer available. Examples are coal, natural gas, and oil—the so-called hydrocarbon fuels.

The demand for natural resources as inputs into production is based on the same principle of marginal revenue product as the demand for labor (and the demand for capital). But the supply of a natural resource is special. Let's look first at the supply of a renewable natural resource.

The Supply of a Renewable Natural Resource

The quantity of land and other renewable natural resources is fixed. The quantity supplied cannot be changed by individual decisions. People can vary the amount of land they own. But when one person buys some land, another person

FIGURE 11   The Supply of Land

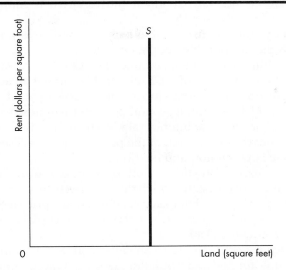

The supply of a given piece of land is perfectly inelastic. No matter what the rent, no more land than the quantity that exists can be supplied.

sells it. The aggregate quantity of land supplied of any particular type and in any particular location is fixed, regardless of the decisions of any individual. This fact means that the supply of each particular piece of land is perfectly inelastic. Figure 11 illustrates such a supply. Regardless of the rent, the quantity of land supplied on Chicago's "Magnificent Mile" is a fixed number of square feet.

Because the supply of land is fixed regardless of its rent, rent is determined by demand. The greater the demand for a specific piece of land, the higher is its rent.

Expensive land can be, and is, used more intensively than inexpensive land. For example, high-rise buildings enable land to be used more intensively. However, to use land more intensively, it has to be combined with another factor of production: capital. An increase in the amount of capital per block of land does not change the supply of land itself.

Although the supply of each type of land is fixed and its supply is perfectly inelastic, each individual firm, operating in competitive land markets, faces an elastic supply of land. For example, Fifth Avenue in New York City has a fixed amount of land, but Doubleday, the bookstore, could rent some space from Saks, the department store. Each firm can rent the quantity of land that it demands at the going rent, as determined in the marketplace. So, provided that land markets are competitive, firms are price takers in these markets, just as they are in the markets for other productive resources.

The Supply of a Nonrenewable Natural Resource

The *stock* of a natural resource is the quantity in existence at a given time. This quantity is fixed and is independent of the price of the resource. The *known* stock of a natural resource is the quantity that has been discovered. This quantity increases over time because advances in technology enable ever less accessible sources to be discovered. Both of these *stock* concepts influence the price of a nonrenewable natural resource. But the influence is indirect. The direct influence on price is the rate at which the resource is supplied for use in production—called the *flow* supply.

The flow supply of a nonrenewable natural resource is *perfectly elastic* at a price that equals the present value of the expected price next period.

To see why, think about the economic choices of Saudi Arabia, a country that possesses a large inventory of oil. Saudi Arabia can sell an additional billion barrels of oil right now and use the income it receives to buy U.S. bonds. Or it can keep the billion barrels in the ground and sell them next year. If it sells the oil and buys bonds, it earns the interest rate on the bonds. If it keeps the oil and sells it next year, it earns the amount of the price increase or loses the amount of the price decrease between now and next year.

If Saudi Arabia expects the price of oil to rise next year by a percentage that *equals* the current interest rate, the price that it expects next year equals $(1 + r)$ multiplied by this year's price. For example, if this year's price is $60 a barrel and the interest rate is 5 percent a year ($r = 0.05$), then next year's expected price is $1.05 \times \$60$, which equals $63 a barrel.

With the price expected to rise to $63 next year, Saudi Arabia is indifferent between selling now for $60 and not selling now but waiting until next year and selling for $63. Saudi Arabia expects to make the same return either way. So at $60 a barrel, Saudi Arabia will sell whatever quantity is demanded.

But if Saudi Arabia expects the price to rise next year by a percentage that *exceeds* the current interest rate, then Saudi Arabia expects to make a bigger return by hanging on to the oil than by selling the oil and buying bonds. So it keeps the oil and sells none. And if Saudi Arabia expects the price to rise next year by a percentage that is *less than* the current interest rate, the bond gives a bigger return than the oil, so Saudi Arabia sells as much oil as it can this year.

The minimum price at which Saudi Arabia is willing to sell oil is the present value of the expected future price. At this price, it will sell as much oil as buyers demand. So its supply is perfectly elastic.

Price and the Hotelling Principle

Figure 12 shows the equilibrium in a nonrenewable natural resource market. Because flow supply is perfectly elastic at the present value of next period's expected price, the actual price of the natural resource equals the present value of next period's expected price. Also, because the current price equals the present value of the expected future price, the price of the resource is expected to rise at a rate equal to the interest rate.

The proposition that the price of a resource is expected to rise at a rate equal to the interest rate is called the *Hotelling Principle*. It was first realized by Harold Hotelling, a mathematician and economist at Columbia University. But as Fig. 13 shows, *actual* prices do not follow the path *predicted* by the Hotelling Principle. Why do the prices of nonrenewable natural resources sometimes fall rather than follow their expected path and increase over time?

The key reason is that the future is unpredictable. Expected technological change is reflected in the price of a natural resource. But a previously unexpected new technology that leads to the discovery or the more efficient use of a nonrenewable natural resource causes its price to fall. Over the years, as technology has advanced, we have become more efficient in our use of nonrenewable natural resources. And we haven't just become more efficient. We've become more efficient than we expected to.

FIGURE 12 A Nonrenewable Natural Resource Market

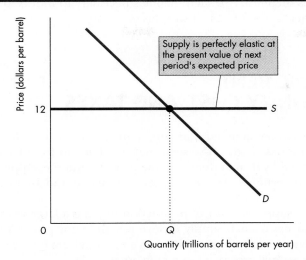

The flow supply of a nonrenewable natural resource is perfectly elastic at the *present value* of next period's expected price. The demand for a nonrenewable natural resource is determined by its marginal revenue product. The price is determined by supply and equals the *present value* of next period's expected price.

FIGURE 13 Falling Resource Prices

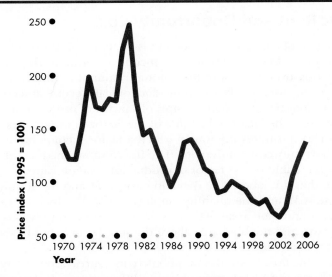

The prices of metals (here a price index that measures the average of the prices of aluminum, copper, iron ore, lead, manganese, nickel, silver, tin, and zinc) have tended to fall over time, not rise as predicted by the Hotelling Principle. The reason is that unanticipated advances in technology have decreased the cost of extracting resources and greatly increased the exploitable known reserves.

Source: *International Financial Statistics* (various issues), Washington, DC: International Monetary Fund.

People supply factors of production to earn an income. But some people earn enormous incomes. Are such incomes necessary to induce people to work and supply other factors? Let's answer this question.

7   ECONOMIC RENT, OPPORTUNITY COST, AND TAXES

You've now seen how demand and supply in factor markets determine factor prices and quantities. And you've seen that the demand for a factor of production is determined by its marginal revenue product and the supply of a factor of production is determined by the resources available and by people's choices about their use.

People who supply a factor of production that has a large marginal revenue product or that has a small supply receive a high factor price. And the people who supply a factor of production that has a small marginal revenue product or that has a large supply receive a low factor price.

The elasticity of supply of a factor of production determines the extent to which its income represents the opportunity cost of using that factor. And this same elasticity determines how the burden of a tax in a factor market is shared between the supplier and the user of the factor. We're now going to explore these issues beginning with the distinction between economic rent and opportunity cost.

Economic Rent and Opportunity Cost

The total income of a factor of production is made up of its economic rent and its opportunity cost. **Economic rent** is the income received by the owner of a factor of production over and above the amount required to induce that owner to offer the factor for use. Any factor of production can receive an economic rent. The income required to induce the supply of a factor of production is the opportunity cost of using the factor—the value of the factor in its next best use.

Figure 14(a) illustrates the way in which a factor income has an economic rent and opportunity cost component. The figure shows the market for a factor of production. It could be *any* factor of production—labor, capital, or land—but we'll suppose that it is labor. The demand curve is *D*, and the supply curve is *S*. The wage rate is *W*, and the quantity employed is *C*. The income earned is the sum of the gray and blue areas. The gray area below the supply curve measures opportunity cost, and the blue area above the supply curve but below the factor price measures economic rent.

To see why the area below the supply curve measures opportunity cost, recall that a supply curve can be interpreted in two different ways. It shows the quantity supplied at a given price, and it shows the minimum price at which a given quantity is willingly supplied. If suppliers receive only the minimum amount required to induce them to supply each unit of the factor, they will be paid a different price for each unit. The prices will trace the supply curve, and the income received will be entirely opportunity cost—the gray area in Fig. 14(a).

The concept of economic rent is similar to that of producer surplus (see the reading on efficiency and equity). Economic rent is the price a person receives for the use of a factor minus the minimum price at which a given quantity of the factor is willingly supplied.

FIGURE 14 Economic Rent and Opportunity Cost

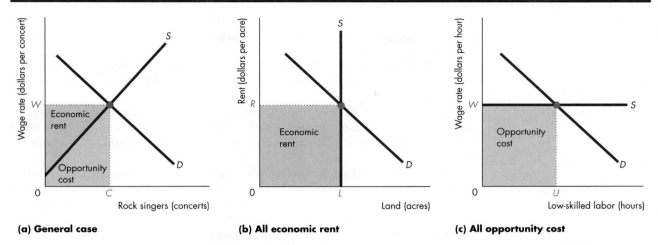

(a) General case **(b) All economic rent** **(c) All opportunity cost**

When the supply curve of a factor slopes upward—the general case—as in part (a), part of the factor income is economic rent (the blue area) and part is opportunity cost (the gray area). When the supply of a factor is perfectly inelastic (the supply curve is vertical), as in part (b), the entire factor income is economic rent. When the supply of the factor is perfectly elastic, as in part (c), the factor's entire income is opportunity cost.

Economic rent is *not* the same thing as the "rent" that a farmer pays for the use of some land or the "rent" that you pay for your apartment. Everyday "rent" is a price paid for the services of land or a building. *Economic rent* is a component of the income received by any factor of production.

The portion of the factor income that consists of economic rent depends on the elasticity of the supply of the factor. When the supply of a factor is perfectly inelastic, its entire income is economic rent. Most of the income received by Garth Brooks and Pearl Jam is economic rent. Also, a large part of Katie Couric's income is economic rent. When the supply of a factor of production is perfectly elastic, none of its income is economic rent. Most of Demetrio Luna's income from window cleaning is opportunity cost. In general, when supply is neither perfectly elastic nor perfectly inelastic, like that illustrated in Fig. 14(a), some part of the factor income is economic rent and the other part is opportunity cost.

Figure 14(b) shows the market for a parcel of land in New York City. The quantity of land is fixed in size at L acres. Therefore the supply curve of the land is vertical—perfectly inelastic. No matter what the rent on the land is, there is no way of increasing the quantity that can be supplied. Suppose that the demand curve in Fig. 14(b) shows the marginal revenue product of this block of land. Then it commands a rent of R. The entire income accruing to the owner of the land is the blue area in the figure. This income is *economic rent*.

Figure 14(c) shows the market for low-skilled labor in a poor country such as India or China. A large quantity of labor is available for work at the going wage rate (in this case, W). The supply of labor is perfectly elastic. The entire income earned by these workers is opportunity cost. They receive no economic rent.

Implications of Economic Rent for Taxes

The share of the burden of a tax and the inefficiency created by a tax depend on the elasticity of supply. If supply is perfectly inelastic, the burden of a tax is borne entirely by the supplier (see the reading on markets in action). So if a tax is imposed on the income of a factor of production with a perfectly inelastic supply, the supplier bears the entire tax. Also, if supply is perfectly inelastic, the tax has no effect on the quantity supplied and no effect on efficiency. The only effect of the tax is to transfer buying power from the factor owner to the government.

But notice that the situation in which a tax has no effect on efficiency is when the entire factor income is economic rent. Taxing economic rent is efficient.

If the supply of a factor of production is not perfectly inelastic, a tax on that factor's income is borne at least partly by the buyer. Also, because the buyer faces a higher factor price, the quantity demanded decreases and an inefficiency arises.

But now notice that this situation in which a tax brings inefficiency is when some of the factor income is an opportunity cost. In the extreme case in which the buyer pays the entire tax, the entire factor income is opportunity cost and none is economic rent.

Reading Between the Lines looks at the market for college football coaches and compares it with the market for professors.

READING BETWEEN THE LINES

Labor Markets in Action

THE NEW YORK TIMES, November 9, 2005

An Awkward Coexistence on Campus

It is worth a take-home exam to discover how the brains behind higher education have lost their minds in the pursuit of football superiority.

Were they hypnotized by the numbing metronome of hook 'em Horns hand signals or snake-charmed by the Super Bowl rings on the fingers of Charlie Weis? Were they paid off by boosters who buy their socks and yachts only in team colors or simply sucked into a devious three-legged race to be one of two teams in the B.C.S. title game?

All of the above has conspired to lead university caretakers into establishing the $3 million club for college coaches. After Notre Dame handed a 10-year extension to Weis last week reportedly worth $30 to $40 million, the N.C.A.A. reached a new level in fiscal lunacy.

Where is intelligent life on campus? At the University of Texas, there is a cosmic star, but he is not named Mack Brown. He is called Big Steve by Texas students and ponders the energy of empty space, but he doesn't dash through gaping holes opened by the offensive line.

Steven Weinberg is a Texas physics professor who grew up in the Bronx, taught at Harvard and won the Nobel Prize in 1979 before being wooed to Texas three years later in one of the university's most famous hires this side of Darrell Royal. . . .

Somehow, Mack Brown's $2.1 million salary still gets paid. As The Austin-American Statesman has reported, Weinberg is the university's highest-paid faculty member, at around $400,000 by most accounts. Upon his arrival, he was rumored to have had his salary contractually linked to that of the head football coach. If only, he says. . . .

Essence of the Story

► Charlie Weis, head football coach at the University of Notre Dame, has a 10-year contract that is reported to be worth between $30 to $40 million—more than $3 million a year.

► Steven Weinberg, a physics professor at the University of Texas who won the Nobel Prize in 1979, is reported to be the university's highest-paid faculty member, with a salary of about $400,000 a year.

Economic Analysis

► The market for college football coaches is competitive.

► The market for professors is also competitive.

► The demand for both coaches and professors is determined by the marginal revenue product of each group.

▶ The marginal revenue product of a coach depends on the coach's ability to win games and the additional revenue that the college or university can raise from its alumni and other contributors when its football team is successful.

▶ The marginal revenue product of a professor depends on the professor's ability to attract students and research funding.

▶ For any given quantity of coaches and professors, the marginal revenue product of a professor almost certainly exceeds that of a coach.

▶ But the equilibrium wage rate of a coach and that of a professor depend on the marginal revenue product of each group and on the supply of each.

▶ The supply of coaches is small and probably inelastic.

▶ The supply of professors is large and most likely elastic.

▶ The supply of coaches is inelastic because few people have the talent demanded by this specialized activity.

▶ The supply of professors is elastic because they are generally well-educated people who can do many alternative jobs.

▶ Equilibrium in the market for coaches occurs at a higher wage rate and a much smaller quantity than does the equilibrium in the market for professors.

▶ Figure 15 shows the two markets. Notice that there is a break in the *x*-axis because the quantity of professors is much greater than that of coaches.

FIGURE 15   The Markets for Coaches and Professors

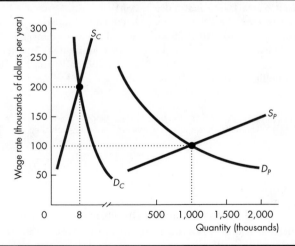

▶ The demand curve for coaches is D_C, and the demand curve for professors is D_P. The supply curve of coaches is S_C, and the supply curve of professors is S_P.

▶ The equilibrium quantity of coaches is 8,000, and the equilibrium quantity of professors is 1 million.

▶ The equilibrium wage rate of a coach is $200,000 a year, and the equilibrium wage rate of a professor is $100,000 a year.

▶ Because the supply of coaches is inelastic, a large part of their income is economic rent.

▶ But colleges and universities can't lower the wage rate of a coach because each school faces a perfectly elastic supply of coaches at the going market-determined equilibrium wage rate.

▶ Some coaches, such as Charlie Weis, and some professors, such as Steven Weinberg, earn much more than the average coach and the average professor in the figure because these individuals are exceptional and the supply of truly outstanding coaches and professors is smaller than the supply of average coaches and average professors.

SUMMARY

- ▶ The demand for and supply of a factor of production determines the equilibrium factor price and factor income.

- ▶ Factor income changes in the same direction as a change in the demand for the factor. The effect of a change in the supply of a factor on factor income depends on the elasticity of demand.

- ▶ The marginal revenue product of labor determines the demand for labor.

- ▶ The quantity of labor supplied increases as the wage rate increases, but at high wage rates, the supply curve eventually bends backward.

- ▶ Wage rates increase because demand increases by more than supply.

- ▶ A labor union can raise the wage rate by restricting the supply or increasing the demand for labor.

- ▶ A monopsony can lower the wage rate below the competitive level.

- ▶ A minimum wage in monopsony can increase employment and raise the wage rate.

- ▶ The capital market determines the interest rate on the financial resources that are used to buy physical capital.

- ▶ To make an investment decision, a firm compares the *present value* of the marginal revenue product of capital with the expenditure on capital.

- ▶ The higher the interest rate, the greater is the amount of saving and the quantity of capital supplied.

- ▶ Capital market equilibrium determines the real interest rate.

- ▶ The demand for natural resources is determined by marginal revenue product.

- ▶ The supply of land is inelastic.

- ▶ The flow supply of nonrenewable natural resources is perfectly elastic at a price equal to the present value of the expected future price.

- ▶ The price of nonrenewable natural resources is expected to rise at a rate equal to the interest rate but fluctuates and sometimes falls.

- ▶ Economic rent is the income above opportunity cost earned by the owner of a factor of production.

- ▶ When the supply of a factor is perfectly inelastic, its entire income is made up of economic rent, and when supply is perfectly elastic, the entire income is made up of opportunity cost.

- ▶ A tax on economic rent is an efficient tax.

PRACTICE PROBLEMS FOR READING 21

1. The marginal revenue product of labor is *most likely* the additional:

   A. product generated by adding one more unit of labor.

   B. revenue generated by adding one more unit of labor.

   C. product generated by each laborer when technology improves.

2. Which of the following is *least likely* to cause a change in the demand curve for labor?

   A. Technology.

   B. Other factor prices.

   C. An increase in the wage rate.

3. All else equal, according to the income effect and the substitution effect, an increase in the wage rate will *most likely* have what effect on the supply of labor?

   A. The income effect and the substitution effect will both increase the supply of labor.

   B. The income effect increases, but the substitution effect decreases the supply of labor.

   C. The income effect decreases, but the substitution effect increases the supply of labor.

4. The main factors that determine the quantity of capital supplied are *least likely* to include:

   A. expenses.

   B. interest rates.

   C. expected future income.

SOLUTIONS FOR READING 21

1. B is correct. The marginal revenue product of labor is the additional revenue generated by adding one more unit of labor.

2. C is correct. An increase in the wage rate would result in a movement along the demand curve for labor, not a change in the demand curve for labor.

3. C is correct. According to the income effect, an increase in the wage rate will increase the demand for leisure and decrease the quantity of labor supplied. According to the substitution effect, an increase in the wage rate will increase the opportunity cost of leisure, resulting in an increase in the quantity of labor supplied.

4. A is correct. Expenses are not a main factor that determines savings and savings dictates the quantity of capital supplied. The factors that determine savings are income, interest rates, and expected future income.

MONITORING JOBS AND THE PRICE LEVEL

by Michael Parkin

LEARNING OUTCOMES

The candidate should be able to:	Mastery
a. define an unemployed person and interpret the main labor market indicators;	☐
b. define aggregate hours and real wage rates and explain their relation to gross domestic product (GDP);	☐
c. explain the types of unemployment, full employment, the natural rate of unemployment, and the relation between unemployment and real GDP;	☐
d. explain and calculate the consumer price index (CPI) and the inflation rate, describe the relation between the CPI and the inflation rate, and explain the main sources of CPI bias.	☐

VITAL SIGNS   1

Each month, we chart the course of unemployment as a measure of U.S. economic health. How do we measure unemployment? What does the unemployment rate tell us? Is it a reliable vital sign for the economy?

Every month, we also chart the number of people working, the number of hours they work, and the wages they receive. Are most new jobs full time or part time? And are they high-wage jobs or low-wage jobs?

As the U.S. economy expanded after 2002, job growth was weak and questions about the health of the labor market became of vital importance to millions of American families. We put the spotlight on the labor market during the past few years in *Reading Between the Lines* at the end of this reading.

Economics, Eighth Edition, by Michael Parkin. Copyright © 2008 by Pearson Education. Reprinted with permission of Pearson Education, publishing as Pearson Addison Wesley.

Having a good job that pays a decent wage is only half of the equation that translates into a good standard of living. The other half is the cost of living. We track the cost of the items that we buy with another number that is published every month, the Consumer Price Index, or CPI. What is the CPI? How is it calculated? And does it provide a reliable guide to the changes in our cost of living?

These are the questions we study in this reading. We begin by looking at the way we measure employment and unemployment.

2   JOBS AND WAGES

The state of the labor market has a large impact on our incomes and our lives. We become concerned when jobs are hard to find and more relaxed when they are plentiful. But we want a good job, which means that we want a well-paid and interesting job. You are now going to learn how economists track the health of the labor market.

Population Survey

Every month, the U.S. Census Bureau surveys 60,000 households and asks a series of questions about the age and job market status of the members of each household. This survey is called the Current Population Survey. The Census Bureau uses the answers to describe the anatomy of the labor force.

Figure 1 shows the population categories used by the Census Bureau and the relationships among the categories.

The population divides into two broad groups: the working-age population and others who are too young to work or who live in institutions and are unable to work. The **working-age population** is the total number of people aged 16 years and over who are not in jail, hospital, or some other form of institutional care.

The Census Bureau divides the working-age population into two groups: those in the labor force and those not in the labor force. It also divides the labor force into two groups: the employed and the unemployed. So the **labor force** is the sum of the employed and the unemployed.

To be counted as employed in the Current Population Survey, a person must have either a full-time job or a part-time job. To be counted as *un*employed, a person must be available for work and must be in one of three categories:

1. Without work but has made specific efforts to find a job within the previous four weeks

2. Waiting to be called back to a job from which he or she has been laid off

3. Waiting to start a new job within 30 days

Anyone surveyed who satisfies one of these three criteria is counted as unemployed. People in the working-age population who are neither employed nor unemployed are classified as not in the labor force.

In 2006, the population of the United States was 299.3 million. There were 70.6 million people under 16 years of age or living in institutions. The working-age population was 228.7 million. Of this number, 76.1 million were not in the labor force. Most of these people were in school full time or had retired from work. The remaining 152.6 million people made up the U.S. labor force. Of these, 145.3 million were employed and 7.3 million were unemployed.

FIGURE 1   Population Labor Force Categories

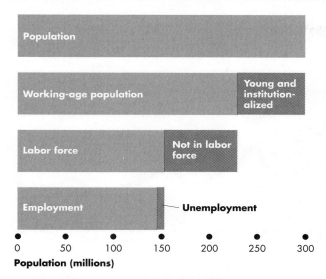

The total population is divided into the working-age population and the young and institutionalized. The working-age population is divided into those in the labor force and those not in the labor force. The labor force is divided into the employed and the unemployed.

Source: Bureau of Labor Statistics.

Three Labor Market Indicators

The Census Bureau calculates three indicators of the state of the labor market, which are shown in Fig. 2. They are

► The unemployment rate
► The labor force participation rate
► The employment-to-population ratio

The Unemployment Rate

The amount of unemployment is an indicator of the extent to which people who want jobs can't find them. The **unemployment rate** is the percentage of the people in the labor force who are unemployed. That is,

$$\text{Unemployment rate} = \frac{\text{Number of people unemployed}}{\text{Labor force}} \times 100$$

and

$$\text{Labor force} = \frac{\text{Number of people employed} +}{\text{Number of people unemployed.}}$$

In 2006, the number of people employed was 145.3 million and the number unemployed was 7.3 million. By using the above equations, you can verify that the

FIGURE 2   Employment, Unemployment, and the Labor Force: 1961–2006

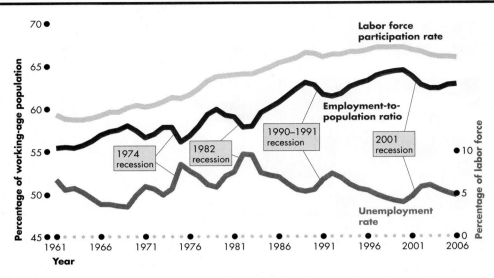

The unemployment rate increases in recessions and decreases in expansions. The labor force participation rate and the employment-to-population ratio have upward trends and fluctuate with the business cycle. The employment-to-population ratio fluctuates more than the labor force participation rate and reflects cyclical fluctuations in the unemployment rate. Fluctuations in the labor force participation rate arise mainly because of discouraged workers.

Source: Bureau of Labor Statistics.

labor force was 152.6 million (145.3 million plus 7.3 million) and the unemployment rate was 4.8 percent (7.3 million divided by 152.6 million, multiplied by 100).

Figure 2 shows the unemployment rate (graphed in gray and plotted against the right-hand scale) and two other labor market indicators from 1961 to 2006. The unemployment rate averaged 5.9 percent and it reached peak values at the end of the recessions of 1974, 1982, 1990–1991, and 2001.

The Labor Force Participation Rate

The number of people who join the labor force is an indicator of the willingness of people of working age to take jobs. The **labor force participation rate** is the percentage of the working-age population who are members of the labor force. That is,

$$\frac{\text{Labor force}}{\text{participation rate}} = \frac{\text{Labor force}}{\text{Working-age population}} \times 100.$$

In 2006, the labor force was 152.6 million and the working-age population was 228.7 million. By using the above equation, you can calculate the labor force participation rate. It was 66.7 percent (152.6 million divided by 228.7 million, multiplied by 100).

Figure 2 shows the labor force participation rate (graphed in light blue and plotted against the left-hand scale). It had an upward trend before 2000. But it fell slightly after 2000. It has also had some mild fluctuations, which result from unsuccessful job seekers becoming discouraged workers.

Discouraged workers are people who are available and willing to work but have not made specific efforts to find a job within the previous four weeks. These workers often temporarily leave the labor force during a recession and reenter during an expansion and become active job seekers.

The Employment-to-Population Ratio

The number of people of working age who have jobs is an indicator of both the availability of jobs and the degree of match between people's skills and jobs. The **employment-to-population ratio** is the percentage of people of working age who have jobs. That is,

$$\text{Employment-to-population ratio} = \frac{\text{Number of people employed}}{\text{Working-age population}} \times 100.$$

In 2006, the number of people employed was 145.3 million and the working-age population was 228.7 million. By using the above equation, you can calculate the employment-to-population ratio. It was 63.5 percent (145.3 million divided by 228.7 million, multiplied by 100).

Figure 2 shows the employment-to-population ratio (graphed in dark blue and plotted against the left-hand scale). This indicator follows the same trends as the participation rate: upward before 2000 and downward after 2000. The increase before 2000 means that the U.S. economy created jobs at a faster rate than the working-age population grew. This indicator also fluctuates, and its fluctuations coincide with but are opposite to those in the unemployment rate. The employment-to-population ratio falls during a recession and increases during an expansion.

Why did the labor force participation rate and the employment-to-population ratio increase up to 2000 and then decrease? Women have driven these upward trends. Figure 3 shows that between 1961 and 2000, the female labor force participation rate increased from 38 percent to 60 percent. Shorter work hours, higher productivity, and an increased emphasis on white-collar jobs expanded the job opportunities and wages available to women. At the same time, technological

FIGURE 3   The Changing Face of the Labor Market

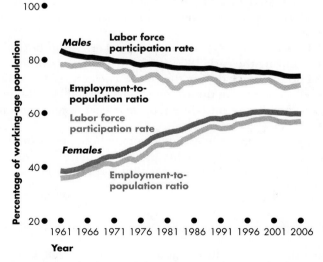

The upward trends in the labor force participation rate and the employment-to-population ratio are accounted for mainly by the increasing participation of women in the labor market. The male labor force participation rate and employment-to-population ratio have decreased.

Source: Bureau of Labor Statistics.

advances increased productivity in the home, which freed up women's time and enabled them to take jobs outside the home. After 2000, the upward path ended.

Men have slowed the upward trend and turned the trend downward after 2000. Between 1961 and 2000, the male labor force participation rate decreased from 83 percent to 75 percent, and by 2006, it was 73 percent.

Male labor force participation decreased because increasing numbers of men are remaining in school longer and because some are retiring earlier.

Aggregate Hours

The three labor market indicators that we've just examined are useful signs of the health of the economy and directly measure what matters to most people: jobs. But these three indicators don't tell us the quantity of labor used to produce real GDP, and we cannot use them to calculate the productivity of labor. The productivity of labor is significant because it influences the wages people earn.

The reason the number of people employed does not measure the quantity of labor employed is that all jobs are not the same. People in part-time jobs might work just a few hours a week. People in full-time jobs work around 35 to 40 hours a week. And some people regularly work overtime. For example, a 7-11 store might hire six students who work for three hours a day each. Another 7-11 store might hire two full-time workers who work nine hours a day each. The number of people employed in these two stores is eight, but the total hours worked by six of the eight is the same as the total hours worked by the other two. To determine the total amount of labor used to produce real GDP, we measure labor in hours rather than in jobs. **Aggregate hours** are the total number of hours worked by all the people employed, both full time and part time, during a year.

Figure 4(a) shows aggregate hours in the U.S. economy from 1961 to 2006. Like the employment-to-population ratio, aggregate hours have an upward trend. But aggregate hours have not grown as quickly as has the number of people employed. Between 1961 and 2006, the number of people employed in the U.S. economy increased by 120 percent. During that same period, aggregate hours increased by 90 percent. Why the difference? Because average hours per worker decreased.

Figure 4(b) shows average hours per worker. After hovering at almost 39 hours a week during the early 1960s, average hours per worker decreased to a bit less than 34 hours a week during the 2000s. The average workweek shortened partly because of a decrease in the average hours worked by full-time workers but also because the number of part-time jobs increased faster than the number of full-time jobs.

Fluctuations in aggregate hours and average hours per worker line up with the business cycle. Figure 4 highlights the past four recessions, during which aggregate hours decreased and average hours per worker decreased more quickly than trend.

Real Wage Rate

The **real wage rate** is the quantity of goods and services that an hour's work can buy. It is equal to the money wage rate (dollars per hour) divided by the price level. If we use the GDP deflator to measure the price level, the real wage rate is expressed in 2000 dollars because the GDP deflator is 100 in 2000. The real wage rate is a significant economic variable because it measures the reward for labor.

What has happened to the real wage rate in the United States? Figure 5 answers this question. It shows three measures of the average hourly real wage rate in the U.S. economy between 1961 and 2006.

FIGURE 4   Aggregate Hours: 1961–2006

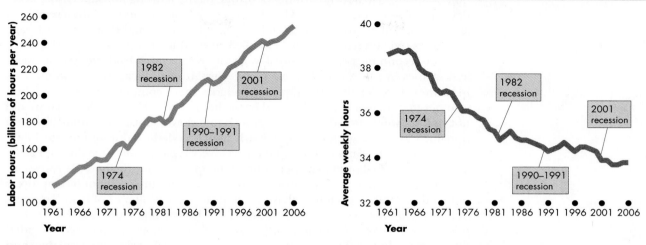

(a) Aggregate hours   **(b) Average weekly hours per person**

Aggregate hours in part (a) measure the total labor used to produce real GDP more accurately than does the number of people employed because an increasing proportion of jobs are part time. Between 1961 and 2006, aggregate hours increased by 90 percent. Fluctuations in aggregate hours coincide with the business cycle. Aggregate hours have increased at a slower rate than the number of jobs because the average workweek in part (b) has shortened.

Sources: Bureau of Labor Statistics and the author's calculations.

FIGURE 5   Real Wage Rates: 1961–2006

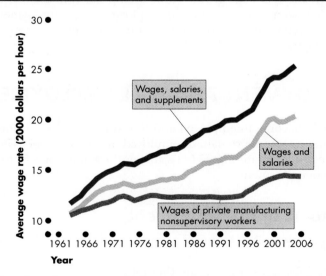

The average hourly real wage rate of private manufacturing nonsupervisory workers peaked in 1978, was constant through 1993, increased through 2001, and then remained constant. Broader measures of real wage rates increased, but all show a growth slowdown during the 1970s.

Sources: Bureau of Economic Analysis, Bureau of Labor Statistics, and the author's calculations.

The first measure of the real wage rate is the Department of Labor's calculation of the average hourly earnings of private manufacturing nonsupervisory workers. This measure increased to $12.44 in 1978 (in 2000 dollars) and then remained almost constant at around $12.30 for 15 years. From the mid-1990s, the real wage rate increased and reached $14.44 by 2003, after which it again stopped rising.

The second measure of the real wage rate is calculated by dividing total wages and salaries in the *National Income and Product Accounts* by aggregate hours. This measure is broader than the first and includes the incomes of all types of labor, whether their rate of pay is calculated by the hour or not. This broader measure did not stop growing after 1978, but its growth rate slowed during the mid-1970s and remained low through the early 1980s. It then speeded up during the late 1980s, sagged during the early 1990s, and then grew very rapidly from 1996 through 2000. This measure of labor income per hour fell temporarily during the 2001 recession.

Fringe benefits such as pension contributions and the payment by employers of health insurance premiums have become an increasing part of labor compensation. Figure 5 shows a third measure of the hourly real wage rate that reflects this trend. It is *total labor compensation*—wages, salaries, *and supplements*—divided by aggregate hours. This measure is the most comprehensive one available, and it shows that the real wage rate increased almost every year until 2000, then flatten before increasing again.

The data in Fig. 5 show us that no matter how we measure the real wage rate, its growth rate slowed during the 1970s. This slowdown in wage growth coincided with a slowdown in productivity growth—in the growth rate of real GDP per hour of work. The average real wage rate of workers in manufacturing was the most severely affected by the productivity growth slowdown, but the broader measures also slowed.

The fall in hourly compensation on the broader measures during the 2001 recession is unusual but not unknown. A small decrease occurred during the 1974 recession and real wage growth slowed temporarily in the other recessions.

You've now seen how we measure employment, unemployment, and real wage rate. Your next task is to study the anatomy of unemployment and see why it never disappears, even at full employment.

3   UNEMPLOYMENT AND FULL EMPLOYMENT

How do people become unemployed and how does a period of unemployment end? How long do people remain unemployed on the average? Who is at greatest risk of becoming unemployed? Let's answer these questions by looking at the anatomy of unemployment.

The Anatomy of Unemployment

People become unemployed if they

1. Lose their jobs and search for another job.
2. Leave their jobs and search for another job.
3. Enter or reenter the labor force to search for a job.

People end a spell of unemployment if they

1. Are hired or recalled.
2. Withdraw from the labor force.

FIGURE 6   Labor Market Flows

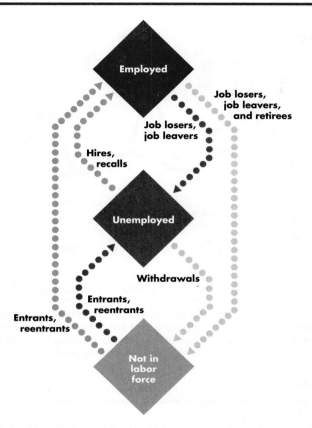

Unemployment results from employed people losing or leaving their jobs (job losers and job leavers) and from people entering the labor force (entrants and reentrants). Unemployment ends because people get hired or recalled or because they withdraw from the labor force.

People who are laid off, either permanently or temporarily, from their jobs are called *job losers*. Some job losers become unemployed, but some immediately withdraw from the labor force. People who voluntarily quit their jobs are called *job leavers*. Like job losers, some job leavers become unemployed and search for a better job while others either withdraw from the labor force temporarily or permanently retire from work. People who enter or reenter the labor force are called *entrants* and *reentrants*. Entrants are mainly people who have just left school. Some entrants get a job right away and are never unemployed, but many spend time searching for their first job, and during this period, they are unemployed. Reentrants are people who have previously withdrawn from the labor force. Most of these people are formerly discouraged workers. Figure 6 shows these labor market flows.

Let's see how much unemployment arises from the three different ways in which people can become unemployed.

The Sources of Unemployment

Figure 7 shows unemployment by reason for becoming unemployed. Job losers are the biggest source of unemployment. On the average, they account for around half of total unemployment. Also, their number fluctuates a great deal. At

FIGURE 7   Unemployment by Reason

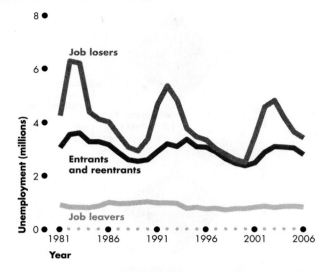

Everyone who is unemployed is a job loser, a job leaver, or an entrant or reentrant into the labor force. Most unemployment results from job loss. The number of job losers fluctuates more closely with the business cycle than do the numbers of job leavers and entrants and reentrants. Entrants and reentrants are the second most common type of unemployed people. Their number fluctuates with the business cycle because of discouraged workers. Job leavers are the least common type of unemployed people.

Source: Bureau of Labor Statistics.

the trough of the recession of 1990–1991, on any given day, more than 5 million of the 9.4 million unemployed were job losers. In contrast, at the business cycle peak in March 2001, only 3.3 million of the 6 million unemployed were job losers.

Entrants and reentrants also make up a large component of the unemployed. Their number fluctuates but more mildly than the fluctuations in the number of job losers.

Job leavers are the smallest and most stable source of unemployment. On any given day, fewer than 1 million people are unemployed because they are job leavers. The number of job leavers is remarkably constant. To the extent that this number fluctuates, it does so in line with the business cycle: A slightly larger number of people leave their jobs in good times than in bad times.

The Duration of Unemployment

Some people are unemployed for a week or two, and others are unemployed for periods of a year or more. The longer the spell of unemployment, the greater is the personal cost to the unemployed. The average duration of unemployment varies over the business cycle. Figure 8 compares the duration of unemployment close to a business cycle peak in 2000, when the unemployment rate was low, with that close to a business cycle trough in 2002, when the unemployment rate was high. In 2000, when the unemployment rate hit a low of 4 percent, 45 percent of the unemployed were in that situation for less than 5 weeks and only 11 percent of the unemployed were jobless for more than 27 weeks. In 2002, when unemployment approached 5.8 percent, only 35 percent of the unemployed found a new job in less than 5 weeks and 18 percent were unemployed for more than 27 weeks. At both low and high unemployment rates, about 30 percent of the unemployed take between 5 weeks and 14 weeks to find a job.

FIGURE 8   Unemployment by Duration

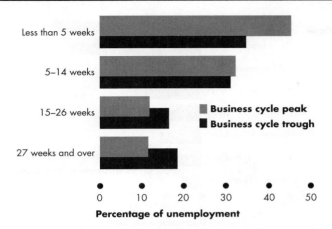

Close to a business cycle peak in 2000, when the unemployment rate was 4 percent, 45 percent of unemployment lasted for less than 5 weeks and 30 percent lasted for 5 to 14 weeks. So 75 percent of unemployment lasted for less than 15 weeks and 25 percent lasted for 15 weeks or more.

Close to a business cycle trough in 2002, when the unemployment rate was 5.8 percent, 35 percent of unemployment lasted for less than 5 weeks and 31 percent lasted for 5 to 14 weeks. So 66 percent of unemployment lasted for less than 15 weeks, and 34 percent lasted for 15 weeks or more.

Source: Bureau of Labor Statistics.

The Demographics of Unemployment

Figure 9 shows unemployment rates for different demographic groups. The figure shows that high unemployment rates occur among young workers and also among blacks. In the business cycle trough in 2002, the unemployment rate of black teenage males was 42 percent. Even in 2000, when the unemployment rate was 4 percent, the black teenage unemployment rates were more than 20 percent. The unemployment rates for white teenagers are less than half those of black teenagers. The racial differences also exist for workers aged 20 years and over. The highest unemployment rates that whites 20 years and over experience are lower than the lowest rates experienced by the other groups.

Why are teenage unemployment rates so high? There are three reasons. First, young people are still in the process of discovering what they are good at and trying different lines of work. So they leave their jobs more frequently than do older workers. Second, firms sometimes hire teenagers on a short-term trial basis. So the rate of job loss is higher for teenagers than for other people. Third, most teenagers are in school and not in the labor force. This fact means that the percentage of the teenage population that is unemployed is much lower than the percentage of the teenage labor force that is unemployed. In 2003, for example, 1 million teenagers were unemployed and 6 million were employed. So the teenage unemployment rate (all races) was 14 percent. But 9 million teenagers were in school. If we considered being in school to be the equivalent of having a job and measured teenage unemployment as a percentage of the teenage labor force plus the school population, we would record that 6 percent of teenagers are unemployed.

FIGURE 9   Unemployment by Demographic Group

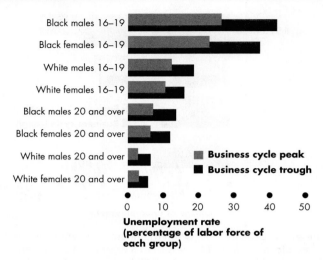

Black teenagers experience unemployment rates that average twice those of white teenagers, and teenage unemployment rates are much higher than those for people aged 20 years and over. Even in a business cycle trough, when unemployment is at its highest rate, only 6 percent of whites aged 20 years and over are unemployed.

Source: Bureau of Labor Statistics.

Types of Unemployment

Unemployment is classified into three types that are based on its origins. They are

► Frictional
► Structural
► Cyclical

Frictional Unemployment

The unemployment that arises from normal labor turnover—from people entering and leaving the labor force and from the ongoing creation and destruction of jobs—is **frictional unemployment**. Frictional unemployment is a permanent and healthy phenomenon in a dynamic, growing economy.

The unending flow of people into and out of the labor force and the processes of job creation and job destruction create the need for people to search for jobs and for businesses to search for workers. There are always businesses with unfilled jobs and people seeking jobs. Look in your local newspaper, and you will see that there are always some jobs being advertised. Businesses don't usually hire the first person who applies for a job, and unemployed people don't usually take the first job that comes their way. Instead, both firms and workers spend time searching out what they believe will be the best match available. By this process of search, people can match their own skills and interests with the available jobs and find a satisfying job and a good income. While these unemployed people are searching, they are frictionally unemployed.

The amount of frictional unemployment depends on the rate at which people enter and reenter the labor force and on the rate at which jobs are created and destroyed. During the 1970s, the amount of frictional unemployment increased as a consequence of the postwar baby boom that began during the 1940s. By the late 1970s, the baby boom had created a bulge in the number of people leaving school. As these people entered the labor force, the amount of frictional unemployment increased.

The amount of frictional unemployment is influenced by unemployment compensation. The greater the number of unemployed people covered by unemployment insurance and the more generous the unemployment benefit they receive, the longer is the average time taken in job search and the greater is the amount of frictional unemployment. In the United States in 2005, 35 percent of the unemployed received unemployment benefit. And the average benefit check was $266 a week. Canada and Western Europe have more generous benefits than those in the United States and have higher unemployment rates.

Structural Unemployment

The unemployment that arises when changes in technology or international competition change the skills needed to perform jobs or change the locations of jobs is **structural unemployment**. Structural unemployment usually lasts longer than frictional unemployment because workers must usually retrain and possibly relocate to find a job. For example, when a steel plant in Gary, Indiana, is automated, some jobs in that city are eliminated. Meanwhile, new jobs for security guards, retail clerks, and life-insurance salespeople are created in Chicago, Indianapolis, and other cities. The unemployed former steelworkers remain unemployed for several months until they move, retrain, and get one of these jobs. Structural unemployment is painful, especially for older workers for whom the best available option might be to retire early or take a lower-skilled, lower-paying job.

At some times, the amount of structural unemployment is modest. At other times, it is large, and at such times, structural unemployment can become a serious long-term problem. It was especially large during the late 1970s and early 1980s. During those years, oil price hikes and an increasingly competitive international environment destroyed jobs in traditional U.S. industries, such as auto and steel, and created jobs in new industries, such as electronics and bioengineering, as well as in banking and insurance. Structural unemployment was also present during the early 1990s as many businesses and governments "downsized."

Cyclical Unemployment

The fluctuating unemployment over the business cycle is **cyclical unemployment**. Cyclical unemployment increases during a recession and decreases during an expansion. An autoworker who is laid off because the economy is in a recession and who gets rehired some months later when the expansion begins has experienced cyclical unemployment.

Full Employment

There is always *some* unemployment—someone looking for a job or laid off and waiting to be recalled. So what do we mean by *full employment*? **Full employment** occurs when there is no cyclical unemployment or, equivalently, when all the unemployment is frictional and structural. The divergence of the unemployment rate from full employment is cyclical unemployment. The unemployment rate at full employment is called the **natural unemployment rate**.

There can be a lot of unemployment at full employment, and the term "full employment" is an example of a technical economic term that does not correspond with everyday language. The term "natural unemployment rate" is another technical economic term whose meaning does not correspond with everyday language. For most people—especially for unemployed workers—there is nothing *natural* about unemployment.

So why do economists call a situation with a lot of unemployment one of "full employment"? And why is the unemployment at full employment called "natural"?

The reason is that the economy is a complex mechanism that is always changing. In 2006, the U.S. economy employed 145 million people. More than 2.5 million workers retired during that year, and more than 3 million new workers entered the labor force. All these people worked in some 20 million businesses that produced goods and services valued at more than $13 trillion. Some of these businesses downsized and failed, and others expanded. This process of change creates frictions and dislocations that are unavoidable. And they create unemployment.

There is not much controversy about the existence of a natural unemployment rate. Nor is there much disagreement that it changes. The natural unemployment rate arises from the existence of frictional and structural unemployment, and it fluctuates because the frictions and the amount of structural change fluctuate.

But economists don't agree about the size of the natural unemployment rate and the extent to which it fluctuates. Some economists believe that the natural unemployment rate fluctuates frequently and that at times of rapid demographic and technological change, the natural unemployment rate can be high. Others think that the natural unemployment rate changes slowly.

Real GDP and Unemployment over the Cycle

The quantity of real GDP at full employment is called **potential GDP**. Over the business cycle, real GDP fluctuates around potential GDP and the unemployment rate fluctuates around the natural unemployment rate. Figure 10 illustrates these fluctuations in the United States between 1981 and 2006—real GDP in part (a) and the unemployment rate in part (b).

When the economy is at full employment, the unemployment rate equals the natural unemployment rate and real GDP equals potential GDP. When the unemployment rate is less than the natural unemployment rate, real GDP is greater than potential GDP. And when the unemployment rate is greater than the natural unemployment rate, real GDP is less than potential GDP.

Figure 10(b) shows one view of the natural unemployment rate. Keep in mind that economists do not know the magnitude of the natural unemployment rate and the natural rate shown in the figure is only one estimate. It shows that the natural unemployment rate was 6.2 percent in 1981 and that it fell steadily through the 1980s and 1990s to 5.2 percent by 1996. This estimate of the natural unemployment rate in the United States is one that many, but not all, economists would accept.

Your final task in this reading is to learn about another vital sign that gets monitored every month: the Consumer Price Index (CPI). What is the CPI, how do we measure it, and what does it mean?

FIGURE 10   Unemployment and Real GDP

(a) Real GDP   (b) Unemployment rate

As real GDP fluctuates around potential GDP (part a), the unemployment rate fluctuates around the natural unemployment rate (part b). At the end of the deep 1982 recession, the unemployment rate reached almost 10 percent. At the end of the milder 1990–1991 and 2001 recessions, unemployment peaked at lower rates. The natural unemployment rate decreased somewhat during the 1980s and 1990s.

Sources: Bureau of Economic Analysis, Bureau of Labor Statistics, and Congressional Budget Office.

THE CONSUMER PRICE INDEX   4

The Bureau of Labor Statistics (BLS) calculates the Consumer Price Index every month. The **Consumer Price Index (CPI)** is a measure of the average of the prices paid by urban consumers for a fixed "basket" of consumer goods and services. What you learn in this section will help you to make sense of the CPI and relate it to your own economic life. The CPI tells you what has happened to the value of the money in your pocket.

Reading the CPI Numbers

The CPI is defined to equal 100 for a period called the **reference base period**. Currently, the reference base period is 1982–1984. That is, for the average of the 36 months from January 1982 through December 1984, the CPI equals 100.

In June 2006, the CPI was 202.9. This number tells us that the average of the prices paid by urban consumers for a fixed market basket of consumer goods and services was 102.9 percent higher in 2006 than it was on the average during 1982–1984.

In June 2006, the CPI was 202.9. A year earlier, it was 194.5. These numbers tell us that the index of the prices paid by urban consumers for a fixed basket of consumer goods and services increased between 2005 and 2006 by 8.4 points, or by 4.3 percent.

Constructing the CPI

Constructing the CPI is a huge operation that involves three stages:

► Selecting the CPI basket
► Conducting the monthly price survey
► Calculating the CPI

The CPI Basket

The first stage in constructing the CPI is to select what is called the *CPI basket*. This "basket" contains the goods and services represented in the index and the relative importance attached to each of them. The idea is to make the relative importance of the items in the CPI basket the same as that in the budget of an average urban household. For example, because people spend more on housing than on bus rides, the CPI places more weight on the price of housing than on the price of bus rides.

The BLS uses two baskets and calculates two CPIs. One, called CPI-U, measures the average price paid by *all* urban households. The other, called CPI-W, measures the average price paid by urban wage earners and clerical workers. Here, we will focus on CPI-U, the broader measure.

To determine the spending patterns of households and to select the CPI basket, the BLS conducts a Consumer Expenditure Survey. This survey is costly and so is undertaken infrequently. Today's CPI basket is based on data gathered in a Consumer Expenditure Survey of 2001–2002. Until 1998, the CPI basket was based on a 1982–1984 Consumer Expenditure Survey but the BLS now updates the CPI basket more frequently.

Until 1998, the time period covered by the Consumer Expenditure Survey was also the reference base period. But now, when the BLS updates the CPI basket, it retains 1982–1984 as the reference base period.

Figure 11 shows the CPI basket at the end of 2005. The basket contains around 80,000 goods and services arranged in the eight large groups shown in the figure. The most important item in a household's budget is housing, which accounts for 42 percent of total expenditure. Transportation comes next at 18 percent. Third in relative importance are food and beverages at 15 percent. These three groups account for three quarters of the average household budget. Medical care and recreation each take 6 percent, and education and communication take 5 percent. Another 4 percent is spent on other goods and services, and apparel (clothing and footwear) takes 4 percent.

The BLS breaks down each of these categories into smaller ones. For example, the education and communication category breaks down into textbooks and supplies, tuition, telephone services, and personal computer services.

As you look at the relative importance of the items in the CPI basket, remember that they apply to the *average* household. *Individual* households are spread around the average. Think about your own expenditure and compare the basket of goods and services you buy with the CPI basket.

The Monthly Price Survey

Each month, BLS employees check the prices of the 80,000 goods and services in the CPI basket in 30 metropolitan areas. Because the CPI aims to measure price *changes*, it is important that the prices recorded each month refer to exactly the same item. For example, suppose the price of a box of jelly beans has increased

FIGURE 11   The CPI Basket

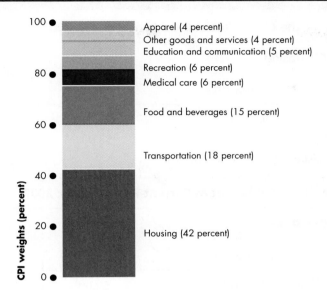

The CPI basket consists of the items that an average urban household buys. It consists mainly of housing (42 percent), transportation (18 percent), and food and beverages (15 percent). All other items add up to 25 percent of the total.

Sources: United States Census Bureau and Bureau of Labor Statistics.

but a box now contains more beans. Has the price of jelly beans increased? The BLS employee must record the details of changes in quality or packaging so that price changes can be isolated from other changes.

Once the raw price data are in hand, the next task is to calculate the CPI.

Calculating the CPI

The CPI calculation has three steps:

1. Find the cost of the CPI basket at base-period prices.

2. Find the cost of the CPI basket at current-period prices.

3. Calculate the CPI for the base period and the current period.

We'll work through these three steps for a simple example. Suppose the CPI basket contains only two goods and services: oranges and haircuts. We'll construct an annual CPI rather than a monthly CPI with the reference base period 2006 and the current period 2007.

Table 1 shows the quantities in the CPI basket and the prices in the base period and current period.

Part (a) contains the data for the base period. In that period, consumers bought 10 oranges at $1 each and 5 haircuts at $8 each. To find the cost of the CPI basket in the base-period prices, multiply the quantities in the CPI basket by the base-period prices. The cost of oranges is $10 (10 at $1 each), and the cost of haircuts is $40 (5 at $8 each). So total cost in the base period of the CPI basket is $50 ($10 + $40).

TABLE 1   The CPI: A Simplified Calculation

(a) The Cost of the CPI Basket at Base-Period Prices: 2006

CPI Basket			
Item	Quantity	Price	Cost of CPI Basket
Oranges	10	$1.00	$10
Haircuts	5	$8.00	$40
Cost of CPI basket at base-period prices			$50

(b) The Cost of the CPI Basket at Current-Period Prices: 2007

CPI Basket			
Item	Quantity	Price	Cost of CPI Basket
Oranges	10	$2.00	$20
Haircuts	5	$10.00	$50
Cost of CPI basket at current-period prices			$70

Part (b) contains the price data for the current period. The price of an orange increased from $1 to $2, which is a 100 percent increase—($1 ÷ $1) × 100 = 100. The price of a haircut increased from $8 to $10, which is a 25 percent increase—($2 ÷ $8) × 100 = 25.

The CPI provides a way of averaging these price increases by comparing the cost of the basket rather than the price of each item. To find the cost of the CPI basket in the current period, 2007, multiply the quantities in the basket by their 2007 prices. The cost of oranges is $20 (10 at $2 each), and the cost of haircuts is $50 (5 at $10 each). So total cost of the fixed CPI basket at current-period prices is $70 ($20 + $50).

You've now taken the first two steps toward calculating the CPI: calculating the cost of the CPI basket in the base period and the current period. The third step uses the numbers you've just calculated to find the CPI for 2006 and 2007.

The formula for the CPI is

$$\text{CPI} = \frac{\text{Cost of CPI basket at current-period prices}}{\text{Cost of CPI basket at base-period prices}} \times 100.$$

In Table 1, you established that in 2006, the cost of the CPI basket was $50 and in 2007, it was $70. You also know that the base period is 2006. So the cost of the CPI basket at base-year prices is $50. If we use these numbers in the CPI formula, we can find the CPI for 2006 and 2007. For 2006, the CPI is

$$\text{CPI in 2006} = \frac{\$50}{\$50} \times 100 = 100.$$

For 2007, the CPI is

$$\text{CPI in 2007} = \frac{\$70}{\$50} \times 100 = 140.$$

The principles that you've applied in this simplified CPI calculation apply to the more complex calculations performed every month by the BLS.

Measuring Inflation

A major purpose of the CPI is to measure *changes* in the cost of living and in the value of money. To measure these changes, we calculate the **inflation rate**, which is the annual percentage change in the price level. To calculate the inflation rate, we use the formula:

$$\text{Inflation rate} = \frac{(\text{CPI this year} - \text{CPI last year})}{\text{CPI last year}} \times 100.$$

We can use this formula to calculate the inflation rate in 2006. The CPI in June 2006 was 202.9, and the CPI in June 2005 was 194.5. So the inflation rate during the twelve months to June 2006 was

$$\text{Inflation rate} = \frac{(202.9 - 194.5)}{194.5} \times 100 = 4.3\%.$$

Figure 12 shows the CPI and the inflation rate in the United States during the 35 years between 1971 and 2006. The two parts of the figure are related.

FIGURE 12 The CPI and the Inflation Rate

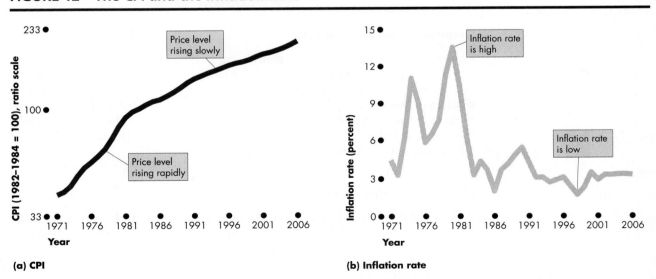

(a) CPI

(b) Inflation rate

In part (a), the CPI (the price level) has increased every year. In part (b), the inflation rate has averaged 4.8 percent a year. During the 1970s and early 1980s, the inflation rate was high and sometimes exceeded 10 percent a year. But after 1983, the inflation rate fell to an average of 3 percent a year.

Source: Bureau of Labor Statistics.

Figure 12 shows that when the price *level* in part (a) rises rapidly, the inflation rate in part (b) is high, and when the price level in part (a) rises slowly, the inflation rate in part (b) is low. Notice in part (a) that the CPI increased every year during this period. During the late 1970s and 1980, the CPI was increasing rapidly, but its rate of increase slowed during the 1980s, 1990s, and 2000s.

The CPI is not a perfect measure of the price level, and changes in the CPI probably overstate the inflation rate. Let's look at the sources of bias.

The Biased CPI

The main sources of bias in the CPI are

► New goods bias
► Quality change bias
► Commodity substitution bias
► Outlet substitution bias

New Goods Bias

If you want to compare the price level in 2007 with that in 1977, you must somehow compare the price of a computer today with that of a typewriter in 1977. Because a PC is more expensive than a typewriter was, the arrival of the PC puts an upward bias into the CPI and its inflation rate.

Quality Change Bias

Cars, CD players, and many other items get better every year. Part of the rise in the prices of these items is a payment for improved quality and is not inflation. But the CPI counts the entire price rise as inflation and so overstates inflation.

Commodity Substitution Bias

Changes in relative prices lead consumers to change the items they buy. For example, if the price of beef rises and the price of chicken remains unchanged, people buy more chicken and less beef. Suppose they switch from beef to chicken on a scale that provides the same amount of protein and the same enjoyment as before and their expenditure is the same as before. The price of protein has not changed. But because it ignores the substitution of chicken for beef, the CPI says the price of protein has increased.

Outlet Substitution Bias

When confronted with higher prices, people use discount stores more frequently and convenience stores less frequently. This phenomenon is called *outlet substitution*. The CPI surveys do not monitor outlet substitutions.

The Magnitude of the Bias

You've reviewed the sources of bias in the CPI. But how big is the bias? This question was tackled in 1996 by a Congressional Advisory Commission on the Consumer Price Index chaired by Michael Boskin, an economics professor at

Stanford University. This commission said that the CPI overstates inflation by 1.1 percentage points a year. That is, if the CPI reports that inflation is 3.1 percent a year, most likely inflation is actually 2 percent a year.

Some Consequences of the Bias

The bias in the CPI distorts private contracts and increases government outlays. Many private agreements, such as wage contracts, are linked to the CPI. For example, a firm and its workers might agree to a three-year wage deal that increases the wage rate by 2 percent a year *plus* the percentage increase in the CPI. Such a deal ends up giving the workers more real income than the firm intended.

Close to a third of federal government outlays, including Social Security checks, are linked directly to the CPI. And while a bias of 1 percent a year seems small, accumulated over a decade it adds up to almost a trillion dollars of additional expenditures.

Reducing the Bias

To reduce the bias in the CPI, the BLS now undertakes consumer spending surveys at more frequent intervals and is experimenting with a chained CPI.

You've now completed your study of the measurement of macroeconomic performance. Your task in the following readings is to learn what determines that performance and how policy actions might improve it. But first, take a close-up look at the jobless recovery of 2002 and 2003 in *Reading Between the Lines*.

5

READING BETWEEN THE LINES

Jobs in the 2002–2006 Expansion

THE LOS ANGELES TIMES, APRIL 8, 2006

Solid Growth for U.S. Payrolls

The U.S. economy turned in a solid performance last month, adding a net 211,000 new jobs and driving the unemployment rate back to its lowest point in the current expansion, the government reported Friday.

March's unemployment rate fell to 4.7%—down from 4.8%—matching the level of two months earlier. That was the lowest rate since July 2001, when the economy was in recession.

The job gain exceeded economists' consensus forecast by 21,000. But the Labor Department revised downward its estimates of job growth in the prior two months by 34,000.

All major economic sectors added jobs in March except manufacturing, which lost 5,000. . . .

Friday's job report provided the latest evidence that the economy had rebounded strongly from a slump at the end of last year. . . .

The Bush administration, however, trumpeted the employment report as a rare and welcome piece of political good news. Within an hour of its release, President Bush said "These millions of new jobs are evidence of an economic resurgence that is strong, broad and benefiting all Americans." . . .

The administration made much of the fact that the March job report sent the economy's total job gain above 5 million since the low point in August 2003. The economy has added jobs at a rate of 167,000 a month since then.

By contrast, however, the economy generated 240,000 jobs a month during the second half of the 1990s. Job creation during the entire decade of the 1990s proceeded at an average of 180,000 a month—faster than in the current expansion even though the decade began with the 1990–91 recession. . . .

Essence of the Story

▶ The U.S. economy added a net 211,000 new jobs in March 2006.

▶ The unemployment rate fell to 4.7 percent, the lowest since July 2001.

▶ President Bush said that the job numbers were evidence of a strong economic resurgence.

▶ The administration emphasized that the economy had added jobs at a rate of 167,000 a month since August 2003.

▶ The economy generated 240,000 jobs a month during the second half of the 1990s.

▶ Job creation during the entire decade of the 1990s averaged 180,000 a month.

Economic Analysis

▶ This news article reports the number of jobs created in March 2006 and the average number of jobs created each month between 2003 and 2006, and during the 1990s expansion.

▶ The figures show the job creation performance of the U.S. economy during the expansion of 2002–2006 and place it in a longer-term historical perspective.

▶ In Fig. 13, the *y*-axis shows the level of employment as a percentage of its level at the business cycle trough and the *x*-axis shows the number of months since the business cycle trough.

▶ By March 2006, the expansion had been running for 54 months (4½ years).

▶ The blue line in the figure shows the growth of employment during the 2002–2006 expansion.

▶ In March 2006, employment was only 6.5 percent higher than it had been at the cycle trough in November 2001.

▶ The gray line in the figure shows the growth of employment on the average during the previous five expansions.

▶ On the average, after 54 months of expansion, employment has expanded by 12 percent—almost double that of the current expansion.

▶ The shaded area shows the range of experience over the previous five expansions.

▶ You can see that the current expansion follows the weakest of the previous ones.

▶ Figure 14 shows the same comparison for the unemployment rate.

▶ In an average expansion, the unemployment rate falls after 54 months to 70 percent of its trough level.

▶ But in the current expansions, the unemployment rate actually increased and after 18 months stood at 10 percent *above* its trough level.

▶ Again, the current expansion is the weakest of the past six expansions.

▶ The slow job recovery arises partly from a weaker-than-average recovery of production and partly from an increase in output per worker.

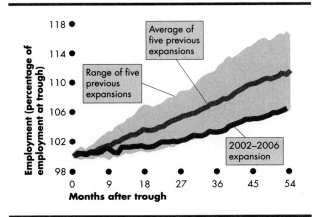

FIGURE 13   Employment during the 2002–2006 Expansion

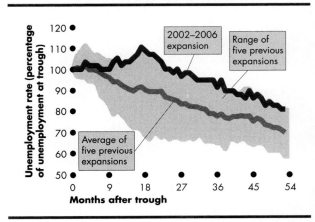

FIGURE 14   The Unemployment Rate during the 2002–2006 Expansion

SUMMARY

- ▶ The unemployment rate averaged 5.9 percent between 1961 and 2006. It increases in recessions and decreases in expansions.
- ▶ The labor force participation rate and the employment-to-population ratio have an upward trend and fluctuate with the business cycle.
- ▶ The labor force participation rate has increased for females and decreased for males.
- ▶ Aggregate hours have an upward trend, and they fluctuate with the business cycle.
- ▶ Real hourly wage rates grow, but their growth rates slowed during the 1970s.
- ▶ People are constantly entering and leaving the state of unemployment.
- ▶ The duration of unemployment fluctuates over the business cycle. But the demographic patterns of unemployment are constant.
- ▶ Unemployment can be frictional, structural, or cyclical.
- ▶ When all unemployment is frictional and structural, the unemployment rate equals the natural unemployment rate, the economy is at full employment, and real GDP equals potential GDP.
- ▶ Over the business cycle, real GDP fluctuates around potential GDP and the unemployment rate fluctuates around the natural unemployment rate.
- ▶ The Consumer Price Index (CPI) is a measure of the average of the prices paid by urban consumers for a fixed basket of consumer goods and services.
- ▶ The CPI is defined to equal 100 for a reference base period—currently 1982–1984.
- ▶ The inflation rate is the percentage change in the CPI from one period to the next.
- ▶ Changes in the CPI probably overstate the inflation rate because of the bias that arises from new goods, quality changes, commodity substitution, and outlet substitution.
- ▶ The bias in the CPI distorts private contracts and increases government outlays.

PRACTICE PROBLEMS FOR READING 22

1. Which of the following is *least likely* to be classified as unemployed? A person who:

    A. is not working, and is not currently looking for work.

    B. is not working, but will start a new job within 30 days.

    C. is not working, but has recently attempted to find work.

2. Workers who voluntarily leave one job to seek another are classified under which type of unemployment?

    A. Cyclical.

    B. Frictional.

    C. Structural.

3. The natural rate of unemployment is equal to:

    A. cyclical unemployment.

    B. cyclical plus structural unemployment.

    C. frictional plus structural unemployment.

4. Full employment occurs when:

    A. cyclical unemployment is zero.

    B. both cyclical and frictional unemployment are zero.

    C. both structural and frictional unemployment are zero.

SOLUTIONS FOR READING 22

1. A is correct. A person who is not working and is not currently looking for work (a discouraged worker) is not classified as unemployed.

2. B is correct. A worker who has voluntarily left one job and is seeking another is classified as part of frictional unemployment.

3. C is correct. The natural rate of unemployment is equal to frictional unemployment plus structural unemployment, and occurs when cyclical unemployment equals zero. This is, also, termed in economics as full employment.

4. A is correct. Full employment, by definition, occurs when there is no cyclical unemployment.

AGGREGATE SUPPLY AND AGGREGATE DEMAND

by Michael Parkin

LEARNING OUTCOMES

The candidate should be able to:	Mastery
a. explain the factors that influence real GDP and long-run and short-run aggregate supply, explain movement along the long-run and short-run aggregate supply curves (LAS and SAS), and discuss the reasons for changes in potential GDP and aggregate supply;	☐
b. explain the components of and the factors that affect real GDP demanded, describe the aggregate demand curve and why it slopes downward, and explain the factors that can change aggregate demand;	☐
c. differentiate between short-run and long-run macroeconomic equilibrium and explain how economic growth, inflation, and changes in aggregate demand and supply influence the macroeconomic equilibrium;	☐
d. compare and contrast the classical, Keynesian, and monetarist schools of macroeconomics.	☐

PRODUCTION AND PRICES   1

Production grows and prices rise. But the pace at which production grows and prices rise is uneven. In 1997, measured by real GDP, production grew by 4.5 percent. At this growth rate, real GDP doubles in about 16 years. But in 2001, growth slowed to less than 1 percent, a rate that takes about 70 years for real GDP to double!

Similarly, during recent years, prices have increased at rates ranging from less than 2 percent to almost 4 percent. An inflation rate of 2 percent a year is barely noticed. But at 4 percent a year, inflation becomes a problem, not least because people begin to wonder where it is heading next.

Economics, Eighth Edition, by Michael Parkin. Copyright © 2008 by Pearson Education. Reprinted with permission of Pearson Education, publishing as Pearson Addison Wesley.

The uneven pace of economic growth and inflation—the business cycle—is the subject of this reading. Here, you will discover the forces that bring fluctuations in the pace of real GDP growth and inflation and associated fluctuations in employment and unemployment.

This reading explains a *model* of real GDP and the price level—the *aggregate supply–aggregate demand model* or *AS–AD model*. This model represents the consensus view of macroeconomists on how real GDP and the price level are determined. The model provides a framework for understanding the forces that make our economy expand, that bring inflation, and that cause business cycle fluctuations. The *AS–AD* model also provides a framework within which we can see the range of views of macroeconomists in different schools of thought.

2 THE MACROECONOMIC LONG RUN AND SHORT RUN

The economy is constantly bombarded by events that move real GDP away from potential GDP and employment away from full employment. Natural shocks, such as Hurricane Katrina, and shocks that are born from a clash of cultures and ideologies, such as terrorist attacks, lower real GDP and employment and send the unemployment rate above the natural rate. Technological shocks, such as the discovery and widespread application of computer and related information technologies, raise real GDP and employment and lower the unemployment rate.

Whatever the source of a shock or its direction, once it hits, real GDP and employment begin an adjustment process. The long run is like an anchor point around which the economy tosses and turns like a boat on an ocean. We're now going to study those tosses and turns. But first, let's be clear about the distinction between the macroeconomic long run and short run.

The Macroeconomic Long Run

The **macroeconomic long run** is a time frame that is sufficiently long for the real wage rate to have adjusted to achieve full employment: real GDP equals potential GDP, unemployment is at the natural rate, the price level is proportional to the quantity of money, and the inflation rate equals the money growth rate minus the real GDP growth rate.

The Macroeconomic Short Run

The **macroeconomic short run** is a period during which some *money* prices are sticky so that real GDP might be below, above, or at potential GDP and the unemployment rate might be above, below, or at the natural unemployment rate.

The aggregate supply–aggregate demand model that you are about to study explains the behavior of real GDP and the price level in the short run. It also explains how the economy adjusts to eventually restore long-run equilibrium and full employment.

We'll begin by learning about aggregate supply.

AGGREGATE SUPPLY 3

The *quantity of real GDP supplied* (*Y*) is the total quantity that firms plan to produce during a given period. This quantity depends on the quantity of labor employed; the quantity of capital, both physical and human; and the state of technology.

At any given time, the quantity of capital and the state of technology are fixed. They depend on decisions that were made in the past. The population is also fixed. But the quantity of labor is not fixed. It depends on decisions made by people and firms about the supply of and demand for labor.

The labor market can be in any one of three states: at full employment, above full employment, or below full employment.

The quantity of real GDP at full employment is *potential GDP*, which depends on the full-employment quantity of labor, the quantity of capital, and the state of technology. Over the business cycle, employment fluctuates around full employment and real GDP fluctuates around potential GDP.

To study aggregate supply in different states of the labor market, we distinguish two time frames for aggregate supply:

▶ Long-run aggregate supply
▶ Short-run aggregate supply

Long-Run Aggregate Supply

Long-run aggregate supply is the relationship between the quantity of real GDP supplied and the price level in the long run when real GDP equals potential GDP. The long-run aggregate supply curve in Fig. 1 illustrates this relationship.

FIGURE 1 Long-Run Aggregate Supply

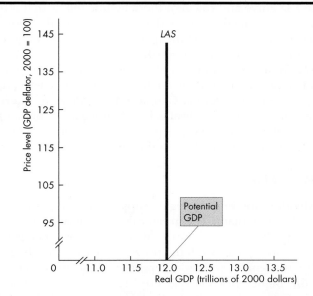

The long-run aggregate supply curve (*LAS*) shows the relationship between potential GDP and the price level. Potential GDP is independent of the price level, so the *LAS* curve is vertical at potential GDP.

The long-run aggregate supply curve is the vertical line at potential GDP labeled *LAS*. Along the long-run aggregate supply curve, as the price level changes, real GDP remains at potential GDP, which in Fig. 1 is $12 trillion. The long-run aggregate supply curve is always vertical and is always located at potential GDP.

The long-run aggregate supply curve is vertical because potential GDP is independent of the price level. The reason for this independence is that a movement along the *LAS* curve is accompanied by a change in *two* sets of prices: the prices of goods and services—the price level—and the prices of the factors of production, most notably, the money wage rate. A 10 percent increase in the prices of goods and services is matched by a 10 percent increase in the money wage rate. Because the price level and the money wage rate change by the same percentage, the *real wage rate* remains constant at its full-employment equilibrium level. So when the price level changes and the real wage rate remains constant, employment remains constant and real GDP remains constant at potential GDP.

Production at a Pepsi Plant

You can see more clearly why real GDP remains constant when all prices change by the same percentage by thinking about production decisions at a Pepsi bottling plant. The plant is producing the quantity of Pepsi that maximizes profit. If the price of Pepsi and the wage rate of workers at the bottling plant rise by the same percentage, the firm has no incentive to change production.

Short-Run Aggregate Supply

Short-run aggregate supply is the relationship between the quantity of real GDP supplied and the price level when the money wage rate, the prices of other resources, and potential GDP remain constant. The short-run aggregate supply curve in Fig. 2 illustrates this relationship as the short-run aggregate supply curve *SAS* and the short-run aggregate supply schedule. Each point on the *SAS* curve corresponds to a row of the short-run aggregate supply schedule. For example, point *A* on the *SAS* curve and row *A* of the schedule tell us that if the price level is 105, the quantity of real GDP supplied is $11 trillion. In the short run, a rise in the price level brings an increase in the quantity of real GDP supplied. The short-run aggregate supply curve slopes upward.

With a given money wage rate, there is one price level at which the real wage rate is at its full-employment equilibrium level. At this price level, the quantity of real GDP supplied equals potential GDP and the *SAS* curve intersects the *LAS* curve. In this example, that price level is 115. At price levels higher than 115, the quantity of real GDP supplied exceeds potential GDP; at price levels below 115, the quantity of real GDP supplied is less than potential GDP.

Back at the Pepsi Plant

You can see why the short-run aggregate supply curve slopes upward by returning to the Pepsi bottling plant. The greater the rate of production, the higher is the marginal cost. The plant maximizes its profit by producing the quantity at which price equals marginal cost. If the price of Pepsi rises while the money wage rate and other costs remain constant, Pepsi has an incentive to increase production because the higher price covers the higher marginal cost. And because Pepsi is in business to maximize its profit, it increases production.

Similarly, if the price of Pepsi falls while the money wage rate and other costs remain constant, Pepsi can avoid a loss by decreasing production. The lower price weakens the incentive to produce, so Pepsi decreases production.

FIGURE 2   Short-Run Aggregate Supply

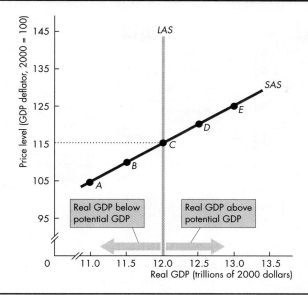

	Price Level (GDP Deflator)	Real GDP Supplied (Trillions of 2000 Dollars)
A	105	11.0
B	110	11.5
C	115	12.0
D	120	12.5
E	125	13.0

The short-run aggregate supply curve, *SAS,* and the short-run aggregate supply schedule show the relationship between the quantity of real GDP supplied and the price level when the money wage rate, other factor prices, and potential GDP remain the same. A rise in the price level brings an increase in the quantity of real GDP supplied: the short-run aggregate supply curve slopes upward.

At the price level that makes the given money wage rate equal the full-employment equilibrium real wage rate, the quantity of real GDP supplied equals potential GDP and the *SAS* curve intersects the *LAS* curve. Here, that price level is 115. At price levels higher than 115, the quantity of real GDP supplied exceeds potential GDP; at price levels below 115, the quantity of real GDP supplied is less than potential GDP.

What's true for Pepsi bottlers is true for the producers of all goods and services. When all prices rise, the *price level rises.* If the price level rises and the money wage rate and other factor prices remain constant, all firms increase production and the quantity of real GDP supplied increases. A fall in the price level has the opposite effect and decreases real GDP.

Movements along the *LAS* and *SAS* Curves

Figure 3 summarizes what you've just learned about the *LAS* and *SAS* curves. When the price level, the money wage rate, and other factor prices rise by the same percentage, relative prices remain constant and the quantity of real GDP supplied equals potential GDP. There is a *movement along* the *LAS* curve.

FIGURE 3 Movements along the Aggregate Supply Curves

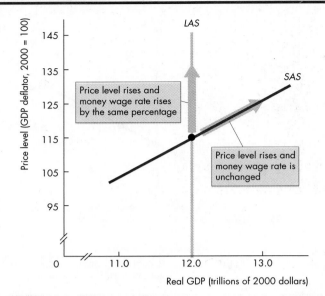

A rise in the price level with no change in the money wage rate and other factor prices brings an increase in the quantity of real GDP supplied and a movement along the short-run aggregate supply curve, *SAS*.

A rise in the price level with equal percentage increases in the money wage rate and other factor prices keeps the quantity of real GDP supplied constant at potential GDP and brings a movement along the long-run aggregate supply curve, *LAS*.

When the price level rises but the money wage rate and other factor prices remain the same, the quantity of real GDP supplied increases and there is a *movement along* the *SAS* curve.

Let's next study the influences that bring changes in aggregate supply.

Changes in Aggregate Supply

You've just seen that a change in the price level brings a movement along the aggregate supply curves but does not change aggregate supply. Aggregate supply changes when influences on production plans other than the price level change. Let's begin by looking at factors that change potential GDP.

Changes in Potential GDP

When potential GDP changes, aggregate supply changes. An increase in potential GDP increases both long-run aggregate supply and short-run aggregate supply.

Figure 4 shows these effects of an increase in potential GDP. Initially, the long-run aggregate supply curve is LAS_0 and the short-run aggregate supply curve is SAS_0. If an increase in the full-employment quantity of labor, an increase in the quantity of capital, or an advance in technology increases potential GDP to $13 trillion, long-run aggregate supply increases and the long-run aggregate supply curve shifts rightward to LAS_1. Short-run aggregate supply also increases, and the short-run aggregate supply curve shifts rightward to SAS_1. The two supply curves shift by the same amount only if the full-employment price level remains constant, which we will assume to be the case.

FIGURE 4 A Change in Potential GDP

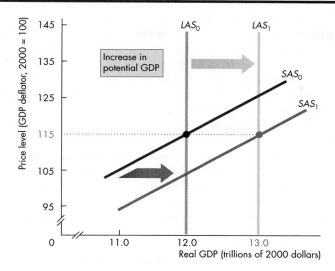

An increase in potential GDP increases both long-run aggregate supply and short-run aggregate supply and shifts both aggregate supply curves rightward from LAS_0 to LAS_1 and from SAS_0 to SAS_1.

Potential GDP can increase for any of three reasons:

▶ The full-employment quantity of labor increases.

▶ The quantity of capital increases.

▶ Technology advances.

Let's look at these influences on potential GDP and the aggregate supply curves.

An Increase in the Full-Employment Quantity of Labor A Pepsi bottling plant that employs 100 workers bottles more Pepsi than does an otherwise identical plant that employs 10 workers. The same is true for the economy as a whole. The larger the quantity of labor employed, the greater is real GDP.

Over time, potential GDP increases because the labor force increases. But (with constant capital and technology) *potential* GDP increases only if the full-employment quantity of labor increases. Fluctuations in employment over the business cycle bring fluctuations in real GDP. But these changes in real GDP are fluctuations around potential GDP. They are not changes in potential GDP and long-run aggregate supply.

An Increase in the Quantity of Capital A Pepsi bottling plant with two production lines bottles more Pepsi than does an otherwise identical plant that has only one production line. For the economy, the larger the quantity of capital, the more productive is the labor force and the greater is its potential GDP. Potential GDP per person in the capital-rich United States is vastly greater than that in capital-poor China and Russia.

Capital includes *human capital.* One Pepsi plant is managed by an economics major with an MBA and has a labor force with an average of 10 years of experience. This plant produces a larger output than does an otherwise identical plant that is managed by someone with no business training or experience and that has a young labor force that is new to bottling. The first plant has a greater amount of human capital than the second. For the economy as a whole, the larger the quantity of *human capital*—the skills that people have acquired in school and through on-the-job training—the greater is potential GDP.

An Advance in Technology   A Pepsi plant that has pre-computer age machines produces less than one that uses the latest robot technology. Technological change enables firms to produce more from any given amount of inputs. So even with fixed quantities of labor and capital, improvements in technology increase potential GDP.

Technological advances are by far the most important source of increased production over the past two centuries. As a result of technological advances, one farmer in the United States today can feed 100 people and one autoworker can produce almost 14 cars and trucks in a year.

Let's now look at the effects of changes in the money wage rate.

Changes in the Money Wage Rate and Other Factor Prices

When the money wage rate (or the money price of any other factor of production such as oil) changes, short-run aggregate supply changes but long-run aggregate supply does not change.

Figure 5 shows the effect of an increase in the money wage rate. Initially, the short-run aggregate supply curve is SAS_0. A rise in the money wage rate *decreases* short-run aggregate supply and shifts the short-run aggregate supply curve leftward to SAS_2.

A rise in the money wage rate decreases short-run aggregate supply because it increases firms' costs. With increased costs, the quantity that firms are willing

FIGURE 5   A Change in the Money Wage Rate

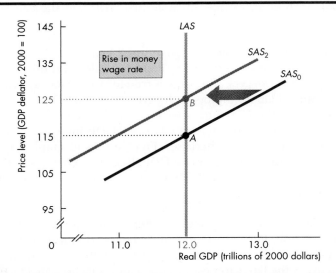

A rise in the money wage rate decreases short-run aggregate supply and shifts the short-run aggregate supply curve leftward from SAS_0 to SAS_2. A rise in the money wage rate does not change potential GDP, so the long-run aggregate supply curve does not shift.

to supply at each price level decreases, which is shown by a leftward shift of the *SAS* curve.

A change in the money wage rate does not change long-run aggregate supply because on the *LAS* curve, the change in the money wage rate is accompanied by an equal percentage change in the price level. With no change in *relative* prices, firms have no incentive to change production and real GDP remains constant at potential GDP. With no change in potential GDP, the long-run aggregate supply curve remains at *LAS*.

What Makes the Money Wage Rate Change?

The money wage rate can change for two reasons: departures from full employment and expectations about inflation. Unemployment above the natural rate puts downward pressure on the money wage rate, and unemployment below the natural rate puts upward pressure on the money wage rate. An expected increase in the inflation rate makes the money wage rate rise faster, and an expected decrease in the inflation rate slows the rate at which the money wage rate rises.

AGGREGATE DEMAND 4

The quantity of real GDP demanded is the sum of the real consumption expenditure (C), investment (I), government expenditure (G), and exports (X) minus imports (M). That is,

$$Y = C + I + G + X - M.$$

The *quantity of real GDP demanded* is the total amount of final goods and services produced in the United States that people, businesses, governments, and foreigners plan to buy.

These buying plans depend on many factors. Some of the main ones are

► The price level
► Expectations
► Fiscal policy and monetary policy
► The world economy

We first focus on the relationship between the quantity of real GDP demanded and the price level. To study this relationship, we keep all other influences on buying plans the same and ask: How does the quantity of real GDP demanded vary as the price level varies?

The Aggregate Demand Curve

Other things remaining the same, the higher the price level, the smaller is the quantity of real GDP demanded. This relationship between the quantity of real GDP demanded and the price level is called **aggregate demand**. Aggregate demand is described by an *aggregate demand schedule* and an *aggregate demand curve*.

FIGURE 6   Aggregate Demand

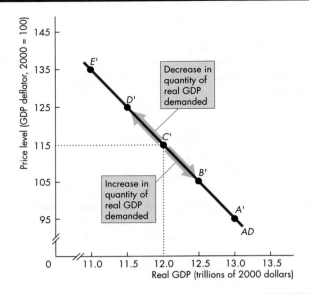

	Price Level (GDP Deflator)	Real GDP Demanded (Trillions of 2000 Dollars)
A′	95	13.0
B′	105	12.5
C′	115	12.0
D′	125	11.5
E′	135	11.0

The aggregate demand curve (*AD*) shows the relationship between the quantity of real GDP demanded and the price level. The aggregate demand curve is based on the aggregate demand schedule in the table. Each point *A′* through *E′* on the curve corresponds to the row in the table identified by the same letter. When the price level is 115, the quantity of real GDP demanded is $12 trillion, as shown by point *C′* in the figure. A change in the price level, when all other influences on aggregate buying plans remain the same, brings a change in the quantity of real GDP demanded and a movement along the *AD* curve.

Figure 6 shows an aggregate demand curve (*AD*) and an aggregate demand schedule. Each point on the *AD* curve corresponds to a row of the schedule. For example, point *C′* on the *AD* curve and row *C′* of the schedule tell us that if the price level is 115, the quantity of real GDP demanded is $12 trillion.

The aggregate demand curve slopes downward for two reasons:

► Wealth effect
► Substitution effects

Wealth Effect

When the price level rises but other things remain the same, *real* wealth decreases. Real wealth is the amount of money in the bank, bonds, stocks, and other assets that people own, measured not in dollars but in terms of the goods and services that the money, bonds, and stock will buy.

People save and hold money, bonds, and stocks for many reasons. One reason is to build up funds for education expenses. Another reason is to build up enough funds to meet possible medical expenses or other big bills. But the biggest reason is to build up enough funds to provide a retirement income.

If the price level rises, real wealth decreases. People then try to restore their wealth. To do so, they must increase saving and, equivalently, decrease current consumption. Such a decrease in consumption is a decrease in aggregate demand.

Maria's Wealth Effect   You can see how the wealth effect works by thinking about Maria's buying plans. Maria lives in Moscow, Russia. She has worked hard all summer and saved 20,000 rubles (the ruble is the currency of Russia), which she plans to spend attending graduate school when she has finished her economics degree. So Maria's wealth is 20,000 rubles. Maria has a part-time job, and her income from this job pays her current expenses. The price level in Russia rises by 100 percent, and now Maria needs 40,000 rubles to buy what 20,000 once bought. To try to make up some of the fall in value of her savings, Maria saves even more and cuts her current spending to the bare minimum.

Substitution Effects

When the price level rises and other things remain the same, interest rates rise. The reason is related to the wealth effect that you've just studied. A rise in the price level decreases the real value of the money in people's pockets and bank accounts. With a smaller amount of real money around, banks and other lenders can get a higher interest rate on loans. But faced with higher interest rates, people and businesses delay plans to buy new capital and consumer durable goods and cut back on spending.

This substitution effect involves substituting goods in the future for goods in the present and is called an *intertemporal* substitution effect—a substitution across time. Saving increases to increase future consumption.

To see this intertemporal substitution effect more clearly, think about your own plan to buy a new computer. At an interest rate of 5 percent a year, you might borrow $2,000 and buy the new computer. But at an interest rate of 10 percent a year, you might decide that the payments would be too high. You don't abandon your plan to buy the computer, but you decide to delay your purchase.

A second substitution effect works through international prices. When the U.S. price level rises and other things remain the same, U.S.-made goods and services become more expensive relative to foreign-made goods and services. This change in *relative prices* encourages people to spend less on U.S.-made items and more on foreign-made items. For example, if the U.S. price level rises relative to the Canadian price level, Canadians buy fewer U.S.-made cars (U.S. exports decrease) and Americans buy more Canadian-made cars (U.S. imports increase). U.S. GDP decreases.

Maria's Substitution Effects   In Moscow, Russia, Maria makes some substitutions. She was planning to trade in her old motor scooter and get a new one. But with a higher price level and higher interest rates, she decides to make her old scooter last one more year. Also, with the prices of Russian goods sharply increasing, Maria substitutes a low-cost dress made in Malaysia for the Russian-made dress she had originally planned to buy.

Changes in the Quantity of Real GDP Demanded

When the price level rises and other things remain the same, the quantity of real GDP demanded decreases—a movement up along the aggregate demand curve as shown by the arrow in Fig. 6. When the price level falls and other things remain the same, the quantity of real GDP demanded increases—a movement down the aggregate demand curve.

We've now seen how the quantity of real GDP demanded changes when the price level changes. How do other influences on buying plans affect aggregate demand?

Changes in Aggregate Demand

A change in any factor that influences buying plans other than the price level brings a change in aggregate demand. The main factors are

► Expectations
► Fiscal policy and monetary policy
► The world economy

Expectations

An increase in expected future income increases the amount of consumption goods (especially big-ticket items such as cars) that people plan to buy today and increases aggregate demand.

An increase in the expected future inflation rate increases aggregate demand because people decide to buy more goods and services at today's relatively lower prices.

An increase in expected future profits increases the investment that firms plan to undertake today and increases aggregate demand.

Fiscal Policy and Monetary Policy

The government's attempt to influence the economy by setting and changing taxes, making transfer payments, and purchasing goods and services is called **fiscal policy**. A tax cut or an increase in transfer payments—for example, unemployment benefits or welfare payments—increases aggregate demand. Both of these influences operate by increasing households' *disposable* income. **Disposable income** is aggregate income minus taxes plus transfer payments. The greater the disposable income, the greater is the quantity of consumption goods and services that households plan to buy and the greater is aggregate demand.

Government expenditure on goods and services is one component of aggregate demand. So if the government spends more on spy satellites, schools, and highways, aggregate demand increases.

Monetary policy consists of changes in interest rates and in the quantity of money in the economy. The quantity of money is determined by the Federal Reserve (the Fed) and the banks (in a process described in the reading on money, the price level, and inflation and the reading on monetary policy). An increase in the quantity of money in the economy increases aggregate demand. To see why money affects aggregate demand, imagine that the Fed borrows the army's helicopters, loads them with millions of new $10 bills, and sprinkles them like confetti across the nation. People gather the newly available money and plan to spend some of it. So the quantity of goods and services demanded increases.

But people don't plan to spend all the new money. They plan to save some of it and lend it to others through the banks. Interest rates fall, and with lower interest rates, people plan to buy more consumer durables and firms plan to increase their investment.

The World Economy

Two main influences that the world economy has on aggregate demand are the exchange rate and foreign income. The *exchange rate* is the amount of a foreign currency that you can buy with a U.S. dollar. Other things remaining the same, a rise in the exchange rate decreases aggregate demand. To see how the exchange rate influences aggregate demand, suppose that the exchange rate is 1.20 euros per U.S. dollar. A Nokia cell phone made in Finland costs 120 euros, and an equivalent Motorola phone made in the United States costs $110. In U.S. dollars, the Nokia phone costs $100, so people around the world buy the cheaper phone from Finland. Now suppose the exchange rate falls to 1 euro per U.S. dollar. The Nokia phone now costs $120 and is more expensive than the Motorola phone. People will switch from the Nokia phone to the Motorola phone. U.S. exports will increase and U.S. imports will decrease, so U.S. aggregate demand will increase.

An increase in foreign income increases U.S. exports and increases U.S. aggregate demand. For example, an increase in income in Japan and Germany increases Japanese and German consumers' and producers' planned expenditures on U.S.-produced goods and services.

Shifts of the Aggregate Demand Curve

When aggregate demand changes, the aggregate demand curve shifts. Figure 7 shows two changes in aggregate demand and summarizes the factors that bring about such changes.

Aggregate demand increases and the aggregate demand curve shifts rightward from AD_0 to AD_1 when expected future income, inflation, or profit increases; government expenditure on goods and services increases; taxes are cut; transfer payments increase; the quantity of money increases and interest rates fall; the exchange rate falls; or foreign income increases.

Aggregate demand decreases and the aggregate demand curve shifts leftward from AD_0 to AD_2 when expected future income, inflation, or profit decreases; government expenditure on goods and services decreases; taxes increase; transfer payments decrease; the quantity of money decreases and interest rates rise; the exchange rate rises; or foreign income decreases.

MACROECONOMIC EQUILIBRIUM   **5**

The purpose of the aggregate supply–aggregate demand model is to explain changes in real GDP and the price level. To achieve this purpose, we combine aggregate supply and aggregate demand and determine macroeconomic equilibrium. There is a macroeconomic equilibrium for each of the time frames for aggregate supply: a long-run equilibrium and a short-run equilibrium. Long-run equilibrium is the state toward which the economy is heading. Short-run equilibrium is the normal state of the economy as it fluctuates around potential GDP.

We'll begin our study of macroeconomic equilibrium by looking first at the short run.

FIGURE 7   Changes in Aggregate Demand

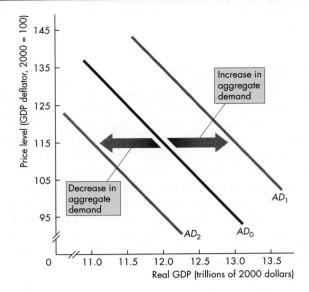

Aggregate demand

Decreases if:

▶ Expected future income, inflation, or profits decrease

▶ Fiscal policy decreases government expenditure, increases taxes, or decreases transfer payments

▶ Monetary policy decreases the quantity of money and increases interest rates

▶ The exchange rate increases or foreign income decreases

Increases if:

▶ Expected future income, inflation, or profits increase

▶ Fiscal policy increases government expenditure, decreases taxes, or increases transfer payments

▶ Monetary policy increases the quantity of money and decreases interest rates

▶ The exchange rate decreases or foreign income increases

Short-Run Macroeconomic Equilibrium

The aggregate demand curve tells us the quantity of real GDP demanded at each price level, and the short-run aggregate supply curve tells us the quantity of real GDP supplied at each price level. **Short-run macroeconomic equilibrium** occurs when the quantity of real GDP demanded equals the quantity of real GDP supplied. That is, short-run macroeconomic equilibrium occurs at the point of intersection of the *AD* curve and the *SAS* curve. Figure 8 shows such an equilibrium at a price level of 115 and real GDP of $12 trillion (points *C* and *C′*).

To see why this position is the equilibrium, think about what happens if the price level is something other than 115. Suppose, for example, that the price level is 125 and that real GDP is $13 trillion (at point *E* on the *SAS* curve). The quantity of real GDP demanded is less than $13 trillion, so firms are unable to sell all their output. Unwanted inventories pile up, and firms cut both production and prices. Production and prices are cut until firms can sell all their output. This situation occurs only when real GDP is $12 trillion and the price level is 115.

FIGURE 8 Short-Run Equilibrium

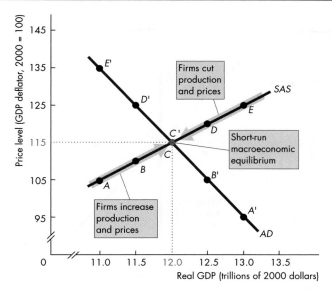

Short-run macroeconomic equilibrium occurs when real GDP demanded equals real GDP supplied—at the intersection of the aggregate demand curve (*AD*) and the short-run aggregate supply curve (*SAS*). Here, such an equilibrium occurs at points *C* and *C'*, where the price level is 115 and real GDP is $12 trillion. If the price level is 125 and real GDP is $13 trillion (point *E*), firms will not be able to sell all their output. They will decrease production and cut prices. If the price level is 105 and real GDP is $11 trillion (point *A*), people will not be able to buy all the goods and services they demand. Firms will increase production and raise their prices. Only when the price level is 115 and real GDP is $12 trillion can firms sell all that they produce and can people buy all the goods and services they demand. This is the short-run macroeconomic equilibrium.

Now suppose the price level is 105 and real GDP is $11 trillion (at point *A* on the *SAS* curve). The quantity of real GDP demanded exceeds $11 trillion, so firms are unable to meet the demand for their output. Inventories decrease, and customers clamor for goods and services. So firms increase production and raise prices. Production and prices increase until firms can meet the demand for their output. This situation occurs only when real GDP is $12 trillion and the price level is 115.

In the short run, the money wage rate is fixed. It does not adjust to move the economy to full employment. So in the short run, real GDP can be greater than or less than potential GDP. But in the long run, the money wage rate does adjust and real GDP moves toward potential GDP. We are going to study this adjustment process. But first, let's look at the economy in long-run equilibrium.

Long-Run Macroeconomic Equilibrium

Long-run macroeconomic equilibrium occurs when real GDP equals potential GDP—equivalently, when the economy is on its *long-run* aggregate supply curve. Figure 9 shows the long-run macroeconomic equilibrium, which occurs at the intersection of the *AD* curve and the *LAS* curve (the blue curves). Long-run macroeconomic equilibrium comes about because the money wage rate adjusts. Potential GDP and aggregate demand determine the price level, and the price level influences the money wage rate. In long-run equilibrium, the money wage

FIGURE 9   Long-Run Equilibrium

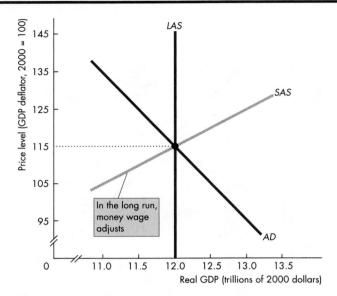

In long-run macroeconomic equilibrium, real GDP equals potential GDP. So long-run equilibrium occurs where the aggregate demand curve *AD* intersects the long-run aggregate supply curve *LAS*. In the long run, aggregate demand determines the price level and has no effect on real GDP. The money wage rate adjusts in the long run, so the *SAS* curve intersects the *LAS* curve at the long-run equilibrium price level.

rate has adjusted to put the (gray) *SAS* curve through the long-run equilibrium point.

We'll look at this money wage adjustment process later in this reading. But first, let's see how the *AS–AD* model helps us to understand economic growth and inflation.

Economic Growth and Inflation

Economic growth occurs because over time, the quantity of labor grows, capital is accumulated, and technology advances. These changes increase potential GDP and shift the *LAS* curve rightward. Figure 10 shows such a shift. The growth rate of potential GDP is determined by the pace at which labor grows, capital is accumulated, and technology advances.

Inflation occurs when over time, the increase in aggregate demand is greater than the increase in long-run aggregate supply. That is, inflation occurs if the *AD* curve shifts rightward by more than the rightward shift in the *LAS* curve. Figure 10 shows such shifts.

If aggregate demand increased at the same pace as long-run aggregate supply, we would experience real GDP growth with no inflation.

In the long run, the main influence on aggregate demand is the growth rate of the quantity of money. At times when the quantity of money increases rapidly, aggregate demand increases quickly and the inflation rate is high. When the growth rate of the quantity of money slows, other things remaining the same, the inflation rate eventually decreases.

Our economy experiences periods of growth and inflation, like those shown in Fig. 10. But it does not experience *steady* growth and *steady* inflation. Real GDP

FIGURE 10   Economic Growth and Inflation

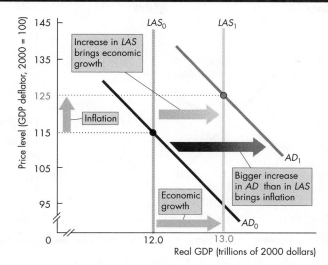

Economic growth is the persistent increase in potential GDP. Economic growth is shown as an ongoing rightward shift of the *LAS* curve. Inflation is the persistent rise in the price level. Inflation occurs when the increase in aggregate demand is greater than the increase in long-run aggregate supply.

fluctuates around potential GDP in a business cycle, and inflation fluctuates. When we study the business cycle, we ignore economic growth. By doing so, we can see the business cycle more clearly.

The Business Cycle

The business cycle occurs because aggregate demand and short-run aggregate supply fluctuate but the money wage rate does not adjust quickly enough to keep real GDP at potential GDP. Figure 11 shows three types of short-run macroeconomic equilibrium.

In part (a), there is a below full-employment equilibrium. A **below full-employment equilibrium** is a macroeconomic equilibrium in which potential GDP exceeds real GDP. The gap between real GDP and potential GDP is the **output gap**. When potential GDP exceeds real GDP, the output gap is also called a **recessionary gap**. This name reminds us that a gap has opened up between potential GDP and real GDP either because the economy has experienced a recession or because real GDP, while growing, has grown more slowly than potential GDP.

The below full-employment equilibrium shown in Fig. 11(a) occurs where the aggregate demand curve AD_0 intersects the short-run aggregate supply curve SAS_0 at a real GDP of $11.8 trillion. Potential GDP is $12 trillion, so the recessionary gap is $0.2 trillion. The U.S. economy was in a situation similar to that shown in Fig. 11(a) in the early 2000s.

Figure 11(b) is an example of **full-employment equilibrium**, in which real GDP equals potential GDP. In this example, the equilibrium occurs where the aggregate demand curve AD_1 intersects the short-run aggregate supply curve SAS_1 at an actual and potential GDP of $12 trillion. The U.S. economy was in a situation such as that shown in Fig. 11(b) in 1998.

FIGURE 11   The Business Cycle

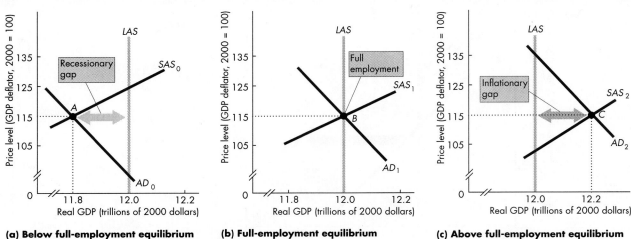

(a) Below full-employment equilibrium   **(b) Full-employment equilibrium**   **(c) Above full-employment equilibrium**

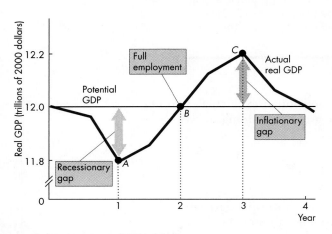

(d) Fluctuations in real GDP

Part (a) shows a below full-employment equilibrium in year 1; part (b) shows a full-employment equilibrium in year 2; and part (c) shows an above full-employment equilibrium in year 3. Part (d) shows how real GDP fluctuates around potential GDP in a business cycle.

In year 1, a recessionary gap exists and the economy is at point *A* (in parts a and d). In year 2, the economy is at full employment and the economy is at point *B* (in parts b and d). In year 3, an inflationary gap exists and the economy is at point *C* (in parts c and d).

Figure 11(c) shows an above full-employment equilibrium. An **above full-employment equilibrium** is a macroeconomic equilibrium in which real GDP exceeds potential GDP. When real GDP exceeds potential GDP, the output gap is called an **inflationary gap**. This name reminds us that a gap has opened up between real GDP and potential GDP and that this gap creates inflationary pressure.

The above full-employment equilibrium shown in Fig. 11(c) occurs where the aggregate demand curve AD_2 intersects the short-run aggregate supply curve SAS_2 at a real GDP of $12.2 trillion. There is an inflationary gap of $0.2 trillion. The U.S. economy was in a situation similar to that depicted in Fig. 11(c) in 1999 and 2000.

The economy moves from one type of macroeconomic equilibrium to another as a result of fluctuations in aggregate demand and in short-run aggregate supply. These fluctuations produce fluctuations in real GDP. Figure 11(d) shows how real GDP fluctuates around potential GDP.

Let's now look at some of the sources of these fluctuations around potential GDP.

FIGURE 12 An Increase in Aggregate Demand

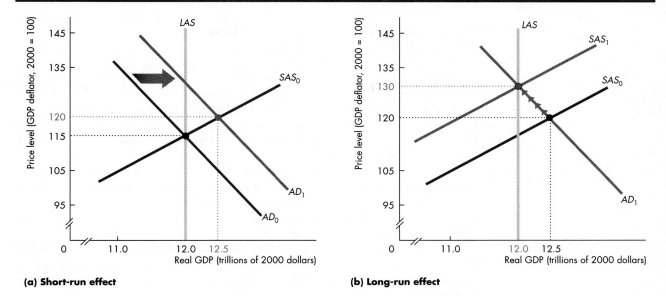

(a) Short-run effect

(b) Long-run effect

An increase in aggregate demand shifts the aggregate demand curve from AD_0 to AD_1. In short-run equilibrium, real GDP increases to \$12.5 trillion and the price level rises to 120. In this situation, an inflationary gap exists. In the long run, the money wage rate rises and the short-run aggregate supply curve shifts leftward in part (b). As short-run aggregate supply decreases, the SAS curve shifts from SAS_0 to SAS_1 and intersects the aggregate demand curve AD_1 at higher price levels and real GDP decreases. Eventually, the price level rises to 130 and real GDP decreases to \$12 trillion—potential GDP.

Fluctuations in Aggregate Demand

One reason real GDP fluctuates around potential GDP is that aggregate demand fluctuates. Let's see what happens when aggregate demand increases.

Figure 12(a) shows an economy at full employment. The aggregate demand curve is AD_0, the short-run aggregate supply curve is SAS_0, and the long-run aggregate supply curve is LAS. Real GDP equals potential GDP at \$12 trillion, and the price level is 115.

Now suppose that the world economy expands and that the demand for U.S.-produced goods increases in Japan and Europe. The increase in U.S. exports increases aggregate demand in the United States, and the aggregate demand curve shifts rightward from AD_0 to AD_1 in Fig. 12(a).

Faced with an increase in demand, firms increase production and raise prices. Real GDP increases to \$12.5 trillion, and the price level rises to 120. The economy is now in an above full-employment equilibrium. Real GDP exceeds potential GDP, and there is an inflationary gap.

The increase in aggregate demand has increased the prices of all goods and services. Faced with higher prices, firms have increased their output rates. At this stage, prices of goods and services have increased but the money wage rate has not changed. (Recall that as we move along a short-run aggregate supply curve, the money wage rate is constant.)

The economy cannot produce in excess of potential GDP forever. Why not? What are the forces at work that bring real GDP back to potential GDP?

Because the price level has increased and the money wage rate is unchanged, workers have experienced a fall in the buying power of their wages and firms' profits have increased. In these circumstances, workers demand higher wages and firms, anxious to maintain their employment and output levels, meet those demands. If firms do not raise the money wage rate, they will either lose workers or have to hire less productive ones.

As the money wage rate rises, the short-run aggregate supply curve begins to shift leftward. In Fig. 12(b), the short-run aggregate supply curve shifts from SAS_0 toward SAS_1. The rise in the money wage rate and the shift in the SAS curve produce a sequence of new equilibrium positions. Along the adjustment path, real GDP decreases and the price level rises. The economy moves up along its aggregate demand curve as shown by the arrowheads in the figure.

Eventually, the money wage rate rises by the same percentage as the price level. At this time, the aggregate demand curve AD_1 intersects SAS_1 at a new full-employment equilibrium. The price level has risen to 130, and real GDP is back where it started, at potential GDP.

A decrease in aggregate demand has effects similar but opposite to those of an increase in aggregate demand. That is, a decrease in aggregate demand shifts the aggregate demand curve leftward. Real GDP decreases to less than potential GDP, and a recessionary gap emerges. Firms cut prices. The lower price level increases the purchasing power of wages and increases firms' costs relative to their output prices because the money wage rate is unchanged. Eventually, the money wage rate falls and the short-run aggregate supply curve shifts rightward.

Let's now work out how real GDP and the price level change when aggregate supply changes.

Fluctuations in Aggregate Supply

Fluctuations in short-run aggregate supply can bring fluctuations in real GDP around potential GDP. Suppose that initially real GDP equals potential GDP. Then there is a large but temporary rise in the price of oil. What happens to real GDP and the price level?

Figure 13 answers this question. The aggregate demand curve is AD_0, the short-run aggregate supply curve is SAS_0, and the long-run aggregate supply curve is LAS. Real GDP is $12 trillion, which equals potential GDP, and the price level is 115. Then the price of oil rises. Faced with higher energy and transportation costs, firms decrease production. Short-run aggregate supply decreases, and the short-run aggregate supply curve shifts leftward to SAS_1. The price level rises to 125, and real GDP decreases to $11.5 trillion. Because real GDP decreases, the economy experiences recession. Because the price level increases, the economy experiences inflation. A combination of recession and inflation, called **stagflation**, actually occurred in the United States in the mid-1970s and early 1980s. But events like this are not common.

When the price of oil returns to its original level, the economy returns to full employment.

We can use the $AS–AD$ model to explain and illustrate the views of the alternative schools of thought in macroeconomics. That is your next task.

6   MACROECONOMIC SCHOOLS OF THOUGHT

Macroeconomics is an active field of research, and much remains to be learned about the forces that make our economy grow and fluctuate. There is a greater degree of consensus and certainty about economic growth and inflation—the longer-term trends in real GDP and the price level—than there is about the business cycle—the short-term fluctuations in these variables. Here, we'll look only at differences of view about short-term fluctuations.

FIGURE 13   A Decrease in Aggregate Supply

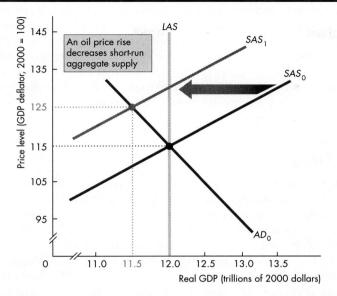

An increase in the price of oil decreases short-run aggregate supply and shifts the short-run aggregate supply curve from SAS_0 to SAS_1. Real GDP falls from $12 trillion to $11.5 trillion, and the price level increases from 115 to 125. The economy experiences stagflation.

The aggregate supply–aggregate demand model that you've studied in this reading provides a good foundation for understanding the range of views that macroeconomists hold about this topic. But what you will learn here is just a first glimpse at the scientific controversy and debate. We'll return to these issues at various points later in the volume and deepen your appreciation of the alternative views.

Classification usually requires simplification. And classifying macroeconomists is no exception to this general rule. The classification that we'll use here is simple, but it is not misleading. We're going to divide macroeconomists into three broad schools of thought and examine the views of each group in turn. The groups are

► Classical
► Keynesian
► Monetarist

The Classical View

A **classical** macroeconomist believes that the economy is self-regulating and always at full employment. The term "classical" derives from the name of the founding school of economics that includes Adam Smith, David Ricardo, and John Stuart Mill.

A **new classical** view is that business cycle fluctuations are the efficient responses of a well-functioning market economy that is bombarded by shocks that arise from the uneven pace of technological change.

The classical view can be understood in terms of beliefs about aggregate demand and aggregate supply.

Aggregate Demand Fluctuations

In the classical view, technological change is the most significant influence on both aggregate demand and aggregate supply. For this reason, classical macroeconomists don't use the *AS–AD* framework. But their views can be interpreted in this framework. A technological change that increases the productivity of capital brings an increase in aggregate demand because firms increase their expenditure on new plant and equipment. A technological change that lengthens the useful life of existing capital decreases the demand for new capital, which decreases aggregate demand.

Aggregate Supply Response

In the classical view, the money wage rate that lies behind the short-run aggregate supply curve is instantly and completely flexible. The money wage rate adjusts so quickly to maintain equilibrium in the labor market that real GDP always adjusts to equal potential GDP.

Potential GDP itself fluctuates for the same reasons that aggregate demand fluctuates: technological change. When the pace of technological change is rapid, potential GDP increases quickly and so does real GDP. And when the pace of technological change slows, so does the growth rate of potential GDP.

Classical Policy

The classical view of policy emphasizes the potential for taxes to stunt incentives and create inefficiency. By minimizing the disincentive effects of taxes, employment, investment, and technological advance are at their efficient levels and the economy expands at an appropriate and rapid pace.

The Keynesian View

A **Keynesian** macroeconomist believes that left alone, the economy would rarely operate at full employment and that to achieve and maintain full employment, active help from fiscal policy and monetary policy is required.

The term "Keynesian" derives from the name of one of the twentieth century's most famous economists, John Maynard Keynes.

The Keynesian view is based on beliefs about the forces that determine aggregate demand and short-run aggregate supply.

Aggregate Demand Fluctuations

In the Keynesian view, *expectations* are the most significant influence on aggregate demand. And expectations are based on herd instinct, or what Keynes himself called "animal spirits." A wave of pessimism about future profit prospects can lead to a fall in aggregate demand and plunge the economy into recession.

Aggregate Supply Response

In the Keynesian view, the money wage rate that lies behind the short-run aggregate supply curve is extremely sticky in the downward direction. Basically, the money wage rate doesn't fall. So if there is a recessionary gap, there is no automatic mechanism for getting rid of it. If it were to happen, a fall in the money wage rate would increase short-run aggregate supply and restore full employment. But the money wage rate doesn't fall, so the economy remains stuck in recession.

A modern version of the Keynesian view known as the **new Keynesian** view holds not only that the money wage rate is sticky but also that prices of goods and services are sticky. With a sticky price level, the short-run aggregate supply curve is horizontal at a fixed price level.

Policy Response Needed

The Keynesian view calls for fiscal policy and monetary policy to actively offset changes in aggregate demand that bring recession.

By stimulating aggregate demand in a recession, full employment can be restored.

The Monetarist View

A **monetarist** is a macroeconomist who believes that the economy is self-regulating and that it will normally operate at full employment, provided that monetary policy is not erratic and that the pace of money growth is kept steady.

The term "monetarist" was coined by an outstanding twentieth-century economist, Karl Brunner, to describe his own views and those of Milton Friedman.

The monetarist view can be interpreted in terms of beliefs about the forces that determine aggregate demand and short-run aggregate supply.

Aggregate Demand Fluctuations

In the monetarist view, *the quantity of money* is the most significant influence on aggregate demand. And the quantity of money is determined by the Federal Reserve (the Fed). If the Fed keeps money growing at a steady pace, aggregate demand fluctuations will be minimized and the economy will operate close to full employment. But if the Fed decreases the quantity of money or even just slows its growth rate too abruptly, the economy will go into recession. In the monetarist view, all recessions result from inappropriate monetary policy.

Aggregate Supply Response

The monetarist view of short-run aggregate supply is the same as the Keynesian view: the money wage rate is sticky. If the economy is in recession, it will take an unnecessarily long time for it to return unaided to full employment.

Monetarist Policy

The monetarist view of policy is the same as the classical view on fiscal policy. Taxes should be kept low to avoid disincentive effects that decrease potential GDP. Provided that the quantity of money is kept on a steady growth path, no active stabilization is needed to offset changes in aggregate demand.

To complete your study of the aggregate supply–aggregate demand model, take a look at the U.S. economy in 2006 through the eyes of this model in *Reading Between the Lines.*

7 READING BETWEEN THE LINES

Aggregate Supply and Aggregate Demand in Action

THE NEW YORK TIMES, MAY 26, 2006

Revised Growth Data Eases Inflation Fear

Concerns the economy might have overheated in the first quarter eased yesterday after revised economic growth figures showed that expansion was indeed strong, but not too strong. . . .

The Commerce Department said yesterday that the nation's gross domestic product expanded 5.3 percent in the first quarter, up from the 4.8 percent first reported last month. That is the fastest rate of growth since 2003. Still, many expected a growth rate of 5.8 percent, according to a survey of economists by Bloomberg News.

But instead of showing signs that inflation was even more of a problem in the first quarter than initially thought, the revised numbers suggested fairly tame price pressures. Consumer spending, which accounts for the bulk of the gross domestic product, contributed 3.63 percentage points to the overall 5.3 percent growth. Initially, the government said consumer spending contributed slightly more.

And core consumer spending, which excludes energy and food, rose 2 percent in the first quarter—unchanged from the first report. Investors looking for signs that inflationary pressures had ebbed were also reassured by a letter to the chairman of the Congressional Joint Economic Committee, from Ben S. Bernanke, the Federal Reserve chairman, that said core inflation appeared stable. . . .

Although his tone was upbeat, Mr. Bernanke did not indicate what the Fed might do when it meets late next month to discuss raising the benchmark short-term interest rate. "Of course, inflation expectations will remain low only so long as the Federal Reserve demonstrates its commitment to price stability," he wrote. . . .

Essence of the Story

▶ Real GDP grew at a 5.3 percent annual rate during the first quarter of 2006, the fastest since 2003.

▶ Consumer spending (the largest component of GDP) contributed 3.63 percentage points to the overall growth.

▶ Federal Reserve chairman Ben S. Bernanke eased concerns about inflation.

▶ He said that core inflation appeared to be stable and low but would remain so only as long as the Federal Reserve demonstrates commitment to price stability.

▶ The data showed a strong expansion but eased fears that the economy might have overheated.

Economic Analysis

▶ U.S. real GDP grew at a 5.3 percent annual rate during the first quarter of 2006, the fastest since the spectacular 8.2 percent annual growth rate in 2003.

▶ Real GDP had increased steadily throughout 2005 and the inflation rate was steady.

▶ In 2006, most forecasters were confident that real GDP growth was not greater than the growth of potential GDP and that there was little fear of inflation breaking out.

▶ The Congressional Budget Office (CBO) estimate of potential GDP and its implied output gap are consistent with this view.

▶ Despite the strong growth, the CBO estimated that real GDP was below potential GDP—that there was a recessionary gap—in 2006.

▶ Figure 14 illustrates the CBO estimate of the recessionary gap through 2005 and in the first quarter of 2006.

FIGURE 14   Actual and Potential Real GDP

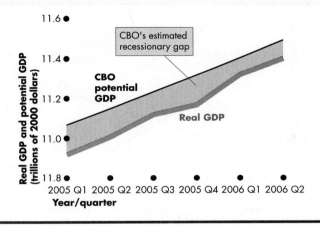

▶ Real GDP (the blue line) grew faster than potential GDP (the black line), so the recessionary gap narrowed. But it didn't disappear.

▶ Another number estimated by the CBO places a question mark on the output gap estimate.

▶ The CBO's estimate of the natural unemployment rate suggests that by mid-2005, the economy was at full employment and that by 2006, there was an inflationary gap.

▶ Figure 15 shows the actual unemployment rate and the CBO's estimate of the natural rate.

▶ Whether inflation is likely to remain constant, increase, or decrease depends on the output gap.

▶ Figure 16 illustrates the three possibilities.

▶ In the second quarter of 2006, real GDP was $11.4 trillion and the price level was 116 at the intersection of the short-run aggregate supply curve *SAS* and the aggregate demand curve *AD*.

FIGURE 15   Actual and Natural Unemployment Rate

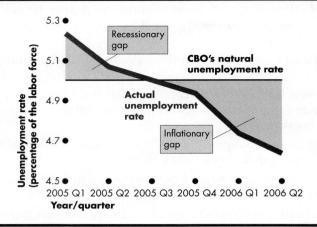

FIGURE 16   Aggregate Supply and Aggregate Demand in 2006

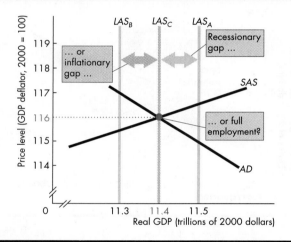

▶ The CBO estimate of potential GDP was $11.5 trillion with the long-run aggregate supply curve at LAS_A.

▶ If the CBO's estimate of the natural unemployment rate provides a better estimate of the output gap, the LAS curve might be LAS_B.

▶ But with stable inflation, it seems more likely that the economy is actually at full employment with the LAS curve at LAS_C.

SUMMARY

► The macroeconomic long run is a time frame in which prices adjust to achieve full employment.

► The macroeconomic short run is a time frame in which some money prices are sticky so that the economy might be below, at, or above full employment.

► In the long run, the quantity of real GDP supplied is potential GDP.

► In the short run, a rise in the price level increases the quantity of real GDP supplied.

► A change in potential GDP changes long-run and short-run aggregate supply. A change in the money wage rate changes only short-run aggregate supply.

► A rise in the price level decreases the quantity of real GDP demanded.

► Changes in expected future income, inflation, and profits; in fiscal policy and monetary policy; and in world real GDP and the exchange rate change aggregate demand.

► Aggregate demand and short-run aggregate supply determine real GDP and the price level.

► In the long run, real GDP equals potential GDP and aggregate demand determines the price level.

► The business cycle occurs because aggregate demand and aggregate supply fluctuate.

► Classical economists believe that the economy is self-regulating and always at full employment.

► Keynesian economists believe that full employment can be achieved only with active policy.

► Monetarist economists believe that recessions result from inappropriate monetary policy.

PRACTICE PROBLEMS FOR READING 23

1. Which of the following is *least likely* to result in an increase in potential GDP?

   A. An advance in technology.

   B. An increase in the money wage rate.

   C. An increase in the quantity of capital.

2. All else equal, aggregate demand is *most likely* to decrease in response to a decrease in:

   A. interest rates.

   B. federal tax revenues.

   C. expected corporate profits.

3. Assuming the economy is operating at full employment, what is the *most likely* long-run effect of an increase in government spending on the price level and real GDP?

   A. The price level and real GDP will both increase.

   B. The price level will increase, but there will be no change in real GDP.

   C. The price level will not change, but there will be an increase in real GDP.

4. Of the following factors, the factor that does not explain the downward slope of the aggregate demand curve is *most likely*:

   A. the wealth effect.

   B. substitution effects.

   C. technological advances.

5. An inflationary gap is *most likely* to occur:

   A. during periods of stagflation.

   B. when real GDP exceeds potential GDP.

   C. when real GDP is below potential GDP.

6. The belief that the economy is self-regulating is *least* associated with:

   A. classical macroeconomics.

   B. Keynesian macroeconomics.

   C. monetarist macroeconomics.

7. Which of the following is independent of the price level?

   A. The aggregate demand curve (AD).

   B. The long-run aggregate supply curve (LAS).

   C. The short-run aggregate supply curve (SAS).

SOLUTIONS FOR READING 23

1. B is correct. Potential GDP will not change in response to an increase in the money wage rate.

2. C is correct. Aggregate demand is expected to decrease if corporate profits decrease because firms will have less money to spend on investment in capital equipment.

3. B is correct. If an economy is operating at full employment, the long-run effect of an increase in government spending is to increase the price level while real GDP will be unchanged at the full employment level.

4. C is correct. The aggregate demand curve slopes downward for two reasons: wealth effect and substitution effects. Technological advances are likely to have an impact on aggregate supply to a far greater degree than their impact on aggregate demand.

5. B is correct. When real GDP exceeds potential GDP, the output gap is called an inflationary gap.

6. B is correct. A Keynesian macroeconomist believes that left alone, the economy would rarely operate at full employment and that to achieve and maintain full employment, active help from fiscal policy and monetary policy is required.

7. B is correct. The long-run aggregate supply curve (LAS) is independent of the price level.

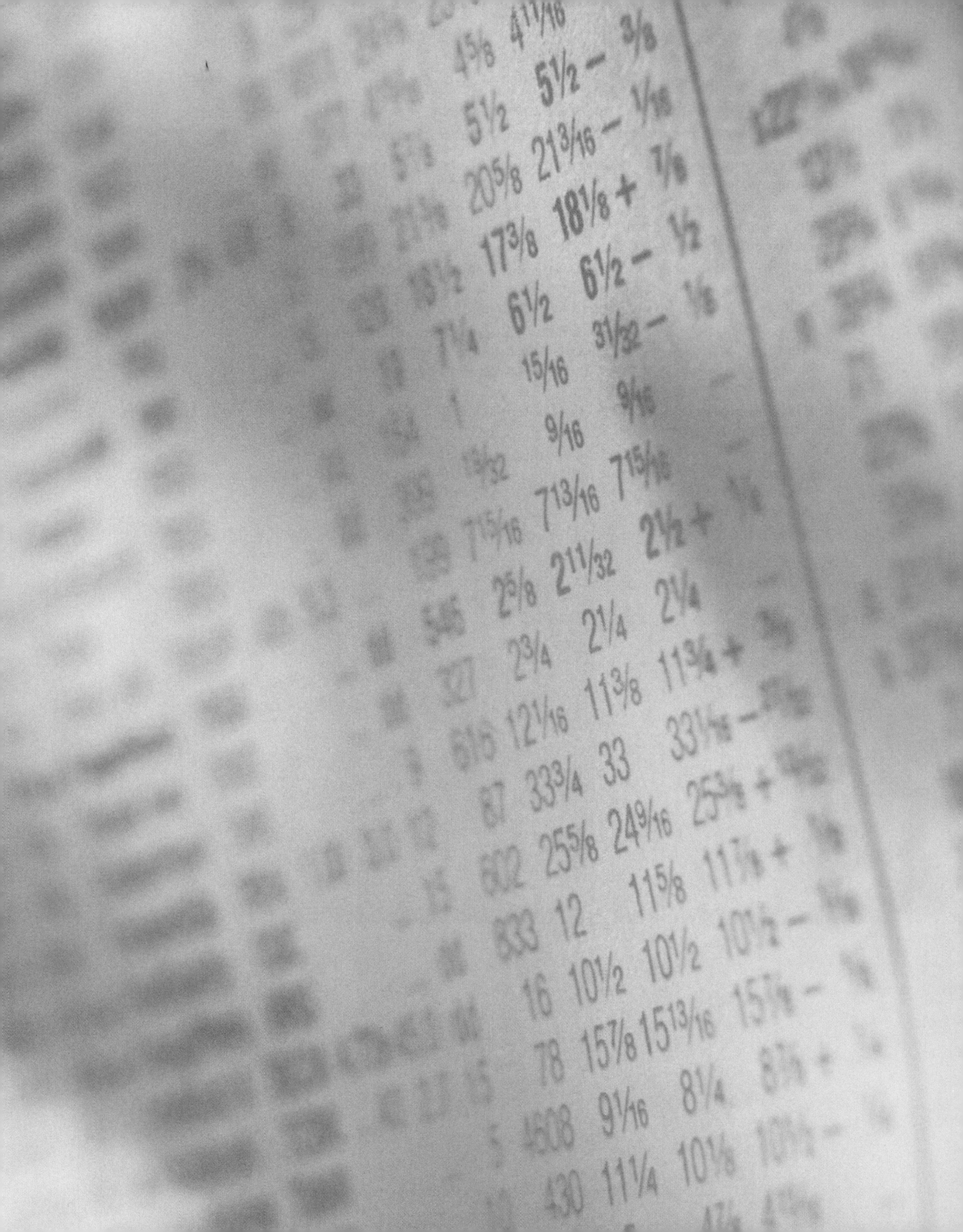

45⅛ 4 11/16

5½ **5½** − ⅜

5½ 2 13/16 − 1/16

20⅝ 18⅛ **+** ⅞

17⅜ **18⅛ +** ⅞

6½ **6½** − ½

7¼ **6½** 3 1/32 − ⅛

15/16

9/16 9/16

7 15/16 7 13/16 7 15/16

7 15/16 7 13/16

2⅝ 2 11/32 **2½ +**

2¾ 2¼ 2¼

12 1/16 11⅜ **11¼ +**

33¾ 33 33 1/16 −

25⅝ 24 9/16 25⅝ +

12 11⅝ 11⅞ +

16 10½ 10½ 10⅛ −

78 15⅞ 15 13/16 15⅞ +

9 1/16 8¼ 8⅛ +

11¼ 10⅛

STUDY SESSION 6
ECONOMICS:
Monetary and Fiscal Economics

This study session focuses on the monetary sector of an economy. It examines the functions of money and how it is created, highlighting the special role of the central bank within an economy. Supply and demand for resources, such as labor and capital, and goods are strongly interrelated. This study session describes circumstances when this relationship may lead to inflation or unemployment and how these concepts relate to the business cycle.

READING ASSIGNMENTS

Reading 24   Money, the Price Level, and Inflation
Economics, Eighth Edition, by Michael Parkin

Reading 25   U.S. Inflation, Unemployment, and Business Cycles
Economics, Eighth Edition, by Michael Parkin

Reading 26   Fiscal Policy
Economics, Eighth Edition, by Michael Parkin

Reading 27   Monetary Policy
Economics, Eighth Edition, by Michael Parkin

Reading 28   An Overview of Central Banks
International Economic Indicators and Central Banks,
by Anne Dolganos Picker

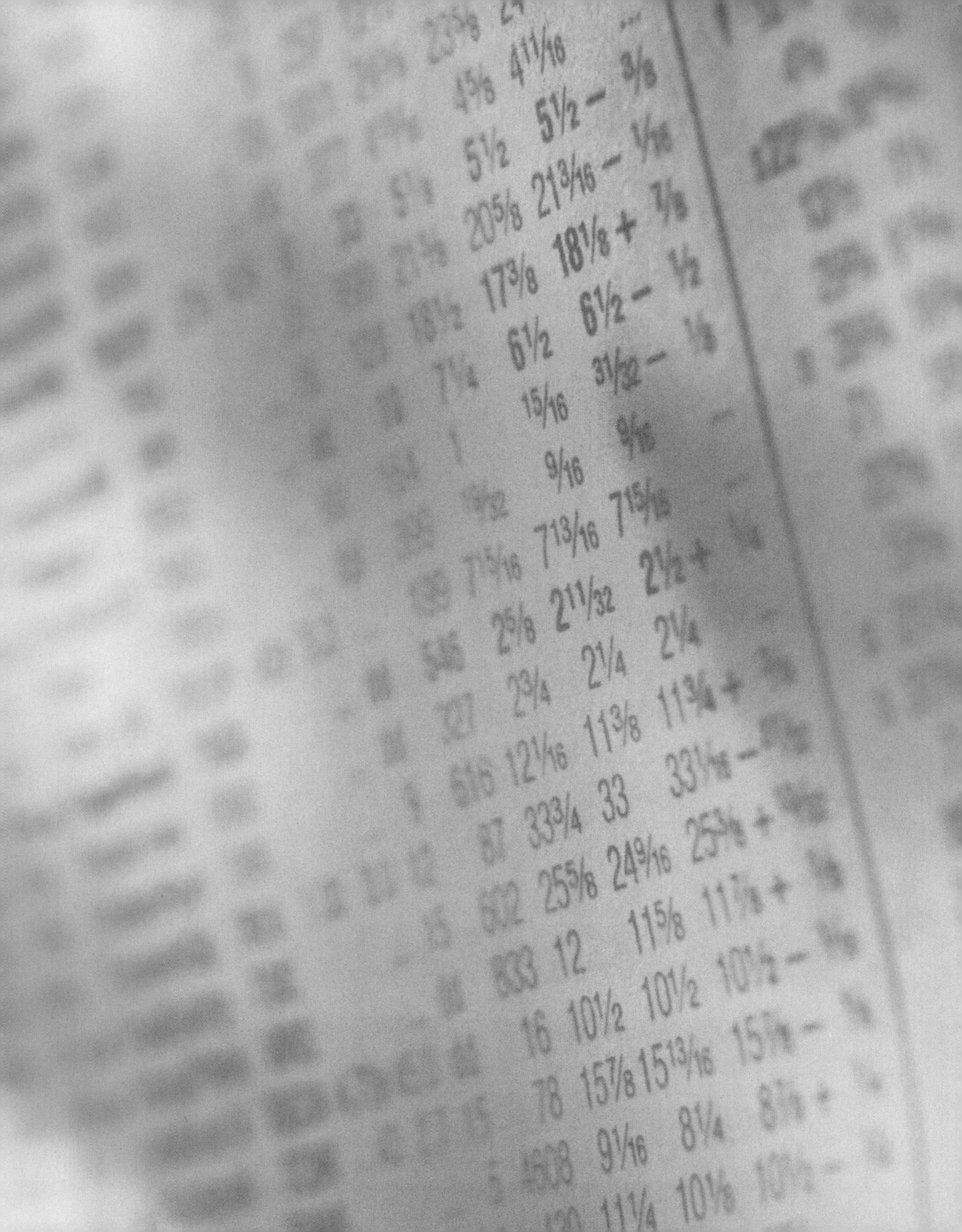

23⅜ 24
4⅝ 4¹¹⁄₁₆
4⅝ 4¹¹⁄₁₆ 5½ − ⅜
5½ 5½ − ⅛
20⅝ 21¹³⁄₁₆ − ⅛
17⅜ 18⅛ + ⅞
18½ 6½ − ½
7½ 6½ 31⁄32 − ⅛
15⁄16 9⅛
9⁄16
7¹³⁄₁₆ 7¹⁵⁄₁₆
7¹⁵⁄₁₆ 7¹³⁄₁₆ 7¹⁵⁄₁₆
2⅝ 2¹¹⁄32 2½ +
2¾ 2¼ 2¼
12¹⁄₁₆ 11⅜ 11¾ +
33¾ 33 33⅛ −
25⅝ 24⁹⁄₁₆ 25⅜ +
12 11⅝ 11⅞ +
10½ 10½ 10⅛ −
15⅞ 15¹³⁄₁₆ 15⅛ −
9¹⁄₁₆ 8¼ 8⅛ +
11¼ 10⅛

MONEY, THE PRICE LEVEL, AND INFLATION
by Michael Parkin

LEARNING OUTCOMES

The candidate should be able to: Mastery

a. explain the functions of money;   ☐

b. describe the components of the M1 and M2 measures of money and   ☐
discuss why checks and credit cards are not counted as money;

c. describe the economic functions of and differentiate among the various   ☐
depository institutions and explain the impact of financial regulation,
deregulation, and innovation;

d. explain the goals of the U.S. Federal Reserve (Fed) in conducting   ☐
monetary policy and how the Fed uses its policy tools to control the
quantity of money, and describe the assets and liabilities on the Fed's
balance sheet;

e. discuss the creation of money, including the role played by excess   ☐
reserves, and calculate the amount of loans a bank can generate, given
new deposits;

f. describe the monetary base and explain the relation among the   ☐
monetary base, the money multiplier, and the quantity of money;

g. explain the factors that influence the demand for money and describe   ☐
the demand for money curve, including the effects of changes in real
GDP and financial innovation;

h. explain interest rate determination and the short-run and long-run   ☐
effects of money on real GDP;

i. discuss the quantity theory of money and its relation to aggregate   ☐
supply and aggregate demand.

Economics, Eighth Edition, by Michael Parkin. Copyright © 2008 by Pearson Education. Reprinted with permission
of Pearson Education, publishing as Pearson Addison Wesley.

1

MONEY MAKES THE WORLD GO AROUND

Money, like fire and the wheel, has been around for a long time. And it has taken many forms. Money was wampum (beads made from shells) for North American Indians, whale's teeth for Fijians, and tobacco for early American colonists. Cakes of salt served as money in Ethiopia and Tibet. Today, when we want to buy something, we use coins or dollar bills, write a check, or present a debit card or a credit card. Soon, we'll be using a "smart card" that keeps track of spending and that our pocket computer can read. Are all these things money?

When we deposit some coins or notes into a bank, is that still money? And what happens when the bank lends the money we've deposited to someone else? How can we get our money back if it has been lent out?

The quantity of money in our economy is regulated by the Federal Reserve—the Fed. How does the Fed influence the quantity of money? And what happens if the Fed creates too much money or too little money?

In this reading, we study the functions of money, the banks that create it, the Federal Reserve and its influence on the quantity of money, and the long-run consequences of changes in the quantity of money. In *Reading Between the Lines* at the end of the reading, we look at a spectacular example of money and inflation in action in the African nation Zimbabwe.

2

WHAT IS MONEY?

What do wampum, tobacco, and nickels and dimes have in common? They are all examples of **money**, which is defined as any commodity or token that is generally acceptable as a means of payment. A **means of payment** is a method of settling a debt. When a payment has been made, there is no remaining obligation between the parties to a transaction. So what wampum, tobacco, and nickels and dimes have in common is that they have served (or still do serve) as the means of payment. Money serves three other functions:

▶ Medium of exchange
▶ Unit of account
▶ Store of value

Medium of Exchange

A *medium of exchange* is any object that is generally accepted in exchange for goods and services. Without a medium of exchange, goods and services must be exchanged directly for other goods and services—an exchange called **barter**. Barter requires a *double coincidence of wants*, a situation that rarely occurs. For example, if you want a hamburger, you might offer a CD in exchange for it. But you must find someone who is selling hamburgers and who wants your CD.

A medium of exchange overcomes the need for a double coincidence of wants. And money acts as a medium of exchange because people with something to sell will always accept money in exchange for it. But money isn't the only medium of exchange. You can buy with a credit card. But a credit card isn't money. It doesn't make a final payment, and the debt it creates must eventually be settled by using money.

Unit of Account

A *unit of account* is an agreed measure for stating the prices of goods and services. To get the most out of your budget, you have to figure out whether seeing one more movie is worth its opportunity cost. But that cost is not dollars and cents. It is the number of ice-cream cones, sodas, or cups of coffee that you must give up. It's easy to do such calculations when all these goods have prices in terms of dollars and cents (see Table 1). If a movie costs $6 and a six-pack of soda costs $3, you know right away that seeing one more movie costs you 2 six-packs of soda. If jelly beans are 50¢ a pack, one more movie costs 12 packs of jelly beans. You need only one calculation to figure out the opportunity cost of any pair of goods and services.

TABLE 1   The Unit of Account Function of Money Simplifies Price Comparisons

Good	Price in Money Units	Price in Units of Another Good
Movie	$6.00 each	2 six-packs of soda
Soda	$3.00 per six-pack	2 ice-cream cones
Ice cream	$1.50 per cone	3 packs of jelly beans
Jelly beans	$0.50 per pack	2 sticks of gum
Gum	$0.25 per stick	1 local phone call

Money as a unit of account: The price of a movie is $6 and the price of a stick of gum is 25¢, so the opportunity cost of a movie is 24 sticks of gum ($6.00 ÷ 25¢ = 24).

No unit of account: You go to a movie theater and learn that the price of a movie is 2 six-packs of soda. You go to a candy store and learn that a pack of jelly beans costs 2 sticks of gum. But how many sticks of gum does seeing a movie cost you? To answer that question, you go to the convenience store and find that a six-pack of soda costs 2 ice-cream cones. Now you head for the ice-cream shop, where an ice-cream cone costs 3 packs of jelly beans. Now you get out your pocket calculator: 1 movie costs 2 six-packs of soda, or 4 ice-cream cones, or 12 packs of jelly beans, or 24 sticks of gum!

But imagine how troublesome it would be if your local movie theater posted its price as 2 six-packs of soda, the convenience store posted the price of a six-pack of soda as 2 ice-cream cones, the ice-cream shop posted the price of an ice-cream cone as 3 packs of jelly beans, and the candy store priced a pack of jelly beans as 2 sticks of gum! Now how much running around and calculating will you have to do to figure out how much that movie is going to cost you in terms of the soda, ice cream, jelly beans, or gum that you must give up to see it? You get the answer for soda right away from the sign posted on the movie theater. But for all the other goods, you're going to have to visit many different stores to establish the price of each commodity in terms of another and then calculate prices in units that are relevant for your own decision. Cover up the column labeled "Price in money units" in Table 1 and see how hard it is to figure out the number of local phone calls it costs to see one movie. It's enough to make a person swear off movies! You can see how much simpler it is if all the prices are expressed in dollars and cents.

Store of Value

Money is a *store of value* in the sense that it can be held and exchanged later for goods and services. If money were not a store of value, it could not serve as a means of payment.

Money is not alone in acting as a store of value. A house, a car, and a work of art are other examples.

The more stable the value of a commodity or token, the better it can act as a store of value and the more useful it is as money. No store of value has a completely stable value. The value of a house, a car, or a work of art fluctuates over time. The value of the commodities and tokens that are used as money also fluctuate over time. And when there is inflation, their values persistently fall.

Because inflation brings a falling value of money, a low inflation rate is needed to make money as useful as possible as a store of value.

Money in the United States Today

In the United States today, money consists of

► Currency
► Deposits at banks and other depository institutions

Currency

The notes and coins held by individuals and businesses are known as **currency**. Notes are money because the government declares them so with the words "This note is legal tender for all debts, public and private." You can see these words on every dollar bill. Notes and coins *inside* banks are not counted as money.

Deposits

Deposits at banks and other depository institutions such as savings and loan associations are also money. Deposits are money because they can be used to make payments.

Official Measures of Money

The two main official measures of money in the United States today are known as M1 and M2. Figure 1 shows the items that make up these two measures. **M1** consists of currency and traveler's checks plus checking deposits owned by individuals and businesses. M1 does *not* include currency held by banks, and it does not include currency and checking deposits owned by the U.S. government. **M2** consists of M1 plus time deposits, savings deposits, and money market mutual funds and other deposits. You can see that M2 is almost five times as large as M1. You can also see that currency is a small part of our money.

Are M1 and M2 Really Money?

Money is the means of payment. So the test of whether an asset is money is whether it serves as a means of payment. Currency passes the test. But what about deposits? Checking deposits are money because they can be transferred from one

FIGURE 1   Two Measures of Money

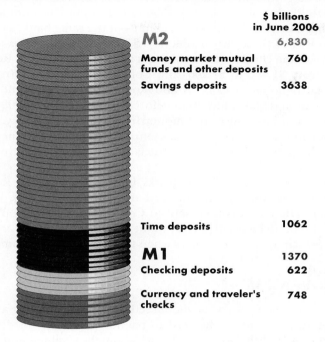

	$ billions in June 2006
M2	6,830
Money market mutual funds and other deposits	760
Savings deposits	3638
Time deposits	1062
M1	1370
Checking deposits	622
Currency and traveler's checks	748

M1   ► Currency and traveler's checks

    ► Checking deposits at commercial banks, savings and loan associations, savings banks, and credit unions

M2   ► M1

    ► Time deposits

    ► Savings deposits

    ► Money market mutual funds and other deposits

Source: The Federal Reserve Board.

person to another by writing a check or using a debit card. Such a transfer of ownership is equivalent to handing over currency. Because M1 consists of currency plus checking deposits and each of these is a means of payment, *M1 is money*.

But what about M2? Some of the savings deposits in M2 are just as much a means of payment as the checking deposits in M1. You can use the ATM at the grocery store checkout or gas station and transfer funds directly from your savings account to pay for your purchase. But some savings deposits are not means of payment. These deposits are known as liquid assets. *Liquidity* is the property of being easily convertible into a means of payment without loss in value. Because the deposits in M2 that are not means of payment are quickly and easily converted into a means of payment—into currency or checking deposits—they are counted as money.

Deposits Are Money but Checks Are Not

In defining money, we include, along with currency, deposits at banks and other depository institutions. But we do not count the checks that people write as money. Why are deposits money and checks not?

To see why deposits are money but checks are not, think about what happens when Colleen buys some roller-blades for $200 from Rocky's Rollers. When Colleen goes to Rocky's shop, she has $500 in her deposit account at the Laser Bank. Rocky has $1,000 in his deposit account—at the same bank, as it happens. The total deposits of these two people are $1,500. Colleen writes a check for $200. Rocky takes the check to the bank right away and deposits it. Rocky's bank balance rises from $1,000 to $1,200, and Colleen's balance falls from $500 to $300. The total deposits of Colleen and Rocky are still the same as before: $1,500. Rocky now has $200 more than before, and Colleen has $200 less.

This transaction has transferred money from Colleen to Rocky. The check itself was never money. There wasn't an extra $200 worth of money while the check was in circulation. The check instructs the bank to transfer money from Colleen to Rocky.

If Colleen and Rocky use different banks, there is an extra step. Rocky's bank credits the check to Rocky's account and then takes the check to a check-clearing center. The check is then sent to Colleen's bank, which pays Rocky's bank $200 and then debits Colleen's account $200. This process can take a few days, but the principles are the same as when two people use the same bank.

Credit Cards Are Not Money

So checks are not money. But what about credit cards? Isn't having a credit card in your wallet and presenting the card to pay for your roller-blades the same thing as using money? Why aren't credit cards somehow valued and counted as part of the quantity of money?

When you pay by check, you are frequently asked to prove your identity by showing your driver's license. It would never occur to you to think of your driver's license as money. It's just an ID card. A credit card is also an ID card but one that lets you take out a loan at the instant you buy something. When you sign a credit card sales slip, you are saying, "I agree to pay for these goods when the credit card company bills me." Once you get your statement from the credit card company, you must make at least the minimum payment due. To make that payment, you need money—you need to have currency or a checking deposit to pay the credit card company. So although you use a credit card when you buy something, the credit card is not the *means of payment* and it is not money.

We've seen that the main component of money in the United States is deposits at banks and other depository institutions. Let's take a closer look at these institutions.

3   DEPOSITORY INSTITUTIONS

A firm that takes deposits from households and firms and makes loans to other households and firms is called a **depository institution**. The deposits of three types of depository institutions make up the nation's money:

► Commercial banks
► Thrift institutions
► Money market mutual funds

Commercial Banks

A *commercial bank* is a firm that is licensed by the Comptroller of the Currency (at the U.S. Treasury) or by a state agency to receive deposits and make loans. About 8,000 commercial banks operate in the United States today.

Profit and Prudence: A Balancing Act

The aim of a bank is to maximize the net worth of its stockholders. To achieve this objective, the interest rate at which a bank lends exceeds the interest rate at which it borrows. But a bank must perform a delicate balancing act. Lending is risky, and the more a bank ties up its deposits in high-risk, high-interest rate loans, the bigger is its chance of not being able to repay its depositors. And if depositors perceive a high risk of not being repaid, they withdraw their funds and create a crisis for the bank. So a bank must be prudent in the way it uses its deposits, balancing security for the depositors against profit for its stockholders.

Reserves and Loans

To achieve security for its depositors, a bank divides the funds it receives in deposits into two parts: reserves and loans. *Reserves* are the cash in a bank's vault plus its deposits at Federal Reserve banks. (We'll study the Federal Reserve banks later in this reading.) The cash in a bank's vaults is a reserve to meet its depositors' demands for currency. This cash keeps the ATM replenished after you and your friends raid it for money for a midnight pizza. The account of a bank at the Federal Reserve is similar to your own bank account. Banks use these accounts to receive and make payments. A commercial bank deposits cash into or draws cash out of its account at the Federal Reserve and writes checks on that account to settle debts with other banks.

If a bank kept all its deposits as reserves, it wouldn't make any profit. In fact, a bank keeps only a small fraction of its funds in reserves and lends the rest. A bank has three types of assets:

1. *Liquid assets* are U.S. government Treasury bills and commercial bills. These assets are the banks' first line of defense if they need cash. Liquid assets can be sold and instantly converted into cash with virtually no risk of loss. Because they are virtually risk free, they have a low interest rate.

2. *Investment securities* are longer-term U.S. government bonds and other bonds. These assets can be sold quickly and converted into cash but at prices that fluctuate. Because their prices fluctuate, these assets are riskier than liquid assets, but they also have a higher interest rate.

3. Loans are commitments of fixed amounts of money for agreed-upon periods of time. Most bank loans are made to corporations to finance the purchase of capital equipment and inventories and to households— personal loans—to finance consumer durable goods, such as cars or boats. The outstanding balances on credit card accounts are also bank loans. Loans are the riskiest assets of a bank because they cannot be converted into cash until they are due to be repaid. And some borrowers default and never repay. Because they are the riskiest of a bank's assets, loans carry the highest interest rate.

Thrift Institutions

The thrift institutions are

► Savings and loan associations
► Savings banks
► Credit unions

Savings and Loan Association

A *savings and loan association* (S&L) is a depository institution that receives checking and savings deposits and that makes personal, commercial, and home-purchase loans.

Savings Bank

A *savings bank* is a depository institution that accepts savings deposits and makes mostly home-purchase loans. Some savings banks (called *mutual* savings banks) are owned by their depositors.

Credit Union

A *credit union* is a depository institution owned by a social or economic group such as a firm's employees that accepts savings deposits and makes mostly personal loans.

Money Market Mutual Funds

A *money market mutual fund* is a fund operated by a financial institution that sells shares in the fund and holds liquid assets such as U.S. Treasury bills or short-term commercial bills.

Money market mutual fund shares act like bank deposits. Shareholders can write checks on their money market mutual fund accounts. But there are restrictions on most of these accounts. For example, the minimum deposit accepted might be $2,500, and the smallest check a depositor is permitted to write might be $500.

The Economic Functions of Depository Institutions

All depository institutions make a profit from the spread between the interest rate they pay on deposits and the interest rate at which they lend. Why can depository institutions get deposits at a low interest rate and lend at a higher one? What services do they perform that make their depositors willing to put up with a low interest rate and their borrowers willing to pay a higher one?

Depository institutions provide four main services that people are willing to pay for:

► Creating liquidity
► Minimizing the cost of obtaining funds
► Minimizing the cost of monitoring borrowers
► Pooling risk

Creating Liquidity

Depository institutions create liquidity. *Liquid assets* are those that are easily convertible into money with little loss of value. Some of the liabilities of depository institutions are themselves money; others are highly liquid assets that are easily converted into money.

Depository institutions create liquidity by borrowing short and lending long. *Borrowing short* means taking deposits but standing ready to repay them on short notice (and even on no notice in the case of checking deposits). *Lending long* means making loan commitments for a prearranged, and often quite long, period of time. For example, when a person makes a deposit with a savings and loan association, that deposit can be withdrawn at any time. But the S&L makes a lending commitment for perhaps more than 20 years to a homebuyer.

Minimizing the Cost of Obtaining Funds

Finding someone from whom to borrow can be a costly business. Imagine how troublesome it would be if there were no depository institutions. A firm that was looking for $1 million to buy a new factory would probably have to hunt around for several dozen people from whom to borrow to acquire enough funds for its capital project. Depository institutions lower the costs of this search. The firm that needs $1 million can go to a single depository institution to obtain those funds. The depository institution has to borrow from a large number of people, but it's not doing that just for this one firm and the million dollars it wants to borrow. The depository institution can establish an organization that is capable of raising funds from a large number of depositors and can spread the cost of this activity over a large number of borrowers.

Minimizing the Cost of Monitoring Borrowers

Lending money is a risky business. There's always a danger that the borrower will not repay. Most of the money that is lent gets used by firms to invest in projects that they hope will return a profit. But sometimes those hopes are not fulfilled. Checking up on the activities of a borrower and ensuring that the best possible decisions are being made for making a profit and avoiding a loss are costly and specialized activities. Imagine how costly it would be if each household that lent money to a firm had to incur the costs of monitoring that firm directly. By depositing funds with a depository institution, households avoid those costs. The depository institution performs the monitoring activity by using specialized resources that have a much lower cost than what the households would incur if they had to undertake the activity individually.

Pooling Risk

As we noted above, lending money is risky. There is always a chance of not being repaid—of default. Lending to a large number of different individuals can reduce the risk of default. In such a situation, if one person defaults on a loan, it is a nuisance but not a disaster. In contrast, if only one person borrows and that person defaults on the loan, the entire loan is a write-off. Depository institutions enable people to pool risk in an efficient way. Thousands of people lend money to any one institution, and, in turn, the institution relends the money to hundreds, perhaps thousands, of individual firms. If any one firm defaults on its loan, that default is spread across all the people who deposited money with the institution, and no individual depositor is left exposed to a high degree of risk.

Financial Innovation

The deposits that form the bulk of the nation's money are financial products and depository institutions are constantly seeking ways to improve their products and earn larger profits. The process of developing new financial products is called *financial innovation.* The aim of financial innovation is to lower the cost of deposits or to increase the return from lending or, more simply, to increase the profit from financial intermediation. The three main influences on financial innovation are

► Economic environment
► Technology
► Regulation

The pace of financial innovation was remarkable during the 1980s and 1990s, and all three of these forces played a role.

Economic Environment

During the late 1970s and early 1980s, a high inflation rate brought high interest rates. For example, the interest rate on home-purchase loans was as high as 15 percent a year.

High inflation and high interest rates created an incentive for financial innovation. Traditionally, house purchases were financed by loans at a guaranteed interest rate. The high interest rates of the early 1980s brought high borrowing costs for S&Ls. But because they were committed to low fixed interest rates on their outstanding home-purchase loans, the industry incurred severe losses.

To overcome this situation, the S&Ls developed variable interest rate mortgages—loans on which the interest rate would change in response to changing economic conditions. The creation of variable interest rate mortgages has taken some of the risk out of long-term lending for house purchases.

Technology

The major technological change of the 1980s and 1990s was the development of low-cost computing and long-distance communication. These new technologies had profound effects on financial products and led to much financial innovation.

Some examples of financial innovation that resulted from these new technologies are the widespread use of credit cards and the spread of daily interest deposit accounts.

The cost of keying in transactions data and of calculating interest on deposits or on outstanding credit card balances was too great to make these financial products widely available before the 1980s. But with today's technologies, these products are highly profitable for banks and widely used.

Regulation

A good deal of financial innovation takes place to avoid regulation. For example, a regulation known as Regulation Q prevented banks from paying interest on checking deposits. This restriction created an incentive for the banks to devise new types of deposits on which checks could be written and interest paid, thereby getting around the regulation.

Financial Innovation and Money

Financial innovation has brought changes in the composition of the nation's money. Checking deposits at S&Ls, savings banks, and credit unions have become an increasing percentage of M1 while checking deposits at commercial banks have become a decreasing percentage. The composition of M2 has also changed as savings deposits have decreased, while time deposits and money market mutual funds have expanded.

You now know what money is and that the bulk of the nation's money is deposits in banks and other institutions. Your next task is to learn about the Federal Reserve System and the ways in which it can influence the quantity of money.

THE FEDERAL RESERVE SYSTEM   4

The central bank of the United States is the **Federal Reserve System** (usually called the **Fed**). A **central bank** is a bank's bank and a public authority that regulates a nation's depository institutions and controls the quantity of money. As the banks' bank, the Fed provides banking services to commercial banks such as Citibank. A central bank is not a citizens' bank. That is, the Fed does not provide general banking services for businesses and individual citizens.

The Fed's Goals and Targets

The Fed conducts the nation's *monetary policy*, which means that it adjusts the quantity of money in circulation. The Fed's goals are to keep inflation in check, maintain full employment, moderate the business cycle, and contribute toward achieving long-term growth. Complete success in the pursuit of these goals is impossible, and the Fed's more modest goal is to improve the performance of the economy and to get closer to the goals than a hands-off approach would achieve. Whether the Fed succeeds in improving economic performance is a matter on which there is a range of opinion.

In pursuit of its ultimate goals, the Fed pays close attention to interest rates and pays special attention to one interest rate, the **federal funds rate**, which is the interest rate that the banks charge each other on overnight loans of reserves. The Fed sets a target for the federal funds rate that is consistent with its ultimate goals and then takes actions to achieve its target.

This section examines the Fed's policy tools. Later in this reading, we look at the long-run effects of the Fed's actions, and in the reading on monetary policy, we look at the short-run context in which the Fed conducts monetary policy. We begin by describing the structure of the Fed.

The Structure of the Fed

The key elements in the structure of the Federal Reserve System are

▶ The Board of Governors
▶ The regional Federal Reserve banks
▶ The Federal Open Market Committee

The Board of Governors

The Board of Governors has seven members, who are appointed by the President of the United States and confirmed by the Senate, each for a 14-year term. The terms are staggered so that one seat on the board becomes vacant every two years. The President appoints one of the board members as chairman for a term of four years, which is renewable.

The Federal Reserve Banks

There are 12 Federal Reserve banks, one for each of 12 Federal Reserve districts shown in Fig. 2. These Federal Reserve banks provide check-clearing services to commercial banks and other depository institutions, hold the reserve accounts of commercial banks, lend reserves to banks, and issue the bank notes that circulate as currency.

One of the district banks, the Federal Reserve Bank of New York (known as the New York Fed), occupies a special place in the Federal Reserve System because it implements the policy decisions of the Federal Open Market Committee.

FIGURE 2   The Federal Reserve System

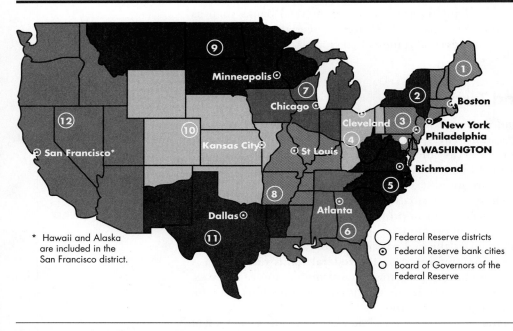

The nation is divided into 12 Federal Reserve districts, each having a Federal Reserve bank. (Some of the larger districts also have branch banks.) The Board of Governors of the Federal Reserve System is located in Washington, D.C.

* Hawaii and Alaska are included in the San Francisco district.

○ Federal Reserve districts
◉ Federal Reserve bank cities
○ Board of Governors of the Federal Reserve

Source: Federal Reserve Bulletin.

The Federal Open Market Committee

The **Federal Open Market Committee** (FOMC) is the main policymaking organ of the Federal Reserve System. The FOMC consists of the following voting members:

▶ The chairman and the other six members of the Board of Governors
▶ The president of the Federal Reserve Bank of New York
▶ The presidents of the other regional Federal Reserve banks (of whom, on a yearly rotating basis, only four vote)

The FOMC meets approximately every six weeks to review the state of the economy and to decide the actions to be carried out by the New York Fed.

The Fed's Power Center

A description of the formal structure of the Fed gives the impression that power in the Fed resides with the Board of Governors. In practice, it is the chairman of the Board of Governors who has the largest influence on the Fed's monetary policy actions, and some remarkable individuals have held this position. The current chairman is Ben Bernanke, a former economics professor at Princeton University, who was appointed by President George W. Bush in 2006. Bernanke's predecessors were Alan Greenspan (1987–2006) and Paul Volker (1979–1987).

The chairman's power and influence stem from three sources. First, it is the chairman who controls the agenda and who dominates the meetings of the FOMC. Second, day-to-day contact with a large staff of economists and other technical experts provides the chairman with detailed background briefings on monetary policy issues. Third, the chairman is the spokesperson for the Fed and the main point of contact of the Fed with the President and government and with foreign central banks and governments.

The Fed's Policy Tools

The Federal Reserve System has many responsibilities, but we'll examine its single most important one: regulating the amount of money floating around in the United States. How does the Fed control the quantity of money? It does so by adjusting the reserves of the banking system. Also, it is by adjusting the reserves of the banking system and by standing ready to make loans to banks that the Fed is able to prevent bank failures. The Fed uses three main policy tools to achieve its objectives:

► Required reserve ratios
► Discount rate
► Open market operations

Required Reserve Ratios

All depository institutions are required to hold a minimum percentage of deposits as reserves. This minimum percentage is known as a **required reserve ratio**. The Fed determines a required reserve ratio for each type of deposit. In 2006, banks were required to hold minimum reserves equal to 3 percent of checking deposits between $7.8 million and $48.3 million and 10 percent of these deposits in excess of $48.3 million. The required reserves on other types of deposits are zero.

Discount Rate

The **discount rate** is the interest rate at which the Fed stands ready to lend reserves to depository institutions. A change in the discount rate is proposed to the FOMC by the Board of Directors of at least one of the 12 Federal Reserve banks and is approved by the Board of Governors.

Open Market Operations

An **open market operation** is the purchase or sale of government securities—U.S. Treasury bills and bonds—by the Federal Reserve System in the open market. When the Fed conducts an open market operation, it makes a transaction with a bank or some other business but it does not transact with the federal government.

Figure 3 summarizes the structure and policy tools of the Fed. To understand how the tools work, we need to know about the Fed's balance sheet.

FIGURE 3   The Structure of the Fed

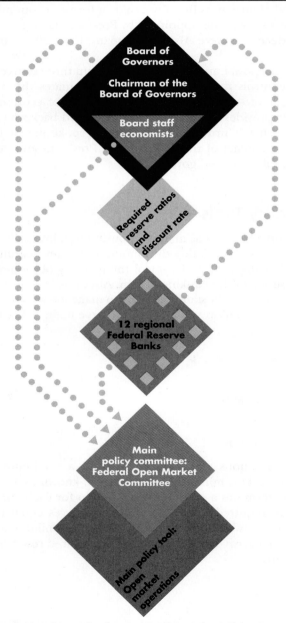

The Board of Governors sets required reserve ratios and, on the proposal of the 12 Federal Reserve banks, sets the discount rate. The Board of Governors and presidents of the regional Federal Reserve banks sit on the FOMC to determine open market operations.

TABLE 2 The Fed's Balance Sheet, June 2006			
Assets **(Billions of Dollars)**		**Liabilities** **(Billions of Dollars)**	
Gold and foreign exchange	13	Federal Reserve notes	754
U.S. government securities*	762	Banks' deposits	21
Loans to banks	—		—
Total assets	775	Total liabilities	775

*Includes other (net) assets.
Source: Federal Reserve Board.

The Fed's Balance Sheet

Table 2 shows the balance sheet of the Federal Reserve System for June 2006. The assets on the left side are what the Fed owns, and the liabilities on the right side are what it owes. The Fed's assets are

1. Gold and foreign exchange
2. U.S. government securities
3. Loans to banks

Gold and foreign exchange are the Fed's holdings of international reserves, which consist of deposits at other central banks and an account called Special Drawing Rights, which the Fed holds at the International Monetary Fund.

The Fed's major assets are U.S. government securities. These securities are short-term Treasury bills and long-term Treasury bonds.

When the banks are short of reserves, they can borrow reserves from the Fed. These borrowed reserves are an asset, "loans to banks," in the Fed's balance sheet.

The Fed's assets are the backing for its liabilities:

1. Federal Reserve notes
2. Banks' deposits

The Federal Reserve notes are the dollar bills that we use in our daily transactions. Some of these notes are held by the public; others are in the tills and vaults of banks and other financial institutions. Banks' deposits are part of the banks' reserves.

You might be wondering why Federal Reserve notes are considered a liability of the Fed. When bank notes were invented, they gave their owner a claim on the gold reserves of the issuing bank. Such notes were *convertible paper money*. The holder of such a note could convert the note on demand into gold (or some other commodity such as silver) at a guaranteed price. So when a bank issued a note, it was holding itself liable to convert that note into gold or silver. Modern bank notes are nonconvertible. A *nonconvertible note* is a bank note that is not convertible into any commodity and that obtains its value by government order and is called "fiat money." Such notes are the legal liability of the bank that issues them, and they are backed by holdings of securities and loans. Federal Reserve notes are backed by the Fed's holdings of U.S. government securities.

The Fed's liabilities together with coins in circulation (coins are issued by the Treasury and are not liabilities of the Fed) make up the monetary base. That is, the **monetary base** is the sum of Federal Reserve notes, coins, and banks' deposits at the Fed. The monetary base is so named because it acts like a base that supports the nation's money. When the monetary base changes, so does the quantity of money, as you're about to see.

Next, we're going to see how the banking system—the banks and the Fed—creates money.

<table><tr><td>5</td></tr></table>

HOW BANKS CREATE MONEY

Banks create money. But this doesn't mean that they have smoke-filled back rooms in which counterfeiters are busily working. Remember, most money is deposits, not currency. What banks create is deposits, and they do so by making loans.

Creating Deposits by Making Loans

The easiest way to see that banks create deposits is to think about what happens when Andy, who has a Visa card issued by Citibank, uses his card to buy a tank of gas from Chevron. When Andy signs the card sales slip, he takes a loan from Citibank and obligates himself to repay the loan at a later date. At the end of the business day, a Chevron clerk takes a pile of signed credit card sales slips, including Andy's, to Chevron's bank. For now, let's assume that Chevron also banks at Citibank. The bank immediately credits Chevron's account with the value of the slips (minus the bank's commission).

You can see that these transactions have created a bank deposit and a loan. Andy has increased the size of his loan (his credit card balance), and Chevron has increased the size of its bank deposit. And because deposits are money, Citibank has created money.

If, as we've just assumed, Andy and Chevron use the same bank, no further transactions take place. But the outcome is essentially the same when two banks are involved. If Chevron's bank is the Bank of America, then Citibank uses its reserves to pay the Bank of America. Citibank has an increase in loans and a decrease in reserves; the Bank of America has an increase in reserves and an increase in deposits. And the banking system as a whole has an increase in loans and deposits and no change in reserves.

If Andy had swiped his card at an automatic payment pump, all these transactions would have occurred at the time he filled his tank, and the quantity of money would have increased by the amount of his purchase (minus the bank's commission for conducting the transactions).

Three factors limit the quantity of deposits that the banking system can create:

► The monetary base
► Desired reserves
► Desired currency holdings

The Monetary Base

You've seen that the *monetary base* is the sum of Federal Reserve notes, coins, and banks' deposits at the Fed. The size of the monetary base limits the total quantity of money that the banking system can create because banks have a desired level of reserves, households and firms have a desired level of currency holding, and both of these desired holdings of the monetary base depend on the quantity of money.

Desired Reserves

A bank's *actual* **reserves** consist of the notes and coins in its vaults and its deposit at the Federal Reserve. A bank uses its reserves to meet depositors' demand for currency and to make payments to other banks.

You've also seen that banks don't have $100 of reserves for every $100 that people have deposited with them. If the banks did behave that way, they wouldn't earn any profit.

Banks today have reserves of $3 for every $100 of M1 deposits and 60¢ for every $100 of M2 deposits. Most of these reserves are currency. You saw in the previous section that reserves in the form of deposits at the Federal Reserve are tiny. But there's no need for panic. These reserve levels are adequate for ordinary business needs.

The fraction of a bank's total deposits that are held in reserves is called the **reserve ratio**. So with reserves of $3 for every $100 of M1 deposits, the M1 reserve ratio is 0.03 or 3 percent, and with reserves of 60¢ for every $100 of M2 deposits, the M2 reserve ratio is 0.006 or 0.6 percent.

A bank's desired reserves are the reserves that it wishes to hold. The banks are required to hold a level of reserves that does not fall below a specified percentage of total deposits. This percentage is the *required reserve ratio*.

The **desired reserve ratio** is the ratio of reserves to deposits that a bank wants to hold. This ratio exceeds the required reserve ratio by an amount that the banks determine to be prudent on the basis of their daily business requirements.

A bank's reserve ratio changes when its customers make a deposit or a withdrawal. If a bank's customer makes a deposit, reserves and deposits increase by the same amount, so the bank's reserve ratio increases. Similarly, if a bank's customer makes a withdrawal, reserves and deposits decrease by the same amount, so the bank's reserve ratio decreases.

A bank's **excess reserves** are its actual reserves minus its desired reserves. Whenever the banking system as a whole has excess reserves, the banks are able to create money. Banks increase their loans and deposits when they have excess reserves and they decrease their loans and deposits when they are short of reserves—when desired reserves exceed actual reserves.

But the greater the desired reserve ratio, the smaller is the quantity of deposits and money that the banking system can create from a given amount of monetary base.

Desired Currency Holding

We hold our money in the form of currency and bank deposits. The proportion of money held as currency isn't constant but at any given time, people have a definite view as to how much they want to hold in each form of money.

In 2006, for every dollar of M1 deposits held, we held $1.20 of currency and for every dollar of M2 deposits, we held 12¢ of currency.

Because households and firms want to hold some proportion of their money in the form of currency, when the total quantity of bank deposits increases, so does the quantity of currency that they want to hold. Because desired currency holding increases when deposits increase, currency leaves the banks when loans are made and deposits increase. We call the leakage of currency from the banking system the *currency drain*. And we call the ratio of currency to deposits the **currency drain ratio**.

The greater the currency drain ratio, the smaller is the quantity of deposits and money that the banking system can create from a given amount of monetary base.

The Money Creation Process

The money creation process begins when the monetary base increases and the banking system has excess reserves. These excess reserves come from a purchase of securities by the Fed from a bank. (The reading on monetary policy explains exactly how the Fed conducts such a purchase, called an open-market operation.)

When the Fed buys securities from a bank, the bank's reserves increase but its deposits do not change. So the bank has excess reserves and it lends those excess reserves. A sequence of events then plays out.

The sequence, which keeps repeating until all the reserves are desired and no excess reserves are being held, has nine steps. They are

1. Banks have excess reserves.
2. Banks lend excess reserves.
3. Bank deposits increase.
4. The quantity of money increases.
5. New money is used to make payments.
6. Some of the new money remains on deposit.
7. Some of the new money is a *currency drain*.
8. Desired reserves increase because deposits have increased.
9. Excess reserves decrease but remain positive.

The sequence repeats in a series of rounds, but each round begins with a smaller quantity of excess reserves than did the previous one. The process continues until excess reserves have finally been eliminated. Figure 4 illustrates this process.

To make the process of money creation more concrete, let's work through an example for a banking system in which each bank has a desired reserve ratio of 10 percent and the currency drain ratio is 50 percent or 0.5. (Although these ratios are larger than the ones in the U.S. economy, they make the process end more quickly and enable you to see more clearly the principles at work.)

Figure 5 will keep track of the numbers. The process begins when all the banks have zero excess reserves except one bank, and it has excess reserves of $100,000. When the bank lends $100,000 of excess reserves, $33,333 drains off and is held outside the banks as currency. The other $66,667 remains in the banks as deposits. The quantity of money has now increased by $100,000—the increase in deposits plus the increase in currency holdings.

The increased bank deposits of $66,667 generate an increase in desired reserves of 10 percent of that amount, which is $6,667. Actual reserves have

FIGURE 4   How the Banking System Creates Money by Making Loans

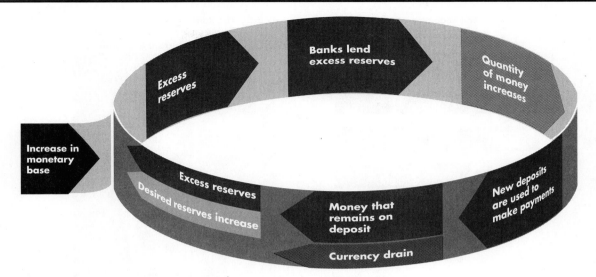

The Federal Reserve increases the monetary base which increases bank reserves and creates excess reserves. Banks lend the excess reserves, new deposits are created, and the quantity of money increases. New deposits are used to make payments. Some of the new money remains on deposit at banks and some leaves the banks in a currency drain. The increase in bank deposits increases banks' desired reserves. But the banks still have excess reserves, though less than before. The process repeats until excess reserves have been eliminated.

increased by the same amount as the increase in deposits: $66,667. So the banks now have excess reserves of $60,000. At this stage, we have gone around the circle shown in Fig. 4 once. The process we've just described repeats but begins with excess reserves of $60,000. Figure 5 shows the next two rounds. At the end of the process, the quantity of money has increased by a multiple of the increase in the monetary base. In this case, the increase is $250,000, which is 2.5 times the increase in the monetary base.

The Money Multiplier

The sequence in Fig. 5 is the first four stages of the process that finally reaches the totals shown in the final row of the running tally. To figure out the entire process, look closely at the numbers in the figure. The initial increase in reserves is $100,000 (call it A). At each stage, the loan is 60 percent (0.6) of the previous loan and the quantity of money increases by 0.6 of the previous increase. Call that proportion $L(L = 0.6)$. We can write down the complete sequence for the increase in the quantity of money as

$$A + AL + AL^2 + AL^3 + AL^4 + AL^5 + \ldots .$$

FIGURE 5   The Money Creation Process: An Example

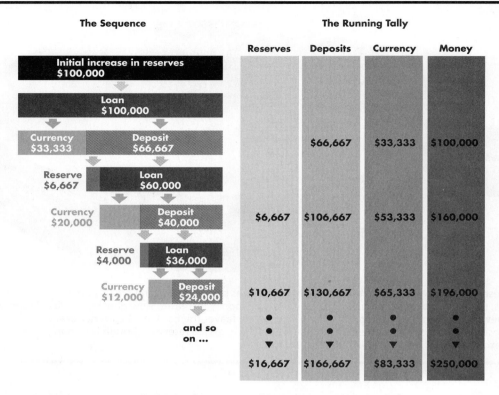

When the Fed provides the banks with $100,000 of additional reserves, the banks lend those reserves. Of the amount lent, $33,333 (50 percent of deposits) leaves the banks in a currency drain and $66,667 remains on deposit. With additional deposits, desired reserves increase by $6,667 (10 percent desired reserve ratio) and the banks lend $60,000. Of this amount, $20,000 leaves the banks in a currency drain and $40,000 remains on deposit. The process repeats until the banks have created enough deposits to eliminate their excess reserves. An additional $100,000 of reserves creates $250,000 of money.

Remember, L is a fraction, so at each stage in this sequence, the amount of new loans and new money gets smaller. The total value of loans made and money created at the end of the process is the sum of the sequence, which is[1]

$$A / (1 - L).$$

---

[1] The sequence of values is called a convergent geometric series. To find the sum of a series such as this, begin by calling the sum S. Then write the sum as

$$S = A + AL + AL^2 + AL^3 + AL^4 + AL^5 + \ldots$$

Multiply by L to get,

$$LS = AL + AL^2 + AL^3 + AL^4 + AL^5 + \ldots$$

and then subtract the second equation from the first to get

$$S(1 - L) = A$$

or

$$S = A / (1 - L).$$

If we use the numbers from the example, the total increase in the quantity of money is

$100,000 + 60,000 + 36,000 + . . .

= $100,000 (1 + 0.6 + 0.36 + . . .)

= $100,000 (1 + 0.6 + 0.6^2 + . . .)

= $100,000 × 1/(1 − 0.6)

= $100,000 × 1/(0.4)

= $100,000 × 2.5

= $250,000.

The **money multiplier** is the ratio of the change in the quantity of money to the change in monetary base. Here, the monetary base increased by $100,000 and the quantity of money increased by $250,000 so the money multiplier is 2.5.

The magnitude of the money multiplier depends on the desired reserve ratio and the currency drain ratio. Call the monetary base MB and the quantity of money M. When there are no excess reserves,

MB = Desired currency holding + Desired reserves.

Also,

M = Deposits + Desired currency holding.

Call the currency drain ratio a and the desired reserve ratio b. Then

Desired currency holding = a × Deposits

Desired reserves = b × Deposits

MB = $(a + b)$ × Deposits

M = $(1 + a)$ × Deposits.

Call the change in monetary base ΔMB and the change in the quantity of money ΔM. Then

ΔMB = $(a + b)$ × Change in deposits

ΔM = $(1 + a)$ × Change in deposits.

Divide the above equation for ΔM by the one for ΔMB, and you see that the money multiplier, which is the ratio of ΔM to ΔMB, is

Money multiplier = $(1 + a)/(a + b)$.

If we use the values of the example summarized in Fig. 5, $a = 0.5$ and $b = 0.1$, the

Money multiplier = $(1 + 0.5)/(0.5 + 0.1)$.

= 1.5/0.6 = 2.5.

The U.S. Money Multiplier

The money multiplier in the United States can be found by using the formula above along with the values of *a* and *b* in the U.S. economy.

Because we have two definitions of money, M1 and M2, we have two money multipliers. The numbers for M1 in 2006 are *a* = 1.20 and *b* = 0.03. So

$$\text{M1 multiplier} = (1 + 1.20)/(1.20 + 0.03)$$
$$= 2.20/1.23 = 1.8.$$

For M2 in 2006, *a* = 0.12 and *b* = 0.006, so

$$\text{M2 multiplier} = (1 + 0.12)/(0.12 + 0.006)$$
$$= 1.12/0.126 = 8.9.$$

You now know how money gets created. Your next task is to study the demand and supply in the "market" for money and money market equilibrium.

6　THE MARKET FOR MONEY

There is no limit to the amount of money we would like to *receive* in payment for our labor or as interest on our savings. But there *is* a limit to how big an inventory of money—the money in our wallet or in a deposit account at the bank—we would like to *hold* and neither spend nor use to buy assets that generate an income. The *quantity of money demanded* is the inventory of money that people plan to hold. The quantity of money held must equal the quantity supplied, and the forces that bring about this equality in the money market have powerful effects on the economy, as you will see in the rest of this reading.

But first, we need to explain what determines the amount of money that people plan to hold.

The Influences on Money Holding

The quantity of money that people plan to hold depends on four main factors:

► The price level
► The *nominal* interest rate
► Real GDP
► Financial innovation

The Price Level

The quantity of money measured in dollars is *nominal money*. The quantity of nominal money demanded is proportional to the price level, other things remaining the same. If the price level rises by 10 percent, people hold 10 percent more nominal money than before, other things remaining the same. If you hold $20 to buy your weekly movies and soda, you will increase your money holding to $22 if the prices of movies and soda—and your wage rate—increase by 10 percent.

The quantity of money measured in constant dollars (for example, in 2000 dollars) is *real money*. Real money is equal to nominal money divided by the price level and is the quantity of money measured in terms of what it will buy. In the above example, when the price level rises by 10 percent and you increase your money holding by 10 percent, your *real* money holding is constant. Your $22 at the new price level buys the same quantity of goods and is the same quantity of *real money* as your $20 at the original price level. The quantity of real money demanded is independent of the price level.

The Nominal *Interest Rate*

A fundamental principle of economics is that as the opportunity cost of something increases, people try to find substitutes for it. Money is no exception. The higher the opportunity cost of holding money, other things remaining the same, the smaller is the quantity of real money demanded. The nominal interest rate on other assets minus the nominal interest rate on money is the opportunity cost of holding money.

   The interest rate that you earn on currency and checking deposits is zero. So the opportunity cost of holding these items is the nominal interest rate on other assets such as a savings bond or Treasury bill. By holding money instead, you forgo the interest that you otherwise would have received.

   Money loses value because of inflation. So why isn't the inflation rate part of the cost of holding money? It is. Other things remaining the same, the higher the expected inflation rate, the higher is the nominal interest rate.

Real GDP

The quantity of money that households and firms plan to hold depends on the amount they are spending, and the quantity of money demanded in the economy as a whole depends on aggregate expenditure—real GDP.

   Again, suppose that you hold an average of $20 to finance your weekly purchases of movies and soda. Now imagine that the prices of these goods and of all other goods remain constant but that your income increases. As a consequence, you now spend more and you also keep a larger amount of money on hand to finance your higher volume of expenditure.

Financial Innovation

Technological change and the arrival of new financial products change the quantity of money held. Financial innovations include

1. Daily interest checking deposits
2. Automatic transfers between checking and saving deposits
3. Automatic teller machines
4. Credit cards and debit cards
5. Internet banking and bill paying

These innovations have occurred because of the development of computing power that has lowered the cost of calculations and record keeping.

   We summarize the effects of the influences on money holding by using a demand for money curve.

The Demand for Money

The **demand for money** is the relationship between the quantity of real money demanded and the nominal interest rate when all other influences on the amount of money that people wish to hold remain the same.

Figure 6 shows a demand for money curve, *MD*. When the interest rate rises, everything else remaining the same, the opportunity cost of holding money rises and the quantity of real money demanded decreases—there is a movement up along the demand for money curve. Similarly, when the interest rate falls, the opportunity cost of holding money falls, and the quantity of real money demanded increases—there is a movement down along the demand for money curve.

When any influence on money holding other than the interest rate changes, there is a change in the demand for money and the demand for money curve shifts. Let's study these shifts.

FIGURE 6   The Demand for Money

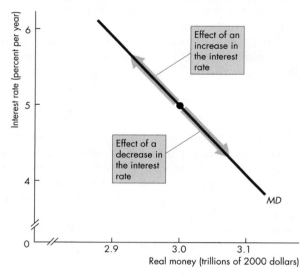

The demand for money curve, *MD*, shows the relationship between the quantity of real money that people plan to hold and the interest rate, other things remaining the same. The interest rate is the opportunity cost of holding money. A change in the interest rate brings a movement along the demand for money curve.

Shifts in the Demand for Money Curve

A change in real GDP or financial innovation changes the demand for money and shifts the demand curve for real money.

Figure 7 illustrates the change in the demand for money. A decrease in real GDP decreases the demand for money and shifts the demand curve leftward from MD_0 to MD_1. An increase in real GDP has the opposite effect: It increases the demand for money and shifts the demand curve rightward from MD_0 to MD_2.

The influence of financial innovation on the demand for money curve is more complicated. It decreases the demand for currency and might increase the demand for some types of deposits and decrease the demand for others. But generally, financial innovation decreases the demand for money.

We'll look at the effects of changes in real GDP and financial innovation by studying the demand for money in the United States.

FIGURE 7   Changes in the Demand for Money

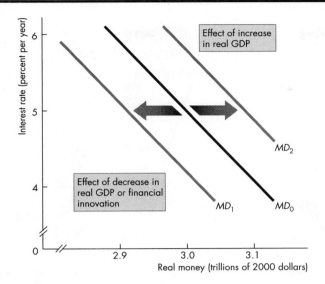

A decrease in real GDP decreases the demand for money. The demand curve shifts leftward from MD_0 to MD_1. An increase in real GDP increases the demand for money. The demand curve shifts rightward from MD_0 to MD_2. Financial innovation generally decreases the demand for money.

The Demand for Money in the United States

Figure 8 shows the relationship between the interest rate and the quantity of real money demanded in the United States from 1970 to 2005. Each dot shows the interest rate and the real money held in a given year. In 1970, the demand for M1 curve, in part (a), was MD_0. During the early 1970s, the spread of credit cards decreased the demand for M1 (currency and checking deposits) and shifted the demand for M1 curve leftward to MD_1. But over the years, real GDP growth increased the demand for M1, and by 1994, the demand for M1 curve had shifted rightward to MD_2. A continued increase in the use of credit cards and the spread of ATMs decreased the demand for M1 and shifted the demand curve leftward again during the 1990s and 2000s to MD_3.

In 1970, the demand for M2 curve, in part (b) was MD_0. New interest-bearing deposits increased the demand for M2 from 1970 through 1989 and shifted the demand curve rightward to MD_1. But between 1989 and 1994, innovations in financial products that compete with deposits of all kinds occurred and the demand for M2 decreased. The demand for M2 curve shifted leftward to MD_2. After 1994, the expanding economy brought rising real GDP and the demand for M2 increased. By 2005, the demand for M2 curve was MD_3.

You now know what determines the demand for money. And you've seen how the banking system creates money. Let's now see how the money market reaches an equilibrium in the short run and in the long run.

Money Market Equilibrium

Money market equilibrium occurs when the quantity of money demanded equals the quantity of money supplied. The adjustments that occur to bring money market equilibrium are fundamentally different in the short run and the

FIGURE 8   The Demand for Money in the United States

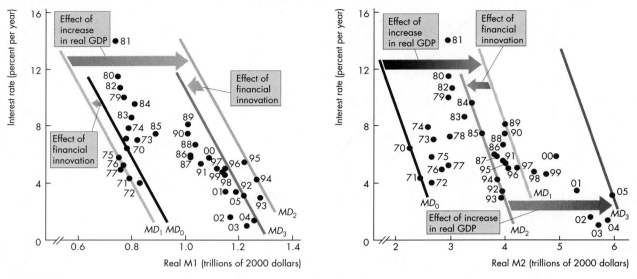

(a) M1 demand   **(b) M2 demand**

The dots show the quantity of real money and the interest rate in each year between 1970 and 2005. In 1970, the demand for M1 curve was MD_0 in part (a). The demand for M1 decreased during the early 1970s because of financial innovation, and the demand curve shifted leftward to MD_1. But real GDP growth increases the demand for M1, and by 1994, the demand curve had shifted rightward to MD_2. Further financial innovation decreased the demand for M1 during the 1990s and 2000s and shifted the demand curve leftward again to MD_3.

    In 1970, the demand for M2 curve was MD_0 in part (b). The growth of real GDP increased the demand for M2, and by 1989, the demand curve had shifted rightward to MD_1. During the early 1990s, new substitutes for M2 decreased the demand for M2 and the demand curve shifted leftward to MD_2. But during the late 1990s, rapid growth of real GDP increased the demand for M2. By 2005, the demand curve had shifted rightward to MD_3.

Sources: Bureau of Economic Analysis and Federal Reserve Board.

long run. Our primary focus here is the long run. But we need to say a little bit about the short run so that you can appreciate how the long-run equilibrium comes about.

Short-Run Equilibrium

The quantity of money supplied is determined by the actions of the banks and the Fed. Each day, the Fed adjusts the quantity of money to hit its interest rate target. In Fig. 9, with demand for money curve *MD*, if the Fed wants the interest rate to be 5 percent, it adjusts the quantity of money so that the quantity of real money supplied is $3.0 trillion and the supply of money curve is *MS*.

    The equilibrium interest rate is 5 percent. If the interest rate were 6 percent, people would want to hold less money than exists. They would buy bonds, bid up their price, and lower the interest rate. If the interest rate were 4 percent, people would want to hold more money than exists. They would sell bonds, bid down their price, and raise the interest rate.

Long-Run Equilibrium

In the long run, supply and demand in the loanable funds market determines the interest rate. The nominal interest rate equals the equilibrium real interest

FIGURE 9   Money Market Equilibrium

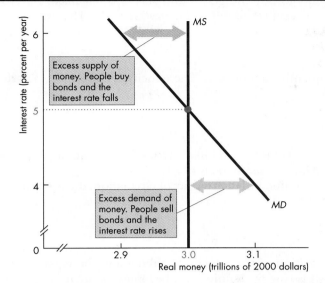

Money market equilibrium occurs when the quantity of money demanded equals the quantity supplied.

   Short run: In the short run, the quantity of real money and real GDP are given and the interest rate adjusts to achieve equilibrium, here 5 percent a year.

   Long run: In the long run, supply and demand in the loanable funds market determines the interest rate, real GDP equals potential GDP, and the price level adjusts to make the quantity of real money supplied equal the quantity demanded, here $3 trillion.

rate plus the expected inflation rate. Real GDP, which influences the demand for money, equals potential GDP. So the only variable that is left to adjust in the long run is the price level. The price level adjusts to make the quantity of real money supplied equal to the quantity demanded. If the Fed changes the nominal quantity of money, the price level changes (in the long run) by the same percentage as the percentage change in the quantity of nominal money. In the long run, the change in the price level is proportional to the change in the quantity of money.

   Let's explore the long-run link between money and the price level a bit more thoroughly.

THE QUANTITY THEORY OF MONEY   7

In the long run, the price level adjusts to make the quantity of real money demanded equal the quantity supplied. A special theory of the price level and inflation—the quantity theory of money—explains this long-run adjustment of the price level.

   The **quantity theory of money** is the proposition that in the long run, an increase in the quantity of money brings an equal percentage increase in the price level. To explain the quantity theory of money, we first need to define *the velocity of circulation.*

The **velocity of circulation** is the average number of times a dollar of money is used annually to buy the goods and services that make up GDP. But GDP equals the price level (P) multiplied by *real* GDP (Y). That is,

GDP $= PY$.

Call the quantity of money M. The velocity of circulation, V, is determined by the equation

$V = PY/M$.

For example, if GDP is \$1,000 billion ($PY =$ \$1,000 billion) and the quantity of money is \$250 billion, the velocity of circulation is 4.

From the definition of the velocity of circulation, the *equation of exchange* tells us how M, V, P, and Y are connected. This equation is

$MV = PY$.

Given the definition of the velocity of circulation, the equation of exchange is always true—it is true by definition. It becomes the quantity theory of money if the quantity of money does not influence the velocity of circulation or real GDP. In this case, the equation of exchange tells us that in the long run, the price level is determined by the quantity of money. That is,

$P = M(V/Y)$,

where (V/Y) is independent of M. So a change in M brings a proportional change in P.

We can also express the equation of exchange in growth rates,[2] in which form it states that

$$\frac{\text{Money}}{\text{growth rate}} + \frac{\text{Rate of}}{\text{velocity change}} = \frac{\text{Inflation}}{\text{rate}} + \frac{\text{Real GDP}}{\text{growth rate}}$$

Solving this equation for the inflation rate gives

$$\frac{\text{Inflation}}{\text{rate}} = \frac{\text{Money}}{\text{growth rate}} + \frac{\text{Rate of}}{\text{velocity change}} - \frac{\text{Real GDP}}{\text{growth rate}}$$

In the long run, the rate of velocity change is not influenced by the money growth rate. More strongly, in the long run, the rate of velocity change is approx-

---

[2] To obtain this equation, begin with

$MV = PY$

and then changes in these variables are related by the equation

$\Delta MV + M\Delta V = \Delta PY + P\Delta Y$

Divide this equation by the equation of exchange to obtain

$\Delta M/M + \Delta V/V = \Delta P/P + \Delta Y/Y$

The term $\Delta M/M$ is the money growth rate, $\Delta V/V$ is the rate of velocity change, $\Delta P/P$ is the inflation rate, and $\Delta Y/Y$ is the real GDP growth rate.

imately zero. With this assumption, the inflation rate in the long run is determined as

$$\text{Inflation rate} = \text{Money growth rate} - \text{Real GDP growth rate}.$$

In the long run, fluctuations in the money growth rate minus the real GDP growth rate bring equal fluctuations in the inflation rate.

Also, in the long run, with the economy at full employment, real GDP equals potential GDP, so the real GDP growth rate equals the potential GDP growth rate. This growth rate might be influenced by inflation but the influence is most likely small, and the quantity theory assumes that it is zero. So the real GDP growth rate is given and doesn't change when the money growth rate changes—inflation is correlated with money growth.

Evidence on the Quantity Theory of Money

Figure 10 summarizes some U.S. evidence on the quantity theory of money. The figure reveals that on the average, as predicted by the quantity theory of money, the inflation rate fluctuates in line with fluctuations in the money growth rate minus the real GDP growth rate.

Figure 11 shows two scatter diagrams of the inflation rate and the money growth rate for 134 countries in part(a) and for those countries with inflation rates below 20 percent a year in part (b). You can see a general tendency for money growth and inflation to be correlated but the quantity theory (the gray lines) does not predict inflation precisely.

The correlation between money growth and inflation isn't perfect. Nor does it tell us that money growth *causes* inflation. Money growth might cause inflation;

FIGURE 10   U.S. Money Growth and Inflation

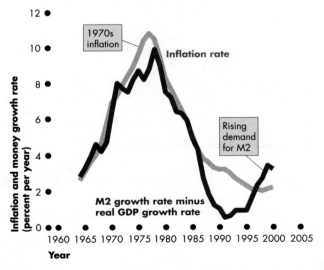

On the average, the inflation rate and money growth rate minus real GDP growth are correlated—they rise and fall together.

Sources: Federal Reserve and Bureau of Labor Statistics.

FIGURE 11   Money Growth and Inflation in the World

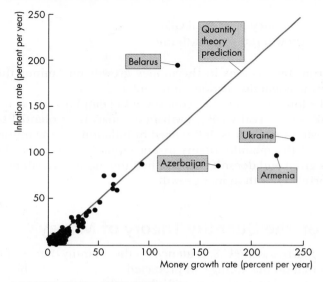

(a) 134 Countries: 1990–2005

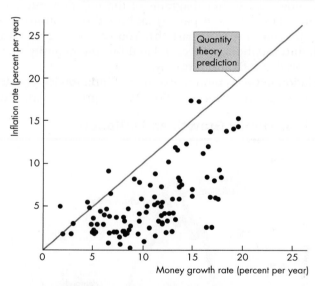

(b) 104 Lower-inflation countries: 1990–2005

Inflation and money growth in 134 countries in part (a) and low-inflation countries in part (b) show a clear positive relationship between money growth and inflation.

Sources: International Financial Statistics Yearbook, 2006 and International Monetary Fund, World Economic Outlook, April 2006.

inflation might cause money growth; or some third variable might cause both inflation and money growth.

You now know what money is, how banks create it, and how the quantity of money influences the interest rate in the short run and the price level in the long run. *Reading Between the Lines* rounds out the reading by looking at the quantity theory of money in action in Zimbabwe today.

READING BETWEEN THE LINES   8

The Quantity Theory of Money in Zimbabwe

THE NEW YORK TIMES, APRIL 25, 2006

Zimbabwe's Prices Rise 900%, Turning Staples into Luxuries

How bad is inflation in Zimbabwe? Well, consider this: at a supermarket near the center of this tatterdemalion capital, toilet paper costs $417.

No, not per roll. Four hundred seventeen Zimbabwean dollars is the value of a single two-ply sheet. A roll costs $145,750—in American currency, about 69 cents.

The price of toilet paper, like everything else here, soars almost daily, spawning jokes about an impending better use for Zimbabwe's $500 bill, now the smallest in circulation.

But what is happening is no laughing matter. For untold numbers of Zimbabweans, toilet paper—and bread, margarine, meat, even the once ubiquitous morning cup of tea—have become unimaginable luxuries. All are casualties of the hyperinflation that is roaring toward 1,000 percent a year, a rate usually seen only in war zones.

Zimbabwe has been tormented this entire decade by both deep recession and high inflation, but in recent months the economy seems to have abandoned whatever moorings it had left. The national budget for 2006 has already been largely spent. Government services have started to crumble.

The purity of Harare's drinking water, siphoned from a lake downstream of its sewer outfall, has been unreliable for months, and dysentery and cholera swept the city in December and January. The city suffers rolling electrical blackouts. Mounds of uncollected garbage pile up on the streets of the slums.

Zimbabwe's inflation is hardly history's worst—in Weimar Germany in 1923, prices quadrupled each month, compared with doubling about once every three or four months in Zimbabwe. That said, experts agree that Zimbabwe's inflation is currently the world's highest, and has been for some time. . . .

Essence of the Story

► In April 2006, in Zimbabwe, a single two-ply sheet of toilet paper cost $417 and a roll cost $145,750 (in Zimbabwe dollars).

► Zimbabwe is suffering a 1,000 percent per year inflation.

► The government had spent its 2006 budget by April, and public services were crumbling.

► Zimbabwe's inflation isn't the highest in history, but it is the highest in the world today.

Economic Analysis

▶ The quantity theory of money explains inflation trends. A low growth rate of the quantity of money keeps inflation low. A rapid growth rate of the quantity of money brings a high inflation rate.

▶ The quantity theory of money is most visible when money growth is rapid and the inflation rate is high.

▶ Zimbabwe has the highest inflation rate in the world today, so it provides a good example of the quantity theory of money in action.

▶ During 2006, the inflation rate averaged close to 1,000 percent a year and exceeded that rate in some months.

▶ To appreciate an inflation rate of 1,000 percent a year, translate it to a monthly inflation rate. Every month, on the average, prices rise by 20 percent. A cup of coffee that costs $3 in January costs $9 in June and $27 in December!

▶ When people expect prices to rise rapidly, they expect the money they hold to fall in value rapidly. So they spend and hold goods rather than money.

▶ The velocity of circulation begins to rise. The velocity of circulation is independent of the quantity of money but not independent of the money growth rate.

▶ Figure 12 shows the inflation rate and money growth rate record in Zimbabwe since 2000.

FIGURE 12   Money Growth and Inflation

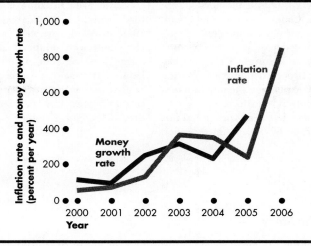

▶ Between 2000 and 2005, the money growth rate increased from a bit more than 100 percent a year to 475 percent a year. (The Reserve Bank of Zimbabwe—the country's central bank—stopped reporting the money data in 2006.)

▶ The inflation rate increased slowly at first, from about 50 percent a year in 2000 to 100 percent a year in 2002.

► In 2003, the inflation rate took off as people started to dump their dollars and scramble to buy goods and services before their prices increased too much.

► The inflation rate continued to increase until it hit 1,000 percent a year in some months of 2006.

► By 2006, prices had risen to the point that even a small item such as a sheet of toilet paper cost hundreds of dollars and a big item such as a pair of jeans cost $10,000,000!

► To cope with all the zeroes, the Reserve Bank of Zimbabwe launched "Project Sunrise," which redefined the Zimbabwe dollar by knocking off three zeroes.

► In new dollars, a pair of jeans cost only $10,000!

► The bank notes issued by the Reserve Bank of Zimbabwe are time limited and worthless after December 31, 2006, when they will be replaced by some other "new" dollars.

► Knocking off three zeroes doesn't solve Zimbabwe's inflation problem. It only makes it a bit easier to live with.

► An inflation such as Zimbabwe's doesn't happen because the central bank wants to create inflation. It occurs because the government can't raise enough tax revenue, so the central bank makes loans to the government, which means that the government spends newly created money.

Courtesy of AP Images/Tsvangirayi Mukwazhi

SUMMARY

► Money is the means of payment. It functions as a medium of exchange, a unit of account, and a store of value.

► Today, money consists of currency and deposits.

► Commercial banks, S&Ls, savings banks, credit unions, and money market mutual funds are depository institutions whose deposits are money.

► Depository institutions provide four main economic services: They create liquidity, minimize the cost of obtaining funds, minimize the cost of monitoring borrowers, and pool risks.

► The Federal Reserve System is the central bank of the United States.

► The Fed influences the quantity of money by setting the required reserve ratio, the discount rate, and by conducting open market operations.

► Banks create money by making loans.

► The total quantity of money that can be created depends on the monetary base, the desired reserve ratio, and the currency drain ratio.

► The quantity of money demanded is the amount of money that people plan to hold.

► The quantity of real money equals the quantity of nominal money divided by the price level.

► The quantity of real money demanded depends on the nominal interest rate, real GDP, and financial innovation. A rise in the nominal interest rate brings a decrease in the quantity of real money demanded.

► In the short run, the Fed sets the quantity of money to hit a target nominal interest rate.

► In the long run, the loanable funds market determines the interest rate and money market equilibrium determines the price level.

► The quantity theory of money is the proposition that money growth and inflation move up and down together in the long run.

► The U.S. and international evidence is consistent with the quantity theory, on the average.

PRACTICE PROBLEMS FOR READING 24

1. Which of the following is *least likely* a component of the M2 money supply?

   A. Savings deposits.

   B. Traveler's checks.

   C. Currency held by banks.

2. The amount of new money that can be created by a commercial bank is *most likely* limited by the amount of that bank's:

   A. actual reserves.

   B. excess reserves.

   C. required reserves.

3. If the monetary authority wants to slow the growth of an economy, its *least* appropriate action will be to increase:

   A. reserve requirements.

   B. the federal funds rate.

   C. purchases of government securities.

4. What is the *most likely* effect of financial innovation and increasing real GDP, respectively, on the demand for money?

	Financial Innovation	Increasing Real GDP
A.	Increase	Increase
B.	Increase	Decrease
C.	Decrease	Increase

5. If the Federal Reserve increases the money supply, the *least likely* short-run effect is a decrease in:

   A. interest rates.

   B. imported goods.

   C. investment spending.

SOLUTIONS FOR READING 24

1. C is correct. The M2 measure of the money supply does not include currency held by banks.

2. B is correct. The amount of new money that a bank can create is limited to the amount of that bank's excess reserves.

3. C is correct. To slow an economy, the monetary authority will want to raise interest rates by being a net seller of government securities.

4. C is correct. Financial innovation generally causes a decrease in the demand for money, while an increase in real GDP causes an increase in the demand for money.

5. C is correct. If the Federal Reserve increases the money supply, investment spending should increase as a result of interest rates decreasing.

U.S. INFLATION, UNEMPLOYMENT, AND BUSINESS CYCLES

by Michael Parkin

LEARNING OUTCOMES

The candidate should be able to:	Mastery
a. differentiate between inflation and the price level;	☐
b. describe and distinguish among the factors resulting in demand-pull and cost-push inflation and describe the evolution of demand-pull and cost-push inflationary processes;	☐
c. explain the costs of anticipated inflation;	☐
d. explain the relation among inflation, nominal interest rates, and the demand and supply of money;	☐
e. explain the impact of inflation on unemployment and describe the short-run and long-run Phillips curve, including the effect of changes in the natural rate of unemployment;	☐
f. explain how economic growth, inflation, and unemployment affect the business cycle;	☐
g. describe mainstream business cycle theory and real business cycle (RBC) theory and distinguish between them, including the role of productivity changes.	☐

INFLATION PLUS UNEMPLOYMENT EQUALS MISERY!   1

Back in the 1970s, when inflation was raging at a double-digit rate, economist Arthur M. Okun proposed what he called the Misery Index. Misery, he suggested, could be measured as the sum of the inflation rate and the unemployment rate. At its peak, in 1980, the Misery Index hit 21. In 2006, it was 9. At its lowest, in 1964 and again in 1999, the Misery Index was 6.

Inflation and unemployment make us miserable for good reasons. We care about inflation because it raises our cost of living. And we care about unemployment because either it hits us directly and takes our jobs or it scares us into thinking that we might lose our jobs.

We want rapid income growth, low unemployment, and low inflation. But can we have all these things at the same time? Or do we face a tradeoff among them?

This reading applies the *aggregate supply–aggregate demand model* that you studied in the reading on aggregate supply and aggregate demand to explain the patterns in inflation and output that occur in our economy. The reading also looks at a related model, the Phillips curve, which illustrates a short-run tradeoff between inflation and unemployment. The reading then applies the classical model to explain how business cycle fluctuations can arise from the normal working of the economy and independently of fluctuations in cost-push forces or aggregate demand.

We begin by looking at the evolving U.S. economy. At the end of the reading, in *Reading Between the Lines*, we examine the state of the economy in 2006 as some people began to fear both inflation and recession.

2   THE EVOLVING U.S. ECONOMY

Real GDP and the price level are continually changing. Let's see how we can use the aggregate supply–aggregate demand model of the reading on aggregate supply and aggregate demand to explain these changes.

Imagine the economy as a video and think of the aggregate supply–aggregate demand figure as a freeze-frame. We can run this video—run an instant replay—but keep our finger on the freeze-frame button and look at some important parts of the previous action. Let's run the video from 1960.

Figure 1 shows the economy in 1960 at the point of intersection of its aggregate demand curve, AD_{60}, and short-run aggregate supply curve, SAS_{60}. Real GDP was $2.5 trillion, and the GDP deflator was 21. In 1960, real GDP equaled potential GDP—the economy was on its long-run aggregate supply curve, LAS_{60}.

By 2005, the economy had reached the point marked by the intersection of the aggregate demand curve AD_{05} and the short-run aggregate supply curve SAS_{05}. Real GDP was $11.1 trillion, and the GDP deflator was 112. The Congressional Budget Office estimated potential GDP in 2005 to be $11.3 trillion, so equilibrium real GDP was less than potential GDP on LAS_{05}.

The path traced by the blue and gray dots in Fig. 1 shows three key features:

▶ Economic growth
▶ Inflation
▶ Business cycles

Economic Growth

Over the years, real GDP grows—shown in Fig. 1 by the rightward movement of the dots. The faster real GDP grows, the larger is the horizontal distance between successive dots. Potential GDP grows because the quantity of labor grows and because capital accumulation (physical capital and human capital) and technological change increase labor productivity.

FIGURE 1 Economic Growth, Inflation, and Cycles: 1960–2005

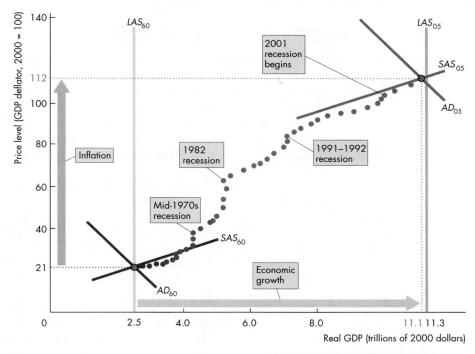

Each point shows the price level and real GDP in a given year. In 1960, the aggregate demand curve, AD_{60}, and the short-run aggregate supply curve, SAS_{60}, determined these variables. Each point is generated by the gradual shifting of the AD and SAS curves. By 2005, the curves were AD_{05} and SAS_{05}, respectively.

Real GDP grew quickly and inflation was moderate during the 1960s; real GDP growth sagged in 1974–1975 and again in 1982. Inflation was rapid during the 1970s but slowed after the 1982 recession. From 1982 to 1989, real GDP growth was strong. A recession began in 1991, and a further strong and sustained expansion then followed until the 2001 recession. The recovery after 2001 was weak at first.

Sources: Bureau of Economic Analysis and Congressional Budget Office.

These forces that bring economic growth were strongest during the 1960s. They strengthened again during the 1990s. But during the 1970s, early 1980s, and early 2000s, economic growth was slow.

Inflation

The price level rises over the years—shown in Fig. 1 by the upward movement of the points. The larger the rise in the price level, the larger is the vertical distance between successive dots in the figure. The main force generating the persistent increase in the price level is a tendency for aggregate demand to increase at a faster pace than the increase in potential GDP. All of the factors that increase aggregate demand and shift the aggregate demand curve influence the pace of inflation. But one factor—the growth of the quantity of money—is the main source of *persistent* increases in aggregate demand and persistent inflation.

Business Cycles

Over the years, the economy grows and shrinks in cycles—shown in Fig. 1 by the wavelike pattern made by the dots, with the recessions highlighted. The cycles arise because both the expansion of short-run aggregate supply and the growth of aggregate demand do not proceed at a fixed, steady pace.

The Evolving Economy: 1960–2005

From 1960 to 1967, real GDP growth was rapid and inflation was low. This was a period of rapid increases in potential GDP and of moderate increases in aggregate demand. The pace of inflation increased in the late 1960s.

In the mid-1970s, a series of massive oil price increases decreased short-run aggregate supply and rapid increases in the quantity of money increased aggregate demand. The decrease in short-run aggregate supply was greater than the increase in aggregate demand and the result was a combination of rapid inflation *and* recession—stagflation.

The rest of the 1970s saw high inflation—the price level increased quickly—but slow real GDP growth. By 1980, inflation was a major problem and the Fed decided to take strong action. The Fed drove interest rates to previously unknown levels and decreased aggregate demand. By 1982, the decrease in aggregate demand put the economy in a deep recession.

During the years 1983–1990, capital accumulation and steady technological change resulted in a sustained increase in potential GDP. Wage growth was moderate, the price of oil fell, and short-run aggregate supply increased. Aggregate demand growth kept pace with the growth of potential GDP. Sustained but steady growth in aggregate supply and aggregate demand kept real GDP growing and inflation steady. The economy moved from a recession in 1982 to above full employment in 1990.

The economy was in this condition when a decrease in aggregate demand led to the 1991 recession. The economy again embarked on a path of expansion through 2001. During the late 1990s and 2000, the expansion increased real GDP to a level that exceeded potential GDP and took employment to above full employment. Then in late 2000 and early 2001, aggregate demand decreased and another recession occurred. This recession was mild and was followed by a slow recovery. By 2005, although real GDP had grown, it remained below potential GDP.

You've seen how the *AS–AD* model can provide an account of the forces that move real GDP and the price level to bring economic growth, inflation, and business cycles. We're now going to use this model to explore the cycles in inflation and real GDP more closely. We're then going to use a related model (the Phillips curve) that focuses on the tradeoff between unemployment and inflation. But the *AS–AD* and Phillips curve models are not the only ones that economists use to study cycles. We'll end this reading by looking at an alternative real business cycle theory that extends the classical model and applies it to explain cycles as well as growth in a unified framework.

3   INFLATION CYCLES

In the long run, inflation is a monetary phenomenon. It occurs if the quantity of money grows faster than potential GDP. But in the short run, many factors can start an inflation, and real GDP and the price level interact. To study these interactions, we distinguish two sources of inflation:

► Demand-pull inflation
► Cost-push inflation

Demand-Pull Inflation

An inflation that starts because aggregate demand increases is called **demand-pull inflation**. Demand-pull inflation can be kicked off by *any* of the factors that change aggregate demand. Examples are a cut in the interest rate, an increase in the quantity of money, an increase in government expenditure, a tax cut, an increase in exports, or an increase in investment stimulated by an increase in expected future profits.

Initial Effect of an Increase in Aggregate Demand

Suppose that last year the price level was 115 and real GDP was \$12 trillion. Potential GDP was also \$12 trillion. Figure 2(a) illustrates this situation. The aggregate demand curve is AD_0, the short-run aggregate supply curve is SAS_0, and the long-run aggregate supply curve is LAS.

FIGURE 2   A Demand-Pull Rise in the Price Level

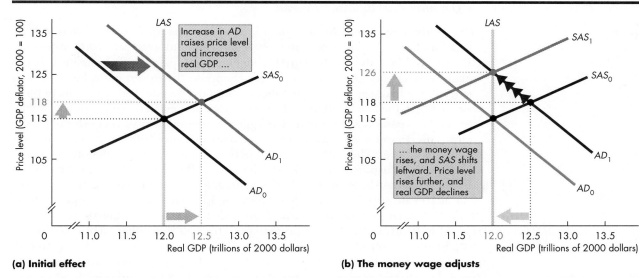

(a) Initial effect

(b) The money wage adjusts

In part (a), the aggregate demand curve is AD_0, the short-run aggregate supply curve is SAS_0, and the long-run aggregate supply curve is LAS. The price level is 115, and real GDP is \$12 trillion, which equals potential GDP. Aggregate demand increases to AD_1. The price level rises to 118, and real GDP increases to \$12.5 trillion.

   In part (b), starting from above full employment, the money wage rate begins to rise and the short-run aggregate supply curve shifts leftward toward SAS_1. The price level rises further, and real GDP returns to potential GDP.

Now suppose that the Fed cuts the interest rate and increases the quantity of money and aggregate demand increases to AD_1. With no change in potential GDP and no change in the money wage rate, the long-run aggregate supply curve and the short-run aggregate supply curve remain at LAS and SAS_0, respectively.

The price level and real GDP are determined at the point where the aggregate demand curve AD_1 intersects the short-run aggregate supply curve. The price level rises to 118, and real GDP increases above potential GDP to \$12.5 trillion.

Unemployment falls below its natural rate. The economy is at an above full-employment equilibrium and there is an inflationary gap. The next step in the unfolding story is a rise in the money wage rate.

Money Wage Rate Response

Real GDP cannot remain above potential GDP forever. With unemployment below its natural rate, there is a shortage of labor. In this situation, the money wage rate begins to rise. As it does so, short-run aggregate supply decreases and the *SAS* curve starts to shift leftward. The price level rises further, and real GDP begins to decrease.

With no further change in aggregate demand—that is, the aggregate demand curve remains at AD_1—this process ends when the short-run aggregate supply curve has shifted to SAS_1 in Fig. 2(b). At this time, the price level has increased to 126 and real GDP has returned to potential GDP of $12 trillion, the level from which it started.

A Demand-Pull Inflation Process

The events that we've just described bring a *one-time rise in the price level*, not an inflation. For inflation to proceed, aggregate demand must *persistently* increase.

The only way in which aggregate demand can persistently increase is if the quantity of money persistently increases. Suppose the government has a budget deficit that it finances by selling bonds. Also suppose that the Fed buys some of these bonds. When the Fed buys bonds, it creates more money. In this situation, aggregate demand increases year after year. The aggregate demand curve keeps shifting rightward. This persistent increase in aggregate demand puts continual upward pressure on the price level. The economy now experiences demand-pull inflation.

Figure 3 illustrates the process of demand-pull inflation. The starting point is the same as that shown in Fig. 2. The aggregate demand curve is AD_0, the short-run aggregate supply curve is SAS_0, and the long-run aggregate supply curve is *LAS*. Real GDP is $12 trillion, and the price level is 115. Aggregate demand increases, shifting the aggregate demand curve to AD_1. Real GDP increases to $12.5 trillion, and the price level rises to 118. The economy is at an above full-employment equilibrium. There is a shortage of labor, and the money wage rate rises. The short-run aggregate supply curve shifts to SAS_1. The price level rises to 126, and real GDP returns to potential GDP.

But the Fed increases the quantity of money again, and aggregate demand continues to increase. The aggregate demand curve shifts rightward to AD_2. The price level rises further to 130, and real GDP again exceeds potential GDP at $12.5 trillion. Yet again, the money wage rate rises and decreases short-run aggregate supply. The *SAS* curve shifts to SAS_2, and the price level rises further, to 138. As the quantity of money continues to grow, aggregate demand increases and the price level rises in an ongoing demand-pull inflation process.

The process you have just studied generates inflation—an ongoing process of a rising price level.

Demand-Pull Inflation in Kalamazoo

You may better understand the inflation process that we've just described by considering what is going on in an individual part of the economy, such as a Kalamazoo soda-bottling plant. Initially, when aggregate demand increases, the demand for soda increases and the price of soda rises. Faced with a higher price, the soda

FIGURE 3   A Demand-Pull Inflation Spiral

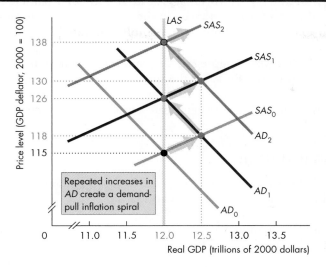

Each time the quantity of money increases, aggregate demand increases and the aggregate demand curve shifts rightward from AD_0 to AD_1 to AD_2, and so on. Each time real GDP increases above potential GDP, the money wage rate rises and the short-run aggregate supply curve shifts leftward from SAS_0 to SAS_1 to SAS_2, and so on. The price level rises from 115 to 118, 126, 130, 138, and so on. There is a demand-pull inflation spiral. Real GDP fluctuates between $12 trillion and $12.5 trillion.

plant works overtime and increases production. Conditions are good for workers in Kalamazoo, and the soda factory finds it hard to hang on to its best people. To do so, it offers a higher money wage rate. As the wage rate rises, so do the soda factory's costs.

What happens next depends on aggregate demand. If aggregate demand remains constant, the firm's costs increase but the price of soda does not increase as quickly as its costs. So the firm cuts production. Eventually, the money wage rate and costs increase by the same percentage as the rise in the price of soda. In real terms, the soda factory is in the same situation as it was initially. It produces the same amount of soda and employs the same amount of labor as before the increase in demand.

But if aggregate demand continues to increase, so does the demand for soda and the price of soda rises at the same rate as wages. The soda factory continues to operate above full employment, and there is a persistent shortage of labor. Prices and wages chase each other upward in a demand-pull inflation spiral.

Demand-Pull Inflation in the United States

A demand-pull inflation like the one you've just studied occurred in the United States during the late 1960s. In 1960, inflation was a moderate 2 percent a year, but its rate increased slowly to 3 percent by 1966. Then, in 1967, a large increase in government expenditure on the Vietnam War and an increase in spending on social programs, together with an increase in the growth rate of the quantity of money, increased aggregate demand more quickly. Consequently, the rightward shift of the aggregate demand curve speeded up and the price level increased more quickly. Real GDP moved above potential GDP, and the unemployment rate fell below its natural rate.

With unemployment below its natural rate, the money wage rate started to rise more quickly and the short-run aggregate supply curve shifted leftward. The Fed responded with a further increase in the money growth rate, and a demand-pull inflation spiral unfolded. By 1970, the inflation rate had reached 5 percent a year.

For the next few years, aggregate demand grew even more quickly and the inflation rate kept rising. By 1974, the inflation rate had reached 11 percent a year.

Next, let's see how shocks to aggregate supply can create cost-push inflation.

Cost-Push Inflation

An inflation that is kicked off by an increase in costs is called **cost-push inflation**. The two main sources of cost increases are

1. An increase in the money wage rate
2. An increase in the money prices of raw materials

At a given price level, the higher the cost of production, the smaller is the amount that firms are willing to produce. So if the money wage rate rises or if the prices of raw materials (for example, oil) rise, firms decrease their supply of goods and services. Aggregate supply decreases, and the short-run aggregate supply curve shifts leftward.[1] Let's trace the effects of such a decrease in short-run aggregate supply on the price level and real GDP.

Initial Effect of a Decrease in Aggregate Supply

Suppose that last year the price level was 115 and real GDP was $12 trillion. Potential real GDP was also $12 trillion. Figure 4(a) illustrates this situation. The aggregate demand curve was AD_0, the short-run aggregate supply curve was SAS_0, and the long-run aggregate supply curve was *LAS*. In the current year, the world's oil producers form a price-fixing organization that strengthens their market power and increases the relative price of oil. They raise the price of oil, and this action decreases short-run aggregate supply. The short-run aggregate supply curve shifts leftward to SAS_1. The price level rises to 122, and real GDP decreases to $11.5 trillion. The economy is at a below full-employment equilibrium and there is a recessionary gap.

This event is a *one-time rise in the price level*. It is not inflation. In fact, a supply shock on its own cannot cause inflation. Something more must happen to enable a one-time supply shock, which causes a one-time rise in the price level, to be converted into a process of ongoing inflation. The quantity of money must persistently increase. And it sometimes does increase, as you will now see.

Aggregate Demand Response

When real GDP decreases, unemployment rises above its natural rate. In such a situation, there is often an outcry of concern and a call for action to restore full

---

[1] Some cost-push forces, such as an increase in the price of oil accompanied by a decrease in the availability of oil, can also decrease long-run aggregate supply. We'll ignore such effects here and examine cost-push factors that change only short-run aggregate supply. Later in the reading, we study the effects of shocks to long-run aggregate supply.

FIGURE 4   Cost-Push Rise in the Price Level

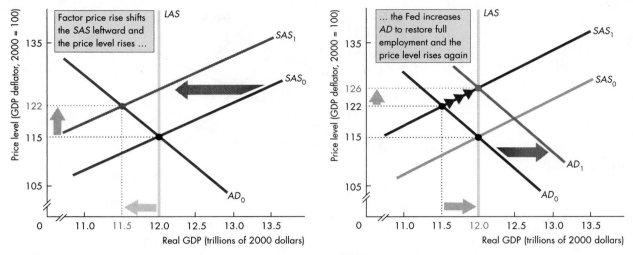

(a) Initial cost push   **(b) The Fed responds**

Initially, the aggregate demand curve is AD_0, the short-run aggregate supply curve is SAS_0, and the long-run aggregate supply curve is LAS. A decrease in aggregate supply (for example, resulting from a rise in the world price of oil) shifts the short-run aggregate supply curve to SAS_1. The economy moves to the point where the short-run aggregate supply curve SAS_1 intersects the aggregate demand curve AD_0. The price level rises to 122, and real GDP decreases to \$11.5 trillion.

In part (b), if the Fed responds by increasing aggregate demand to restore full employment, the aggregate demand curve shifts rightward to AD_1. The economy returns to full employment, but the price level rises further to 126.

employment. Suppose that the Fed cuts the interest rate and increases the quantity of money. Aggregate demand increases. In Fig. 4(b), the aggregate demand curve shifts rightward to AD_1 and full employment is restored. But the price level rises further to 126.

A Cost-Push Inflation Process

The oil producers now see the prices of everything they buy increasing. So OPEC increases the price of oil again to restore its new high relative price. Figure 5 continues the story. The short-run aggregate supply curve now shifts to SAS_2. The price level rises and real GDP decreases.

The price level rises further, to 134, and real GDP decreases to \$11.5 trillion. Unemployment increases above its natural rate. If the Fed responds yet again with an increase in the quantity of money, aggregate demand increases and the aggregate demand curve shifts to AD_2. The price level rises even higher—to 138—and full employment is again restored. A cost-push inflation spiral results. The combination of a rising price level and decreasing real GDP is called **stagflation**.

You can see that the Fed has a dilemma. If it does not respond when OPEC raises the price of oil, the economy remains below full employment. If the Fed increases the quantity of money to restore full employment, it invites another oil price hike that will call forth yet a further increase in the quantity of money.

If the Fed responds to each oil price hike by increasing the quantity of money, inflation will rage along at a rate decided by OPEC. But if the Fed keeps the lid on money growth, the economy remains below full employment.

FIGURE 5   A Cost-Push Inflation Spiral

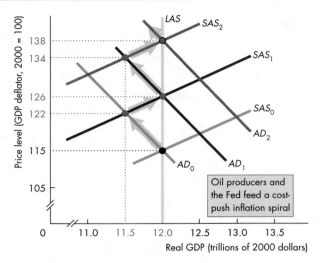

Each time a cost increase occurs, the short-run aggregate supply curve shifts leftward from SAS_0 to SAS_1 to SAS_2, and so on. Each time real GDP decreases below potential GDP, the Fed increases the quantity of money and the aggregate demand curve shifts rightward from AD_0 to AD_1 to AD_2, and so on. The price level rises from 115 to 122, 126, 134, 138, and so on. There is a cost-push inflation spiral. Real GDP fluctuates between $12 trillion and $11.5 trillion.

Cost-Push Inflation in Kalamazoo

What is going on in the Kalamazoo soda-bottling plant when the economy is experiencing cost-push inflation?

When the oil price increases, so do the costs of bottling soda. These higher costs decrease the supply of soda, increasing its price and decreasing the quantity produced. The soda plant lays off some workers.

This situation persists until either the Fed increases aggregate demand or the price of oil falls. If the Fed increases aggregate demand, the demand for soda increases and so does its price. The higher price of soda brings higher profits, and the bottling plant increases its production. The soda factory rehires the laid-off workers.

Cost-Push Inflation in the United States

A cost-push inflation like the one you've just studied occurred in the United States during the 1970s. It began in 1974 when the Organization of the Petroleum Exporting Countries (OPEC) raised the price of oil fourfold. The higher oil price decreased aggregate supply, which caused the price level to rise more quickly and real GDP to shrink. The Fed then faced a dilemma: Would it increase the quantity of money and accommodate the cost-push forces, or would it keep aggregate demand growth in check by limiting money growth? In 1975, 1976, and 1977, the Fed repeatedly allowed the quantity of money to grow quickly and inflation proceeded at a rapid rate. In 1979 and 1980, OPEC was again able to push oil prices higher. On that occasion, the Fed decided not to respond to the oil price hike with an increase in the quantity of money. The result was a recession but also, eventually, a fall in inflation.

Expected Inflation

If inflation is expected, the fluctuations in real GDP that accompany demand-pull and cost-push inflation that you've just studied don't occur. Instead, inflation proceeds as it does in the long run, with real GDP equal to potential GDP and unemployment at its natural rate. Figure 6 explains why.

FIGURE 6   Expected Inflation

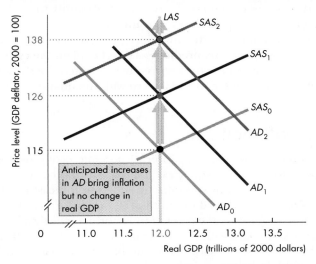

Potential real GDP is $12 trillion. Last year, aggregate demand was AD_0 and the short-run aggregate supply curve was SAS_0. The actual price level was the same as the expected price level: 115. This year, aggregate demand is expected to increase to AD_1 and the price level is expected to rise from 115 to 126. As a result, the money wage rate rises and the short-run aggregate supply curve shifts to SAS_1. If aggregate demand actually increases as expected, the actual aggregate demand curve AD_1 is the same as the expected aggregate demand curve. Real GDP is $12 trillion, and the actual price level rises to 126. The inflation is expected. Next year, the process continues with aggregate demand increasing as expected to AD_2 and the money wage rate rising to shift the short-run aggregate supply curve to SAS_2. Again, real GDP remains at $12 trillion, and the price level rises, as expected, to 138.

Suppose that last year the aggregate demand curve was AD_0, the aggregate supply curve was SAS_0, and the long-run aggregate supply curve was LAS. The price level was 115, and real GDP was $12 trillion, which is also potential GDP.

To keep things as simple as possible, suppose that potential GDP does not change, so the LAS curve doesn't shift. Also suppose that aggregate demand is *expected to increase* to AD_1.

In anticipation of this increase in aggregate demand, the money wage rate rises and the short-run aggregate supply curve shifts leftward. If the money wage rate rises by the same percentage as the price level is expected to rise, the short-run aggregate supply curve for next year is SAS_1.

If aggregate demand turns out to be the same as expected, the aggregate demand curve is AD_1. The short-run aggregate supply curve, SAS_1, and AD_1 determine the actual price level at 126. Between last year and this year, the price level increased from 115 to 126 and the economy experienced an inflation rate equal to that expected. If this inflation is ongoing, aggregate demand increases (as expected) in the following year and the aggregate demand curve shifts to AD_2. The money wage rate rises to reflect the expected inflation, and the short-run aggregate supply curve shifts to SAS_2. The price level rises, as expected, to 138.

What caused this inflation? The immediate answer is that because people expected inflation, the money wage rate increased and the price level increased. But the expectation was correct. Aggregate demand was expected to increase, and it did increase. It is the actual and expected increase in aggregate demand that caused the inflation.

An expected inflation at full employment is exactly the process that the quantity theory of money predicts. To review the quantity theory of money, see the reading on money, the price level, and inflation.

This broader account of the inflation process and its short-run effects explains why the quantity theory predictions don't explain the cycles in inflation. Only if aggregate demand growth is correctly forecasted does the economy follow the course described in Fig. 6 and accord with the quantity theory of money.

Forecasting Inflation

To anticipate inflation, people must forecast it. Some economists who work for macroeconomic forecasting agencies, banks, insurance companies, labor unions, and large corporations specialize in inflation forecasting. The best forecast available is one that is based on all the relevant information and is called a **rational expectation**. A rational expectation is not necessarily a correct forecast. It is simply the best forecast with the information available. It will often turn out to be wrong, but no other forecast that could have been made with the information available could do better.

Inflation and the Business Cycle

When the inflation forecast is correct, the economy operates at full employment. If aggregate demand grows faster than expected, real GDP moves above potential GDP, the inflation rate exceeds its expected rate, and the economy behaves like it does in a demand-pull inflation. If aggregate demand grows more slowly than expected, real GDP falls below potential GDP, the inflation rate slows, and the economy behaves like it does in a cost-push inflation.

4   INFLATION AND UNEMPLOYMENT: THE PHILLIPS CURVE

Another way of studying inflation cycles focuses on the relationship and the short-run tradeoff between inflation and unemployment, a relationship called the **Phillips curve**—so named because it was first suggested by New Zealand economist A. W. Phillips.

Why do we need another way of studying inflation? What is wrong with the AS–AD explanation of the fluctuations in inflation and real GDP? The first answer to both questions is that we often want to study changes in both the expected and actual inflation rates and for this purpose the Phillips curve provides a simpler tool and clearer insights than what the AS–AD model provides. The second answer to both questions is that we often want to study changes in the short-run tradeoff between inflation and real economic activity (real GDP and unemployment) and again, the Phillips curve serves this purpose well.

To begin our explanation of the Phillips curve, we distinguish between two time frames (similar to the two aggregate supply time frames). We study

▶ The short-run Phillips curve
▶ The long-run Phillips curve

The Short-Run Phillips Curve

The **short-run Phillips curve** shows the relationship between inflation and unemployment, holding constant:

1. The expected inflation rate
2. The natural unemployment rate

You've just seen what determines the expected inflation rate.

Figure 7 shows a short-run Phillips curve, *SRPC*. Suppose that the expected inflation rate is 10 percent a year and the natural unemployment rate is 6 percent, point *A* in the figure. A short-run Phillips curve passes through this point. If inflation rises above its expected rate, unemployment falls below its natural rate. This joint movement in the inflation rate and the unemployment rate is illustrated as a movement up along the short-run Phillips curve from point *A* to point *B*. Similarly, if inflation falls below its expected rate, unemployment rises above its natural rate. In this case, there is movement down along the short-run Phillips curve from point *A* to point *C*.

The short-run Phillips curve is like the short-run aggregate supply curve. A movement along the *SAS* curve that brings a higher price level and an increase in

FIGURE 7   A Short-Run Phillips Curve

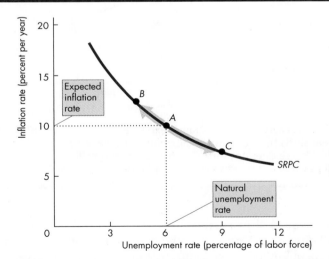

The short-run Phillips curve (*SRPC*) shows the relationship between inflation and unemployment at a given expected inflation rate and a given natural unemployment rate. With an expected inflation rate of 10 percent a year and a natural unemployment rate of 6 percent, the short-run Phillips curve passes through point *A*.

An unexpected increase in aggregate demand lowers unemployment and increases the inflation rate—a movement up along the short-run Phillips curve to point *B*. An unexpected decrease in aggregate demand increases unemployment and lowers the inflation rate—a movement down along the short-run Phillips curve to point *C*.

real GDP is equivalent to a movement along the short-run Phillips curve from *A* to *B* that brings an increase in the inflation rate and a decrease in the unemployment rate.

Similarly, a movement along the *SAS* curve that brings a lower price level and a decrease in real GDP is equivalent to a movement along the short-run Phillips curve from *A* to *C* that brings a decrease in the inflation rate and an increase in the unemployment rate.

The Long-Run Phillips Curve

The **long-run Phillips curve** shows the relationship between inflation and unemployment when the actual inflation rate equals the expected inflation rate. The long-run Phillips curve is vertical at the natural unemployment rate. In Fig. 8, it is the vertical line *LRPC*. The long-run Phillips curve tells us that any expected inflation rate is possible at the natural unemployment rate. This proposition is consistent with the *AS–AD* model, which predicts that when inflation is expected, real GDP equals potential GDP and unemployment is at its natural rate.

FIGURE 8   Short-Run and Long-Run Phillips Curves

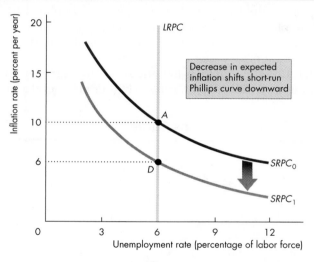

The long-run Phillips curve is *LRPC*. A fall in expected inflation from 10 percent a year to 6 percent a year shifts the short-run Phillips curve downward from $SRPC_0$ to $SRPC_1$. The long-run Phillips curve does not shift. The new short-run Phillips curve intersects the long-run Phillips curve at the new expected inflation rate—point *D*.

The short-run Phillips curve intersects the long-run Phillips curve at the expected inflation rate. A change in the expected inflation rate shifts the short-run Phillips curve but it does not shift the long-run Phillips curve.

In Fig. 8, if the expected inflation rate is 10 percent a year, the short-run Phillips curve is $SRPC_0$. If the expected inflation rate falls to 6 percent a year, the short-run Phillips curve shifts downward to $SRPC_1$. The vertical distance by which the short-run Phillips curve shifts from point *A* to point *D* is equal to the change in the expected inflation rate. If the actual inflation rate also falls from 10 percent to 6 percent, there is a movement down the long-run Phillips curve from *A* to *D*. An increase in the expected inflation rate has the opposite effect to that shown in Fig. 8.

The other source of a shift in the Phillips curve is a change in the natural unemployment rate.

Changes in the Natural Unemployment Rate

The natural unemployment rate changes for many reasons. A change in the natural unemployment rate shifts both the short-run and long-run Phillips curves. Figure 9 illustrates such shifts. If the natural unemployment rate increases from 6 percent to 9 percent, the long-run Phillips curve shifts from $LRPC_0$ to $LRPC_1$, and if expected inflation is constant at 10 percent a year, the short-run Phillips curve shifts from $SRPC_0$ to $SRPC_1$. Because the expected inflation rate is constant, the short-run Phillips curve $SRPC_1$ intersects the long-run curve $LRPC_1$ (point *E*) at the same inflation rate at which the short-run Phillips curve $SRPC_0$ intersects the long-run curve $LRPC_0$ (point *A*).

FIGURE 9   A Change in the Natural Unemployment Rate

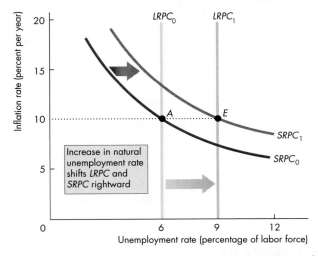

A change in the natural unemployment rate shifts both the short-run and long-run Phillips curves. An increase in the natural unemployment rate from 6 percent to 9 percent shifts the Phillips curves rightward to $SRPC_1$ and $LRPC_1$. The new long-run Phillips curve intersects the new short-run Phillips curve at the expected inflation rate—point *E*.

The U.S. Phillips Curve

Figure 10(a) is a scatter diagram of the inflation rate and the unemployment rate since 1961. We can interpret the data in terms of the shifting short-run Phillips curve in Fig. 10(b). During the 1960s, the short-run Phillips curve was $SRPC_0$, with a natural unemployment rate of 4.5 percent and an expected inflation rate of 2 percent a year (point *A*). During the early 1970s, the short-run Phillips curve was $SRPC_1$ with a natural unemployment rate of 5 percent and an expected inflation rate of 6 percent a year (point *B*). During the late 1970s, the natural unemployment rate increased to 8 percent (point *C*) and the short-run

FIGURE 10   Phillips Curves in the United States

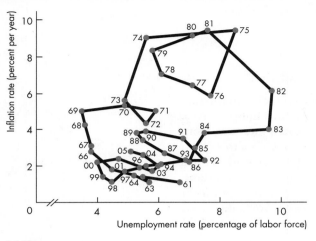

(a) Time sequence

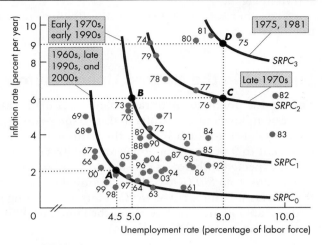

(b) Four Phillips curves

In part (a), each dot represents the combination of inflation and unemployment for a particular year. Part (b) interprets the data with a shifting short-run Phillips curve. The black dots *A, B, C,* and *D* show the combination of the natural unemployment rate and the expected inflation rate in different periods. The short-run Phillips curve was $SRPC_0$ during the 1960s and the late 1990s and early 2000s. It was $SRPC_1$ during the early 1970s and early 1990s, $SRPC_2$ during the late 1970s, and $SRPC_3$ (briefly) in 1975 and 1981.

Sources: Bureau of Labor Statistics and the author's calculations and assumptions.

Phillips curve was $SRPC_2$. And briefly in 1975 and again in 1981, the expected inflation rate surged to 9 percent a year (point *D*) and the short-run Phillips curve was $SRPC_3$. During the 1980s and 1990s, the expected inflation rate and the natural unemployment rate decreased and the short-run Phillips curve shifted leftward. By the early 1990s, it was back at $SRPC_1$. And by the mid-1990s, it was again $SRPC_0$, where it has remained into the 2000s.

5   BUSINESS CYCLES

Business cycles are easy to describe but hard to explain and business cycle theory remains unsettled and a source of controversy. We'll look at two approaches to understanding business cycles:

▶ Mainstream business cycle theory

▶ Real business cycle theory

Mainstream Business Cycle Theory

The mainstream business cycle theory is that potential GDP grows at a steady rate while aggregate demand grows at a fluctuating rate. Because the money wage rate is sticky, if aggregate demand grows faster than potential GDP, real GDP moves above potential GDP and an inflationary gap emerges. And if aggregate

FIGURE 11   The Mainstream Business Cycle Theory

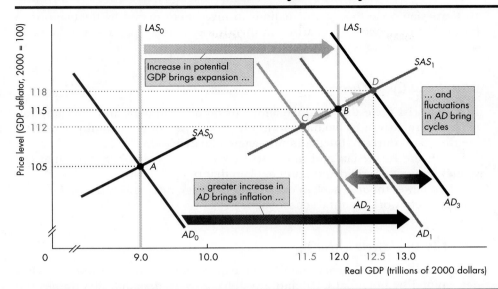

In a business cycle expansion, potential GDP increases and the *LAS* curve shifts rightward from LAS_0 to LAS_1. A greater than expected increase in aggregate demand brings inflation.

If the aggregate demand curve shifts to AD_1, the economy remains at full employment. If the aggregate demand curve shifts to AD_2, a recessionary gap arises. If the aggregate demand curve shifts to AD_3, an inflationary gap arises.

demand grows slower than potential GDP, real GDP moves below potential GDP and a recessionary gap emerges. If aggregate demand decreases, real GDP also decreases in a recession.

Figure 11 illustrates this cycle theory. Initially, actual and potential GDP are $9 trillion, and the long-run aggregate supply curve is LAS_0. Aggregate demand curve is AD_0, and the price level is 105. The economy is at full employment at point *A*.

An expansion occurs when potential GDP increases and the *LAS* curve shifts rightward to LAS_1. During an expansion, aggregate demand also increases, and usually by more than potential GDP, so the price level rises. Assume that in the current expansion, the price level is expected to rise to 115 and that the money wage rate has been set on that expectation. The short-run aggregate supply curve is SAS_1.

If aggregate demand increases to AD_1, real GDP increases to $12 trillion, the new level of potential GDP, and the price level rises, as expected, to 115. The economy remains at full employment but now at point *B*.

If aggregate demand increases more slowly to AD_2, real GDP grows by less than potential GDP and the economy moves to point *C*, with real GDP at $11.5 trillion and the price level at 112. Real GDP growth is slower and inflation is lower than expected.

If aggregate demand increases more quickly to AD_3, real GDP grows by more than potential GDP and the economy moves to point *D*, with real GDP at $12.5 trillion and the price level at 118. Real GDP growth is faster and inflation is higher than expected.

Growth, inflation, and business cycles arise from the relentless increases in potential GDP, faster (on the average) increases in aggregate demand, and fluctuations in the pace of aggregate demand growth.

This mainstream theory comes in a number of special forms that differ in what is regarded as the source of fluctuations in aggregate demand growth and the source of money wage stickiness.

Keynesian Cycle Theory

In **Keynesian cycle theory**, fluctuations in investment driven by fluctuations in business confidence—summarized in the phrase "animal spirits"—are the main source of fluctuations in aggregate demand.

Monetarist Cycle Theory

In **monetarist cycle theory**, fluctuations in both investment and consumption expenditure, driven by fluctuations in the growth rate of the quantity of money, are the main source of fluctuations in aggregate demand.

Both the Keynesian and monetarist cycle theories simply assume that the money wage rate is rigid and don't explain that rigidity.

Two newer theories seek to explain money wage rate rigidity and to be more careful about working out its consequences.

New Classical Cycle Theory

In **new classical cycle theory**, the rational expectation of the price level, which is determined by potential GDP and *expected* aggregate demand, determines the money wage rate and the position of the *SAS* curve. In this theory, only *unexpected* fluctuations in aggregate demand bring fluctuations in real GDP around potential GDP.

New Keynesian Cycle Theory

The **new Keynesian cycle theory** emphasizes the fact that today's money wage rates were negotiated at many past dates, which means that *past* rational expectations of the current price level influence the money wage rate and the position of the *SAS* curve. In this theory, both unexpected and currently expected fluctuations in aggregate demand bring fluctuations in real GDP around potential GDP.

The mainstream cycle theories don't rule out the possibility that occasionally an aggregate supply shock might occur. An oil price rise, a widespread drought, a major hurricane, or another natural disaster, could, for example, bring a recession. But supply shocks are not the normal source of fluctuations in the mainstream theories. In contrast, real business cycle theory puts supply shocks at center stage.

Real Business Cycle Theory

The newest theory of the business cycle, known as **real business cycle theory** (or RBC theory), regards random fluctuations in productivity as the main source of economic fluctuations. These productivity fluctuations are assumed to result mainly from fluctuations in the pace of technological change, but they might also have other sources, such as international disturbances, climate fluctuations, or natural disasters. The origins of RBC theory can be traced to the rational expectations revolution set off by Robert E. Lucas, Jr., but the first demonstrations of the power of this theory were given by Edward Prescott and Finn Kydland and by John Long and Charles Plosser. Today, RBC theory is part of a broad research agenda called dynamic general equilibrium analysis, and hundreds of young macroeconomists do research on this topic.

We'll explore RBC theory by looking first at its impulse and then at the mechanism that converts that impulse into a cycle in real GDP.

The RBC Impulse

The impulse in RBC theory is the growth rate of productivity that results from technological change. RBC theorists believe this impulse to be generated mainly by the process of research and development that leads to the creation and use of new technologies.

To isolate the RBC theory impulse, economists use growth accounting. Figure 12 shows the RBC impulse for the United States from 1960 through 2005. You can see that fluctuations in productivity growth are correlated with real GDP fluctuations.

FIGURE 12   The Real Business Cycle Impulse

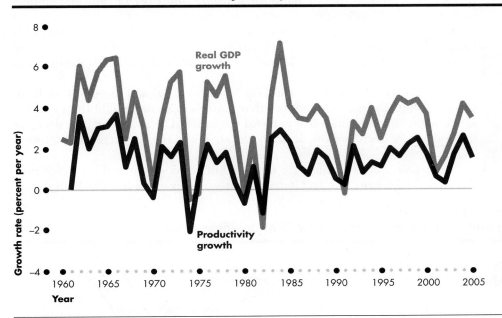

The real business cycle is caused by changes in technology that bring fluctuations in the growth rate of productivity. The fluctuations in productivity growth shown here are calculated by using growth accounting (the one third rule) to remove the contribution of capital accumulation to productivity growth. Productivity fluctuations are correlated with real GDP fluctuations. Economists are not sure what the productivity variable actually measures or what causes it to fluctuate.

Sources: Bureau of Economic Analysis and author's assumptions and calculations.

Most of the time, technological change is steady and productivity grows at a moderate pace. But sometimes productivity growth speeds up, and occasionally productivity *decreases*—labor becomes less productive, on the average. A period of rapid productivity growth brings a business cycle expansion, and a *decrease* in productivity triggers a recession.

It is easy to understand why technological change brings productivity growth. But how does it *decrease* productivity? All technological change eventually increases productivity. But if initially, technological change makes a sufficient amount of existing capital—especially human capital—obsolete, productivity temporarily decreases. At such a time, more jobs are destroyed than created and more businesses fail than start up.

The RBC Mechanism

Two effects follow from a change in productivity that gets an expansion or a contraction going:

1. Investment demand changes.

2. The demand for labor changes.

We'll study these effects and their consequences during a recession. In an expansion, they work in the direction opposite to what is described here.

Technological change makes some existing capital obsolete and temporarily decreases productivity. Firms expect the future profits to fall and see their labor productivity falling. With lower profit expectations, they cut back their purchases of new capital, and with lower labor productivity, they plan to lay off some workers. So the initial effect of a temporary fall in productivity is a decrease in investment demand and a decrease in the demand for labor.

Figure 13 illustrates these two initial effects of a decrease in productivity. Part (a) shows the effects of a decrease in investment demand in the loanable funds market. The demand for loanable funds is DLF and the supply of loanable funds is SLF. Initially, the demand for loanable funds is DLF_0 and the equilibrium quantity of funds is $2 trillion at a real interest rate of 6 percent a year. A decrease in productivity decreases investment demand, and the demand for loanable funds curve DLF shifts leftward to DLF_1. The real interest rate falls to 4 percent a year, and the equilibrium quantity of loanable funds decreases to $1.7 trillion.

Figure 13(b) shows the demand for labor curve LD and the supply of labor curve LS. Initially, the demand for labor curve is LD_0, and equilibrium employment is 200 billion hours a year at a real wage rate of $35 an hour. The decrease in productivity decreases the demand for labor, and the LD curve shifts leftward to LD_1.

Before we can determine the new level of employment and real wage rate, we need to take a ripple effect into account—the key effect in RBC theory.

FIGURE 13   Loanable Funds and Labor Markets in a Real Business Cycle

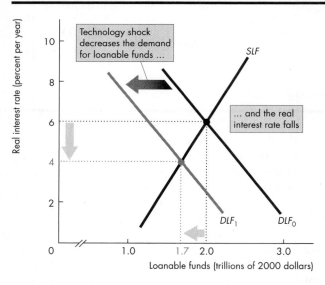

(a) Loanable funds and interest rate

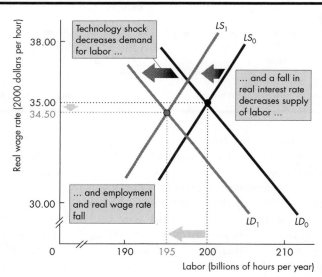

(b) Labor and wage rate

In part (a), the supply of loanable funds SLF and initial demand for loanable funds DLF_0 determine the real interest rate at 6 percent a year. In part (b), the initial demand for labor LD_0 and supply of labor, LS_0, determine the real wage rate at $35 an hour and employment at 200 billion hours. A technological change temporarily decreases productivity, and both the demand for loanable funds and the demand for labor decrease. The two demand curves shift leftward to DLF_1 and LD_1. In part (a), the real interest rate falls to 4 percent a year. In part (b), the fall in the real interest rate decreases the supply of labor (the when-to-work decision) and the supply of labor curve shifts leftward to LS_1. Employment decreases to 195 billion hours, and the real wage rate falls to $34.50 an hour. A recession is underway.

The Key Decision: When to Work?

According to RBC theory, people decide *when* to work by doing a cost-benefit calculation. They compare the return from working in the current period with the *expected* return from working in a later period. You make such a comparison every day in school. Suppose your goal in this course is to get an A. To achieve this goal, you work hard most of the time. But during the few days before the midterm and final exams, you work especially hard. Why? Because you believe that the return from studying close to the exam is greater than the return from studying when the exam is a long time away. So during the term, you take time off for the movies and other leisure pursuits, but at exam time, you study every evening and weekend.

RBC theory says that workers behave like you. They work fewer hours, sometimes zero hours, when the real wage rate is temporarily low, and they work more hours when the real wage rate is temporarily high. But to properly compare the current wage rate with the expected future wage rate, workers must use the real interest rate. If the real interest rate is 6 percent a year, a real wage of $1 an hour earned this week will become $1.06 a year from now. If the real wage rate is expected to be $1.05 an hour next year, today's real wage of $1 looks good. By working longer hours now and shorter hours a year from now, a person can get a 1 percent higher real wage. But suppose the real interest rate is 4 percent a year. In this case, $1 earned now is worth $1.04 next year. Working fewer hours now and more next year is the way to get a 1 percent higher real wage.

So the when-to-work decision depends on the real interest rate. The lower the real interest rate, other things remaining the same, the smaller is the supply of labor today. Many economists believe this *intertemporal substitution* effect to be of negligible size. RBC theorists believe that the effect is large, and it is the key feature of the RBC mechanism.

You saw in Fig. 13(a) that the decrease in the demand for loanable funds lowers the real interest rate. This fall in the real interest rate lowers the return to current work and decreases the supply of labor.

In Fig. 13(b), the labor supply curve shifts leftward to LS_1. The effect of the decrease in productivity on the demand for labor is larger than the effect of the fall in the real interest rate on the supply of labor. That is, the *LD* curve shifts farther leftward than does the *LS* curve. As a result, the real wage rate falls to $34.50 an hour and employment decreases to 195 billion hours. A recession has begun and is intensifying.

What Happened to Money?

The name *real* business cycle theory is no accident. It reflects the central prediction of the theory. Real things, not nominal or monetary things, cause business cycles. If the quantity of money changes, aggregate demand changes. But if there is no real change—with no change in the use of resources and no change in potential GDP—the change in the quantity of money changes only the price level. In RBC theory, this outcome occurs because the aggregate supply curve is the *LAS* curve, which pins real GDP down at potential GDP, so when aggregate demand changes, only the price level changes.

Cycles and Growth

The shock that drives the business cycle of RBC theory is the same as the force that generates economic growth: technological change. On the average, as technology advances, productivity grows. But it grows at an uneven pace. RBC theory says that there are frequent shocks to productivity that are mostly positive but that are occasionally negative.

Criticisms and Defenses of RBC Theory

The three main criticisms of RBC theory are that 1) the money wage rate *is* sticky, and to assume otherwise is at odds with a clear fact; 2) intertemporal substitution is too weak a force to account for large fluctuations in labor supply and employment with small real wage rate changes; and 3) productivity shocks are as likely to be caused by *changes in aggregate demand* as by technological change.

If the fluctuations in productivity are caused by aggregate demand fluctuations, then the traditional aggregate demand theories are needed to explain them. Fluctuations in productivity do not cause business cycles but are caused by them!

Building on this theme, the critics point out that the so-called productivity fluctuations that growth accounting measures are correlated with changes in the growth rate of money and other indicators of changes in aggregate demand.

The defenders of RBC theory claim that the theory explains the macroeconomic facts about business cycles and is consistent with the facts about economic growth. In effect, a single theory explains *both growth and cycles*. The growth accounting exercise that explains slowly changing trends also explains the more frequent business cycle swings. Its defenders also claim that RBC theory is consistent with a wide range of *micro*economic evidence about labor supply decisions, labor demand and investment demand decisions, and information on the distribution of income between labor and capital.

You can complete your study of inflation and the business cycle in *Reading Between the Lines*, which reviews the tradeoff between inflation and unemployment in the United States in 2006.

READING BETWEEN THE LINES   6

The Short-Run Inflation–Unemployment Tradeoff in 2006

THE NEW YORK TIMES, JUNE 15, 2006

A Modest Rise Still Amplifies Inflation Fears

. . . After taking over as Fed chairman this year, Ben S. Bernanke indicated that he believed the underlying rate of inflation should not exceed 2 percent a year. That tough goal, which most other Fed policy makers share, reflects a major shift in attitude about the risks of inflation.

Much as the 1930s Depression seared an entire generation of Americans who lived through it, the stagflation of the 1970s and the acute recession of the early 1980s indelibly marked an entire generation of economists.

"It's a complete regime change," said Barry P. Bosworth, a top economic adviser to President Jimmy Carter during the worst years of soaring inflation.

"Back then, we were arguing about the trade-off between unemployment and inflation, and we weren't clear about which one was more important," he explained. "Today, there is no question: you cannot run the economy without the primacy of the goal of price stability."

These days, the Fed's goal is to reduce "inflation expectations," even though the effect could be to slow down an economy that already seems to be slowing, to send another icy chill through the housing market and possibly to increase unemployment. All that, even though hourly wages have barely kept up with consumer prices, which, including energy and food costs, rose 0.4 percent in May, leaving them 4.2 percent higher than a year earlier.

The effort to keep inflation so low is not without controversy, however. Some argue that the Fed should tolerate a slightly higher range, worrying that if the Fed establishes a narrow comfort zone of zero to 2 percent, it runs the risk of something worse—actual deflation—if the economy hits a bump in the road. . . .

Essence of the Story

► The Fed wants to keep the inflation rate close to 2 percent a year.

► The stagflation of the 1970s and the recession of the early 1980s have left an indelible mark on Bernanke's generation of economists.

► During the 1970s, economists were arguing about the tradeoff between unemployment and inflation and weren't clear about which one was more important.

► Today, economists agree that the primary goal is price stability.

► The Fed wants to lower inflation expectations, even if the effect is to slow further an already slowing economy.

► Some economists think the Fed should tolerate a slightly higher inflation rate because a negative shock might bring deflation.

Economic Analysis

► The inflation rate (CPI) in July 2006 was 0.4 percent, which translates to an annual inflation rate of almost 5 percent.

► The unemployment rate in July 2006 was 4.7 percent.

► The Congressional Budget Office's estimate of the natural unemployment rate is 5.5 percent.

► Using this estimate of the natural rate, the economy was in an above-full employment equilibrium in the summer of 2006.

► Figure 14 illustrates the state of the U.S. economy in July 2006 using the Phillips curve model.

FIGURE 14   The Phillips Curves

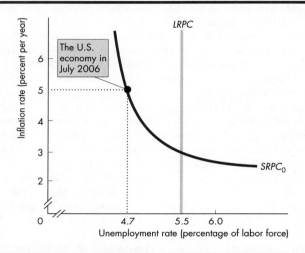

► The long-run Phillips curve is *LRPC* at the natural unemployment rate of 5.5 percent.

► The short-run Phillips curve is $SRPC_0$, which is based on an assumed expected inflation rate of 3 percent a year.

► The actual inflation rate exceeds the expected inflation rate.

► If the Fed takes no action and if the economy doesn't slow on its own, the expected inflation rate will rise and the short-run Phillips curve will shift upward and make the trade-off between inflation and unemployment more unfavorable.

► Figure 15 shows what happens if the Fed slows the growth rate of aggregate demand and pushes the unemployment rate up.

► The inflation rate slows and the economy moves down the short-run Phillips curve $SRPC_0$.

► Figure 16 shows the longer run effects of slowing inflation.

► When the unemployment rate rises above the natural rate, the inflation rate slows to less than the expected inflation rate.

► Eventually, the expected inflation rate begins to fall, and the short-run Phillips curve shifts downward.

FIGURE 15 The Fed Decreases the Money Growth Rate

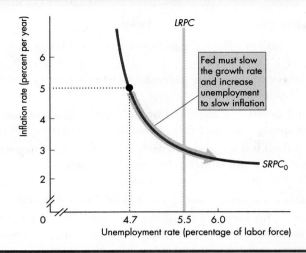

FIGURE 16 In the Long Run, Inflation Slows

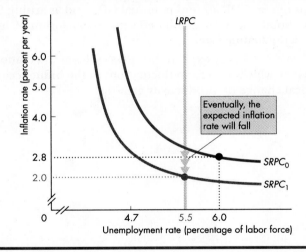

▶ If the Fed can lower the expected inflation rate to 2 percent a year, the short-run Phillips curve shifts downward to $SRPC_1$.

▶ It is unlikely that a negative shock would bring deflation, as the article says some fear.

▶ But if the Fed failed to act to lower the inflation rate, it is most likely that inflation expectations would become unanchored and increase.

SUMMARY

- ▶ Potential GDP grows.
- ▶ Inflation persists because aggregate demand grows faster than potential GDP.
- ▶ Business cycles occur because potential GDP and aggregate demand change at an uneven pace.
- ▶ Demand-pull inflation is triggered by an increase in aggregate demand and fueled by ongoing money growth. Real GDP cycles above full employment.
- ▶ Cost-push inflation is triggered by an increase in the money wage rate or raw material prices and is fueled by ongoing money growth. Real GDP cycles below full employment in a stagflation.
- ▶ When inflation is expected correctly, real GDP remains at potential GDP.
- ▶ The short-run Phillips curve shows the tradeoff between inflation and unemployment when the expected inflation rate and the natural unemployment rate are constant.
- ▶ The long-run Phillips curve, which is vertical, shows that when the actual inflation rate equals the expected inflation rate, the unemployment rate equals the natural unemployment rate.
- ▶ The mainstream business cycle theory explains business cycles as fluctuations of real GDP around potential GDP and as arising from a steady expansion of potential GDP combined with an expansion of aggregate demand at a fluctuating rate.
- ▶ Real business cycle theory explains business cycles as fluctuations of potential GDP, which arise from fluctuations in the influence of technological change on productivity growth.

PRACTICE PROBLEMS FOR READING 25

1. An analyst gathered the following year-end price level data for an economy:

Year End	Price Level
2000	174.0
2004	190.3
2005	196.8

The economy's annual inflation rate for 2005 and the compounded annual inflation rate for the 2000–2005 period are *closest* to:

	2005 Inflation	2000–2005 Inflation
A.	3.42%	2.49%
B.	3.42%	2.62%
C.	6.50%	2.49%

2. Assuming an economy is operating at full employment, which of the following is *least likely* to contribute to demand-pull inflation? An increase in:

   A. the quantity of money.

   B. government purchases.

   C. government borrowing.

3. If the inflation rate is greater than anticipated, are workers and lenders *most likely* to gain or lose relative to employers and borrowers, respectively?

   A. Workers and lenders will both lose.

   B. Workers will gain, but lenders will lose.

   C. Workers will lose, but lenders will gain.

4. Which of the following can lead to demand-pull inflation?

   A. An increase in exports.

   B. A decrease in government expenditures.

   C. An increase in the prices of raw materials.

5. When analyzing Gross Domestic Product (GDP), which condition is indicative of a recessionary gap? When potential GDP is:

   A. above real GDP.

   B. below real GDP.

   C. equal to real GDP.

SOLUTIONS FOR READING 25

1. A is correct. Inflation for 2005 = (196.8/190.3) − 1 = 1.0342 − 1 = 3.42% or (196.8 − 190.3)/190.3 = 3.42%. The compound annual inflation for 2000–2005 is found using a financial calculator. Inputs are $PV = -174.0$, $FV = 196.8$, $N = 5$, $PMT = 0$, and compute $I/Y = 2.49\%$.

2. C is correct. Government borrowing is unlikely to contribute to demand-pull inflation because it would result in increased interest rates (crowding-out effect) which would tend to slow the economy's growth.

3. A is correct. If inflation is greater than anticipated, then 1) the real wage rate falls and workers lose relative to employers, and 2) the borrower makes loan payments with deflated dollars, which causes the lender to lose relative to the borrower.

4. A is correct. An increase in exports reflects an increase in aggregate demand that causes inflation.

5. A is correct. A recessionary gap is when potential GDP is above real GDP.

FISCAL POLICY
by Michael Parkin

LEARNING OUTCOMES

The candidate should be able to:

	Mastery
a. explain supply side effects on employment, potential GDP, and aggregate supply, including the income tax and taxes on expenditure, and describe the Laffer curve and its relation to supply side economics;	☐
b. discuss the sources of investment finance and the influence of fiscal policy on capital markets, including the crowding-out effect;	☐
c. discuss the generational effects of fiscal policy, including generational accounting and generational imbalance;	☐
d. discuss the use of fiscal policy to stabilize the economy, including the effects of the government expenditure multiplier, the tax multiplier, and the balanced budget multiplier;	☐
e. explain the limitations of discretionary fiscal policy, and differentiate between discretionary fiscal policy and automatic stabilizers.	☐

BALANCING ACTS ON CAPITOL HILL

1

OPTIONAL SEGMENT BEGINS

In 2007, the federal government planned to collect in taxes 18.2 cents of every dollar Americans earned and to spend 21.1 cents of every dollar that Americans earned. So the government planned a deficit of almost 3 cents of every dollar earned—a total deficit of $370 billion. Federal government deficits are not new. Aside from the four years 1998–2001, the government's budget has been in deficit every year since 1970. Deficits bring debts, and your share of the federal government's debt is around $29,000.

What are the effects of taxes on the economy? Do they harm employment and production?

Does it matter if the government doesn't balance its books? What are the effects of an ongoing government deficit and accumulating debt? Do they slow economic growth? Do they impose a burden on future generations—on you and your children?

What are the effects of government spending on the economy? Does a dollar spent by the government on goods and services have the same effect as a dollar spent by someone else? Does it create jobs, or does it destroy them?

These are the fiscal policy issues that you will study in this reading. In *Reading Between the Lines* at the end of the reading, we look at the federal budget in 2007 and compare it with that of 2000, the last year of the Clinton administration.

2   THE FEDERAL BUDGET

The annual statement of the outlays and tax revenues of the government of the United States together with the laws and regulations that approve and support those outlays and tax revenues make up the **federal budget**. The federal budget has two purposes:

1. To finance the activities of the federal government
2. To achieve macroeconomic objectives

The first purpose of the federal budget was its only purpose before the Great Depression years of the 1930s. The second purpose arose as a reaction to the Great Depression. The use of the federal budget to achieve macroeconomic objectives such as full employment, sustained economic growth, and price level stability is called **fiscal policy**. It is on this second purpose that we focus in this reading.

The Institutions and Laws

Fiscal policy is made by the President and Congress on an annual timeline that is shown in Fig. 1 for the 2007 budget.

The Roles of the President and Congress

The President *proposes* a budget to Congress each February and, after Congress has passed the budget acts in September, either signs those acts into law or vetoes the *entire* budget bill. The President does not have the veto power to eliminate specific items in a budget bill and approve others—known as a *line-item veto*. Many state governors have long had line-item veto authority, and Congress attempted to grant these powers to the President of the United States in 1996. But in a 1998 Supreme Court ruling, the line-item veto for the President was declared unconstitutional. Although the President proposes and ultimately approves the budget, the task of making the tough decisions on spending and taxes rests with Congress.

Congress begins its work on the budget with the President's proposal. The House of Representatives and the Senate develop their own budget ideas in their respective House and Senate Budget Committees. Formal conferences between the two houses eventually resolve differences of view, and a series of spending acts and an overall budget act are usually passed by both houses before the start of the

FIGURE 1   The Federal Budget Timeline in Fiscal 2007

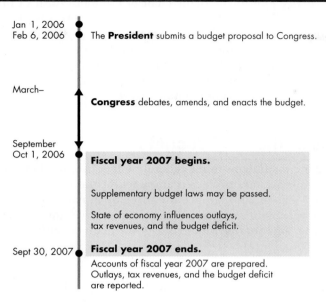

The federal budget process begins with the President's proposals in February. Congress debates and amends these proposals and enacts a budget before the start of the fiscal year on October 1. The President signs the budget acts into law or vetoes the entire budget bill. Throughout the fiscal year, Congress might pass supplementary budget laws. The budget outcome is calculated after the end of the fiscal year.

fiscal year. A *fiscal year* is a year that runs from October 1 to September 30 in the next calendar year. *Fiscal* 2007 is the fiscal year that *begins* on October 1, 2006.

During a fiscal year, Congress often passes supplementary budget laws, and the budget outcome is influenced by the evolving state of the economy. For example, if a recession begins, tax revenues fall and welfare payments increase.

The Employment Act of 1946

Fiscal policy operates within the framework of the landmark **Employment Act of 1946** in which Congress declared that

> . . . it is the continuing policy and responsibility of the Federal Government to use all practicable means . . . to coordinate and utilize all its plans, functions, and resources . . . to promote maximum employment, production, and purchasing power.

This act recognized a role for government actions to keep unemployment low, the economy expanding, and inflation in check. The *Full Employment and Balanced Growth Act of 1978*, more commonly known as the *Humphrey-Hawkins Act*, went farther than the Employment Act of 1946 and set a specific target of 4 percent for the unemployment rate. But this target has never been treated as an unwavering policy goal. Under the 1946 act, the President must describe the current economic situation and the policies he believes are needed in the annual *Economic Report of the President*, which the Council of Economic Advisers writes.

The Council of Economic Advisers

The President's Council of Economic Advisers was established in the Employment Act of 1946. The Council consists of a chairperson and two other members, all of whom are economists on a one- or two-year leave from their regular university or public service jobs. In 2006, the chair of President Bush's Council of Economic Advisers was Edward P. Lazear of Stanford University. The **Council of Economic Advisers** monitors the economy and keeps the President and the public well informed about the current state of the economy and the best available forecasts of where it is heading. This economic intelligence activity is one source of data that informs the budget-making process.

Let's look at the most recent federal budget.

Highlights of the 2007 Budget

Table 1 shows the main items in the federal budget proposed by President Bush for 2007. The numbers are projected amounts for the fiscal year beginning on October 1, 2006—fiscal 2007. Notice the three main parts of the table: *Tax revenues* are the government's receipts, *outlays* are the government's payments, and the *deficit* is the amount by which the government's outlays exceed its tax revenues.

Tax Revenues

Tax revenues were projected to be $2,521 billion in fiscal 2007. These revenues come from four sources:

1. Personal income taxes
2. Social security taxes
3. Corporate income taxes
4. Indirect taxes

TABLE 1   Federal Budget in Fiscal 2007

Item	Projections (Billions of Dollars)	
Tax Revenues	**2,521**	
Personal income taxes		1,098
Social security taxes		949
Corporate income taxes		297
Indirect taxes		177
Outlays	**2,891**	
Transfer payments		1,738
Expenditure on goods and services		837
Debt interest		316
Deficit	**370**	

Source: *Budget of the United States Government, Fiscal Year 2007*, Table 14.1.

The largest source of revenue is *personal income taxes*, which in 2007 are expected to be $1,098 billion. These taxes are paid by individuals on their incomes. The second largest source is *social security taxes*. These taxes are paid by workers and their employers to finance the government's social security programs. Third in size are *corporate income taxes*. These taxes are paid by companies on their profits. Finally, the smallest source of federal revenue is what are called *indirect taxes*. These taxes are on the sale of gasoline, alcoholic beverages, and a few other items.

Outlays

Outlays are classified in three categories:

1. Transfer payments
2. Expenditure on goods and services
3. Debt interest

The largest item of outlays, *transfer payments*, are payments to individuals, businesses, other levels of government, and the rest of the world. In 2007, this item is expected to be $1,738 billion. It includes Social Security benefits, Medicare and Medicaid, unemployment checks, welfare payments, farm subsidies, grants to state and local governments, aid to developing countries, and dues to international organizations such as the United Nations. Transfer payments, especially those for Medicare and Medicaid, are sources of persistent growth in government expenditures and are a major source of concern and political debate.

Expenditure on goods and services is the expenditure on final goods and services, and in 2007, it is expected to total $837 billion. This expenditure, which includes that on national defense, homeland security, research on cures for AIDS, computers for the Internal Revenue Service, government cars and trucks, federal highways, and dams, has decreased in recent years. This component of the federal budget is the *government expenditure on goods and services* that appears in the circular flow of expenditure and income and in the National Income and Product Accounts.

Debt interest is the interest on the government debt. In 2007, this item is expected to be $316 billion—about 10 percent of total expenditure. This interest payment is large because the government has a debt of more than $4 trillion, which has arisen from many years of budget deficits during the 1970s, 1980s, 1990s, and 2000s.

Surplus or Deficit

The government's budget balance is equal to tax revenues minus outlays.

Budget balance = Tax revenues − Outlays.

If tax revenues exceed outlays, the government has a **budget surplus**. If outlays exceed tax revenues, the government has a **budget deficit**. If tax revenues equal outlays, the government has a **balanced budget**. In fiscal 2007, with projected outlays of $2,891 billion and tax revenues of $2,521 billion, the government projected a budget deficit of $370 billion.

Big numbers like these are hard to visualize and hard to compare over time. To get a better sense of the magnitude of tax revenues, outlays, and the deficit, we often express them as percentages of GDP. Expressing them in this way lets us see how large government is relative to the size of the economy and also helps us to study *changes* in the scale of government over time.

How typical is the federal budget of 2007? Let's look at the recent history of the budget.

The Budget in Historical Perspective

Figure 2 shows the government's tax revenues, outlays, and budget surplus or deficit since 1980. Through 1997, there was a budget deficit. The federal government began running a deficit in 1970, and the 1983 deficit shown in the figure was the highest on record at 5.2 percent of GDP. The deficit declined through 1989 but climbed again during the 1990–1991 recession. During the 1990s expansion, the deficit gradually shrank, and in 1998, the first budget surplus since 1969 emerged. But by 2002, the budget was again in deficit.

Why did the budget deficit grow during the 1980s and vanish in the late 1990s? The answer lies in the changes in outlays and tax revenues. But which components of outlays and tax revenues changed to swell and then shrink the deficit? Let's look at tax revenues and outlays in a bit more detail.

FIGURE 2   The Budget Surplus and Deficit

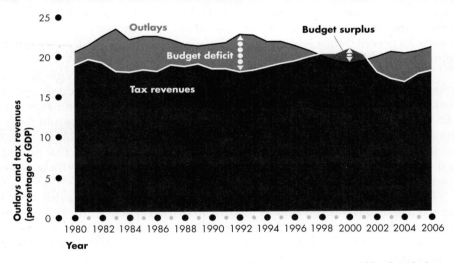

The figure records the federal government's outlays, tax revenues, and budget balance from 1980 to 2006. During the 1980s, a large and persistent budget deficit arose from the combination of falling tax revenues and rising outlays. In 1998, rising tax revenues and falling outlays (as percentages of GDP) created a budget surplus, but a deficit emerged again in 2002 as expenditure on security increased and taxes were cut.

Source: *Budget of the United States Government, Fiscal Year 2007*, Table 14.2.

Tax Revenues

Figure 3(a) shows the components of tax revenues as percentages of GDP from 1980 to 2006. Cuts in corporate and personal income taxes lowered total tax revenues between 1983 and 1986. The decline resulted from tax cuts that had been passed during 1981. From 1986 through 1991, tax revenues did not change much as a percentage of GDP. Personal income tax payments increased through the 1990s but fell sharply after 2000.

FIGURE 3   Federal Government Tax Revenues and Outlays

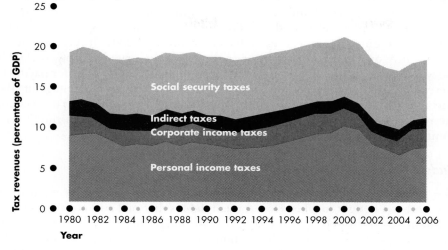

(a) Tax revenues

(b) Outlays

In part (a), revenues from personal and corporate income taxes as a percentage of GDP were approximately constant during the 1980s, increased during the 1990s, and decreased sharply from 2000 to 2004 but then increased again. The other components of tax revenues remained steady.

In part (b), expenditure on goods and services as a percentage of GDP decreased through 2001 but then increased because expenditure on security-related goods and services increased sharply after 2001. Transfer payments increased over the entire period. Debt interest held steady during the 1980s and decreased during the 1990s and 2000s, helped by a shrinking budget deficit during the 1990s and low interest rates during 2002 and 2003.

Source: *Budget of the United States Government, Fiscal Year 2007,* Table 14.2.

Outlays

Figure 3(b) shows the components of government outlays as percentages of GDP from 1980 to 2006. Total outlays decreased slightly through 1989, increased during the early 1990s, decreased steadily until 2000, and then increased again. Expenditure on goods and services decreased through 2001. It increased when expenditure on security-related goods and services increased sharply in 2002 in the wake of the attacks that occurred on September 11, 2001. Transfer payments increased over the entire period. Debt interest was a constant percentage of GDP during the 1980s and fell slightly during the late 1990s and 2000s. To understand the role of debt interest, we need to see the connection between the government's budget balance and debt.

Budget Balance and Debt

The government borrows when it has a budget deficit and makes repayments when it has a budget surplus. **Government debt** is the total amount that the government has borrowed. It is the sum of past budget deficits minus the sum of past budget surpluses. A government budget deficit increases government debt. A persistent budget deficit feeds itself: The budget deficit leads to increased borrowing; increased borrowing leads to larger interest payments; and larger interest payments lead to a larger deficit. That is the story of the increasing budget deficit during the 1970s and 1980s.

Figure 4 shows two measures of government debt since 1940. Gross debt includes the amounts that the government owes to future generations in social security payments. Net debt is the debt held by the public, and it excludes social security obligations.

FIGURE 4   The Federal Government Debt

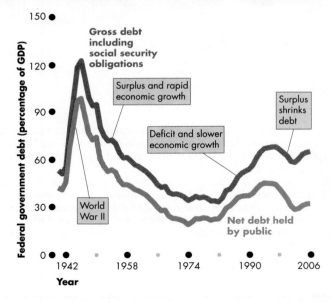

Gross and net government debt (the accumulation of past budget deficits less past budget surpluses) was at its highest at the end of World War II. Debt as a percentage of GDP fell through 1974 but then started to increase. After a further brief decline during the late 1970s, it exploded during the 1980s and continued to increase through 1995, after which it fell. After 2002, it began to rise again.

Source: Budget of the United States Government, Fiscal Year 2007, Table 7.1.

Government debt (as a percentage of GDP) was at an all-time high at the end of World War II. Budget surpluses and rapid economic growth lowered the debt-to-GDP ratio through 1974. Small budget deficits increased the debt-to-GDP ratio slightly through the 1970s, and large budget deficits increased it dramatically during the 1980s and the 1990–1991 recession. The growth rate of the debt-to-GDP ratio slowed as the economy expanded during the mid-1990s, fell when the budget went into surplus in the late 1990s and early 2000s, and began to rise again as the budget turned in deficit.

Debt and Capital

Businesses and individuals incur debts to buy capital—assets that yield a return. In fact, the main point of debt is to enable people to buy assets that will earn a return that exceeds the interest paid on the debt. The government is similar to individuals and businesses in this regard. Much government expenditure is on public assets that yield a return. Highways, major irrigation schemes, public schools and universities, public libraries, and the stock of national defense capital all yield a social rate of return that probably far exceeds the interest rate the government pays on its debt.

But total government debt, which exceeds $4 trillion, is four times the value of the government's capital stock. So some government debt has been incurred to finance public consumption expenditure and transfer payments, which do not have a social return. Future generations bear the cost of this debt.

How does the U.S. government budget balance compare with those in other countries?

The U.S. Government Budget in Global Perspective

Figure 5 places the U.S. government budget of 2006 in a global perspective. In that year, almost all countries had budget deficits. Summing the deficits of all the governments, the world as a whole had a deficit of 3 percent of world GDP—a total government deficit of close to $2 trillion.

The government of Japan had the largest deficit, as a percentage of GDP. The United States, Italy, and Germany came next, followed by the developing countries. Of the other advanced economies, the United Kingdom, France, and the entire European Union had large deficits.

Even the newly industrialized economies of Asia (Hong Kong, South Korea, Singapore, and Taiwan) had deficits. The other advanced countries as a group and Canada had surpluses in 2006.

State and Local Budgets

The *total government* sector of the United States includes state and local governments as well as the federal government. In 2005, when federal government outlays were about $2,500 billion, state and local outlays were almost $1,700 billion. Most of these expenditures were on public schools, colleges, and universities ($550 billion); local police and fire services; and roads.

It is the combination of federal, state, and local government tax revenues, outlays, and budget deficits that influences the economy. But state and local budgets are not designed to stabilize the aggregate economy or to make it more efficient. So sometimes, when the federal government cuts taxes or outlays, state and local governments do the reverse and, to a degree, cancel out the effects of the federal actions. For example, during 2001, when federal taxes began to decrease as a percentage of GDP, state and local taxes increased.

FIGURE 5   Government Budgets around the World in 2006

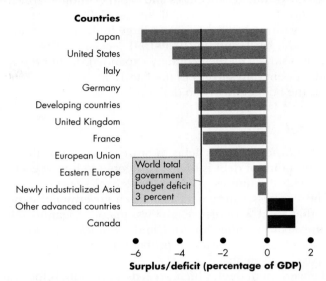

Countries

Japan
United States
Italy
Germany
Developing countries
United Kingdom
France
European Union
Eastern Europe
Newly industrialized Asia
Other advanced countries
Canada

World total government budget deficit 3 percent

Surplus/deficit (percentage of GDP)

−6   −4   −2   0   2

Governments in most countries had budget deficits in 2006. The largest ones were in Japan, followed by the United States, Italy, and Germany. The developing countries, the United Kingdom, and France also had large deficits. Other advanced economies and Canada had budget surpluses.

Source: International Monetary Fund, *World Economic Outlook*, April 2006.

Now that you know what the federal budget is and what the main components of tax revenues and outlay are, it is time to study the *effects* of fiscal policy. We'll begin by learning about the effects of taxes on employment, aggregate supply, and potential GDP. Then we'll study the effects of budget deficits and see how fiscal policy brings redistribution across generations. Finally, we'll look at the demand-side effects of fiscal policy and see how it provides a tool for stabilizing the business cycle.

OPTIONAL SEGMENT
ENDS

3

THE SUPPLY SIDE: EMPLOYMENT AND POTENTIAL GDP

Fiscal policy has important effects on employment, potential GDP, and aggregate supply that we'll now examine. These effects are known as **supply-side effects**, and economists who believe these effects to be large ones are generally referred to as *supply-siders*. To study these effects, we'll begin with a refresher on how full employment and potential GDP are determined in the absence of taxes. Then we'll introduce an income tax and see how it changes the economic outcome.

Full Employment and Potential GDP

At full employment, the real wage rate adjusts to make the quantity of labor demanded equal the quantity of labor supplied. Potential GDP is the real GDP that the full-employment quantity of labor produces.

FIGURE 6 The Effects of the Income Tax on Aggregate Supply

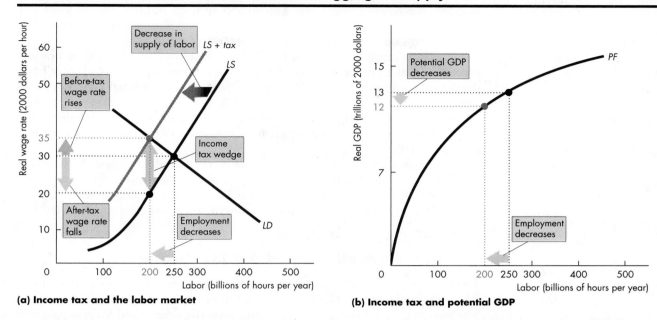

(a) Income tax and the labor market

(b) Income tax and potential GDP

In part (a), with no income tax, the real wage rate is $30 an hour and employment is 250 billion hours. In part (b), potential GDP is $13 trillion. An income tax shifts the supply of labor curve leftward to *LS* + *tax*. The before-tax wage rate rises to $35 an hour, the after-tax wage rate falls to $20 an hour, and the quantity of labor employed decreases to 200 billion hours. With less labor, potential GDP decreases.

Figure 6 illustrates a full-employment situation. In part (a), the demand for labor curve is *LD*, the supply of labor curve is *LS*. At a real wage rate of $30 an hour and 250 billion hours of labor a year employed, the economy is at full employment.

In Fig. 6(b), the production function is *PF*. When 250 billion hours of labor are employed, real GDP—which is also potential GDP—is $13 trillion.

Let's now see how an income tax changes potential GDP.

The Effects of the Income Tax

The tax on labor income influences potential GDP and aggregate supply by changing the full-employment quantity of labor. The income tax weakens the incentive to work and drives a wedge between the take-home wage of workers and the cost of labor to firms. The result is a smaller quantity of labor and a lower potential GDP.

Figure 6 shows this outcome. In the labor market, the income tax has no effect on the demand for labor, which remains at *LD*. The reason is that the quantity of labor that firms plan to hire depends only on how productive labor is and what it costs—its real wage rate.

But the supply of labor *does* change. With no income tax, the real wage rate is $30 an hour and 250 billion hours of labor a year are employed. An income tax weakens the incentive to work and decreases the supply of labor. The reason is that for each dollar of before-tax earnings, workers must pay the government an amount determined by the income tax code. So workers look at the after-tax wage rate when they decide how much labor to supply. An income tax shifts the supply curve leftward to *LS* + *tax*. The vertical distance between the *LS* curve and the *LS* + *tax* curve measures the amount of income tax. With the smaller supply of labor, the *before-tax* wage rate rises to $35 an hour but the *after-tax* wage rate falls to $20 an hour. The gap created between the before-tax and after-tax wage rates is called the **tax wedge**.

The new equilibrium quantity of labor employed is 200 billion hours a year—less than in the no-tax case. Because the full-employment quantity of labor decreases, so does potential GDP. And a decrease in potential GDP decreases aggregate supply.

In this example, the tax rate is high—$15 tax on a $35 wage rate, about 43 percent. A lower tax rate would have a smaller effect on employment and potential GDP.

An increase in the tax rate to above 43 percent would decrease the supply of labor by more than the decrease shown in Fig. 6. Equilibrium employment and potential GDP would also decrease still further. A tax cut would increase the supply of labor, increase equilibrium employment, and increase potential GDP.

Taxes on Expenditure and the Tax Wedge

The tax wedge that we've just considered is only a part of the wedge that affects labor-supply decisions. Taxes on consumption expenditure add to the wedge. The reason is that a tax on consumption raises the prices paid for consumption goods and services and is equivalent to a cut in the real wage rate.

The incentive to supply labor depends on the goods and services that an hour of labor can buy. The higher the taxes on goods and services and the lower the after-tax wage rate, the less is the incentive to supply labor. If the income tax rate is 25 percent and the tax rate on consumption expenditure is 10 percent, a dollar earned buys only 65 cents worth of goods and services. The tax wedge is 35 percent.

Some Real World Tax Wedges

Edward C. Prescott of Arizona State University, who shared the 2004 Nobel Prize for Economic Science, has estimated the tax wedges for a number of countries. The U.S. tax wedge is a combination of 13 percent tax on consumption and 32 percent tax on incomes. The income tax rate includes Social Security taxes and is a *marginal* tax rate.

Among the industrial countries, the U.S. tax wedge is relatively small. Prescott estimates that in France, taxes on consumption are 33 percent and taxes on incomes are 49 percent. The estimates for the United Kingdom fall between those for the United States and France. Figure 7 shows these components of the tax wedges in the three countries.

Does the Tax Wedge Matter?

According to Prescott's estimates, the tax wedge has a powerful effect on employment and potential GDP. Potential GDP in France is 14 percent below that of the United States (per person), and the entire difference can be attributed to the difference in the tax wedge in the two countries.

Potential GDP in the United Kingdom is 41 percent below that of the United States (per person), and about a third of the difference arises from the different tax wedges. (The rest is due to different productivities.)

FIGURE 7   Three Tax Wedges

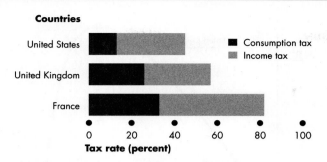

Tax rates are much higher in France and the United Kingdom than in the United States and can account for much of the difference in potential GDP per person.

Source: Edward C. Prescott, *American Economic Review*, 2003.

Tax Revenues and the Laffer Curve

An interesting consequence of the effect of a tax on employment is that a higher tax *rate* does not always bring greater tax *revenue*. A higher tax rate brings in more revenue per dollar earned. But because a higher tax rate decreases the number of dollars earned, two forces operate in opposite directions on the tax revenue collected.

The relationship between the tax rate and the amount of tax revenue collected is called the **Laffer curve**. The curve is so named because Arthur B. Laffer, a member of President Reagan's Economic Policy Advisory Board, drew such a curve on a table napkin and launched the idea that tax *cuts* could *increase* tax revenue.

Figure 8 shows a Laffer curve. The tax *rate* is on the *x*-axis, and total tax *revenue* is on the *y*-axis. For tax rates below *T**, an increase in the tax rate increases tax revenue; at *T**, tax revenue is maximized; and a tax rate increase above *T**, decreases tax revenue.

Most people think that the United States is on the upward-sloping part of the Laffer curve. So is the United Kingdom. But France might be close to the maximum point or perhaps even beyond it.

The Supply-Side Debate

Before 1980, few economists paid attention to the supply-side effects of taxes on employment and potential GDP. Then, when Ronald Reagan took office as President, a group of supply-siders began to argue the virtues of cutting taxes. Arthur Laffer was one of them. Laffer and his supporters were not held in high esteem among mainstream economists, but they were influential for a period. They correctly argued that tax cuts would increase employment and increase output. But they incorrectly argued that tax cuts would increase tax revenues and decrease the budget deficit. For this prediction to be correct, the United States would have had to be on the "wrong" side of the Laffer curve. Given that U.S. tax rates are among the lowest in the industrial world, it is unlikely that this condition was met. And when the Reagan administration did cut taxes, the budget deficit increased, a fact that reinforces this view.

FIGURE 8   A Laffer Curve

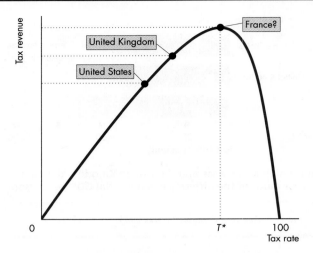

A Laffer curve shows the relationship between the tax rate and tax revenues. For tax rates below T^*, an increase in the tax rate increases tax revenue. At the tax rate T^*, tax revenue is maximized. For tax rates above T^*, an increase in the tax rate decreases tax revenue.

Supply-side economics became tarnished because of its association with Laffer and came to be called "voodoo economics." But mainstream economists, including Martin Feldstein, a Harvard professor who was Reagan's chief economic advisor, recognized the power of tax cuts as incentives but took the standard view that tax cuts without spending cuts would swell the budget deficit and bring serious further problems. This view is now widely accepted by economists of all political persuasions.

You now know the effects of taxes on potential GDP. The effects that we've studied influence the *level* of real GDP but not its *growth rate*. We're now going to look at the effects of taxes and the budget deficit on saving and investment, which in turn influence the pace of economic growth.

4   THE SUPPLY SIDE: INVESTMENT, SAVING, AND ECONOMIC GROWTH

Investment is financed by national saving and borrowing from the rest of the world, and the real interest rate adjusts in the loanable funds market to coordinate saving and lending and investment and borrowing plans. Investment increases the capital stock and contributes to real GDP growth.

We're now going to see how a government budget deficit changes the equilibrium in the loanable funds market. We'll begin by reviewing the sources of investment finance.

The Sources of Investment Finance

GDP equals the sum of consumption expenditure, C, investment, I, government expenditure on goods and services, G, and net exports, $(X - M)$. That is,

$$GDP = C + I + G + (X - M).$$

GDP also equals the sum of consumption expenditure, saving, S, and net taxes, T. That is,

$$GDP = C + S + T.$$

By combining these two ways of looking at GDP, you can see that

$$I + G + (X - M) = S + T$$

or

$$I = S + (T - G) + (M - X).$$

This equation tells us that investment, I, is financed by saving, S, government saving, $T - G$, and borrowing from the rest of the world, $(M - X)$. Saving and borrowing from the rest of the world are the private sources of saving, PS, and

$$PS = S + (M - X).$$

Investment is equal to the sum of private saving and government saving. That is,

$$I = PS + (T - G).$$

► If T exceeds G, the government sector has a budget surplus and government saving is positive.

► If G exceeds T, the government sector has a budget deficit and government saving is negative.

When the government sector has a budget surplus, it contributes toward financing investment. But when the government sector has a budget deficit, it competes with businesses for private saving.

Figure 9 shows the sources of investment finance in the United States from 1973 to 2005. It shows that during the 1990s, a sharp increase in investment was financed by an increase in borrowing from the rest of the world and a decrease in the government deficit. During the 2000s, private saving and borrowing from the rest of the world financed both investment and a growing government deficit.

Fiscal policy influences investment and saving in two ways:

► Taxes affect the incentive to save and change the supply of loanable funds.

► Government saving—the budget surplus or deficit—is a component of total saving and the supply of loanable funds.

FIGURE 9   **Financing U.S. Investment**

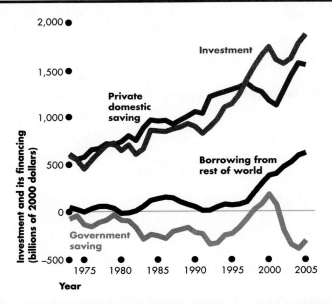

During the 1990s, rising U.S. investment was financed by a rise in borrowing from the rest of the world and a fall in the budget deficit. During the 2000s, U.S. investment and a rising budget deficit were financed by a surge in borrowing from the rest of the world and a rise in private saving.

Sources: Bureau of Economic Analysis and Office of Management and Budget.

Taxes and the Incentive to Save

A tax on interest income weakens the incentive to save and drives a wedge between the after-tax interest rate earned by savers and the interest rate paid by firms. These effects are analogous to those of a tax on labor income. But they are more serious for two reasons.

First, a tax on labor income lowers the quantity of labor employed and lowers potential GDP, while a tax on capital income lowers the quantity of saving and investment and *slows the growth rate of real GDP*. A tax on capital income creates a Lucas wedge—an ever widening gap between potential GDP and the potential GDP that might have been.

Second, the true tax rate on interest income is much higher than that on labor income because of the way in which inflation and taxes on interest income interact. We'll examine this interaction before we study the effects of taxes on saving and investment.

Tax Rate on Real Interest Rate

The interest rate that influences investment and saving plans is the *real after-tax interest rate*. The real *after-tax* interest rate subtracts the income tax paid on interest income from the real interest rate. But the taxes depend on the nominal interest rate, not the real interest rate. So the higher the inflation rate, the higher is the true tax rate on interest income. Here is an example. Suppose the real interest rate is 4 percent a year and the tax rate is 40 percent.

If there is no inflation, the nominal interest rate equals the real interest rate. The tax on 4 percent interest is 1.6 percent (40 percent of 4 percent), so the real after-tax interest rate is 4 percent minus 1.6 percent, which equals 2.4 percent.

If the inflation rate is 6 percent a year, the nominal interest rate is 10 percent. The tax on 10 percent interest is 4 percent (40 percent of 10 percent), so the real after-tax interest rate is 4 percent minus 4 percent, which equals zero. The true tax rate in this case is not 40 percent but 100 percent!

Effect of Income Tax on Saving and Investment

In Fig. 10, initially there are no taxes. Also, the government has a balanced budget. The demand for loanable funds curve, which is also the investment demand curve, is *DLF*. The supply of loanable funds curve, which is also the saving supply curve, is *SLF*. The equilibrium interest rate is 3 percent a year, and the quantity of funds borrowed and lent is $2 trillion a year.

FIGURE 10   The Effects of a Tax on Capital Income

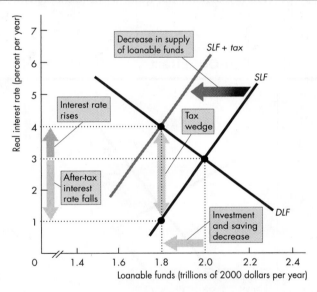

The demand for loanable funds and investment demand curve is *DLF*, and the supply of loanable funds and saving supply curve is *SLF*. With no income tax, the real interest rate is 3 percent a year and investment is $2 trillion. An income tax shifts the supply curve leftward to *SLF + tax*. The interest rate rises to 4 percent a year, the after-tax interest rate falls to 1 percent a year, and investment decreases to $1.8 trillion. With less investment, the real GDP growth rate decreases.

A tax on interest income has no effect on the demand for loanable funds. The quantity of investment and borrowing that firms plan to undertake depends only on how productive capital is and what it costs—its real interest rate. But a tax on interest income weakens the incentive to save and lend and decreases the supply of loanable funds. For each dollar of before-tax earnings, savers must pay the government an amount determined by the tax code. So savers look at the after-tax real interest rate when they decide how much to save.

When a tax is imposed, saving decreases and the supply of loanable funds curve shifts leftward to *SLF + tax*. The amount of tax payable is measured by the vertical distance between the *SLF* curve and the *SLF + tax* curve. With this smaller supply of loanable funds, the interest rate rises to 4 percent a year but the *after-tax* interest rate falls to 1 percent a year. A tax wedge is driven between the interest rate and the after-tax interest rate, and the equilibrium quantity of loanable funds decreases. Saving and investment also decrease.

The effects of the income tax on saving and investment are likely to be large. And at a high inflation rate, these effects are likely to be especially large.

You've seen how taxes affect private saving. Let's now see how government saving affects the loanable funds market.

Government Saving

Government saving is positive when the government has a budget surplus, negative when it has a budget deficit, and zero when it has a balanced budget.

In Fig. 11, *DLF* is the demand of loanable funds curve. The curve labeled *PSLF* is the *private* supply of loanable funds generated by private saving. With a balanced government budget, the *PSLF* curve is the market supply curve, the real interest rate is 4 percent a year, and the quantity of loanable funds, saving, and investment are $1.8 trillion a year.

FIGURE 11   A Crowding-Out Effect

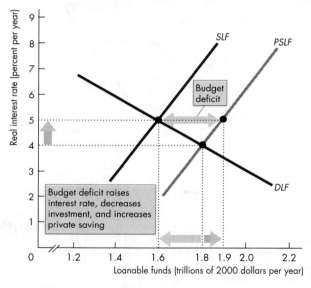

The demand for loanable funds curve is *DLF*, and the private supply of loanable funds is *PSLF*. With a balanced government budget, the real interest rate is 4 percent a year and investment is $1.8 trillion a year. A government budget deficit is negative government saving (dissaving). We subtract the budget deficit from private saving to determine the supply of loanable funds curve *SLF*. The real interest rate rises, investment decreases (is crowded out), and private saving increases.

When the government has a budget deficit, we must subtract the budget deficit from private saving to find the supply of loanable funds—the curve labeled *SLF*. The horizontal distance between the *PSLF* curve and the *SLF* curve is government saving, which in this example is a negative $0.3 trillion. (This number, like all the other numbers in Fig. 11, is similar to the actual value in the United States in 2006.)

The effect of negative government saving, which is also called *dissaving*, is to decrease the supply of loanable funds and increase the real interest rate. The quantity of loanable funds demanded and the investment that it finances decrease. In Fig. 11, with a government deficit of $0.3 trillion, the supply of loanable funds curve shifts leftward and the real interest rate rises from 4 percent to 5 percent a year. The equilibrium quantity of borrowing and investment decrease from $1.8 trillion to $1.6 trillion. Investment does not decrease by the full amount of the government deficit because the higher real interest rate induces an increase in private saving. In Fig. 11, private saving increases by $0.1 trillion to $1.9 trillion.

The tendency for a government budget deficit to decrease investment is called a **crowding-out effect**. By raising the real interest rate, the government budget deficit crowds out private investment. A government budget surplus has the opposite effect to what we've just seen. It increases the supply of loanable funds, lowers the real interest rate, and increases investment.

In the crowding-out case, the *quantity of private saving* changes because the real interest rate changes. There is a movement along the *PSLF* curve. But the private supply of loanable funds does not change. That is, the *PSLF* curve does not shift. But suppose that a change in government saving changes private saving and shifts the *PSLF* curve. This possibility is called the Ricardo-Barro effect, so named because it was first suggested by the English economist David Ricardo in the eighteenth century and refined by Robert J. Barro of Harvard University during the 1970s and 1980s. **Ricardo-Barro equivalence** is the proposition that taxes and government borrowing are equivalent—budget deficit has no effect on the real interest rate or investment.

The reasoning behind Ricardo-Barro equivalence is the following. A government that has a budget deficit must sell bonds to pay for the goods and services that are not paid for by taxes. And the government must pay interest on those bonds. It must also collect more taxes *in the future* to pay the interest on the larger quantity of bonds that are outstanding. Taxpayers are rational and have good foresight. They can see that their taxes will be higher in the future and so their disposable income will be lower. Lower expected future disposable income increases saving. And if taxpayers want to neutralize the effects of the budget deficit on their own consumption plans, they increase their own saving by the same amount that the government is dissaving through its deficit.

This outcome is extreme and probably does not actually occur. Taxpayers probably respond in the *direction* suggested by Ricardo and Barro but not in the *amount* they suggest. So the effect of a budget deficit probably lies between the case shown in Fig. 11 and the Ricardo-Barro case. A budget deficit increases the real interest rate and partly crowds out private investment, but it also induces an increase in private saving in anticipation of higher future taxes.

You now know how a government budget deficit influences saving and investment. Because a budget deficit crowds out investment, it slows the growth rate of real GDP. Next we'll look at the effects of fiscal policy on intergenerational redistribution.

GENERATIONAL EFFECTS OF FISCAL POLICY   5

Is a budget deficit a burden on future generations? If it is, how will the burden be borne? And is the budget deficit the only burden on future generations? What about the deficit in the Social Security fund? Does it matter who owns the bonds that the government sells to finance its deficit? What about the bonds owned by foreigners? Won't repaying those bonds impose a bigger burden than repaying bonds owned by Americans?

To answer questions like these, we use a tool called **generational accounting**— an accounting system that measures the lifetime tax burden and benefits of each generation. This accounting system was developed by Alan Auerbach of the University of Pennsylvania and Laurence Kotlikoff of Boston University. Generational accounts for the United States have been prepared by Jagadeesh Gokhale of the Federal Reserve Bank of Cleveland and Kent Smetters of the University of Pennsylvania.

Generational Accounting and Present Value

Income taxes and social security taxes are paid by people who have jobs. Social security benefits are paid to people after they retire. So to compare taxes and benefits, we must compare the value of taxes paid by people during their working years with the benefits received in their retirement years. To compare the value of an amount of money at one date with that at a later date, we use the concept of present value. A **present value** is an amount of money that, if invested today, will grow to equal a given future amount when the interest that it earns is taken into account. We can compare dollars today with dollars in 2030 or any other future year by using present values.

For example, if the interest rate is 5 percent a year, $1,000 invested today will grow, with interest, to $11,467 after 50 years. So the present value (in 2006) of $11,467 in 2056 is $1,000.

By using present values, we can assess the magnitude of the government's debts to older Americans in the form of pensions and medical benefits.

But the assumed interest rate and growth rate of taxes and benefits critically influence the answers we get. For example, at an interest rate of 3 percent a year, the present value (in 2006) of $11,467 in 2056 is $2,616. The lower the interest rate, the greater is the present value of a given future amount.

Because there is uncertainty about the proper interest rate to use to calculate present values, plausible alternative numbers are used to estimate a range of present values.

Using generational accounting and present values, economists have studied the situation facing the federal government arising from its social security obligations. And they have found a time bomb!

The Social Security Time Bomb

When social security was introduced in the New Deal of the 1930s, today's demographic situation was not envisaged. The age distribution of the U.S. population today is dominated by the surge in the birth rate after World War II that created what is called the "baby boom generation." There are 77 million "baby boomers."

In 2008, the first of the baby boomers will start collecting Social Security pensions and in 2011, they will become eligible for Medicare benefits. By 2030, all the baby boomers will have retired and, compared to 2006, the population supported by social security will have doubled.

Under the existing Social Security laws, the federal government has an obligation to these citizens to pay pensions and Medicare benefits on an already declared scale. These obligations are a debt owed by the government and are just as real as the bonds that the government issues to finance its current budget deficit.

To assess the full extent of the government's obligations, economists use the concept of fiscal imbalance. **Fiscal imbalance** is the present value of the government's commitments to pay benefits minus the present value of its tax revenues. Fiscal imbalance is an attempt to measure the scale of the government's true liabilities.

Gokhale and Smetters estimated that the fiscal imbalance was $45 trillion in 2003. (Using alternative assumptions about interest rates and growth rates, the number might be as low as $29 trillion or as high as $65 trillion.) To put the $45 trillion in perspective, note that U.S. GDP in 2003 was $11 trillion. So the fiscal imbalance was 4 times the value of one year's production.

How can the federal government meet its social security obligations? Gokhale and Smetters consider four alternative fiscal policy changes that might be made:

▶ Raise income taxes

▶ Raise social security taxes

▶ Cut social security benefits

▶ Cut federal government discretionary spending

They estimated that starting in 2003 and making only one of these changes, income taxes would need to be raised by 69 percent, or social security taxes raised by 95 percent, or social security benefits cut by 56 percent. Even if the government stopped all its discretionary spending, including that on national defense, it would not be able to pay its bills.

Of course, by combining the four measures, the pain from each could be lessened. But the pain would still be severe. And worse, delay makes all these numbers rise. With no action, the fiscal imbalance climbs from the $45 trillion of 2003 to $54 trillion in 2008.

Generational Imbalance

A fiscal imbalance must eventually be corrected and when it is, people either pay higher taxes or receive lower benefits. The concept of generational imbalance tells us who will pay. **Generational imbalance** is the division of the fiscal imbalance between the current and future generations, assuming that the current generation will enjoy the existing levels of taxes and benefits.

Figure 12 shows an estimate of how the fiscal imbalance is distributed across the current (born before 1988) and future (born in or after 1988) generations. It also shows that the major source of the imbalances is Medicare. Social Security pension benefits create a fiscal imbalance, but these benefits will be more than fully paid for by the current generation. But the current generation will pay less than 50 percent of its Medicare costs, and the balance will fall on future generations. If we sum all the items, the current generation will pay 43 percent and future generations will pay 57 percent of the fiscal imbalance.

Because the estimated fiscal imbalance is so large, it is not possible to predict how it will be resolved. But we can predict that the outcome will involve both lower benefits and higher taxes. One of these taxes could be the inflation tax—paying bills with new money and creating inflation. But the Fed will resist inflation being used to deal with the imbalance, as you will see in the reading on monetary policy.

FIGURE 12   Fiscal and Generational Imbalances

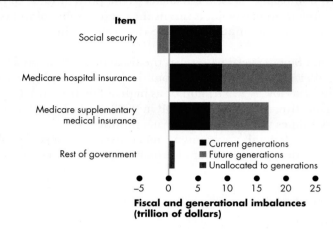

The bars show the scale of the fiscal imbalance. The largest component is the more than $20 trillion of Medicare benefits. These benefits are also the main component of the generational imbalance. Social security pensions are paid for entirely by the current generation.

Source: Jagadeesh Gokhale and Kent Smetters, *Fiscal and Generational Imbalances: New Budget Measures for New Budget Priorities*, Washington, D.C.: The AEI Press, April 2003.

International Debt

So far in our discussion of government deficits and debts, we've ignored the role played by the rest of the world. We'll conclude this discussion by considering the role and magnitude of international debt.

You've seen that borrowing from the rest of the world is one source of investment finance. And you've also seen that this source of investment finance became larger during the late 1990s and 2000s.

How large is the contribution of the rest of the world? How much investment have we paid for by borrowing from the rest of the world? And how much U.S. government debt is held abroad?

Table 2 answers these questions. In June 2006, the United States had a net debt to the rest of the world of $5.2 trillion. Of that debt, $2.2 trillion was U.S. government debt. U.S. corporations had used $4.4 trillion of foreign funds ($2.1 trillion in bonds and $2.3 trillion in equities). More than half of the outstanding government debt is held by foreigners.

The international debt of the United States is important because, when that debt is repaid, the United States will transfer real resources to the rest of the world. Instead of running a large net exports deficit, the United States will need a surplus of exports over imports. To make a surplus possible, U.S. saving must increase and consumption must decrease. Some tough choices lie ahead.

You now know how economists assess fiscal imbalance and how they divide the cost of covering an imbalance across generations. And you've seen the extent and implication of U.S. debt held in the rest of the world. We conclude this reading by looking at fiscal policy as a tool for stabilizing the business cycle.

TABLE 2	What the United States Owed the Rest of the World in June 2006

	$ Trillions
(a) U.S. Liabilities	
Deposits in U.S. banks	0.8
U.S. government securities	2.2
U.S. corporate bonds	2.1
U.S. corporate equities	2.3
Other (net)	–2.2
Total	5.2
(b) U.S. Government Securities	
Held by rest of world	2.2
Held in the United States	1.9
Total	4.1

Source: Federal Reserve Board.

STABILIZING THE BUSINESS CYCLE

6

Fiscal policy actions influence both aggregate supply and aggregate demand. Policies that seek to stabilize the business cycle work by changing aggregate demand.

▶ Discretionary or
▶ Automatic

A fiscal action initiated by an act of Congress is called **discretionary fiscal policy**. It requires a change in a spending program or in a tax law. For example, an increase in defense spending or a cut in the income tax rate is a discretionary fiscal policy.

A fiscal action that is triggered by the state of the economy is called **automatic fiscal policy**. For example, an increase in unemployment induces an increase in payments to the unemployed. A fall in incomes induces a decrease in tax revenues.

Changes in government expenditure and changes in taxes have multiplier effects on aggregate demand, which we'll now study.

Government Expenditure Multiplier

The **government expenditure multiplier** is the magnification effect of a change in government expenditure on goods and services on aggregate demand. Government expenditure is a component of aggregate expenditure, so when government expenditure changes, aggregate demand changes. Real GDP changes and induces a change in consumption expenditure, which brings a further change in aggregate expenditure. A multiplier process ensues.

A Homeland Security Multiplier

The terrorist attacks of September 11, 2001, brought a reappraisal of the nation's homeland security requirements and an increase in government expenditure. This increase initially increased the incomes of producers of airport and border security equipment and security workers. Better-off security workers increased their consumption expenditure. With rising revenues, other businesses in all parts of the nation boomed and expanded their payrolls. A second round of increased consumption expenditure increased incomes yet further. This multiplier effect helped to end the 2001 recession.

The Autonomous Tax Multiplier

The **autonomous tax multiplier** is the magnification effect of a change in autonomous taxes on aggregate demand. A *decrease* in taxes *increases* disposable income, which increases consumption expenditure. A decrease in taxes works like an increase in government expenditure. But the magnitude of the autonomous tax multiplier is smaller than the government expenditure multiplier. The reason is that a $1 tax cut generates *less than* $1 of additional expenditure. The marginal propensity to consume determines the increase in consumption expenditure induced by a tax cut. For example, if the marginal propensity to consume is 0.75, then a $1 tax cut increases consumption expenditure by only 75 cents. In this case, the tax multiplier is 0.75 times the magnitude of the government expenditure multiplier.

A Bush Tax Cut Multiplier

Congress enacted the Bush tax cut package that lowered taxes starting in 2002. These tax cuts had a multiplier effect. With more disposable income, people increased consumption expenditure. This spending increased other people's incomes, which spurred yet more consumption expenditure. Like the increase in security expenditures, the tax cut and its multiplier effect helped to end the 2001 recession.

The Balanced Budget Multiplier

The **balanced budget multiplier** is the magnification effect on aggregate demand of a *simultaneous* change in government expenditure and taxes that leaves the budget balance unchanged. The balanced budget multiplier is positive because a $1 increase in government expenditure increases aggregate demand by more than a $1 increase in taxes decreases aggregate demand. So when both government expenditure and taxes increase by $1, aggregate demand increases.

Discretionary Fiscal Stabilization

If real GDP is below potential GDP, discretionary fiscal policy might be used in an attempt to restore full employment. The government might increase its expenditure on goods and services, cut taxes, or do some of both. These actions would increase aggregate demand. If they were timed correctly and were of the correct magnitude, they could restore full employment. Figure 13 shows how. Potential GDP is $12 trillion, but real GDP is below potential at $11 trillion and

FIGURE 13   Expansionary Fiscal Policy

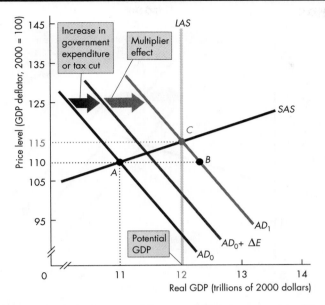

Potential GDP is $12 trillion, real GDP is $11 trillion, and there is a $1 trillion recessionary gap. An increase in government expenditure or a tax cut increases expenditure by ΔE. The multiplier increases induced expenditure. The AD curve shifts rightward to AD_1, the price level rises to 115, real GDP increases to $12 trillion, and the recessionary gap is eliminated.

there is a $1 trillion *recessionary gap* (see the reading on aggregate supply and aggregate demand). To restore full employment, the government takes a discretionary fiscal policy action. An increase in government expenditure or a tax cut increases aggregate expenditure by ΔE. If this were the only change in spending plans, the AD curve would become $AD_0 + \Delta E$ in Fig. 13. But the fiscal policy action sets off a multiplier process, which increases consumption expenditure. As the multiplier process plays out, aggregate demand increases further and the AD curve shifts rightward to AD_1.

With no change in the price level, the economy would move from point A to point B on AD_1. But the increase in aggregate demand combined with the upward-sloping SAS curve brings a rise in the price level. The economy moves to point C, and the economy returns to full employment.

Figure 14 illustrates the opposite case in which discretionary fiscal policy is used to eliminate inflationary pressure. The government decreases its expenditure on goods and services or raises taxes to decrease aggregate demand. In the figure, the fiscal policy action decreases aggregate expenditure by ΔE and the AD curve shifts to $AD_0 - \Delta E$. The initial decrease in aggregate expenditure sets off a multiplier process, which decreases consumption expenditure. The multiplier process decreases aggregate demand further and the AD curve shifts leftward to AD_1.

With no change in the price level, the economy would move from point A to point B on AD_1 in Fig. 14. But the decrease in aggregate demand combined with the upward-sloping SAS curve brings a fall in the price level. So the economy moves to point C, where the inflationary gap has been eliminated, inflation has been avoided, and the economy is back at full employment.

FIGURE 14   Contractionary Fiscal Policy

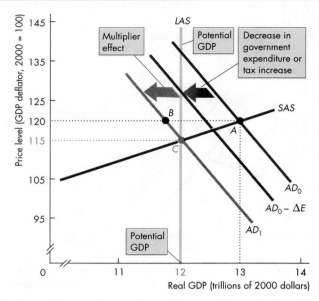

Potential GDP is $12 trillion, real GDP is $13 trillion, and there is a $1 trillion inflationary gap. A decrease in government expenditure or a rise in taxes decreases expenditure by ΔE. The multiplier decreases induced expenditure. The AD curve shifts leftward to AD_1, the price level falls to 115, real GDP decreases to $12 trillion, and the inflationary gap is eliminated.

Figures 13 and 14 make fiscal policy look easy: Calculate the recessionary gap or the inflationary gap and the multiplier, change government expenditure or taxes, and eliminate the gap. In reality, things are not that easy.

Limitations of Discretionary Fiscal Policy

The use of discretionary fiscal policy is seriously hampered by three time lags:

► Recognition lag
► Law-making lag
► Impact lag

Recognition Lag

The recognition lag is the time it takes to figure out that fiscal policy actions are needed. This process has two aspects: assessing the current state of the economy and forecasting its future state.

Law-Making Lag

The law-making lag is the time it takes Congress to pass the laws needed to change taxes or spending. This process takes time because each member of Congress has a different idea about what is the best tax or spending program to change, so long debates and committee meetings are needed to reconcile conflicting views. The economy might benefit from fiscal stimulation today, but by the time Congress acts, a different fiscal medicine is needed.

Impact Lag

The impact lag is the time it takes from passing a tax or spending change to its effects on real GDP being felt. This lag depends partly on the speed with which government agencies can act and partly on the timing of changes in spending plans by households and businesses.

Economic forecasting has improved in recent years, but it remains inexact and subject to error. So because of these three time lags, discretionary fiscal action might end up moving real GDP *away* from potential GDP and creating the very problems it seeks to correct.

Let's now look at automatic fiscal policy.

Automatic Stabilizers

Automatic fiscal policy is a consequence of tax revenues and outlays that fluctuate with real GDP. These features of fiscal policy are called **automatic stabilizers** because they work to stabilize real GDP without explicit action by the government. Their name is borrowed from engineering and conjures up images of shock absorbers, thermostats, and sophisticated devices that keep airplanes and ships steady in turbulent air and seas.

Induced Taxes

On the revenues side of the budget, tax laws define tax *rates*, not tax *dollars*. Tax dollars paid depend on tax rates and incomes. But incomes vary with real GDP, so tax revenues depend on real GDP. Taxes that vary with real GDP are called **induced taxes**. When real GDP increases in an expansion, wages and profits rise, so the taxes on these incomes—induced taxes—rise. When real GDP decreases in a recession, wages and profits fall, so the induced taxes on these incomes fall.

Needs-Tested Spending

On the outlays side of the budget, the government creates programs that pay benefits to suitably qualified people and businesses. The spending on such programs is called **needs-tested spending**, and it results in transfer payments that depend on the economic state of individual citizens and businesses. When the economy is in a recession, unemployment is high and the number of people experiencing economic hardship increases, and needs-tested spending on unemployment benefits and food stamps also increases. When the economy expands, unemployment falls, the number of people experiencing economic hardship decreases, and needs-tested spending decreases.

Induced taxes and needs-tested spending decrease the multiplier effects of changes in autonomous expenditure (such as investment and exports). So they moderate both expansions and recessions and make real GDP more stable. They achieve this outcome by weakening the link between real GDP and disposable income and so reduce the effect of a change in real GDP on consumption expenditure. When real GDP increases, induced taxes increase and needs-tested spending decreases, so disposable income does not increase by as much as the increase in real GDP. As a result, consumption expenditure does not increase by as much as it otherwise would and the multiplier effect is reduced.

We can see the effects of automatic stabilizers by looking at the way in which the government budget deficit fluctuates over the business cycle.

FIGURE 15 The Business Cycle and the Budget Deficit

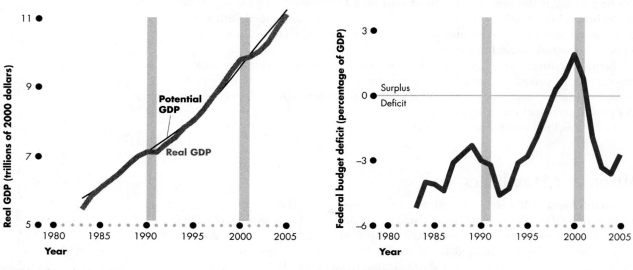

(a) Growth and recessions

(b) Federal budget deficit

As real GDP fluctuates around potential GDP (part a), the budget deficit fluctuates (part b). During a recession (shaded years), tax revenues decrease, transfer payments increase, and the budget deficit increases. The deficit also increases *before* a recession as real GDP growth slows and *after* a recession before real GDP growth speeds up.

Sources: Bureau of Economic Analysis, Congressional Budget Office, and Office of Management and the Budget.

Budget Deficit over the Business Cycle

Figure 15 shows the business cycle in part (a) and fluctuations in the budget deficit in part (b) between 1983 and 2005. Both parts highlight recessions by shading those periods. By comparing the two parts of the figure, you can see the relationship between the business cycle and the budget deficit. When the economy is in an expansion, the budget deficit declines. (In the figure, a declining deficit means a deficit that is getting closer to zero.) As the expansion slows before the recession begins, the budget deficit increases. It continues to increase during the recession and for a period after the recession is over. Then, when the expansion is well under way, the budget deficit declines again.

The budget deficit fluctuates with the business cycle because both tax revenues and outlays fluctuate with real GDP. As real GDP increases during an expansion, tax revenues increase and transfer payments decrease, so the budget deficit automatically decreases. As real GDP decreases during a recession, tax revenues decrease and transfer payments increase, so the budget deficit automatically increases. Fluctuations in investment and exports have a multiplier effect on real GDP. But fluctuations in the budget deficit decrease the swings in disposable income and make the multiplier effect smaller. They dampen both expansions and recessions.

Cyclical and Structural Balances

Because the government budget balance fluctuates with the business cycle, we need a method of measuring the balance that tells us whether it is a temporary cyclical phenomenon or a persistent phenomenon. A temporary cyclical surplus or deficit vanishes when full employment returns. A persistent surplus or deficit requires government action to remove it.

FIGURE 16   Cyclical and Structural Surpluses and Deficits

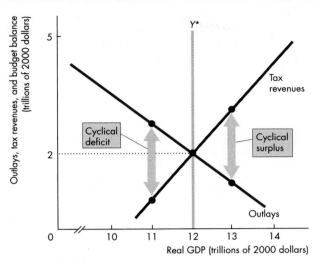

(a) Cyclical deficit and cyclical surplus

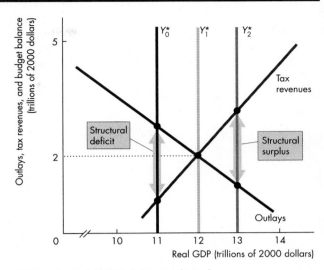

(b) Structural deficit and structural surplus

In part (a), potential GDP is $12 trillion. When real GDP is less than potential GDP, the budget is in a *cyclical deficit*. When real GDP exceeds potential GDP, the budget is in a *cyclical surplus*. The government has a *balanced budget* when real GDP equals potential GDP. In part (b), if real GDP and potential GDP are $11 trillion, there is a *structural deficit*. But if real GDP and potential GDP are $13 trillion, there is a *structural surplus*.

To determine whether the budget balance is persistent or temporary and cyclical, economists have developed the concepts of the structural budget balance and the cyclical budget balance. The **structural surplus or deficit** is the budget balance that would occur if the economy were at full employment and real GDP were equal to potential GDP. The **cyclical surplus or deficit** is the actual surplus or deficit minus the structural surplus or deficit. That is, the cyclical surplus or deficit is the part of the budget balance that arises purely because real GDP does not equal potential GDP. For example, suppose that the budget deficit is $100 billion. And suppose that economists have determined that there is a structural deficit of $25 billion. Then there is a cyclical deficit of $75 billion.

Figure 16 illustrates the concepts of the cyclical surplus or deficit and the structural surplus or deficit. The dark blue curve shows government outlays. The outlays curve slopes downward because transfer payments, a component of government outlays, decreases as real GDP increases. The dark gray curve shows tax revenues. The tax revenues curve slopes upward because most components of tax revenues increase as incomes and real GDP increase.

In Fig. 16(a), potential GDP is $12 trillion. If real GDP equals potential GDP, the government has a *balanced budget*. Outlays and tax revenues each equal $2 trillion. If real GDP is less than potential GDP, outlays exceed tax revenues and there is a *cyclical deficit*. If real GDP is greater than potential GDP, outlays are less than tax revenues and there is a *cyclical surplus*.

In Fig. 16(b), if both real GDP and potential GDP are $11 trillion ($Y_0^*$), the government has a budget deficit and it is a *structural deficit*. If both real GDP and potential GDP are $12 trillion ($Y_1^*$), the budget is balanced—a *structural balance* of zero. If both real GDP and potential GDP are $13 trillion ($Y_2^*$), the government has a budget surplus and it is a *structural surplus*.

The U.S. federal budget is a structural deficit and has been in that state since the early 1970s. The structural deficit decreased from 1992 to 2000 and was almost eliminated in 2000. But since 2000, the structural deficit has increased. The cyclical deficit is estimated to be small relative to the structural deficit.

The federal government faces some tough fiscal policy challenges.

You've seen how fiscal policy influences potential GDP, the growth rate of real GDP, and real GDP fluctuations. *Reading Between the Lines* looks further at the 2007 budget and contrasts it with fiscal policy in the Clinton years.

READING BETWEEN THE LINES   7

Fiscal Policy Today

THE NEW YORK TIMES, APRIL 6, 2006

80% of Budget Effectively Off Limits to Cuts

. . . Since President Bush took office, overall federal spending has risen 33 percent, twice as fast as under President Bill Clinton and faster than any other president since Lyndon B. Johnson.

But the biggest growth has come in areas that Republicans, by and large, have supported: the military, domestic security and the biggest expansion of Medicare in 40 years.

The military and so-called entitlement programs like Medicare now account for about four-fifths of the government's $2.7 trillion budget, and they are set to keep increasing much faster than inflation or the economy. Given the political realities, they are effectively off limits for now to budget cutters.

With tax cuts putting a squeeze on government revenues, almost all the battle to shrink the budget deficit is therefore focused on the less than one-fifth of government spending that goes to domestic "discretionary" pro-grams like education, scientific research, national parks and space programs.

Spending on domestic discretionary programs—the ones that Congress must appropriate money for each year—climbed 31 percent from 2001 through 2005.

A result is a pitched battle over tiny corners of budget—whether to shift $7 billion out of more than $500 billion in military spending into health and education programs—rather than to attack the broader issues.

If House Republican leaders get their way, for example, Congress would trim about $6.8 billion over the next five years from the expected growth in entitlement programs like Medicare and Medicaid.

But those savings would be obliterated by the $385 billion in additional spending over five years for the Medicare prescription drug benefits that the Republican-led Congress passed in 2003. . . .

Essence of the Story

▶ Federal spending has increased by 33 percent since 2000.

▶ This percentage increase is twice that of the 1990s under President Bill Clinton and the fastest since the 1960s under President Lyndon B. Johnson.

▶ The biggest growth has been in expenditure on the military, domestic security, and Medicare.

▶ The military and entitlement programs account for 80 percent of the $2.7 trillion budget and are off limits for cuts.

▶ Tax cuts have decreased government revenues, so spending must be cut.

► The spending cuts that are under consideration are swamped by the growth in spending over the next five years for the Medicare prescription drug benefits that Congress passed in 2003.

Economic Analysis

► The news article compares expenditure growth during the Bush years with that during the Clinton years.

► Figure 17 shows the broad facts about the federal budget in 2000 and 2007. The 2000 numbers are those for the last Clinton year, and the 2007 numbers are for the current year.

FIGURE 17   Bush and Clinton Budgets in Billions of Dollars

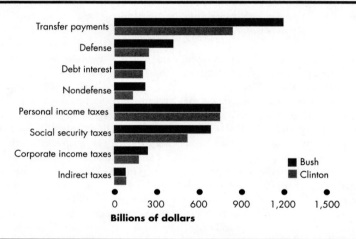

► Outlays have increased substantially. Transfer payments increased by $484 billion; defense spending increased by $234 billion; and other expenditures increased by $121 billion. Total outlays were up by $1,039 billion.

► Tax revenues increased by much less than outlays. Personal income taxes *decreased* by $2 billion. Corporate income taxes increased by $91 billion, and social security taxes and indirect taxes increased by $224 billion. Total taxes increased by $480 billion.

► The balance of the federal budget turned from a surplus of $189 billion in 2000 to a deficit of $370 billion in 2007.

► Figure 18 expresses the budget data as percentages of GDP. This way of looking at the budget highlights the allocation of resources between the federal government and the rest of the economy.

► Relative to GDP, the increase in outlays is small. You can see that transfer payments and nondefense expenditures increased by more than the increase in defense expenditures.

► Figure 18 also highlights the decrease in personal income taxes. These tax cuts and the consequent swing from surplus to deficit are the major fiscal policy events of the Bush administration.

► These fiscal policy actions have supply-side effects on the labor market and capital market, generational effects, and stabilization effects.

FIGURE 18   Bush and Clinton Budgets as Percentages of GDP

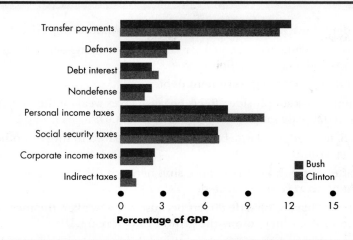

- ▶ The swing from surplus to deficit, a swing of $559 billion, has been financed by a $300 billion *increase* in borrowing from the rest of the world and a $259 billion crowding out of private expenditures.

- ▶ The tax cuts have positive supply-side effects, but the government spending increase has a negative crowding-out effect.

- ▶ The increased deficit increases the burden that is transferred to future generations.

- ▶ The combined spending increase and tax cut increased aggregate demand and helped to bring the economy back from recession.

- ▶ But according to the Congressional Budget Office, real GDP remained below potential GDP in 2006.

You're the Voter

- ▶ Do you think the current federal fiscal policy is appropriate?

- ▶ Would you vote for further tax cuts and spending cuts or for tax and spending increases or for tax increases and spending cuts? Explain.

SUMMARY

- ► The federal budget is used to achieve macroeconomic objectives.
- ► Tax revenues can exceed, equal, or fall short of outlays—the budget can be in surplus, balanced, or deficit.
- ► Budget deficits create government debt.
- ► Fiscal policy has supply-side effects because taxes weaken the incentive to work and decrease employment and potential GDP.
- ► The U.S. tax wedge is large but it is small compared to those of other industrial countries.
- ► The Laffer curve shows the relationship between the tax rate and the amount of tax revenue collected.
- ► Fiscal policy has supply-side effects because taxes weaken the incentive to save and invest, which lowers the growth rate of real GDP.
- ► A government budget deficit raises the real interest rate and crowds out some investment.
- ► If the Ricardo-Barro equivalence proposition is correct, a government budget deficit has no crowding-out effect.
- ► Generational accounting measures the lifetime tax burden and benefits of each generation.
- ► In 2003, the U.S. fiscal imbalance was estimated to be $45 trillion—4 times the value of one year's production.
- ► Future generations will pay for 57 percent of the benefits of the current generation.
- ► About half of U.S. government debt is held by the rest of the world.
- ► Fiscal stabilization can be discretionary or automatic.
- ► Discretionary changes in government expenditure or taxes can change aggregate demand but are hampered by law-making lags and the difficulty of correctly diagnosing and forecasting the state of the economy.
- ► Automatic changes in fiscal policy moderate the business cycle.

PRACTICE PROBLEMS FOR READING 26

1. The crowding-out effect *most likely* occurs when increased government spending and subsequent budget deficits cause:

    A. interest rates to increase, which reduces investment spending.

    B. an increase in the imports and a decrease in the exports of goods and services.

    C. the Federal Reserve to increase the money supply resulting in demand-pull inflation.

2. According to the tax multiplier and the balanced budget multiplier, respectively, which will *most likely* result in the greatest increase in aggregate demand—a tax cut or a government purchases increase of the same size?

    A. Tax cut.

    B. Purchases increase.

    C. Both have equal impact.

3. In the presence of automatic stabilizers, as an economy slides into a recession:

    A. tax receipts decrease.

    B. the government increases tax rates.

    C. the government decreases tax rates.

4. If the consumption tax is 10% and income tax is 20%, the tax wedge is *closest* to:

    A. 10%.

    B. 20%.

    C. 30%.

5. The Laffer curve illustrates the relationship between:

    A. the tax rate and tax revenue.

    B. labor and the real wage rate.

    C. labor and real Gross Domestic Product (GDP).

SOLUTIONS FOR READING 26

1. A is correct. The crowding-out effect occurs when government borrowing to finance budget deficits causes an increase in interest rates, which crowds out private borrowing for capital investment spending.

2. B is correct. Because of consumers' marginal propensity to save, part of any increase in disposable income resulting from a tax cut will be saved thereby reducing the potential impact of the tax cut on aggregate demand. On the other hand, 100 percent of the increase in government purchases will accrue to aggregate demand.

3. A is correct. As the economy slides in to a recession, the decline in wages and profits reduces taxable income, thereby reducing tax receipts.

4. C is correct. The tax wedge is the difference between the before-tax and after-tax wage, which includes income tax and consumption tax.

5. A is correct. The Laffer curve measures the relationship between the tax rate and tax revenue.

MONETARY POLICY
by Michael Parkin

LEARNING OUTCOMES

The candidate should be able to:	Mastery
a. discuss the goals of U.S. monetary policy and the Federal Reserve's (Fed's) means for achieving the goals, including how the Fed operationalizes those goals;	☐
b. describe how the Fed conducts monetary policy and explain the Fed's decision-making strategy, including an instrument rule, a targeting rule, open-market operations, and the market for reserves;	☐
c. discuss monetary policy's transmission mechanism (chain of events) between changing the federal funds rate and achieving the ultimate monetary policy goal when fighting either inflation or recession, and explain loose links and time lags in the adjustment process;	☐
d. describe alternative monetary policy strategies and explain why they have been rejected by the Fed.	☐

WHAT CAN MONETARY POLICY DO?

1

At eight regularly scheduled meetings a year, the Federal Reserve announces whether the interest rate will rise, fall, or remain constant until the next decision date. And every business day, the Federal Reserve Bank of New York operates in financial markets to implement the Fed's decision and ensure that its target interest rate is achieved. Financial market traders and economic journalists watch the economy for clues about what the Fed will decide at its next meeting.

How does the Fed make its interest rate decision? What exactly does the New York Fed do every day to keep the interest rate where it wants it? And how do the Fed's interest rate changes influence the economy? Can the Fed speed up

Economics, Eighth Edition, by Michael Parkin. Copyright © 2008 by Pearson Education. Reprinted with permission of Pearson Education, publishing as Pearson Addison Wesley.

459

economic growth and lower unemployment by lowering the interest rate and keep inflation in check by raising the interest rate?

The Fed's monetary policy strategy gradually evolves. And the current strategy isn't the only one that might be used. Is the current monetary policy strategy the best one? What are the benefits and what are the risks associated with the alternative monetary policy strategies?

You learned about the functions of the Federal Reserve and its long-run effects on the price level and inflation rate in the reading on money, the price level, and inflation. In this reading, you will learn about the Fed's monetary policy in both the long run and the short run. You will learn how the Fed influences the interest rate and how the interest rate influences the economy. You will also review the alternative ways in which monetary policy might be conducted. In *Reading Between the Lines* at the end of the reading, you will see the dilemma that the Fed sometimes faces as it tries to steer a steady course between inflation and recession.

2 MONETARY POLICY OBJECTIVES AND FRAMEWORK

A nation's monetary policy objectives and the framework for setting and achieving those objectives stem from the relationship between the central bank and the government.

We'll describe the objectives of U.S. monetary policy and the framework and assignment of responsibility for achieving those objectives.

Monetary Policy Objectives

The objectives of monetary policy are ultimately political. The objectives of U.S. monetary policy are set out in the mandate of the Board of Governors of the Federal Reserve System, which is defined by the Federal Reserve Act of 1913 and its subsequent amendments.

Federal Reserve Act

The Fed's mandate was most recently clarified in amendments to the Federal Reserve Act passed by Congress in 2000. The 2000 law states that mandate in the following words:

> The Board of Governors of the Federal Reserve System and the Federal Open Market Committee shall maintain long-run growth of the monetary and credit aggregates commensurate with the economy's long-run potential to increase production, so as to promote effectively the goals of maximum employment, stable prices, and moderate long-term interest rates.

Goals and Means

This description of the Fed's monetary policy objectives has two distinct parts: a statement of the goals, or ultimate objectives, and a prescription of the means by which the Fed should pursue its goals.

Goals of Monetary Policy

The goals are "maximum employment, stable prices, and moderate long-term interest rates." In the long run, these goals are in harmony and reinforce each other. But in the short run, these goals might come into conflict. Let's examine these goals a bit more closely.

Achieving the goal of "maximum employment" means attaining the maximum sustainable growth rate of potential GDP and keeping real GDP close to potential GDP. It also means keeping the unemployment rate close to the natural unemployment rate.

Achieving the goal of "stable prices" means keeping the inflation rate low (and perhaps close to zero).

Achieving the goal of "moderate long-term interest rates" means keeping long-term *nominal* interest rates close to (or even equal to) long-term *real* interest rates.

Price stability is the key goal. It is the source of maximum employment and moderate long-term interest rates. Price stability provides the best available environment for households and firms to make the saving and investment decisions that bring economic growth. So price stability encourages the maximum sustainable growth rate of potential GDP.

Price stability delivers moderate long-term interest rates because the nominal interest rate reflects the inflation rate. The nominal interest rate equals the real interest rate plus the inflation rate. With stable prices, the nominal interest rate is close to the real interest rate, and most of the time, this rate is likely to be moderate.

In the short run, the Fed faces a tradeoff between inflation and interest rates and between inflation and real GDP, employment, and unemployment. Taking an action that is designed to lower the inflation rate and achieve stable prices might mean raising interest rates, which lowers employment and real GDP and increases the unemployment rate in the short run.

Means for Achieving the Goals

The 2000 law instructs the Fed to pursue its goals by "maintain[ing] long-run growth of the monetary and credit aggregates commensurate with the economy's long-run potential to increase production." You can perhaps recognize this statement as being consistent with the quantity theory of money that you studied in the reading on money, the price level, and inflation. The "economy's long-run potential to increase production" is the growth rate of potential GDP. The "monetary and credit aggregates" are the quantities of money and loans. By keeping the growth rate of the quantity of money in line with the growth rate of potential GDP, the Fed is expected to be able to maintain full employment and keep the price level stable.

To pursue the goals of monetary policy, the Fed must make the general concepts of price stability and maximum employment precise and operational.

Operational "Stable Prices" Goal

The Fed uses the Consumer Price Index (CPI) to determine whether the goal of stable prices is being achieved. But the Fed pays closest attention to the *core CPI*—the CPI excluding food and fuel. The rate of increase in the core CPI is the **core inflation rate**.

The Fed focuses on the core inflation rate because it is less volatile than the total CPI inflation rate and the Fed believes that it provides a better indication of whether price stability is being achieved.

FIGURE 1   Operational Price Stability Goal: Core Inflation

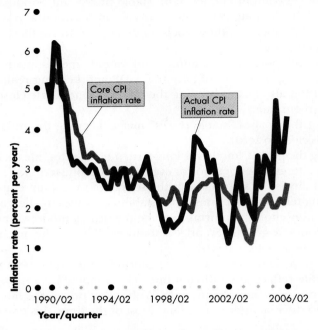

The CPI inflation rate fluctuates more than the core inflation rate. If a 1 to 2 percent core inflation rate is price stability, the Fed has achieved stable prices in 1999 and between 2002 and 2005. In all the other years, the inflation rate was above the level consistent with price stability.

Source: Bureau of Labor Statistics.

Figure 1 shows the core inflation rate alongside the total CPI inflation rate since 1990. You can see why the Fed says that the core rate is a better indicator. Its fluctuations are smoother and represent a sort of trend through the wider fluctuations in total CPI inflation.

The Fed has not defined price stability. But it almost certainly doesn't regard price stability as meaning a core inflation rate equal to zero. Former Fed Chairman Alan Greenspan suggests that "price stability is best thought of as an environment in which inflation is so low and stable over time that it does not materially enter into the decisions of households and firms." He also believes that a "specific numerical inflation target would represent an unhelpful and false precision."[1]

Ben Bernanke, Alan Greenspan's successor, has been more precise and suggested that a core inflation rate of between 1 and 2 percent a year is the equivalent of price stability. This rate takes account of the upward bias in the CPI measure of inflation that you met in the reading on monitoring jobs and the price level.

Operational "Maximum Employment" Goal

The Fed regards stable prices (a core inflation rate of 1 to 2 percent a year) as the primary goal of monetary policy and as a means to achieving the other two goals. But the Fed also pays attention to the business cycle and tries to steer a

---

[1] Alan Greenspan, "Transparency in Monetary Policy," *Federal Reserve of St. Louis Review*, 84(4), 5–6, July/August 2002.

steady course between inflation and recession. To gauge the state of output and employment relative to full employment, the Fed looks at a large number of indicators that include the labor force participation rate, the unemployment rate, measures of capacity utilization, activity in the housing market, the stock market, and regional information gathered by the regional Federal Reserve Banks. All these data are summarized in the Fed's *Beige Book*.

While the Fed considers a vast range of data, one number stands out as a summary of the overall state of aggregate demand relative to potential GDP. That number is the *output gap*—the percentage deviation of real GDP from potential GDP.

When the output gap is positive, it is an inflationary gap that brings an increase in the inflation rate. And when the output gap is negative, it is a recessionary gap that results in lost output and in employment being below its full-employment equilibrium level. So the Fed tries to minimize the output gap.

Responsibility for Monetary Policy

Who is responsible for monetary policy in the United States? What are the roles of the Fed, the Congress, and the President?

The Role of the Fed

The Federal Reserve Act makes the Board of Governors of the Federal Reserve System and the Federal Open Market Committee (FOMC) responsible for the conduct of monetary policy. We described the composition of the FOMC in the reading on money, the price level, and inflation. The FOMC makes a monetary policy decision at eight scheduled meetings each year and communicates its decision with a brief explanation. Three weeks after an FOMC meeting, the full minutes are published.

The Role of Congress

Congress plays no role in making monetary policy decisions but the Federal Reserve Act requires the Board of Governors to report on monetary policy to Congress. The Fed makes two reports each year, one in February and another in July. These reports and the Fed chairman's testimony before Congress along with the minutes of the FOMC communicate the Fed's thinking on monetary policy to lawmakers and the public.

The Role of the President

The formal role of the President of the United States is limited to appointing the members and the Chairman of the Board of Governors. But some Presidents— Richard Nixon was one—have tried to influence Fed decisions.

You now know the objectives of monetary policy and can describe the framework and assignment of responsibility for achieving those objectives. Your next task is to see how the Federal Reserve conducts its monetary policy.

3   THE CONDUCT OF MONETARY POLICY

In this section, we describe the way in which the Federal Reserve conducts its monetary policy and we explain the Fed's monetary policy strategy. We evaluate the Fed's strategy in the final section of this reading, where we describe and compare alternative monetary policy strategies.

Choosing a Policy Instrument

A **monetary policy instrument** is a variable that the Fed can directly control or closely target. As the sole issuer of the monetary base, the Fed is a monopoly. Like all monopolies, it can fix the quantity of its product and leave the market to determine the price; or it can fix the price of its product and leave the market to choose the quantity.

The first decision is whether to fix the price of U.S. money on the foreign exchange market—the exchange rate. A country that operates a fixed exchange rate cannot pursue an independent monetary policy. The United States has a flexible exchange rate and pursues an independent monetary policy.

Even with a flexible exchange rate, the Fed still has a choice of policy instrument. It can decide to target the monetary base or a short-term interest rate. While the Fed can set either of these two variables, it cannot set both. The value of one is the consequence of the other. If the Fed decided to decrease the monetary base, the interest rate would rise. If the Fed decided to raise the interest rate, the monetary base would decrease. So the Fed must decide which of these two variables to target.

The Federal Funds Rate

The Fed's choice of monetary policy instrument, which is the same choice as that made by most other major central banks, is a short-term interest rate. Given this choice, the Fed permits the exchange rate and the quantity of money to find their own equilibrium values and has no preset views about what those values should be.

The interest rate that the Fed targets is the **federal funds rate**, which is the interest rate on overnight loans that banks make to each other.

Figure 2 shows the federal funds rate since 1990. You can see that the federal funds rate was 8.25 percent in 1990 and that it was increased to 6.5 percent in 2000. In both of these periods of a high federal funds rate, the Fed wanted to take actions that lowered the inflation rate.

Between 2002 and 2004, the federal funds rate was set at historically low levels. The reason is that with inflation well anchored close to 2 percent a year, the Fed was less concerned about inflation than it was about recession so it wanted to lean in the direction of avoiding recession.

Although the Fed can change the federal funds rate by any (reasonable) amount that it chooses, it normally changes the federal funds rate by only a quarter of a percentage point.[2]

How does the Fed decide the appropriate level for the federal funds rate? And how, having made that decision, does the Fed move the federal funds rate to its target level? We'll now answer these two questions.

---

[2] A quarter of a percentage point is also called 25 *basis points*. A basis point is one hundredth of one percentage point.

FIGURE 2   The Federal Funds Rate

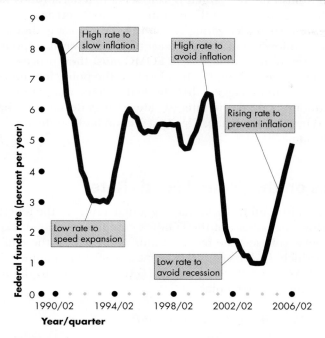

The Fed sets a target for the federal funds rate and then takes actions to keep the rate close to its target. When the Fed wants to slow inflation, it takes actions that raise the federal funds rate. When inflation is low and the Fed wants to avoid recession, it takes actions that lower the federal funds rate.

Source: Board of Governors of the Federal Reserve System.

The Fed's Decision-Making Strategy

Two alternative decision-making strategies might be used. They are summarized by the terms:

► Instrument rule
► Targeting rule

Instrument Rule

An **instrument rule** is a decision rule for monetary policy that sets the policy instrument at a level that is based on the current state of the economy. The best-known instrument rule is the *Taylor rule*, in which the instrument is the federal funds rate and the rule is to make the federal funds rate respond by formula to the inflation rate and the output gap. (We describe the Taylor rule on the next page.)

To implement the Taylor instrument rule, the FOMC would simply get the best estimates available of the current inflation rate and output gap and then mechanically calculate the level at which to set the federal funds rate.

Targeting Rule

A **targeting rule** is a decision rule for monetary policy that sets the policy instrument at a level that makes the forecast of the ultimate policy goal equal to its target. If the ultimate policy goal is a 2 percent inflation rate and the instrument is the federal funds rate, the targeting rule sets the federal funds rate at a level that makes the forecast of the inflation rate equal to 2 percent.

To implement such a targeting rule, the FOMC must gather and process a large amount of information about the economy, the way it responds to shocks, and the way it responds to policy. The FOMC must then process all these data and come to a judgment about the best level for the policy instrument.

The FOMC minutes suggest that the Fed follows a targeting rule strategy. But some economists think the interest rate settings decided by the FOMC are well described by the Taylor rule. The next section looks at the influences on the federal funds rate.

Influences on the Federal Funds Rate

Stanford economist John B. Taylor has suggested a rule for the federal funds that he says describes the *outcome* of the FOMC's complex decision-making deliberations. The **Taylor rule** sets the federal funds rate (*FFR*) at the equilibrium real interest rate (which Taylor says is 2 percent a year) plus amounts based on the inflation rate (*INF*), and the output gap (*GAP*) according to the following formula (all the values are percentages):

$$FFR = 2 + INF + 0.5(INF - 2) + 0.5GAP$$

In other words, the Taylor rule sets the federal funds rate at 2 percent plus the inflation rate plus one half of the deviation of inflation from its implicit target of 2 percent, plus one half of the output gap.

Taylor says that if the Fed followed this rule, the economy would perform better than it has performed historically. But he also says that the Fed comes close to following this rule.

Figure 3 shows how close the Fed has come to using the Taylor rule. Part (a) shows the extent to which the inflation rate has exceeded 2 percent a year—the extent to which the Fed has missed the goal of price stability. This variable has a downward trend. Part (b) shows the output gap—the extent to which the Fed missed its maximum employment goal. This variable cycles. Part (c) shows the federal funds rate that would have been set based on parts (a) and (b) if the Taylor rule had been followed (the dark gray line) and the federal funds rate decisions of the FOMC (the blue line).

You can see that between 1991 and 1994, the Fed set the federal funds rate at a lower level than what the Taylor rule would have achieved. Between 1992 and 1994, the gap between the Fed's decision and the Taylor rule was especially wide. The reason for the discrepancy is that during the 1990–1991 recession, the Fed placed a greater weight on achieving the goal of "maximum employment" and a lower weight on lowering the inflation rate. In contrast, the Taylor rule places equal weight on the deviation of inflation from its target and the output gap.

After 9/11, the Fed also lowered the federal funds rate by more than what the Taylor rule required to ensure that financial markets did not collapse during a period of increased uncertainty and pessimism.

We've now described the Fed's monetary policy instrument and the FOMC's strategy for setting it. We next see how the Fed hits its instrument target.

FIGURE 3   Influences on the Federal Funds Rate

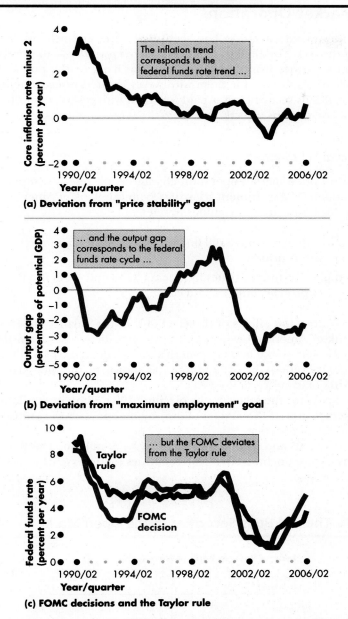

(a) Deviation from "price stability" goal

(b) Deviation from "maximum employment" goal

(c) FOMC decisions and the Taylor rule

The downward trend in the federal funds rate follows the downward trend in the inflation rate toward 2 percent in part (a), and the cycles in the federal funds rate follow the cycles in the output gap in part (b), but the FOMC decision in part (c) does not exactly match the Taylor rule formula.

Sources: Board of Governors of the Federal Reserve System, Congressional Budget Office, and Bureau of Labor Statistics.

Hitting the Federal Funds Rate Target: Open Market Operations

Once an interest rate decision has been made, the Fed achieves its target by instructing the New York Fed to make *open market operations*—to purchase or sell government securities from or to a commercial bank or the public. When the Fed buys securities, it pays for them with newly created reserves held by banks. When the Fed sells securities, it is paid for them with reserves held by banks. So open market operations directly influence the reserves of banks.

An Open Market Purchase

To see how an open market operation changes bank reserves, suppose the Fed buys $100 million of government securities from the Bank of America. When the Fed makes this transaction, two things happen:

1. The Bank of America has $100 million less securities, and the Fed has $100 million more securities.

2. The Fed pays for the securities by placing $100 million in the Bank of America's deposit account at the Fed.

Figure 4 shows the effects of these actions on the balance sheets of the Fed and the Bank of America. Ownership of the securities passes from the Bank of America to the Fed, so the Bank of America's assets decrease by $100 million and the Fed's assets increase by $100 million, as shown by the blue arrow running from the Bank of America to the Fed.

The Fed pays for the securities by placing $100 million in the Bank of America's reserve account at the Fed, as shown by the gray arrow running from the Fed to the Bank of America.

The Fed's assets and liabilities increase by $100 million. The Bank of America's total assets are unchanged: It sold securities to increase its reserves.

FIGURE 4   The Fed Buys Securities in the Open Market

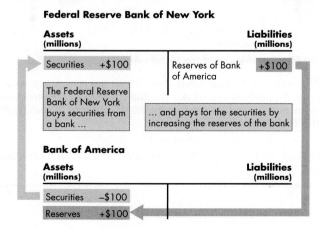

When the Fed buys securities in the open market, it creates bank reserves. Fed assets and liabilities increase, and the selling bank exchanges securities for reserves.

An Open Market Sale

If the Fed *sells* $100 million of government securities in the open market:

1. The Bank of America has $100 million more securities, and the Fed has $100 million less securities.
2. The Bank of America pays for the securities by using $100 million of its reserves deposit account at the Fed.

   Figure 5 shows the effects of these actions on the balance sheets of the Fed and the Bank of America. Ownership of the securities passes from the Fed to the Bank of America, so the Fed's assets decrease by $100 million and the Bank of America's assets increase by $100 million, as shown by the blue arrow running from the Fed to the Bank of America.

   The Bank of America uses $100 million of its reserves to pay for the securities, as the gray arrow running from the Bank of America to the Fed shows.

   Both the Fed's assets and liabilities decrease by $100 million. The Bank of America's total assets are unchanged: It has used reserves to buy securities.

FIGURE 5   The Fed Sells Securities in the Open Market

Federal Reserve Bank of New York

Assets (millions)		Liabilities (millions)	
Securities	−$100	Reserves of Bank of America	−$100

The Federal Reserve Bank of New York sells securities to a bank ...

... and the bank uses its reserves to pay for the securities

Bank of America

Assets (millions)		Liabilities (millions)
Securities	+$100	
Reserves	−$100	

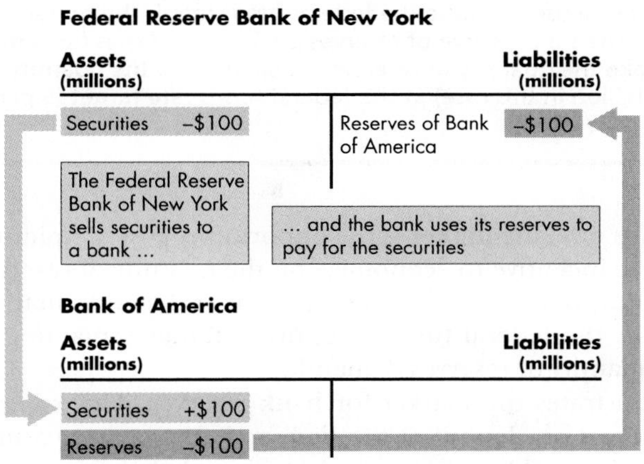

When the Fed sells securities in the open market, it reduces bank reserves. Fed assets and liabilities decrease, and the buying bank exchanges reserves for securities.

Equilibrium in the Market for Reserves

To see how an open market operation changes the federal funds rate, we must see what happens in the federal funds market—the market in which banks lend to and borrow from each other overnight—and in the market for bank reserves.

The higher the federal funds rate, the greater is the quantity of overnight loans supplied and the smaller is the quantity of overnight loans demanded in the federal funds market. The equilibrium federal funds rate balances the quantities demanded and supplied.

An equivalent way of looking at the forces that determine the federal funds rate is to consider the demand for and supply of bank reserves. Banks hold reserves to meet the required reserve ratio and so that they can make payments. But reserves are costly to hold. The alternative to holding reserves is to lend them in the federal funds market and earn the federal funds rate. The higher

FIGURE 6   The Market for Bank Reserves

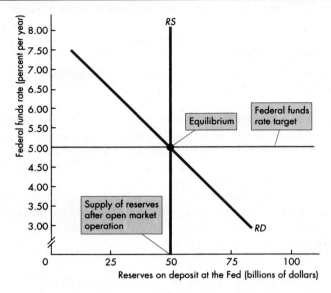

The demand curve for reserves is *RD*. The quantity of reserves demanded decreases as the federal funds rate rises because the federal funds rate is the opportunity cost of holding reserves. The supply curve of reserves is *RS*. The Fed uses open market operations to make the quantity of reserves supplied equal the quantity of reserves demanded ($50 billion in this case) at the federal funds rate target (5 percent a year in this case).

the federal funds rate, the higher is the opportunity cost of holding reserves and the greater is the incentive to economize on the quantity of reserves held.

So the quantity of reserves demanded by banks depends on the federal funds rate. The higher the federal funds rate, other things remaining the same, the smaller is the quantity of reserves demanded.

Figure 6 illustrates the market for bank reserves. The *x*-axis measures the quantity of reserves on deposit at the Fed, and the *y*-axis measures the federal funds rate. The demand for reserves is the curve labeled *RD*.

The Fed's open market operations determine the supply of reserves, which is shown by the supply curve *RS*. To decrease reserves, the Fed conducts an open market sale. To increase reserves, the Fed conducts an open market purchase.

Equilibrium in the market for bank reserves determines the federal funds rate where the quantity of reserves demanded by the banks equals the quantity of reserves supplied by the Fed. By using open market operations, the Fed adjusts the supply of reserves to keep the federal funds rate on target.

4   MONETARY POLICY TRANSMISSION

You've seen that the Fed's goal is to keep the price level stable (keep the inflation rate around 2 percent a year) and to achieve maximum employment (keep the output gap close to zero). And you've seen how the Fed can use its power to set the federal funds rate at its desired level. We're now going to trace the events that follow a change in the federal funds rate and see how those events lead to the ultimate policy goal. We'll begin with a quick overview of the transmission process and then look at each step a bit more closely.

Quick Overview

When the Fed lowers the federal funds rate, other short-term interest rates and the exchange rate also fall. The quantity of money and the supply of loanable funds increase. The long-term real interest rate falls. The lower real interest rate increases consumption expenditure and investment. And the lower exchange rate makes U.S. exports cheaper and imports more costly. So net exports increase. Easier bank loans reinforce the effect of lower interest rates on aggregate expenditure. Aggregate demand increases, which increases real GDP and the price level relative to what they would have been. Real GDP growth and inflation speed up.

When the Fed raises the federal funds rate, as the sequence of events that we've just reviewed plays out, the effects are in the opposite directions.

Figure 7 provides a schematic summary of these ripple effects for both a cut and a rise in the federal funds rate.

These ripple effects stretch out over a period of between one and two years. The interest rate and exchange rate effects are immediate. The effects on money and bank loans follow in a few weeks and run for a few months. Real long-term interest rates change quickly and often in anticipation of the short-term interest rate changes. Spending plans change and real GDP growth slows after about one year. And the inflation rate changes between one year and two years after the

FIGURE 7   The Ripple Effects of a Change in the Federal Funds Rate

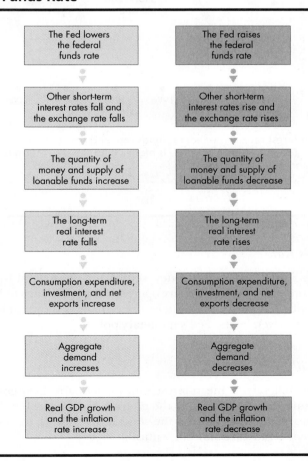

change in the federal funds rate. But these time lags are not entirely predictable and can be longer or shorter.

We're going to look at each stage in the transmission process, starting with the interest rate effects.

Interest Rate Changes

The first effect of a monetary policy decision by the FOMC is a change in the federal funds rate. Other interest rates then change. These interest rate effects occur quickly and relatively predictably.

Figure 8 shows the fluctuations in three interest rates: the federal funds rate, the short-term bill rate, and the long-term bond rate.

FIGURE 8   Three Interest Rates

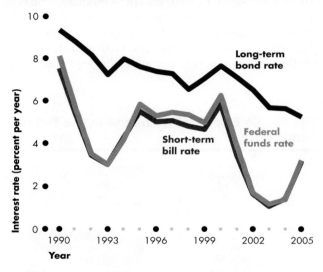

The short-term interest rates—the federal funds rate and the short-term bill rate—move closely together. The long-term bond rate is higher than the short-term rates, and it fluctuates less than the short-term rates.

Source: Board of Governors of the Federal Reserve System.

Federal Funds Rate

As soon as the FOMC announces a new setting for the federal funds rate, the New York Fed undertakes the necessary open market operations to hit the target. There is no doubt about where the interest rate changes shown in Fig. 8 are generated. They are driven by the Fed's monetary policy.

Short-Term Bill Rate

The short-term bill rate is the interest rate paid by the U.S. government on 3-month Treasury bills. It is similar to the interest rate paid by U.S. businesses on short-term loans. Notice how closely the short-term bill rate follows the federal funds rate. The two rates are almost identical.

A powerful substitution effect keeps these two interest rates close. Commercial banks have a choice about how to hold their short-term liquid assets. And an overnight loan to another bank is a close substitute for short-term securities such as Treasury bills. If the interest rate on Treasury bills is higher than the federal funds rate, the quantity of overnight loans supplied decreases and the demand for Treasury bills increases. The price of Treasury bills rises and the interest rate falls.

Similarly, if the interest rate on Treasury bills is lower than the federal funds rate, the quantity of overnight loans supplied increases and the demand for Treasury bills decreases. The price of Treasury bills falls, and the interest rate rises.

When the interest rate on Treasury bills is close to the federal funds rate, there is no incentive for a bank to switch between making an overnight loan and buying Treasury bills. Both the Treasury bill market and the federal funds market are in equilibrium.

The Long-Term Bond Rate

The long-term bond rate is the interest rate paid on bonds issued by large corporations. It is this interest rate that businesses pay on the loans that finance their purchase of new capital and that influences their investment decisions.

Two features of the long-term bond rate stand out: It is higher than the short-term rates, and it fluctuates less than the short-term rates.

The long-term interest rate is higher than the two short-term rates because long-term loans are riskier than short-term loans. To provide the incentive that brings forth a supply of long-term loans, lenders must be compensated for the additional risk. Without compensation for the additional risk, only short-term loans would be supplied.

The long-term interest rate fluctuates less than the short-term rates because it is influenced by expectations about future short-term interest rates as well as current short-term interest rates. The alternative to borrowing or lending long term is to borrow or lend using a sequence of short term securities. If the long-term interest rate exceeds the expected average of future short-term interest rates, people will lend long term and borrow short term. The long-term interest rate will fall. And if the long-term interest rate is below the expected average of future short-term interest rates, people will borrow long term and lend short term. The long-term interest rate will rise.

These market forces keep the long-term interest rate close to the expected average of future short-term interest rates (plus a premium for the extra risk associated with long-term loans). And the expected average future short-term interest rate fluctuates less than the current short-term interest rate.

Exchange Rate Fluctuations

The exchange rate responds to changes in the interest rate in the United States relative to the interest rates in other countries—*the U.S. interest rate differential.*

When the Fed raises the federal funds rate, the U.S. interest rate differential rises and, other things remaining the same, the U.S. dollar appreciates. And when the Fed lowers the federal funds rate, the U.S. interest rate differential falls and, other things remaining the same, the U.S. dollar depreciates.

Many factors other than the U.S. interest rate differential influence the exchange rate, so when the Fed changes the federal funds rate, the exchange rate does not usually change in exactly the way it would with other things remaining the same. So while monetary policy influences the exchange rate, many other factors also make the exchange rate change.

Money and Bank Loans

The quantity of money and bank loans change when the Fed changes the federal funds rate target. A rise in the federal funds rate decreases the quantity of money and bank loans, and a fall in the federal funds rate increases the quantity of money and bank loans. These changes occur for two reasons: The quantity of deposits and loans created by the banking system changes and the quantity of money demanded changes.

You've seen that to change the federal funds rate, the Fed must change the quantity of bank reserves. A change in the quantity of bank reserves changes the monetary base, which in turn changes the quantity of deposits and loans that the banking system can create. A rise in the federal funds rate decreases reserves and decreases the quantity of deposits and bank loans created; and a fall in the federal funds rate increases reserves and increases the quantity of deposits and bank loans created.

The quantity of money created by the banking system must be held by households and firms. The change in the interest rate changes the quantity of money demanded. A fall in the interest rate increases the quantity of money demanded, and a rise in the interest rate decreases the quantity of money demanded.

A change in the quantity of money and the supply of bank loans directly affects consumption and investment plans. With more money and easier access to loans, consumers and firms spend more. With less money and loans harder to get, consumers and firms spend less.

The Long-Term Real Interest Rate

Demand and supply in the market for loanable funds determine the long-term *real interest rate*, which equals the long-term *nominal* interest rate minus the expected inflation rate. The long-term real interest rate influences expenditure decisions.

In the long run, demand and supply in the loanable funds market depend only on real forces—on saving and investment decisions. But in the short run, when the price level is not fully flexible, the supply of loanable funds is influenced by the supply of bank loans. Changes in the federal funds rate change the supply of bank loans, which changes the supply of loanable funds and changes the interest rate in the loanable funds market.

A fall in the federal funds rate that increases the supply of bank loans increases the supply of loanable funds and lowers the equilibrium real interest rate. A rise in the federal funds rate that decreases the supply of bank loans decreases the supply of loanable funds and raises the equilibrium real interest rate.

These changes in the real interest rate, along with the other factors we've just described, change expenditure plans.

Expenditure Plans

The ripple effects that follow a change in the federal funds rate change three components of aggregate expenditure:

► Consumption expenditure
► Investment
► Net exports

Consumption Expenditure

Other things remaining the same, the lower the real interest rate, the greater is the amount of consumption expenditure and the smaller is the amount of saving.

Investment

Other things remaining the same, the lower the real interest rate, the greater is the amount of investment.

Net Exports

Other things remaining the same, the lower the interest rate, the lower is the exchange rate and the greater are exports and the smaller are imports.

So eventually, a cut in the federal funds rate increases aggregate expenditure and a rise in the federal funds rate curtails aggregate expenditure. These changes in aggregate expenditure plans change aggregate demand, real GDP, and the price level.

The Change in Aggregate Demand, Real GDP, and the Price Level

The final link in the transmission chain is a change in aggregate demand and a resulting change in real GDP and the price level. By changing real GDP and the price level relative to what they would have been without a change in the federal funds rate, the Fed influences its ultimate goals: the inflation rate and the output gap.

The Fed Fights Recession

If inflation is low and real GDP is below potential GDP, the Fed takes actions that are designed to restore full employment. Figure 9 shows the effects of the Fed's actions, starting in the market for bank reserves and ending in the market for real GDP.

Market for Bank Reserves

In Fig. 9(a), which shows the market for bank reserves, the FOMC lowers the target federal funds rate from 5 percent to 4 percent a year. To achieve the new target, the New York Fed buys securities and increases the supply of reserves of the banking system from RS_0 to RS_1.

Money Market

With increased reserves, the banks create deposits by making loans and the supply of money increases. The short-term interest rate falls and the quantity of money demanded increases. In Fig. 9(b), the supply of money increases from MS_0 to MS_1, the interest rate falls from 5 percent to 4 percent a year and the quantity of money increases from $3 trillion to $3.1 trillion. The interest rate in the money market and the federal funds rate are kept close to each other by the powerful substitution effect described on p. 473.

FIGURE 9   The Fed Fights Recession

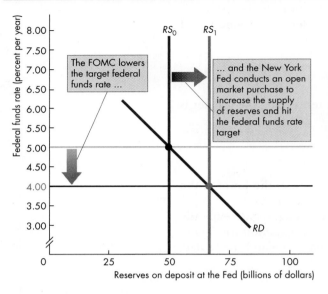

(a) The market for bank reserves

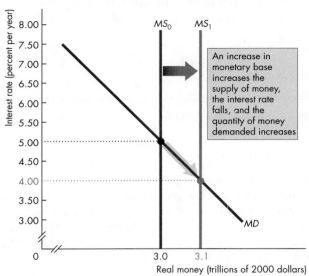

(b) Money market

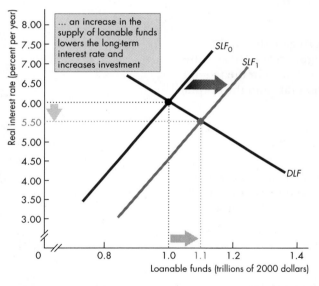

(c) The market for loanable funds

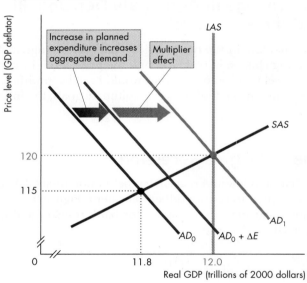

(d) Real GDP and the price level

In part (a), the FOMC lowers the federal funds rate target from 5 percent to 4 percent. The New York Fed buys securities in an open market operation and increases the supply of reserves from RS_0 to RS_1 to hit the new federal funds rate target.

In part (b), the supply of money increases from MS_0 to MS_1, the short-term interest rate falls, and the quantity of money demanded increases. The short-term interest rate and the federal funds rate change by similar amounts.

In part (c), an increase in the supply of bank loans increases the supply of loanable funds from SLF_0 to SLF_1 and the real interest rate falls. Investment increases.

In part (d), aggregate planned expenditure increases. The aggregate demand curve shifts to $AD_0 + \Delta E$ and eventually it shifts rightward to AD_1. Real GDP increases to potential GDP, and the price level rises.

Loanable Funds Market

Banks create money by making loans. In the long run, an increase in the supply of bank loans is matched by a rise in the price level and the quantity of *real* loans is unchanged. But in the short run, with a sticky price level, an increase in the supply of bank loans increases the supply of (real) loanable funds.

In Fig. 9(c), the supply of loanable funds curve shifts rightward from SLF_0 to SLF_1. With the demand for loanable funds at DLF, the real interest rate falls from 6 percent to 5.5 percent a year. (We're assuming a zero inflation rate so that the real interest rate equals the nominal interest rate.) The long-term interest rate changes by a smaller amount than the change in the short-term interest rate.

The Market for Real GDP

Figure 9(d) shows aggregate demand and aggregate supply—the demand for and supply of real GDP. Potential GDP is $12 trillion, where LAS is located. The short-run aggregate supply curve is SAS, and initially, the aggregate demand curve is AD_0. Real GDP is $11.8 trillion, which is less than potential GDP, so there is a recessionary gap. The Fed is reacting to this recessionary gap.

The increase in the supply of loans and the decrease in the real interest rate increase aggregate planned expenditure. (Not shown in the figure, a fall in the interest rate lowers the exchange rate, which increases net exports and aggregate planned expenditure.) The increase in aggregate expenditure, ΔE, increases aggregate demand and shifts the aggregate demand curve rightward to $AD_0 + \Delta E$. A multiplier process begins. The increase in expenditure increases income, which induces an increase in consumption expenditure. Aggregate demand increases further, and the aggregate demand curve eventually shifts rightward to AD_1.

The new equilibrium is at full employment. Real GDP is equal to potential GDP. The price level rises to 120 and then becomes stable at that level. So after a one-time adjustment, there is price stability.

In this example, we have given the Fed a perfect hit at achieving full employment and keeping the price level stable. It is unlikely that the Fed would be able to achieve the precision of this example. If the Fed stimulated demand by too little and too late, the economy would experience a recession. And if the Fed hit the gas pedal too hard, it would push the economy from recession to inflation.

The Fed Fights Inflation

If the inflation rate is too high and real GDP is above potential GDP, the Fed takes actions that are designed to lower the inflation rate and restore price stability. Figure 10 shows the effects of the Fed's actions starting in the market for reserves and ending in the market for real GDP.

Market for Bank Reserves

In Fig. 10(a), which shows the market for bank reserves, the FOMC raises the target federal funds rate from 5 percent to 6 percent a year. To achieve the new target, the New York Fed sells securities and decreases the supply of reserves of the banking system from RS_0 to RS_1.

FIGURE 10   The Fed Fights Inflation

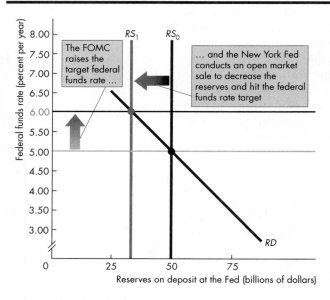

(a) The market for bank reserves

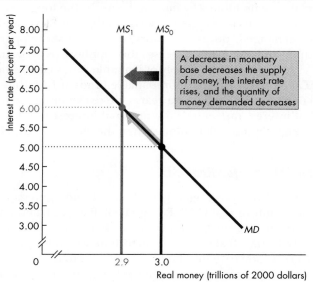

(b) Money market

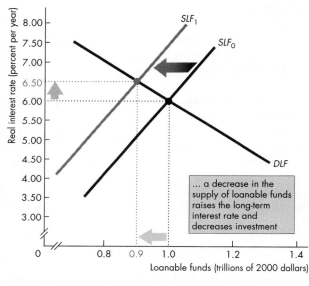

(c) The market for loanable funds

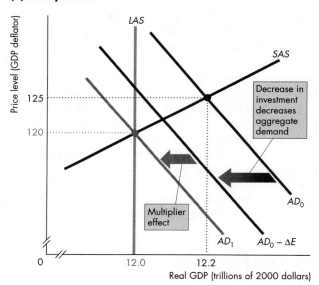

(d) Real GDP and the price level

In part (a), the FOMC raises the federal funds rate from 5 percent to 6 percent. The New York Fed sells securities in an open market operation to decrease the supply of reserves from RS_0 to RS_1 and hit the new federal funds rate target.

In part (b), the supply of money decreases from MS_0 to MS_1, the short-term interest rate rises, and the quantity of money demanded decreases. The short-term interest rate and the federal funds rate change by similar amounts.

In part (c), a decrease in the supply of bank loans decreases the supply of loanable funds from SLF_0 to SLF_1 and the real interest rate rises. Investment decreases.

In part (d), aggregate planned expenditure decreases. Aggregate demand decreases and the AD curve shifts leftward from AD_0 to AD_1. Real GDP decreases to potential GDP, and the price level falls.

Money Market

With decreased reserves, the banks shrink deposits by decreasing loans and the supply of money decreases. The short-term interest rate rises and the quantity of money demanded decreases. In Fig. 10(b), the supply of money decreases from MS_0 to MS_1, the interest rate rises from 5 percent to 6 percent a year and the quantity of money decreases from $3 trillion to $2.9 trillion.

Loanable Funds Market

With a decrease in reserves, banks must decrease the supply of loans. The supply of (real) loanable funds decreases, and the supply of loanable funds curve shifts leftward in Fig. 10(c) from SLF_0 to SLF_1. With the demand for loanable funds at DLF, the real interest rate rises from 6 percent to 6.5 percent a year. (Again, we're assuming a zero inflation rate so that the real interest rate equals the nominal interest rate.)

The Market for Real GDP

Figure 10(d) shows aggregate demand and aggregate supply in the market for real GDP. Potential GDP is $12 trillion where LAS is located. The short-run aggregate supply curve is SAS and initially the aggregate demand is AD_0. Now, real GDP is $12.2 trillion, which is greater than potential GDP, so there is an inflationary gap. The Fed is reacting to this inflationary gap.

The increase in the short-term interest rate, the decrease in the supply of bank loans, and the increase in the real interest rate decrease aggregate planned expenditure. (Not shown in the figures, a rise in the interest rate raises the exchange rate, which decreases net exports and aggregate planned expenditure.)

The decrease in aggregate expenditure, ΔE, decreases aggregate demand and shifts the aggregate demand curve to $AD_0 - \Delta E$. A multiplier process begins. The decrease in expenditure decreases income, which induces a decrease in consumption expenditure. Aggregate demand decreases further, and the aggregate demand curve eventually shifts leftward to AD_1.

The economy returns to full employment. Real GDP is equal to potential GDP. The price level falls to 120 and then becomes stable at that level. So after a one-time adjustment, there is price stability.

Again, in this example, we have given the Fed a perfect hit at achieving full employment and keeping the price level stable. If the Fed decreased aggregate demand by too little and too late, the economy would have remained with an inflationary gap and the inflation rate would have moved above the rate that is consistent with price stability. And if the Fed hit the brakes too hard, it would push the economy from inflation to recession.

Loose Links and Long and Variable Lags

The ripple effects of monetary policy that we've just analyzed with the precision of an economic model are, in reality, very hard to predict and anticipate.

To achieve its goals of price stability and full employment, the Fed needs a combination of good judgment and good luck. Too large an interest rate cut in an underemployed economy can bring inflation, as it did during the 1970s. And too large an interest rate rise in an inflationary economy can create unemployment, as it did in 1981 and 1991.

Loose links in the chain that runs from the federal funds rate to the ultimate policy goals make unwanted policy outcomes inevitable. And time lags that are both long and variable add to the Fed's challenges.

Loose Link from Federal Funds Rate to Spending

The real long-term interest rate that influences spending plans is linked only loosely to the federal funds rate. Also, the response of the *real* long-term interest rate to a change in the nominal interest rate depends on how inflation expectations change. And the response of expenditure plans to changes in the real interest rate depend on many factors that make the response hard to predict.

Time Lags in the Adjustment Process

The Fed is especially handicapped by the fact that the monetary policy transmission process is long and drawn out. Also, the economy does not always respond in exactly the same way to a policy change. Further, many factors other than policy are constantly changing and bringing new situations to which policy must respond.

A Final Reality Check

You've studied the theory of monetary policy. Does it really work in the way we've described? It does. And Fig. 11 provides some evidence to support this claim.

FIGURE 11   Interest Rates and Real GDP Growth

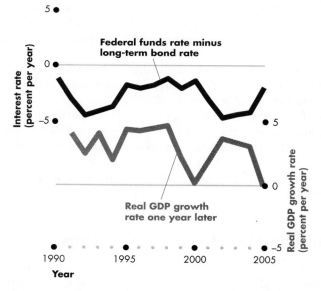

When the federal funds rate rises relative to the long-term bond rate, the real GDP growth rate usually slows about one year later. Similarly, when the federal funds rate falls relative to the long-term bond rate, the real GDP growth rate speeds up about one year later.

Sources: Interest rates, see Fig. 8; real GDP growth, Bureau of Economic Analysis.

In Fig. 11, the blue line shows the federal funds rate that the Fed targets minus the long-term bond rate. We can view the gap between the long-term bond rate and the federal funds rate as a measure of how hard the Fed is trying to steer a change in course. When the federal funds rate falls relative to the long-term bond rate, the Fed is trying to stimulate real GDP growth. When the federal funds rate rises relative to the long-term bond rate, the Fed is trying to restrain inflation and slow real GDP growth.

The gray line in Fig. 11 is the real GDP growth rate *one year later.* You can see that when the FOMC raises the federal funds rate, the real GDP growth rate slows one year later. And when the Fed lowers the federal funds rate, the real GDP growth rate speeds up one year later.

Not shown in Fig. 11, the inflation rate increases and decreases corresponding to the fluctuations in the real GDP growth rate. But the effects on the inflation rate take even longer.

You've seen how the Fed operates and the effects of its actions. We close this reading by looking at alternative ways in which the Fed could operate.

ALTERNATIVE MONETARY POLICY STRATEGIES   5

So far in this reading, we've described and analyzed the Fed's method of conducting monetary policy. But the Fed does have choices among alternative monetary policy strategies. We're going to end our discussion of monetary policy by examining the alternatives and explaining why the Fed has rejected them in favor of the interest rate strategy that we've described.

You've seen that we can summarize monetary policy strategies in two broad categories: *instrument rules* and *targeting rules.* And you've seen that the Fed uses a *targeting rule* strategy but one that comes close to being the same as the Taylor rule, an instrument rule for the federal funds rate. So the Fed has rejected a pure or simple instrument rule. It has also rejected some other possible instrument and targeting rules.

The Fed might have chosen any of four alternative monetary policy strategies: One of them is an instrument rule, and three are alternative targeting rules. The four alternatives are

▶ Monetary base instrument rule
▶ Money targeting rule
▶ Exchange rate targeting rule
▶ Inflation rate targeting rule

Monetary Base Instrument Rule

Although the Fed uses open market operations to hit its federal funds rate target, it could instead shoot for a target level of the monetary base.

The idea of using a rule to set the monetary base has been suggested by Carnegie-Mellon University economist Bennet T. McCallum, and a monetary base rule bears his name.

The **McCallum rule** makes the growth rate of the monetary base respond to the long-term average growth rate of real GDP and medium-term changes in the velocity of circulation of the monetary base.

The rule is based on the *quantity theory of money* (see the reading on money, the price level, and inflation). McCallum's idea is that by making the monetary base grow at a rate equal to a target inflation rate plus the long-term real GDP growth rate minus the medium-term growth rate of the velocity of circulation of the monetary base, inflation will be kept close to target and the economy will be kept close to full employment.

The McCallum rule has some advantages over the Taylor rule. To target the interest rate using the Taylor rule, the Fed must estimate the long-run equilibrium real interest rate and the output gap.

In the Taylor rule, the long-run equilibrium real interest rate is 2 percent a year. The federal funds rate is set at this level if the inflation rate and output gap are zero. But if the long-run equilibrium real interest rate is not 2 percent a year, the Taylor rule would set the interest rate either too high on the average and bring persistent recession or too low on the average and bring persistent and accelerating inflation.

Similarly, if the Fed overestimated the output gap, it would set the federal funds rate too high on the average and bring persistent recession. And if the Fed underestimated the output gap, it would set the federal funds rate too low on the average and bring persistent inflation.

Because the McCallum rule doesn't react to either the real interest rate or the output gap, the McCallum rule doesn't suffer from the problems of the Taylor rule.

A disadvantage of the McCallum rule compared to the Taylor rule is that it relies on the demand for money and demand for monetary base being reasonably stable.

The Fed believes that shifts in the demand for money and the demand for monetary base would bring large fluctuations in the interest rate, which in turn would bring large fluctuations in aggregate demand.

Money Targeting Rule

As long ago as 1948, Nobel Laureate Milton Friedman proposed a targeting rule for the quantity of money. Friedman's **k-percent rule** makes the quantity of money grow at a rate of *k* percent a year, where *k* equals the growth rate of potential GDP.

Like the McCallum rule, Friedman's *k*-percent rule relies on a stable demand for money, which translates to a stable velocity of circulation. Friedman had examined data on money and nominal GDP and argued that the velocity of circulation of money was one of the most stable macroeconomic variables and that it could be exploited to deliver a stable price level and small business cycle fluctuations.

Friedman's idea remained just that until the 1970s, when inflation increased to more than 10 percent a year in the United States and to much higher rates in some other major countries.

During the mid-1970s, in a bid to end the inflation, the central banks of most major countries adopted the *k*-percent rule for the growth rate of the quantity of money. The Fed, too, began to pay close attention to the growth rates of money aggregates, including M1 and M2.

Inflation rates fell during the early 1980s in the countries that had adopted a *k*-percent rule. But one by one, these countries abandoned the *k*-percent rule.

Money targeting works when the demand for money is stable and predictable—when the velocity of circulation is stable. But in the world of the 1980s, and possibly in the world of today, technological change in the banking system leads to large and unpredictable fluctuations in the demand for money, which make the use of monetary targeting unreliable. With monetary targeting, aggregate demand fluctuates because the demand for money fluctuates. With interest rate targeting, aggregate demand is insulated from fluctuations in the demand for money (and the velocity of circulation).

Exchange Rate Targeting Rule

The Fed could, if it wished to do so, intervene in the foreign exchange market to target the exchange rate. A fixed exchange rate is one possible exchange rate target. The Fed could fix the value of the U.S. dollar against a basket of other currencies such as the *trade-weighted index*.

But with a fixed exchange rate, a country has no control over its inflation rate. The reason is that for internationally traded goods, *purchasing power parity* moves domestic prices in line with foreign prices. If a computer chip costs $100 in Los Angeles and if the exchange rate is 120 yen per $1.00, then the computer chip will sell for 12,000 yen (ignoring local tax differences) in Tokyo. If this purchasing power parity didn't prevail, it would be possible to earn a profit by buying at the lower price and selling at the higher price. This trading would compete away the profit and price difference.

So prices of traded goods (and in the long run the prices of all goods and services) must rise at the same rate in the United States as they do on the average in the other countries against which the value of the U.S. dollar is fixed.

The Fed could avoid a direct inflation link by using a *crawling peg exchange rate* as a means of achieving an inflation target. To do so, the Fed would make the exchange rate change at a rate equal to the U.S. inflation rate minus the target inflation rate. If other countries have an average inflation rate of 3 percent a year and the United States wants an inflation rate of 2 percent a year, the Fed would make the U.S. dollar appreciate at a rate of 1 percent a year against the trade-weighted index of other currencies.

Some developing countries that have an inflation problem use this monetary policy strategy to lower the inflation rate. The main reason for choosing this method is that these countries don't have well-functioning markets for bonds and overnight loans, so they cannot use the policy approach that relies on these features of a banking system.

A major disadvantage of a crawling peg to target the inflation rate is that the real exchange rate often changes in unpredictable ways. The **real exchange rate** between the United States and its trading partners is the relative price of the GDP basket of goods and services in the United States with respect to that in other countries. U.S. GDP contains a larger proportion of high-technology products and services than GDP in other countries contain. So when the relative prices of these items change, our real exchange rate changes. With a crawling peg targeting the inflation rate, we would need to be able to identify changes in the real exchange rate and offset them. This task is difficult to accomplish.

Inflation Rate Targeting Rule

Inflation rate targeting is a monetary policy strategy in which the central bank makes a public commitment

1. To achieve an explicit inflation target
2. To explain how its policy actions will achieve that target

Of the alternatives to the Fed's current strategy, inflation targeting is the most likely to be considered. In fact, some economists see it as a small step from what the Fed currently does. For these reasons, we'll explain this policy strategy in a bit of detail. Which countries practice inflation targeting, how do they do it, and what does it achieve?

Inflation Targeters

Several major central banks practice inflation targeting and have done so since the mid-1990s. The best examples of central banks that use inflation targeting are the Bank of England, Bank of Canada, the Reserve Bank of New Zealand, and the Swedish Riksbank. The European Central Bank also practices inflation targeting. Japan and the United States are the most prominent major industrial economies that do not use this monetary policy strategy. But it is interesting to note that when the chairman of the Board of Governors of the Federal Reserve System, Ben Bernanke, and a member of the Board of Governors, Frederic S. Mishkin, were economics professors (at Princeton University and Columbia University, respectively), they did research together and wrote important articles and books on this topic. And their general conclusion was that inflation targeting is a sensible way in which to conduct monetary policy.

How Inflation Targeting Is Conducted

Inflation targets are specified in terms of a range for the CPI inflation rate. This range is typically between 1 percent and 3 percent a year, with an aim to achieve an average inflation rate of 2 percent per year. Because the lags in the operation of monetary policy are long, if the inflation rate falls outside the target range, the expectation is that the central bank will move the inflation rate back on target over the next two years.

All the inflation-targeting central banks use the overnight interest rate (the equivalent of the federal funds rate) as the policy instrument. And they use open market operations as the tool for achieving the desired overnight rate.

To explain their policy actions, inflation targeters publish an inflation report that describes the current state of the economy and its expected evolution over the next two years. The report also explains the central bank's current policy and how and why the central bank expects that its policy will achieve the inflation target.

What Does Inflation Targeting Achieve?

The goals of inflation targeting are to state clearly and publicly the goals of monetary policy, to establish a framework of accountability, and to keep the inflation rate low and stable while maintaining a high and stable level of employment.

There is wide agreement that inflation targeting achieves its first two goals. And the inflation reports of inflation targeters have raised the level of discussion and understanding of the monetary policy process.

It is less clear whether inflation targeting does better than the implicit targeting that the Fed currently pursues in achieving low and stable inflation. The Fed's own record, without a formal inflation target, has been impressive over the past several years.

But monetary policy is about managing inflation expectations. And it seems clear that an explicit inflation target that is taken seriously and toward which policy actions are aimed and explained is a sensible way to manage expectations.

It is when the going gets tough that inflation targeting has the greatest attraction. It is difficult to imagine a serious inflation-targeting central bank permitting inflation to take off in the way that it did during the 1970s. And it is difficult to imagine deflation and ongoing recession such as Japan has endured for the past 10 years if monetary policy is guided by an explicit inflation target.

The debate on inflation targeting will continue!

Why Rules?

You might be wondering why all monetary policy strategies involve rules. Why doesn't the Fed just do what seems best every day, month, and year, at its discretion? The answer lies in what you've just read. Monetary policy is about managing inflation expectations. In both financial markets and labor markets, people must make long-term commitments. So these markets work best when plans are based on correctly anticipated inflation outcomes. A well-understood monetary policy rule helps to create an environment in which inflation is easier to forecast and manage.

As you complete your study of monetary policy, take a look at *Reading Between the Lines* and see the Fed's policy challenge in 2006.

6

READING BETWEEN THE LINES

Monetary Policy in Action

THE NEW YORK TIMES, AUGUST 9, 2006

In a Policy Shift, the Fed Halts a 2-Year String of Rate Increases

. . . After 17 consecutive increases [one] at each meeting since June 2004, the central bank voted to hold its benchmark interest rate steady at 5.25 percent. Policy makers suggested that they wanted more time to see where the economy was headed before deciding whether further increases might be necessary.

In a statement accompanying its decision, the Fed acknowledged that inflation had accelerated. But it predicted that slowing economic growth—led by the retreat of the housing market—would lead to smaller consumer price increases before long.

. . . The shift amounts to a bet by the Federal Reserve's chairman, Ben S. Bernanke, on an elusive goal in monetary policy: a "soft landing" in which the economy slows enough to cool spending and ease inflationary pressures but not enough to cause a big jump in unemployment.

. . . Many economists said they disagreed with the Fed's sanguine outlook, saying that prices and wages were both climbing significantly faster than just a year ago and showed no signs of slowing yet.

. . . Mr. Bernanke, both before and after he became Fed chairman, has said that his definition of price stability is a "core" inflation rate—excluding prices for energy and food—of 1 to 2 percent. But by the Fed's preferred measure of core inflation prices are about 2.9 percent higher than one year ago. That is the biggest year-over-year jump in 11 years.

. . . Laurence H. Meyer, a former Fed governor and now an economic forecaster at Macroeconomic Advisers, predicted that it would take more than a soft landing to reduce inflation significantly. For that to happen, he said, unemployment would have to rise for a sustained period. . . .

Essence of the Story

► In the summer of 2006, the core inflation rate was 2.9 percent.

► At its meeting on August 8, 2006, the Fed noted that the inflation rate was too high but said that it would fall without a further rise in the interest rate.

► So the Fed decided to hold the federal funds rate target at 5.25 percent.

► The hope was that the inflation rate would fall with no big jump in unemployment in a "soft landing."

► Many economists disagreed with the Fed and said that inflation showed no signs of slowing.

► Economist Laurence H. Meyer predicted that it would take more than a soft landing to reduce inflation, and that unemployment would have to rise for a sustained period.

Economic Analysis

► In mid-2006, the core inflation rate was above the rate consistent with price stability.

► Figure 12 illustrates the situation in the second quarter of 2006 compared with the second quarter of 2005.

FIGURE 12   Real GDP and Inflation 2005 to 2006

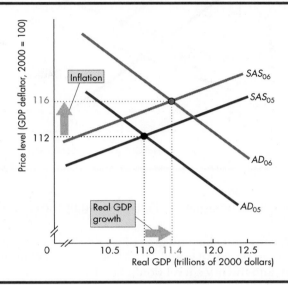

► In 2005, the aggregate demand curve was AD_{05}, the short-run aggregate supply curve was SAS_{05}, real GDP was \$11 trillion, and the price level was 112.

► In 2006, the aggregate demand curve was AD_{06}, the short-run aggregate supply curve was SAS_{06}, real GDP was \$11.4 trillion, and the price level was 116.

► During the year, real GDP had grown by about 3.6 percent and the price level measured by the GDP deflator had increased by 3.6 percent.

► The core inflation rate was just below 3 percent a year. In this situation, the Fed wanted to lower the inflation rate.

► But the Fed faces an uncertain future and must set the interest rate based on its best forecast of how the economy will evolve over the coming year.

► In the summer of 2006, the Fed expected the economy to slow and the inflation rate to decrease with no further monetary policy action. So the Fed kept the federal funds rate constant.

► Some economists thought that the Fed was incorrect and that further interest rate increases would be necessary to slow an economy that is growing too rapidly.

► Figure 13 illustrates the situation in the second quarter of 2007 if the Fed was wrong and inflation persisted at too high a rate.

► By mid-2007, the aggregate demand curve would be AD_{07}, the short-run aggregate supply curve would be SAS_{07}, real GDP would be \$11.9 trillion, and the price level would be 122.

FIGURE 13   Possibilities for 2006 to 2007

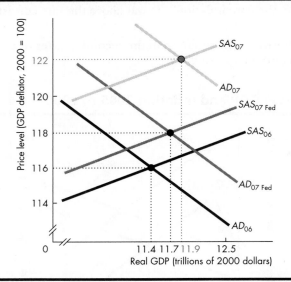

► Figure 13 also illustrates what the Fed expected by the second quarter of 2007.

► By mid-2007, aggregate demand growth would slow to AD_{07Fed}, the short-run aggregate supply curve would be SAS_{07Fed}, real GDP would be $11.7 trillion, and the price level would be 118.

► The inflation rate and real GDP growth rate would have slowed, and inflation would be back in the range consistent with price stability.

You're the Voter

► Do you think the Fed was right to hold the interest rate constant in August 2006?

► If you were a member of the FOMC, what interest rate setting would you vote for today? Explain your decision.

SUMMARY

► The Federal Reserve Act requires the Fed to use monetary policy to achieve maximum employment, stable prices, and moderate long-term interest rates.

► The goal of stable prices delivers maximum employment and low interest rates in the long run but can conflict with the other goals in the short run.

► The Fed translates the goal of stable prices as an inflation rate of between 1 and 2 percent per year.

► The FOMC has the responsibility for the conduct of monetary policy, but the Fed reports to the public and to Congress.

► The Fed's monetary policy instrument is the federal funds rate.

► The Fed sets the federal funds rate target and announces changes on eight dates each year.

► An *instrument rule* for monetary policy makes the instrument respond predictably to the state of the economy. The Fed does *not* use a mechanical instrument rule.

► A *targeting rule* for monetary policy sets the instrument to make the forecast of the inflation rate equal to the target inflation rate. The Fed *does* use such a rule, but its actions are similar to an instrument rule.

► The Fed hits its federal funds rate target by using open market operations.

► By buying or selling government securities in the open market, the Fed is able to change bank reserves and change the federal funds rate.

► A change in the federal funds rate changes other interest rates, the exchange rate, the quantity of money and loans, aggregate demand, and eventually real GDP and the price level.

► Changes in the federal funds rate change real GDP about one year later and change the inflation rate with an even longer time lag.

► The main alternatives to setting the federal funds rate are a monetary base instrument rule, a money targeting rule, an exchange rate targeting rule, or an inflation rate targeting rule.

► Rules dominate discretion in monetary policy because they better enable the central bank to manage inflation expectations.

PRACTICE PROBLEMS FOR READING 27

1. Which of the following is *least likely* a policy instrument that the Fed can directly control or closely target?

   A. Discount rate.

   B. Inflation rate.

   C. Commercial bank deposits at the Federal Reserve Banks.

2. Which of the following actions is *most* consistent with the goals of monetary policy?

   A. Decreasing the natural unemployment rate to zero.

   B. Keeping real Gross Domestic Product (GDP) close to potential GDP.

   C. Increasing the difference between long-term nominal interest rates and long-term real rates.

3. Core inflation is the rate of increase in the:

   A. Consumer Price Index.

   B. Consumer Price Index excluding fuel.

   C. Consumer Price Index excluding fuel and food.

4. An increase in the inflation rate is *most likely* indicated when the output gap is:

   A. zero.

   B. positive.

   C. negative.

5. When the Federal Reserve Bank of New York buys government securities from a commercial bank, the commercial bank:

   A. receives an equivalent amount in reserves.

   B. has an increase in liabilities that is offset by an equal increase in assets due to receiving reserves.

   C. has an increase in liabilities that is offset by an equal increase in equity due to receiving reserves.

SOLUTIONS FOR READING 27

1. B is correct. The possible intermediate targets of monetary policy are the monetary aggregates (M1 and M2), the monetary base, and the federal funds rate. The Fed cannot closely control inflation.

2. B is correct. One of the goals of monetary policy is to achieve maximum employment, which is consistent with keeping real GDP and potential GDP as near as possible in level.

3. C is correct. Core inflation is the rate of increase in the Consumer Price Index less food and fuel.

4. B is correct. A positive output gap is indicative of inflation (output gap equals percentage deviation of real GDP from potential GDP).

5. A is correct. The bank receives an equivalent amount in reserves (i.e., from the bank's perspective, an asset is exchanged for a different asset).

$4\frac{5}{8}$ $4\frac{11}{16}$ $-\frac{3}{8}$

$5\frac{1}{2}$ $5\frac{1}{2}$ $-$

$20\frac{5}{8}$ $21\frac{13}{16}$ $-\frac{1}{16}$

$17\frac{3}{8}$ **$18\frac{1}{8}$ $+$ $\frac{7}{8}$**

$18\frac{1}{2}$ $6\frac{1}{2}$ **$6\frac{1}{2}$ $-$ $\frac{1}{2}$**

$7\frac{1}{4}$ $6\frac{1}{2}$ $3\frac{1}{32}$ $-$ $\frac{1}{8}$

$15\frac{1}{16}$ $\frac{9}{16}$

$\frac{9}{16}$

$7\frac{15}{16}$ $7\frac{13}{16}$ $7\frac{15}{16}$

$7\frac{15}{16}$ $7\frac{13}{16}$ **$2\frac{1}{2}$ $+$**

$2\frac{5}{8}$ $2\frac{11}{32}$

$2\frac{3}{4}$ $2\frac{1}{4}$ $2\frac{1}{4}$

$12\frac{1}{16}$ $11\frac{3}{8}$ $11\frac{3}{4}$ $+$

$33\frac{3}{4}$ 33 $33\frac{1}{8}$ $-$

$25\frac{5}{8}$ $24\frac{9}{16}$ $25\frac{3}{8}$ $+$

12 $11\frac{5}{8}$ $11\frac{7}{8}$ $+$

16 $10\frac{1}{2}$ $10\frac{1}{2}$ $10\frac{1}{8}$ $-$

78 $15\frac{7}{8}$ $15\frac{13}{16}$ $15\frac{3}{8}$ $-$

$9\frac{1}{16}$ $8\frac{1}{4}$ $8\frac{3}{4}$ $+$

$11\frac{1}{4}$ $10\frac{1}{8}$

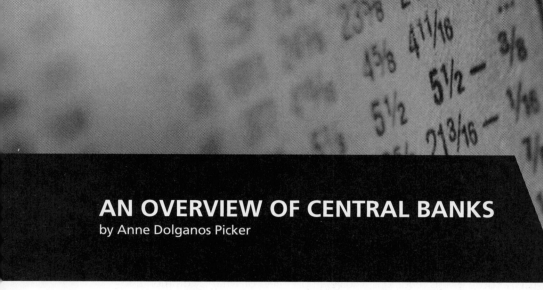

AN OVERVIEW OF CENTRAL BANKS
by Anne Dolganos Picker

LEARNING OUTCOMES

The candidate should be able to:	Mastery
a. identify the functions of a central bank;	☐
b. discuss monetary policy and the tools utilized by central banks to carry out monetary policy.	☐

Central banks everywhere have several things in common regardless of where they are located. They are a banker's bank, a place where banks can seek relief in turbulent times. They usually are issuers and custodians of the currency, and protect it from everything including forgery to runs on its value. Many have regulatory powers as well. And most importantly, they make monetary policy decisions.

Financial market participants view central banks' monetary policy decisions and their timing as one of the primary inputs to the investment decision-making process. Central bank decisions impact interest rates, and interest rates have a direct effect on the cost of doing business and therefore profits. Their role in setting interest rates directly is relatively new and it is only in the last 15 to 20 years that central banks have targeted them directly. For example, the Federal Reserve (Fed) began to set the federal funds rate directly in June 1989 rather than targeting monetary aggregates (M1, M2, M3). Previously, money supply was increased/decreased to achieve the desired interest rate. And there were also periods in the 1980s and before when the Fed targeted the fed funds rate even more overtly and no announcement was made. Instead, Fed watchers would have to pore over the weekly money supply data to see if there had been a policy change.

International Economic Indicators and Central Banks, Anne Dolganos Picker. Copyright © 2007 by John Wiley & Sons. All rights reserved. Used under license from John Wiley & Sons, Inc.

493

There are many commonalities—and differences—in the business of central banking. They include the way each bank adjusts interest rates, how economic data are used to help make informed decisions, differing interpretations and uses of inflation targeting, central bank cooperation both with other central banks and financial regulators, and the list goes on. And while policies may seem similar, often terminology will differ. Some of the banks are relatively transparent in their decision making while others remain opaque. Each bank applies common central bank policies in a way that is unique to their political and social environment. A key policy tool for many—but not all—central banks is inflation targeting. But we will get to that later in this reading.

The purpose of this reading is to give an overview of what is common and different about the Banks. The Banks covered are the European Central Bank (ECB), Bank of England, Bank of Japan (BoJ), Bank of Canada, Reserve Bank of Australia (RBA) and the People's Bank of China (PBOC).

1   A FASCINATION WITH CENTRAL BANKS

Central Bank Watching—A Major Financial Market Occupation

The U.S. Federal Reserve's (Fed's) pronouncements are sliced and diced for any hints regarding policy that would affect the economy and the financial markets. And it is no different for "other" central banks. Investors in other particular geographic areas behave in much the same way as watchers in the United States. In fact, like the Fed, these other central banks can impact financial markets worldwide. Investors everywhere watch the BoJ for assurances that deflation has ended in Japan. Investors in Europe hope that the ECB will not increase rates by too much and cut off its nascent recovery. And Canadian investors watch Bank of Canada policy as they weigh the relative merit of Canadian versus U.S. investment payoffs. Bank of England watchers are wondering if interest rates can accommodate the inflationary pressures of crude oil prices and tight labor markets while at the same time, not squashing consumer demand.

Investors care about a bank's independence from political pressures. For example, the ECB did not respond to persistent and intense political pressure to lower interest rates despite anemic growth and the stronger euro during 2004 and 2005. The ECB is the newest central bank and wanted to show how free of political interference it is—political rhetoric is bound to make it do the opposite.

The BoJ used to be part of the Ministry of Finance (MoF). Now it is fiercely independent and fends off any interference from the Ministry or, for that matter, any other part of the Japanese government. It struggled over policy especially in the late 1990s and early 2000s while the economy was in the depths of a recession. And in early 2006 when it was apparent to the central bank that deflation was ending and the economy had recovered and was out of recession, the Bank staved off an avalanche of political rhetoric and proceeded to begin the normalization of its policies. The Bank continues to act for the Ministry of Finance in the currency markets, usually selling yen for dollars to deflate the yen's value.

Central bank policies provide guidance for investors. Interest rate policies provide the broad umbrella under which business is done and the banks' announcements are broadly watched and anticipated by market players. The Bank of Canada meets about every six weeks; the Bank of England, ECB, and Reserve Bank of Australia meet monthly; and the BoJ, about every three weeks, while the PBOC meets quarterly. But all can hold emergency meetings should the situation arise. Virtually all the central banks held emergency meetings in the aftermath of the terrorist attacks on September 11, 2001, for example.

A quick word about the Fed—even though I have not included the U.S. central bank within the scope of this book. (See Evelina Tainer's marvelous description of the Federal Reserve in her third edition of *Using Economic Indicators to Improve Investment Analysis.* Hoboken, NJ: John Wiley & Sons, 2006.) I would be remiss not to mention the worldwide impact of Fed policy moves. Given the U.S. position as the world's primary engine of growth, a brief recent example of its impact on global markets should be sufficient. In the run up to the Federal Open Market Committee (FOMC) meeting in May 2004, world financial markets became transfixed as they waited for the decision on interest rate policy. When the post-meeting statement indicated that an interest rate increase would occur soon, equity markets in Europe and Asia swooned but the dollar rose on the news.

"Carry trade" became a popular form of trading in the low-interest-rate years of the early 2000s. Investors took full advantage of interest rate spreads between countries to borrow in a low-interest-rate country and then invest the funds in a higher-interest-rate country. For example, when U.S. interest rates were 1 percent, it was fashionable to borrow here and invest elsewhere—perhaps Australia, where rates were as much as 425 basis points higher at that time. As U.S. rates began to climb, the paradigm changed, investors borrowed in Europe, where rates were 2 percent and below most other countries, or in Japan, where zero interest rates prevailed.

Central Bank Tasks

Regardless of which central bank you are talking about, they all have essentially the same functions. They:

► Set monetary policy.
► Determine how the economy behaves.
► Respond to economic and financial market conditions within their jurisdiction.
► Control money supply.
► Regulate the banking system.
► Issue currency (The Federal Reserve is the exception. The U.S. Treasury prints U.S. currency while the Fed puts it into circulation.)

A Primer on How Monetary Policy Works

Setting policy by directly changing interest rates is a relatively new tool for central banks. For example, the Federal Open Market Committee (FOMC) began setting targets for the fed funds rate in June 1989. And other central banks soon followed.

When a central bank decides to change the official interest rate their goal is to eventually influence the overall level of consumer and business expenditures. Beginning in November 2003 and ending in August 2004, for example, the Bank of England increased interest rates five times with the explicit intent of slowing down the housing market, where prices were skyrocketing. At the same time, they wanted to cool torrid consumer spending. The Bank uses the interest rate at which they lend to financial institutions or "repo" as the mechanism to adjust rates. When the Bank moves the "repo" rate up or down, it triggers changes in a whole gamut of interest rates, including those set by commercial banks, building societies, and other institutions for their own savers and borrowers. Interest rate changes affect financial asset prices for bonds and equities as well. The exchange rate for a country's currency can also feel the reverberations of an interest rate change, especially when it goes against traders' expectations. In short, lowering or raising interest rates affects spending throughout the economy.

Saving is less attractive and borrowing more attractive when interest rates are reduced. This in turn stimulates spending. Recent U.S. experience with lower-than-normal interest rates is a good example of what cheap money can do. But lower interest rates can have a negative influence on both consumers' and firms' cash flow. Lower interest rates reduce savings (interest) income as well as the interest payments due on loans. Lower interest rates can boost the prices of assets such as equities and houses. Higher house prices enable existing home owners to extend their mortgages in order to finance higher consumption. Higher share prices raise households' wealth and can increase their willingness to spend. The opposite occurs when interest rates are increased.

The exchange rate can be pressured by interest rate changes. The widening (or narrowing) of the spread between interest rates in two countries impacts investment flows between the two and the consequent demand for their currencies. For example, if the United Kingdom's interest rate was higher relative to those in the U.S. it would give British investors a higher return on assets relative to their foreign currency equivalents, tending to make U.K. assets more attractive. This was particularly true during 2003 and 2004 when the fed funds rate rested at 1 percent and the Bank of England was in the process of increasing its key interest rate to 4.75 percent.

Fluctuations in currencies also can influence consumer and business demand in a variety of ways but usually via international trade. Again let us use the United Kingdom as an example. In theory, the wider spread in the country's favor should raise the value of the pound sterling, reduce the price of imports, and reduce demand for U.K. goods and services abroad. However, the impact of interest rates on the exchange rate is, unfortunately, seldom that predictable. The only thing predictable about the foreign exchange market is its unpredictability!

Some of these influences can work more quickly than others. And the overall effect of monetary policy will be more rapid if it is credible. But, in general, there are time lags before changes in interest rates work their way through to spending and saving decisions, and longer still before they affect consumer prices. It is estimated that the maximum effect on output can take up to about one year while the maximum impact of a change in interest rates on consumer price inflation takes up to about two years. So interest rates have to be set based on judgments about what inflation might be—not what it is today.

Interest Rates Come with a Variety of Names

Central banks have a variety of names for their policy-making interest rate even though they are basically similar and the goal is the same—to increase or decrease what banks must pay to borrow and thereby affect the whole gamut of interest rates available to borrowers. But regardless of what it is called, interest is payment for the use of borrowed money.

The one most familiar to investors is the federal (fed) funds rate. The fed funds rate is the interest rate charged by one depository institution on an overnight sale of immediately available funds (balances at the Federal Reserve) to another depository institution. The rate can vary from depository institution to depository institution and from day to day. The target fed funds rate is set by the FOMC. By setting a target fed funds rate and using monetary policy tools, that is, open market operations, discount window lending, and reserve requirements, to achieve that target rate, the Federal Reserve and the FOMC seek "to promote effectively the goals of maximum employment, stable prices, and moderate long-term interest rates," as required by the Federal Reserve Act.

The discount rate is the rate at which central banks lend or discount eligible paper. It is also known as the bank rate. In the United States, the discount rate is usually changed at the same time as the fed funds rate upon the request of the 12 regional Federal Reserve Banks. The Bank of Japan targets its discount rate as its policy-setting rate and uses the discount rate as its policy rate for uncollateralized loans.

One of the more common terms is *repo rate* or *repurchase rate*. It is generally used to refer to the interest rate on securities repurchase agreements used by central banks to influence domestic money markets. For example, an overnight repo is used by the Bank of England to adjust interest rates.

The overnight rate is the interest rate at which major financial institutions may borrow/lend overnight or one-day funds among themselves. This is common in Canada.

The Reserve Bank of Australia uses the cash rate. The *cash rate* is the rate charged on overnight loans between financial intermediaries and exerts a powerful influence on other interest rates. It forms the base on which the structure of other interest rates is built. The cash rate is determined in the money market by the interaction of demand for and supply of overnight funds.

Looking for the Magic Formula for Monetary Policy

What is the best way to operate monetary policy in order to provide the conditions for sustainable growth? Over the years, central banks tried to find the magic combination of policies that would sustain growth. They would work for a while and then become problematic. First, central banks tried fixing exchange rates to gold and some tried fixing or pegging their exchange rates to those of other countries. Some central banks tried to target credit or the growth of monetary aggregates, while many relied solely on their own judgment. Suffice it to say that all have their problems.

Many banks now think that the best way for monetary policy to promote sustainable economic growth is to anchor expectations in the future purchasing power of money. Bitter experience has proven that when monetary policy chases short-term goals, mistakes are made, uncertainty is increased, and fluctuations in economic activity are aggravated. Now, focusing on domestic price stability is thought to be the best contribution monetary policy can make to economic stabilization and sustainable long-term growth. But only time will tell if it is the panacea its supporters think it is.

2   INFLATION TARGETING

New Zealand, the first country to adopt inflation targeting, did so with strong support and fairly specific instructions from its legislature. The Reserve Bank of New Zealand Act of 1989 established the basic framework, giving the central bank the objective of "achieving and maintaining stability in the general level of prices," with "regard for the efficiency and soundness of the financial system." The act provided that the government and Reserve Bank jointly determine the specific inflation target and other policy objectives through Policy Target Agreements. The first of these agreements defined price stability as a range of 0 percent to 2 percent in New Zealand's consumer price index, set a goal of achieving price stability in two years, and gave conditions that could justify breaching its inflation targeting range. Several changes since then have widened the price stability range and have introduced additional objectives, such as output growth stability. These modifications have made New Zealand's inflation targeting much more flexible.

Canada followed New Zealand in 1991. The United Kingdom adopted a form of targeting in 1992, while Australia and Sweden followed in 1993. Subsequently, Finland and Spain adopted inflation targeting (before becoming members of the European Monetary Union) and in the last few years several developing countries have adopted this approach. Although the European Central Bank does not identify itself as an inflation-targeting regime, the Maastricht Treaty set price stability as the ECB's primary objective, and the ECB has set an explicit numerical target for inflation.

The 1990s were a period of considerable reform and innovation in central banks around the world. Many new central banks were established, while many already established banks were given greater independence from their governments, often in exchange for a clear commitment to meet specific targets for inflation.

Governmental involvement, although important, was somewhat less explicit for Chile, Canada, and the United Kingdom. When Chile adopted inflation targeting in 1990, the move was preceded by new central bank legislation. In 1991, a joint announcement by the Canadian government and the Bank of Canada stated its target. This announcement along with the subsequent joint announcements established a target range for price stability but left the details and the responsibility for policy in the hands of the Bank. In the United Kingdom, which adopted inflation targeting in 1992, the Chancellor of the Exchequer announced the inflation goal. Though the Bank of England later gained independence, the Chancellor still sets policy goals for the Bank annually in his budget message.

There was less explicit governmental involvement in the next group of inflation targeting countries. In Sweden, which adopted inflation targeting in 1993, the government had previously announced that controlling inflation was an overriding goal for the Riksbank. At the Reserve Bank of Australia, its Governor, using broad and previously delegated authority, announced its change to inflation targeting in a speech. Norway's Norges Bank operates under a governmental mandate declaring that the long-term objective of monetary policy is to maintain the domestic and international value of its currency. The European Central Bank operates under the authority delegated to it by the Maastricht Treaty establishing the European Community with the primary goal of price stability.

What Is Inflation Targeting?

Most major central banks' primary monetary policy goal is to contain inflation. That is, a specific number or range in which inflation or price increases must remain is set. Other goals such as sustained growth are secondary in many cases. However, two major central banks have shunned inflation targeting so far—the Bank of Japan and the U.S. Federal Reserve. While they both agree that price stability is of paramount importance, they have other goals as well.

U.S. monetary policy focuses on encouraging economic growth and achieving full employment while containing inflation. It has been under pressure to consider using an inflation target as a way to make policy more transparent. Prior to being named chairman in 2006, Ben Bernanke was a leading exponent of inflation targeting during his term on the Board of Governors. The Federal Reserve Act calls on the Fed to maintain growth of credit and the money supply "commensurate with the economy's long-run potential to increase production, so as to promote effectively the goals of maximum employment, stable prices, and moderate long-term interest rates." The Fed's mandate states directly that monetary policy should aim at having the U.S. economy operate at full capacity.

The Bank of Japan has thus far spurned official inflation targeting despite pressures from the government. The suggestion implied that if the BoJ fixed an inflation target, the economy would rid itself of deflation. In the first quarter of 2006, the Bank's inflation measure, the CPI, was no longer declining—much to the consternation of government officials, who hoped for zero interest rates a while longer to finance their astronomical fiscal deficit cheaply.

Inflation targeting generally identifies price stability as the primary objective in monetary policy. An explicit numerical target for inflation is set, including a time period over which any deviation from the target is to be eliminated. Some variations do provide escape clauses related to the pace of return to price stability. While the theme is common, there are various ways in which the target can be defined. But they boil down to either a range or a specific numerical target or a combination of both. Some are dogmatic in pursuing the target, while others are more flexible and include other considerations besides inflation into their monetary policy objective.

Three Examples of Inflation Targeting

The three more prominent monetary policies that rely on inflation targeting are those of the European Central Bank and the Banks of England and Canada. The ECB is mandated by treaty to target inflation, while the Bank of England has its inflation target set annually by the Chancellor of the Exchequer in his budget message. The Bank of Canada's target range is decided jointly by the Bank and the government every five years. Both the ECB and Bank of England use a specific numerical inflation target—2 percent, but with a difference. While the ECB sets a ceiling above which inflation should not climb, the Bank of England tends toward its target but allows for symmetry around it with a range of plus or minus 1 percent around the target. Should inflation exceed/drop more than the 1 percent, the Governor is required to write a letter or remit to the Chancellor explaining why this happened. The Bank of Canada uses a range of 1 to 3 percent and tends toward the 2 percent midpoint.

Measures of Inflation for Targeting Purposes

The various central banks tend to use different measures of inflation for policy purposes. And all are calculated somewhat differently. The ECB uses the harmonized index of consumer prices (HICP), the inflation measure for the European Union. The Bank of England recently changed its inflation measure from the retail price index excluding mortgage interest payments (RPIX) to one modeled after the HICP and called the CPI. The Bank of Canada uses a consumer price index but it is formulated differently from those used by the U.K. and EU. Most use a core measure of consumer prices, but do not always exclude the same items. They all, however, use a year-on-year percent change measure. The United States has several consumer price measures, but former Fed Chairman Alan Greenspan preferred the personal consumption expenditure (PCE) deflator that is calculated as part of gross domestic product (GDP) rather than the CPI, believing that it better reflects the actual change in the cost of living. The Fed monitors the PCE excluding food and energy, and it is one of the variables they forecast in their annual statement. But they also keep an eye on the CPI.

In a 2005 speech, Bank of Canada Governor David Dodge provided insight to the Canadian interpretation of inflation targeting. He explained the Bank's choice of the CPI as its particular inflation measure. Among the reasons he cited was that the CPI was familiar to Canadians and choosing a well-known indicator makes it easier to be accountable to the population and provide an explanation for the Bank's actions. Because the volatility of some CPI components can cause sharp month-to-month fluctuations, the Bank uses a core inflation measure as an operational guide. The core strips out the eight most volatile components, along with the effect of changes in indirect taxes on the rest of the index to give a better understanding of inflation's trend.

He also said that the Bank uses a symmetric target and is not focused on a specific numerical target. Dodge emphasized that policy makers worry equally about inflation falling below target and about it rising above target. The symmetry provides an answer to charges that central banks target inflation at the expense of growth. Paying close attention to the deviation from target promotes timely action in response to both positive and negative demand shocks. Businesses and individuals can make long-range economic plans with increased confidence because the Bank guards against both deflation and inflation.

In the Bank's view, inflation targeting is very helpful in terms of accountability. If inflation persistently deviates from the target, it is committed to explaining the reasons why this is so, what will be done to return it to target, and how long the process should take.

The Actual Practice of Inflation Targeting

The Bank of Canada probably has the vaguest legal mandate. Its statute requires it to regulate "credit and currency in the best interests of the economic life of the nation." Despite the absence of a precise legal mandate, the details of the Bank's monetary policy objectives are reached by agreement between the Bank and the Department of Finance. The current agreement, which is renewed every five years, sets price stability as monetary policy's principal objective and sets the range for inflation as 1 percent to 3 percent, with the midpoint as the explicit target.

The Reserve Bank of Australia has a mandate most closely resembling the United States, but it is even broader and more open-ended. And although the country is considered an inflation-targeting country, it has a dual mandate rather than a hierarchical one. Their legislative mandate as stated in the Reserve Bank

Act is "to [promote] stability of the currency of Australia; [maintain] full employment in Australia; and [foster] economic prosperity and welfare of the people of Australia." The explicit inflation target is 2 percent to 3 percent and is set by the central bank. It applies to the average inflation rate over a business cycle rather than a specific time horizon.

The mandate of the Bank of England is set out in Article 11 of the Bank of England Act. It sets monetary policy objectives "to maintain price stability" and "subject to that, to support the economic policy of Her Majesty's Government, including its objectives for growth and employment." The explicit target, which is set by the Chancellor of the Exchequer annually in his budget message, is currently 2 percent. The Governor of the Bank of England must write a letter to the Chancellor if inflation deviates by more than 1 percentage point from the target.

The European Central Bank was established by the Maastricht Treaty, which identifies price stability as the principal objective. Article 105 of the Maastricht Treaty states that "the primary objective of the [European System of Central Banks (ESCB)] shall be to maintain price stability." The objectives mentioned include "sustainable and non-inflationary growth," a "high level of employment," and "raising the standard of living" among member states. The ECB's Governing Council sets the explicit numerical inflation target, which is a ceiling of 2 percent.

INTER-CENTRAL BANK COOPERATION   **3**

Bank for International Settlements

Cooperation between the world's central banks is visible at times of crisis, although it certainly is not limited to only those times. Cooperation is particularly apparent through the Bank for International Settlements (BIS), an international organization that fosters international monetary and financial cooperation and serves as a bank for central banks. It was established on May 17, 1930, and is the world's oldest international financial organization. The BIS provides a forum to promote discussion and policy analysis among central banks and within the international financial community; a center for economic and monetary research; a prime counterparty for central banks in their financial transactions; and an agent or trustee in connection with international financial operations. The head office is in Basel, Switzerland, and there are two representative offices: in Hong Kong and in Mexico City.

Crisis management was apparent in the immediate aftermath of the terrorist attack on the New York World Trade Center on September 11, 2001, as central banks sought to assure global liquidity in the financial markets. In the immediate aftermath, the Bank of Canada matched the Federal Reserve's 125-basis-point interest rate reduction in September and October, while the Bank of England reduced rates by 50 basis points. The Bank of Japan had no place to go with interest rates already at near zero. The Reserve Bank of Australia also lowered rates by 50 basis points. The European Central Bank lagged the others, gradually reducing rates by 50 basis points in September and then another 25 basis points in November.

Group of Five, then Seven

To further international cooperation, the finance ministers and central bank chairs of the major industrial countries meet periodically to discuss common economic and financial issues. The Group of Five, originally consisting of the

United States, Japan, the United Kingdom, Germany, and France, met for the first time in 1975, and in 1976 were joined by Canada and Italy. The meetings expanded to include heads of state on an annual basis usually in June or July. The finance ministers and central bank chairs generally meet quarterly. Financial markets usually pay close attention to the statements that emanate from these meetings. For example, the April 2006 meeting statement saying that Asian countries should allow their currencies to rise in value was interpreted by currency traders to mean that the U.S. dollar should decline, much to the consternation of Asian governments, who prefer a lower currency value to promote their exports.

PRACTICE PROBLEM FOR READING 28

1. Why are some items extracted from broad-based price indices for the purpose of inflation targeting? The extracted items:

    A. generate too much volatility.

    B. are not measured with sufficient accuracy.

    C. are not considered items to be applicable to households.

SOLUTION FOR READING 28

1. A is correct. The extracted items (e.g., food and fuel) create too much volatility.

A priori probability A probability based on logical analysis rather than on observation or personal judgment.

Abandonment option The ability to terminate a project at some future time if the financial results are disappointing.

Abnormal return The amount by which a security's actual return differs from its expected return, given the security's risk and the market's return.

Above full-employment equilibrium A macroeconomic equilibrium in which real GDP exceeds potential GDP.

Absolute dispersion The amount of variability present without comparison to any reference point or benchmark.

Absolute frequency The number of observations in a given interval (for grouped data).

Accelerated book build An offering of securities by an investment bank acting as principal that is accomplished in only one or two days.

Accelerated methods of depreciation Depreciation methods that allocate a relatively large proportion of the cost of an asset to the early years of the asset's useful life.

Account With the accounting systems, a formal record of increases and decreases in a specific asset, liability, component of owners' equity, revenue, or expense.

Account format A method of presentation of accounting transactions in which effects on assets appear at the left and effects on liabilities and equity appear at the right of a central dividing line; also known as T-account format.

Accounting profit (income before taxes or pretax income) Income as reported on the income statement, in accordance with prevailing accounting standards, before the provisions for income tax expense.

Accounting risk The risk associated with accounting standards that vary from country to country or with any uncertainty about how certain transactions should be recorded.

Accounts payable Amounts that a business owes to its vendors for goods and services that were purchased from them but which have not yet been paid.

Accounts receivable turnover Ratio of sales on credit to the average balance in accounts receivable.

Accrual basis Method of accounting in which the effect of transactions on financial condition and income are recorded when they occur, not when they are settled in cash.

Accrued expenses (accrued liabilities) Liabilities related to expenses that have been incurred but not yet paid as of the end of an accounting period—an example of an accrued expense is rent that has been incurred but not yet paid, resulting in a liability "rent payable."

Accrued interest Interest earned but not yet paid.

Accumulated benefit obligation Under U.S. GAAP, a measure used in estimating a defined-benefit pension plan's liabilities, defined as "the actuarial present value of benefits (whether vested or non-vested) attributed by the pension benefit formula to employee service rendered before a specified date and based on employee service and compensation (if applicable) prior to that date."

Accumulated depreciation An offset to property, plant, and equipment (PPE) reflecting the amount of the cost of PPE that has been allocated to current and previous accounting periods.

Acquiring company, or acquirer The company in a merger or acquisition that is acquiring the target.

Acquisition The purchase of some portion of one company by another; the purchase may be for assets, a definable segment of another entity, or the purchase of an entire company.

Acquisition method A method of accounting for a business combination where the acquirer is required to measure each identifiable asset and liability at fair value. This method was the result of a joint project of the IASB and FASB aiming at convergence in standards for the accounting of business combinations.

Active factor risk The contribution to active risk squared resulting from the portfolio's different-than-benchmark exposures relative to factors specified in the risk model.

Active investment An approach to investing in which the investor seeks to outperform a given benchmark.

Active return The return on a portfolio minus the return on the portfolio's benchmark.

Active risk The standard deviation of active returns.

Active risk squared The variance of active returns; active risk raised to the second power.

Active specific risk or asset selection risk The contribution to active risk squared resulting from the portfolio's active weights on individual assets as those weights interact with assets' residual risk.

Active strategy In reference to short-term cash management, an investment strategy characterized by monitoring and attempting to capitalize on market conditions to optimize the risk and return relationship of short-term investments.

Activity ratios (asset utilization or operating efficiency ratios) Ratios that measure how efficiently a company performs day-to-day tasks, such as the collection of receivables and management of inventory.

Addition rule for probabilities A principle stating that the probability that A or B occurs (both occur) equals the probability that A occurs, plus the probability that B occurs, minus the probability that both A and B occur.

Add-on interest A procedure for determining the interest on a bond or loan in which the interest is added onto the face value of a contract.

Adjusted beta Historical beta adjusted to reflect the tendency of beta to be mean reverting.

Adjusted R^2 A measure of goodness-of-fit of a regression that is adjusted for degrees of freedom and hence does not automatically increase when another independent variable is added to a regression.

Agency costs Costs associated with the conflict of interest present when a company is managed by non-owners. Agency costs result from the inherent conflicts of interest between managers and equity owners.

Agency costs of equity The smaller the stake that managers have in the company, the less is their share in bearing the cost of excessive perquisite consumption or not giving their best efforts in running the company.

Agency problem, or principal-agent problem A conflict of interest that arises when the agent in an agency relationship has goals and incentives that differ from the principal to whom the agent owes a fiduciary duty.

Agency relationships An arrangement whereby someone, an agent, acts on behalf of another person, the principal.

Aggregate demand The relationship between the quantity of real GDP demanded and the price level.

G-1

Aggregate hours The total number of hours worked by all the people employed, both full time and part time, during a year.

Aging schedule A breakdown of accounts into categories of days outstanding.

Allocationally efficient Said of a market, a financial system, or an economy that promotes the allocation of resources to their highest value uses.

Allowance for bad debts An offset to accounts receivable for the amount of accounts receivable that are estimated to be uncollectible.

All-or-nothing (AON) orders An order that includes the instruction to trade only if the trade fills the entire quantity (size) specified.

Alternative hypothesis The hypothesis accepted when the null hypothesis is rejected.

Alternative investment markets Market for investments other than traditional securities investments (i.e., traditional common and preferred shares and traditional fixed income instruments). The term usually encompasses direct and indirect investment in real estate (including timberland and farmland) and commodities (including precious metals); hedge funds, private equity, and other investments requiring specialized due diligence.

Alternative trading systems (electronic communications networks or multilateral trading facilities) Trading venues that function like exchanges but that do not exercise regulatory authority over their subscribers except with respect to the conduct of the subscribers' trading in their trading systems.

American depository receipt A U.S. dollar-denominated security that trades like a common share on U.S. exchanges.

American depository shares The underlying shares on which American depository receipts are based. They trade in the issuing company's domestic market.

American option An option that can be exercised at any time until its expiration date.

Amortization The process of allocating the cost of intangible long-term assets having a finite useful life to accounting periods; the allocation of the amount of a bond premium or discount to the periods remaining until bond maturity.

Amortizing and accreting swaps A swap in which the notional principal changes according to a formula related to changes in the underlying.

Analysis of variance (ANOVA) The analysis of the total variability of a dataset (such as observations on the dependent variable in a regression) into components representing different sources of variation; with reference to regression, ANOVA provides the inputs for an F-test of the significance of the regression as a whole.

Annual percentage rate The cost of borrowing expressed as a yearly rate.

Annuity A finite set of level sequential cash flows.

Annuity due An annuity having a first cash flow that is paid immediately.

Anticipation stock Excess inventory that is held in anticipation of increased demand, often because of seasonal patterns of demand.

Antidilutive With reference to a transaction or a security, one that would increase earnings per share (EPS) or result in EPS higher than the company's basic EPS—antidilutive securities are not included in the calculation of diluted EPS.

Arbitrage 1) The simultaneous purchase of an undervalued asset or portfolio and sale of an overvalued but equivalent asset or portfolio, in order to obtain a riskless profit on the price differential. Taking advantage of a market inefficiency in a risk-free manner. 2) The condition in a financial market in which equivalent assets or combinations of assets sell for two different prices, creating an opportunity to profit at no risk with no commitment of money. In a well-functioning financial market, few arbitrage opportunities are possible. 3) A risk-free operation that earns an expected positive net profit but requires no net investment of money.

Arbitrage opportunity An opportunity to conduct an arbitrage; an opportunity to earn an expected positive net profit without risk and with no net investment of money.

Arbitrage portfolio The portfolio that exploits an arbitrage opportunity.

Arbitrageurs Traders who engage in arbitrage (see *arbitrage*).

Arithmetic mean The sum of the observations divided by the number of observations.

Arms index, also called **TRIN** A flow of funds indicator applied to a broad stock market index to measure the relative extent to which money is moving into or out of rising and declining stocks.

Arrears swap A type of interest rate swap in which the floating payment is set at the end of the period and the interest is paid at that same time.

Asian call option A European-style option with a value at maturity equal to the difference between the stock price at maturity and the average stock price during the life of the option, or $0, whichever is greater.

Ask (offer) The price at which a dealer or trader is willing to sell an asset, typically qualified by a maximum quantity (ask size).

Ask size The maximum quantity of an asset that pertains to a specific ask price from a trader. For example, if the ask for a share issue is $30 for a size of 1,000 shares, the trader is offering to sell at $30 up to 1,000 shares.

Asset allocation The process of determining how investment funds should be distributed among asset classes.

Asset beta The unlevered beta; reflects the business risk of the assets; the asset's systematic risk.

Asset class A group of assets that have similar characteristics, attributes, and risk/return relationships.

Asset purchase An acquisition in which the acquirer purchases the target company's assets and payment is made directly to the target company.

Asset retirement obligations (AROs) The fair value of the estimated costs to be incurred at the end of a tangible asset's service life. The fair value of the liability is determined on the basis of discounted cash flows.

Asset-based loan A loan that is secured with company assets.

Asset-based valuation models Valuation based on estimates of the market value of a company's assets.

Assets Resources controlled by an enterprise as a result of past events and from which future economic benefits to the enterprise are expected to flow.

Assignment of accounts receivable The use of accounts receivable as collateral for a loan.

Asymmetric information The differential of information between corporate insiders and outsiders regarding the company's performance and prospects. Managers typically have more information about the company's performance and prospects than owners and creditors.

At the money An option in which the underlying value equals the exercise price.

Autocorrelation The correlation of a time series with its own past values.

Automated Clearing House An electronic payment network available to businesses, individuals, and financial institutions in the United States, U.S. Territories, and Canada.

Automatic fiscal policy A fiscal policy action that is triggered by the state of the economy.

Automatic stabilizers Mechanisms that stabilize real GDP without explicit action by the government.

Autonomous tax multiplier The magnification effect of a change in taxes on aggregate demand.

Autoregressive (AR) model A time series regressed on its own past values, in which the independent variable is a lagged value of the dependent variable.

Available-for-sale investments Debt and equity securities not classified as either held-to-maturity or held-for-trading securities. The investor is willing to sell but not actively planning to sell. In general, available-for-sale securities are reported at fair value on the balance sheet.

Average cost pricing rule A rule that sets price to cover cost including normal profit, which means setting the price equal to average total cost.

Average fixed cost Total fixed cost per unit of output.

Average product The average product of a factor of production. It equals total product divided by the quantity of the factor employed.

Average total cost Total cost per unit of output.

Average variable cost Total variable cost per unit of output.

Backtesting With reference to portfolio strategies, the application of a strategy's portfolio selection rules to historical data to assess what would have been the strategy's historical performance.

Backward integration A merger involving the purchase of a target ahead of the acquirer in the value or production chain; for example, to acquire a supplier.

Backwardation A condition in the futures markets in which the benefits of holding an asset exceed the costs, leaving the futures price less than the spot price.

Balance sheet (statement of financial position or statement of financial condition) The financial statement that presents an entity's current financial position by disclosing resources the entity controls (its assets) and the claims on those resources (its liabilities and equity claims), as of a particular point in time (the date of the balance sheet).

Balance sheet ratios Financial ratios involving balance sheet items only.

Balanced budget A government budget in which tax revenues and outlays are equal.

Balanced budget multiplier The magnification effect on aggregate demand of a simultaneous change in government expenditure and taxes that leaves the budget balanced.

Balance-sheet-based accruals ratio The difference between net operating assets at the end and the beginning of the period compared to the average net operating assets over the period.

Balance-sheet-based aggregate accruals The difference between net operating assets at the end and the beginning of the period.

Bank discount basis A quoting convention that annualizes, on a 360-day year, the discount as a percentage of face value.

Bar chart A price chart with four bits of data for each time interval—the high, low, opening, and closing prices. A vertical line connects the high and low. A cross-hatch left indicates the opening price and a cross-hatch right indicates the close.

Bargain purchase When a company is acquired and the purchase price is less than the fair value of the net assets. The current treatment of the excess of fair value over the purchase price is different under IFRS and U.S. GAAP. The excess is never accounted for as negative goodwill.

Barriers to entry Legal or natural constraints that protect a firm from potential competitors.

Barter The direct exchange of one good or service for other goods and services.

Basic EPS Net earnings available to common shareholders (i.e., net income minus preferred dividends) divided by the weighted average number of common shares outstanding.

Basis point value (BPV) Also called *present value of a basis point* or *price value of a basis point* (PVBP), the change in the bond price for a 1 basis point change in yield.

Basis swap 1) An interest rate swap involving two floating rates. 2) A swap in which both parties pay a floating rate.

Basket of listed depository receipts An exchange-traded fund (ETF) that represents a portfolio of depository receipts.

Bayes' formula A method for updating probabilities based on new information.

Bear hug A tactic used by acquirers to circumvent target management's objections to a proposed merger by submitting the proposal directly to the target company's board of directors.

Bear spread An option strategy that involves selling a put with a lower exercise price and buying a put with a higher exercise price. It can also be executed with calls.

Behavioral finance A field of finance that examines the psychological variables that affect and often distort the investment decision making of investors, analysts, and portfolio managers.

Behind the market Said of prices specified in orders that are worse than the best current price; e.g., for a limit buy order, a limit price below the best bid.

Below full-employment equilibrium A macroeconomic equilibrium in which potential GDP exceeds real GDP.

Benchmark A comparison portfolio; a point of reference or comparison.

Benchmark error The use of an inappropriate or incorrect benchmark to assess and compare portfolio returns and management.

Benchmark portfolio A comparison portfolio or index that represents the persistent and prominent investment characteristics of the securities in an actual portfolio.

Bernoulli random variable A random variable having the outcomes 0 and 1.

Bernoulli trial An experiment that can produce one of two outcomes.

Best bid The highest bid in the market.

Best efforts offering An offering of a security using an investment bank in which the investment bank, as agent for the issuer, promises to use its best efforts to sell the offering but does not guarantee that a specific amount will be sold.

Best offer The lowest offer (ask price) in the market.

Beta A measure of systematic risk that is based on the covariance of an asset's or portfolio's return with the return of the overall market.

Bid price The price at which a dealer or trader is willing to buy an asset, typically qualified by a maximum quantity.

Bid size The maximum quantity of an asset that pertains to a specific bid price from a trader.

Big tradeoff The conflict between equality and efficiency.

Bilateral monopoly A situation in which a single seller (a monopoly) faces a single buyer (a monopsony).

Binomial model A model for pricing options in which the underlying price can move to only one of two possible new prices.

Binomial random variable The number of successes in n Bernoulli trials for which the probability of success is constant for all trials and the trials are independent.

Binomial tree The graphical representation of a model of asset price dynamics in which, at each period, the asset moves up with probability p or down with probability $(1 - p)$.

Black market   An illegal market in which the price exceeds the legally imposed price ceiling.

Block   Orders to buy or sell that are too large for the liquidity ordinarily available in dealer networks or stock exchanges.

Block brokers   A broker (agent) that provides brokerage services for large-size trades.

Blue chip companies   Widely held large market capitalization companies that are considered financially sound and are leaders in their respective industry or local stock market.

Bollinger Bands   A price-based technical analysis indicator consisting of a moving average plus a higher line representing the moving average plus a set number of standard deviations from average price (for the same number of periods as used to calculate the moving average) and a lower line that is a moving average minus the same number of standard deviations.

Bond equivalent yield   A calculation of yield that is annualized using the ratio of 365 to the number of days to maturity. Bond equivalent yield allows for the restatement and comparison of securities with different compounding periods.

Bond option   An option in which the underlying is a bond; primarily traded in over-the-counter markets.

Bond yield plus risk premium approach   An estimate of the cost of common equity that is produced by summing the before-tax cost of debt and a risk premium that captures the additional yield on a company's stock relative to its bonds. The additional yield is often estimated using historical spreads between bond yields and stock yields.

Bond-equivalent basis   A basis for stating an annual yield that annualizes a semiannual yield by doubling it.

Bond-equivalent yield   The yield to maturity on a basis that ignores compounding.

Bonding costs   Costs borne by management to assure owners that they are working in the owners' best interest (e.g., implicit cost of non-compete agreements).

Book building   Investment bankers' process of compiling a "book" or list of indications of interest to buy part of an offering.

Book value (or **carrying value**)   The net amount shown for an asset or liability on the balance sheet; book value may also refer to the company's excess of total assets over total liabilities.

Book value equity per share   The amount of book value (also called carrying value) of common equity per share of common stock, calculated by dividing the book value of shareholders' equity by the number of shares of common stock outstanding.

Bootstrapping earnings   An increase in a company's earnings that results as a consequence of the idiosyncrasies of a merger transaction itself rather than because of resulting economic benefits of the combination.

Bottom-up analysis   With reference to investment selection processes, an approach that involves selection from all securities within a specified investment universe, i.e., without prior narrowing of the universe on the basis of macroeconomic or overall market considerations.

Box spread   An option strategy that combines a bull spread and a bear spread having two different exercise prices, which produces a risk-free payoff of the difference in the exercise prices.

Break point   In the context of the weighted average cost of capital (WACC), a break point is the amount of capital at which the cost of one or more of the sources of capital changes, leading to a change in the WACC.

Breakeven point   The number of units produced and sold at which the company's net income is zero (revenues = total costs).

Breakup value   The value that can be achieved if a company's assets are divided and sold separately.

Breusch–Pagan test   A test for conditional heteroskedasticity in the error term of a regression.

Broker   1) An agent who executes orders to buy or sell securities on behalf of a client in exchange for a commission. 2) *See* Futures commission merchants.

Broker–dealer   A financial intermediary (often a company) that may function as a principal (dealer) or as an agent (broker) depending on the type of trade.

Brokered market   A market in which brokers arrange trades among their clients.

Budget deficit   A government's budget balance that is negative—outlays exceed tax revenues.

Budget surplus   A government's budget balance that is positive—tax revenues exceed outlays.

Bull spread   An option strategy that involves buying a call with a lower exercise price and selling a call with a higher exercise price. It can also be executed with puts.

Business risk   The risk associated with operating earnings. Operating earnings are uncertain because total revenues and many of the expenditures contributed to produce those revenues are uncertain.

Butterfly spread   An option strategy that combines two bull or bear spreads and has three exercise prices.

Buy side firm   An investment management company or other investor that uses the services of brokers or dealers (i.e., the client of the sell side firms).

Buyout fund   A fund that buys all the shares of a public company so that, in effect, the company becomes private.

Call   An option that gives the holder the right to buy an underlying asset from another party at a fixed price over a specific period of time.

Call market   A market in which trades occur only at a particular time and place (i.e., when the market is called).

Call money rate   The interest rate that buyers pay for their margin loan.

Callable (or redeemable) **common shares**   Shares that give the issuing company the option (or right), but not the obligation, to buy back the shares from investors at a call price that is specified when the shares are originally issued.

Candlestick chart   A price chart with four bits of data for each time interval. A candle indicates the opening and closing price for the interval. The body of the candle is shaded if the opening price was higher than the closing price, and the body is clear if the opening price was lower than the closing price. Vertical lines known as wicks or shadows extend from the top and bottom of the candle to indicate the high and the low prices for the interval.

Cannibalization   Cannibalization occurs when an investment takes customers and sales away from another part of the company.

Cap   1) A contract on an interest rate, whereby at periodic payment dates, the writer of the cap pays the difference between the market interest rate and a specified cap rate if, and only if, this difference is positive. This is equivalent to a stream of call options on the interest rate. 2) A combination of interest rate call options designed to hedge a borrower against rate increases on a floating-rate loan.

Capital allocation line (CAL)   A graph line that describes the combinations of expected return and standard deviation of return available to an investor from combining the optimal portfolio of risky assets with the risk-free asset.

Capital asset pricing model (CAPM)   An equation describing the expected return on any asset (or portfolio) as a linear function of its beta relative to the market portfolio.

Capital budgeting   The allocation of funds to relatively long-range projects or investments.

Capital market expectations   An investor's expectations concerning the risk and return prospects of asset classes.

Capital market line (CML) The line with an intercept point equal to the risk-free rate that is tangent to the efficient frontier of risky assets; represents the efficient frontier when a risk-free asset is available for investment.

Capital markets Financial markets that trade securities of longer duration, such as bonds and equities.

Capital rationing A capital rationing environment assumes that the company has a fixed amount of funds to invest.

Capital structure The mix of debt and equity that a company uses to finance its business; a company's specific mixture of long-term financing.

Capitalized inventory costs Costs of inventories including costs of purchase, costs of conversion, other costs to bring the inventories to their present location and condition, and the allocated portion of fixed production overhead costs.

Caplet Each component call option in a cap.

Capped swap A swap in which the floating payments have an upper limit.

Captive finance subsidiary A wholly-owned subsidiary of a company that is established to provide financing of the sales of the parent company.

Carrying amount (book value) The amount at which an asset or liability is valued according to accounting principles.

Cartel A group of firms that has entered into a collusive agreement to restrict output and increase prices and profits.

Cash In accounting contexts, cash on hand (e.g., petty cash and cash not yet deposited to the bank) and demand deposits held in banks and similar accounts that can be used in payment of obligations.

Cash basis Accounting method in which the only relevant transactions for the financial statements are those that involve cash.

Cash conversion cycle (net operating cycle) A financial metric that measures the length of time required for a company to convert cash invested in its operations to cash received as a result of its operations; equal to days of inventory on hand + days of sales outstanding – number of days of payables.

Cash equivalents Very liquid short-term investments, usually maturing in 90 days or less.

Cash flow additivity principle The principle that dollar amounts indexed at the same point in time are additive.

Cash flow at risk (CFAR) A variation of VAR that reflects the risk of a company's cash flow instead of its market value.

Cash flow from operations (cash flow from operating activities or operating cash flow) The net amount of cash provided from operating activities.

Cash flow statement (statement of cash flows) A financial statement that reconciles beginning-of-period and end-of-period balance sheet values of cash; consists of three parts: cash flows from operating activities, cash flows from investing activities, and cash flows from financing activities.

Cash offering A merger or acquisition that is to be paid for with cash; the cash for the merger might come from the acquiring company's existing assets or from a debt issue.

Cash price or spot price The price for immediate purchase of the underlying asset.

Cash ratio A liquidity ratio calculated as (cash + short-term marketable investments) divided by current liabilities; measures a company's ability to meet its current obligations with just the cash and cash equivalents on hand.

Cash settlement A procedure used in certain derivative transactions that specifies that the long and short parties engage in the equivalent cash value of a delivery transaction.

Cash-flow-statement-based accruals ratio The difference between reported net income on an accrual basis and the cash flows from operating and investing activities compared to the average net operating assets over the period.

Cash-flow-statement-based aggregate accruals The difference between reported net income on an accrual basis and the cash flows from operating and investing activities.

CBOE Volatility Index A measure of near-term market volatility as conveyed by S&P 500 stock index option prices.

Central bank A bank's bank and a public authority that regulates the nation's depository institutions and controls the quantity of money.

Central limit theorem A result in statistics that states that the sample mean computed from large samples of size n from a population with finite variance will follow an approximate normal distribution with a mean equal to the population mean and a variance equal to the population variance divided by n.

Centralized risk management or companywide risk management When a company has a single risk management group that monitors and controls all of the risk-taking activities of the organization. Centralization permits economies of scale and allows a company to use some of its risks to offset other risks. (See also *enterprise risk management*.)

Chain rule of forecasting A forecasting process in which the next period's value as predicted by the forecasting equation is substituted into the right-hand side of the equation to give a predicted value two periods ahead.

Change in polarity principle A tenet of technical analysis that once a support level is breached, it becomes a resistance level. The same holds true for resistance levels; once breached, they become support levels.

Chart of accounts A list of accounts used in an entity's accounting system.

Cheapest to deliver A bond in which the amount received for delivering the bond is largest compared with the amount paid in the market for the bond.

Cherry-picking When a bankrupt company is allowed to enforce contracts that are favorable to it while walking away from contracts that are unfavorable to it.

Classical A macroeconomist who believes that the economy is self-regulating and that it is always at full employment.

Classified balance sheet A balance sheet organized so as to group together the various assets and liabilities into subcategories (e.g., current and noncurrent).

Clean-surplus accounting The bottom-line income reflects all changes in shareholders' equity arising from other than owner transactions. In the absence of owner transactions, the change in shareholders' equity should equal net income. No adjustments such as translation adjustments bypass the income statement and go directly to shareholders equity.

Clearing instructions Instructions that indicate how to arrange the final settlement ("clearing") of a trade.

Clearinghouse An entity associated with a futures market that acts as middleman between the contracting parties and guarantees to each party the performance of the other.

Clientele effect The preference some investors have for shares that exhibit certain characteristics.

Closed-end fund A mutual fund in which no new investment money is accepted. New investors invest by buying existing shares, and investors in the fund liquidate by selling their shares to other investors.

Closeout netting Netting the market values of *all* derivative contracts between two parties to determine one overall value owed by one party to another in the event of bankruptcy.

Coefficient of variation (CV) The ratio of a set of observations' standard deviation to the observations' mean value.

Cointegrated Describes two time series that have a long-term financial or economic relationship such that they do not diverge from each other without bound in the long run.

Collar An option strategy involving the purchase of a put and sale of a call in which the holder of an asset gains protection below a certain level, the exercise price of the put, and pays for it by giving up gains above a certain level, the exercise price of the call. Collars also can be used to provide protection against rising interest rates on a floating-rate loan by giving up gains from lower interest rates.

Collusive agreement An agreement between two (or more) producers to restrict output, raise the price, and increase profits.

Combination A listing in which the order of the listed items does not matter.

Command system A method of allocating resources by the order (command) of someone in authority. In a firm a managerial hierarchy organizes production.

Commercial paper Unsecured short-term corporate debt that is characterized by a single payment at maturity.

Committed lines of credit A bank commitment to extend credit up to a pre-specified amount; the commitment is considered a short-term liability and is usually in effect for 364 days (one day short of a full year).

Commodity forward A contract in which the underlying asset is oil, a precious metal, or some other commodity.

Commodity futures Futures contracts in which the underlying is a traditional agricultural, metal, or petroleum product.

Commodity option An option in which the asset underlying the futures is a commodity, such as oil, gold, wheat, or soybeans.

Commodity swap A swap in which the underlying is a commodity such as oil, gold, or an agricultural product.

Common shares A type of security that represent an ownership interest in a company.

Common size statements Financial statements in which all elements (accounts) are stated as a percentage of a key figure such as revenue for an income statement or total assets for a balance sheet.

Common-size analysis The restatement of financial statement items using a common denominator or reference item that allows one to identify trends and major differences; an example is an income statement in which all items are expressed as a percent of revenue.

Company analysis Analysis of an individual company.

Company fundamental factors Factors related to the company's internal performance, such as factors relating to earnings growth, earnings variability, earnings momentum, and financial leverage.

Company share-related factors Valuation measures and other factors related to share price or the trading characteristics of the shares, such as earnings yield, dividend yield, and book-to-market value.

Comparable company A company that has similar business risk; usually in the same industry and preferably with a single line of business.

Competitive strategy A company's plans for responding to the threats and opportunities presented by the external environment.

Complement In probability, with reference to an event *S*, the event that *S* does not occur; in economics, a good that is used in conjunction with another good.

Complete markets Informally, markets in which the variety of distinct securities traded is so broad that any desired payoff in a future state-of-the-world is achievable.

Completed contract A method of revenue recognition in which the company does not recognize any revenue until the contract is completed; used particularly in long-term construction contracts.

Component cost of capital The rate of return required by suppliers of capital for an individual source of a company's funding, such as debt or equity.

Compounding The process of accumulating interest on interest.

Comprehensive income The change in equity of a business enterprise during a period from nonowner sources; includes all changes in equity during a period except those resulting from investments by owners and distributions to owners; comprehensive income equals net income plus other comprehensive income.

Conditional expected value The expected value of a stated event given that another event has occurred.

Conditional heteroskedasticity Heteroskedasticity in the error variance that is correlated with the values of the independent variable(s) in the regression.

Conditional probability The probability of an event given (conditioned on) another event.

Conditional variances The variance of one variable, given the outcome of another.

Confidence interval A range that has a given probability that it will contain the population parameter it is intended to estimate.

Conglomerate merger A merger involving companies that are in unrelated businesses.

Consistency A desirable property of estimators; a consistent estimator is one for which the probability of estimates close to the value of the population parameter increases as sample size increases.

Consistent With reference to estimators, describes an estimator for which the probability of estimates close to the value of the population parameter increases as sample size increases.

Consolidation The combining of the results of operations of subsidiaries with the parent company to present financial statements as if they were a single economic unit. The asset, liabilities, revenues and expenses of the subsidiaries are combined with those of the parent company, eliminating intercompany transactions.

Constant maturity swap or CMT swap A swap in which the floating rate is the rate on a security known as a constant maturity treasury or CMT security.

Constant maturity treasury or CMT A hypothetical U.S. Treasury note with a constant maturity. A CMT exists for various years in the range of 2 to 10.

Constant returns to scale Features of a firm's technology that lead to constant long-run average cost as output increases. When constant returns to scale are present, the *LRAC* curve is horizontal.

Constituent securities With respect to an index, the individual securities within an index.

Consumer Price Index (CPI) An index that measures the average of the prices paid by urban consumers for a fixed "basket" of the consumer goods and services.

Consumer surplus The value (or marginal benefit) of a good minus the price paid for it, summed over the quantity bought.

Contango A situation in a futures market where the current futures price is greater than the current spot price for the underlying asset.

Contestable market A market in which firms can enter and leave so easily that firms in the market face competition from potential entrants.

Contingent claims Derivatives in which the payoffs occur if a specific event occurs; generally referred to as options.

Continuation patterns A type of pattern used in technical analysis to predict the resumption of a market trend that was in place prior to the formation of a pattern.

Continuous market A market where stocks are priced and traded continuously by an auction process or by dealers when the market is open.

Continuous random variable A random variable for which the range of possible outcomes is the real line (all real numbers between $-\infty$ and $+\infty$ or some subset of the real line).

Continuous time Time thought of as advancing in extremely small increments.

Continuous trading market A market in which trades can be arranged and executed any time the market is open.

Continuously compounded return The natural logarithm of 1 plus the holding period return, or equivalently, the natural logarithm of the ending price over the beginning price.

Contra account An account that offsets another account.

Contribution margin The amount available for fixed costs and profit after paying variable costs; revenue minus variable costs.

Controlling interest An investment where the investor exerts control over the investee, typically by having a greater than 50 percent ownership in the investee.

Convenience yield The nonmonetary return offered by an asset when the asset is in short supply, often associated with assets with seasonal production processes.

Conventional cash flow A conventional cash flow pattern is one with an initial outflow followed by a series of inflows.

Convergence In technical analysis, a term that describes the case when an indicator moves in the same manner as the security being analyzed.

Conversion factor An adjustment used to facilitate delivery on bond futures contracts in which any of a number of bonds with different characteristics are eligible for delivery.

Convertible debt Debt with the added feature that the bond-holder has the option to exchange the debt for equity at pre-specified terms.

Convertible preference shares A type of equity security that entitles shareholders to convert their shares into a specified number of common shares.

Cooperative equilibrium The outcome of a game in which the players make and share the monopoly profit.

Core inflation rate A measure of inflation based on the core CPI—the CPI excluding food and fuel.

Corporate governance The system of principles, policies, procedures, and clearly defined responsibilities and accountabilities used by stakeholders to overcome the conflicts of interest inherent in the corporate form.

Corporate raider A person or organization seeking to profit by acquiring a company and reselling it, or seeking to profit from the takeover attempt itself (e.g. greenmail).

Corporation A legal entity with rights similar to those of a person. The chief officers, executives, or top managers act as agents for the firm and are legally entitled to authorize corporate activities and to enter into contracts on behalf of the business.

Correlation A number between -1 and $+1$ that measures the co-movement (linear association) between two random variables.

Correlation analysis The analysis of the strength of the linear relationship between two data series.

Correlation coefficient A number between -1 and $+1$ that measures the consistency or tendency for two investments to act in a similar way. It is used to determine the effect on portfolio risk when two assets are combined.

Cost averaging The periodic investment of a fixed amount of money.

Cost of capital The rate of return that suppliers of capital require as compensation for their contribution of capital.

Cost of carry The cost associated with holding some asset, including financing, storage, and insurance costs. Any yield received on the asset is treated as a negative carrying cost.

Cost of carry model A model for pricing futures contracts in which the futures price is determined by adding the cost of carry to the spot price.

Cost of debt The cost of debt financing to a company, such as when it issues a bond or takes out a bank loan.

Cost of goods sold For a given period, equal to beginning inventory minus ending inventory plus the cost of goods acquired or produced during the period.

Cost of preferred stock The cost to a company of issuing preferred stock; the dividend yield that a company must commit to pay preferred stockholders.

Cost recovery method A method of revenue recognition in which the seller does not report any profit until the cash amounts paid by the buyer—including principal and interest on any financing from the seller—are greater than all the seller's costs for the merchandise sold.

Cost structure The mix of a company's variable costs and fixed costs.

Cost-push inflation An inflation that results from an initial increase in costs.

Council of Economic Advisers The President's council whose main work is to monitor the economy and keep the President and the public well informed about the current state of the economy and the best available forecasts of where it is heading.

Counterparty risk The risk that the other party to a contract will fail to honor the terms of the contract.

Coupon rate The interest rate promised in a contract; this is the rate used to calculate the periodic interest payments.

Covariance A measure of the co-movement (linear association) between two random variables.

Covariance matrix A matrix or square array whose entries are covariances; also known as a variance–covariance matrix.

Covariance stationary Describes a time series when its expected value and variance are constant and finite in all periods and when its covariance with itself for a fixed number of periods in the past or future is constant and finite in all periods.

Covered call An option strategy involving the holding of an asset and sale of a call on the asset.

Covered interest arbitrage A transaction executed in the foreign exchange market in which a currency is purchased (sold) and a forward contract is sold (purchased) to lock in the exchange rate for future delivery of the currency. This transaction should earn the risk-free rate of the investor's home country.

Credit With respect to double-entry accounting, a credit records increases in liability, owners' equity, and revenue accounts or decreases in asset accounts; with respect to borrowing, the willingness and ability of the borrower to make promised payments on the borrowing.

Credit analysis The evaluation of credit risk; the evaluation of the creditworthiness of a borrower or counterparty.

Credit derivatives A contract in which one party has the right to claim a payment from another party in the event that a specific credit event occurs over the life of the contract.

Credit risk or default risk The risk of loss caused by a counterparty's or debtor's failure to make a promised payment.

Credit scoring model A statistical model used to classify borrowers according to creditworthiness.

Credit spread option An option on the yield spread on a bond.

Credit swap   A type of swap transaction used as a credit derivative in which one party makes periodic payments to the other and receives the promise of a payoff if a third party defaults.

Credit VAR, Default VAR, or Credit at Risk   A variation of VAR that reflects credit risk.

Credit-linked notes   Fixed-income securities in which the holder of the security has the right to withhold payment of the full amount due at maturity if a credit event occurs.

Credit-worthiness   The perceived ability of the borrower to pay what is owed on the borrowing in a timely manner; it represents the ability of a company to withstand adverse impacts on its cash flows.

Cross elasticity of demand   The responsiveness of the demand for a good to a change in the price of a substitute or complement, other things remaining the same. It is calculated as the percentage change in the quantity demanded of the good divided by the percentage change in the price of the substitute or complement.

Crossing networks   Trading systems that match buyers and sellers who are willing to trade at prices obtained from other markets.

Cross-product netting   Netting the market values of all contracts, not just derivatives, between parties.

Cross-sectional analysis   Analysis that involves comparisons across individuals in a group over a given time period or at a given point in time.

Cross-sectional data   Observations over individual units at a point in time, as opposed to time-series data.

Crowding-out effect   The tendency for a government budget deficit to decrease investment.

Cumulative distribution function   A function giving the probability that a random variable is less than or equal to a specified value.

Cumulative preference shares   Preference shares for which any dividends that are not paid accrue and must be paid in full before dividends on common shares can be paid.

Cumulative relative frequency   For data grouped into intervals, the fraction of total observations that are less than the value of the upper limit of a stated interval.

Cumulative voting   Voting that allows shareholders to direct their total voting rights to specific candidates, as opposed to having to allocate their voting rights evenly among all candidates.

Currency   The notes and coins held by individuals and businesses.

Currency drain ratio   The ratio of currency to deposits.

Currency forward   A forward contract in which the underlying is a foreign currency.

Currency option   An option that allows the holder to buy (if a call) or sell (if a put) an underlying currency at a fixed exercise rate, expressed as an exchange rate.

Currency swap   A swap in which each party makes interest payments to the other in different currencies.

Current assets, or liquid assets   Assets that are expected to be consumed or converted into cash in the near future, typically one year or less.

Current cost   With reference to assets, the amount of cash or cash equivalents that would have to be paid to buy the same or an equivalent asset today; with reference to liabilities, the undiscounted amount of cash or cash equivalents that would be required to settle the obligation today.

Current credit risk   The risk associated with the possibility that a payment currently due will not be made.

Current exchange rate   For accounting purposes, the spot exchange rate on the balance sheet date.

Current liabilities   Short-term obligations, such as accounts payable, wages payable, or accrued liabilities, that are expected to be settled in the near future, typically one year or less.

Current rate method   Approach to translating foreign currency financial statements for consolidation in which all assets and liabilities are translated at the current exchange rate. The current rate method is the prevalent method of translation.

Current ratio   A liquidity ratio calculated as current assets divided by current liabilities.

Current taxes payable   Tax expenses that have been recognized and recorded on a company's income statement but which have not yet been paid.

Cyclical company   A company whose profits are strongly correlated with the strength of the overall economy.

Cyclical stock   The shares (stock) of a company whose earnings have above-average sensitivity to the business cycle.

Cyclical surplus or deficit   The actual surplus or deficit minus the structural surplus or deficit.

Cyclical unemployment   The fluctuating unemployment over the business cycle.

Daily settlement   See *Marking to market*.

Dark pools   Alternative trading systems that do not display the orders that their clients send to them.

Data mining (or **data snooping**)   The practice of determining a model by extensive searching through a dataset for statistically significant patterns.

Day order   An order that is good for the day on which it is submitted. If it has not been filled by the close of business, the order expires unfilled.

Day trader   A trader holding a position open somewhat longer than a scalper but closing all positions at the end of the day.

Days of inventory on hand (DOH)   An activity ratio equal to the number of days in the period divided by inventory turnover over the period.

Days of sales outstanding (DSO)   An activity ratio equal to the number of days in the period divided by receivables turnover.

Dead cross   A technical analysis term that describes a situation where a short-term moving average crosses from above a longer-term moving average to below it; this movement is considered bearish.

Dead-hand provision   A poison pill provision that allows for the redemption or cancellation of a poison pill provision only by a vote of continuing directors (generally directors who were on the target company's board prior to the takeover attempt).

Deadweight loss   A measure of inefficiency. It is equal to the decrease in total surplus that results from an inefficient level of production.

Dealers   A financial intermediary that acts as a principal in trades.

Dealing securities   Securities held by banks or other financial intermediaries for trading purposes.

Debit   With respect to double-entry accounting, a debit records increases of asset and expense accounts or decreases in liability and owners' equity accounts.

Debt covenants   Agreements between the company as borrower and its creditors.

Debt incurrence test   A financial covenant made in conjunction with existing debt that restricts a company's ability to incur additional debt at the same seniority based on one or more financial tests or conditions.

Debt rating approach   A method for estimating a company's before-tax cost of debt based upon the yield on comparably rated bonds for maturities that closely match that of the company's existing debt.

Debt ratings   An objective measure of the quality and safety of a company's debt based upon an analysis of the company's ability to pay the promised cash flows, as well as an analysis of any indentures.

Debt with warrants   Debt issued with warrants that give the bondholder the right to purchase equity at prespecified terms.

Debt-to-assets ratio　A solvency ratio calculated as total debt divided by total assets.

Debt-to-capital ratio　A solvency ratio calculated as total debt divided by total debt plus total shareholders' equity.

Debt-to-equity ratio　A solvency ratio calculated as total debt divided by total shareholders' equity.

Decentralized risk management　A system that allows individual units within an organization to manage risk. Decentralization results in duplication of effort but has the advantage of having people closer to the risk be more directly involved in its management.

Deciles　Quantiles that divide a distribution into 10 equal parts.

Decision rule　With respect to hypothesis testing, the rule according to which the null hypothesis will be rejected or not rejected; involves the comparison of the test statistic to rejection point(s).

Declaration date　The day that the corporation issues a statement declaring a specific dividend.

Deductible temporary differences　Temporary differences that result in a reduction of or deduction from taxable income in a future period when the balance sheet item is recovered or settled.

Deep in the money　Options that are far in-the-money.

Deep out of the money　Options that are far out-of-the-money.

Default risk premium　An extra return that compensates investors for the possibility that the borrower will fail to make a promised payment at the contracted time and in the contracted amount.

Defensive company　A company whose revenues and profits are least affected by fluctuations in the overall economic activity.

Defensive interval ratio　A liquidity ratio that estimates the number of days that an entity could meet cash needs from liquid assets; calculated as (cash + short-term marketable investments + receivables) divided by daily cash expenditures.

Defensive stock　The shares (stock) of a company whose earnings have below-average sensitivity to the business cycle.

Deferred tax assets　A balance sheet asset that arises when an excess amount is paid for income taxes relative to accounting profit. The taxable income is higher than accounting profit and income tax payable exceeds tax expense. The company expects to recover the difference during the course of future operations when tax expense exceeds income tax payable.

Deferred tax liabilities　A balance sheet liability that arises when a deficit amount is paid for income taxes relative to accounting profit. The taxable income is less than the accounting profit and income tax payable is less than tax expense. The company expects to eliminate the liability over the course of future operations when income tax payable exceeds tax expense.

Defined-benefit pension plans　Plan in which the company promises to pay a certain annual amount (defined benefit) to the employee after retirement. The company bears the investment risk of the plan assets.

Defined-contribution pension plans　Individual accounts to which an employee and typically the employer makes contributions, generally on a tax-advantaged basis. The amounts of contributions are defined at the outset, but the future value of the benefit is unknown. The employee bears the investment risk of the plan assets.

Definitive merger agreement　A contract signed by both parties to a merger that clarifies the details of the transaction, including the terms, warranties, conditions, termination details, and the rights of all parties.

Degree of confidence　The probability that a confidence interval includes the unknown population parameter.

Degree of financial leverage (DFL)　The ratio of the percentage change in net income to the percentage change in operating income; the sensitivity of the cash flows available to owners when operating income changes.

Degree of operating leverage (DOL)　The ratio of the percentage change in operating income to the percentage change in units sold; the sensitivity of operating income to changes in units sold.

Degree of total leverage　The ratio of the percentage change in net income to the percentage change in units sold; the sensitivity of the cash flows to owners to changes in the number of units produced and sold.

Degrees of freedom (df)　The number of independent observations used.

Delivery　A process used in a deliverable forward contract in which the long pays the agreed-upon price to the short, which in turn delivers the underlying asset to the long.

Delivery option　The feature of a futures contract giving the short the right to make decisions about what, when, and where to deliver.

Delta　The relationship between the option price and the underlying price, which reflects the sensitivity of the price of the option to changes in the price of the underlying.

Delta hedge　An option strategy in which a position in an asset is converted to a risk-free position with a position in a specific number of options. The number of options per unit of the underlying changes through time, and the position must be revised to maintain the hedge.

Delta-normal method　A measure of VAR equivalent to the analytical method but that refers to the use of delta to estimate the option's price sensitivity.

Demand for money　The relationship between the quantity of money demanded and the interest rate when all other influences on the amount of money that people wish to hold remain the same.

Demand-pull inflation　An inflation that results from an initial increase in aggregate demand.

Dependent　With reference to events, the property that the probability of one event occurring depends on (is related to) the occurrence of another event.

Dependent variable　The variable whose variation about its mean is to be explained by the regression; the left-hand-side variable in a regression equation.

Depository institution　A firm that takes deposits from households and firms and makes loans to other households and firms.

Depository institutions　Commercial banks, savings and loan banks, credit unions, and similar institutions that raise funds from depositors and other investors and lend it to borrowers.

Depository receipt　A security that trades like an ordinary share on a local exchange and represents an economic interest in a foreign company.

Depreciation　The process of systematically allocating the cost of long-lived (tangible) assets to the periods during which the assets are expected to provide economic benefits.

Derivative　A financial instrument whose value depends on the value of some underlying asset or factor (e.g., a stock price, an interest rate, or exchange rate).

Derivative pricing rule　A pricing rule used by crossing networks in which a price is taken (derived) from the price that is current in the asset's primary market.

Derivatives dealers　Commercial and investment banks that make markets in derivatives.

Derived demand　Demand for a factor of production, which is derived from the demand for the goods and services produced by that factor.

Descriptive statistics　The study of how data can be summarized effectively.

Designated fair value instruments Financial instruments that an entity chooses to measure at fair value per IAS 39 or SFAS 159. Generally, the election to use the fair value option is irrevocable.

Desired reserve ratio The ratio of reserves to deposits that banks want to hold.

Diff swaps A swap in which the payments are based on the difference between interest rates in two countries but payments are made in only a single currency.

Diffuse prior The assumption of equal prior probabilities.

Diluted EPS The EPS that would result if all dilutive securities were converted into common shares.

Diluted shares The number of shares that would be outstanding if all potentially dilutive claims on common shares (e.g., convertible debt, convertible preferred stock, and employee stock options) were exercised.

Diminishing balance method An accelerated depreciation method, i.e., one that allocates a relatively large proportion of the cost of an asset to the early years of the asset's useful life.

Diminishing marginal returns The tendency for the marginal product of an additional unit of a factor of production to be less than the marginal product of the previous unit of the factor.

Direct debit program An arrangement whereby a customer authorizes a debit to a demand account; typically used by companies to collect routine payments for services.

Direct financing lease A type of finance lease, from a lessor perspective, where the present value of the lease payments (lease receivable) equals the carrying value of the leased asset. The revenues earned by the lessor are financing in nature.

Direct format (direct method) With reference to the cash flow statement, a format for the presentation of the statement in which cash flow from operating activities is shown as operating cash receipts less operating cash disbursements.

Direct write-off method An approach to recognizing credit losses on customer receivables in which the company waits until such time as a customer has defaulted and only then recognizes the loss.

Dirty-surplus accounting Accounting in which some income items are reported as part of stockholders' equity rather than as gains and losses on the income statement; certain items of comprehensive income bypass the income statement and appear as direct adjustments to shareholders' equity.

Dirty-surplus items Direct adjustments to shareholders' equity that bypass the income statement.

Disbursement float The amount of time between check issuance and a check's clearing back against the company's account.

Discount To reduce the value of a future payment in allowance for how far away it is in time; to calculate the present value of some future amount. Also, the amount by which an instrument is priced below its face value.

Discount interest A procedure for determining the interest on a loan or bond in which the interest is deducted from the face value in advance.

Discount rate The interest rate at which the Fed stands ready to lend reserves to depository institutions.

Discounted cash flow analysis In the context of merger analysis, it is an estimate of a target company's value found by discounting the company's expected future free cash flows to the present.

Discouraged workers People who are available and willing to work but have not made specific effort to find a job in the previous four weeks.

Discrete random variable A random variable that can take on at most a countable number of possible values.

Discrete time Time thought of as advancing in distinct finite increments.

Discretionary fiscal policy A fiscal action that is initiated by an act of Congress.

Discriminant analysis A multivariate classification technique used to discriminate between groups, such as companies that either will or will not become bankrupt during some time frame.

Discriminatory pricing rule A pricing rule used in continuous markets in which the limit price of the order or quote that first arrived determines the trade price.

Diseconomies of scale Features of a firm's technology that lead to rising long-run average cost as output increases.

Dispersion The variability around the central tendency.

Display size The size of an order displayed to public view.

Disposable income Aggregate income minus taxes plus transfer payments.

Divergence In technical analysis, a term that describes the case when an indicator moves differently from the security being analyzed.

Diversification ratio The ratio of the standard deviation of an equally weighted portfolio to the standard deviation of a randomly selected security.

Divestiture The sale, liquidation, or spin-off of a division or subsidiary.

Dividend A distribution paid to shareholders based on the number of shares owned.

Dividend discount model (DDM) A present value model that estimates the intrinsic value of an equity share based on the present value of its expected future dividends.

Dividend discount model based approach An approach for estimating a country's equity risk premium. The market rate of return is estimated as the sum of the dividend yield and the growth rate in dividends for a market index. Subtracting the risk-free rate of return from the estimated market return produces an estimate for the equity risk premium.

Dividend payout policy The strategy a company follows with regard to the amount and timing of dividend payments.

Dividend payout ratio The ratio of cash dividends paid to earnings for a period.

Dividend yield Annual dividends per share divided by share price.

Dividends per share The dollar amount of cash dividends paid during a period per share of common stock.

Divisor A number (denominator) used to determine the value of a price return index. It is initially chosen at the inception of an index and subsequently adjusted by the index provider, as necessary, to avoid changes in the index value that are unrelated to changes in the prices of its constituent securities.

Dominant strategy equilibrium A Nash equilibrium in which the best strategy for each player is to cheat (deny) regardless of the strategy of the other player.

Double bottoms In technical analysis, a reversal pattern that is formed when the price reaches a low, rebounds, and then sells off back to the first low level; used to predict a change from a downtrend to an uptrend.

Double declining balance depreciation An accelerated depreciation method that involves depreciating the asset at double the straight-line rate. This rate is multiplied by the book value of the asset at the beginning of the period (a declining balance) to calculate depreciation expense.

Double taxation Corporate earnings are taxed twice when paid out as dividends. First, corporate earnings are taxed regardless of whether they will be distributed as dividends or retained at the corporate level, and second, dividends are taxed again at the individual shareholder level.

Double top In technical analysis, a reversal pattern that is formed when an uptrend reverses twice at roughly the same high price level; used to predict a change from an uptrend to a downtrend.

Double-entry accounting The accounting system of recording transactions in which every recorded transaction affects at least two accounts so as to keep the basic accounting equation (assets = liabilities + owners' equity) in balance.

Down transition probability The probability that an asset's value moves down in a model of asset price dynamics.

Downstream A transaction between two affiliates, an investor company and an associate company such that the investor company records a profit on its income statement. An example is a sale of inventory by the investor company to the associate.

Drag on liquidity When receipts lag, creating pressure from the decreased available funds.

Dummy variable A type of qualitative variable that takes on a value of 1 if a particular condition is true and 0 if that condition is false.

Duopoly A market structure in which two producers of a good or service compete.

DuPont analysis An approach to decomposing return on investment, e.g., return on equity, as the product of other financial ratios.

Duration A measure of an option-free bond's average maturity. Specifically, the weighted average maturity of all future cash flows paid by a security, in which the weights are the present value of these cash flows as a fraction of the bond's price. A measure of a bond's price sensitivity to interest rate movements.

Dutch Book theorem A result in probability theory stating that inconsistent probabilities create profit opportunities.

Dynamic hedging A strategy in which a position is hedged by making frequent adjustments to the quantity of the instrument used for hedging in relation to the instrument being hedged.

Earnings at risk (EAR) A variation of VAR that reflects the risk of a company's earnings instead of its market value.

Earnings expectation management Attempts by management to influence analysts' earnings forecasts.

Earnings game Management's focus on reporting earnings that meet consensus estimates.

Earnings management activity Deliberate activity aimed at influencing reporting earnings numbers, often with the goal of placing management in a favorable light; the opportunistic use of accruals to manage earnings.

Earnings per share The amount of income earned during a period per share of common stock.

Earnings surprise The portion of a company's earnings that is unanticipated by investors and, according to the efficient market hypothesis, merits a price adjustment.

Economic depreciation The change in the market value of capital over a given period.

Economic efficiency A situation that occurs when the firm produces a given output at the least cost.

Economic exposure The risk associated with changes in the relative attractiveness of products and services offered for sale, arising out of the competitive effects of changes in exchange rates.

Economic order quantity–reorder point An approach to managing inventory based on expected demand and the predictability of demand; the ordering point for new inventory is determined based on the costs of ordering and carrying inventory, such that the total cost associated with inventory is minimized.

Economic profit A firm's total revenue minus its total cost.

Economic rent Any surplus—consumer surplus, producer surplus or economic profit. The income received by the owner of a factor of production over and above the amount required to induce that owner to offer the factor for use.

Economies of scale Features of a firm's technology that lead to a falling long-run average cost as output increases. In reference to mergers, it is the savings achieved through the consolidation of operations and elimination of duplicate resources.

Economies of scope Decreases in average total cost that occur when a firm uses specialized resources to produce a range of goods and services.

Effective annual rate The amount by which a unit of currency will grow in a year with interest on interest included.

Effective annual yield (EAY) An annualized return that accounts for the effect of interest on interest; EAY is computed by compounding 1 plus the holding period yield forward to one year, then subtracting 1.

Effective interest rate The borrowing rate or market rate that a company incurs at the time of issuance of a bond.

Efficiency In statistics, a desirable property of estimators; an efficient estimator is the unbiased estimator with the smallest variance among unbiased estimators of the same parameter.

Efficiency wage A real wage rate that is set above the equilibrium wage rate and that balances the costs and benefits of this higher wage rate to maximize the firm's profit.

Efficient frontier The portion of the minimum-variance frontier beginning with the global minimum-variance portfolio and continuing above it; the graph of the set of portfolios offering the maximum expected return for their level of variance of return.

Efficient portfolio A portfolio offering the highest expected return for a given level of risk as measured by variance or standard deviation of return.

Elastic demand Demand with a price elasticity greater than 1; other things remaining the same, the percentage change in the quantity demanded exceeds the percentage change in price.

Elasticity A measure of sensitivity; the incremental change in one variable with respect to an incremental change in another variable.

Elasticity of supply The responsiveness of the quantity supplied of a good to a change in its price, other things remaining the same.

Electronic funds transfer The use of computer networks to conduct financial transactions electronically.

Elliott wave theory A technical analysis theory that claims that the market follows regular, repeated waves or cycles.

Empirical probability The probability of an event estimated as a relative frequency of occurrence.

Employment Act of 1946 A landmark Congressional act that recognizes a role for government actions to keep unemployment low, the economy expanding, and inflation in check.

Employment-to-population ratio The percentage of people of working age who have jobs.

Enhanced derivatives products companies (EDPC) A type of subsidiary engaged in derivatives transactions that is separated from the parent company in order to have a higher credit rating than the parent company.

Enterprise risk management A form of *centralized risk management* that typically encompasses the management of a broad variety of risks, including insurance risk.

Enterprise value A measure of a company's total market value from which the value of cash and short-term investments have been subtracted.

Equal weighting An index weighting method in which an equal weight is assigned to each constituent security at inception.

Equitizing cash A strategy used to replicate an index. It is also used to take a given amount of cash and turn it into an equity position while maintaining the liquidity provided by the cash.

Equity   Assets less liabilities; the residual interest in the assets after subtracting the liabilities.

Equity carve-out   A form of restructuring that involves the creation of a new legal entity and the sale of equity in it to outsiders.

Equity forward   A contract calling for the purchase of an individual stock, a stock portfolio, or a stock index at a later date at an agreed-upon price.

Equity method   A basis for reporting investment income in which the investing entity recognizes a share of income as earned rather than as dividends when received. These transactions are typically reflected in Investments in Associates or Equity Method Investments.

Equity options   Options on individual stocks; also known as stock options.

Equity risk premium   The expected return on equities minus the risk-free rate; the premium that investors demand for investing in equities.

Equity swap   A swap transaction in which at least one cash flow is tied to the return to an equity portfolio position, often an equity index.

Error autocorrelation   The autocorrelation of the error term.

Error term   The portion of the dependent variable that is not explained by the independent variable(s) in the regression.

Estimate   The particular value calculated from sample observations using an estimator.

Estimated (or fitted) parameters   With reference to regression analysis, the estimated values of the population intercept and population slope coefficient(s) in a regression.

Estimation   With reference to statistical inference, the subdivision dealing with estimating the value of a population parameter.

Estimator   An estimation formula; the formula used to compute the sample mean and other sample statistics are examples of estimators.

Eurodollar   A dollar deposited outside the United States.

European-style option (or **European option**)   An option that can only be exercised on its expiration date.

Event   Any outcome or specified set of outcomes of a random variable.

Excess kurtosis   Degree of peakedness (fatness of tails) in excess of the peakedness of the normal distribution.

Excess reserves   A bank's actual reserves minus its desired reserves.

Exchange for physicals (EFP)   A permissible delivery procedure used by futures market participants, in which the long and short arrange a delivery procedure other than the normal procedures stipulated by the futures exchange.

Exchange ratio   The number of shares that target stockholders are to receive in exchange for each of their shares in the target company.

Exchanges   Places where traders can meet to arrange their trades.

Ex-dividend   Trading ex-dividend refers to shares that no longer carry the right to the next dividend payment.

Ex-dividend date   The first date that a share trades without (i.e. "ex") the dividend.

Execution instructions   Instructions that indicate how to fill an order.

Exercise or exercising the option   The process of using an option to buy or sell the underlying.

Exercise date   The day that employees actually exercise the options and convert them to stock.

Exercise price (strike price, striking price, or strike)   The fixed price at which an option holder can buy or sell the underlying.

Exercise rate or strike rate   The fixed rate at which the holder of an interest rate option can buy or sell the underlying.

Exercise value   The value obtained if an option is exercised based on current conditions.

Exhaustive   Covering or containing all possible outcomes.

Expected value   The probability-weighted average of the possible outcomes of a random variable.

Expensed   Taken as a deduction in arriving at net income.

Expenses   Outflows of economic resources or increases in liabilities that result in decreases in equity (other than decreases because of distributions to owners); reductions in net assets associated with the creation of revenues.

Experience curve   A curve that shows the direct cost per unit of good or service produced or delivered as a typically declining function of cumulative output.

Expiration date   The date on which a derivative contract expires.

Exposure to foreign exchange risk   The risk of a change in value of an asset or liability denominated in a foreign currency due to a change in exchange rates.

External diseconomies   Factors outside the control of a firm that raise the firm's costs as the industry produces a larger output.

External economies   Factors beyond the control of a firm that lower the firm's costs as the industry produces a larger output.

External growth   Company growth in output or sales that is achieved by buying the necessary resources externally (i.e., achieved through mergers and acquisitions).

Externality   The effect of an investment on other things besides the investment itself.

Extra or **special dividend**   A dividend paid by a company that does not pay dividends on a regular schedule, or a dividend that supplements regular cash dividends with an extra payment.

Face value (also principal, par value, stated value, or maturity value)   The amount of cash payable by a company to the bondholders when the bonds mature; the promised payment at maturity separate from any coupon payment.

Factor   A common or underlying element with which several variables are correlated.

Factor risk premium (or **factor price**)   The expected return in excess of the risk-free rate for a portfolio with a sensitivity of 1 to one factor and a sensitivity of 0 to all other factors.

Factor sensitivity (also **factor betas** or **factor loadings**)   A measure of the response of return to each unit of increase in a factor, holding all other factors constant.

Fair market value   The market price of an asset or liability that trades regularly.

Fair value   The amount at which an asset could be exchanged, or a liability settled, between knowledgeable, willing parties in an arm's-length transaction; the price that would be received to sell an asset or paid to transfer a liability in an orderly transaction between market participants.

Federal budget   The annual statement of the outlays and tax revenues of the government of the United States, together with the laws and regulations that approve and support those outlays and taxes.

Federal funds rate   The interest rate that the banks charge each other on overnight loans.

Federal Open Market Committee   The main policy-making organ of the Federal Reserve System.

Federal Reserve System (the Fed)   The central bank of the United States.

Fibonacci sequence   A sequence of numbers starting with 0 and 1, and then each subsequent number in the sequence is the sum of the two preceding numbers. In Elliott Wave Theory, it is believed that market waves follow patterns that are the ratios of the numbers in the Fibonacci sequence.

Fiduciary call A combination of a European call and a risk-free bond that matures on the option expiration day and has a face value equal to the exercise price of the call.

FIFO method The first in, first out, method of accounting for inventory, which matches sales against the costs of items of inventory in the order in which they were placed in inventory.

Finance lease (capital lease) Essentially, the purchase of some asset by the buyer (lessee) that is directly financed by the seller (lessor).

Financial analysis The process of selecting, evaluating, and interpreting financial data in order to formulate an assessment of a company's present and future financial condition and performance.

Financial distress Heightened uncertainty regarding a company's ability to meet its various obligations because of lower or negative earnings.

Financial flexibility The ability to react and adapt to financial adversities and opportunities.

Financial futures Futures contracts in which the underlying is a stock, bond, or currency.

Financial leverage The extent to which a company can effect, through the use of debt, a proportional change in the return on common equity that is greater than a given proportional change in operating income; also, short for the financial leverage ratio.

Financial leverage ratio A measure of financial leverage calculated as average total assets divided by average total equity.

Financial reporting quality The accuracy with which a company's reported financials reflect its operating performance and their usefulness for forecasting future cash flows.

Financial risk The risk that environmental, social, or governance risk factors will result in significant costs or other losses to a company and its shareholders; the risk arising from a company's obligation to meet required payments under its financing agreements.

Financing activities Activities related to obtaining or repaying capital to be used in the business (e.g., equity and long-term debt).

Firm An economic unit that hires factors of production and organizes those factors to produce and sell goods and services.

First-differencing A transformation that subtracts the value of the time series in period $t-1$ from its value in period t.

First-order serial correlation Correlation between adjacent observations in a time series.

Fiscal imbalance The present value of the government's commitments to pay benefits minus the present value of its tax revenues.

Fiscal policy The government's attempt to achieve macroeconomic objectives such as full employment, sustained long-term economic growth, and price level stability by setting and changing tax rates, making transfer payments, and purchasing goods and services.

Fixed asset turnover An activity ratio calculated as total revenue divided by average net fixed assets.

Fixed charge coverage A solvency ratio measuring the number of times interest and lease payments are covered by operating income, calculated as (EBIT + lease payments) divided by (interest payments + lease payments).

Fixed costs Costs that remain at the same level regardless of a company's level of production and sales.

Fixed price tender offer Offer made by a company to repurchase a specific number of shares at a fixed price that is typically at a premium to the current market price.

Fixed rate perpetual preferred stock Nonconvertible, noncallable preferred stock that has a fixed dividend rate and no maturity date.

Fixed-income forward A forward contract in which the underlying is a bond.

Flags A technical analysis continuation pattern formed by parallel trendlines, typically over a short period.

Flip-in pill A poison pill takeover defense that dilutes an acquirer's ownership in a target by giving other existing target company shareholders the right to buy additional target company shares at a discount.

Flip-over pill A poison pill takeover defense that gives target company shareholders the right to purchase shares of the acquirer at a significant discount to the market price, which has the effect of causing dilution to all existing acquiring company shareholders.

Float In the context of customer receipts, the amount of money that is in transit between payments made by customers and the funds that are usable by the company.

Float factor An estimate of the average number of days it takes deposited checks to clear; average daily float divided by average daily deposit.

Float-adjusted market-capitalization weighting An index weighting method in which the weight assigned to each constituent security is determined by adjusting its market capitalization for its market float.

Floating-rate loan A loan in which the interest rate is reset at least once after the starting date.

Floor A combination of interest rate put options designed to hedge a lender against lower rates on a floating-rate loan.

Floor traders or locals Market makers that buy and sell by quoting a bid and an ask price. They are the primary providers of liquidity to the market.

Floored swap A swap in which the floating payments have a lower limit.

Floorlet Each component put option in a floor.

Flotation cost Fees charged to companies by investment bankers and other costs associated with raising new capital.

Foreign currency transactions Transactions that are denominated in a currency other than a company's functional currency.

Foreign exchange gains (or losses) Gains (or losses) that occur when the exchange rate changes between the investor's currency and the currency that foreign securities are denominated in.

Forward contract An agreement between two parties in which one party, the buyer, agrees to buy from the other party, the seller, an underlying asset at a later date for a price established at the start of the contract.

Forward integration A merger involving the purchase of a target that is farther along the value or production chain; for example, to acquire a distributor.

Forward price or forward rate The fixed price or rate at which the transaction scheduled to occur at the expiration of a forward contract will take place. This price is agreed on at the initiation date of the contract.

Forward rate agreement (FRA) A forward contract calling for one party to make a fixed interest payment and the other to make an interest payment at a rate to be determined at the contract expiration.

Forward swap A forward contract to enter into a swap.

Four-firm concentration ratio A measure of market power that is calculated as the percentage of the value of sales accounted for by the four largest firms in an industry.

Free cash flow The actual cash that would be available to the company's investors after making all investments necessary to maintain the company as an ongoing enterprise (also referred to as free cash flow to the firm); the internally generated funds that can be distributed to the company's investors (e.g., shareholders and bondholders) without impairing the value of the company.

Free cash flow hypothesis   The hypothesis that higher debt levels discipline managers by forcing them to make fixed debt service payments and by reducing the company's free cash flow.

Free cash flow to equity   The cash flow available to a company's common shareholders after all operating expenses, interest, and principal payments have been made, and necessary investments in working and fixed capital have been made.

Free cash flow to the firm   The cash flow available to the company's suppliers of capital after all operating expenses have been paid and necessary investments in working capital and fixed capital have been made.

Free float   The number of shares that are readily and freely tradable in the secondary market.

Free-cash-flow-to-equity models   Valuation models based on discounting expected future free cash flow to equity.

Frequency distribution   A tabular display of data summarized into a relatively small number of intervals.

Frequency polygon   A graph of a frequency distribution obtained by drawing straight lines joining successive points representing the class frequencies.

Frictional unemployment   The unemployment that arises from normal labor turnover—from people entering and leaving the labor force and from the ongoing creation and destruction of jobs.

Friendly transaction   A potential business combination that is endorsed by the managers of both companies.

Full employment   A situation in which the quantity of labor demanded equals the quantity supplied. At full employment, there is no cyclical unemployment—all unemployment is frictional and structural.

Full-employment equilibrium   A macroeconomic equilibrium in which real GDP equals potential GDP.

Full price   The price of a security with accrued interest.

Functional currency   The currency of the primary economic environment in which an entity operates.

Fundamental analysis   The examination of publicly available information and the formulation of forecasts to estimate the intrinsic value of assets.

Fundamental beta   A beta that is based at least in part on fundamental data for a company.

Fundamental factor models   A multifactor model in which the factors are attributes of stocks or companies that are important in explaining cross-sectional differences in stock prices.

Fundamental (or intrinsic) value   The underlying or true value of an asset based on an analysis of its qualitative and quantitative characteristics.

Fundamental weighting   An index weighting method in which the weight assigned to each constituent security is based on its underlying company's size. It attempts to address the disadvantages of market-capitalization weighting by using measures that are independent of the constituent security's price.

Future value (FV)   The amount to which a payment or series of payments will grow by a stated future date.

Futures commission merchants (FCMs)   Individuals or companies that execute futures transactions for other parties off the exchange.

Futures contract   A variation of a forward contract that has essentially the same basic definition but with some additional features, such as a clearinghouse guarantee against credit losses, a daily settlement of gains and losses, and an organized electronic or floor trading facility.

Futures exchange   A legal corporate entity whose shareholders are its members. The members of the exchange have the privilege of executing transactions directly on the exchange.

Gains   Asset inflows not directly related to the ordinary activities of the business.

Game theory   A tool that economists use to analyze strategic behavior—behavior that takes into account the expected behavior of others and the recognition of mutual interdependence.

Gamma   A numerical measure of how sensitive an option's delta is to a change in the underlying.

Generalized least squares   A regression estimation technique that addresses heteroskedasticity of the error term.

Generational accounting   An accounting system that measures the lifetime tax burden and benefits of each generation.

Generational imbalance   The division of the fiscal imbalance between the current and future generations, assuming that the current generation will enjoy the existing levels of taxes and benefits.

Geometric mean   A measure of central tendency computed by taking the nth root of the product of n non-negative values.

Giro system   An electronic payment system used widely in Europe and Japan.

Global depository receipt   A depository receipt that is issued outside of the company's home country and outside of the United States.

Global minimum-variance portfolio   The portfolio on the minimum-variance frontier with the smallest variance of return.

Global registered share   A common share that is traded on different stock exchanges around the world in different currencies.

Golden cross   A technical analysis term that describes a situation where a short-term moving average crosses from below a longer-term moving average to above it; this movement is considered bullish.

Good-on-close (market on close)   An execution instruction specifying that an order can only be filled at the close of trading.

Good-on-open   An execution instruction specifying that an order can only be filled at the opening of trading.

Good-till-cancelled order   An order specifying that it is valid until the entity placing the order has cancelled it (or, commonly, until some specified amount of time such as 60 days has elapsed, whichever comes sooner).

Goodwill   An intangible asset that represents the excess of the purchase price of an acquired company over the value of the net assets acquired.

Government debt   The total amount that the government has borrowed. It equals the sum of past budget deficits minus the sum of past budget surpluses.

Government expenditure multiplier   The magnification effect of a change in government expenditure on goods and services on equilibrium expenditure and real GDP.

Grant date   The day that options are granted to employees; usually the date that compensation expense is measured if both the number of shares and option price are known.

Greenmail   The purchase of the accumulated shares of a hostile investor by a company that is targeted for takeover by that investor, usually at a substantial premium over market price.

Gross profit (gross margin)   Sales minus the cost of sales (i.e., the cost of goods sold for a manufacturing company).

Gross profit margin   The ratio of gross profit to revenues.

Grouping by function   With reference to the presentation of expenses in an income statement, the grouping together of expenses serving the same function, e.g. all items that are costs of goods sold.

Grouping by nature   With reference to the presentation of expenses in an income statement, the grouping together of expenses by similar nature, e.g., all depreciation expenses.

Growth cyclical　A term sometimes used to describe companies that are growing rapidly on a long-term basis but that still experience above-average fluctuation in their revenues and profits over the course of a business cycle.

Growth investors　With reference to equity investors, investors who seek to invest in high-earnings-growth companies.

Growth option or expansion option　The ability to make additional investments in a project at some future time if the financial results are strong.

Harmonic mean　A type of weighted mean computed by averaging the reciprocals of the observations, then taking the reciprocal of that average.

Head and shoulders pattern　In technical analysis, a reversal pattern that is formed in three parts: a left shoulder, head, and right shoulder; used to predict a change from an uptrend to a downtrend.

Hedge fund　A historically loosely regulated, pooled investment vehicle that may implement various investment strategies.

Hedge funds　Private investment vehicles that typically use leverage, derivatives, and long and short investment strategies.

Hedge ratio　The relationship of the quantity of an asset being hedged to the quantity of the derivative used for hedging.

Hedging　A general strategy usually thought of as reducing, if not eliminating, risk.

Held-for-trading securities (trading securities)　Debt or equity financial assets bought with the intention to sell them in the near term, usually less than three months; securities that a company intends to trade.

Held-to-maturity investments　Debt (fixed-income) securities that a company intends to hold to maturity; these are presented at their original cost, updated for any amortization of discounts or premiums.

Herding　Clustered trading that may or may not be based on information.

Herfindahl–Hirschman Index　A measure of market concentration that is calculated by summing the squared market shares for competing companies in an industry; high HHI readings or mergers that would result in large HHI increases are more likely to result in regulatory challenges.

Heteroskedastic　With reference to the error term of a regression, having a variance that differs across observations.

Heteroskedasticity　The property of having a nonconstant variance; refers to an error term with the property that its variance differs across observations.

Heteroskedasticity-consistent standard errors　Standard errors of the estimated parameters of a regression that correct for the presence of heteroskedasticity in the regression's error term.

Hidden order　An order that is exposed not to the public but only to the brokers or exchanges that receive it.

Histogram　A bar chart of data that have been grouped into a frequency distribution.

Historical cost　In reference to assets, the amount paid to purchase an asset, including any costs of acquisition and/or preparation; with reference to liabilities, the amount of proceeds received in exchange in issuing the liability.

Historical equity risk premium approach　An estimate of a country's equity risk premium that is based upon the historical averages of the risk-free rate and the rate of return on the market portfolio.

Historical exchange rates　For accounting purposes, the exchange rates that existed when the assets and liabilities were initially recorded.

Historical method　A method of estimating VAR that uses data from the returns of the portfolio over a recent past period and compiles this data in the form of a histogram.

Historical simulation (or back simulation)　Another term for the historical method of estimating VAR. This term is somewhat misleading in that the method involves not a *simulation* of the past but rather what *actually happened* in the past, sometimes adjusted to reflect the fact that a different portfolio may have existed in the past than is planned for the future.

Holder-of-record date　The date that a shareholder listed on the corporation's books will be deemed to have ownership of the shares for purposes of receiving an upcoming dividend; two business days after the ex-dividend date.

Holding period return　The return that an investor earns during a specified holding period; a synonym for total return.

Holding period yield (HPY)　The return that an investor earns during a specified holding period; holding period return with reference to a fixed-income instrument.

Homogeneity of expectations　The assumption that all investors have the same economic expectations and thus have the same expectations of prices, cash flows, and other investment characteristics.

Homogenization　Creating a contract with standard and generally accepted terms, which makes it more acceptable to a broader group of participants.

Homoskedasticity　The property of having a constant variance; refers to an error term that is constant across observations.

Horizontal analysis　Common-size analysis that involves comparing a specific financial statement with that statement in prior or future time periods; also, cross-sectional analysis of one company with another.

Horizontal common-size analysis　A form of common-size analysis in which the accounts in a given period are used as the benchmark or base period, and every account is restated in subsequent periods as a percentage of the base period's same account.

Horizontal merger　A merger involving companies in the same line of business, usually as competitors.

Hostile transaction　An attempt to acquire a company against the wishes of the target's managers.

Hurdle rate　The rate of return that must be met for a project to be accepted.

Hypothesis　With reference to statistical inference, a statement about one or more populations.

Hypothesis testing　With reference to statistical inference, the subdivision dealing with the testing of hypotheses about one or more populations.

Iceberg order　An order in which the display size is less than the order's full size.

Identifiable intangible　An intangible that can be acquired singly and is typically linked to specific rights or privileges having finite benefit periods (e.g., a patent or trademark).

If-converted method　A method for accounting for the effect of convertible securities on earnings per share (EPS) that specifies what EPS would have been if the convertible securities had been converted at the beginning of the period, taking account of the effects of conversion on net income and the weighted average number of shares outstanding.

Immediate or cancel order (fill or kill)　An order that is valid only upon receipt by the broker or exchange. If such an order cannot be filled in part or in whole upon receipt, it cancels immediately.

Impairment　Diminishment in value as a result of carrying (book) value exceeding fair value and/or recoverable value.

Impairment of capital rule　A legal restriction that dividends cannot exceed retained earnings.

Implicit rental rate　The firm's opportunity cost of using its own capital.

Implied repo rate   The rate of return from a cash-and-carry transaction implied by the futures price relative to the spot price.

Implied volatility   The volatility that option traders use to price an option, implied by the price of the option and a particular option-pricing model.

Implied yield   A measure of the yield on the underlying bond of a futures contract implied by pricing it as though the underlying will be delivered at the futures expiration.

Imputation   In reference to corporate taxes, a system that imputes, or attributes, taxes at only one level of taxation. For countries using an imputation tax system, taxes on dividends are effectively levied only at the shareholder rate. Taxes are paid at the corporate level but they are *attributed* to the shareholder. Shareholders deduct from their tax bill their portion of taxes paid by the company.

Incentive system   A method of organizing production that uses a market-like mechanism inside the firm.

Income   Increases in economic benefits in the form of inflows or enhancements of assets, or decreases of liabilities that result in an increase in equity (other than increases resulting from contributions by owners).

Income elasticity of demand   The responsiveness of demand to a change in income, other things remaining the same. It is calculated as the percentage change in the quantity demanded divided by the percentage change in income.

Income statement (statement of operations or profit and loss statement)   A financial statement that provides information about a company's profitability over a stated period of time.

Income tax paid   The actual amount paid for income taxes in the period; not a provision, but the actual cash outflow.

Income tax payable   The income tax owed by the company on the basis of taxable income.

Income tax recoverable   The income tax expected to be recovered, from the taxing authority, on the basis of taxable income. It is a recovery of previously remitted taxes or future taxes owed by the company.

Income trust   A type of equity ownership vehicle established as a trust issuing ownership shares known as units.

Incremental cash flow   The cash flow that is realized because of a decision; the changes or increments to cash flows resulting from a decision or action.

Independent   With reference to events, the property that the occurrence of one event does not affect the probability of another event occurring.

Independent and identically distributed (IID)   With respect to random variables, the property of random variables that are independent of each other but follow the identical probability distribution.

Independent projects   Independent projects are projects whose cash flows are independent of each other.

Independent variable   A variable used to explain the dependent variable in a regression; a right-hand-side variable in a regression equation.

Index amortizing swap   An interest rate swap in which the notional principal is indexed to the level of interest rates and declines with the level of interest rates according to a predefined schedule. This type of swap is frequently used to hedge securities that are prepaid as interest rates decline, such as mortgage-backed securities.

Index option   An option in which the underlying is a stock index.

Indexing   An investment strategy in which an investor constructs a portfolio to mirror the performance of a specified index.

Indifference curve   The graph of risk–return combinations that an investor would be willing to accept to maintain a given level of utility.

Indirect format (indirect method)   With reference to cash flow statements, a format for the presentation of the statement which, in the operating cash flow section, begins with net income then shows additions and subtractions to arrive at operating cash flow.

Induced taxes   Taxes that vary with real GDP.

Industry   A group of companies offering similar products and/or services.

Industry analysis   The analysis of a specific branch of manufacturing, service, or trade.

Inelastic demand   A demand with a price elasticity between 0 and 1; the percentage change in the quantity demanded is less than the percentage change in price.

Inflation premium   An extra return that compensates investors for expected inflation.

Inflation rate   The annual percentage change in the price level.

Inflation rate targeting   A monetary policy strategy in which the central bank makes a public commitment to achieve an explicit inflation rate and to explain how its policy actions will achieve that target.

Inflationary gap   The amount by which real GDP exceeds potential GDP.

Information ratio (IR)   Mean active return divided by active risk.

Information cascade   The transmission of information from those participants who act first and whose decisions influence the decisions of others.

Information-motivated traders   Traders that trade to profit from information that they believe allows them to predict future prices.

Informationally efficient market   A market in which asset prices reflect new information quickly and rationally.

Initial margin   The amount that must be deposited in a clearing-house account when entering into a futures contract.

Initial margin requirement   The margin requirement on the first day of a transaction as well as on any day in which additional margin funds must be deposited.

Initial public offering (IPO)   The first issuance of common shares to the public by a formerly private corporation.

In-sample forecast errors   The residuals from a fitted time-series model within the sample period used to fit the model.

Instability in the minimum-variance frontier   The characteristic of minimum-variance frontiers that they are sensitive to small changes in inputs.

Installment   Said of a sale in which proceeds are to be paid in installments over an extended period of time.

Installment method (installment-sales method)   With respect to revenue recognition, a method that specifies that the portion of the total profit of the sale that is recognized in each period is determined by the percentage of the total sales price for which the seller has received cash.

Instrument rule   A decision rule for monetary policy that sets the policy instrument at a level that is based on the current state of the economy.

Intangible assets   Assets lacking physical substance, such as patents and trademarks.

Interest coverage   A solvency ratio calculated as EBIT divided by interest payments.

Interest rate   A rate of return that reflects the relationship between differently dated cash flows; a discount rate.

Interest rate call   An option in which the holder has the right to make a known interest payment and receive an unknown interest payment.

Interest rate cap or cap   A series of call options on an interest rate, with each option expiring at the date on which the floating loan rate will be reset, and with each option having the same exercise rate. A cap in general can have an underlying other than an interest rate.

Interest rate collar   A combination of a long cap and a short floor, or a short cap and a long floor. A collar in general can have an underlying other than an interest rate.

Interest rate floor or floor   A series of put options on an interest rate, with each option expiring at the date on which the floating loan rate will be reset, and with each option having the same exercise rate. A floor in general can have an underlying other than the interest rate.

Interest rate forward   See *Forward rate agreement*.

Interest rate option   An option in which the underlying is an interest rate.

Interest rate parity   A formula that expresses the equivalence or parity of spot and forward rates, after adjusting for differences in the interest rates.

Interest rate put   An option in which the holder has the right to make an unknown interest payment and receive a known interest payment.

Interest rate swap   A swap in which the underlying is an interest rate. Can be viewed as a currency swap in which both currencies are the same and can be created as a combination of currency swaps.

Intergenerational data mining   A form of data mining that applies information developed by previous researchers using a dataset to guide current research using the same or a related dataset.

Intermarket analysis   A field within technical analysis that combines analysis of major categories of securities—namely, equities, bonds, currencies, and commodities—to identify market trends and possible inflections in a trend.

Internal rate of return (IRR)   The discount rate that makes net present value equal 0; the discount rate that makes the present value of an investment's costs (outflows) equal to the present value of the investment's benefits (inflows).

Interquartile range   The difference between the third and first quartiles of a dataset.

Interval   With reference to grouped data, a set of values within which an observation falls.

Interval scale   A measurement scale that not only ranks data but also gives assurance that the differences between scale values are equal.

In-the-money   Options that, if exercised, would result in the value received being worth more than the payment required to exercise.

Inventory   The unsold units of product on hand.

Inventory blanket lien   The use of inventory as collateral for a loan. Though the lender has claim to some or all of the company's inventory, the company may still sell or use the inventory in the ordinary course of business.

Inventory turnover   An activity ratio calculated as cost of goods sold divided by average inventory.

Inverse floater   A floating-rate note or bond in which the coupon is adjusted to move opposite to a benchmark interest rate.

Investing activities   Activities which are associated with the acquisition and disposal of property, plant, and equipment; intangible assets; other long-term assets; and both long-term and short-term investments in the equity and debt (bonds and loans) issued by other companies.

Investment banks   Financial intermediaries that provide advice to their mostly corporate clients and help them arrange transactions such as initial and seasoned securities offerings.

Investment opportunity schedule   A graphical depiction of a company's investment opportunities ordered from highest to lowest expected return. A company's optimal capital budget is found where the investment opportunity schedule intersects with the company's marginal cost of capital.

Investment policy statement (IPS)   A written planning document that describes a client's investment objectives and risk tolerance over a relevant time horizon, along with constraints that apply to the client's portfolio.

Investment strategy   A set of rules, guidelines, or procedures that is used to analyze and select securities and manage portfolios.

IRR rule   An investment decision rule that accepts projects or investments for which the IRR is greater than the opportunity cost of capital.

January effect (also **turn-of-the-year effect**)   Calendar anomaly that stock market returns in January are significantly higher compared to the rest of the months of the year, with most of the abnormal returns reported during the first five trading days in January.

Joint probability   The probability of the joint occurrence of stated events.

Joint probability function   A function giving the probability of joint occurrences of values of stated random variables.

Joint venture   An entity (partnership, corporation, or other legal form) where control is shared by two or more entities called venturers.

Just-in-time method   Method of managing inventory that minimizes in-process inventory stocks.

Keynesian   A macroeconomist who believes that left alone, the economy would rarely operate at full employment and that to achieve full employment, active help from fiscal policy and monetary policy is required.

Keynesian cycle theory   A theory that fluctuations in investment driven by fluctuations in business confidence—summarized in the phrase "animal spirits"—are the main source of fluctuations in aggregate demand.

Kondratieff wave   A 54-year long economic cycle postulated by Nikolai Kondratieff.

***k*-percent rule**   A rule that makes the quantity of money grow at a rate of k percent a year, where k equals the growth rate of potential GDP.

***k*th Order autocorrelation**   The correlation between observations in a time series separated by k periods.

Kurtosis   The statistical measure that indicates the peakedness of a distribution.

Labor force   The sum of the people who are employed and who are unemployed.

Labor force participation rate   The percentage of the working-age population who are members of the labor force.

Labor union   An organized group of workers whose purpose is to increase wages and to influence other job conditions.

Laddering strategy   A form of active strategy which entails scheduling maturities on a systematic basis within the investment portfolio such that investments are spread out equally over the term of the ladder.

Laffer curve   The relationship between the tax rate and the amount of tax revenue collected.

Law of diminishing returns   As a firm uses more of a variable input, with a given quantity of other inputs (fixed inputs), the marginal product of the variable input eventually diminishes.

Law of one price   The condition in a financial market in which two equivalent financial instruments or combinations of financial instruments can sell for only one price. Equivalent to the principle that no arbitrage opportunities are possible.

Lead underwriter   The lead investment bank in a syndicate of investment banks and broker–dealers involved in a securities underwriting.

Legal monopoly A market structure in which there is one firm and entry is restricted by the granting of a public franchise, government license, patent, or copyright.

Legal risk The risk that failures by company managers to effectively manage a company's environmental, social, and governance risk exposures will lead to lawsuits and other judicial remedies, resulting in potentially catastrophic losses for the company; the risk that the legal system will not enforce a contract in case of dispute or fraud.

Legislative and regulatory risk The risk that governmental laws and regulations directly or indirectly affecting a company's operations will change with potentially severe adverse effects on the company's continued profitability and even its long-term sustainability.

Leptokurtic Describes a distribution that is more peaked than a normal distribution.

Lessee The party obtaining the use of an asset through a lease.

Lessor The owner of an asset that grants the right to use the asset to another party.

Level of significance The probability of a Type I error in testing a hypothesis.

Leverage In the context of corporate finance, leverage refers to the use of fixed costs within a company's cost structure. Fixed costs that are operating costs (such as depreciation or rent) create operating leverage. Fixed costs that are financial costs (such as interest expense) create financial leverage.

Leveraged buyout (LBO) A transaction whereby the target company management team converts the target to a privately held company by using heavy borrowing to finance the purchase of the target company's outstanding shares.

Leveraged floating-rate note or leveraged floater A floating-rate note or bond in which the coupon is adjusted at a multiple of a benchmark interest rate.

Leveraged recapitalization A post-offer takeover defense mechanism that involves the assumption of a large amount of debt that is then used to finance share repurchases; the effect is to dramatically change the company's capital structure while attempting to deliver a value to target shareholders in excess of a hostile bid.

Liabilities Present obligations of an enterprise arising from past events, the settlement of which is expected to result in an outflow of resources embodying economic benefits; creditors' claims on the resources of a company.

Life-cycle stage The stage of the life cycle: embryonic, growth, shakeout, mature, declining.

LIFO layer liquidation (LIFO liquidation) With respect to the application of the LIFO inventory method, the liquidation of old, relatively low-priced inventory; happens when the volume of sales rises above the volume of recent purchases so that some sales are made from relatively old, low-priced inventory.

LIFO method The last in, first out, method of accounting for inventory, which matches sales against the costs of items of inventory in the reverse order the items were placed in inventory (i.e., inventory produced or acquired last are assumed to be sold first).

LIFO reserve The difference between inventory reported at FIFO and inventory reported at LIFO (FIFO inventory value less LIFO inventory value).

Likelihood The probability of an observation, given a particular set of conditions.

Limit down A limit move in the futures market in which the price at which a transaction would be made is at or below the lower limit.

Limit move A condition in the futures markets in which the price at which a transaction would be made is at or beyond the price limits.

Limit order Instructions to a broker or exchange to obtain the best price immediately available when filling an order, but in no event accept a price higher than a specified (limit) price when buying or accept a price lower than a specified (limit) price when selling.

Limit order book The book or list of limit orders to buy and sell that pertains to a security.

Limit pricing The practice of setting the price at the highest level that inflicts a loss on an entrant.

Limit up A limit move in the futures market in which the price at which a transaction would be made is at or above the upper limit.

Line chart In technical analysis, a plot of price data, typically closing prices, with a line connecting the points.

Linear (arithmetic) scale A scale in which equal distances correspond to equal absolute amounts.

Linear association A straight-line relationship, as opposed to a relationship that cannot be graphed as a straight line.

Linear interpolation The estimation of an unknown value on the basis of two known values that bracket it, using a straight line between the two known values.

Linear regression Regression that models the straight-line relationship between the dependent and independent variable(s).

Linear trend A trend in which the dependent variable changes at a constant rate with time.

Liquid An asset that can be easily converted into cash in a short period of time at a price close to fair market value.

Liquid market Said of a market in which traders can buy or sell with low total transaction costs when they want to trade.

Liquidating dividend A dividend that is a return of capital rather than a distribution from earnings or retained earnings.

Liquidation To sell the assets of a company, division, or subsidiary piecemeal, typically because of bankruptcy; the form of bankruptcy that allows for the orderly satisfaction of creditors' claims after which the company ceases to exist.

Liquidity The ability to purchase or sell an asset quickly and easily at a price close to fair market value. The ability to meet short-term obligations using assets that are the most readily converted into cash.

Liquidity premium An extra return that compensates investors for the risk of loss relative to an investment's fair value if the investment needs to be converted to cash quickly.

Liquidity ratios Financial ratios measuring the company's ability to meet its short-term obligations.

Liquidity risk The risk that a financial instrument cannot be purchased or sold without a significant concession in price due to the size of the market.

Living wage An hourly wage rate that enables a person who works a 40-hour work week to rent adequate housing for not more than 30 percent of the amount earned.

Load fund A mutual fund in which, in addition to the annual fee, a percentage fee is charged to invest in the fund and/or for redemptions from the fund.

Local currency The currency of the country where a company is located.

Lockbox system A payment system in which customer payments are mailed to a post office box and the banking institution retrieves and deposits these payments several times a day, enabling the company to have use of the fund sooner than in a centralized system in which customer payments are sent to the company.

Locked limit A condition in the futures markets in which a transaction cannot take place because the price would be beyond the limits.

Logarithmic scale A scale in which equal distances represent equal proportional changes in the underlying quantity.

Logit model A qualitative-dependent-variable multiple regression model based on the logistic probability distribution.

Log-linear model With reference to time-series models, a model in which the growth rate of the time series as a function of time is constant.

Log-log regression model A regression that expresses the dependent and independent variables as natural logarithms.

London Interbank Offer Rate (LIBOR) The Eurodollar rate at which London banks lend dollars to other London banks; considered to be the best representative rate on a dollar borrowed by a private, high-quality borrower.

Long The buyer of a derivative contract. Also refers to the position of owning a derivative.

Long position A position in an asset or contract in which one owns the asset or has an exercisable right under the contract.

Long run A period of time in which the quantities of all resources can be varied.

Longitudinal data Observations on characteristic(s) of the same observational unit through time.

Long-lived assets (or long-term assets) Assets that are expected to provide economic benefits over a future period of time, typically greater than one year.

Long-run aggregate supply The relationship between the quantity of real GDP supplied and the price level in the long run when real GDP equals potential GDP.

Long-run average cost curve The relationship between the lowest attainable average total cost and output when both plant size and labor are varied.

Long-run industry supply curve A curve that shows how the quantity supplied by an industry varies as the market price varies after all the possible adjustments have been made, including changes in plant size and the number of firms in the industry.

Long-run macroeconomic equilibrium A situation that occurs when real GDP equals potential GDP—the economy is on its long-run aggregate supply curve.

Long-run Phillips curve A curve that shows the relationship between inflation and unemployment when the actual inflation rate equals the expected inflation rate.

Long-term contract A contract that spans a number of accounting periods.

Long-term debt-to-assets ratio The proportion of a company's assets that is financed with long-term debt.

Long-term equity anticipatory securities (LEAPS) Options originally created with expirations of several years.

Long-term liability An obligation that is expected to be settled, with the outflow of resources embodying economic benefits, over a future period generally greater than one year.

Look-ahead bias A bias caused by using information that was unavailable on the test date.

Losses Asset outflows not directly related to the ordinary activities of the business.

Lower bound The lowest possible value of an option.

M1 A measure of money that consists of currency and traveler's checks plus checking deposits owned by individuals and businesses.

M2 A measure of money that consists of M1 plus time deposits, savings deposits, and money market mutual funds, and other deposits.

M^2 A measure of what a portfolio would have returned if it had taken on the same total risk as the market index.

Macaulay duration The duration without dividing by 1 plus the bond's yield to maturity. The term, named for one of the economists who first derived it, is used to distinguish the calculation from modified duration. (See also *modified duration*.)

Macroeconomic factor A factor related to the economy, such as the inflation rate, industrial production, or economic sector membership.

Macroeconomic factor model A multifactor model in which the factors are surprises in macroeconomic variables that significantly explain equity returns.

Macroeconomic long run A time frame that is sufficiently long for the real wage rate to have adjusted to achieve full employment: real GDP equal to potential GDP, unemployment equal to the natural unemployment rate, the price level is proportional to the quantity of money, and the inflation rate equal to the money growth rate minus the real GDP growth rate.

Macroeconomic short run A period during which some money prices are sticky and real GDP might be below, above, or at potential GDP and unemployment might be above, below, or at the natural rate of unemployment.

Maintenance margin The minimum amount that is required by a futures clearinghouse to maintain a margin account and to protect against default. Participants whose margin balances drop below the required maintenance margin must replenish their accounts.

Maintenance margin requirement The margin requirement on any day other than the first day of a transaction.

Management buyout (MBO) An event in which a group of investors consisting primarily of the company's existing management purchase all of its outstanding shares and take the company private.

Managerialism theories Theories that posit that corporate executives are motivated to engage in mergers to maximize the size of their company rather than shareholder value.

Manufacturing resource planning (MRP) The incorporation of production planning into inventory management. A MRP analysis provides both a materials acquisition schedule and a production schedule.

Margin call A notice to deposit additional cash or securities in a margin account.

Margin loan Money borrowed from a broker to purchase securities.

Marginal cost The opportunity cost of producing one more unit of a good or service. It is the best alternative forgone. It is calculated as the increase in total cost divided by the increase in output.

Marginal cost pricing rule A rule that sets the price of a good or service equal to the marginal cost of producing it.

Marginal product The increase in total product that results from a one-unit increase in the variable input, with all other inputs remaining the same. It is calculated as the increase in total product divided by the increase in the variable input employed, when the quantities of all other inputs are constant.

Marginal revenue The change in total revenue that results from a one-unit increase in the quantity sold. It is calculated as the change in total revenue divided by the change in quantity sold.

Marginal revenue product The change in total revenue that results from employing one more unit of a factor of production (labor) while the quantity of all other factors remains the same. It is calculated as the increase in total revenue divided by the increase in the quantity of the factor (labor).

Market A means of bringing buyers and sellers together to exchange goods and services.

Market anomaly Change in the price or return of a security that cannot directly be linked to current relevant information known in the market or to the release of new information into the market.

Market bid–ask spread The difference between the best bid and the best offer.

Market float The number of shares that are available to the investing public.

Market model   A regression equation that specifies a linear relationship between the return on a security (or portfolio) and the return on a broad market index.

Market order   Instructions to a broker or exchange to obtain the best price immediately available when filling an order.

Market power   The ability to influence the market, and in particular the market price, by influencing the total quantity offered for sale.

Market price of risk   The slope of the capital market line, indicating the market risk premium for each unit of market risk.

Market rate   The rate demanded by purchasers of bonds, given the risks associated with future cash payment obligations of the particular bond issue.

Market risk   The risk associated with interest rates, exchange rates, and equity prices.

Market risk premium   The expected excess return on the market over the risk-free rate.

Market value   The price at which an asset or security can currently be bought or sold in an open market.

Marketable limit order   A buy limit order in which the limit price is placed above the best offer, or a sell limit order in which the limit price is placed below the best bid. Such orders generally will partially or completely fill right away.

Market-capitalization weighting (or value weighting)   An index weighting method in which the weight assigned to each constituent security is determined by dividing its market capitalization by the total market capitalization (sum of the market capitalization) of all securities in the index.

Market-oriented investors   With reference to equity investors, investors whose investment disciplines cannot be clearly categorized as value or growth.

Marking to market   A procedure used primarily in futures markets in which the parties to a contract settle the amount owed daily. Also known as the *daily settlement*.

Markowitz decision rule   A decision rule for choosing between two investments based on their means and variances.

Markowitz efficient frontier   The graph of the set of portfolios offering the maximum expected return for their level of risk (standard deviation of return).

Mark-to-market   The revaluation of a financial asset or liability to its current market value or fair value.

Matching principle   The accounting principle that expenses should be recognized when the associated revenue is recognized.

Matching strategy   An active investment strategy that includes intentional matching of the timing of cash outflows with investment maturities.

Materiality   The condition of being of sufficient importance so that omission or misstatement of the item in a financial report could make a difference to users' decisions.

Matrix pricing   In the fixed income markets, to price a security on the basis of valuation-relevant characteristics (e.g. debt-rating approach).

Maturity premium   An extra return that compensates investors for the increased sensitivity of the market value of debt to a change in market interest rates as maturity is extended.

McCallum rule   A rule that makes the growth rate of the monetary base respond to the long-term average growth rate of real GDP and medium-term changes in the velocity of circulation of the monetary base.

Mean   The sum of all values in a distribution or dataset, divided by the number of values summed; a synonym of arithmetic mean.

Mean absolute deviation   With reference to a sample, the mean of the absolute values of deviations from the sample mean.

Mean excess return   The average rate of return in excess of the risk-free rate.

Mean rate of return   The average rate of return on an investment over time.

Mean reversion   The tendency of a time series to fall when its level is above its mean and rise when its level is below its mean; a mean-reverting time series tends to return to its long-term mean.

Mean–variance analysis   An approach to portfolio analysis using expected means, variances, and covariances of asset returns.

Means of payment   A method of settling a debt.

Measure of central tendency   A quantitative measure that specifies where data are centered.

Measure of location   A quantitative measure that describes the location or distribution of data; includes not only measures of central tendency but also other measures such as percentiles.

Measurement scales   A scheme of measuring differences. The four types of measurement scales are nominal, ordinal, interval, and ratio.

Median   The value of the middle item of a set of items that has been sorted into ascending or descending order; the 50th percentile.

Merger   The absorption of one company by another; that is, two companies become one entity and one or both of the pre-merger companies ceases to exist as a separate entity.

Mesokurtic   Describes a distribution with kurtosis identical to that of the normal distribution.

Minimum efficient scale   The smallest quantity of output at which the long-run average cost curve reaches its lowest level.

Minimum wage   A regulation that makes the hiring of labor below a specified wage rate illegal. The lowest wage at which a firm may legally hire labor.

Minimum-variance frontier   The graph of the set of portfolios that have minimum variance for their level of expected return.

Minimum-variance portfolio   The portfolio with the minimum variance for each given level of expected return.

Minority active investments   Investments in which investors exert significant influence, but not control, over the investee. Typically, the investor has 20 to 50% ownership in the investee.

Minority interest (noncontrolling interest)   The proportion of the ownership of a subsidiary not held by the parent (controlling) company.

Minority passive investments (passive investments)   Investments in which the investor has no significant influence or control over the operations of the investee.

Mismatching strategy   An active investment strategy whereby the timing of cash outflows is not matched with investment maturities.

Mixed factor models   Factor models that combine features of more than one type of factor model.

Mixed offering   A merger or acquisition that is to be paid for with cash, securities, or some combination of the two.

Modal interval   With reference to grouped data, the most frequently occurring interval.

Mode   The most frequently occurring value in a set of observations.

Model risk   The use of an inaccurate pricing model for a particular investment, or the improper use of the right model.

Model specification   With reference to regression, the set of variables included in the regression and the regression equation's functional form.

Modern portfolio theory (MPT)   The analysis of rational portfolio choices based on the efficient use of risk.

Modified duration   A measure of a bond's price sensitivity to interest rate movements. Equal to the Macaulay duration of a bond divided by one plus its yield to maturity.

Momentum oscillators   A graphical representation of market sentiment that is constructed from price data and calculated so that it oscillates either between a high and a low or around some number.

Monetarist   A macroeconomist who believes that the economy is self-regulating and that it will normally operate at full employment, provided that monetary policy is not erratic and that the pace of money growth is kept steady.

Monetarist cycle theory   A theory that fluctuations in both investment and consumption expenditure, driven by fluctuations in the growth rate of the quantity of money, are the main source of fluctuations in aggregate demand.

Monetary assets and liabilities   Assets and liabilities with value equal to the amount of currency contracted for, a fixed amount of currency. Examples are cash, accounts receivable, mortgages receivable, accounts payable, bonds payable, and mortgages payable. Inventory is not a monetary asset. Most liabilities are monetary.

Monetary base   The sum of Federal Reserve notes, coins and banks' deposits at the Fed.

Monetary policy   The Fed conducts the nation's monetary policy by changing interest rates and adjusting the quantity of money.

Monetary policy instrument   A variable that the Fed can control directly or closely target.

Monetary/nonmonetary method   Approach to translating foreign currency financial statements for consolidation in which monetary assets and liabilities are translated at the current exchange rate. Nonmonetary assets and liabilities are translated at historical exchange rates (the exchange rates that existed when the assets and liabilities were acquired).

Money   Any commodity or token that is generally acceptable as the means of payment.

Money market   The market for short-term debt instruments (one-year maturity or less).

Money market yield (or CD equivalent yield)   A yield on a basis comparable to the quoted yield on an interest-bearing money market instrument that pays interest on a 360-day basis; the annualized holding period yield, assuming a 360-day year.

Money multiplier   The ratio of the change in the quantity of money to the change in the monetary base.

Moneyness   The relationship between the price of the underlying and an option's exercise price.

Money-weighted rate of return   The internal rate of return on a portfolio, taking account of all cash flows.

Monitoring costs   Costs borne by owners to monitor the management of the company (e.g., board of director expenses).

Monopolistic competition   A market structure in which a large number of firms compete by making similar but slightly different products.

Monopoly   A market structure in which there is one firm, which produces a good or service that has no close substitutes and in which the firm is protected from competition by a barrier preventing the entry of new firms.

Monopsony   A market in which there is a single buyer.

Monte Carlo simulation method   An approach to estimating a probability distribution of outcomes to examine what might happen if particular risks are faced. This method is widely used in the sciences as well as in business to study a variety of problems.

Moving average   The average of the closing price of a security over a specified number of periods. With each new period, the average is recalculated.

Moving-average convergence/divergence oscillator (MACD)   A momentum oscillator that is constructed based on the difference between short-term and long-term moving averages of a security's price.

Multicollinearity   A regression assumption violation that occurs when two or more independent variables (or combinations of independent variables) are highly but not perfectly correlated with each other.

Multiple linear regression model   A linear regression model with two or more independent variables.

Multiple R   The correlation between the actual and forecasted values of the dependent variable in a regression.

Multiplication rule for probabilities   The rule that the joint probability of events A and B equals the probability of A given B times the probability of B.

Multiplier models (or **market multiple models**)   Valuation models based on share price multiples or enterprise value multiples.

Multi-factor model   A model that explains a variable in terms of the values of a set of factors.

Multi-market index   An index comprised of indices from different countries, designed to represent multiple security markets.

Multi-step format   With respect to the format of the income statement, a format that presents a subtotal for gross profit (revenue minus cost of goods sold).

Multivariate distribution   A probability distribution that specifies the probabilities for a group of related random variables.

Multivariate normal distribution   A probability distribution for a group of random variables that is completely defined by the means and variances of the variables plus all the correlations between pairs of the variables.

Mutual fund   A professionally managed investment pool in which investors in the fund typically each have a pro-rata claim on the income and value of the fund.

Mutually exclusive events   Events such that only one can occur at a time.

Mutually exclusive projects   Mutually exclusive projects compete directly with each other. For example, if Projects A and B are mutually exclusive, you can choose A or B, but you cannot choose both.

***n* Factorial**   For a positive integer n, the product of the first n positive integers; 0 factorial equals 1 by definition. n factorial is written as $n!$.

Nash equilibrium   The outcome of a game that occurs when player A takes the best possible action given the action of player B and player B takes the best possible action given the action of player A.

Natural monopoly   A monopoly that occurs when one firm can supply the entire market at a lower price than two or more firms can.

Natural unemployment rate   The unemployment rate when the economy is at full employment. There is no cyclical unemployment; all unemployment is frictional, structural, and seasonal.

Needs-tested spending   Government spending on programs that pay benefits to suitably qualified people and businesses.

Negative serial correlation   Serial correlation in which a positive error for one observation increases the chance of a negative error for another observation, and vice versa.

Net asset balance sheet exposure   When assets translated at the current exchange rate are greater in amount than liabilities translated at the current exchange rate. Assets exposed to translation gains or losses exceed the exposed liabilities.

Net book value The remaining (undepreciated) balance of an asset's purchase cost. For liabilities, the face value of a bond minus any unamortized discount, or plus any unamortized premium.

Net income (loss) The difference between revenue and expenses; what remains after subtracting all expenses (including depreciation, interest, and taxes) from revenue.

Net liability balance sheet exposure When liabilities translated at the current exchange rate are greater than assets translated at the current exchange rate. Liabilities exposed to translation gains or losses exceed the exposed assets.

Net operating assets The difference between operating assets (total assets less cash) and operating liabilities (total liabilities less total debt).

Net operating cycle An estimate of the average time that elapses between paying suppliers for materials and collecting cash from the subsequent sale of goods produced.

Net operating profit less adjusted taxes, or NOPLAT A company's operating profit with adjustments to normalize the effects of capital structure.

Net present value (NPV) The present value of an investment's cash inflows (benefits) minus the present value of its cash outflows (costs).

Net profit margin (profit margin or return on sales) An indicator of profitability, calculated as net income divided by revenue; indicates how much of each dollar of revenues is left after all costs and expenses.

Net realizable value Estimated selling price in the ordinary course of business less the estimated costs necessary to make the sale.

Net revenue Revenue after adjustments (e.g., for estimated returns or for amounts unlikely to be collected).

Netting When parties agree to exchange only the net amount owed from one party to the other.

New classical A macroeconomist who holds the view that business cycle fluctuations are the efficient responses of a well-functioning market economy bombarded by shocks that arise from the uneven pace of technological change.

New classical cycle theory A rational expectations theory of the business cycle that regards unexpected fluctuations in aggregate demand as the main source of fluctuations of real GDP around potential GDP.

New-issue DRP (scrip dividend schemes) Dividend reinvestment plan in which the company meets the need for additional shares by issuing them instead of purchasing them.

New Keynesian A macroeconomist who holds the view that not only is the money wage rate sticky but also that the prices of goods and services are sticky.

New Keynesian cycle theory A rational expectations theory of the business cycle that regards unexpected and currently expected fluctuations in aggregate demand as the main source of fluctuations of real GDP around potential GDP.

Node Each value on a binomial tree from which successive moves or outcomes branch.

No-load fund A mutual fund in which there is no fee for investing in the fund or for redeeming fund shares, although there is an annual fee based on a percentage of the fund's net asset value.

Nominal rate A rate of interest based on the security's face value.

Nominal risk-free interest rate The sum of the real risk-free interest rate and the inflation premium.

Nominal scale A measurement scale that categorizes data but does not rank them.

Nonconventional cash flow In a nonconventional cash flow pattern, the initial outflow is not followed by inflows only, but the cash flows can flip from positive (inflows) to negative (outflows) again (or even change signs several times).

Non-cumulative preference shares Preference shares for which dividends that are not paid in the current or subsequent periods are forfeited permanently (instead of being accrued and paid at a later date).

Noncurrent Not due to be consumed, converted into cash, or settled within one year after the balance sheet date.

Noncurrent assets Assets that are expected to benefit the company over an extended period of time (usually more than one year).

Non-current liability An obligation that broadly represents a probable sacrifice of economic benefits in periods generally greater than one year in the future.

Non-cyclical A company whose performance is largely independent of the business cycle.

Nondeliverable forwards (NDFs) Cash-settled forward contracts, used predominately with respect to foreign exchange forwards.

Nonlinear relation An association or relationship between variables that cannot be graphed as a straight line.

Nonmonetary assets and liabilities Assets and liabilities that are not monetary assets and liabilities. Nonmonetary assets include inventory, fixed assets, and intangibles, and nonmonetary liabilities include deferred revenue.

Nonparametric test A test that is not concerned with a parameter, or that makes minimal assumptions about the population from which a sample comes.

Non-participating preference shares Preference shares that do not entitle shareholders to share in the profits of the company. Instead, shareholders are only entitled to receive a fixed dividend payment and the par value of the shares in the event of liquidation.

Nonrenewable natural resources Natural resources that can be used only once and that cannot be replaced once they have been used.

Nonstationarity With reference to a random variable, the property of having characteristics such as mean and variance that are not constant through time.

Nonsystematic risk Unique risk that is local or limited to a particular asset or industry that need not affect assets outside of that asset class.

Normal backwardation The condition in futures markets in which futures prices are lower than expected spot prices.

Normal contango The condition in futures markets in which futures prices are higher than expected spot prices.

Normal distribution A continuous, symmetric probability distribution that is completely described by its mean and its variance.

Normal profit The return that an entrepreneur can expect to receive on the average.

Notes payable Amounts owed by a business to creditors as a result of borrowings that are evidenced by (short-term) loan agreements.

n-Period moving average The average of the current and immediately prior $n - 1$ values of a time series.

NPV rule An investment decision rule that states that an investment should be undertaken if its NPV is positive but not undertaken if its NPV is negative.

Null hypothesis The hypothesis to be tested.

Number of days of inventory An activity ratio equal to the number of days in a period divided by the inventory ratio for the period; an indication of the number of days a company ties up funds in inventory.

Number of days of payables An activity ratio equal to the number of days in a period divided by the payables turnover ratio for the period; an estimate of the average number of days it takes a company to pay its suppliers.

Number of days of receivables　Estimate of the average number of days it takes to collect on credit accounts.

Objective probabilities　Probabilities that generally do not vary from person to person; includes a priori and objective probabilities.

Off-balance sheet financing　Arrangements that do not result in additional liabilities on the balance sheet but nonetheless create economic obligations.

Off-market FRA　A contract in which the initial value is intentionally set at a value other than zero and therefore requires a cash payment at the start from one party to the other.

Offsetting　A transaction in exchange-listed derivative markets in which a party re-enters the market to close out a position.

Oligopoly　A market structure in which a small number of firms compete.

One-sided hypothesis test (or one-tailed hypothesis test)　A test in which the null hypothesis is rejected only if the evidence indicates that the population parameter is greater than (smaller than) θ_0. The alternative hypothesis also has one side.

Open market operation　The purchase or sale of government securities—U.S. Treasury bills and bonds—by the Federal Reserve in the open market.

Open-end fund　A mutual fund that accepts new investment money and issues additional shares at a value equal to the net asset value of the fund at the time of investment.

Open-market DRP　Dividend reinvestment plan in which the company purchases shares in the open market to acquire the additional shares credited to plan participants.

Operating activities　Activities that are part of the day-to-day business functioning of an entity, such as selling inventory and providing services.

Operating breakeven　The number of units produced and sold at which the company's operating profit is zero (revenues = operating costs).

Operating cycle　A measure of the time needed to convert raw materials into cash from a sale; it consists of the number of days of inventory and the number of days of receivables.

Operating lease　An agreement allowing the lessee to use some asset for a period of time; essentially a rental.

Operating leverage　The use of fixed costs in operations.

Operating profit (operating income)　A company's profits on its usual business activities before deducting taxes.

Operating profit margin (operating margin)　A profitability ratio calculated as operating income (i.e., income before interest and taxes) divided by revenue.

Operating return on assets (operating ROA)　A profitability ratio calculated as operating income divided by average total assets.

Operating risk　The risk attributed to the operating cost structure, in particular the use of fixed costs in operations; the risk arising from the mix of fixed and variable costs; the risk that a company's operations may be severely affected by environmental, social, and governance risk factors.

Operationally efficient　Said of a market, a financial system, or an economy that has relatively low transaction costs.

Operations risk or **operational risk**　The risk of loss from failures in a company's systems and procedures (for example, due to computer failures or human failures) or events completely outside the control of organizations (which would include "acts of God" and terrorist actions).

Opportunity cost　The value that investors forgo by choosing a particular course of action; the value of something in its best alternative use.

Opportunity set　The set of assets available for investment.

Optimal capital structure　The capital structure at which the value of the company is maximized.

Optimizer　A specialized computer program or a spreadsheet that solves for the portfolio weights that will result in the lowest risk for a specified level of expected return.

Option (or option contract)　A financial instrument that gives one party the right, but not the obligation, to buy or sell an underlying asset from or to another party at a fixed price over a specific period of time. Also referred to as contingent claims.

Option price, option premium, or premium　The amount of money a buyer pays and seller receives to engage in an option transaction.

Order　A specification of what instrument to trade, how much to trade, and whether to buy or sell.

Order precedence hierarchy　With respect to the execution of orders to trade, a set of rules that determines which orders execute before other orders.

Order-driven markets　A market (generally an auction market) that uses rules to arrange trades based on the orders that traders submit; in their pure form, such markets do not make use of dealers.

Ordinal scale　A measurement scale that sorts data into categories that are ordered (ranked) with respect to some characteristic.

Ordinary annuity　An annuity with a first cash flow that is paid one period from the present.

Ordinary least squares (OLS)　An estimation method based on the criterion of minimizing the sum of the squared residuals of a regression.

Ordinary shares (common stock or common shares)　Equity shares that are subordinate to all other types of equity (e.g., preferred equity).

Organic growth　Company growth in output or sales that is achieved by making investments internally (i.e., excludes growth achieved through mergers and acquisitions).

Orthogonal　Uncorrelated; at a right angle.

Other comprehensive income　Items of comprehensive income that are not reported on the income statement; comprehensive income minus net income.

Other post-retirement benefits　Promises by the company to pay benefits in the future, other than pension benefits, such as life insurance premiums and all or part of health care insurance for its retirees.

Other receivables　Amounts owed to the company from parties other than customers.

Outcome　A possible value of a random variable.

Outliers　Small numbers of observations at either extreme (small or large) of a sample.

Out-of-sample forecast errors　The differences between actual and predicted value of time series outside the sample period used to fit the model.

Out-of-sample test　A test of a strategy or model using a sample outside the time period on which the strategy or model was developed.

Out-of-the-money　Options that, if exercised, would require the payment of more money than the value received and therefore would not be currently exercised.

Output gap　Real GDP minus potential GDP.

Overbought　A market condition in which market sentiment is thought to be unsustainably bullish.

Overnight index swap (OIS)   A swap in which the floating rate is the cumulative value of a single unit of currency invested at an overnight rate during the settlement period.

Oversold   A market condition in which market sentiment is thought to be unsustainably bearish.

Owners' equity   The excess of assets over liabilities; the residual interest of shareholders in the assets of an entity after deducting the entity's liabilities.

Paired comparisons test   A statistical test for differences based on paired observations drawn from samples that are dependent on each other.

Paired observations   Observations that are dependent on each other.

Pairs arbitrage trade   A trade in two closely related stocks involving the short sale of one and the purchase of the other.

Panel data   Observations through time on a single characteristic of multiple observational units.

Parameter   A descriptive measure computed from or used to describe a population of data, conventionally represented by Greek letters.

Parameter instability   The problem or issue of population regression parameters that have changed over time.

Parametric test   Any test (or procedure) concerned with parameters or whose validity depends on assumptions concerning the population generating the sample.

Partial regression coefficients or partial slope coefficients   The slope coefficients in a multiple regression.

Participating preference shares   Preference shares that entitle shareholders to receive the standard preferred dividend plus the opportunity to receive an additional dividend if the company's profits exceed a pre-specified level.

Partnership   A business owned and operated by more than one individual.

Passive investment   A buy and hold approach in which an investor does not make portfolio changes based on short-term expectations of changing market or security performance.

Passive strategy   In reference to short-term cash management, it is an investment strategy characterized by simple decision rules for making daily investments.

Payables turnover   An activity ratio calculated as purchases divided by average trade payables.

Payer swaption   A swaption that allows the holder to enter into a swap as the fixed-rate payer and floating-rate receiver.

Payment date   The day that the company actually mails out (or electronically transfers) a dividend payment.

Payment netting   A means of settling payments in which the amount owed by the first party to the second is netted with the amount owed by the second party to the first; only the net difference is paid.

Payoff   The value of an option at expiration.

Payoff matrix   A table that shows the payoffs for every possible action by each player for every possible action by each other player.

Payout   Cash dividends and the value of shares repurchased in any given year.

Payout policy   A company's set of principles guiding payouts.

Payout ratio   The percentage of total earnings paid out in dividends in any given year (in per-share terms, DPS/EPS).

Pecking order theory   The theory that managers take into account how their actions might be interpreted by outsiders and thus order their preferences for various forms of corporate financing. Forms of financing that are least visible to outsiders (e.g., internally generated funds) are most preferable to managers and those that are most visible (e.g., equity) are least preferable.

Peer group   A group of companies engaged in similar business activities whose economics and valuation are influenced by closely related factors.

Pennants   A technical analysis continuation pattern formed by trendlines that converge to form a triangle, typically over a short period.

Per unit contribution margin   The amount that each unit sold contributes to covering fixed costs—that is, the difference between the price per unit and the variable cost per unit.

Percentage-of-completion   A method of revenue recognition in which, in each accounting period, the company estimates what percentage of the contract is complete and then reports that percentage of the total contract revenue in its income statement.

Percentiles   Quantiles that divide a distribution into 100 equal parts.

Perfect collinearity   The existence of an exact linear relation between two or more independent variables or combinations of independent variables.

Perfect competition   A market in which there are many firms each selling an identical product; there are many buyers; there are no restrictions on entry into the industry; firms in the industry have no advantage over potential new entrants; and firms and buyers are well informed about the price of each firm's product.

Perfect price discrimination   Price discrimination that extracts the entire consumer surplus.

Perfectly elastic demand   Demand with an infinite price elasticity; the quantity demanded changes by an infinitely large percentage in response to a tiny price change.

Perfectly inelastic demand   Demand with a price elasticity of zero; the quantity demanded remains constant when the price changes.

Performance appraisal   The evaluation of risk-adjusted performance; the evaluation of investment skill.

Performance evaluation   The measurement and assessment of the outcomes of investment management decisions.

Performance guarantee   A guarantee from the clearinghouse that if one party makes money on a transaction, the clearinghouse ensures it will be paid.

Performance measurement   The calculation of returns in a logical and consistent manner.

Period costs   Costs (e.g., executives' salaries) that cannot be directly matched with the timing of revenues and which are thus expensed immediately.

Periodic rate   The quoted interest rate per period; the stated annual interest rate divided by the number of compounding periods per year.

Permanent differences   Differences between tax and financial reporting of revenue (expenses) that will not be reversed at some future date. These result in a difference between the company's effective tax rate and statutory tax rate and do not result in a deferred tax item.

Permutation   An ordered listing.

Perpetuity   A perpetual annuity, or a set of never-ending level sequential cash flows, with the first cash flow occurring one period from now.

Pet projects   Projects in which influential managers want the corporation to invest. Often, unfortunately, pet projects are selected without undergoing normal capital budgeting analysis.

Phillips curve   A curve that shows a relationship between inflation and unemployment.

Plain vanilla swap An interest rate swap in which one party pays a fixed rate and the other pays a floating rate, with both sets of payments in the same currency.

Platykurtic Describes a distribution that is less peaked than the normal distribution.

Point and figure chart A technical analysis chart that is constructed with columns of X's alternating with columns of O's such that the horizontal axis represents only the number of changes in price without reference to time or volume.

Point estimate A single numerical estimate of an unknown quantity, such as a population parameter.

Point of sale Systems that capture transaction data at the physical location in which the sale is made.

Poison pill A pre-offer takeover defense mechanism that makes it prohibitively costly for an acquirer to take control of a target without the prior approval of the target's board of directors.

Poison puts A pre-offer takeover defense mechanism that gives target company bondholders the right to sell their bonds back to the target at a pre-specified redemption price, typically at or above par value; this defense increases the need for cash and raises the cost of the acquisition.

Pooled estimate An estimate of a parameter that involves combining (pooling) observations from two or more samples.

Pooling of interests accounting method A method of accounting in which combined companies were portrayed as if they had always operated as a single economic entity. Called pooling of interests under U.S. GAAP and uniting of interests under IFRS. (No longer allowed under U.S. GAAP or IFRS.)

Population All members of a specified group.

Population mean The arithmetic mean value of a population; the arithmetic mean of all the observations or values in the population.

Population standard deviation A measure of dispersion relating to a population in the same unit of measurement as the observations, calculated as the positive square root of the population variance.

Population variance A measure of dispersion relating to a population, calculated as the mean of the squared deviations around the population mean.

Portfolio performance attribution The analysis of portfolio performance in terms of the contributions from various sources of risk.

Portfolio planning The process of creating a plan for building a portfolio that is expected to satisfy a client's investment objectives.

Portfolio possibilities curve A graphical representation of the expected return and risk of all portfolios that can be formed using two assets.

Position The quantity of an asset that an entity owns or owes.

Position trader A trader who typically holds positions open overnight.

Positive serial correlation Serial correlation in which a positive error for one observation increases the chance of a positive error for another observation, and a negative error for one observation increases the chance of a negative error for another observation.

Posterior probability An updated probability that reflects or comes after new information.

Potential credit risk The risk associated with the possibility that a payment due at a later date will not be made.

Potential GDP The value of production when all the economy's labor, capital, land, and entrepreneurial ability are fully employed; the quantity of real GDP at full employment.

Power of a test The probability of correctly rejecting the null—that is, rejecting the null hypothesis when it is false.

Precautionary stocks A level of inventory beyond anticipated needs that provides a cushion in the event that it takes longer to replenish inventory than expected or in the case of greater than expected demand.

Preference shares (or preferred stock) A type of equity interest which ranks above common shares with respect to the payment of dividends and the distribution of the company's net assets upon liquidation. They have characteristics of both debt and equity securities.

Preferred stock A form of equity (generally non-voting) that has priority over common stock in the receipt of dividends and on the issuer's assets in the event of a company's liquidation.

Pre-investing The strategy of using futures contracts to enter the market without an immediate outlay of cash.

Prepaid expense A normal operating expense that has been paid in advance of when it is due.

Present (price) value of a basis point (PVBP) The change in the bond price for a 1 basis point change in yield. Also called *basis point value* (BPV).

Present value (PV) The present discounted value of future cash flows: For assets, the present discounted value of the future net cash inflows that the asset is expected to generate; for liabilities, the present discounted value of the future net cash outflows that are expected to be required to settle the liabilities.

Present value models (or **discounted cash flow models**) Valuation models that estimate the intrinsic value of a security as the present value of the future benefits expected to be received from the security.

Presentation currency The currency in which financial statement amounts are presented.

Pretax margin A profitability ratio calculated as earnings before taxes divided by revenue.

Price ceiling A regulation that makes it illegal to charge a price higher than a specified level.

Price discovery A feature of futures markets in which futures prices provide valuable information about the price of the underlying asset.

Price discrimination The practice of selling different units of a good or service for different prices or of charging one customer different prices for different quantities bought.

Price elasticity of demand A units-free measure of the responsiveness of the quantity demanded of a good to a change in its price, when all other influences on buyers' plans remain the same.

Price floor A regulation that makes it illegal to trade at a price lower than a specified level.

Price limits Limits imposed by a futures exchange on the price change that can occur from one day to the next.

Price multiple A ratio that compares the share price with some sort of monetary flow or value to allow evaluation of the relative worth of a company's stock.

Price priority The principle that the highest priced buy orders and the lowest priced sell orders execute first.

Price relative A ratio of an ending price over a beginning price; it is equal to 1 plus the holding period return on the asset.

Price return Measures *only* the price appreciation or percentage change in price of the securities in an index or portfolio.

Price return index (or **price index**) An index that reflects *only* the price appreciation or percentage change in price of the constituent securities.

Price taker A firm that cannot influence the price of the good or service it produces.

Price to book value A valuation ratio calculated as price per share divided by book value per share.

Price to cash flow A valuation ratio calculated as price per share divided by cash flow per share.

Price to sales A valuation ratio calculated as price per share divided by sales per share.

Price weighting An index weighting method in which the weight assigned to each constituent security is determined by dividing its price by the sum of all the prices of the constituent securities.

Price/earnings (P/E) ratio The ratio of share price to earnings per share.

Priced risk Risk for which investors demand compensation for bearing (e.g. equity risk, company-specific factors, macroeconomic factors).

Price-setting option The operational flexibility to adjust prices when demand varies from forecast. For example, when demand exceeds capacity, the company could benefit from the excess demand by increasing prices.

Price-weighted index An index in which the weight on each constituent security is determined by dividing its price by the sum of all the prices of the constituent securities.

Primary market The market where securities are first sold and the issuers receive the proceeds.

Principal The amount of funds originally invested in a project or instrument; the face value to be paid at maturity.

Principal–agent problem The problem of devising compensation rules that induce an *agent* to act in the best interest of a *principal*.

Principal business activity The business activity from which a company derives a majority of its revenues and/or earnings.

Prior probabilities Probabilities reflecting beliefs prior to the arrival of new information.

Private equity securities Securities that are not listed on public exchanges and have no active secondary market. They are issued primarily to institutional investors via non-public offerings, such as private placements.

Private investment in public equity An investment in the equity of a publicly traded firm that is made at a discount to the market value of the firm's shares.

Private placement When corporations sell securities directly to a small group of qualified investors, usually with the assistance of an investment bank.

Probability A number between 0 and 1 describing the chance that a stated event will occur.

Probability density function A function with non-negative values such that probability can be described by areas under the curve graphing the function.

Probability distribution A distribution that specifies the probabilities of a random variable's possible outcomes.

Probability function A function that specifies the probability that the random variable takes on a specific value.

Probit model A qualitative-dependent-variable multiple regression model based on the normal distribution.

Producer surplus The price of a good minus its minimum supply-price, summed over the quantity sold.

Product differentiation Making a product slightly different from the product of a competing firm.

Production quota An upper limit to the quantity of a good that may be produced in a specified period.

Production-flexibility The operational flexibility to alter production when demand varies from forecast. For example, if demand is strong, a company may profit from employees working overtime or from adding additional shifts.

Profitability ratios Ratios that measure a company's ability to generate profitable sales from its resources (assets).

Project sequencing To defer the decision to invest in a future project until the outcome of some or all of a current project is known. Projects are sequenced through time, so that investing in a project creates the option to invest in future projects.

Projected benefit obligation Under U.S. GAAP, a measure used in estimating a defined-benefit pension plan's liabilities, defined as "the actuarial present value as of a date of all benefits attributed by the pension benefit formula to employee service rendered prior to that date. The projected benefit obligation is measured using assumptions as to future compensation if the pension benefit formula is based on those future compensation levels."

Property, plant, and equipment Tangible assets that are expected to be used for more than one period in either the production or supply of goods or services, or for administrative purposes.

Proportionate consolidation A method of accounting for joint ventures where the venturer's share of the assets, liabilities, income and expenses of the joint venture are combined on a line-by-line basis with similar items on the venturer's financial statements.

Protective put An option strategy in which a long position in an asset is combined with a long position in a put.

Provision In accounting, a liability of uncertain timing or amount.

Proxy fight An attempt to take control of a company through a shareholder vote.

Proxy statement A public document that provides the material facts concerning matters on which shareholders will vote.

Pseudo-random numbers Numbers produced by random number generators.

Pull on liquidity When disbursements are paid too quickly or trade credit availability is limited, requiring companies to expend funds before they receive funds from sales that could cover the liability.

Purchase method A method of accounting for a business combination where the acquiring company allocates the purchase price to each asset acquired and liability assumed at fair value. If the purchase price exceeds the allocation, the excess is recorded as goodwill.

Purchased in-process research and development costs The costs of research and development in progress at an acquired company.

Purchasing power gain A gain in value caused by changes in price levels. Monetary liabilities experience purchasing power gains during periods of inflation.

Purchasing power loss A loss in value caused by changes in price levels. Monetary assets experience purchasing power losses during periods of inflation.

Pure discount instruments Instruments that pay interest as the difference between the amount borrowed and the amount paid back.

Pure factor portfolio A portfolio with sensitivity of 1 to the factor in question and a sensitivity of 0 to all other factors.

Pure-play method A method for estimating the beta for a company or project; it requires using a comparable company's beta and adjusting it for financial leverage differences.

Put An option that gives the holder the right to sell an underlying asset to another party at a fixed price over a specific period of time.

Put–call parity An equation expressing the equivalence (parity) of a portfolio of a call and a bond with a portfolio of a put and the underlying, which leads to the relationship between put and call prices.

Put–call–forward parity The relationship among puts, calls, and forward contracts.

Put/call ratio A technical analysis indicator that evaluates market sentiment based upon the volume of put options traded divided by the volume of call options traded for a particular financial instrument.

Putable common shares Common shares that give investors the option (or right) to sell their shares (i.e., "put" them) back to the issuing company at a price that is specified when the shares are originally issued.

***p*-Value** The smallest level of significance at which the null hypothesis can be rejected; also called the marginal significance level.

Qualifying special purpose entities Under U.S. GAAP, a special purpose entity structured to avoid consolidation that must meet qualification criteria.

Qualitative dependent variables Dummy variables used as dependent variables rather than as independent variables.

Quantile (or fractile) A value at or below which a stated fraction of the data lies.

Quantity theory of money The proposition that in the long run, an increase in the quantity of money brings an equal percentage increase in the price level.

Quartiles Quantiles that divide a distribution into four equal parts.

Quick assets Assets that can be most readily converted to cash (e.g., cash, short-term marketable investments, receivables).

Quick ratio, or acid test ratio A stringent measure of liquidity that indicates a company's ability to satisfy current liabilities with its most liquid assets, calculated as (cash + short-term marketable investments + receivables) divided by current liabilities.

Quintiles Quantiles that divide a distribution into five equal parts.

Quote-driven market A market in which dealers acting as principals facilitate trading.

Random number An observation drawn from a uniform distribution.

Random number generator An algorithm that produces uniformly distributed random numbers between 0 and 1.

Random variable A quantity whose future outcomes are uncertain.

Random walk A time series in which the value of the series in one period is the value of the series in the previous period plus an unpredictable random error.

Range The difference between the maximum and minimum values in a dataset.

Ratio scales A measurement scale that has all the characteristics of interval measurement scales as well as a true zero point as the origin.

Ratio spread An option strategy in which a long position in a certain number of options is offset by a short position in a certain number of other options on the same underlying, resulting in a risk-free position.

Rational expectation The most accurate forecast possible, a forecast that uses all the available information, including knowledge of the relevant economic forces that influence the variable being forecasted.

Real business cycle theory A theory of the business cycle that regards random fluctuations in productivity as the main source of economic fluctuations.

Real exchange rate The relative price of foreign-made goods and services to U.S.-made goods and services.

Real risk-free interest rate The single-period interest rate for a completely risk-free security if no inflation were expected.

Real wage rate The quantity of goods and services that an hour's work can buy. It is equal to the money wage rate divided by the price level and multiplied by 100.

Realizable value (settlement value) With reference to assets, the amount of cash or cash equivalents that could currently be obtained by selling the asset in an orderly disposal; with reference to liabilities, the undiscounted amount of cash or cash equivalents expected to be paid to satisfy the liabilities in the normal course of business.

Realized capital gains The gains resulting from the sale of an asset that has appreciated in value.

Rebalancing Adjusting the weights of the constituent securities in an index.

Rebalancing policy The set of rules that guide the process of restoring a portfolio's asset class weights to those specified in the strategic asset allocation.

Receivables turnover An activity ratio equal to revenue divided by average receivables.

Receiver swaption A swaption that allows the holder to enter into a swap as the fixed-rate receiver and floating-rate payer.

Recessionary gap The amount by which potential GDP exceeds real GDP.

Reference base period The period in which the CPI is defined to be 100.

Regime With reference to a time series, the underlying model generating the times series.

Regression coefficients The intercept and slope coefficient(s) of a regression.

Regulatory risk The risk associated with the uncertainty of how derivative transactions will be regulated or with changes in regulations.

Rejection point (or critical value) A value against which a computed test statistic is compared to decide whether to reject or not reject the null hypothesis.

Relative dispersion The amount of dispersion relative to a reference value or benchmark.

Relative frequency With reference to an interval of grouped data, the number of observations in the interval divided by the total number of observations in the sample.

Relative strength analysis A comparison of the performance of one asset with the performance of another asset or a benchmark based on changes in the ratio of the securities' respective prices over time.

Relative strength index A technical analysis momentum oscillator that compares a security's gains with its losses over a set period.

Renewable natural resources Natural resources that can be used repeatedly without depleting what is available for future use.

Rent ceiling A regulation that makes it illegal to charge a rent higher than a specified level.

Rent seeking The pursuit of wealth by capturing economic rent—consumer surplus, producer surplus, or economic profit.

Reorganization Agreements made by a company in bankruptcy under which a company's capital structure is altered and/or alternative arrangements are made for debt repayment; U.S. Chapter 11 bankruptcy. The company emerges from bankruptcy as a going concern.

Replacement value The market value of a swap.

Report format With respect to the format of a balance sheet, a format in which assets, liabilities, and equity are listed in a single column.

Reputational risk The risk that a company will suffer an extended diminution in market value relative to other companies in the same industry due to a demonstrated lack of concern for environmental, social, and governance risk factors.

Required reserve ratio The minimum percentage of deposits that banks are required to hold as reserves.

Reserve ratio The fraction of a bank's total deposits that are held in reserves.

Reserves A bank's reserves consist of notes and coins in its vaults plus its deposit at the Federal Reserve.

Residual autocorrelations   The sample autocorrelations of the residuals.

Residual claim   The owners' remaining claim on the company's assets after the liabilities are deducted.

Residual dividend approach   A dividend payout policy under which earnings in excess of the funds necessary to finance the equity portion of company's capital budget are paid out in dividends.

Residual loss   Agency costs that are incurred despite adequate monitoring and bonding of management.

Resistance   In technical analysis, a price range in which selling activity is sufficient to stop the rise in the price of a security.

Retail method   An inventory accounting method in which the sales value of an item is reduced by the gross margin to calculate the item's cost.

Retracement   In technical analysis, a reversal in the movement of a security's price such that it is counter to the prevailing longer-term price trend.

Return on assets (ROA)   A profitability ratio calculated as net income divided by average total assets; indicates a company's net profit generated per dollar invested in total assets.

Return on common equity (ROCE)   A profitability ratio calculated as (net income − preferred dividends) divided by average common equity; equal to the return on equity ratio when no preferred equity is outstanding.

Return on equity (ROE)   A profitability ratio calculated as net income divided by average shareholders' equity.

Return on total capital   A profitability ratio calculated as EBIT divided by the sum of short- and long-term debt and equity.

Return-generating model   A model that can provide an estimate of the expected return of a security given certain parameters and estimates of the values of the independent variables in the model.

Revaluation   The process of valuing long-lived assets at fair value, rather than at cost less accumulated depreciation. Any resulting profit or loss is either reported on the income statement and/or through equity under revaluation surplus.

Revenue   The amount charged for the delivery of goods or services in the ordinary activities of a business over a stated period; the inflows of economic resources to a company over a stated period.

Reversal patterns   A type of pattern used in technical analysis to predict the end of a trend and a change in direction of the security's price.

Reverse stock split   A reduction in the number of shares outstanding with a corresponding increase in share price, but no change to the company's underlying fundamentals.

Revolving credit agreements   The strongest form of short-term bank borrowing facilities; they are in effect for multiple years (e.g., 3–5 years) and may have optional medium-term loan features.

Rho   The sensitivity of the option price to the risk-free rate.

Ricardo-Barro equivalence   The proposition that taxes and government borrowing are equivalent—a budget deficit has no effect on the real interest rate or investment.

Risk averse   The assumption that an investor will choose the least risky alternative.

Risk aversion   The degree of an investor's inability and unwillingness to take risk.

Risk budgeting   The establishment of objectives for individuals, groups, or divisions of an organization that takes into account the allocation of an acceptable level of risk.

Risk governance   The setting of overall policies and standards in risk management.

Risk management   The process of identifying the level of risk an entity wants, measuring the level of risk the entity currently has, taking actions that bring the actual level of risk to the desired level of risk, and monitoring the new actual level of risk so that it continues to be aligned with the desired level of risk.

Risk premium   The expected return on an investment minus the risk-free rate.

Risk tolerance   The amount of risk an investor is willing and able to bear to achieve an investment goal.

Risk-neutral probabilities   Weights that are used to compute a binomial option price. They are the probabilities that would apply if a risk-neutral investor valued an option.

Risk-neutral valuation   The process by which options and other derivatives are priced by treating investors as though they were risk neutral.

Robust   The quality of being relatively unaffected by a violation of assumptions.

Robust standard errors   Standard errors of the estimated parameters of a regression that correct for the presence of heteroskedasticity in the regression's error term.

Root mean squared error (RMSE)   The square root of the average squared forecast error; used to compare the out-of-sample forecasting performance of forecasting models.

Roy's safety first criterion   A criterion asserting that the optimal portfolio is the one that minimizes the probability that portfolio return falls below a threshold level.

Rule of 72   The principle that the approximate number of years necessary for an investment to double is 72 divided by the stated interest rate.

Safety stock   A level of inventory beyond anticipated needs that provides a cushion in the event that it takes longer to replenish inventory than expected or in the case of greater than expected demand.

Safety-first rules   Rules for portfolio selection that focus on the risk that portfolio value will fall below some minimum acceptable level over some time horizon.

Sales   Generally, a synonym for revenue; "sales" is generally understood to refer to the sale of goods, whereas "revenue" is understood to include the sale of goods or services.

Sales returns and allowances   An offset to revenue reflecting any cash refunds, credits on account, and discounts from sales prices given to customers who purchased defective or unsatisfactory items.

Sales risk   Uncertainty with respect to the quantity of goods and services that a company is able to sell and the price it is able to achieve; the risk related to the uncertainty of revenues.

Sales-type lease   A type of finance lease, from a lessor perspective, where the present value of the lease payments (lease receivable) exceeds the carrying value of the leased asset. The revenues earned by the lessor are operating (the profit on the sale) and financing (interest) in nature.

Salvage value (or residual value)   The amount the company estimates that it can sell the asset for at the end of its useful life.

Sample   A subset of a population.

Sample excess kurtosis   A sample measure of the degree of a distribution's peakedness in excess of the normal distribution's peakedness.

Sample kurtosis   A sample measure of the degree of a distribution's peakedness.

Sample mean   The sum of the sample observations, divided by the sample size.

Sample selection bias   Bias introduced by systematically excluding some members of the population according to a particular attribute—for example, the bias introduced when data availability leads to certain observations being excluded from the analysis.

Sample skewness   A sample measure of degree of asymmetry of a distribution.

Sample standard deviation   The positive square root of the sample variance.

Sample statistic or **statistic**   A quantity computed from or used to describe a sample.

Sample variance   A sample measure of the degree of dispersion of a distribution, calculated by dividing the sum of the squared deviations from the sample mean by the sample size (n) minus 1.

Sampling   The process of obtaining a sample.

Sampling distribution   The distribution of all distinct possible values that a statistic can assume when computed from samples of the same size randomly drawn from the same population.

Sampling error   The difference between the observed value of a statistic and the quantity it is intended to estimate.

Sampling plan   The set of rules used to select a sample.

Sandwich spread   An option strategy that is equivalent to a short butterfly spread.

Sarbanes–Oxley Act   An act passed by the U.S. Congress in 2002 that created the Public Company Accounting Oversight Board (PCAOB) to oversee auditors.

Scalper   A trader who offers to buy or sell futures contracts, holding the position for only a brief period of time. Scalpers attempt to profit by buying at the bid price and selling at the higher ask price.

Scatter plot   A two-dimensional plot of pairs of observations on two data series.

Scenario analysis   Analysis that shows the changes in key financial quantities that result from given (economic) events, such as the loss of customers, the loss of a supply source, or a catastrophic event; a risk management technique involving examination of the performance of a portfolio under specified situations. Closely related to stress testing.

Screening   The application of a set of criteria to reduce a set of potential investments to a smaller set having certain desired characteristics.

Search activity   The time spent looking for someone with whom to do business.

Seasoned offering   An offering in which an issuer sells additional units of a previously issued security.

Seats   Memberships in a derivatives exchange.

Secondary market   The market where securities are traded among investors.

Secondary precedence rules   Rules that determine how to rank orders placed at the same time.

Sector   A group of related industries.

Sector indices   Indices that represent and track different economic sectors—such as consumer goods, energy, finance, health care, and technology—on either a national, regional, or global basis.

Sector neutralizing   Measure of financial reporting quality by subtracting the mean or median ratio for a given sector group from a given company's ratio.

Securities Act of 1933   An act passed by the U.S. Congress in 1933 that specifies the financial and other significant information that investors must receive when securities are sold, prohibits misrepresentations, and requires initial registration of all public issuances of securities.

Securities Exchange Act of 1934   An act passed by the U.S. Congress in 1934 that created the Securities and Exchange Commission (SEC), gave the SEC authority over all aspects of the securities industry, and empowered the SEC to require periodic reporting by companies with publicly traded securities.

Securities offering   A merger or acquisition in which target shareholders are to receive shares of the acquirer's common stock as compensation.

Security characteristic line   A plot of the excess return of a security on the excess return of the market.

Security market index   A portfolio of securities representing a given security market, market segment, or asset class.

Security market line (SML)   The graph of the capital asset pricing model.

Security selection   The process of selecting individual securities; typically, security selection has the objective of generating superior risk-adjusted returns relative to a portfolio's benchmark.

Segment debt ratio   Segment liabilities divided by segment assets.

Segment margin   Segment profit (loss) divided by segment revenue.

Segment ROA   Segment profit (loss) divided by segment assets.

Segment turnover   Segment revenue divided by segment assets.

Self-investment limits   With respect to investment limitations applying to pension plans, restrictions on the percentage of assets that can be invested in securities issued by the pension plan sponsor.

Sell side firm   A broker or dealer that sells securities to and provides independent investment research and recommendations to investment management companies.

Semideviation   The positive square root of semivariance (sometimes called semistandard deviation).

Semilogarithmic   Describes a scale constructed so that equal intervals on the vertical scale represent equal rates of change, and equal intervals on the horizontal scale represent equal amounts of change.

Semi-strong-form efficient market hypothesis   The belief that security prices reflect all publicly known and available information.

Semivariance   The average squared deviation below the mean.

Sensitivity analysis   Analysis that shows the range of possible outcomes as specific assumptions are changed.

Separately managed account (SMA)   An investment portfolio managed exclusively for the benefit of an individual or institution.

Serially correlated   With reference to regression errors, errors that are correlated across observations.

Service period   The period benefited by the employee's service, usually the period between the grant date and the vesting date.

Settlement date or payment date   The date on which the parties to a swap make payments.

Settlement period   The time between settlement dates.

Settlement price   The official price, designated by the clearinghouse, from which daily gains and losses will be determined and marked to market.

Settlement risk   When settling a contract, the risk that one party could be in the process of paying the counterparty while the counterparty is declaring bankruptcy.

Share repurchase   A transaction in which a company buys back its own shares. Unlike stock dividends and stock splits, share repurchases use corporate cash.

Shark repellents   A pre-offer takeover defense mechanism involving the corporate charter (e.g., staggered boards of directors and supermajority provisions).

Sharpe ratio   The average return in excess of the risk-free rate divided by the standard deviation of return; a measure of the average excess return earned per unit of standard deviation of return.

Shelf registration   A registration of an offering well in advance of the offering; the issuer may not sell all shares registered in a single transaction.

Short   The seller of a derivative contract. Also refers to the position of being short a derivative.

Short position   A position in an asset or contract in which one has sold an asset one does not own, or in which a right under a contract can be exercised against oneself.

Short run   The period of time in which the quantity of at least one factor of production is fixed and the quantities of the other factors can be varied. The fixed factor is usually capital—that is, the firm has a given plant size.

Shortfall risk   The risk that portfolio value will fall below some minimum acceptable level over some time horizon.

Short-run aggregate supply   The relationship between the quantity of real GDP supplied and the price level when the money wage rate, the prices of other resources, and potential GDP remain constant.

Short-run industry supply curve   A curve that shows the quantity supplied by the industry at each price when the plant size of each firm and the number of firms in the industry remain the same.

Short-run macroeconomic equilibrium   A situation that occurs when the quantity of real GDP demanded equals the quantity of real GDP supplied—at the point of intersection of the *AD* curve and the *SAS* curve.

Short-run Phillips curve   A curve that shows the tradeoff between inflation and unemployment, when the expected inflation rate and the natural unemployment rate remain the same.

Short selling   A transaction in which borrowed securities are sold with the intention to repurchase them at a lower price at a later date and return them to the lender.

Shutdown point   The output and price at which the firm just covers its total variable cost. In the short run, the firm is indifferent between producing the profit-maximizing output and shutting down temporarily.

Signal   An action taken by an informed person (or firm) to send a message to uninformed people or an action taken outside a market that conveys information that can be used by the market.

Simple interest   The interest earned each period on the original investment; interest calculated on the principal only.

Simple random sample   A subset of a larger population created in such a way that each element of the population has an equal probability of being selected to the subset.

Simple random sampling   The procedure of drawing a sample to satisfy the definition of a simple random sample.

Simulation   Computer-generated sensitivity or scenario analysis that is based on probability models for the factors that drive outcomes.

Simulation trial   A complete pass through the steps of a simulation.

Single-payment loan   A loan in which the borrower receives a sum of money at the start and pays back the entire amount with interest in a single payment at maturity.

Single-price monopoly   A monopoly that must sell each unit of its output for the same price to all its customers.

Single-step format   With respect to the format of the income statement, a format that does not subtotal for gross profit (revenue minus cost of goods sold).

Skewed   Not symmetrical.

Skewness   A quantitative measure of skew (lack of symmetry); a synonym of skew.

Sole proprietorship   A business owned and operated by a single person.

Solvency   With respect to financial statement analysis, the ability of a company to fulfill its long-term obligations.

Solvency ratios   Ratios that measure a company's ability to meet its long-term obligations.

Sovereign yield spread   An estimate of the country spread (country equity premium) for a developing nation that is based on a comparison of bonds yields in country being analyzed and a developed country. The sovereign yield spread is the difference between a government bond yield in the country being analyzed, denominated in the currency of the developed country, and the Treasury bond yield on a similar maturity bond in the developed country.

Spearman rank correlation coefficient   A measure of correlation applied to ranked data.

Special purpose entity (special purpose vehicle or variable interest entity)   A non-operating entity created to carry out a specified purpose, such as leasing assets or securitizing receivables; can be a corporation, partnership, trust, limited liability, or partnership formed to facilitate a specific type of business activity.

Specific identification method   An inventory accounting method that identifies which specific inventory items were sold and which remained in inventory to be carried over to later periods.

Spin-off   A form of restructuring in which shareholders of the parent company receive a proportional number of shares in a new, separate entity; shareholders end up owning stock in two different companies where there used to be one.

Split-off   A form of restructuring in which shareholders of the parent company are given shares in a newly created entity in exchange for their shares of the parent company.

Split-rate   In reference to corporate taxes, a split-rate system taxes earnings to be distributed as dividends at a different rate than earnings to be retained. Corporate profits distributed as dividends are taxed at a lower rate than those retained in the business.

Sponsored depository receipt   A type of depository receipt in which the foreign company whose shares are held by the depository has a direct involvement in the issuance of the receipts.

Spot markets   Markets that trade assets for immediate delivery.

Spread   An option strategy involving the purchase of one option and sale of another option that is identical to the first in all respects except either exercise price or expiration.

Spurious correlation   A correlation that misleadingly points towards associations between variables.

Stagflation   The combination of inflation and recession.

Standard cost   With respect to inventory accounting, the planned or target unit cost of inventory items or services.

Standard deviation   The positive square root of the variance; a measure of dispersion in the same units as the original data.

Standard normal distribution (or unit normal distribution)   The normal density with mean (μ) equal to 0 and standard deviation (σ) equal to 1.

Standardized beta   With reference to fundamental factor models, the value of the attribute for an asset minus the average value of the attribute across all stocks, divided by the standard deviation of the attribute across all stocks.

Standardizing   A transformation that involves subtracting the mean and dividing the result by the standard deviation.

Standing limit orders   A limit order at a price below market and which therefore is waiting to trade.

Stated annual interest rate or quoted interest rate   A quoted interest rate that does not account for compounding within the year.

Stated rate (nominal rate or coupon rate)   The rate at which periodic interest payments are calculated.

Statement of cash flows (cash flow statement)   A financial statement that reconciles beginning-of-period and end-of-period balance sheet values of cash; provides information about an entity's cash inflows and cash outflows as they pertain to operating, investing, and financing activities.

Statement of changes in shareholders' equity (statement of owners' equity)   A financial statement that reconciles the beginning-of-period and end-of-period balance sheet values of shareholders' equity; provides information about all factors affecting shareholders' equity.

Statement of retained earnings   A financial statement that reconciles beginning-of-period and end-of-period balance sheet values of retained income; shows the linkage between the balance sheet and income statement.

Static trade-off theory of capital structure   A theory pertaining to a company's optimal capital structure; the optimal level of debt is found at the point where additional debt would cause the costs of financial distress to increase by a greater amount than the benefit of the additional tax shield.

Statistic   A quantity computed from or used to describe a sample of data.

Statistical factor models   A multifactor model in which statistical methods are applied to a set of historical returns to determine portfolios that best explain either historical return covariances or variances.

Statistical inference   Making forecasts, estimates, or judgments about a larger group from a smaller group actually observed; using a sample statistic to infer the value of an unknown population parameter.

Statistically significant   A result indicating that the null hypothesis can be rejected; with reference to an estimated regression coefficient, frequently understood to mean a result indicating that the corresponding population regression coefficient is different from 0.

Statistics   The science of describing, analyzing, and drawing conclusions from data; also, a collection of numerical data.

Statutory merger   A merger in which one company ceases to exist as an identifiable entity and all its assets and liabilities become part of a purchasing company.

Statutory voting   A common method of voting where each share represents one vote.

Stock dividend (also **bonus issue of shares**)   A type of dividend in which a company distributes additional shares of its common stock to shareholders instead of cash.

Stock grants   The granting of stock to employees as a form of compensation.

Stock options (stock option grants)   The granting of stock options to employees as a form of compensation.

Stock purchase   An acquisition in which the acquirer gives the target company's shareholders some combination of cash and securities in exchange for shares of the target company's stock.

Stock-out losses   Profits lost from not having sufficient inventory on hand to satisfy demand.

Stop order (or **stop-loss order**)   An order in which a trader has specified a stop price condition.

Storage costs or carrying costs   The costs of holding an asset, generally a function of the physical characteristics of the underlying asset.

Straddle   An option strategy involving the purchase of a put and a call with the same exercise price. A straddle is based on the expectation of high volatility of the underlying.

Straight-line method   A depreciation method that allocates evenly the cost of a long-lived asset less its estimated residual value over the estimated useful life of the asset.

Strangle   A variation of a straddle in which the put and call have different exercise prices.

Strap   An option strategy involving the purchase of two calls and one put.

Strategic analysis   Analysis of the competitive environment with an emphasis on the implications of the environment for corporate strategy.

Strategic asset allocation   The set of exposures to IPS-permissible asset classes that is expected to achieve the client's long-term objectives given the client's investment constraints.

Strategic groups   Groups sharing distinct business models or catering to specific market segments in an industry.

Strategies   All the possible actions of each player in a game.

Stratified random sampling   A procedure by which a population is divided into subpopulations (strata) based on one or more classification criteria. Simple random samples are then drawn from each stratum in sizes proportional to the relative size of each stratum in the population. These samples are then pooled.

Stress testing   A set of techniques for estimating losses in extremely unfavorable combinations of events or scenarios.

Strip   An option strategy involving the purchase of two puts and one call.

Strong-form efficient market hypothesis   The belief that security prices reflect all public and private information.

Structural surplus or deficit   The budget balance that would occur if the economy were at full employment and real GDP were equal to potential GDP.

Structural unemployment   The unemployment that arises when changes in technology or international competition change the skills needed to perform jobs or change the locations of jobs.

Structured note   A variation of a floating-rate note that has some type of unusual characteristic such as a leverage factor or in which the rate moves opposite to interest rates.

Subjective probability   A probability drawing on personal or subjective judgment.

Subsidiary merger   A merger in which the company being purchased becomes a subsidiary of the purchaser.

Subsidy   A payment made by the government to a producer.

Sunk cost   A cost that has already been incurred.

Supply-side effects   The effects of fiscal policy on employment, potential GDP, and aggregate supply.

Support   In technical analysis, a price range in which buying activity is sufficient to stop the decline in the price of a security.

Support level   A price at which investors consider a security to be an attractive investment and are willing to buy, even in the wake of a sharp decline.

Surprise   The actual value of a variable minus its predicted (or expected) value.

Survey approach   An estimate of the equity risk premium that is based upon estimates provided by a panel of finance experts.

Survivorship bias   The bias resulting from a test design that fails to account for companies that have gone bankrupt, merged, or are otherwise no longer reported in a database.

Sustainable growth rate   The rate of dividend (and earnings) growth that can be sustained over time for a given level of return on equity, keeping the capital structure constant and without issuing additional common stock.

Swap (or **swap contract**)   An agreement between two parties to exchange a series of future cash flows.

Swap spread The difference between the fixed rate on an interest rate swap and the rate on a Treasury note with equivalent maturity; it reflects the general level of credit risk in the market.

Swaption An option to enter into a swap.

Symmetry principle A requirement that people in similar situations be treated similarly.

Synthetic call The combination of puts, the underlying, and risk-free bonds that replicates a call option.

Synthetic forward contract The combination of the underlying, puts, calls, and risk-free bonds that replicates a forward contract.

Synthetic index fund An index fund position created by combining risk-free bonds and futures on the desired index.

Synthetic put The combination of calls, the underlying, and risk-free bonds that replicates a put option.

Systematic factors Factors that affect the average returns of a large number of different assets.

Systematic risk Risk that affects the entire market or economy; it cannot be avoided and is inherent in the overall market. Systematic risk is also known as non diversifiable or market risk.

Systematic sampling A procedure of selecting every kth member until reaching a sample of the desired size. The sample that results from this procedure should be approximately random.

Tactical asset allocation The decision to deliberately deviate from the strategic asset allocation in an attempt to add value based on forecasts of the near-term relative performance of asset classes.

Takeover A merger; the term may be applied to any transaction, but is often used in reference to hostile transactions.

Takeover premium The amount by which the takeover price for each share of stock must exceed the current stock price in order to entice shareholders to relinquish control of the company to an acquirer.

Tangible assets Long-term assets with physical substance that are used in company operations, such as land (property), plant, and equipment.

Target balance A minimum level of cash to be held available—estimated in advance and adjusted for known funds transfers, seasonality, or other factors.

Target capital structure A company's chosen proportions of debt and equity.

Target company or **target** The company in a merger or acquisition that is being acquired.

Target payout ratio A strategic corporate goal representing the long-term proportion of earnings that the company intends to distribute to shareholders as dividends.

Target semideviation The positive square root of target semivariance.

Target semivariance The average squared deviation below a target value.

Targeting rule A decision rule for monetary policy that sets the policy instrument at a level that makes the forecast of the ultimate policy target equal to the target.

Tax base (tax basis) The amount at which an asset or liability is valued for tax purposes.

Tax expense An aggregate of an entity's income tax payable (or recoverable in the case of a tax benefit) and any changes in deferred tax assets and liabilities. It is essentially the income tax payable or recoverable if these had been determined based on accounting profit rather than taxable income.

Tax incidence The division of the burden of the tax between the buyer and the seller.

Tax loss carry forward A taxable loss in the current period that may be used to reduce future taxable income.

Tax risk The uncertainty associated with tax laws.

Tax wedge The gap between the before-tax and after-tax wage rates.

Taxable income The portion of an entity's income that is subject to income taxes under the tax laws of its jurisdiction.

Taxable temporary differences Temporary differences that result in a taxable amount in a future period when determining the taxable profit as the balance sheet item is recovered or settled.

Taylor rule A rule that sets the federal funds rate at the equilibrium real interest rate (which Taylor says is 2 percent a year) plus amounts based on the inflation rate and the output gap.

t-Distribution A symmetrical distribution defined by a single parameter, degrees of freedom, that is largely used to make inferences concerning the mean of a normal distribution whose variance is unknown.

Technical analysis A form of security analysis that uses price and volume data, which is often displayed graphically, in decision making.

Technological efficiency A situation that occurs when the firm produces a given output by using the least amount of inputs.

Technology Any method of producing a good or service.

Temporal method A variation of the monetary/nonmonetary translation method that requires not only monetary assets and liabilities, but also nonmonetary assets and liabilities that are measured at their current value on the balance sheet date to be translated at the current exchange rate. Assets and liabilities are translated at rates consistent with the timing of their measurement value. This method is typically used when the functional currency is other than the local currency.

Tender offer A public offer whereby the acquirer invites target shareholders to submit ("tender") their shares in return for the proposed payment.

Tenor The original time to maturity on a swap.

Terminal stock value (or **terminal value**) The expected value of a share at the end of the investment horizon—in effect, the expected selling price.

Termination date The date of the final payment on a swap; also, the swap's expiration date.

Test statistic A quantity, calculated based on a sample, whose value is the basis for deciding whether or not to reject the null hypothesis.

Theta The rate at which an option's time value decays.

Time series A set of observations on a variable's outcomes in different time periods.

Time to expiration The time remaining in the life of a derivative, typically expressed in years.

Time value or speculative value The difference between the market price of the option and its intrinsic value, determined by the uncertainty of the underlying over the remaining life of the option.

Time value decay The loss in the value of an option resulting from movement of the option price toward its payoff value as the expiration day approaches.

Time value of money The principles governing equivalence relationships between cash flows with different dates.

Time-period bias The possibility that when we use a time-series sample, our statistical conclusion may be sensitive to the starting and ending dates of the sample.

Time-series data Observations of a variable over time.

Time-weighted rate of return The compound rate of growth of one unit of currency invested in a portfolio during a stated measurement period; a measure of investment performance that is not sensitive to the timing and amount of withdrawals or additions to the portfolio.

Top-down analysis With reference to investment selection processes, an approach that starts with macro selection (i.e., identifying attractive geographic segments and/or industry segments) and then addresses selection of the most attractive investments within those segments.

Total asset turnover An activity ratio calculated as revenue divided by average total assets.

Total cost The cost of all the productive resources that a firm uses.

Total fixed cost The cost of the firm's fixed inputs.

Total invested capital The sum of market value of common equity, book value of preferred equity, and face value of debt.

Total probability rule A rule explaining the unconditional probability of an event in terms of probabilities of the event conditional on mutually exclusive and exhaustive scenarios.

Total probability rule for expected value A rule explaining the expected value of a random variable in terms of expected values of the random variable conditional on mutually exclusive and exhaustive scenarios.

Total product The total output produced by a firm in a given period of time.

Total return Measures the price appreciation, or percentage change in price of the securities in an index or portfolio, plus any income received over the period.

Total return index An index that reflects the price appreciation or percentage change in price of the constituent securities plus any income received since inception.

Total return swap A swap in which one party agrees to pay the total return on a security. Often used as a credit derivative, in which the underlying is a bond.

Total revenue The value of a firm's sales. It is calculated as the price of the good multiplied by the quantity sold.

Total revenue test A method of estimating the price elasticity of demand by observing the change in total revenue that results from a change in the price, when all other influences on the quantity sold remain the same.

Total variable cost The cost of all the firm's variable inputs.

Tracking error The standard deviation of the difference in returns between an active investment portfolio and its benchmark portfolio; also called tracking error volatility, tracking risk, and active risk.

Tracking portfolio A portfolio having factor sensitivities that are matched to those of a benchmark or other portfolio.

Tracking risk (tracking error) The standard deviation of the differences between a portfolio's returns and its benchmark's returns; a synonym of active risk.

Trade credit A spontaneous form of credit in which a purchaser of the goods or service is financing its purchase by delaying the date on which payment is made.

Trade receivables (commercial receivables or accounts receivable) Amounts customers owe the company for products that have been sold as well as amounts that may be due from suppliers (such as for returns of merchandise).

Trading securities (held-for-trading securities) Securities held by a company with the intent to trade them.

Traditional investment markets Markets for traditional investments, which include all publicly traded debts and equities and shares in pooled investment vehicles that hold publicly traded debts and/or equities.

Transaction exposure The risk of a change in value between the transaction date and the settlement date of an asset or liability denominated in a foreign currency.

Transactions motive In the context of inventory management, the need for inventory as part of the routine production–sales cycle.

Translation exposure The risk associated with the conversion of foreign financial statements into domestic currency.

Treasury shares Shares that were issued and subsequently repurchased by the company.

Treasury stock method A method for accounting for the effect of options (and warrants) on earnings per share (EPS) that specifies what EPS would have been if the options and warrants had been exercised and the company had used the proceeds to repurchase common stock.

Tree diagram A diagram with branches emanating from nodes representing either mutually exclusive chance events or mutually exclusive decisions.

Trend A long-term pattern of movement in a particular direction.

Treynor ratio A measure of risk-adjusted performance that relates a portfolio's excess returns to the portfolio's beta.

Triangle patterns In technical analysis, a continuation chart pattern that forms as the range between high and low prices narrows, visually forming a triangle.

Trimmed mean A mean computed after excluding a stated small percentage of the lowest and highest observations.

Triple bottoms In technical analysis, a reversal pattern that is formed when the price forms three troughs at roughly the same price level; used to predict a change from a downtrend to an uptrend.

Triple tops In technical analysis, a reversal pattern that is formed when the price forms three peaks at roughly the same price level; used to predict a change from an uptrend to a downtrend.

Trust receipt arrangement The use of inventory as collateral for a loan. The inventory is segregated and held in trust, and the proceeds of any sale must be remitted to the lender immediately.

t-Test A hypothesis test using a statistic (t-statistic) that follows a t-distribution.

Two-fund separation theorem The theory that all investors regardless of taste, risk preferences, and initial wealth will hold a combination of two portfolios or funds: a risk-free asset and an optimal portfolio of risky assets.

Two-sided hypothesis test (or two-tailed hypothesis test) A test in which the null hypothesis is rejected in favor of the alternative hypothesis if the evidence indicates that the population parameter is either smaller or larger than a hypothesized value.

Type I error The error of rejecting a true null hypothesis.

Type II error The error of not rejecting a false null hypothesis.

Unbiasedness Lack of bias. A desirable property of estimators, an unbiased estimator is one whose expected value (the mean of its sampling distribution) equals the parameter it is intended to estimate.

Unbilled revenue (accrued revenue) Revenue that has been earned but not yet billed to customers as of the end of an accounting period.

Unclassified balance sheet A balance sheet that does not show subtotals for current assets and current liabilities.

Unconditional heteroskedasticity Heteroskedasticity of the error term that is not correlated with the values of the independent variable(s) in the regression.

Unconditional probability (or marginal probability) The probability of an event *not* conditioned on another event.

Underlying An asset that trades in a market in which buyers and sellers meet, decide on a price, and the seller then delivers the asset to the buyer and receives payment. The underlying is the asset or other derivative on which a particular derivative is based. The market for the underlying is also referred to as the spot market.

Underwritten offering   An offering in which the (lead) investment bank guarantees the sale of the issue at an offering price that it negotiates with the issuer.

Unearned fees   Unearned fees are recognized when a company receives cash payment for fees prior to earning them.

Unearned revenue (deferred revenue)   A liability account for money that has been collected for goods or services that have not yet been delivered; payment received in advance of providing a good or service.

Unemployment rate   The number of unemployed people expressed as a percentage of all the people who have jobs or are looking for one. It is the percentage of the labor force who are unemployed.

Unidentifiable intangible   An intangible that cannot be acquired singly and that typically possesses an indefinite benefit period; an example is accounting goodwill.

Unit elastic demand   Demand with a price elasticity of 1; the percentage change in the quantity demanded equals the percentage change in price.

Unit root   A time series that is not covariance stationary is said to have a unit root.

Uniting of interests method   A method of accounting in which combined companies were portrayed as if they had always operated as a single economic entity. Called pooling of interests under U.S. GAAP and uniting of interests under IFRS. (No longer allowed under U.S. GAAP or IFRS.)

Units-of-production method   A depreciation method that allocates the cost of a long-lived asset based on actual usage during the period.

Univariate distribution   A distribution that specifies the probabilities for a single random variable.

Unlimited funds   An unlimited funds environment assumes that the company can raise the funds it wants for all profitable projects simply by paying the required rate of return.

Unsponsored depository receipt   A type of depository receipt in which the foreign company whose shares are held by the depository has no involvement in the issuance of the receipts.

Up transition probability   The probability that an asset's value moves up.

Upstream   A transaction between two affiliates, an investor company and an associate company such that the associate company records a profit on its income statement. An example is a sale of inventory by the associate to the investor company.

Utilitarianism   A principle that states that we should strive to achieve "the greatest happiness for the greatest number of people."

Validity instructions   Instructions which indicate when the order may be filled.

Valuation   The process of determining the value of an asset or service.

Valuation allowance   A reserve created against deferred tax assets, based on the likelihood of realizing the deferred tax assets in future accounting periods.

Valuation ratios   Ratios that measure the quantity of an asset or flow (e.g., earnings) in relation to the price associated with a specified claim (e.g., a share or ownership of the enterprise).

Value   The amount for which one can sell something, or the amount one must pay to acquire something.

Value at risk (VAR)   A money measure of the minimum value of losses expected during a specified time period at a given level of probability.

Value investors   With reference to equity investors, investors who are focused on paying a relatively low share price in relation to earnings or assets per share.

Value stocks   Stocks that appear to be undervalued for reasons besides earnings growth potential. These stocks are usually identified based on high dividend yields, low *P/E* ratios, or low price-to-book ratios.

Value (market-capitalization) weighted index   An index in which the weight on each constituent security is determined by dividing its market capitalization by the total market capitalization (the sum of the market capitalization) of all the securities in the index.

Variable costs   Costs that fluctuate with the level of production and sales.

Variance   The expected value (the probability-weighted average) of squared deviations from a random variable's expected value.

Variation margin   Additional margin that must be deposited in an amount sufficient to bring the balance up to the initial margin requirement.

Vega   The relationship between option price and volatility.

Velocity of circulation   The average number of times a dollar of money is used annually to buy the goods and services that make up GDP.

Venture capital   Investments that provide "seed" or start-up capital, early-stage financing, or mezzanine financing to companies that are in the early stages of development and require additional capital for expansion.

Venture capital fund   A fund for private equity investors that provides financing for development-stage companies.

Venturers   The owners of a joint venture. Each is active in the management and shares control of the joint venture.

Vertical analysis   Common-size analysis using only one reporting period or one base financial statement; for example, an income statement in which all items are stated as percentages of sales.

Vertical common-size analysis   The most common type of common-size analysis, in which the accounts in a given period are compared to a benchmark item in that same year.

Vertical merger   A merger involving companies at different positions of the same production chain; for example, a supplier or a distributor.

Vested benefit obligation   Under U.S. GAAP, a measure used in estimating a defined-benefit pension plan's liabilities, defined as the "actuarial present value of vested benefits."

Vested benefits   Future benefits promised to the employee regardless of continuing service. Benefits typically vest after a specified period of service or a specified period of service combined with age.

Vesting date   The date that employees can first exercise stock options; vesting can be immediate or over a future period.

Volatility   As used in option pricing, the standard deviation of the continuously compounded returns on the underlying asset.

Vote by proxy   A mechanism that allows a designated party—such as another shareholder, a shareholder representative, or management—to vote on the shareholder's behalf.

Warehouse receipt arrangement   The use of inventory as collateral for a loan; similar to a trust receipt arrangement except there is a third party (i.e., a warehouse company) that supervises the inventory.

Weak-form efficient market hypothesis   The belief that security prices fully reflect all past market data, which refers to all historical price and volume trading information.

Weighted average cost method   An inventory accounting method that averages the total cost of available inventory items over the total units available for sale.

Weighted mean   An average in which each observation is weighted by an index of its relative importance.

Weighted-average cost of capital　A weighted average of the after-tax required rates of return on a company's common stock, preferred stock, and long-term debt, where the weights are the fraction of each source of financing in the company's target capital structure.

White knight　A third party that is sought out by the target company's board to purchase the target in lieu of a hostile bidder.

White squire　A third party that is sought out by the target company's board to purchase a substantial minority stake in the target—enough to block a hostile takeover without selling the entire company.

White-corrected standard errors　A synonym for robust standard errors.

Winner's curse　The tendency for the winner in certain competitive bidding situations to overpay, whether because of over-estimation of intrinsic value, emotion, or information asymmetries.

Winsorized mean　A mean computed after assigning a stated percent of the lowest values equal to one specified low value, and a stated percent of the highest values equal to one specified high value.

Working capital　The difference between current assets and current liabilities.

Working capital management　The management of a company's short-term assets (such as inventory) and short-term liabilities (such as money owed to suppliers).

Working capital turnover　A comparison of revenues with working capital to produce a measure that shows how efficiently working capital is employed.

Working-age population　The total number of people aged 15 years and over.

Yield　The actual return on a debt security if it is held to maturity.

Yield beta　A measure of the sensitivity of a bond's yield to a general measure of bond yields in the market that is used to refine the hedge ratio.

Yield spread　The difference between the yield on a bond and the yield on a default-free security, usually a government note, of the same maturity. The yield spread is primarily determined by the market's perception of the credit risk on the bond.

Yield to maturity　The annual return that an investor earns on a bond if the investor purchases the bond today and holds it until maturity.

Zero-cost collar　A transaction in which a position in the underlying is protected by buying a put and selling a call with the premium from the sale of the call offsetting the premium from the purchase of the put. It can also be used to protect a floating-rate borrower against interest rate increases with the premium on a long cap offsetting the premium on a short floor.

4⅝ 4¹¹⁄₁₆

5½ 5½ — ⅜

5½ 21³⁄₁₆ — ¹⁄₁₆

20⅝

17⅜ 18⅛ + ⅞

6½ 6½ — ½

7¼ 3¹⁄₃₂ —

15⁄16

9⁄16 ⅝

7¹⁵⁄₁₆ 7¹³⁄₁₆ 7¹⁵⁄₁₆

2⅝ 2¹¹⁄₃₂ 2½ +

2¾ 2¼ 2¼

12¹⁄₁₆ 11⅜ 11¼ +

33¾ 33 33¼ —

25⅝ 24⁹⁄₁₆ 25⅜ +

12 11⅝ 11⅝ +

10½ 10½ 10⅛ —

15⅞ 15¹³⁄₁₆ 15⅞ —

9¹⁄₁₆ 8¼ 8⅛ +

11¼ 10⅛

INDEX